THE NIV®
STANDARD LESSON COMMENTARY®
2003-2004

edited by

RONALD G. DAVIS, RONALD L. NICKELSON,
AND JONATHAN UNDERWOOD

published by
Standard Publishing

Jonathan Underwood, Senior Editor
Cheryl Frey, Associate Editor
Mark A. Taylor, Publisher
Paul D. Learned, Executive Director, Church Resources
Carla J. Crane, Production Manager

Tenth Annual Volume

CINCINNATI, OHIO

Standard
PUBLISHING

CD-ROM AVAILABLE

The *Standard Lesson Commentary*® is available in an electronic format in special editions of the *Standard Lesson Commentary*® (King James edition) and *The NIV*® *Standard Lesson Commentary*®. These editions (order #20004 for KJV and 30004 for NIV®) contain a compact disk for use with Windows®-based computers.

The Libronix Digital Library System is the technology that powers the electronic version of the *Standard Lesson Commentary*®. In addition to the electronic version of the Commentary, other compatible Bibles and Bible reference books are available on the CD-ROM for purchase. The Libronix DLS is from the makers of the Logos Library System (LLS). All LLS books, including previously released LLS versions of the *Standard Lesson Commentary*® work with the Libronix DLS.

SYSTEM REQUIREMENTS
Computer/Processor: Pentium 133MHz (300MHz processor recommended)
CD-ROM Drive: 2x or better
Operating System: Microsoft Windows 95 or later (Will run on Windows 98/98SE/Me/NT 4.0 (SP3)/2000/XP)
Memory: Windows 95/98/Me/NT: 64 MB; Windows 2000/XP: 64 MB (128 MB recommended)
Hard Drive Space: 60 MB Minimum
Screen Resolution: 800x600 or larger

If you have any questions regarding the installation, registration, or activation of this CD-ROM, please contact Logos **Customer Service** at **(800) 875-6467.**
If you have problems with the CD, *Technical Support* is available by telephone at *(360) 679-4496,* by e-mail at *tech@logos.com,* or online at *www.logos.com/support.*

© 2003
STANDARD PUBLISHING
a division of STANDEX INTERNATIONAL Corporation
8121 Hamilton Avenue, Cincinnati, Ohio 45231
Printed in U.S.A.

In This Volume

Special Features

Index of Printed Texts...page 4
Cumulative Index of Printed Texts ....page 5
Uniform Lesson Cycle ....page 10
Lesson Planning Page ....page 14

Fall Quarter, 2003
Faith Faces the World

Writers

Lesson Development ....Orrin Root

Verbal Illustrations.................Charles R. Boatman

Why Teach This Lesson? ....Ronald L. Nickelson

Discovery Learning ....Ronald L. Oakes

What Do You Think? ....Kenneth Goble (1-8),
.....Richard W. Baynes (9-13)

Winter Quarter, 2003-2004
A Child Is Given / Lessons From Life

Writers

Lesson Development ....Dennis Gaertner (1-4),
Terry Clark (5-8), John W. Wade (9-13)

Discovery Learning..............W. Edward Fine (1-7)
...................Alan Weber (8-13)

Verbal Illustrations ....Robert C. Shannon (1-8),
.............Jerran Jackson (9-13)

What Do You Think? ....Kenneth Beck

Why Teach This Lesson? ....Ronald L. Nickelson

Spring Quarter, 2004
Jesus Fulfills His Mission / Living Expectantly

Writers

Lesson Development...........Gary Carpenter (1-3),
David Marvin (4-6), Jon Weatherly (7-9),
Thomas E. Friskney (10-13)

Verbal Illustrations.................Charles R. Boatman

Why Teach This Lesson? ....Ronald L. Nickelson

Discovery Learning........Thomas Hutchison (1-6),
Everett Brewer (7-9), Greg DeLort (10-13)

What Do You Think? .Jonathan Underwood (1-6),
.............Dale Cornett (7-13)

Summer Quarter, 2004
Hold Fast to the Faith / Guidelines for the Church's Ministry

Writers

Lesson Development.............John W. Wade (1-8),
...J. Michael Shannon (9-13)

Verbal Illustrations.....................Rod Huron (1-8),
...............Gene Andrews (9-13)

Why Teach This Lesson? ....Ronald L. Nickelson

Discovery Learning ....Alan Weber (1-8),
.....Richard A. Koffarnus (9-13)

What Do You Think? ....Harold Orndorff (1-8),
Jonathan Underwood (9-13)

Index of Printed Texts, 2003-2004

The printed texts for 2003-2004 are arranged here in the order in which they appear in the Bible. Opposite each reference is the page number on which the lesson that treats the passage begins in this volume.

REFERENCE	PAGE	REFERENCE	PAGE
1 Samuel 1:20	127	Titus 2:7, 8	441
1 Samuel 1:24-28	127	Titus 2:11-15	441
1 Samuel 2:1-8a	127	Titus 3:1-10	441
Esther 3:1-6	215	Hebrews 1:1-9	345
Esther 4:7-16	215	Hebrews 2:1-4	345
Esther 8:3-8	223	Hebrews 2:5-18	353
Esther 9:17-23	223	Hebrews 3:12-19	361
Job 2:1-10	159	Hebrews 4:1, 2	361
Job 9:32-35	167	Hebrews 4:9-13	361
Job 13:20-24	167	Hebrews 4:14-16	369
Job 19:25-27	167	Hebrews 5:1-10	369
Job 23:10-12	167	Hebrews 5:11-14	377
Job 27:2-5	175	Hebrews 6:1-12	377
Job 31:5-15	175	Hebrews 8:6-13	385
Job 31:24-28	175	Hebrews 11:1-13	393
Job 38:1-7	183	Hebrews 12:1-13	401
Job 40:6-9	183	James 1:1-8	17
Job 42:1-6	183	James 1:12-18	17
Ecclesiastes 3:1-15	191	James 1:22-27	25
Ecclesiastes 11:7-10	199	James 2:8, 9	25
Ecclesiastes 12:1-8	199	James 2:14-17	25
Song of Solomon 2:8-13	207	James 3	33
Song of Solomon 7:10-12	207	James 4	41
Song of Solomon 8:6, 7	207	James 5:13-16	25
Matthew 1:18-25	143	1 Peter 1:3-5	49
Matthew 26:3-15	237	1 Peter 1:13-21	49
Matthew 26:20-25	237	1 Peter 2:4-10	49
Matthew 26:36-50	253	1 Peter 2:11, 12	57
Matthew 28:1-15	277	1 Peter 3:13-17	57
Mark 14:53	261	1 Peter 4:7-11	57
Mark 14:55-64	261	1 Peter 5:6-10	57
Mark 15:1, 2	261	2 Peter 1:3-15	65
Mark 15:12-15	261	2 Peter 3:3-18	73
Luke 1:67-80	135	1 John 1:5-10	81
Luke 2:40-52	151	1 John 2:1-6	81
Luke 22:7-23	245	1 John 2:15-17	81
John 19:16b-24	269	1 John 2:29	81
John 19:26-30	269	1 John 3:1	81
1 Thessalonians 1:2-10	285	1 John 3:11-16	89
1 Thessalonians 3:6-10	285	1 John 4:7-16	89
1 Thessalonians 4:13-18	293	1 John 5:1-15	97
1 Thessalonians 5:2-11	293	2 John 4-9	105
2 Thessalonians 1:3, 4	301	3 John 3-12	105
2 Thessalonians 1:11, 12	301	Jude 3, 4	113
2 Thessalonians 2:13-17	301	Jude 8-13	113
2 Thessalonians 3:1-4	301	Jude 16-23	113
1 Timothy 3:1-13	409	Revelation 5:1-10	309
1 Timothy 4:7-16	417	Revelation 7:1-3	317
1 Timothy 5:1-8	417	Revelation 7:9, 10	317
1 Timothy 5:17-19	409	Revelation 7:13-17	317
2 Timothy 2:1-15	425	Revelation 14:6-13	325
2 Timothy 3:1-5	433	Revelation 21:1-7	333
2 Timothy 3:12-17	433	Revelation 21:22-27	333
2 Timothy 4:1-5	433		

Cumulative Index of Printed Texts

A cumulative index for the Scripture passages used in *The NIV Standard Lesson Commentary*® for September, 1998—August, 2004 is presented here for your convenience.

REFERENCE	YEAR	PAGE	REFERENCE	YEAR	PAGE	REFERENCE	YEAR	PAGE
Genesis 1:1, 2	1998-1999	345	Numbers 9:15-23	1999-2000	49	1 Samuel 8:1-9	1998-1999	57
Genesis 1:20-31	1998-1999	345	Numbers 13:1-3	1999-2000	57	1 Samuel 8:19-22	1998-1999	57
Genesis 2:7-9	1998-1999	353	Numbers 13:32, 33	1999-2000	57	1 Samuel 9:1, 2a	2000-2001	49
Genesis 2:15-25	1998-1999	353	Numbers 14:1-4	1999-2000	57	1 Samuel 10:17-26	2000-2001	49
Genesis 3:1-13	1998-1999	17	Numbers 14:20-24	1999-2000	57	1 Samuel 16:1-13	2000-2001	57
Genesis 4:1-16	1998-1999	361	Deut. 1:41-46	1999-2000	65	2 Samuel 1:17-27	2000-2001	65
Genesis 6:5-8	1998-1999	369	Deut. 2:1-8	1999-2000	65	2 Samuel 2:1-7	2000-2001	73
Genesis 7:1-4	1998-1999	369	Deut. 5:6-21	1998-1999	33	2 Samuel 5:1-5	2000-2001	73
Genesis 9:12-17	1998-1999	369	Deut. 6:1-9	1999-2000	73	2 Samuel 7:1-13	2000-2001	81
Genesis 11:31, 32	1998-1999	377	Deut. 6:20-25	1999-2000	73	2 Samuel 7:16	2000-2001	81
Genesis 12:1-9	1998-1999	377	Deut. 8:6-20	1999-2000	81	2 Samuel 11:2-5	2000-2001	89
Genesis 15:1-6	1998-1999	385	Deut. 31:1-8	1999-2000	89	2 Samuel 11:14-18	2000-2001	89
Genesis 17:17-21	1998-1999	385	Deut. 34:5-9	1999-2000	89	2 Samuel 11:26, 27	2000-2001	89
Genesis 21:1-3	1998-1999	385	Joshua 3:7-17	1999-2000	97	2 Samuel 12:13-15	2000-2001	89
Genesis 22:1-14	1998-1999	393	Joshua 4:1-3	1998-1999	41	1 Kings 2:1-4	2000-2001	97
Genesis 25:29-34	1998-1999	401	Joshua 4:8-11	1998-1999	41	1 Kings 3:3-10	2000-2001	97
Genesis 27:30-37	1998-1999	401	Joshua 4:20-24	1998-1999	41	1 Kings 6:37, 38	2000-2001	105
Genesis 27:41	1998-1999	409	Joshua 6:1-5	1999-2000	105	1 Kings 8:22, 23	2000-2001	105
Genesis 28:10-16	1998-1999	409	Joshua 6:15-20	1999-2000	105	1 Kings 8:27-30	2000-2001	105
Genesis 28:18-22	1998-1999	409	Joshua 24:1, 2a	1999-2000	113	1 Kings 9:1-5	2000-2001	105
Genesis 32:9-11	1998-1999	417	Joshua 24:14-25	1999-2000	113	1 Kings 11:1-13a	2000-2001	113
Genesis 32:24-30	1998-1999	417	Judges 2:11-20a	1998-1999	49	1 Kings 12:3-13a	2000-2001	345
Genesis 33:1-4	1998-1999	417	Judges 4:1-9	2000-2001	17	1 Kings 12:16	2000-2001	345
Genesis 37:3, 4	1998-1999	425	Judges 4:14, 15	2000-2001	17	1 Kings 12:20	1998-1999	65
Genesis 37:17b-28	1998-1999	425	Judges 4:17a	2000-2001	17	1 Kings 12:25-33	1998-1999	65
Genesis 41:14-16	1998-1999	433	Judges 4:21, 22a	2000-2001	17	1 Kings 17:1-16	2000-2001	353
Genesis 41:25-40	1998-1999	433	Judges 6:11-14	2000-2001	25	1 Kings 18:20, 21	2000-2001	361
Genesis 44:16-20	1998-1999	441	Judges 7:1-7	2000-2001	25	1 Kings 18:30-39	2000-2001	361
Genesis 44:33, 34	1998-1999	441	Judges 7:20, 21	2000-2001	25	1 Kings 22:15-28	2000-2001	369
Genesis 45:1-7	1998-1999	441	Judges 16:4, 5	2000-2001	33	2 Kings 5:1-14	1998-1999	73
Exodus 2:23-25	1998-1999	25	Judges 16:16, 17	2000-2001	33	2 Kings 17:6-18	2000-2001	441
Exodus 3:1-14	1999-2000	17	Judges 16:19-22	2000-2001	33	2 Chron. 30:1-12	2002-2003	15
Exodus 5:1, 2	1998-1999	25	Judges 16:28-30	2000-2001	33	2 Chron. 33:1-13	2002-2003	23
Exodus 12:29-32	1998-1999	25	Ruth 1:1-8	2001-2002	199	2 Chron. 34:1-4	2002-2003	39
Exodus 13:17-22	1999-2000	25	Ruth 1:16-19a	2001-2002	199	2 Chron. 34:19-21	2002-2003	39
Exodus 14:21, 22	1999-2000	25	Ruth 2:1-3	2001-2002	207	2 Chron. 34:29-33	2002-2003	39
Exodus 14:26-31	1999-2000	25	Ruth 2:8-12	2001-2002	207	2 Chron. 36:11-21	2002-2003	87
Exodus 15:1, 2	1998-1999	25	Ruth 4:13-17	2001-2002	207	Ezra 1	2002-2003	337
Exodus 19:3-6	1999-2000	33	1 Samuel 1:20	2003-2004	127	Ezra 3:1-3	2002-2003	345
Exodus 20:2-4	1999-2000	33	1 Samuel 1:24-28	2003-2004	127	Ezra 3:6b, 7	2002-2003	345
Exodus 20:7, 8	1999-2000	33	1 Samuel 2:1-8a	2003-2004	127	Ezra 3:10-13	2002-2003	345
Exodus 20:12-17	1999-2000	33	1 Samuel 3:2-10	2000-2001	41	Ezra 6:13-22	2002-2003	369
Exodus 40:1-9	1999-2000	41	1 Samuel 3:19-21	2000-2001	41	Nehemiah 1:1-4	2002-2003	377
Exodus 40:34-38	1999-2000	49	1 Samuel 7:3-5	2000-2001	41	Nehemiah 2:4, 5	2002-2003	377
Leviticus 26:2-6a	1999-2000	41	1 Samuel 7:12	2000-2001	41	Nehemiah 2:13	2002-2003	377
Leviticus 26:11-13	1999-2000	41	1 Samuel 7:15-17	1998-1999	57	Nehemiah 2:16-18	2002-2003	377

REFERENCE	YEAR	PAGE
Nehemiah 6:1-9	2002-2003	385
Nehemiah 6:15, 16	2002-2003	385
Nehemiah 8:1-12	2002-2003	393
Nehemiah 8:13-18	1998-1999	113
Nehemiah 9:1-3	1998-1999	113
Nehemiah 10:28-39	2002-2003	401
Esther 3:1-6	2003-2004	215
Esther 4:7-16	2003-2004	215
Esther 8:3-8	2003-2004	223
Esther 9:17-23	2003-2004	223
Job 2:1-10	2003-2004	159
Job 9:32-35	2003-2004	167
Job 13:20-24	2003-2004	167
Job 19:25-27	2003-2004	167
Job 23:10-12	2003-2004	167
Job 27:2-5	2003-2004	175
Job 31:5-15	2003-2004	175
Job 31:24-28	2003-2004	175
Job 38:1-7	2003-2004	183
Job 40:6-9	2003-2004	183
Job 42:1-6	2003-2004	183
Psalm 1:1-6	2001-2002	345
Psalm 8:1-9	2001-2002	393
Psalm 19:7-10	2001-2002	345
Psalm 23:1-6	2001-2002	361
Psalm 32:1-11	2001-2002	401
Psalm 42:1-11	2001-2002	353
Psalm 67:1-5	2001-2002	409
Psalm 73:1-3	1998-1999	89
Psalm 73:12, 13	1998-1999	89
Psalm 73:16-18	1998-1999	89
Psalm 73:21-26	1998-1999	89
Psalm 78:1-8	2001-2002	377
Psalm 82:1-8	2001-2002	369
Psalm 96:1-9	2001-2002	409
Psalm 100:1-5	2001-2002	393
Psalm 104:24-35	2001-2002	385
Psalm 113:5-9	2001-2002	369
Psalm 121:1-8	2001-2002	361
Proverbs 3:13-18	2001-2002	417
Proverbs 4:1-9	2001-2002	417
Proverbs 6:16-28	2001-2002	425
Proverbs 15:1-4	2001-2002	433
Proverbs 15:7, 8	2001-2002	433
Proverbs 17:4-10	2001-2002	433
Proverbs 19:17	2001-2002	441
Proverbs 22:1-4	2001-2002	441
Proverbs 22: 8, 9, 16	2001-2002	441
Proverbs 22:22, 23	2001-2002	441
Proverbs 23:10, 11	2001-2002	441
Ecclesiastes 3:1-15	2003-2004	191
Ecclesiastes 11:7-10	2003-2004	199
Ecclesiastes 12:1-8	2003-2004	199

REFERENCE	YEAR	PAGE
Song of Sol. 2:8-13	2003-2004	207
Song of Sol. 7:10-12	2003-2004	207
Song of Sol. 8:6, 7	2003-2004	207
Isaiah 5:1-8	2000-2001	433
Isaiah 5:11	2000-2001	433
Isaiah 5:18-23	2000-2001	433
Isaiah 6	2000-2001	417
Isaiah 7:1-6	2000-2001	425
Isaiah 7:10-17	2000-2001	425
Isaiah 9:2-7	2001-2002	151
Isaiah 11:1-9	2001-2002	135
Isaiah 40:1-11	2001-2002	143
Isaiah 40:28-31	2001-2002	143
Isaiah 42:1-9	2001-2002	159
Isaiah 49:1-6	2001-2002	127
Isaiah 55:1-9	2001-2002	175
Isaiah 58:1-9a	2001-2002	183
Isaiah 60:1-3	2001-2002	167
Isaiah 61:1-4	2001-2002	167
Isaiah 61:10, 11	2001-2002	167
Isaiah 65:17-25	2001-2002	191
Jeremiah 6:16-21	2002-2003	47
Jeremiah 6:26-30	2002-2003	47
Jeremiah 19:1-4	1998-1999	97
Jeremiah 19:10, 11	1998-1999	97
Jeremiah 21:1, 2	1998-1999	97
Jeremiah 21:8-10	1998-1999	97
Jeremiah 22:13-17	2002-2003	63
Jeremiah 22:21-23	2002-2003	63
Jeremiah 25:1-9	2002-2003	55
Jeremiah 26:12, 13	2002-2003	55
Jeremiah 31:23-34	2002-2003	71
Lam. 1:12-16	2002-2003	95
Lam. 3:22-26	2002-2003	95
Lam. 3:31-33	2002-2003	95
Lam. 3:40	2002-2003	95
Ezekiel 18:1-4	2002-2003	103
Ezekiel 18:20, 21	2002-2003	103
Ezekiel 18:25-32	2002-2003	103
Ezekiel 36:22-32	2002-2003	111
Ezekiel 37:1-11a	1998-1999	105
Ezekiel 37:25-27	1998-1999	105
Daniel 2:26	2002-2003	433
Daniel 2:36-45	2002-2003	433
Daniel 12:1-9	2002-2003	441
Hosea 1:2-11	2000-2001	393
Hosea 2:1-4	2000-2001	393
Hosea 11:1-9	2000-2001	401
Joel 2:1, 2	2002-2003	417
Joel 2:12-14	2002-2003	417
Joel 2:28, 29	2002-2003	417
Amos 1:1, 2	2000-2001	377
Amos 2:4-10	2000-2001	377

REFERENCE	YEAR	PAGE
Amos 4:2-5	2000-2001	385
Amos 5:18-24	2000-2001	385
Amos 6:1	1998-1999	81
Amos 7:7-15	1998-1999	81
Obadiah 1-4	2002-2003	409
Obadiah 10, 11	2002-2003	409
Obadiah 15	2002-2003	409
Obadiah 21	2002-2003	409
Jonah 1:1-7	2001-2002	215
Jonah 1:11-17	2001-2002	215
Jonah 2:1	2001-2002	215
Jonah 2:10	2001-2002	215
Jonah 3:1-5	2001-2002	223
Jonah 3:10	2001-2002	223
Jonah 4:1-5	2001-2002	223
Jonah 4:11	2001-2002	223
Micah 3:5-12	2000-2001	409
Micah 6:3-8	2000-2001	409
Habakkuk 3:2-6	2002-2003	79
Habakkuk 3:16-19	2002-2003	79
Zephaniah 1:12	2002-2003	31
Zephaniah 3:1-7	2002-2003	31
Zephaniah 3:11-15	2002-2003	31
Haggai 1:2-14	2002-2003	353
Zechariah 8:1-13	2002-2003	361
Malachi 3:1-4	2002-2003	425
Malachi 3:16-18	2002-2003	425
Malachi 4:1-6	2002-2003	425
Matthew 1:18-25	2003-2004	143
Matthew 1:1-6	1999-2000	143
Matthew 1:18-21	2002-2003	139
Matthew 1:18-25	1999-2000	143
Matthew 1:18-25	2003-2004	143
Matthew 1:24, 25	2002-2003	139
Matthew 2:1-12	1999-2000	151
Matthew 2:13-15	2002-2003	139
Matthew 2:19-21	2002-2003	139
Matthew 2:23	2002-2003	139
Matthew 3:1-11	2002-2003	155
Matthew 3:1-17	1999-2000	127
Matthew 4:1-16	1999-2000	135
Matthew 4:18-22	1999-2000	159
Matthew 5:1-16	2001-2002	89
Matthew 5:17-20	2001-2002	97
Matthew 5:38-48	2001-2002	97
Matthew 6:1-15	1999-2000	167
Matthew 6:19-34	2001-2002	105
Matthew 7:1-5	2001-2002	113
Matthew 7:12-20	2001-2002	113
Matthew 8:23-27	2001-2002	25
Matthew 9:9-13	1999-2000	159
Matthew 9:18-31	1999-2000	175
Matthew 9:35, 36	1999-2000	175

REFERENCE	YEAR	PAGE
Matthew 10:1-4	1999-2000	159
Matthew 11:7-10	2002-2003	155
Matthew 12:22-32	1999-2000	183
Matthew 12:38-41	1999-2000	183
Matthew 13:1-13	2001-2002	57
Matthew 13:16	2001-2002	57
Matthew 13:34, 35	2001-2002	57
Matthew 14:14-21	2001-2002	25
Matthew 15:21-31	2001-2002	41
Matthew 16:13-23	1998-1999	127
Matthew 18:1-4	1998-1999	175
Matthew 18:21-35	1998-1999	183
Matthew 20:1-16	1999-2000	191
Matthew 20:17-28	1998-1999	175
Matthew 21:1-13	1999-2000	199
Matthew 24:45-51	1999-2000	207
Matthew 25:1-13	1999-2000	207
Matthew 25:31-46	2001-2002	81
Matthew 26:3-15	2003-2004	237
Matthew 26:20-25	2003-2004	237
Matthew 26:36-50	2003-2004	253
Matthew 27:35-54	1999-2000	215
Matthew 28:1-10	1999-2000	223
Matthew 28:1-15	2003-2004	277
Matthew 28:16-20	1999-2000	223
Mark 1:9-26	2002-2003	231
Mark 2:3-17	2002-2003	239
Mark 3:1-6	2001-2002	33
Mark 4:36-41	2002-2003	247
Mark 5:2-13a	2002-2003	247
Mark 5:22-36	2002-2003	295
Mark 5:41, 42	2002-2003	295
Mark 6:1-13	2002-2003	255
Mark 7:1-15	2002-2003	263
Mark 7:24-37	2002-2003	303
Mark 8:27-36	2002-2003	311
Mark 9:2-8	2002-2003	311
Mark 9:14-29	2002-2003	319
Mark 10:17-27	2002-2003	163
Mark 10:35-52	2002-2003	327
Mark 11:1-9	2002-2003	271
Mark 11:15-18	2002-2003	271
Mark 12:28-34	1998-1999	159
Mark 14:12-25	2002-2003	279
Mark 14:53	2003-2004	261
Mark 14:55-64	2003-2004	261
Mark 15:1, 2	2003-2004	261
Mark 15:12-15	2003-2004	261
Mark 15:21-25	2002-2003	287
Mark 15:33-37	2002-2003	287
Mark 16:1-8	2002-2003	287
Luke 1:1-4	1998-1999	135
Luke 1:5-14	2002-2003	123
REFERENCE	YEAR	PAGE
Luke 1:26-38	2000-2001	135
Luke 1:26-38	2002-2003	131
Luke 1:39-45	2002-2003	123
Luke 1:39-55	2000-2001	143
Luke 1:46-49	2002-2003	131
Luke 1:57, 58	2002-2003	123
Luke 1:67-80	2003-2004	135
Luke 2:1	2002-2003	147
Luke 2:1-17	1998-1999	143
Luke 2:4-20	2000-2001	151
Luke 2:4-20	2002-2003	147
Luke 2:25-38	2000-2001	159
Luke 2:40-52	2003-2004	151
Luke 3:2b-18	2000-2001	127
Luke 4:16-30	2000-2001	167
Luke 6:27-31	1998-1999	159
Luke 9:57-62	2000-2001	175
Luke 10:25-37	2001-2002	65
Luke 10:38-42	2002-2003	171
Luke 12:13-21	1998-1999	167
Luke 14:25-33	2000-2001	175
Luke 15:1, 2	2000-2001	183
Luke 15:11-24	2000-2001	183
Luke 16:1-13	2000-2001	191
Luke 18:1-14	2001-2002	73
Luke 18:31-34	2000-2001	199
Luke 19:1-10	2000-2001	199
Luke 22:7-23	2003-2004	245
Luke 22:14-30	2000-2001	207
Luke 22:31-34	2002-2003	187
Luke 22:54-62	2002-2003	187
Luke 23:33-49	2000-2001	215
Luke 24:1-10	2000-2001	285
Luke 24:33-49	2000-2001	223
Luke 24:36-53	1998-1999	151
John 1:1-18	1998-1999	237
John 1:19-34	1998-1999	245
John 2:1-11	2001-2002	17
John 3:1-17	1998-1999	253
John 4:7-15	1998-1999	261
John 4:28-30	1998-1999	261
John 4:39, 40	1998-1999	261
John 6:10-14	1998-1999	285
John 6:26, 27	1998-1999	285
John 6:35-40	1998-1999	285
John 6:47-51	1998-1999	285
John 8:12	1998-1999	293
John 8:21-36	1998-1999	293
John 9:1-12	2001-2002	33
John 9:35-38	2001-2002	33
John 11:1-7	2001-2002	49
John 11:11-15	2001-2002	49
John 11:20-32	2002-2003	171
REFERENCE	YEAR	PAGE
John 11:38-44	2001-2002	49
John 12:23-37	1998-1999	301
John 12:42, 43	1998-1999	301
John 13:1-17	1998-1999	309
John 13:34, 35	1998-1999	159
John 14:15-18	1998-1999	325
John 14:24-26	1998-1999	325
John 15:1-17	1998-1999	317
John 16:7-15	1998-1999	325
John 17:1-5	1998-1999	333
John 17:9-11	1998-1999	333
John 17:15-24	1998-1999	333
John 18:31-38	2002-2003	179
John 19:12-16	2002-2003	179
John 19:16-18	1998-1999	269
John 19:16b-24	2003-2004	269
John 19:26-30	2003-2004	269
John 19:28-30	1998-1999	269
John 20:1	2001-2002	269
John 20:11-17	2001-2002	269
John 20:11-18	1998-1999	269
John 20:19-29	1998-1999	277
John 20:30, 31	1998-1999	237
John 21:17	2002-2003	187
Acts 1:1-14	2000-2001	237
Acts 2:1-4	2000-2001	245
Acts 2:37-47	2000-2001	245
Acts 3:1-10	2000-2001	253
Acts 4:1-4	2000-2001	253
Acts 4:13	2000-2001	253
Acts 4:36, 37	2002-2003	195
Acts 5:27-42	2000-2001	261
Acts 6:1-8	2000-2001	269
Acts 7:55-60	2000-2001	269
Acts 8:1a	2000-2001	269
Acts 8:4-8	2000-2001	277
Acts 8:26-39	2000-2001	277
Acts 9:19b-22	2000-2001	285
Acts 9:26, 27	2002-2003	195
Acts 9:26-28	2000-2001	285
Acts 10:30-40	2000-2001	293
Acts 10:43-48	2000-2001	293
Acts 11:19-30	2000-2001	301
Acts 11:22-26	2002-2003	195
Acts 13:1-3	2000-2001	301
Acts 13:4	2000-2001	309
Acts 13:13-15	2000-2001	309
Acts 13:42-52	2000-2001	309
Acts 15:1, 2	2000-2001	317
Acts 15:6-15a	2000-2001	317
Acts 15:19, 20	2000-2001	317
Acts 15:36-41	2002-2003	195
Acts 16:1-5	2002-2003	211

REFERENCE	YEAR	PAGE
Acts 16:9-15	2000-2001	325
Acts 16:25-33	2000-2001	325
Acts 17:22-34	1998-1999	191
Acts 18:1-4	2002-2003	219
Acts 18:18, 19a	2002-2003	219
Acts 18:24-26	2002-2003	219
Acts 20:17-32	2000-2001	333
Acts 26:12-23	2002-2003	203
Acts 26:27-29	2002-2003	203
Romans 1:1-17	2001-2002	237
Romans 3:1-4	2001-2002	245
Romans 3:9, 10	2001-2002	245
Romans 3:19-31	2001-2002	245
Romans 4:1-5	2001-2002	253
Romans 4:13-25	2001-2002	253
Romans 5:1-11	2001-2002	261
Romans 5:18-21	2001-2002	261
Romans 6:3-11	2001-2002	269
Romans 8:18-28	2001-2002	277
Romans 8:31b-34	2001-2002	277
Romans 8:38, 39	2001-2002	277
Romans 10:1-17	2001-2002	285
Romans 12:1-3	2001-2002	293
Romans 12:9-21	2001-2002	293
Romans 13	1998-1999	199
Romans 14:1-13	2001-2002	301
Romans 15:1, 2	2001-2002	301
Romans 16:3-5a	2002-2003	219
1 Cor. 1:2-17	1999-2000	237
1 Cor. 2:1-16	1999-2000	245
1 Cor. 4:1-13	1999-2000	253
1 Cor. 5	1999-2000	261
1 Cor. 7:1-16	1999-2000	269
1 Cor. 8	1999-2000	277
1 Cor. 11:20-34	1998-1999	207
1 Cor. 12:4-20	1999-2000	285
1 Cor. 12:24b-26	1999-2000	285
1 Cor. 12:31	1999-2000	301
1 Cor. 13	1999-2000	301
1 Cor. 15:1-4	1998-1999	135
1 Cor. 15:20-27	1999-2000	293
1 Cor. 15:35-44	1999-2000	293
1 Cor. 16:19	2002-2003	219
2 Cor. 2:4-17	1999-2000	309
2 Cor. 4:5-18	1999-2000	317
2 Cor. 5:11-21	1998-1999	215
2 Cor. 9:1-13	1999-2000	325
2 Cor. 13	1999-2000	333
Galatians 1:1, 2	2001-2002	309
Galatians 1:6-12	2001-2002	309
Galatians 2:15-21	2001-2002	309

REFERENCE	YEAR	PAGE
Galatians 3:6-9	2001-2002	317
Galatians 3:23-29	2001-2002	317
Galatians 4:1-7	2001-2002	317
Galatians 5:1-15	2001-2002	325
Galatians 5:16-26	2001-2002	333
Galatians 6:1-9	2001-2002	333
Ephesians 1:1-14	1999-2000	377
Ephesians 2:8-22	1999-2000	385
Ephesians 4:1-16	1999-2000	393
Ephesians 5:1-5	1999-2000	401
Ephesians 5:18-29	1999-2000	401
Ephesians 6:1-4	1999-2000	401
Ephesians 6:10-24	1999-2000	409
Philippians 1:12-26	1999-2000	345
Philippians 2:1-13	1999-2000	353
Philippians 2:19-24	2002-2003	211
Philippians 3:7-21	1999-2000	361
Philippians 4:4-19	1999-2000	369
Colossians 1:15-29	1999-2000	417
Colossians 2:6-19	1999-2000	425
Colossians 3:1-17	1999-2000	433
1 Thess. 1:2-10	2003-2004	285
1 Thess. 3:6-10	2003-2004	285
1 Thess. 4:13-18	2003-2004	293
1 Thess. 5:2-11	2003-2004	293
2 Thess. 1:3, 4	2003-2004	301
2 Thess. 1:11, 12	2003-2004	301
2 Thess. 2:13-17	2003-2004	301
2 Thess. 3:1-4	2003-2004	301
1 Timothy 1:1-3	2002-2003	211
1 Timothy 3:1-13	2003-2004	409
1 Timothy 4:7-16	2003-2004	417
1 Timothy 5:1-8	2003-2004	417
1 Timothy 5:17-19	2003-2004	409
2 Timothy 1:3-6	2002-2003	211
2 Timothy 2:1-15	2003-2004	425
2 Timothy 3:1-5	2003-2004	433
2 Timothy 3:12-17	2003-2004	433
2 Timothy 4:1-5	2003-2004	433
2 Timothy 4:19	2002-2003	219
Titus 2:7, 8	2003-2004	441
Titus 2:11-14	1998-1999	223
Titus 2:11-15	2003-2004	441
Titus 3:1-10	2003-2004	441
Philemon 4-21	1999-2000	441
Hebrews 1:1-4	1998-1999	127
Hebrews 1:1-9	2003-2004	345
Hebrews 2:1-4	2003-2004	345
Hebrews 2:5-18	2003-2004	353
Hebrews 3:12-19	2003-2004	361
Hebrews 4:1, 2	2003-2004	361

REFERENCE	YEAR	PAGE
Hebrews 4:9-13	2003-2004	361
Hebrews 4:14-16	2003-2004	369
Hebrews 5:1-10	2003-2004	369
Hebrews 5:11-14	2003-2004	377
Hebrews 6:1-12	2003-2004	377
Hebrews 8:6-13	2003-2004	385
Hebrews 11:1-13	2003-2004	393
Hebrews 12:1-13	2003-2004	401
Hebrews 12:26-29	1998-1999	223
James 1:1-8	2003-2004	17
James 1:12-18	2003-2004	17
James 1:22-27	2003-2004	25
James 2:8, 9	2003-2004	25
James 2:14-17	2003-2004	25
James 3	2003-2004	33
James 4	2003-2004	41
James 5:13-16	2003-2004	25
1 Peter 1:3-5	2003-2004	49
1 Peter 1:13-21	2003-2004	49
1 Peter 2:4-10	2003-2004	49
1 Peter 2:11, 12	2003-2004	57
1 Peter 3:13-17	2003-2004	57
1 Peter 4:7-11	2003-2004	57
1 Peter 5:6-10	2003-2004	57
2 Peter 1:3-15	2003-2004	65
2 Peter 3:3-18	2003-2004	73
1 John 1:1-4	1998-1999	135
1 John 1:5-10	2003-2004	81
1 John 2:1-6	2003-2004	81
1 John 2:15-17	2003-2004	81
1 John 2:29	2003-2004	81
1 John 3:1	2003-2004	81
1 John 3:11-16	2003-2004	89
1 John 4:7-16	2003-2004	89
1 John 5:1-15	2003-2004	97
2 John 4-9	2003-2004	105
3 John 3-12	2003-2004	105
Jude 3, 4	2003-2004	113
Jude 8-13	2003-2004	113
Jude 16-23	2003-2004	113
Revelation 1:17-20	1998-1999	223
Revelation 5:1-10	2003-2004	309
Revelation 7:1-3	2003-2004	317
Revelation 7:9, 10	2003-2004	317
Revelation 7:13-17	2003-2004	317
Revelation 11:15	1998-1999	223
Revelation 14:6-13	2003-2004	325
Revelation 21:1-7	2003-2004	333
Revelation 21:22-27	2003-2004	333

Fall Quarter, 2003

Faith Faces the World

Special Features

		Page
Fifty Years and Beyond		10
Faith With Substance	Orrin Root	11
The World of Early Christianity (Map)		15
Faith Faces the World (Chart)		16

Lessons

Unit 1: Live in Faith

September	7	Faith and Temptation	*James 1:1-8, 12-18*	17
	14	Faith and Action	*James 1:22-27; 2:8, 9, 14-17; 5:13-16*	25
	21	Faith and Wisdom	*James 3*	33
	28	Faith and Attitudes	*James 4*	41

Unit 2: Live in Hope

October	5	Live as God's People	*1 Peter 1:3-5, 13-21; 2:4-10*	49
	12	Set a Good Example	*1 Peter 2:11, 12; 3:13-17; 4:7-11; 5:6-10*	57
	19	Grow in Faith	*2 Peter 1:3-15*	65
	26	Trust God's Promise	*2 Peter 3:3-18*	73

Unit 3: Live as God's Children

November	2	Enjoy Fellowship With God	*1 John 1:5–2:6, 15-17, 29–3:1*	81
	9	Love One Another	*1 John 3:11-16; 4:7-16*	89
	16	Live With Confidence	*1 John 5:1-15*	97

Unit 4: Live With Purpose

November	23	Remain Loyal	*2 John 4-9; 3 John 3-12*	105
	30	Maintain Steadfast Faith	*Jude 3, 4, 8-13, 16-23*	113

About These Lessons

The lessons of the present quarter are about putting faith into practice. Faith is easy to talk about, especially in Sunday school. The next thirteen lessons will encourage and challenge each participant to do more than talk, to take faith beyond the walls of the Sunday school classroom and into the home, the market, the workplace, and everywhere the learner goes.

Sep 7
Sep 14
Sep 21
Sep 28
Oct 5
Oct 12
Oct 19
Oct 26
Nov 2
Nov 9
Nov 16
Nov 23
Nov 30

Fifty Years and Beyond

With the year 2004 the *Standard Lesson Commentary*® is fifty years old. Through the past half-century the Commentary has become one of the most popular Sunday school lesson books in the world. For the past ten years that tradition has been enriched by *The NIV Standard Lesson Commentary*®.

With this fiftieth-anniversary edition of the Lesson Commentary we conclude another six-year study of the Scriptures, following the International Sunday School Lesson plan (see the chart below). It is not the plan that is important, however, but the purpose. For fifty years we have striven to achieve the same purpose as expressed by the apostle Paul: "to fill you with the knowledge of [God's] will through all spiritual wisdom and understanding. . . . in order that you may live a life worthy of the Lord and may please him in every way: bearing fruit in every good work, growing in the knowledge of God" (Colossians 1:9, 10).

We pray that this volume, and every volume published in the future, will help you to see that goal realized in your life and in the lives of your learners.

International Sunday School Lesson Cycle
September, 1998—August, 2004

YEAR	FALL QUARTER (Sept., Oct., Nov.)	WINTER QUARTER (Dec., Jan., Feb.)	SPRING QUARTER (Mar., Apr., May)	SUMMER QUARTER (June, July, Aug.)
1998-1999	God Calls a People to Faithful Living (Old Testament Survey)	God Calls Anew in Jesus Christ (New Testament Survey)	That You May Believe (John)	Genesis: Beginnings (Genesis)
1999-2000	From Slavery to Conquest (Exodus, Leviticus, Numbers, Deuteronomy, Joshua)	Immanuel: God With Us (Matthew)	Helping a Church Confront Crisis (1 and 2 Corinthians)	New Life in Christ (Ephesians, Philippians, Colossians, Philemon)
2000-2001	Rulers of Israel (Judges, 1 and 2 Samuel, 1 Kings 1-11)	Good News of Jesus (Luke)	Continuing Jesus' Work (Acts)	Division and Decline (1 Kings 12-22, 2 Kings 1-17, Isaiah 1-39, Hosea, Amos, Micah)
2001-2002	Jesus' Ministry (Parables, Miracles, Sermon on the Mount)	Light for All People (Isaiah 9:1-7; 11:1-9; 40-66; Ruth, Jonah, Nahum)	The Power of the Gospel (Romans, Galatians)	Worship and Wisdom for Living (Psalms, Proverbs)
2002-2003	Judgment and Exile (2 Kings 18-25, Jeremiah, Lamentations, Ezekiel, Habakkuk, Zephaniah)	Portraits of Faith (Personalities in the New Testament)	Jesus: God's Power in Action (Mark)	God Restores a Remnant (Ezra, Nehemiah, Daniel, Joel, Obadiah, Haggai, Zechariah, Malachi)
2003-2004	Faith Faces the World (James, 1 and 2 Peter, 1, 2, 3 John, Jude)	A Child Is Given (Samuel, John the Baptist, Jesus) Lessons From Life (Esther, Job, Ecclesiastes, Song of Solomon)	Jesus Fulfills His Mission (Death, Burial, and Resurrection Texts) Living Expectantly (1, 2 Thessalonians, Revelation)	Hold Fast to the Faith (Hebrews) Guidelines for the Church's Ministry (1, 2 Timothy, Titus)

Faith With Substance

by Orrin Root

Now faith is being sure of what we hope for and certain of what we do not see" (Hebrews 11:1). Therefore, faith may seem to be at a disadvantage in a world of things seen and touched and enjoyed. But faith is more durable. It will emerge triumphant when the visible world is no more (2 Corinthians 4:18). So in the hearts and minds where faith is strong, faith is triumphant even now (1 John 5:4).

In the next three months our Sunday school lessons will trace some of the adventures of faith, an unseen power in a visible world. If we are "sure of what we hope for" and accept the evidence "of what we do not see," we shall find ourselves growing more confident week by week.

These lessons also will make us more familiar with the seven short books we find in our Bibles between Hebrews and Revelation. Five of the seven were written by Peter and John, apostles of Jesus. The other two were written by James and Jude, half-brothers of Jesus. All of these men were involved in the church from its beginning, and all were well aware of its condition and its problems in the second half of the first century.

For our study the thirteen lessons of the quarter are presented in four units. These are listed below with short previews of the lessons in each unit.

UNIT 1. LIVE IN FAITH

Lesson 1: Faith and Temptation. Some versions of the Bible have *temptations* where the *New International Version* has *trials*. The many troubles that try our strength and our patience and our faith are distressing, but James challenges us to face them with joy because we know they will make better persons of us. Shall we rise to his challenge? Shall we face each distressing problem with delight instead of grim determination?

Lesson 2: Faith and Action. Faith is believing and more than believing. So James challenges us again: "Do not merely listen to the word, and so deceive yourselves. Do what it says" (James 1:22). And he warns us that faith without action is dead (James 2:17). So if our faith is feeble we need to revive it and put it to work. Quick, before it dies!

Lesson 3: Faith and Wisdom. Without faith one may think wisdom is skill in promoting himself and putting others down. This kind of wisdom is "earthly, unspiritual, of the devil" (James 3:15). With faith in God we seek wisdom from him, wisdom that "is first of all pure; then peaceloving, considerate, submissive, full of mercy and good fruit, impartial and sincere" (James 3:17). May we all emerge with more wisdom of that kind!

Lesson 4: Faith and Attitudes. A selfish attitude leads to conflict. Be unselfish (James 4:1). Too much affection for the godless world makes one an enemy of God. Put God first (James 4:4). A proud attitude forfeits God's grace. Be humble before him (James 4:10). Save your hostility for the devil. Resist him and defeat him (James 4:7). A judgmental attitude usurps God's place. Leave judging to him. An arrogant attitude in planning is unwise. Make your plans subject to God's will (James 4:15). Remember that you are just a human being, and God is God.

UNIT 2. LIVE IN HOPE

Lesson 5: Live as God's People. The text of this lesson begins with a burst of praise to God because he in his mercy has brought us to rebirth, by which we

SEPTEMBER

OCTOBER

are his children. As his children we have the hope of eternity, not an eternity of poverty and trouble, but an eternity blessed by the inheritance that falls to the children of the Almighty. If we believe as God's children ought, his power will keep us safe through earth's perils and bring us to that glorious eternity. Responsibility goes with such privilege, of course. We are to be holy, dedicated to God's service, obedient to his will. If we do that, the family of God is pictured as a spiritual house, a royal priesthood, and a holy nation. Then let us all exert ourselves to be holy, as our Father in Heaven is holy (1 Peter 1:15, 16).

Lesson 6: Set a Good Example. Of course, every child of God ought to set a good example for other Christians and everyone else. This not only assures for him a glorious inheritance in eternity; it brings glory to God even now. If our lives are as good as they ought to be, even some of the heathen will give honor and praise to our Father because he teaches us to do right. Since God gives us glory eternal, don't we owe it to him to bring him all the glory we can while we live on earth? Shall we then persist in doing right, even when everything seems to go wrong? Shall we then seek to help our fellow Christians rather than seek their help? This is good for us, and for those we help, and for the glory of God.

Lesson 7: Grow in Faith. In an earlier lesson we heard James say faith is dead unless it makes a difference in what we do. Now we hear Peter name some things that should accompany our faith: goodness, knowledge, self-control, patience, godliness, brotherly kindness, love. All of these help faith make a difference in what we do. They make us fruitful in our Christian service, and ensure our entrance into the everlasting kingdom of our Lord. Peter said he was repeating what the readers had heard before, and meant to keep repeating it as long as he lived on earth. As long as we live on earth, shall we keep on rereading the advice of Peter and other New Testament writers to help us grow in Christian faith and character and action?

Lesson 8: Trust God's Promise. When Jesus was preparing to leave this world, he promised to come again, bringing changes in sky and earth. Thirty years later, scoffers were laughing at that promise. They said the earth had been going along in the same way ever since creation and would continue in the same way. Peter said those scoffers were misinterpreting history. The world had not always gone along in the same way. Once a great flood had drowned most of earth's people. There will be changes greater than that when Jesus comes again. Earth and sky will disappear. But there will be a new creation where righteousness will live. Do we trust the promise? Are we looking for Jesus to come back and getting ready to live with righteousness in the new creation?

UNIT 3. LIVE AS GOD'S CHILDREN

NOVEMBER

Lesson 9: Enjoy Fellowship With God. Darkness is a symbol of ignorance and evil, but God is light. If we have fellowship with him, we are free from darkness. But the call of the godless world is strong, and sometimes we stumble into darkness. Then our advocate is Jesus, who died to atone for our sin. Forgiveness is ready when we turn back to the light. Shall we not guide our lives daily by the Word of God and live in the light?

Lesson 10: Love One Another. The world about us provides abundant examples of hatred, but we know that one who hates his brother is a murderer at heart. We do not take our example from the world, but from Heaven. God so loves us that he sent his Son to die for us; Jesus so loves us that he accepted death. We cannot give our lives as he gave his to atone for others' sins; but shall we not give large parts of our lives in helping the brothers we love?

Lesson 11: Live With Confidence. We believe that Jesus is God's Son and our Savior. Because of that faith we become children of God, and by that same faith we overcome the godless world that would turn us away from God. Because we are obedient children of God, we know that we have eternal life. While we live on this earth we know God will give us what we ask if we ask according to his will. Shall we not then obey God with all confidence, knowing that faith is the victory that overcomes the world?

UNIT 4. LIVE WITH PURPOSE

Lesson 12: Remain Loyal. Writing to a Christian lady, John expressed his joy at seeing some of her children walking in truth. But he warned that many deceivers would like to turn them from that way, and he urged the lady to be loyal to Christ and the truth. In another letter John approved the Christian life of Gaius, especially the help he gave to traveling evangelists. But again he warned that false teachers were opposing the good. Taking these two letters to heart, shall we not examine ourselves to be sure we are loyal to Christ and we are helpers of the good?

Lesson 13: Maintain Steadfast Faith. Writing to Christians like us, Jude warned that many false teachers were trying to turn Christians away from their faith. He urged his readers not only to cling to their faith, but also to contend earnestly for it, not with railing accusations, but with calm reasoning and truth. He urged the long-ago readers and the present readers not only to maintain their own faith, but to help their fellow Christians do the same.

Lesson Planning Page

List the aims here, either directly from the lesson or revised to suit your individual needs.

LESSON AIMS

Begin with an opening activity like the illustration from the beginning of the lesson, "Into the Lesson" from the Discovery Learning page, a discussion question, or some other appropriate opener.

GETTING STARTED

List in order the activities you will use. These include discussion questions, activities from the discovery learning page and the reproducible page—as well as key points from the commentary section.

LESSON DEVELOPMENT

I.

II.

III.

How will you bring the lesson to a climax, stressing the key point and desired action steps?

CONCLUSION & APPLICATION

Dismiss the class with an activity that reinforces the Bible lesson.

CLOSING ACTIVITY

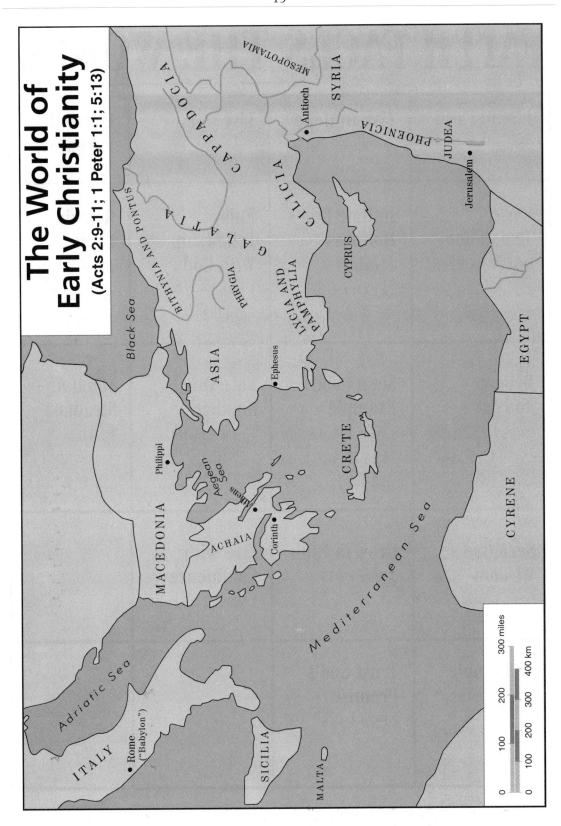

The World of Early Christianity

(Acts 2:9-11; 1 Peter 1:1; 5:13)

MESOPOTAMIA

CAPPADOCIA

SYRIA

Antioch

CILICIA

PHOENICIA

JUDEA

GALATIA

Jerusalem

BITHYNIA AND PONTUS

PHRYGIA

LYCIA AND PAMPHYLIA

CYPRUS

Black Sea

ASIA

Ephesus

CRETE

EGYPT

Philippi

Aegean Sea

Athens

MACEDONIA

ACHAIA

Corinth

Mediterranean Sea

CYRENE

Adriatic Sea

Rome
("Babylon")

ITALY

SICILIA

MALTA

| 0 | 100 | 200 | 300 miles |
| 0 | 100 | 200 | 300 | 400 km |

FAITH FACES THE WORLD

Live in Faith	Live in Hope	Live in Love	Live with Purpose
Resist Temptation James 1:1-8, 12-18	**Imitate God's Holiness** 1 Peter 1:3-5, 13-21; 2:4-10	**Enjoy Fellowship With God** 1 John 1:5–2:6, 15-17, 29–3:1	**Remain Loyal** 2 John 4-9; 3 John 3-12
Believe and Act James 1:22-27; 2:8, 9, 14-17; 5:13-16	**Set a Good Example** 1 Peter 2:11, 12; 3:13-17; 4:7-11; 5:6-10	**Love One Another** 1 John 3:11-16; 4:7-16	**Maintain Steadfast Faith** Jude 3, 4, 8-13, 16-23
Seek God's Wisdom James 3	**Grow in Faith** 2 Peter 1:3-15	**Live With Confidence** 1 John 5:1-15	
Be Humble James 4	**Trust God's Promise** 2 Peter 3:3-18		

Faith Faces the World
Unit 1: Live in Faith
(Lessons 1-4)

FAITH AND TEMPTATION
LESSON 1

WHY TEACH THIS LESSON?

"I can resist anything except temptation!" goes an old wisecrack. Perhaps you've used this lame witticism yourself at a church potluck dinner while reaching for that second piece of pumpkin pie. Some TV commercials boldly encourage us to "give in to temptation" and to "indulge" ourselves. The trials and hardships we undergo in this world should make us want to use their products because, as the commercials say, we've "earned it." So many temptations all around us every day!

But temptation is really nothing to make light of. Physical and spiritual temptations can earn for us eternal destruction (Romans 6:23), and earthly troubles can make us more susceptible to those temptations. Bible writers spend a great deal of effort in wrestling with the problem of temptation to sin (e.g., Romans 7:7-25). Today's lesson brings this struggle to your twenty-first century learners, who also should be trying to persevere under distress and to defeat temptation.

INTRODUCTION

Being a hermit by nature, I was fortunate to have a wife as social as I am unsocial. Thanks to her, both of us had a multitude of friends living near and far away. When we composed our annual "Christmas letter" for them, we had to make five hundred copies.

But to members of our family we wrote a different kind of letter, and we wrote more often. Instead of giving a summary of our lives for a year, each letter spoke of matters of special interest to the person or couple to whom that letter was sent. One copy was enough.

A. LETTERS IN THE NEW TESTAMENT

About one-third of the New Testament consists of letters. Some of those letters are like our letters to family members. Some in that group are addressed to special individuals such as Timothy, Titus, or Philemon. Some are addressed to all the Christians in certain cities such as Rome or Corinth. One is addressed to the Christians in Galatia, a district including a number of cities. These are called "special letters" because each one was specially written for a certain individual or a certain group.

New Testament letters of another group are called "general letters" because the identity of specific recipients is hard to determine; this brings up the possibility that they were written for Christians in general, not for specific individuals or groups. Each of these letters is named for its writer: James, Peter, John, or Jude. Peter wrote two of the general letters, and John wrote three. Second John and 3 John actually are special letters, since one is addressed to a certain lady and her children, and the other to a man named Gaius. But those two very short works are grouped with 1 John among the general letters for convenience. These seven letters appear in the Bible after the book of Hebrews (which itself often is considered to be one of the general letters), and before the final book, Revelation. Our lessons for the fall will be drawn from these books that are called "general letters" or "general epistles."

DEVOTIONAL READING:
2 CORINTHIANS 4:5-11

BACKGROUND SCRIPTURE:
JAMES 1:1-18

PRINTED TEXT:
JAMES 1:1-8, 12-18

LESSON AIMS

After participating in this lesson, each student will be able to:

1. Tell what James says about trials and temptations—and how to achieve victory through them.

2. Explain how to use wisdom from God to overcome temptation.

3. Identify a specific temptation that he or she is experiencing and pray for help to do what is right.

KEY VERSE

Consider it pure joy, my brothers, whenever you face trials of many kinds, because you know that the testing of your faith develops perseverance.
— James 1:2, 3

B. LESSON BACKGROUND

The book of James is not heavy on doctrine as are many other letters in the New Testament. The focus, instead, is on how Christians are to conduct themselves. Of course, the author cannot teach his readers lessons about proper conduct without solid doctrine as a foundation. But here that doctrinal foundation is assumed to be already in place; this allows the author to focus on his main concern: right behavior. As we shall see, much of this letter bears a strong resemblance to things Jesus had to say in his Sermon on the Mount.

I. AUTHOR AND AUDIENCE (JAMES 1:1)

If we pick up a new book dealing with space travel, we look for the name of the author. If he is a well-known writer of fiction, we expect this story to be fiction as well. If the writer is one of those who walked on the moon years ago, perhaps the book will have interesting reminiscences of what it felt like to be literally out of this world. If the new book comes from an official of NASA, we expect to learn something about the latest developments in travel in outer space. So when we know who wrote the book of James perhaps we will know what to expect in the book.

A. THE WRITER (v. 1a)

1a. James, a servant of God and of the Lord Jesus Christ,

Ancient letters customarily begin with the name of the writer. The New Testament notes several men by the name of *James*. Two of Jesus' twelve disciples bore the name: the son of Zebedee and brother of John (Matthew 10:2) and the son of Alphaeus (Matthew 10:3). "James the younger" (Mark 15:40) is generally assumed to be the apostle James, son of Alphaeus. One of Jesus' brothers was also named James (Matthew 13:55; Mark 6:3). Another James is mentioned in Luke 6:16 and Acts 1:13, but nothing more than his relationship to Judas is known.

So who was this James who wrote the letter we are beginning to read? Modestly he calls himself *a servant of God and of the Lord Jesus Christ*. That is also a description of you or me or any active Christian. Most likely this is "James, the Lord's brother" (Galatians 1:19). James is named first among Jesus' brothers in both Matthew and Mark, perhaps indicating that he was the oldest of those siblings.

When Jesus began his ministry, all his siblings must have learned that he was doing miracles (Matthew 4:23-25) and teaching amazing things (7:28, 29). They must have known their brother was the most popular teacher in Israel, for when they went with their mother to talk with him, they found the crowd so big and so tightly packed that they could not reach him. The people of God had replaced them as his family (Luke 8:19-21).

After more than two years of miracles and teaching, Jesus' brothers still did not believe Jesus was Israel's Messiah and the world's Savior (John 7:5). They did not become convinced until he rose from the dead. After that, his brothers were among his disciples in Jerusalem (Acts 1:13, 14). Peter thought highly enough of James to mention him by name (Acts 12:17). Later, Paul named James along with two of the other apostles as pillars of the church (Galatians 2:9). During an important doctrinal debate, it was James who stated the conclusion reached by the apostles, the elders, and the church at Jerusalem (Acts 15:13-29). When we look at the book of James, then, we are seeing a letter from one of the strongest, wisest, and most trusted leaders of the first church in Jerusalem. From such a writer we can expect good counsel, and the inspiration of the Holy Spirit assures us that we shall find no mistakes.

FAITH FACES THE WORLD

Live in Faith	Live in Hope	Live in Love	Live with Purpose
Resist Temptation James 1:1-8, 12-18	Imitate God's Holiness 1 Peter 1:3-5, 13-21; 2:4-10	Enjoy Fellowship With God 1 John 1:5-2:6, 15-17, 29-3:1	Remain Loyal 2 John 4-9; 3 John 3-12
Believe and Act James 1:22-27; 2:8, 9, 14-17; 5:13-16	Set a Good Example 1 Peter 2:11, 12; 3:13-17; 4:7-11; 5:6-10	Love One Another 1 John 3:11-16; 4:7-16	Maintain Steadfast Faith Jude 3, 4, 8-13, 16-25
Seek God's Wisdom James 3	Grow in Faith 2 Peter 1:3-15	Live With Confidence 1 John 5:1-15	
Be Humble James 4	Trust God's Promise 2 Peter 3:3-18		

Use this poster from the Adult Visuals packet to provide an overview of the lessons this quarter.

B. The Readers (v. 1b)

1b. To the twelve tribes scattered among the nations:
Greetings.

Taken literally this would refer to all the Jews living outside their homeland of Palestine. Jews lived in various parts of the sprawling Roman Empire. Acts 2:9-11 lists some of the places from which they came for the feast of Passover in Jerusalem.

However, since those who are expected to read this letter have faith in "our glorious Lord Jesus Christ" (James 2:1), we conclude that James writes it for Jewish Christians in many places outside of Palestine. Certainly it contains good advice for all Christians everywhere, even to us who live two thousand years later.

II. TEMPTATION AND TRIUMPH (JAMES 1:2-8, 12)

After the very short greeting of verse 1, James dives right into the subjects he wants to discuss.

A. Joy in Temptation (v. 2)

2. Consider it pure joy, my brothers, whenever you face trials of many kinds,

Scarcely has the sound of James's greeting died away when he introduces a word that we may prefer not to hear: *trials*. This refers to things, events, or circumstances that test our strength of character. Sometimes the trials and temptations of life entice us to relieve our distress by doing wrong. But James recommends an unusual way of responding to trouble or distress: meet it with joy! (See Matthew 5:12.)

We probably have a hard time imagining ourselves clapping our hands in joy when we break a leg, lose a job, or wreck the car! Such trials test our faith, our patience, and our godly disposition. Trials like this tempt us to do something wrong, such as trying to defraud the insurance company or blaming God for our careless driving. In any case, the disaster is not likely to be greeted with delight. But James is not insane. He is taking the long view, as the next verse shows.

B. Happy Results (vv. 3, 4)

3, 4. . . . because you know that the testing of your faith develops perseverance. Perseverance must finish its work so that you may be mature and complete, not lacking anything.

Catastrophe may indeed test our *faith*. It may tempt us to turn away from God. But if our faith is strong and healthy, it passes the test. Strong faith does not ask, "Where was God when that wild driver rammed me?" Instead, with gratitude this faith says, "Thank God I'm alive." So the test of your faith produces *perseverance*. This word *perseverance* does not suggest that we simply wait out our troubles passively. Instead, it includes the idea of active persistence. We hang in there. We keep on thinking straight, speaking truthfully, and doing right. When perseverance finishes *its work*, we become *mature and complete*, lacking nothing that belongs in Christian character and life. As a result, we emerge from our troubles better people. We are firmer, stronger, more secure in our faith. Isn't that reason enough for the joy recommended in verse 2? (See also v. 12, below.)

When Circumstances Stress Us

Somewhere over Africa on December 29, 2000, British Airways flight 2069 suddenly went out of control. Dr. Mark Jasmine, his wife Mary, and their two daughters were on that flight, heading for a vacation safari.

As the plane fell into a steep dive, it vibrated horribly and parts of the ceiling and luggage from the overhead bins cascaded onto the passengers. The Jasmines

What Do You Think?

"Are we having fun yet?" That question exposes the shallow ambitions of worldly people. What can the church do to help the average Christian seek lasting joy instead of pursuing that which brings only temporary happiness?

What Do You Think?

Many Christians feel that they are failures if they repeatedly have to deal with the same trial or temptation. In what ways can the church effectively teach that these experiences, while potentially dangerous, are not sin in and of themselves, and are also opportunities for growth?

embraced the children, sure that all would die soon. Mary started singing a gospel song by Twila Paris that spoke of God's being in control.

Unbeknownst to most of the passengers, a deranged man had burst into the cockpit and disengaged the autopilot, causing the plane to plunge nineteen thousand feet before the crew could subdue him and bring the plane under control.

Mary Jasmine said later, "I had this island of calm right in the middle of all this chaos . . . the holy presence inside me. . . . Hang onto that place. Call on it regularly, not just when the chips are down. [God's] grace is more than sufficient."

The Jasmine family learned the lesson of today's text: when life's circumstances threaten to destroy us, God will provide not only momentary peace, but lasting, patient trust and confidence in his loving care.   —C. R. B.

C. WISDOM TO WIN (vv. 5-8)

5. If any of you lacks wisdom, he should ask God, who gives generously to all without finding fault, and it will be given to him.

Easily we fall into the foolish habit of blaming someone else for our problems. If we cannot put the blame on the other driver, we put it on God. Why didn't he rescue me from that awful situation? It takes more than human wisdom to see clearly a situation that involves ourselves. So *ask God.* (See also Matthew 7:7.)

When you ask God, you allow him to teach you something through your trials. But you should not expect God to give you a clear understanding against your will. Do your best to see your situation and yourself fairly, impartially. Imagine yourself in someone else's place. How would your conduct look to him? Or imagine someone else in your place. Would you find excuses for her as easily as you find them for yourself?

6. But when he asks, he must believe and not doubt, because he who doubts is like a wave of the sea, blown and tossed by the wind.

Ask wisdom from God, fully expect to receive it, and be willing and eager to accept God's view of the situation even if it makes you look bad. If you waver between your wish for clear understanding and your wish to make yourself look good, you can't be satisfied either with God's clear understanding or your own biased view. You're like a wind-tossed *wave of the sea.*

7, 8. That man should not think he will receive anything from the Lord; he is a double-minded man, unstable in all he does.

So we must make up our minds: Do we want God's clear wisdom or our own self-justifying opinions? God knows what we really want, and that is what we will get. (See also James 4:8.)

D. REWARD OF VICTORY (v. 12)

12. Blessed is the man who perseveres under trial, because when he has stood the test, he will receive the crown of life that God has promised to those who love him.

In verse 2 James urged us to be joyful in the midst of our trials and temptations. Now he looks forward to the end of all those trials and temptations. When their end comes, we shall stand before God as mature Christians, strengthened by every *trial.* By his grace we at long last shall be as Christlike as we have been trying to be throughout our lives. Then we shall be crowned with *life,* endless life, life without trials and temptations, life in the presence of God. Isn't that worth all the struggles you ever have in this earthly life? (See also Matthew 24:13; James 5:11.)

III. EVIL AND GOOD (JAMES 1:13-18)

Sometimes it is hard to trace a matter to its source or to find the cause of a result that is plain before us. When rainfall makes a river overflow its banks, can we

WHAT DO YOU THINK?

It's easy to say we need to ask God for wisdom. It's much harder to remember to do it. Perhaps hardest yet is discerning his answer. How do you do what James is telling us to do in this passage?

WHAT DO YOU THINK?

James seems to describe both the short- and long-term results of dealing successfully with trials and temptations. How can Christians effectively communicate both perspectives?

say that God caused the resulting destruction? Did the devil cause it? (Compare Job 1:6-19.) Or was the owner of the house at fault by foolishly building on a flood plain? In the last part of our text, James gives us some guidelines for our thinking about sources.

A. SOURCES OF EVIL (vv. 13-15)

13. When tempted, no one should say, "God is tempting me." For God cannot be tempted by evil, nor does he tempt anyone;

The word *tempt* has different shades of meaning. "God tested Abraham" (some versions say "tempted") to show to him and to us the depth and power of Abraham's faith (Genesis 22:1-13). But in verse 13 of our text, *tempted* has the meaning that it most often has today. James is saying God does not entice anyone to commit sin. If you are wondering who or what is trying to make you do wrong, here is a starting point for your thinking: God is not doing it.

14. . . . but each one is tempted when, by his own evil desire, he is dragged away and enticed.

Does this shock you? The source of temptation is inside you. It is your *own evil desire*, your own wish. This does not deny the devil's part in temptation (see 1 Peter 5:8). But the devil cannot make you do anything wrong unless some wish of yours cooperates with him. Alert for every opportunity, the devil uses your own wish to entice you into wrongdoing in order to get what you desire. The devil may be stronger than you are, but God is even stronger (1 John 4:4). He will strengthen us in our time of temptation, if we let him.

15. Then, after desire has conceived, it gives birth to sin; and sin, when it is full-grown, gives birth to death.

James draws a vivid, sobering picture of adultery and illicit reproduction. When a person surrenders to the enticement of evil desire (v. 14) the result is an illegitimate conception and *birth* of *sin*—your sin. And when that sin is *full-grown* it is worse than the original *desire*. The sin results in *death*—your death. Now aren't you glad you stood firm against your wish when first it tried to entice you to do wrong? Aren't you glad you resisted its pleading, put it in its place, and refused to do anything wrong? In so doing, you allowed God to save you for eternity.

COSTLY DESIRES

Would you like to travel the world over, but not have to eat any "strange" food or sleep in a stranger's bed every night? You say you want the comforts of home but still want to see exotic sights? When we want our desires to be fulfilled without the normal cost that comes with that fulfillment, usually there's not much help.

But some of us keep trying. How about the possibility of visiting cities around the world, sleeping in our own bed every night, eating our customary diet while doing so, and never having to pay the penalty of discomfort in our travels? Now it can be done! *The World of ResidenSea*, a new cruise ship launched in 2002, is an ocean-going condominium with 110 units ranging from 1,100 to 3,200 square feet each. You may cook in your own kitchen and eat on your own terrace, or you can patronize one of the four restaurants on board. All this for only $2 million to $6.8 million! (But don't forget the 5 percent annual fee that includes all but food and drink.)

Most of us don't have desires as grandiose as that, but what we do want gives us trouble when we don't want to pay the price. When what we want is wrong and the price is too high, James says, "Don't blame God; it's your own fault!" When we allow evil desires to be incubated in our hearts, we should not be surprised that the price is more than we want to pay!   —C. R. B.

HOW TO SAY IT

Abraham. AY-bruh-ham.
Alphaeus. Al-FEE-us.
Corinth. KOR-inth.
Gaius. GAY-us.
Galatia. Guh-LAY-shuh.
Hebrews. HEE-brews.
Jerusalem. Juh-ROO-suh-lem.
Messiah. Meh-SIGH-uh.
Philemon. Fih-LEE-mun or
*   Fye-LEE-mun.*
Titus. TY-tus.

DAILY BIBLE READINGS

Monday, Sept. 1—Persecuted, But Not Abandoned (2 Corinthians 4:5-10)

Tuesday, Sept. 2—Given Over to Death for Jesus' Sake (2 Corinthians 4:11-15)

Wednesday, Sept. 3—In Great Endurance (2 Corinthians 6:3-10)

Thursday, Sept. 4—Suffering That Glorifies God (1 Peter 4:12-19)

Friday, Sept. 5—Faith Must Be Tested (James 1:1-8)

Saturday, Sept. 6—A Crown Awaits One Who Endures (James 1:9-12)

Sunday, Sept. 7—Temptations Come From Our Desires (James 1:13-18)

PRAYER

Our Father in Heaven, it is good to be assured that all things work together for good to them that love you, as Romans 8:28 promises. We do love you, Lord, and we do want to serve you. "Lead us not into temptation." Give us, instead, the wisdom to know what is right and the courage to do it. In Jesus' name, amen.

THOUGHT TO REMEMBER

Trust God and do right.

B. SOURCE OF GOOD (vv. 16-18)

16. Don't be deceived, my dear brothers.

"Make no mistake about this," says James. James already has assured us that God does not tempt anyone (v. 13).

Next he tells us what God does instead. He is the provider of good. James wants us to be fully convinced of this truth.

17. Every good and perfect gift is from above, coming down from the Father of the heavenly lights, who does not change like shifting shadows.

The *gift* that results is *perfect*, complete, all that it ought to be, all the recipients need. Such wonderful generosity is beyond the reach of us ordinary human beings; they are *from above*, from Heaven. In fact, they come *down from the Father* who made *the heavenly lights* (Genesis 1; Psalm 136:7-9). This imagery naturally makes us think of the blazing sun by day and the mellow moon and the sparkling stars by night.

The lights we see above are variable. They are dimmed by clouds and eclipses; they brighten in a clear sky; they cast *shifting shadows* as the time of day passes. But the Father of them all is forever changeless, forever dependable, forever in the good act of giving perfect gifts.

18. He chose to give us birth through the word of truth, that we might be a kind of firstfruits of all he created.

Through *the word of truth*, it is God who grants the power and the right to be born again, born of water and of the Spirit (John 3:3-5). Thus he makes us to be new creatures (2 Corinthians 5:17) and the *firstfruits of all he created*.

When Jesus returns and our salvation is completed in Heaven, the "bondage to decay" shall be no more (Romans 8:21). All of creation, which "has been groaning as in the pains of childbirth right up to the present time" (Romans 8:22) will be renewed (Revelation 21:5).

CONCLUSION

Nearly every scholar who comments on the book of James tells us it is a very practical book. So, what practical advice for daily living have we seen in this lesson?

First, James counsels us to live with joy, especially to find joy in things that trouble and distress us. Those troubles can be beneficial. If we meet them with courage and keep on doing right, they make us better people. Isn't that what we want? And, after all, most of us are not greatly troubled or distressed most of the time. Still, we know God's tomorrow will be better than today if we meet life with courage and keep on doing right. How can we not be filled with joy? How can we not greet each day that brings us closer to eternity?

Second, James tells us to live for victory. One of the things that troubles us is the constant presence of temptation, the urge to do wrong in order to gain some short-term advantage. Don't let it scare you.

With wisdom from God, you can beat the devil. "Resist the devil, and he will flee from you" (James 4:7). More dangerous may be the enemy within you, your own wish to do something wrong (4:1). You can beat that wish with a better one. More than anything else, wish for God's kingdom (Matthew 6:33). That is, wish to be ruled by God, to do his will. And wish for God's righteousness. You can never get that for yourself, but God can give it to you by his gracious forgiveness (1 John 1:9).

Third, James tells us to live for the future. As Paul puts it, "our present sufferings are not worth comparing with the glory that will be revealed in us" (Romans 8:18). Go for the glory!

Discovery Learning

This page contains an alternative lesson plan emphasizing learning activities. Classes desiring such student involvement will find these suggestions helpful. The next page is a reproducible activity page to further enhance discovery learning.

LEARNING GOALS

After this lesson each student will be able to:

1. Tell what James says about trials and temptations—and how to achieve victory through them.

2. Explain how to use wisdom from God to overcome temptation.

3. Identify a specific temptation that he or she is experiencing and pray for help to do what is right.

INTO THE LESSON

Begin by stating, "People respond differently to the same event. For example, some rejoice over the outcome of a football game; others are quite disappointed." To illustrate different reactions to the same event, ask for volunteers to serve in two skit groups of at least two people. Each skit group will illustrate both a positive and a negative response to a particular situation. The first skit group prepares two short skits describing the reaction of parents to their teenage son's car accident. The second skit group shows the reaction of an employee who should have received a job promotion to another employee who actually did. Ask the groups to give the negative reaction first. After both groups have finished, state: "As we have seen, people can react differently to the very same situation. I want you to think about how people react differently to temptation or trials that come. Our text today describes how we should respond if we want to receive eternal life. Turn to the book of James and let's read James 1:1-8, 12-18."

INTO THE WORD

Ask two learners to read the two sections of the text aloud. Make a transparency of the reproducible activity "What Do We Know About This James?" from the next page. State: "To begin our study, we need to identify this James." Move the class into three groups and assign three Scripture references to each. Give the groups five to seven minutes to prepare a response for each one. Ask each group to tell what it has discovered. Then state: "Now let's see what James, the Lord's brother, has to say about trials and temptations." Ask the following questions:

1. How does James say we should respond to trials and temptations? (*"Consider it pure joy," v. 2*)

2. What are the benefits of responding to trials in that way? (*It develops perseverance, v. 3, and that leads to our becoming "mature and complete, not lacking anything," v. 4.*)

3. What does James promise will be the reward for persevering? (*"The crown of life," v. 12*) Discuss why some people "break" under trials while others actually get stronger. The different response is often due to their different focus. People who "break" under trials see only the immediate difficulty. But people who grow stronger see the big picture, the future result, not the present difficulty.

4. What does James say a person should do to know how to face trials? (*"If any of you lacks wisdom, he should ask God," v. 5.*)

5. What determines whether a person's prayer to God is granted? (*"He must believe and not doubt," v. 6.*)

Assign half of the class to each of the following two questions and give about three minutes for them to determine some answers:

1. What qualities or characteristics does James say a person has who perseveres under trials? (*"Wisdom," v. 5; "belief," v. 6; "love," v. 12.*)

2. Why should one never say, "God is tempting me"? (*God does not tempt anyone, v. 13; God gives only good and perfect gifts to man, v. 17; God does not change, v. 17.*) After a time, ask for their answers. State: "The source of temptation is inside us. Our own evil desire leads to our own sin resulting in our own death (vv. 14, 15). We need to know how to resist temptation."

INTO LIFE

No one is exempt from temptation. But how Christians respond determines whether they actually sin. Prior to class make a transparency of the reproducible activity "Build a Barricade Against Temptation" from the next page. Project that transparency before the class. Ask the following question and write the suggested answers on the transparency sheet around the fire: "What would you say are the most common temptations that Christians yield to in our community?" Assign a group of students to each temptation and give a few minutes to determine how Christians should respond. Ask: "In light of what James says to Christians who face temptation, what practical ways can a struggling Christian overcome falling into these temptations?" Ask the groups for recommended solutions. Write their suggestions on the stone blocks of the wall. Encourage them to build a barricade against temptation and close the class by praying for help in applying those practical ways.

What Do We Know About This James?

Read the following Scriptures and write what each one tells us about James.

Galatians 1:19

Mark 6:3

Matthew 4:23-25

Matthew 7:28, 29

Luke 8:19-21

John 7:5

Acts 1:13, 14

Galatians 2:9

Acts 15:13-29

Build a Barricade Against Temptation

What are the most common temptations that Christians yield to in our community? Write the names of several temptations on or near the fire below.

In light of what James says to Christians who face temptation, what practical ways can a struggling Christian overcome falling into these temptations? Write your suggestions on the stone blocks of the wall.

Faith Faces the World

Unit 1: Live in Faith
(Lessons 1-4)

FAITH AND ACTION

LESSON 2

Sep
14

WHY TEACH THIS LESSON?

A few years ago I had a small part in helping to plant a new church. It was quite exciting to see so many people in the area come to our very first service! Soon thereafter, the lead minister began to make follow-up calls on our first-time attendees (which, actually, was everyone if you think about it). One woman he called on was quite candid. She said she was very interested in making our church her family's new spiritual "home," but the problem was her husband. He preferred to place their membership with the well-established church down the street so he could remain "invisible" in their Sunday morning crowd of eight hundred. He wanted to go to church, sit, and do nothing!

Sadly, some of your learners today are infected with such an attitude. Sometimes to ease their conscience they may put more money in the offering plate so the church can afford additional staff members to get the jobs done. But the church only works when each of us works. Today's lesson stresses for your learners the importance of action and the dangers of inaction.

INTRODUCTION

"Wash your hands, boys," Mom called. "We'll have supper in a minute." That was so long ago that our farm home had no running water and no bathroom. My brother beat me to the wash bench just inside the kitchen door. Savoring his victory, he took his time about dipping water from the bucket to the basin and washing his hands. Meanwhile I looked through the screen door at a robin gathering his supper bug by bug from the tiny lawn behind the house. Then the plot thickened. I saw a cat crouching behind a clump of mums, obviously hoping the bird would come close enough to become his supper. Breathless, I watched the little drama of life and death while minutes ticked away. Finally the robin did come within range, and the cat pounced. But the bird was too quick for him. He took flight a scant inch ahead of the slashing claws, and I started breathing again.

At that moment Mom called again: "Come on, boys. Supper's on." We took our places at the table and bowed our heads while Dad spoke a short prayer. Then Mom turned to me with a gentle rebuke: "Go back and wash your hands."

A. FORGETTING AND NEGLECTING

I wish I could say I quickly outgrew the habit of forgetting my duty, but I didn't. Only yesterday, engrossed in lesson 1 of this series, I forgot it was my turn to help distribute the mail in the retirement home where I live. I did not remember until the telephone rang and a good friend gave me the gentle rebuke.

Do we Christians become so engrossed in earning our living and enjoying our lives that we forget our duties to God? I mean the duty of reading his Word and applying it in our daily living, the duty of helping one another at every opportunity, the duty of keeping up an attractive and helpful program of worship in the church and teaching in the Sunday school, the duty of maintaining happy fellowship and mutual encouragement among the saints, the duty of doing "good to all people, especially to those who belong to the family of believers" (Galatians

DEVOTIONAL READING:
MATTHEW 7:21-27

BACKGROUND SCRIPTURE:
JAMES 1:19–2:26; 5:7-20

PRINTED TEXT:
JAMES 1:22-27; 2:8, 9, 14-17;
5:13-16

LESSON AIMS

After participating in this lesson, each student will be able to:

1. List several features of a living and active faith.

2. Explain why faith must be active to be real.

3. Work with others in the class to develop a project that would enable members to help the needy.

KEY VERSE

Do not merely listen to the word, and so deceive yourselves. Do what it says.   —James 1:22

6:10), the duty of sharing the gospel with people who need it, the duty of supporting those who give their full time to various Christian ministries, the duty of being the salt of the earth and the light of the world (Matthew 5:13-16).

Is it also possible that some of us do not *forget* all these duties but *neglect* them anyway? That is even worse than forgetting, for "anyone . . . who knows the good he ought to do and doesn't do it, sins" (James 4:17).

B. LESSON BACKGROUND

As noted in last week's lesson, practical James is interested in what we do. Today he reminds us of our duties and rebukes our neglect of them. The immediate background of our text lies in the verse just before it: "Get rid of all moral filth and the evil that is so prevalent and humbly accept the word planted in you, which can save you" (James 1:21). But James says it is not enough to receive the Word and cherish it in our hearts. We need it to direct the work of our hands.

I. ACCEPTABLE RELIGION (JAMES 1:22-27)

Many people have used or heard the phrase, "That's a dead church." Dead churches are all about us, unfortunately. But James has the solution for bringing dead churches and lifeless Christians back to life.

A. THE CALL TO ACTION (v. 22)

22. Do not merely listen to the word, and so deceive yourselves. Do what it says.

Christian teaching is designed to graft God's Word into our minds and hearts (v. 21), to make it a vital part of our thinking and our emotions. But you are fooling yourself if you think you are a good Christian when you have *the word* in your mind and heart but not in your hands and feet.

B. THE FORGETFUL NON-DOER (vv. 23, 24)

23, 24. Anyone who listens to the word but does not do what it says is like a man who looks at his face in a mirror and, after looking at himself, goes away and immediately forgets what he looks like.

You don't look in a *mirror* just for the privilege of admiring yourself for a few seconds. You look to see if you need to comb your hair, adjust your tie, or renew your makeup. If any of these is needed, you provide it without delay. That is what makes the look in the mirror worthwhile. But some people, even some Christians, hear the Word of God point out some error or sin in their behavior and then go on their way and forget what they just heard! In that case the hearing is worthless. A change to better conduct is what gives value to the hearing.

C. THE BLESSED DOER (v. 25)

25. But the man who looks intently into the perfect law that gives freedom, and continues to do this, not forgetting what he has heard, but doing it—he will be blessed in what he does.

God's Word is called *the perfect law that gives freedom* (see also James 2:12) because those who hear it and obey it are made free (John 8:31, 32). They are made free from the bondage of sin (John 8:34) and free from the punishment of sin (Romans 6:23). If anyone looks into God's Word and changes his conduct to match God's teaching and continues to live by that teaching, *he will be blessed in what he does.* Our godly actions and deeds don't "earn" this blessing, of course, but they do demonstrate the sincerity of our faith (see James 2:17, 18). In his Sermon on the Mount, Jesus also stressed the importance of being a "doer" (see Matthew 5:19; 7:21, 26, 27).

WHAT DO YOU THINK?

James says deception and real Christianity do not mix. What can each Christian do to avoid spiritual self-deception?

Use this poster from the Adult Visuals *packet to illustrate James 1:22.*

NEEDED: AN EXTERNAL REFERENCE POINT

Jerry Dragoo is a biology professor at the University of New Mexico. He dresses in traditional "western" style—cowboy boots, jeans, and a belt with a big, fancy buckle. But instead of the usual silver and turquoise inlays, the buckle features a skunk standing on its front legs, ready to defend itself as only a skunk can do!

Skunks are Dragoo's academic specialty. They are in his lab, his backyard, and there are even three in his home—none of which has been "fixed." He says, "My wife has a problem with that." On his first assignment as a student studying skunks, Dragoo got "sprayed." When he couldn't smell anything, he wondered why people spoke so disparagingly of skunks. But back at school, he was kicked out of the building. Since then he has often been a *persona non grata* and has been ejected from meetings, evicted from his residence, and generally avoided in public, all because he has almost no sense of smell. His work is significant, but it hasn't made people like to be around him!

We all need an external reference point—someone or something that can give us an unbiased evaluation of how we look and act (and smell!). For our actions and thoughts, the Word of God provides that point of reference. However, it is of practical value only if we pay attention to what it says about our lives.   —C. R. B.

D. AN ACTIVE SELF-DISCIPLINE (v. 26)

26. If anyone considers himself religious and yet does not keep a tight rein on his tongue, he deceives himself and his religion is worthless.

Picture a man who goes to church every Sunday, who perhaps leads in prayer when he is asked, and who may even be a deacon. But he fails to control *his tongue*. Perhaps he repeats unfounded gossip. Perhaps he is cruel and loud in judging others. Perhaps he loses his temper and curses. Such a person may fool himself, thinking himself to be a good Christian. He may make some others think he is a genuine and ardent follower of Christ. But when he lets his tongue run wild, he shows that his *religion is worthless*. James will have much more to say about the tongue in 3:1-12.

E. A PURE RELIGION (v. 27)

27. Religion that God our Father accepts as pure and faultless is this: to look after orphans and widows in their distress and to keep oneself from being polluted by the world.

We have just seen one mark of a phony Christian: an unruly tongue. Now we see two marks of a real Christian. First is generosity in taking care of *orphans and widows,* people unable to earn their own living. The Old Testament frequently connects these two groups of people as being some of the most helpless and vulnerable in the ancient world (see Exodus 22:22-24; Deuteronomy 10:18; 14:28, 29; and many others).

Second is keeping oneself morally pure, to avoid *being polluted by the world.* In the Christian's thinking, there is to be none of the world's selfishness or lust. Moral purity is an important theme in the New Testament (see 1 Timothy 5:22; 6:14; Titus 2:12; James 1:21; 2 Peter 1:4; 2:20; 3:14).

II. ACTIVE LOVE AND FAITH (JAMES 2:8, 9, 14-17)

Surely every Christian is aware of the high place love holds in Christianity (see Matthew 22:37-40; 1 John 3:11; 4:7-10). But faith is no less important. "Without faith it is impossible to please God, because anyone who comes to him must believe that he exists and that he rewards those who earnestly seek him" (Hebrews 11:6). Practical James would have us know that love and faith in our hearts and minds are powerless until they find expression in what we do.

WHAT DO YOU THINK?

What is our church doing to help those who are powerless to help themselves? What more ought to be done?

[Use Proverbs 14:31 and James 2:9; 4:17 in your discussion.]

WHAT DO YOU THINK?

A complete Christian, according to James, is one who deals well with temptation (avoids sin) and is known for taking positive action to reach out to others (performs good deeds). How can Christians do both?

DAILY BIBLE READINGS

Monday, Sept. 8—A Good Heart Produces Good (Luke 6:43-49)

Tuesday, Sept. 9—Act on the Word (James 1:19-25)

Wednesday, Sept. 10—Live Out Pure Religion (James 1:26–2:4)

Thursday, Sept. 11—Do Not Show Favoritism (James 2:5-13)

Friday, Sept. 12—Faith and Works Go Together (James 2:14-18)

Saturday, Sept. 13—Live With Patience (James 5:7-12)

Sunday, Sept. 14—Pray for One Another (James 5:13-20)

A. THE KINGLY LAW (v. 8)

8. If you really keep the royal law found in Scripture, "Love your neighbor as yourself," you are doing right.

The *Scripture* James refers to is Leviticus 19:18; see also Matthew 5:43; 19:19; Mark 12:31, 33. Loving *your neighbor as yourself* is *the royal law*, the kingly law. That may mean this law is established by the King of Heaven and earth, the Lord God Almighty. Or it may mean the law itself is the king of laws, ruling over all the other laws that regulate our relationships with others (see Romans 13:8-10). Whichever meaning James intends, we do *right* when we obey it, when we really do love our neighbors as we love ourselves. How well are we doing that?

LIVING (AND DYING) BY THE ROYAL LAW

Adam Mayblum was on the eighty-seventh floor of the north tower of the World Trade Center when a terrorist-commanded plane slammed into the building on September 11, 2001. He made it to safety, and then wrote an e-mail to twenty-five friends, describing his escape from the burning tower. His friends were so moved that they passed the story on to many others. Within twenty-four hours one hundred people whom Mayblum did not know had written to thank him for the story's impact on their lives; within four months one thousand strangers from around the world had written to him.

In his e-mail Mayblum described the smoke and fire at the top, and his conversations with people who did not escape. He also told of meeting the firefighters at the forty-fourth floor as they struggled to the top, sacrificing their lives (as we would learn later) for people they did not know, regardless of their race, nationality, or social station in life.

We don't know how many of those rescue workers were Christians. Some may merely have been doing their duty; others perhaps were simply expressing their humanitarian spirit. Regardless of what motivated them and regardless of what their faith may have been, they were living—and soon to be dying—examples of the royal law of which James speaks. Whether in crisis or in daily life, do we do as well as they in living up to the royal law of our King?   —C. R. B.

B. TRANSGRESSION AGAINST THE KING (v. 9)

9. But if you show favoritism, you sin and are convicted by the law as lawbreakers.

To *show favoritism* is to discriminate, to show more love to one neighbor than to another—perhaps because of who he or she "is" or has. See the example in verses 1-4 of this chapter in which a church welcomes a rich man more cordially than it welcomes a poor man. If we show such partiality instead of loving rich and poor alike, we *sin*. The royal law itself convicts us of transgression against that king of laws and against the great King who made that law. God himself "does not show favoritism" (Acts 10:34), so why should we?

C. DEAD FAITH (vv. 14-17)

14. What good is it, my brothers, if a man claims to have faith but has no deeds? Can such faith save him?

Emphatically the apostle Paul teaches that we are saved by God's grace through our *faith*, not by the good works we do (Romans 3:21-31; Galatians 2:16; Ephesians 2:8, 9). James does not contradict Paul, but adds that genuine *faith* makes a difference in what we do. If we really believe in God and love him, we try to do what he tells us to do (John 14:15). If a person says he or she believes in the God of the Bible, but still goes on in a life of wickedness, we know that that person's faith is fraudulent. Both Paul and James use Abraham as an example of a man with the right kind of faith (Romans 4; James 2:20-24).

15, 16. Suppose a brother or sister is without clothes and daily food. If one of you says to him, "Go, I wish you well; keep warm and well fed," but does nothing about his physical needs, what good is it?

Suppose a fellow Christian is out of a job and out of money. He is hungry; he is cold. Suppose you greet him with a cordial handshake and give him your good wishes, but nothing more. He is still hungry and cold. Your good wishes are worthless without food for the stomach and fuel for the furnace. Likewise, worthless is faith that does nothing but "believe" (cf. James 2:19). Certainly James isn't saying that we should reward lazy people by feeding them (see 2 Thessalonians 3:10). We put faith to work by meeting genuine needs, especially those of fellow Christians (Galatians 6:10; 1 John 3:17, 18).

17. In the same way, faith by itself, if it is not accompanied by action, is dead.

We have been saying that inactive *faith* is phony. Practical James is even more blunt. He says inactive faith is *dead*. What mourning there would be if we would have a mass funeral for all the dead faith in the church!

III. ADVICE FOR SPECIAL CASES (JAMES 5:13-16)

Again we note that James is a practical writer. He knows the specific things that concern his readers, and he has suggestions—actually, requirements from God!—about what to do.

A. The Afflicted (v. 13a)

13a. Is any one of you in trouble? He should pray.

So many things afflict us! There is poverty. There are people who don't like us. There is loss of a loved one. There is loneliness. Whatever your affliction, James says to tell your Heavenly Father about your misery. That in itself may help more than you think it can. In his 1904 book *Quiet Talks on Prayer,* S. D. Gordon observes that, "You can do more than pray, *after* you have prayed. But you can *not* do more than pray *until* you have prayed." Perhaps God will help you make a plan to bring cheer to someone whose affliction is worse than yours. You are sure to feel better as you carry out that plan. Or perhaps you will think of a way to do something good for that person who dislikes you. You'll be surprised to see how much that will help you.

The New Testament stresses the importance of prayer in many places (e.g., Romans 15:30-32). Acts 16:25 demonstrates that we can both pray and sing in the midst of affliction.

B. The Merry (v. 13b)

13b. Is anyone happy? Let him sing songs of praise.

Many of the *happy* folk today choose to celebrate with bawdy songs and booze. The next day they think they will never be happy again. James has a better idea. And see what a collection of *songs of praise* is found in Psalms 103–107! Some of the psalms have been set to music in our modern praise choruses. Or, if you prefer, perhaps you will call family and friends to the piano to sing grand old Christian hymns. If you don't have other songs in mind, look at the index of your hymnbook. And the next day you will be happy still.

C. The Sick (vv. 14, 15)

14. Is any one of you sick? He should call the elders of the church to pray over him and anoint him with oil in the name of the Lord.

Today's *elders* agree about praying for the *sick*, but many are puzzled about anointing *him with oil.* Some obey literally without question: "James says to do it,

How to Say It

Ephesians. Ee-FEE-zhunz.
Galatians. Guh-LAY-shunz.
Hebrews. HEE-brews.

PRAYER

Heavenly Father, we believe in you, we believe in Jesus, and we love you both. Give us wisdom to see what our faith and love ought to be doing, and give us energy and enthusiasm to do it joyfully. In Jesus' name, amen.

WHAT DO YOU THINK?

James makes no provision for passing on confessional information to anyone but God. Does this forbid sharing with another? When would such sharing become gossip, and what steps can the church take both to discourage gossiping and discipline the gossips? [See 2 Corinthians 12:20.]

WHAT DO YOU THINK?

Notice that James does not say, "prayer is powerful." James's requirement is that of persistent prayer coming from a righteous person. How can the church teach both the discipline of prayer as well as the attitudes and actions expected of the one who prays?

[Matthew 6:5-8 and 1 Peter 3:7 may help you in your discussion.]

THOUGHT TO REMEMBER

What you do today is your gift to God.

so we do it." Some note that oil had medicinal value in the ancient world. Since our medical technology has improved, they say, using oil isn't much needed any longer. Still others point out that anointing with oil in the Bible is symbolic for setting things and people apart for God in a special way (cf. Exodus 40:9, 15). They say it should be taken that way here as well.

Others like to avoid debate and let each elder do as he thinks best about anointing the sick. The most important thing is to recognize our need to place ultimate trust in *the Lord* since healing comes from no other.

15. And the prayer offered in faith will make the sick person well; the Lord will raise him up. If he has sinned, he will be forgiven.

Whatever we think about anointing the sick with oil, it is notable that James attributes the outcome to *the prayer offered in faith,* not to the anointing. But a skeptic thinks this promise is far too confident. "Sometimes," says the skeptic, "a *sick person* dies instead of getting *well.*" But the Greek word translated *make . . . well* often refers to salvation in the New Testament. If you think about it, you know death is the best possible recovery for a Christian who is sick. The one who dies is safe from illness forever, safe also from pain and grief and fear. Note the reference to the forgiveness of sins. That is the best part of the promise. This Christian is safe in Heaven for eternity. He or she is raised up far higher than mere restoration to health on earth.

D. THE FAULTY (v. 16)

16. Therefore confess your sins to each other and pray for each other so that you may be healed. The prayer of a righteous man is powerful and effective.

This seems to broaden the instruction given in verse 15. All of us have *sins,* don't we? We can confess them *to each other* instead of only to the elders or other church leaders. All of us, elders or not, can *pray for each other* for healing, either from physical sickness or from moral weakness. If I am troubled by some fault or sin of mine, I can be greatly helped by telling a good Christian friend about it. He can help me keep from continuing or repeating my wrongdoing. If I have to go where I will be tempted, perhaps he can go with me and give me strength. He can pray with me and for me. We do well to keep in mind that the *prayer of a righteous man is powerful and effective,* whether he is an elder or not.

CONCLUSION

James has had some very important things to say to every church in every century. In light of that, are you satisfied with how you're "living out" your Christianity? Do your love and faith just make you feel comfortable in church on Sunday, or do they make you feel uncomfortable until you make some improvements in your Christian living, or until you do something to help someone else?

A year ago, Juan was a ten-year-old immigrant from Mexico. He was in third grade because he was too big for a first-grade seat. He couldn't even do first-grade work because he spoke only Spanish. Joe was working a night shift, so he could tutor Juan. He bought third-grade books, and the two worked together every day after school. After working through the summer Juan was ready for fourth grade.

Jeremy was haunted by the thought that he was not doing enough for the Lord. He planned to be a missionary, but when he talked with advisors at a Bible college, another plan emerged. He kept his well-paying job; he increased his contributions for missions; he sent his two sons to Bible college. Now they are ministers, and Jeremy believes that they are doing twice as much for the Lord as he would be doing if he had become a missionary.

How do these examples affect you?

Discovery Learning

This page contains an alternative lesson plan emphasizing learning activities. Classes desiring such student involvement will find these suggestions helpful. The next page is a reproducible activity page to further enhance discovery learning.

LEARNING GOALS

After this lesson each student will be able to:

1. List several features of a living and active faith.

2. Explain why faith must be active to be real.

3. Work with others in the class to develop a project that would enable members to help the needy.

INTO THE LESSON

Prior to this week's lesson, purchase several packs of different flavors of chewing gum. Open all the packs and slide the foil-wrapped gum sticks out of the paper sleeves. Mix the various sticks of gum and re-insert each foil-wrapped gum stick into a different paper sleeve. Make certain that the label on the paper wrapper does not match the gum in the foil. Next, place the gum sticks back into the packs so that the labels on the sticks of gum match the labels on the packs.

Begin the lesson by holding up the various packs of gum and stating, "To begin the lesson this week, I want each of you to select a stick of gum from these packs." After the gum has made it around the room and everyone has taken a stick of gum, have the learners move their chairs to form groups based on the flavors of gum they chose After the class has moved into small groups, state: "Now, unwrap the gum and chew it (or smell it)."

Project a transparency of the reproducible activity "Ways People Deceive People" from the next page. State: "All of you have been deceived this morning. The gum you selected was not the kind you thought it was. I changed the wrappers to deceive you. Some recognized it; others did not. That's what happens in life. What ways do people deceive others today?" Write suggested answers on the transparency for all to see. After getting some answers, state: "Today's text reveals another kind of deception, self-deception. Turn to James and let's see how Christians sometimes deceive themselves."

INTO THE WORD

Assign James 1:22-27 to group one, James 2:8, 9, 14-17 to group two, and James 5:13-16 to group three. Appoint a member of each group to read the text aloud to the class. For this study activity, prepare the following questions for each group on a separate sheet of paper. Hand the question sheet to each group and state, "Now that we've read the whole lesson Scripture, I'd like each group to discuss the questions you have. After a few min-

utes, I will ask for your answers." (After about eight minutes, have a member of each group give their answers.)

Questions for Group One:

1. What are the characteristics of a living and active faith? (*"Do what the word says,"* 1:22)

2. How does James indicate a person could be self-deceived? (*"Merely listen to the word,"* 1:22; *"does not keep a tight rein on his tongue,"* 1:26.)

3. Describe the two qualities of pure, faultless religion. (*"To look after orphans and widows"* and *"keep oneself from being polluted by the world,"* 1:27.)

4. What causes a person to be blessed by God? (*"Not forgetting what he has heard, but doing it,"* 1:25.)

Questions for Group Two:

1. What physical needs does James say one should meet to show genuine faith? (*Clothes, food,* 2:15, 16.)

2. What happens when Christians show preference to some people over others. (*They sin,* 2:9.)

3. What are the characteristics of a living and active faith? (*"Love your neighbor as yourself,"* 2:8.)

4. Why must faith be active to be real? (*"Faith by itself . . . is dead,"* 2:17.)

Questions for Group Three:

1. What does James recommend that the church do for a sick member? (*Elders are to pray and anoint him with oil,* 5:14.)

2. What should a Christian do about personal failures and faults? (*"Confess your sins to each other and pray,"* 5:16.)

3. What are the characteristics of a living and active faith? (*Pray, sing songs of praise, or worship regardless of circumstances,* 5:13, 14.)

4. Why must faith be active to be real? (*"The prayer of a righteous man is powerful and effective,"* 5:16.)

INTO LIFE

State: "James makes it clear that faith means action! Otherwise, we deceive ourselves and our faith is dead. Now, let's develop a class project to demonstrate our faith to the needy." Ask the class to brainstorm suggested projects and write those on the chalkboard. Next, ask each small group to decide which one they want to do. Give each group a copy of the reproducible activity "Project Planning Sheet" from the next page. Ask the members to plan a specific project to demonstrate their faith. Close the session with a prayer circle asking God's blessing on the projects that have been planned.

Ways People Deceive People

Write in the spaces provided the various ways that people deceive other people.

DECEPTION

DECEPTION

DECEPTION

DECEPTION

DECEPTION

DECEPTION

DECEPTION

Project Planning Sheet

Plan a specific project that you or several of you can work on that will both help someone in need and demonstrate your faith. Write in the details below.

What?
What will you do?

Why?
What is the purpose?
What need will be met?

When?
When can you start?
How long will it take to finish

Where?
Where will this be done? Where will your
group meet to go there together?

Who?
Who will be involved? What specific role
can be assigned to each?

FAITH AND WISDOM

LESSON 3

DEVOTIONAL READING:
COLOSSIANS 1:3-14
BACKGROUND SCRIPTURE:
JAMES 3
PRINTED TEXT:
JAMES 3

Sep
21

WHY TEACH THIS LESSON?

There seems to be many kinds of wisdom in the world. For example, we've all heard of the distinction between being "book smart" and being "street smart." But the type of wisdom we're all exposed to first is what might be called *parental wisdom*. When we came home sobbing because a first-grade classmate ridiculed us our parents taught us to say, "Stick and stones may break my bones, but words will never harm me." As we grew older we came to realize that that's not really true—words can indeed do great harm. But that was the type of comforting wisdom that we needed for the moment, and it got us through a rough spot.

The spiritual wisdom we get from our heavenly Father is always true and always applies. This kind of wisdom gets us through rough spots in our Christian walk—especially as it teaches us to control the tongue and curtail selfish ambition. Spiritual wisdom is what each of your learners desperately needs because it prepares them for eternity. Spiritual wisdom is what today's lesson is all about.

INTRODUCTION

Mary was delighted when husband John remembered her birthday and took her out for a fabulous dinner at their favorite restaurant. The evening was pure joy until Mary began to cough. She smothered the coughs with a napkin, and they were not loud. In fact, they were so quiet that Mary distinctly heard a low-voiced but angry comment from another table: "That coughing! She makes me sick!"

Mary almost strangled in trying to stop coughing, but she failed. She struggled to her feet and staggered from the room, blinded by her streaming tears, tears of mingled grief and rage. John had no choice but to follow, leaving the fabulous dinner unfinished and the pretty little birthday cake untouched.

Mary and John have never seen their favorite restaurant again. Dining out has lost all its charm for Mary. Even on their wedding anniversary, she wants to eat at home. Tears flood her eyes anew when she thinks how she made another diner sick, and how cruelly that diner responded.

And the woman who was sickened? Probably she never gave it a second thought, was not really sick, finished her dinner complacently, and never suspected that she had hurt anyone.

A. WORDS THAT WOUND

There are many words that wound. Some of them are spoken maliciously, with the intention of wounding. More are spoken thoughtlessly or jokingly. But they hurt. Don't you remember a time when you wept over a careless or malicious remark? Worse than that, do you remember when you carelessly or maliciously wounded someone else's spirit with your words? This is not new in the twenty-first century. James took note of it back in century one.

B. LESSON BACKGROUND

Although brought up under the strict standards of Jewish law, James knew that the accepted teachers did not always live by their own teaching (Matthew

LESSON AIMS

After participating in this lesson, each student will be able to:

1. Recall the various sins that are caused by an unwise use of the tongue.

2. Compare the way the tongue is used by one who has "wisdom from below" with that of one with godly wisdom.

3. Create a personal reminder to use wisdom in his or her speech during the coming week.

KEY VERSE:

Who is wise and understanding among you? Let him show it by his good life, by deeds done in the humility that comes from wisdom. —James 3:13

Lesson 3 Notes

23:1-3). Writing to Jewish Christians living abroad among the Gentiles, he also knew about the so-called "wisdom" that continually circulated in the ancient world. In this lesson we shall see how he urged those readers to be careful with their talk: to be always truthful, always sincere, always helpful. We shall see also how he urged them to see the difference between God's wisdom and human wisdom, and to make God's wisdom their own.

I. TEACHERS AND TONGUES (JAMES 3:1-12)

In everyday conversation we answer one another promptly, not taking time to think before we speak. With the best of intentions sometimes we say things that are untrue, unkind, or unhelpful. There will be no conversation if we must stop and think for an hour, or even ten minutes, before we respond. So we need to be armed in advance with Christian truth, principles, and motives—so well armed that we shall rarely lose our way in conversation or teaching.

A. WARNING! (v. 1)
1. Not many of you should presume to be teachers, my brothers, because you know that we who teach will be judged more strictly.

If your Sunday school is constantly trying to enlist more *teachers*, you may be disappointed to see James's advice that *not many* Christians undertake that work. Paul urged Timothy to be training teachers (2 Timothy 2:2). Then why does James advise as he does?

James certainly does not want Christians to be untaught. But he *does* want them to be taught truly, correctly, properly. Teachers in the first-century church had a high status (Acts 13:1; Ephesians 4:11). This status is a dangerous temptation for those thinking that their own wisdom makes them natural teachers. But more is expected of a teacher than of a new Christian, who needs to be taught. The teacher is held to a higher standard, has a greater responsibility, and *will be judged more strictly* for failure.

If our churches need more teachers we certainly must be looking for them; and we must search for people who not only understand Christian teaching and live by it, but also have the ability to teach it clearly and convincingly.

What Do You Think?

James says that teachers will be held to a higher standard. What does that mean for people other than teachers? To what degree are they accountable?

[Matthew 12:36 and Hebrews 13:17 may help your discussion.]

B. STUMBLING (v. 2)
2. We all stumble in many ways. If anyone is never at fault in what he says, he is a perfect man, able to keep his whole body in check.

The fact that *we all stumble in many ways* means that all teachers (including James himself) go astray at some time or other in a variety of ways.

None of us intends to go astray *in what he says*. But sins of the tongue are especially hard to control. Frequently we need to say something quickly, and we fail to take time to think about it. So it's easy to slip up, to say the wrong thing, just as a person walking may accidentally stumble over a rough place in the path. As a result, we say something that we later wish we had not said, or we fail to say what we should have said.

The wrong word seems to slip out so easily, so quickly, so uncontrollably—to be able to *never* be wrong in words spoken is so difficult! But when we become mature in this area, we are *able to keep* the *whole body in check*. What a worthwhile goal for teachers and non-teachers alike!

C. ILLUSTRATIONS AND APPLICATIONS (vv. 3-6)
3. When we put bits into the mouths of horses to make them obey us, we can turn the whole animal.

A "bit" is a small part of a bridle, and a bridle is only as big as the horse's head, and the horse is many times as big as the head. But think about how that tiny bit controls *the whole* horse!

4. Or take ships as an example. Although they are so large and are driven by strong winds, they are steered by a very small rudder wherever the pilot wants to go.

If you have ever seen a ship in dry dock, you may have been surprised to see how *small* the *rudder* was. Yet that little rudder turns a huge ocean liner to the right or the left, wherever *the pilot wants* it *to go*.

5a. Likewise the tongue is a small part of the body, but it makes great boasts.

The tongue is not a large body *part*, and usually it is hidden from sight. Yet the tongue can tell a tremendous truth or a monstrous lie, make or break a friendship, start or stop a war. People such as Hitler, Hussein, and bin Laden led entire nations astray with their tongues.

5b, 6. Consider what a great forest is set on fire by a small spark. The tongue also is a fire, a world of evil among the parts of the body. It corrupts the whole person, sets the whole course of his life on fire, and is itself set on fire by hell.

In bold figures of speech James sets forth the damage done by evil talk. *The tongue . . . is a fire:* that is, a small thing with tremendous destructive power (cf. Proverbs 16:27; 26:21). Some forest fires are started when campers go home without extinguishing their campfires completely. The small smoldering embers that remain ignite a great conflagration that destroys thousands of acres of woodland.

The tongue is like that. Every kind of *evil* in the *world* can be generated by vicious talk (Proverbs 7:21-23; Romans 16:18).

The relation of the tongue to the other *parts of the body* is such that a foul tongue *corrupts the whole person:* dirty talk makes the whole person dirty, corrupt, despicable (cf. Mark 7:15). A fiery tongue *sets the whole course of his life on fire:* it so inflames a person's very being that the effect of his or her life is destructive. We can guess easily the source of the foul talk that defiles and destroys—it comes from *hell*.

D. OUR DOMINION (v. 7)

7. All kinds of animals, birds, reptiles and creatures of the sea are being tamed and have been tamed by man,

A circus is a fascinating illustration of what is written here, and of God's original decree of humanity's dominion (Genesis 1:26). Massive elephants and savage tigers move in smooth harmony at the ringmaster's command, as if they could understand his language. Perhaps your own dog will "sit," "stay," or "come" when you speak the word.

E. THE TONGUE'S FREEDOM (v. 8)

8. . . . but no man can tame the tongue. It is a restless evil, full of deadly poison.

A *man* may control elephants and tigers, and still let his *tongue* escape his control and strike with *deadly poison*. Someone who loses his or her temper is likely to lose control of the tongue at the same time. Even within a loving family circle a tongue liberated by anger may utter ugly sarcasm, cruel criticism, or unjust accusations. Thus the tongue may deeply wound someone dearly loved by the owner of the tongue.

However, let us concede that James uses a bit of hyperbole when he says *no man can tame the tongue*. Some people can and do control their tongues. My own parents were such people. In more than twenty years of living with them, I never heard either of their tongues break free and rant against the other, or against anyone else. Even when they were provoked, their speech was rational,

WHAT DO YOU THINK?

James says that keeping the tongue in check is the first step to keeping all other parts of the body under control. What are some steps to take in controlling the tongue?

[Psalm 119:11, 105 can start your discussion.]

WHAT DO YOU THINK?

Hurtful words spoken by those with differences of opinion often are the root cause of many church fights or splits. How can the church develop ways to help resolve disputes and at the same time help bring to maturity those who would use their tongues in destructive ways?

[Use Proverbs 6:16-19; Matthew 5:23, 24; 18:15-17; Galatians 6:1; 2 Timothy 4:2; and James 3:17, 18 to frame your discussion.]

WHAT DO YOU THINK?

There is an old saying, "You can't unscramble an egg." If a Christian does misspeak, what steps can be taken to reduce the possibility of creating the terrible results listed in verses 5, 6, and 8?

[Use Philippians 2:1-8 to start your discussion. Also compare 2 Timothy 4:2 with Titus 3:10.]

temperate, controlled. We must remember, however, that a hyperbole is not a falsehood. What James says is true even though there are exceptions to it. People do lose control of their tongues. Uncontrolled tongues do rant irrationally, intemperately, even falsely. So what do you do? You keep your own tongue under control. You know you can do it if God helps you. So you pray, as David did (Psalm 39:1-3).

F. THE INCONSISTENT TONGUE (vv. 9-12)

9, 10. With the tongue we praise our Lord and Father, and with it we curse men, who have been made in God's likeness. Out of the same mouth come praise and cursing. My brothers, this should not be.

What an amazing thing—we use our tongues to *praise* the Lord and then turn right around and *curse* people who *have been made* in his image (Genesis 1:26, 27)! Of course, some people have horribly defaced the image of God by their sin. We have to take a stand against evil and rebuke it (Luke 17:3). Sometimes we ought to do that privately (Matthew 18:15); sometimes we have to do it publicly (1 Timothy 5:20). But we do that by using God's Word to point out the right way and show the wrong that has been done, not by cursing the one who has done wrong. Of course, some people really are eternally accursed, but that judgment is not for us to make; it is for the Lord (Matthew 25:41-46).

11, 12. Can both fresh water and salt water flow from the same spring? My brothers, can a fig tree bear olives, or a grapevine bear figs? Neither can a salt spring produce fresh water.

Ancient villages depended on nearby springs to produce usable *water*. So it is with a Christian's talk. The *fig tree* produces *figs* every year, never *olives*, never grapes, never thorns or thistles. That is how you know what kind of a tree it is (Matthew 7:16-20). Likewise a Christian can be identified by his or her talk. It is always good, clean, wholesome, uplifting Christian talk (cf. Ephesians 4:29; 5:4).

CONFLICTING IDENTITIES

In September 2001, San Francisco police arrested a man for robbing eight banks and attempting to rob another. When taken into custody, the man admitted his crimes. He was an unlikely suspect, since in daily life he had a $98,000 job as an air traffic controller. He was known to be very cool under the pressure of his job, a trait he exhibited during his short career as a bank robber. Described by friends as a nice, friendly person, he took his teenage sons and their friends camping and to ball games.

Investigation showed he was unable to make his salary stretch far enough to cover his expenses, which included large bills for alimony, child support, and school tuition. So he apparently allowed another side of himself to grow alongside his law-abiding, family-man persona. The court ordered that he undergo psychiatric evaluation to determine his sanity.

It could be argued that there must be something "insane" about a man who risked a good job and his reputation in everyday life to take up a second, risky and unlawful, identity. But James says we demonstrate a similar type of split in our persona when we let our tongues get out of control. When Christians bless God in worship and curse others elsewhere, it may not be a mark of insanity, but it certainly doesn't make sense.

—C. R. B.

II. WORDS AND WISDOM (JAMES 3:13-18)

After thinking so much about the tongue with its follies and failures, it is fitting to turn our thoughts to wisdom. Wisdom is what every tongue needs to restrain and guide it. But sometimes wisdom is not easily recognized, for human

DAILY BIBLE READINGS

Monday, Sept. 15—*Search for Wisdom (Proverbs 2:1-5)*

Tuesday, Sept. 16—*God Gives Wisdom (Proverbs 2:6-11)*

Wednesday, Sept. 17—*Be Careful to Live Wisely (Ephesians 5:11-17)*

Thursday, Sept. 18—*A Prayer for Wisdom (Colossians 1:9-14)*

Friday, Sept. 19—*Keep the Tongue in Check (James 3:1-6)*

Saturday, Sept. 20—*Bless and Do Not Curse (James 3:7-12)*

Sunday, Sept. 21—*Godly Wisdom Is Pure (James 3:13-18)*

folly likes to masquerade as wisdom, and capable but unwary people may be deceived. With a few well-chosen words, James describes the true wisdom and the phony.

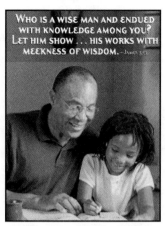

This poster from the Adult Visuals *packet illustrates the Key Verse, James 3:13.*

A. The Proof (v. 13)

13. Who is wise and understanding among you? Let him show it by his good life, by deeds done in the humility that comes from wisdom.

If asked, each one of us would like to state with confidence, "I am a *wise* person who has *understanding.*" But James wants an answer in the form of our *deeds* (works). A person who does foolish things is not wise. If a person is wise, his or her lifestyle is *good,* unselfish, helpful. That good lifestyle is the stage on which each individual work is done. Further, it is done with wise meekness or *humility* (cf. Matthew 5:5). Now, how wise are you?

B. The Lower Wisdom (vv. 14-16)

14. But if you harbor bitter envy and selfish ambition in your hearts, do not boast about it or deny the truth.

Imagine a popular leader in a certain church. Perhaps he is a handsome man with a ready smile and charming manners. With his pleasant ways and flattering words he wins followers easily, but this fellow is winning them for himself rather than for Christ. His heart is full of *bitter envy* of other leaders. Instead of cooperating with them, he belittles them, their opinions, and their plans. In so doing, he generates strife (factionalism) instead of unified fellowship. James warns such a one *not* to *boast*—don't be proud of yourself and your accomplishments and opinions. Speak well of other leaders rather than praising yourself. (This is part of the meekness of v. 13.) Don't exaggerate your own goodness, your own wisdom, your own accomplishment because when you do you *deny the truth.*

15. Such "wisdom" does not come down from heaven but is earthly, unspiritual, of the devil.

The *wisdom* that glorifies self is not God-given. It arises out of *earthly* ambition, selfishness, and the prompting of the devil (cf. 1 Corinthians 1:20; 2:5, 6). One who asks God for wisdom (Proverbs 2:6; James 1:5) is rewarded with the kind described in verse 17 (below).

16. For where you have envy and selfish ambition, there you find disorder and every evil practice.

If *envy and selfish ambition* are prompted by the devil (v. 15), we can be sure they are not good for us. This kind of confusion infected the church at Corinth (2 Corinthians 12:20). But *disorder and every evil practice* please no one but Satan and some victims of his deceit.

C. The Higher Wisdom (vv. 17, 18)

17. But the wisdom that comes from heaven is first of all pure; then peace-loving, considerate, submissive, full of mercy and good fruit, impartial and sincere.

Paul lists the "fruit of the Spirit" in Galatians 5:22, 23. Here, James lists what may be called the "fruit of *wisdom.*" Wisdom that is *pure* has no trace of the phoniness that is earthly, sensual, and devilish. *Peace-loving* wisdom will not produce strife, as selfishness and pride often do. A person of *considerate* wisdom does not try to overpower others and force opinions on them.

A wise person stands firm for truth and righteousness. In matters of opinion, however, this kind of person is *submissive.* This means such a person listens to reason and compromises when appropriate. A wise person shows *mercy* by being kind, helpful, and quick to forgive. Wisdom is evident in a person's *good* fruits or

How to Say It

Corinthians. Kor-IN-thee-unz.
Ephesians. Ee-FEE-zhunz.
Galatians. Guh-LAY-shunz.
Philippians. Fih-LIP-ee-unz.

PRAYER

Our gracious Father in Heaven, we thank you for the clear guidance of your Word, and we thank you for the privilege of using the minds and wisdom you have given us to make decisions in the light of your Word. Give us wisdom day by day according to our need. We pray in Jesus' name, amen.

WHAT DO YOU THINK?

Using the principles in today's lesson, what ingredients do Christians need to make use of in order to be good peacemakers? How can we be peacemakers without becoming doormats, or simply "sweeping things under the rug" to keep people on friendly terms with each other?

THOUGHT TO REMEMBER

"Wisdom is supreme; therefore get wisdom" (Proverbs 4:7).

deeds to others, especially to fellow Christians (Galatians 6:10). Impartiality and sincerity are two of the characteristics of wisdom that is pure.

LIVING WITH INTEGRITY

It seemed like a good idea at the time. A professor at Columbia University Business School decided to do some research on how businesses handle customer complaints. So he wrote—on official university stationery—identical letters of complaint to two hundred and forty restaurants. In the letter he falsely complained that he had contracted food poisoning on an evening when he and his wife had eaten there. The poisoning ruined a "romantic wedding anniversary," and also resulted in his curling up—violently ill—in the fetal position on the floor of their home bathroom all night.

Several restaurants checked their reservation lists for the evening in question and found the professor's claims to be spurious. Although his research was well-intentioned, he was forced to send out letters of apology, admitting his lack of integrity. Then he had to face an academic review board to determine the fate of his career.

James tells us that our manner of life should demonstrate the integrity that comes from living in accordance with the wisdom that comes from above. The Bible is a ready source of instruction as to the kind of attitudes, speech, and actions that are to characterize the life of the Christian. True wisdom will demonstrate itself in relationships that are honest, pure, and straightforward. Do our lives show it?

—C. R. B.

18. Peacemakers who sow in peace raise a harvest of righteousness.

Envying and strife provide the soil where confusion grows along with "every evil work" (v. 16). But wise people that make *peace* find in that peace the soil where they can plant the seeds that grow into *a harvest of righteousness,* their own and that of others. (See also 2 Corinthians 9:10; Philippians 1:11.)

CONCLUSION

As Christians we are called to "put on the full armor of God" (Ephesians 6:10-18) and "fight the good fight of the faith" (1 Timothy 6:12). So we sing "Onward, Christians Soldiers" with our feet tapping in martial tempo. But through the drumbeat we hear Paul urging, "If it is possible, as far as it depends on you, live at peace with everyone" (Romans 12:18). Jesus himself pronounced a blessing on "the peacemakers" in the Sermon on the Mount (Matthew 5:9). Wise indeed is the Christian who knows when to fight and when to make peace.

Of course, we are to resist the devil and drive him back in defeat (James 4:7). Naturally, we are to live in peace with our brothers and sisters in the family of God. But the devil is a master of disguise (2 Corinthians 11:14); and—let's face it—some of God's people stumble into ungodliness. So what do we do?

When there is a clear-cut decision between right and wrong, we choose the right. Example: May a Christian continue to live openly in an adulterous relationship? No, he may not. He must either give up that relationship or give up his membership in the church. That is the teaching of Scripture (1 Corinthians 5).

But some questions are not so readily answered. Example: May our teenagers conduct a series of car washes to pay their way to a Christian camp? The Bible does not say yes or no. Some of us think it is a great idea; some of us think Christian activities should be supported solely by the gifts of Christians (cf. 3 John 7). Each of us may express an opinion, but we do not quarrel to the point of splitting the church. One congregation may take a vote of its members. Another may accept the decision of its elders. In either case, the matter (which is not a doctrinal issue) is settled and peace is unbroken.

To recall our lesson title, this is the way of faith and wisdom.

Discovery Learning

This page contains an alternative lesson plan emphasizing learning activities. Classes desiring such student involvement will find these suggestions helpful. The next page is a reproducible activity page to further enhance discovery learning.

LEARNING GOALS

After participating in this lesson, each student will be able to:

1. Recall the various sins that are caused by an unwise use of the tongue.

2. Compare the way the tongue is used by one who has "wisdom from below" with that of one with godly wisdom.

3. Create a personal reminder to use wisdom in his or her speech during the coming week.

INTO THE LESSON

Prepare the following chart on either a transparency sheet to project or on the board. The title of the chart is, "The Tongue." Below the title there are two columns: left, "Godly Use"; right, "Sinful Use." Draw a horizontal line underneath the column titles and draw a vertical line between the columns. Begin class this week by saying: "Today's lesson focuses on the tongue. To begin the lesson I'd like us to brainstorm both positive and negative uses of the tongue. I've made a chart that has two columns. The tongue can be used in a godly way, but it can also be used in a sinful way. As you think of a use of the tongue, call it out and I'll put it on the appropriate side of the chart." (*Possible godly uses include the following: praying; thanking someone; asking forgiveness; encouraging. Possible sinful uses: lying; gossiping; taking God's name in vain; using profanity.*)

After a few minutes, summarize the godly and sinful ways the tongue is used. Say: "As you see, the tongue can be an instrument of evil, or it can be an instrument of good. Our text today explains the difficulty we have in controlling the tongue, and it suggests what we need to do. Turn to James 3 and let's read our lesson text."

INTO THE WORD

Ask each of six members of the class to read aloud three verses of James 3—today's lesson text. After the Scripture has been read, say, "To help us understand this text, I want us to move into small groups of three students each. In your group, I want you to answer the following questions."

1. List the ten analogies to the tongue that James makes in this passage. (*Bits in horses' mouths, v. 3; rudder of a ship, v. 4; a fire, v. 6; animals, birds, reptiles, creatures of the sea, v. 7; spring, v. 11; fig tree, grapevine, v. 12.*)

2. List the five descriptions of the tongue that James gives. (*"A small part of the body," v. 5; "a fire," "a world of evil," v. 6; "a restless evil," "full of deadly poison," v. 8.*)

Allow several minutes for the groups to look up the answers to these two questions; then ask them to report their findings. As the groups reveal their answers, write them for display.

For this next activity, make enough copies of the reproducible activity "Wisdom: From Below and From Above" from the next page so that each small group may have one. Say: "James makes it perfectly clear that the tongue can be used either in a sinful way or in a godly way. Prepare two lists from James 3:13-18. First, list all the characteristics of the way the tongue is used by one who has 'wisdom from below.' (*"Bitter envy," "selfish ambition," v. 14; "earthly," "unspiritual," "of the devil," v. 15; "disorder," "evil practice," v. 16.*) Second, list all the characteristics of the way the tongue is used by one who has 'wisdom from above.'" (*"Good life," "deeds done in humility," v. 13; "pure," "peaceloving," "considerate," "submissive," "full of mercy," "good fruit," "impartial," "sincere," v. 17.*)

Say, "James says in verse two that a perfect man is one who 'is never at fault in what he says.' To live that way requires wisdom from above. Perhaps we have seen some speech habits we need to overcome. Perhaps we need to be reminded each day to speak with godly wisdom. Let's create a personal reminder to use wisdom in our speech this week."

INTO LIFE

People use all sorts of reminders to make certain specific actions are not forgotten. Prior to this week's lesson, make enough copies of the reproducible activity "Pop-Up Message Reminder" from the next page so that every student may have one. Distribute these reminders to the class, and say: "For the next few minutes, think about how you can apply this concept of godly wisdom in your life this week. Write a personal goal on the lines provided on the message reminder stating what you will either do or not do this week. Then, either type the message into a personal computer program that provides pop-up reminders or put it in a place where you will see it every day."

Close the class time with a prayer that you and your learners will follow God's wisdom.

Wisdom: From Below or From Above

Prepare two lists from James 3:13-18. First, list all the characteristics of the way the tongue is used by one who has "wisdom from below." Second, list all the characteristics of the way the tongue is used by one who has "wisdom from above."

WISDOM FROM BELOW	WISDOM FROM ABOVE

Pop-Up Message Reminder

"But the wisdom that comes from heaven is first of all pure; then peace-loving, considerate, submissive, full of mercy and good fruit, impartial and sincere. Peacemakers who sow in peace raise a harvest of righteousness." James 3:17, 18

Write a personal goal in the space provided stating what you will either do or will avoid this week to apply this wisdom from Heaven into your life. Have it "pop-up" each day this coming week to remind you.

With wisdom from above, I will

Signed _____

FAITH AND ATTITUDES

LESSON 4

DEVOTIONAL READING:
1 PETER 5:1-6

BACKGROUND SCRIPTURE:
JAMES 4:1–5:6

PRINTED TEXT:
JAMES 4:1-17

Sep
28

WHY TEACH THIS LESSON?

For centuries, Bible scholars have argued about "what we're born with." Do we come into the world stained with the guilt of Adam's sin, or not? Do we come into the world with free will, or not? Do we come into the world with impure tendencies, or do we pick those up somewhere along the way? The arguments dealing with the first two questions can fill books. But I can answer the third question quickly: Just look at the attitude of any two-year-old! What you'll see is self-centeredness. Everything is "Mine!" There is little regard for the feelings of others. And when you put two self-centered two-year-olds together, watch out!

Seeing this attitude in young children can, to a point, be amusing. But unspiritual attitudes such as self-centeredness in adults can be deadly to the health of a church. Your learners need to know that wrong attitudes are Satan's best tools! Defeating such attitudes takes self-examination. That's what this lesson is all about.

INTRODUCTION

Brenda and Linda are cousins, but they were born in the same week and they look like identical twins. Although both are girls, their mothers soon learned to dress one in pink and the other in blue when they were to be together at Grandma's. Thus each mom was sure of going home with her own baby.

When the two were old enough to ramble on all fours, it was fascinating to watch their antics as they got acquainted with each other and explored their environment. On Christmas Day Grandma's floor was littered, and the babies went from toy to toy too swiftly to give attention to any. Not surprisingly, both of them chanced to pick up one item at the same time. It was a bright paper Santa Claus designed to be hung in the window, but now on the floor Brenda clung to its head and Linda clung to its feet. There was a brief tug-of-war with wordless sounds of protest. Then Santa was in two pieces, and two little girls were in tears.

A. NO WINNER

How often we see an adult tug-of-war with like results! Neither contestant gets what he or she wants, and both are disappointed. And when the result is decisive and the winner takes all, that may be no better. The loser feels defeated, defrauded, and resentful; the winner learns the victory was not worth the struggle. When will grown-ups learn that cooperation is better than conflict?

B. LESSON BACKGROUND

In last week's lesson James drew a contrast between two kinds of wisdom. The lower kind produces "disorder and every evil practice." The higher kind is "first of all pure; then peace-loving." Our text concluded with this declaration: "Peacemakers who sow in peace raise a harvest of righteousness" (James 3:13-18). But that conclusion is not the end of what James has to say on that subject. This week we shall read more about war and peace, and the attitudes that produce them. As with our previous studies in James, we shall see several parallels to Jesus' "Sermon on the Mount."

LESSON AIMS

After participating in this lesson, each student will be able to:

1. Recall key points from James's warning against evil passions and his call to submission to God.

2. Tell how wrong attitudes can lead to conflicts between Christians.

3. Identify and confess a sinful attitude that has led to a disagreement with another believer.

KEY VERSE

Humble yourselves before the Lord, and he will lift you up.

— James 4:10

LESSON 4 NOTES

WHAT DO YOU THINK?

Bickering among church members often undermines the spirit and effectiveness of the local church. What must the local congregation teach its members in order to reduce the risk of strife within the church?

[You will find passages such as 1 Corinthians 13; Galatians 6:1-5; Ephesians 4:2, 3; and Philippians 2:3, 4 to be helpful in thinking about this question.]

I. CHURCH PROBLEMS (JAMES 4:1-5)

Conflict in the church is as old as the church itself. (See Acts 5:1-11; 9:26-28; and 15:1-31.) As we consider the word of James, we discover some typical sources of church conflict.

A. WRONG DESIRES (v. 1)

1. What causes fights and quarrels among you? Don't they come from your desires that battle within you?

Fights and quarrels—these are strong terms. We cannot think that James's readers were having among them literal wars with swords and spears, however. The first century was the time of the famed "Roman peace." The Romans did not allow such wars among the people they ruled. We must suppose James was writing of church fights such as are all too common among Christians now. Perhaps he used those strong terms to help his readers understand that church fights were really serious matters, matters to be avoided.

Where do *fights* come from, *fights* between individuals and between factions in the church? They often come from our self-centered *desires,* our cravings. Craving for power can lead to competition between two leaders and the groups that follow them. It is bad enough when one person fights with selfish desires and is led to do wrong for personal gain. But the damage can be more than doubled when two talented people both use "no holds barred" tactics to gain popularity and leadership. In 1 Corinthians 1:10-13 Paul pleads with Christians to put an end to such divisions in the church (cf. 3 John 9, 10).

B. BAD RESULTS (vv. 2, 3)

2. You want something but don't get it. You kill and covet, but you cannot have what you want. You quarrel and fight. You do not have, because you do not ask God.

Again we see those strong words, *quarrel, fight,* and *covet.* Now another is added: *kill.* Again we must doubt that it is to be taken literally. It hardly seems possible that Jewish Christians were accustomed to killing one another to gain some advantage in a church fight. Perhaps James was thinking, as John did, that anyone who hates a brother is a murderer at heart, even though never actually killing anyone (1 John 3:15).

But even without bloodshed, a church fight can be tragic. One Christian belittles or denounces another, or two groups defame each other's integrity, and the conflict is almost as disgraceful as a bloody battle would be. Nobody wins. Each fierce fighter or group gains shame instead of honor and prestige. Why don't all the Christians unite in harmonious work for the progress of the church and then *ask God* for success? Instead of that, the battling groups end up taking glory from Christ and giving it to themselves. Surely we do not need to be told that it is futile for such groups to ask the Lord for success!

"HOLY WARS"

We've heard a lot about "holy wars" in recent years, but church fights are not in that category! A few years ago, a minister's stubbornness conspired with the power needs of some of the members to bring the congregation's temperature to "fever level." Some members had unreasonable expectations of the minister; he resisted accommodating their desires in *any* way.

The board chair called a church meeting to allow each side to express its concerns. The rules were as follows: there would be no personal attacks, no one could speak twice until everyone had spoken once, and no action would be taken during that meeting (it was not a business meeting; the purpose was to restore some long-lost communication). Some on each side found those rules *very* hard to live by, since their anger had been seething for a long time.

Opinions were split 45 percent to 45 percent, with 10 percent in the middle wishing the rest would act more like Christians. The minister would have stayed had he been able to count on the support of half of the congregation. Lacking that support, he soon resigned. As a result, several who had sided with the minister also left the church, and many of his opponents dug in to consolidate their gain in power. Many of the rest found themselves helpless to heal the broken spirit of a now declining congregation. Obviously, *no one won the battle.* James is telling us that is what always happens!   —C. R. B.

3. When you ask, you do not receive, because you ask with wrong motives, that you may spend what you get on your pleasures.

The fighters do not get what they want from God because their attitudes, aims, and wants are wrong. They are not concerned about God's kingdom and his righteousness (Matthew 6:33); rather, they are concerned about satisfying their own *pleasures,* their own desires. They want money for their own enjoyment; they want influence and power for their own pride. The Bible speaks to the importance of our motives in other places as well (see 1 Chronicles 28:9; Proverbs 16:2; 1 Corinthians 4:5).

C. CONFLICTING FRIENDSHIPS (vv. 4, 5)

4. You adulterous people, don't you know that friendship with the world is hatred toward God? Anyone who chooses to be a friend of the world becomes an enemy of God.

Now James digs deeper. The cause of those selfish and worldly desires lies in a damaged relationship with God. In the Old Testament Scriptures, so well known to James and the other Jewish Christians, the relationship of God to his people sometimes is pictured as that of husband and wife (e.g., Isaiah 54:5). Israel's idol worship is described as adultery, and God punished her with divorce (Jeremiah 3:6-9). He no longer took care of Israel, and as a result she was destroyed by pagans.

In a similar figure of speech we now see James accusing his readers of giving more devotion to worldly interests than to God, and that is a type of adultery. Perhaps there are cases of "physical" adultery among James's readers, but James is saying those readers are guilty of "spiritual" adultery when they gave their devotion to the godless *world* and its attractions rather than to *God* himself (cf. Revelation 17:1, 2). God wants to be supreme in our hearts and lives. If we give the greater part of it to anyone or anything else, we become God's enemies (Colossians 1:21). So choose which *friend* you want.

5. Or do you think Scripture says without reason that the spirit he caused to live in us envies intensely?

This verse puzzles us because the part that seems to be a quotation from *Scripture* is not found in the Scriptures we know. Was James quoting a Scripture that God has chosen not to preserve except in this very passage? Or are we reading a mistranslation that has crept in along the way? (This verse is not the same in all the ancient manuscripts, so some scholars think the original wording has been lost.)

In any case, we do know the Holy Spirit lives in us if we are Christians (1 Corinthians 3:16). The verse seems to be saying that the Holy Spirit in us longs for our full devotion. (Notice that the footnotes in the NIV have the upper-case "Spirit" as a possible understanding.) God longs so ardently for us that he actually *envies.* Exodus 20:5 says God is jealous over us, so maybe that is the Scripture James had in mind as he wrote this.

WHAT DO YOU THINK?

Many people have become good at shifting blame. The old saying, "The devil made me do it" is an example. How can we teach individuals that the source of their ungodly attitudes lies within themselves?

[Philippians 4:8 may start your thinking in the right direction.]

DAILY BIBLE READINGS

   Monday, Sept. 22—Praise and Offerings to God (Psalm 66:8-15)

   Tuesday, Sept. 23—God Hears a Sincere Heart (Psalm 66:16-20)

   Wednesday, Sept. 24— Warning About Trusting Riches (James 5:1-6)

   Thursday, Sept. 25—Be Clothed in Humility (1 Peter 5: 1-6)

   Friday, Sept. 26—God Gives Grace to the Humble (James 4: 1-6)

   Saturday, Sept. 27—God Exalts the Humble (James 4: 7-12)

   Sunday, Sept. 28—Get Rid of Arrogance (James 4:13-17)

II. GOD'S SOLUTIONS (JAMES 4:6-10)

An old saying goes, "It's not enough to smell a rotten egg, you have to lay a better one!" James doesn't leave his readers condemned with problems—he provides solutions.

A. ACCEPT GOD'S GRACE (v. 6)

6. *But he gives us more grace. That is why Scripture says:*

   "God opposes the proud
   but gives grace to the humble."

God's Spirit living in us does not desert us if we fall short of the full devotion he longs for. In fact, he *gives grace*—more favor than we deserve. This is verified by Proverbs 3:34. James quotes that verse from the Greek translation used by Greek-speaking Jews. That is the reason it does not read quite like our own version of Proverbs 3:34 (see also 1 Peter 5:5). No doubt all of us sometimes fail to follow the leading of the Holy Spirit, who lives in us. With his grace he gives us forgiveness if we are *humble* and willing to receive it (cf. Matthew 5:3). If we are *proud* and defiant in rejecting his leading, we find ourselves in opposition to God Almighty. Nothing could be worse than that!

THE SMARTEST KID IN THE WORLD

For a while, Justin Chapman was the smartest kid in the world. At age three his IQ tested off the charts. At six he scored a record 298-plus. On the SAT math test he scored a perfect 800. He was taking on-line high school classes at age five and enrolled at New York's University of Rochester when he was six. Justin was a celebrity, being interviewed by the governor of New York, appearing in a BBC documentary that focused on young geniuses, and speaking at numerous conferences on the unique needs of gifted children.

Mom, of course, was justly proud of her boy genius and specialized in bragging about him, adding fuel to the fire of his fame. But everything changed when, at age eight, he began to exhibit bizarre behavior and was hospitalized for severe mental problems.

As evidence of psychological pressure on Justin came to light, the court took the boy away from his mother. In hopes of regaining custody, she admitted that she had falsified the IQ scores and stolen a neighbor's SAT scores. She said, "It just happened, and I let things get out of control."

There is no doubt that Justin is very bright. But his mother's exaggerated and misguided pride brought pathetic results in terms of her son's health and well-being. Eventually, God will judge our pride and bring us down. Worse, we often take others with us!

                                          —C. R. B.

B. CHOOSE YOUR MASTER (vv. 7-10)

7. *Submit yourselves, then, to God. Resist the devil, and he will flee from you.*

When we *submit* ourselves *to God*, we follow the leading of his written Word in our hands and his gracious Spirit in our hearts. In verse 1 of our text, James attributes some of our wrongdoing to our own wrong desires. But now James leads us to consider the cause of our wrong wishes. *The devil* is always trying to implant them and encourage them. The devil is like a roaring lion eager to devour us (1 Peter 5:8), but he pretends to be an angel of light (2 Corinthians 11:14). If we are fooled by his pretense, he will lead us into all kinds of wrong thinking, wishing, and doing. But if we recognize his evil influence and *resist* it, he can only take to his heels. We are safe from the devil's wiles if we know the Bible and apply it in our lives.

HOW TO SAY IT

Colossians. Kuh-LOSH-unz.
Corinthians. Kor-IN-thee-unz.
Isaiah. Eye-ZAY-uh.
Jeremiah. Jair-uh-MY-uh.
Leviticus. Leh-VIT-ih-kus.
Nehemiah. NEE-huh-MY-uh.

8. Come near to God and he will come near to you. Wash your hands, you sinners, and purify your hearts, you double-minded.

So you choose God to be your master. You renounce the devil, and you renounce your own devilish desires (cf. Matthew 6:24). But when you decide to serve the Lord, do not try to serve him from afar. Instead, *come near* to him—seek his presence. He is not hard to find, for he is looking for you, too (Acts 17:27). But you will not be comfortable in his presence with those sin-stained *hands.* So *wash your hands* in his loving forgiveness (cf. 1 John 1:9).

Remember, God wants no half-hearted service. So *purify your hearts* if you have been wavering between the call of God and the call of the godless world. A *double-minded* person can expect no blessing from the Lord (James 1:7, 8).

9, 10. Grieve, mourn and wail. Change your laughter to mourning and your joy to gloom. Humble yourselves before the Lord, and he will lift you up.

In Nehemiah 8:9-12, the people are told to stop *mourning* and start rejoicing. Now circumstances call for the opposite to be done. This weeping is for the sinners and the double-minded of verse 8. They (and we) are not to come proudly to the Lord; they are not to hold their heads high and demand his cleansing. Instead, they (and we) are to come with a broken spirit and a contrite heart (Psalm 51:17). Then the Lord will purify hearts and *lift* up those ready to serve him.

III. DON'T TRY TO BE GOD (JAMES 4:11-17)

We have been warned against destructive conflicts with Christian brothers and sisters. We have been warned against our own desires that cause conflicts. We have been warned against the godless world that constantly tries to make us as godless as itself. We have been warned against the devil, who is out to destroy us. But we are exalted by the thought that we have God's Spirit living in us.

Now in the last part of our text we are warned against thinking we are more than we can be. God's friends are not God. Let us not be foolish enough to take on ourselves the judging that only God can do. Let us not be arrogant enough to think we can plan and direct our lives with no thought of God's will.

A. LET GOD BE THE JUDGE (vv. 11, 12)

11. Brothers, do not slander one another. Anyone who speaks against his brother or judges him speaks against the law and judges it. When you judge the law, you are not keeping it, but sitting in judgment on it.

Jesus warns us against judging our fellow Christians (Matthew 5:22; 7:1-5). So does Paul (Romans 14:3, 10, 13). Now we see a like warning from James. Sometimes such warnings are misunderstood. They are taken to mean that we should let a fellow Christian's wrongdoing go on without rebuke. That is a mistake. If a fellow Christian is doing something that is plainly contrary to Bible teaching, we ought to call his or her attention to God's judgment of what he or she is doing (Luke 17:3). We ought to help the person stop the wrongdoing when we can.

First, we take up the issue privately with the wrongdoer (Matthew 18:15). Too often we do just the opposite: we tell the wrongdoer's fault to everyone but the wrongdoer. It becomes common gossip in the church and community, but no one mentions it to the one who could make the needed change!

Passing judgment on fellow Christians is tantamount to speaking *against the law* and sitting in judgment on it. Some careful students conclude that James is alluding to what he calls "the royal law": "Love your neighbor as yourself" (Leviticus 19:18; Matthew 5:43; 19:19; James 2:8). Jesus said that this commandment was one of two upon which hang "all the Law and the Prophets" (Matthew 22:37-40). This one law is the whole law of human relations

Humble yourselves in the sight of the Lord, and he shall lift you up. James 4:10

Display this poster as you discuss James 4:10. It is in the Adult Visuals packet.

condensed into a single statement (Romans 13:8-10). Anyone who speaks evil of his brother is breaking that royal law, and thereby judging it unworthy of obedience—thus speaking evil of it.

12. There is only one Lawgiver and Judge, the one who is able to save and destroy. But you—who are you to judge your neighbor?

The Lord God Almighty is the *one Lawgiver*. Remember that *to save* and *destroy* is his prerogative, not ours (Isaiah 33:22).

B. CONSIDER GOD'S WILL (vv. 13-17)

13. Now listen, you who say, "Today or tomorrow we will go to this or that city, spend a year there, carry on business and make money."

The words *now listen* seem to carry a bit of rebuke for not having thought or acted already. In today's English we sometimes say, "Come on, now!" with the same meaning. Here James calls his readers to rethink the attitude with which they make their plans. In the Roman Empire as today, many in the church are astute business people. It is not unusual for one of them to see a business opportunity in another city and to plan to go there immediately.

14. Why, you do not even know what will happen tomorrow. What is your life? You are a mist that appears for a little while and then vanishes.

In our hearts we know the plans we make are breakable. You may be disabled in a traffic accident. I may drop dead with a heart attack (cf. Luke 12:20). That city to which we plan to go may be so damaged by earthquake, fire, flood, or terrorism that no wise person would conduct business there.

15. Instead, you ought to say, "If it is the Lord's will, we will live and do this or that."

Keeping *the Lord's will* in our planning allows us to maintain a proper perspective. When we do that, we make plans that he can approve of; we ensure that we can make a profit without defrauding anyone. Perhaps you have heard people say, "Lord willing" when they tell of their plans. It is a healthy reminder.

16. As it is, you boast and brag. All such boasting is evil.

The fault of James's readers is not in making business plans. Rather, their problem is in leaving God out of the planning. J. B. Adamson calls this "practical atheism." The arrogant *boasting* in human wisdom, power, and success *is evil.* God's people ought to have him always on their minds, ought to depend on him, ought to serve him, ought to seek his kingdom and his righteousness above their own profit (Matthew 6:33).

17. Anyone, then, who knows the good he ought to do and doesn't do it, sins.

All of James's readers, including us, ought to know that:

1. It is good to control our desires, and not be controlled by them.
2. It is good to seek to be friends of God rather than to be friends of the world.
3. It is good to serve God humbly, not to try to take his place.

So watch your step. If you do not do what you know is *good*, that is *sin*. Failing *to do good* can also be called a "sin of omission."

CONCLUSION

Perhaps we can best conclude this lesson by listing key thoughts from its three main sections.

I. Problems arise in the church when people fail to control their desires. Beware!

II. God, through his Word, provides solutions to those problems. Practice those solutions!

III. God's people are not God; they are his humble servants. Serve him well!

WHAT DO YOU THINK?

How can Christians come to understand the seriousness of the sin of being judgmental? What does Matthew 7:15-20 tell us about our proper role in judging or discerning?

WHAT DO YOU THINK?

The Bible teaches the virtue of being an industrious self-starter (e.g., Proverbs 10:4). On the other hand, James seems to be saying that a person's planning for tomorrow may be fruitless, since God is in control of what will happen. What should the church teach in order to clarify this seeming contradiction?

[Luke 14:28-31 and Romans 15:23-29 can start your thinking.]

WHAT DO YOU THINK?

Over time, most church members unconsciously fall into the habit of emphasizing some types of sin (perhaps "sins of action") over other types (perhaps "sins of inaction" or "attitude"). What can we do to explore this "blind side" in reference to sin?

THOUGHT TO REMEMBER

"He mocks proud mockers but gives grace to the humble" (Proverbs 3:34).

Discovery Learning

*This page contains an alternative lesson plan emphasizing learning activities. Classes
desiring such student involvement will find these suggestions helpful. The next page
is a reproducible activity page to further enhance discovery learning.*

LEARNING GOALS

After this lesson each student will be able to:

1. Recall key points from James's warning against evil passions and his call to submission to God.

2. Tell how wrong attitudes can lead to conflicts between Christians.

3. Identify and confess a sinful attitude that has led to a disagreement with another believer.

INTO THE LESSON

Prepare a scrambled word and sentence activity. The sentence is James 4:7, "Submit yourselves therefore to God." Estimate how many small groups of three students you will have in class. For each group, prepare a set of three three-by-five index cards and place them in an envelope. One card will have "TUMSIB" *(submit)*, one will have "SOVLSERUEY" *(yourselves)*, and the other will have three words "HETN OT ODG" *(then to God)*.

Shuffle the cards before placing them into the envelopes. After moving the class into groups of three, begin class by saying, "Each of these envelopes contains index cards that have one or more scrambled words written on them. When I tell you to begin, take the cards out of the envelope, unscramble the words, and then arrange the words to form a verse from our lesson text today."

Say, "Our lesson text today describes what happens when people have a broken relationship with God and what is necessary to restore that relationship. Open your Bible to James 4."

INTO THE WORD

Prepare three question sheets using the questions given below. Ask someone to read aloud James 4. Then move the class into three groups, giving each group one of the question sheets to answer. Allow about eight minutes for the groups to work. When they have finished, ask each group to tell the answers to their questions.

Group A

1. What are the characteristics of one who has a broken relationship with God (vv. 1-6)? *(Fights, quarrels, evil desires, murder, covetousness, adultery, worldliness, pride, selfishness.)*

2. What does James say explains why believers did not have the things they wanted (vv. 2, 3)? *(They did not ask God; when they did ask, they did so with wrong motives.)*

3. What is a proper attitude for Christians (v. 6)? *(Humility.)*

Group B

1. What should you do to restore a broken relationship with God (vv. 7-10)? *(Use the reproducible activity "Steps to Restoring a Broken Relationship" from the next page to make an overhead transparency. Write these answers on it as the group reports: submit to God; resist the devil; come near to God; wash your hands; purify your hearts; grieve, mourn, wail; humble yourselves.)*

2. What does James say is the source of the wars and fightings among believers (v. 1)? *(Individual desires that lead to sinful deeds.)*

3. What metaphor does James use to describe a person's life (v. 14)? *(A mist that appears and vanishes.)*

Group C

1. What does James call those believers who engage in wars and fightings among themselves (vv. 4, 8, 11)? *(Adulterers, sinners, double-minded; judges of the law rather than doers.)*

2. How should Christians make plans for the future (vv. 13-15)? *(Plans should always be "if it is the Lord's will.")*

3. What does James say indicates sin in a person's life (v. 17)? *(Not doing the good that one knows should be done)*

After discussing the answers, say, "James isn't the only one who dealt with conflicts between Christians. Unfortunately, we all face it too often. This lesson is called, 'Faith and Attitudes' because conflicts often begin with wrong attitudes that lead to sinful behaviors. Let's explore this concept."

INTO LIFE

Use the reproducible activity "Disagreements Between Believers" from the next page and make an overhead transparency. Ask the class to identify wrong attitudes that cause conflicts between Christians. As the ideas are suggested, write them in the left column. Then ask the class to suggest how each attitude may lead to a broken relationship; write the broken relationship in the right column. Ask each student to pick one sinful attitude that has led to a disagreement with another believer. Distribute three-by-five cards and ask each student to write a prayer confessing an attitude that has broken a relationship. Remind learners of James 4:10.

Steps to Restoring a Broken Relationship With God

What should you do to restore a broken relationship with God? Read James 4:7-10, and list a number of steps.

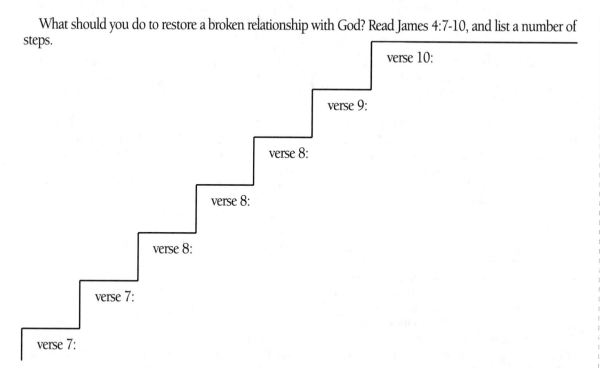

verse 10:

verse 9:

verse 8:

verse 8:

verse 8:

verse 7:

verse 7:

Disagreements Between Believers

Identify wrong attitudes that cause conflicts between Christians; write them in the left column. Then think of how each attitude may lead to a broken relationship; write the broken relationship in the right column.

SINFUL ATTITUDES	BROKEN RELATIONSHIPS

Faith Faces the World

Unit 2: Live in Hope
(Lessons 5-8)

LIVE AS GOD'S PEOPLE

LESSON 5

WHY TEACH THIS LESSON?

Real estate experts say that before you buy a house you should have it inspected. A professional inspector will find the flaws you need to know about ahead of time. Later, you will be wise to have smoke, radon, and carbon monoxide detectors to monitor your home's safety. Many of us will go on to buy water purifiers, air conditioners, and garage door openers to make our houses more livable.

But what about the quality of our "spiritual house"—do we pay as much attention to it? Are we vigilant for cracks of unholiness that may appear in its foundation? Do we monitor the presence of sin on an ongoing basis? Is this house always in order, or is there "spiritual trash" strewn about? Jesus paid a high price (his own life) to buy that house for us, and he continues to be its cornerstone to this day. Today's lesson will help you and your learners keep the spiritual termites out of this house as we learn to "Live as God's People."

INTRODUCTION

"It's not fair," Rob grumbled. "Everybody expects a preacher's kid to be good for nothing." Rob's father, the preacher, answered with a laugh. "Then your work is cut out for you, Robbie," he said. "Your job is to disappoint everybody by being good for something."

This preacher's kid indeed has proven to be good for many things, and he has won increased respect for his father as well as for himself.

A. OUR JOB

This week's lesson title challenges us to "Live as God's People." If anyone expects Christians to be hypocrites, our job is to disappoint that one! When we are sincere, honest, and devoted to the Lord, we win respect not only for ourselves but also for our Father in Heaven. Isn't that what Jesus asks? "Let your light shine before men, that they may see your good deeds and praise your Father in heaven" (Matthew 5:16).

B. LESSON BACKGROUND

After our four lessons from the epistle of James, we now turn to the first of two letters by Simon Peter. Not many heroes of the infant church are better known than this man! He was one of the first of Jesus' disciples (John 1:35-42) and was taught intensively through the years of Jesus' earthly ministry. After Jesus died and rose again, Peter was the one who preached on that memorable Day of Pentecost when the church began its tremendous growth (Acts 2:1-41). Later, God chose Peter as the first to carry the gospel to the Gentiles (Acts 10). We know little about Peter's movements after that, but certainly he remained a tower of strength in the growing church (Galatians 2:9).

I. PRAISE GOD (1 PETER 1:3-5)

Peter probably wrote his first letter in about A.D. 64. That means he had been a Christian for more than thirty years. He wrote from a place he called "Babylon"

DEVOTIONAL READING:
LEVITICUS 19:1-10

BACKGROUND SCRIPTURE:
1 PETER 1:1–2:10

PRINTED TEXT:
1 PETER 1:3-5, 13-21; 2:4-10

Oct
5

LESSON AIMS

After participating in this lesson, each student will be able to:

1. List several qualities that characterize Christians who respond to the challenge of our text.

2. Explain how these qualities help draw others to the Lord.

3. Suggest a course of action that will help him or her to improve on at least one of these qualities.

KEY VERSE

Just as he who called you is holy, so be holy in all you do.
—1 Peter 1:15

(1 Peter 5:13), probably a code word for pagan Rome. He wrote to Christians in Asia Minor (1:1), that large landmass south of the Black Sea and north of the east part of the Mediterranean Sea, where modern Turkey is today.

A. PRAISE GOD FOR OUR HOPE (v. 3)
3. Praise be to the God and Father of our Lord Jesus Christ! In his great mercy he has given us new birth into a living hope through the resurrection of Jesus Christ from the dead,

What a privilege it is to *praise* God, who is *Father of our Lord Jesus Christ!* Since the Father *has given us new birth,* he is our Father as well. Of course God did not beget us in the same way he begot Jesus (Luke 1:26-35). No one else is God's Son in the same way Jesus is. But in another way all Christians are children of God, since he has caused us to be born again as his children (cf. Galatians 3:26, 27). This statement is true not because we have a right to rebirth or deserve it, but it is by *his great mercy* that he gave that rebirth to us when we deserved just the opposite.

By his mercy we are born again, born into *a living hope,* a lively and active hope that will not be disappointed (see the next verse). God brought us to that hope *through the resurrection of Jesus Christ from the dead.* Because we know Jesus had the power to live again and is living still, we know that he has the power to cause us to live again—and to live forever—after our own deaths.

B. PRAISE GOD FOR OUR INHERITANCE (v. 4)
4. . . . and into an inheritance that can never perish, spoil or fade—kept in heaven for you.

Born again as God's children, we are "heirs of God and co-heirs with Christ" (Romans 8:17). Our *inheritance* is secure forever, *kept in Heaven for* us. Inheritance is an important theme in the Bible (e.g., Psalm 37:9; Matthew 5:5; 19:29; 25:34; 1 Peter 3:9).

C. PRAISE GOD FOR OUR SAFEKEEPING (v. 5)
5. . . . who through faith are shielded by God's power until the coming of the salvation that is ready to be revealed in the last time.

Can we be sure of receiving that matchless inheritance that is reserved for us? Yes—and no. *God's power* guarantees it, if we are faithful. It is God who keeps us safe against every attack of the world, the flesh, and the devil. But God does it *through* our *faith,* and the maintenance of our faith is our own responsibility (cf. Hebrews 2:1).

II. PREPARE YOURSELF (1 PETER 1:13-21)
The word *therefore* that begins our next section means that what Peter has to say next is the logical conclusion of what he has said just before. In 1:6-12 (not in our text), he recognizes the trials his readers are suffering. He also reminds them of the reality of their salvation. This leads him to exhort his readers to do certain things and think certain ways.

A. CALL TO HOLINESS (vv. 13-16)
13. Therefore, prepare your minds for action; be self-controlled; set your hope fully on the grace to be given you when Jesus Christ is revealed.

Prepare your minds for action is a loose translation of the more literal "gird up the loins of your mind." In Peter's day a man's daily garb was rather like a modern bathrobe. In preparing to run or to work vigorously, a man would lift the hem of

WHAT DO YOU THINK?

What steps can Christians take to ensure their praise, whether in corporate worship or in personal devotions, is a fitting response to being born into "a living hope," celebrating the Giver of the greatest gift ever received?

(Encourage the students to offer specific suggestions for keeping their focus on what God has done when they worship, and for how to express personal and heart-felt thanks.)

HOW TO SAY IT

Corinthians. Kor-IN-thee-unz.
Deuteronomy. Due-ter-AHN-uh-me.
Ecclesiastes. Ik-LEEZ-ee-AS-teez.
Ephesians. Ee-FEE-zhunz.
Galatians. Guh-LAY-shunz.
Leviticus. Leh-VIT-ih-kus.
Mediterranean. MED-uh-tuh-RAY-nee-un.
Pisa. PEE-zuh.
Zion. ZI-un.

his robe above his knees and tuck it into the belt around his waist. Peter is not asking us to free our legs for a footrace, but to free our minds for proper thinking.

In this context to *be self-controlled* means "to be serious and thoughtful, not careless or facetious." To *set your hope fully* means to hope completely, confidently. Peter is telling us to expect the *grace,* the favor of God, that forgives our sins and welcomes us to Heaven when *Jesus Christ* returns.

14. As obedient children, do not conform to the evil desires you had when you lived in ignorance.

Most of the Christians receiving this letter had been pagans before they had heard the gospel. In their *ignorance* of Christian teaching they had fashioned themselves according to their natural *desires.* But now as Christians they must shape themselves in a different fashion, the fashion of *obedient children* of God. The apostle Paul also wrote to some of these same people to remind them of the life they should have left behind (see Galatians 4:8-11).

15. But just as he who called you is holy, so be holy in all you do;

Holy things and holy people are dedicated to the service of God. Christians must pattern themselves to be like Jesus, to be holy and dedicated to God's service. Holiness is not a part-time job; holiness will affect *all you do.*

16. . . . for it is written: "Be holy, because I am holy."

The call to holiness *is written* more than once in the Old Testament (Leviticus 11:44, 45; 19:2; 20:7). That Testament was given to the people of Israel; now Peter repeats the same call to Christians, whether Jewish or Gentile in background.

APPLYING THE RIGHT PRINCIPLES

Rudolph Giuliani, former mayor of New York City, is most famous for his commanding and comforting presence at the horrendous scene of the terrorist attacks on the World Trade Center on September 11, 2001. However, he had become famous (or infamous, depending on one's politics) for changes he brought about earlier in his tenure as mayor.

Giuliani came to office at a time when the city was crime-ridden and the streets overrun by cast-off derelicts of society. *A New York Times* poll indicated that more than 50 percent of the adults in the city were planning to leave. A decade later, the murder rate was one-third of what it had been, the homeless had been moved into facilities where they could be helped, and street prostitution, drug-dealing, and graffiti had all declined due to aggressive law enforcement. The mayor's promotion of "middle-class values" (in other words, the advocacy of principles of human decency) had made New York City livable again.

Regardless of sociological and political fads that try to make humanity's sinful condition excusable—or even laudable—the biblical values of sobriety, morality, and holiness that Peter advocates are the only principles that will make society work. With anything else, we are merely fooling ourselves.   —C. R. B.

B. CALL TO REVERENCE (vv. 17-21)

17. Since you call on a Father who judges each man's work impartially, live your lives as strangers here in reverent fear.

Wise Solomon concluded a long discussion by saying, "Fear God and keep his commandments, for this is the whole duty of man" (Ecclesiastes 12:13). That does not mean we ought to try to hide from God, as guilty Adam did (Genesis 3:8). We are not tormented by fear as Adam was. When we *call on* the *Father* in prayer, our fear of God is an attitude of reverence and awe.

As we learned in lesson 2, God *judges each man's work impartially,* for he does not discriminate or show favoritism (Acts 10:34). He evaluates us on the basis of our *work* for his kingdom, not on the basis of race or ethnic group.

WHAT DO YOU THINK?

When children are obedient, it is a testimony to the parents' skill in child-rearing. What needs to be done to teach Christians that God is to receive the glory when a person becomes obedient to his commands?

WHAT DO YOU THINK?

Chapter 1 uses many verbs to describe what Christians are to do as a result of being born into God's family. What are some actions a Christian can take to live out each of these?

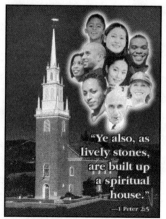

"Ye also, as lively stones, are built up a spiritual house."
—1 Peter 2:5

Drawing from 1 Peter 2:5, this visual illustrates that the church is people, not a building.

18, 19. *For you know that it was not with perishable things such as silver or gold that you were redeemed from the empty way of life handed down to you from your forefathers, but with the precious blood of Christ, a lamb without blemish or defect.*

Before they became Christians, most of Peter's audience had been pagan. Their *way of life* that had been *handed down to* them *from* their *forefathers* was *empty*—concerned with worldly values and false religion, with no hope for eternity. But their Christian redemption has not come about on the basis of *silver or gold. The precious blood of Christ* was required for that. *A lamb* offered in sacrifice had to be perfect, *without blemish or defect* (Leviticus 22:21). "The Lamb of God, who takes away the sin of the world!" (John 1:29) had to be God's faultless Son.

20, 21. *He was chosen before the creation of the world, but was revealed in these last times for your sake. Through him you believe in God, who raised him from the dead and glorified him, and so your faith and hope are in God.*

Before God began to make *the world,* he had a plan for the redemption of people whose own actions would make them slaves of sin and doomed to death. God planned to send his own Son to live a sinless life among sinful people, to take upon himself the punishment that all those sinners deserved, and thus to ransom the sinners from sin and death (Mark 10:45). It was in Peter's time that the Redeemer *was revealed*—was seen and known. This was all according to God's ancient plan. Jesus gave his life to redeem lost sinners today just as much as he did it for those people in Asia Minor who received this letter originally.

Peter's audience had forsaken their old, imaginary gods for Jesus. The real God was the one who *raised him from the dead and glorified him.* Those people of Asia Minor had learned about that, and that was the reason they put their *faith and hope* in God. And don't we put our faith and hope in the same God for the same reasons?

III. YOUR SPIRITUAL HOUSE (1 PETER 2:4-10)

In language mostly literal, the first two parts of our text tell something about what we "do" as God's people. Now Peter switches to figurative language to tell us more about our relationship to Jesus. In his metaphor we appear as things rather than people, but in a way that enhances our human dignity.

A. THE MATERIALS (vv. 4, 5)

4, 5. *As you come to him, the living Stone—rejected by men but chosen by God and precious to him—you also, like living stones, are being built into a spiritual house to be a holy priesthood, offering spiritual sacrifices acceptable to God through Jesus Christ.*

A glance at verse 3 (not in our text) shows that *to him* means to the Lord, to Jesus. In Peter's metaphor, Jesus is *the living Stone* to whom we Christians, as *living stones,* come. As the Christians in Asia Minor came to Jesus and were built *into a spiritual house* (the church), so are we.

Adding to the imagery, Peter notes that we "living stones" are also priests to offer *spiritual sacrifices.* Now that the Old Testament era is past, there is no longer any need for a separate category of priests. We are all priests (Revelation 1:6; 5:10), and Jesus is our Great High Priest (Hebrews 6:20).

Romans 12:1 helps us understand the nature of our spiritual sacrifices. That passage urges us to offer up to God our very bodies—not killed at the altar like ancient sacrifices, but living and serving.

WHAT DO YOU THINK?

Peter describes God's people as being very special, based on what has been accomplished through the sacrifice of Jesus. What can the church do to awaken all its members to practice the unity—character, purpose, and direction—that Peter describes with the figures of speech in 1 Peter 2:5?

B. THE CORNERSTONE (vv. 6-8)

6. *For in Scripture it says:*

> *"See, I lay a stone in Zion,*
> *a chosen and precious cornerstone,*
> *and the one who trusts in him*
> *will never be put to shame."*

The *Scripture* Peter quotes is Isaiah 28:16, a seven-hundred-year-old prophecy of Jesus as a *precious cornerstone*. *Zion* is another name for Jerusalem and the hill on which it stands. Jerusalem had been one of the important places of Jesus' ministry, and the church of which he is the cornerstone began its amazing growth there (Acts 2). Jesus the cornerstone is forever secure, forever dependable.

7. *Now to you who believe, this stone is precious. But to those who do not believe,*

> *"The stone the builders rejected*
> *has become the capstone,"*

This verse alludes to Psalm 118:22, 23. That passage sings of a building *stone* rejected by builders whom God overrules. That *rejected* stone becomes the chief cornerstone, the most important stone in the building. Long before Peter wrote this letter we are reading, he presented that bit of Psalm 118 as a fulfilled prophecy of Jesus (Acts 4:8-12). Jesus was rejected by the official *builders* of Israel—the priests and scholars and teachers. But God overruled them (cf. Mark 12:10, 11).

We who believe in Jesus understand how *precious* he is: the secure cornerstone of the eternal church to which we commit ourselves. No other foundation is necessary or possible (cf. 1 Corinthians 3:10; Ephesians 2:20). *Those who do not believe*, the non-Christians, take their stand with the mistaken builders who rejected him at his first appearance on earth. Unbelievers may be loud in their denial now, but in the end they will be confounded, discredited, and put to shame. This very cornerstone ultimately will crush them (Luke 20:17, 18).

8. *. . . and,*

> *"A stone that causes men to stumble*
> *and a rock that makes them fall."*

They stumble because they disobey the message—which is also what they were destined for.

Peter now cites Isaiah 8:14. The *message*, the good news of Jesus and salvation, was told in Peter's time and is told now in our century. Each person who hears it has the same opportunity to submit to Jesus as Lord. Those who do are built into a spiritual house with him, saved for eternity. Those who refuse *stumble* and *fall* for eternity. God has not *destined* anyone to reject Christ. But those who do reject Christ of their own free will are indeed appointed to stumble over him.

THE ONLY STONE THAT LASTS FOR AGES

The pyramids and Sphinx of Egypt, the Tower of London, the Cathedral of Notre Dame in Paris, the Washington Monument in Washington, D.C.—throughout history, when people have wanted to build an edifice that would last for ages, they have built with stone. Yet these monuments show the effects of time: the pyramids and Sphinx have eroded and the other structures have had to undergo periodic restoration to preserve them.

One of the most striking examples of this need to expend great amounts of effort and money to preserve our monuments is the "Leaning Tower" of Pisa. The

---

WHAT DO YOU THINK?

Our faith is not a blind leap in the dark. Our faith is based on the solidness of Jesus Christ and the historical evidence about him. How can Christians demonstrate in daily life their confidence in this sure foundation (Jesus)?

DAILY BIBLE READINGS

Monday, Sept. 29—God's Treasured Possession (Deuteronomy 7:6-11)

Tuesday, Sept. 30—People Led by a Holy God (Leviticus 19:1-5)

Wednesday, Oct. 1—New Birth Into a Living Hope (1 Peter 1:1-7)

Thursday, Oct. 2—People of a Glorious Joy (1 Peter 1:8-12)

Friday, Oct. 3—Disciplined and Holy People (1 Peter 1:13-21)

Saturday, Oct. 4—People Longing for Spiritual Milk (1 Peter 1:22–2:3)

Sunday, Oct. 5—God's Own People (1 Peter 2:4-10)

190-foot-tall bell tower was begun in 1173. Before the third of its eight levels was completed, however, its foundation had begun to sink, and the tilt began. Through the centuries numerous attempts were made to stop the tilting, all without success. It was not until 1990, after a ten-year, twenty-seven million dollar effort, that engineers finally succeeded in keeping the tower from falling down.

Nothing we build in this life, even when made of the hardest stone, will last forever. It will gradually wear away and ultimately crumble or have to be demolished. But Peter tells us that Christ is a precious, living stone and the only sure foundation for our lives. Some may reject this stone or stumble over it, but those who build their lives on it will never be disappointed. They are incorporated into a spiritual building that will last forever.   —C. R. B.

C. The Building (vv. 9, 10)

9. But you are a chosen people, a royal priesthood, a holy nation, a people belonging to God, that you may declare the praises of him who called you out of darkness into his wonderful light.

We are not only a spiritual house (v. 5), but also *a chosen people,* a group of people related by being born again (1 Peter 1:3). We are *a royal priesthood,* a group of priests (2:5) associated with Jesus the King. As *a holy nation* we are dedicated to God's service. Being *a people belonging to God* indicates that we are a distinctive possession (cf. Exodus 19:5, 6; Deuteronomy 7:6). All these mean that we ought to *declare the praises of him who called us out of darkness into his wonderful light* (cf. Isaiah 43:20, 21).

10. Once you were not a people, but now you are the people of God; once you had not received mercy, but now you have received mercy.

Peter now draws on Hosea 1:6, 9, 10; 2:23. Before becoming Christians, Peter's audience in Asia Minor had been scattered among several nations, with little in common (1 Peter 1:1). As Christians they are all bound together as *the people of God.* Likewise today's Christians are all members of one body (Ephesians 4:4-6). Before we were Christians we *had not received mercy.* We were loaded with the guilt of our sins, doomed to die. But now we *have received mercy* and forgiveness and eternal life (Romans 6:23). Praise God!

CONCLUSION

Through the month of September we read parts of a letter from James. Often we noted that James was a practical man, interested in what we do. Now we are starting to read a letter from Peter. Can we glean from him some practical ideas for our "doing"?

Part 1 of our lesson is about praising God. When you praise a store or a physician, your praise may bring a new customer to the store or a new patient to the doctor. How many non-Christians have been brought to God by your praise of him?

Part 2 of our lessons is about being holy and reverent. We have to do some thinking about that. If we make a big show of being holy as the Pharisees did (Matthew 6:1-6; 23:5-12) we may turn people away from us and from God. But Jesus asks us to let people see our good works so they will glorify our Father in Heaven (5:16). Has anyone become more holy and reverent by following your example?

Part 3 of our lesson is about being built into a spiritual house, the church. What are you in that house? Are you a pillar of strength, like James, Peter, and John (Galatians 2:9)? Or are you an area of weakness, leaning on the strength of others? Can you be stronger?

Discovery Learning

This page contains an alternative lesson plan emphasizing learning activities. Classes desiring such student involvement will find these suggestions helpful. The next page is a reproducible activity page to further enhance discovery learning.

LEARNING GOALS

After participating in this lesson, each student will be able to:

1. List several qualities that characterize Christians who respond to the challenge of our text.

2. Explain how these qualities help draw others to the Lord.

3. Suggest a course of action that will help him or her to improve on at least one of these qualities.

INTO THE LESSON

On a poster board or butcher paper prepare a graffiti poster with the words, "Change is . . ." in big letters in one color. Leave space on the paper for written comments from the class. Place this on the classroom wall and have available broad-tip markers in different colors. After the learners have arrived, say: "Notice the graffiti poster on the wall. The word *change* brings with it many different emotions and thoughts. Think about change for a moment, and then I'd like each of you to come to the poster and write an emotion or thought about change." (*Possible responses include scary, uncomfortable, disliked, resisted, exciting.*) After everyone has added a word or phrase, state: "Let's talk about your responses." Read aloud the responses and ask for clarification or an example. Once these responses have been reviewed, make this transition statement: "This idea of change certainly carries with it much emotion. Yet, our Scripture today makes it clear that change is an expected result of coming to Christ. Open your Bibles to 1 Peter 1, and let's see what changes occurred in those Christians."

INTO THE WORD

Move the class into small groups of four or five. Ask each group to select a reader, and ask the readers to read the lesson Scripture aloud to their own groups. Prior to class, prepare a work sheet for each group with three columns labeled: PAST (What were they?), PRESENT (What are they?), and FUTURE (What will they be or have?). Give a work sheet to each group and ask them to find text descriptions to help answer those questions, and to write those under the appropriate column heading. Allow about fifteen minutes. (*Possible answers include the following: PAST—evil desires, ignorance, v. 14; empty life, v. 18; disobedient, 2:8; in darkness, 2:9; PRESENT—living hope, vv. 3, 13; faith, God's power, v. 5;* prepare minds for action, self-controlled, v. 13; holy, vv. 15, 16; redeemed, v. 18; chosen, precious, 2:4; priesthood, holy nation, people belonging to God, 2:9; FUTURE—inheritance in Heaven, v. 4; salvation, v. 5; revealing of Jesus, v. 13; being built into a spiritual house, 2:5.) When time is up, ask for answers. Point out the radical changes that were made.

Now ask each group to prepare a mock TV interview with some of these Christians to cover the whole transition from past, through the present, and to the future. Have one-third of the groups focus on the past, one-third on the present, and one-third on the future. Ask the groups to write several questions for the interview and to gather some insights into what each of these time periods might have been like to those believers. Allow ten to twelve minutes for this activity and then ask for volunteer groups to demonstrate their interviews before the whole class.

After the "TV news shows" have been completed, move the class back into one large group. Say: "Now that we have a better understanding of the thinking and emotions of these early believers, what qualities from the text characterize Christians?" Make a transparency of the reproducible activity "Magnetic Attraction" from the next page. Write answers on the transparency for all to see. (*Some possible answers to this question are self-controlled, v. 13; obedient, v. 14; holy, v. 15; demonstrate faith and hope, v. 21; declare his praises, 2:9.*) Say, "These qualities that characterize Christians are like a magnet to iron shavings. They attract people to Jesus. Turn to a neighbor and decide how these qualities draw others to the Lord." Ask volunteers to report their answers.

INTO LIFE

Ask each learner to evaluate his or her level of attracting others to Jesus through these qualities. Then ask, "How could a Christian improve some of these qualities? What specific steps we can take to improve one that appears to be weak?" Discuss with the class various suggestions offered. Prior to class, make enough photocopies of the reproducible activity "Action Plan," from the next page, so that each student has one. Ask them to select a quality and identify ways they can improve that quality in their own lives. Ask each learner to complete the worksheet and then ask God to help him or her to grow.

Magnetic Attraction

List below some Christian qualities that help draw people to Jesus, and suggest some ways these qualities are attractive.

ATTRACTIVE CHRISTIAN QUALITIES	HOW THEY DRAW PEOPLE TO CHRIST
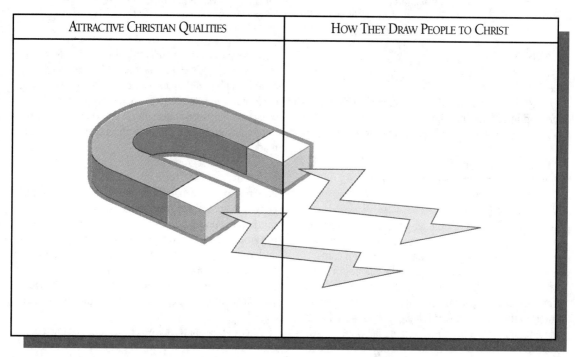	

Action Plan

A quality I need to improve:_____

Specific Steps to Improvement:

1.

2.

3.

4.

5.

SET A GOOD EXAMPLE

LESSON 6

WHY TEACH THIS LESSON?

The ancient Roman politician Cicero (106–43 B.C.) really nailed it when he observed that, "[Our rulers] do more harm by their evil example than by their actual sin." If Cicero were alive today he could comfortably make the very same statement!

Yet no matter how loudly we complain about the bad examples set by politicians, entertainers, and others in the public eye, there's often little we can do to change their behavior. Your learners can, however, control their own actions and the examples they set. Jesus stressed the importance of this when he warned, "Woe to that person through whom [sins] come. It would be better for him to be thrown into the sea with a millstone tied around his neck than for him to cause one of these little ones to sin. So watch yourselves" (Luke 17:1-3). With so much at stake, today's lesson is one that your learners cannot afford to ignore.

INTRODUCTION

A. BAD EXAMPLES

"Follow the Leader" was the game on our country schoolyard, and Jake was the leader. Some of us fell in line reluctantly, for we knew we soon would be shamed by failure to follow. Jake was the tallest boy in school. Easily he jumped high enough to catch the lowest limb of the ash tree and pull himself up among the branches—but only two of the boys could follow him. Beaming with pride, Jake came down and hopped on one foot till half the boys dropped out with weariness. Next, our leader put his hands on the top rail of the fence and vaulted over into the area beside the road. It was against the rules to leave the schoolyard, but all of us vaulted or clambered over the fence. Then Jake tried what was meant to be his greatest stunt. Running at top speed across the road, he leaped over the irrigation ditch beyond it. His feet landed on the other bank, but his body had not quite kept up with his feet. With arms flailing, he fell back into the waist-deep water.

Every boy in the line was happy to see our leader fail. We surrounded him with jests and ridicule as he climbed from the ditch, dripping from head to toe. Then the bell sounded to end our afternoon recess a few minutes early, and we went to form orderly lines in front of the schoolhouse door.

From the top of the steps the teacher faced us with a heavy frown. No questioning was needed; she had been watching from a window. "Jake," she said, "go home and get into some dry clothes. Tell your parents you will be staying after school tomorrow."

So Jake got his bicycle and rode away, while the teacher led us into the schoolroom and gave us a lecture on the peril of following a bad example. I have forgotten the lecture, but I remember the clincher of it. The teacher said, "Next time anyone leaves the schoolyard before four o'clock, he will learn what *that* is for." She jerked a thumb over her shoulder at the big switch on the wall behind her.

Children often begin to smoke, drink, or use illegal drugs because others are doing it. A child usually knows better, but he or she dares not refuse to follow the

DEVOTIONAL READING:
GALATIANS 5:16-26
BACKGROUND SCRIPTURE:
1 PETER 2:11–5:14
PRINTED TEXT:
1 PETER 2:11, 12; 3:13-17; 4:7-11; 5:6-10

LESSON AIMS

After participating in this lesson, each student will be able to:

1. Tell some ways Peter says a Christian can set a good example.

2. Explain why setting a good example is important for the sake of other believers and also unbelievers.

3. Spend time with a new Christian and give him or her guidance and encouragement.

Oct
12

KEY VERSE

Live such good lives among the pagans that, though they accuse you of doing wrong, they may see your good deeds and glorify God on the day he visits us.
—1 Peter 2:12

leader. Sometimes "children" forty or sixty years old do the same thing. They want to be congenial, so they embrace the customs of those around them. In other surroundings, they may fall (or jump!) into customs of double-dealing, fraud, or simple stealing. In yet another environment they may adopt the prevailing customs of infidelity, adultery, and divorce. Too late such folks may discover that evil examples corrupt good character (cf. Proverbs 24:1, 2; 1 Corinthians 15:33).

B. LESSON BACKGROUND

Paul was a wise old Christian made wiser still by the Holy Spirit, who inspired him. He wanted his trainee to be an example to the Christians whom he taught. So Paul told Timothy to be an example "in speech, in life, in love, in spirit, in faith and in purity" (1 Timothy 4:12). What a list! These are the kinds of examples each Christian should set, and that is the background against which we look at the thoughts about example in our text.

I. DO RIGHT FOR GOD'S GLORY (1 PETER 2:11, 12)

First Peter 2:9, 10, the verses just before our text, remind us that as Christians we are a separate people, the people of God, and a holy nation apart from the nations of the world. We are good citizens of the earthly countries where we live (vv. 13, 14 of our text), but our primary citizenship is in Heaven (Philippians 3:20). Our first allegiance is to God, the heavenly King. His standards are our standards, his will is our will.

A. WHAT TO DO (v. 11)

11. Dear friends, I urge you, as aliens and strangers in the world, to abstain from sinful desires, which war against your soul.

Repeating from 1:1, Peter reminds his readers that they are *strangers* in this *world*. This is the mind-set that all Christians must have in order to be able to resist the *sinful desires* that are all around us.

No province in ancient Asia Minor had laws against gluttony, drunkenness, or fornication resulting from such lusts. In fact, many pagans looked forward to the festival of "Bacchanalia," a Roman feast that was little more than a drunken orgy. But Christians do right according to the standards of the heavenly King, not those of the prevailing culture.

B. WHY TO DO IT (v. 12)

12. Live such good lives among the pagans that, though they accuse you of doing wrong, they may see your good deeds and glorify God on the day he visits us.

Pagans of Peter's day often accused Christians *of doing wrong*. Christians will not worship the imaginary gods of their neighbors, so they are called atheists. In some places the emperor is worshiped as a god, so the Christians are accused of rebellion against Rome's government and religion. And Christians are called cannibals because they eat the body of Jesus and drink his blood.

How could Christians defend themselves? It is true that they will worship no god but one. It is true that they, in a symbolic way, eat Jesus' body and drink his blood at Communion. So the Christians' defense is simply to do good so constantly that no one will believe the evil that is spoken against them. A Christian's way of life must be so plainly above reproach that every accusation of wrongdoing falls flat. But beware: if we advertise our goodness, we spoil it. No one admires the Pharisees who did good to be seen by others (Matthew 23:5-11). We do *good deeds* in such a way that those who see what we do will give credit to God rather than to us (Matthew 5:16).

HOW TO SAY IT

Bacchanalia. Bah-keh-NAIL-yuh.
fornication. for-neh-KAY-shun.
Gethsemane. Geth-SEM-uh-nee.
Jeremiah. Jair-uh-MY-uh.
Philippians. Fih-LIP-ee-unz.

Finally, when is the *day he visits us?* God is said to "visit" people for punishment (Isaiah 10:3; Jeremiah 51:18) or for rescue (Genesis 50:24, 25; Ruth 1:6; Psalm 106:4). If Christians perform *good deeds* in such a way as to lead their neighbors to Christ, those neighbors will *glorify God.* So the day any of them becomes a Christian may rightly be called a day God visits them. Or God's day of visitation may be the day Christ returns, giving punishment to those who have not accepted him and salvation to those who have.

II. DO RIGHT IN ALL CIRCUMSTANCES (1 PETER 3:13-17; 4:7-11)

Some of the pagans are accusing Christians of doing wrong (2:12), but the persecution goes beyond name-calling. Peter calls it a "painful trial" (4:12) and indicates that it is being inflicted on Christians elsewhere (5:9). This seems to speak of violent opposition, which the Christians must endure even as Christ endured the suffering inflicted on him (2:21-23). They must not meet violence with violence, but simply go on doing right (3:9-12).

A. BLESSING, FEAR, HEART, AND HOPE (3:13-15)

13, 14. Who is going to harm you if you are eager to do good? But even if you should suffer for what is right, you are blessed. "Do not fear what they fear; do not be frightened."

The best way to prevent *harm,* either to body or to reputation, is simply *to do good.* No one can justly attack you for that.

But sometimes doing right is not enough to keep you from being mistreated. People may abuse you just because your conduct highlights their own evil. In that case their attack is a compliment. Rather than being upset or troubled, rejoice that your right conduct brings forth opposition (Acts 5:41; cf. Isaiah 8:12).

15. But in your hearts set apart Christ as Lord. Always be prepared to give an answer to everyone who asks you to give the reason for the hope that you have. But do this with gentleness and respect,

Your opponents have hurt you in some way—physically, emotionally, or financially. They can't understand why you still smile. So you explain, if you have their attention. In your heart you have sanctified *Christ as Lord.* You have given him first place. In his own time he will reward you. You can wait for his time because he is Lord forever and you will live forever, too. *The hope that you have* will surely be realized, for God is unconquerable.

You explain all this to the questioner *with gentleness* and *respect.* You answer the questioner with reverence before God, who is far above all of us on earth.

B. CONSCIENCE, SHAME, GOD'S WILL, AND SUFFERING (3:16, 17)

16. . . . keeping a clear conscience, so that those who speak maliciously against your good behavior in Christ may be ashamed of their slander.

Keep your *conscience* clear by doing right—doing it so continuously and so obviously that those who falsely *speak maliciously* of your good way of life will be *ashamed* of their falsehood. This repeats and emphasizes what we read in 1 Peter 2:12. The Bible speaks of the importance of conscience in other places as well (e.g., Genesis 20:5, 6; Job 27:6; Acts 23:1; 24:16; 1 Corinthians 4:4; 1 Timothy 1:5; Hebrews 13:18).

LIVING ABOVE CRITICISM

During the Cold War thousands of East Germans escaped Communist repression by crossing into West Berlin. In response to calls for sealing the border, Walter Ulbricht, Communist Party leader, promised in 1961 that it would not happen. Less

WHAT DO YOU THINK?

What can the church do to prepare believers to stand strong when being teased or persecuted? How can Christians can turn trying circumstances into opportunities to introduce others to the Savior?

[See 1 Peter 2:13-25; 4:4, 12-16, 19; and John 15:18-25.]

WHAT DO YOU THINK?

What is a response Christians can prepare in advance to give whenever he or she is being ridiculed or persecuted?

WHAT DO YOU THINK?

Why is "having a good conscience" important to ensure that a Christian's witness sounds and looks credible to unbelievers, particularly those who are hostile?

than two months later the infamous Berlin Wall arose, complete with minefields and watchtowers, to make sure no one escaped from the "worker's paradise."

Democratic Socialists are today's successors to the old Communist Party. They are still condemned for the broken promise regarding the Wall. People are calling on the Party to admit its past inhumanity and apologize for its actions. The past will be hard to live down: evidence of Communism's sins is found in pieces of the Wall in various places around the world and at the Berlin memorial, where a section of the Wall still stands amidst a re-created section of the "death strip" where hundreds were murdered as they tried to escape.

Those sins should long be remembered lest they be committed again. But the evil claims spoken against the church in Peter's day were unfounded. How should Christians respond? Peter says to live so that the charges are obviously groundless, accept the world's attack as proof the church is doing what is right, and share your hope in Christ. Two thousand years later God's plan remains the same for us.

—C. R. B.

WHAT DO YOU THINK?

Suppose a Christian friend is being discriminated against at work because of his faith. After one more episode, he comes to you for advice. "It's just not fair!" he says. Remembering how Jesus was treated, how do you answer?

17. It is better, if it is God's will, to suffer for doing good than for doing evil.

Most would agree that suffering for evildoing is a good thing; perhaps the one suffering will learn to stop *doing evil!* But suffering for *doing good* is more difficult to accept. The constant question in such cases is "why?" The suffering of Job is one example. (See also Judges 6:13.) Peter deals with this issue in more depth in 4:12-19 (not in today's text). Christ suffered and so shall we (but not in all the same ways).

C. SELF-CONTROL, PRAYER, LOVE, AND SIN (4:7-9)

7. The end of all things is near. Therefore be clear minded and self-controlled so that you can pray.

The end of all things speaks of the end of the present creation as associated with the Lord's return (cf. 2 Peter 3:10). We sometimes think that if something is *near,* then we can expect it right away. But *near* can easily indicate that the event can happen at any time. Thus, the Lord's return has been *near* ever since Peter's day—and still it can happen at any time. By encouraging his readers to *be clear minded so that* they *can pray,* perhaps Peter is thinking back to his own failure in this regard in the Garden of Gethsemane (Matthew 26:40, 41).

8. Above all, love each other deeply, because love covers over a multitude of sins.

Love among Christians ought to be felt *deeply;* it should be enthusiastic and constant (see 1 Peter 1:22). Such love *covers over a multitude of sins* in several ways. Such a love "keeps no record of wrongs" (1 Corinthians 13:5); it is able to forgive (Matthew 18:21, 22); it persuades others to stop sinning (James 5:19, 20).

HOW BROTHERS SHOULD TREAT EACH OTHER

Gary Klahr met Steven Barbin when Steven was twenty-one and Gary was twenty-four. They struck up one of those special friendships that seems to "click" automatically. Gary was best man at Steven's wedding. Once he even gave Steven a photograph inscribed, "You are truly my brother."

Twenty-five years later, they discovered from an adoption caseworker that they *really are* brothers! It turns out that they were two of nine children (out of thirteen) whose parents had given them up for adoption. For twenty-five years they had not known the truth but had acted in the spirit of true brotherhood anyway.

We don't always "click" in our relationships with other Christians. In fact, sometimes we have real trouble with them! Peter tells us how to resolve such conflicts: prayerfully, seriously develop good intentions toward others; offer loving forgiveness when it is needed; and demonstrate generous hospitality toward fellow Christians. This is the attitude we show to "best friends," and it *should* characterize our relationships with other Christians. The fact that Peter had to admonish his readers (and us) in this regard indicates how important these Christian graces are for the well-being of the family of God. —C. R. B.

9. Offer hospitality to one another without grumbling.

What Peter stresses here is nothing new (see Romans 12:13; Hebrews 13:2; 3 John 5, 6; contrast 2 John 10, 11), but it does bear repeating. *Hospitality* to fellow Christians is especially important in a time of persecution, and persecution in Asia Minor is severe enough to be called a "painful trial" (1 Peter 4:12). Christians may be afraid to go home because hostile neighbors are waiting to meet them with physical violence. A Christian's home might even be destroyed by a mob of persecutors. The need to offer hope to fellow Christians *without grumbling* is part of our Christian witness as well (see Philippians 2:14).

D. GIFTS, GRACE, SPEAKING, AND SERVING (4:10, 11)

10. Each one should use whatever gift he has received to serve others, faithfully administering God's grace in its various forms.

Whatever spiritual gifts, talents, or abilities you have are gifts from God. God does not give them to us to be used selfishly, however, but for the benefit of others. You can find lists of spiritual gifts in Romans 12; 1 Corinthians 12; and Ephesians 4.

11. If anyone speaks, he should do it as one speaking the very words of God. If anyone serves, he should do it with the strength God provides, so that in all things God may be praised through Jesus Christ. To him be the glory and the power for ever and ever. Amen.

The context of the opening command is that of speech a preacher or teacher uses when we assemble for worship. What sobering challenge it is to ensure that they speak *the very words of God!* This includes knowing, understanding, and following what God says in the Bible. Many who are not called to speak in this way are able to serve, to help others in various ways (v. 10, above). Each helpful Christian should let it be known that it is God who makes him or her able to help. Thus through the Christians and through Christ the credit will be given to God, for *glory* and *power* properly belong to God *for ever and ever.*

III. DO RIGHT WITH AWARENESS (1 PETER 5:6-10)

The title of our lesson is, "Set a Good Example." Naturally this puts strong emphasis on doing right, for that is the way to set a good example. But people who do right face a strong temptation to become proud of their goodness, like the Pharisee whose prayer consisted of telling God how good that Pharisee thought himself to be (Luke 18:11, 12). So the last section of our text reminds us to be humble and trust in God rather than in ourselves.

A. TRUST GOD TO EXALT YOU (v. 6)

6. Humble yourselves, therefore, under God's mighty hand, that he may lift you up in due time.

The word *therefore* looks back to the verse before this, which ends by saying, "God opposes the proud but gives grace to the humble." *Therefore* we had better be among the *humble*, for God's grace is better than anything we can gain for ourselves. As Peter reflects on humility and our coming exaltation, perhaps he is recalling the Master's teaching in this regard of some thirty years before (see Matthew 23:12).

Do Good Deeds

Visual for lessons 6 and 12. *This visual suggests an application of the message of 1 Peter 4:7-11. Have the class suggest other specific acts of love.*

DAILY BIBLE READINGS

Monday, Oct. 6—*Be Zealous in Serving God (Romans 12: 9-18)*

Tuesday, Oct. 7—*Conduct Yourselves Honorably (1 Peter 2:11-17)*

Wednesday, Oct. 8—*Don't Repay Evil for Evil (1 Peter 3: 8-12)*

Thursday, Oct. 9—*Be Ready With a Gentle Defense (1 Peter 3:13-22)*

Friday, Oct. 10—*Live by the Will of God (1 Peter 4:1-6)*

Saturday, Oct. 11—*Maintain Love for One Another (1 Peter 4:7-11)*

Sunday, Oct. 12—*Keep Alert, Resist the Devil (1 Peter 5:7-14)*

PRAYER

Forgive us, Father. How we do dirty ourselves! How we thank you for your cleansing day by day. And for today and tomorrow we pray for faith, wisdom, and courage to walk without fouling ourselves again. In Jesus' name, amen.

WHAT DO YOU THINK?

What can Christians do collectively and individually to protect themselves from the devil's tactics?

WHAT DO YOU THINK?

What other promises can we commit to memory that will keep us from losing heart even in the face of the toughest situations? Why are these promises important?

[Romans 8:26-28; 2 Corinthians 12:7-10; and Philippians 4:19 may start your thinking.]

THOUGHT TO REMEMBER

Be an "example to those who would believe on him and receive eternal life" (1 Timothy 1:16).

B. TRUST GOD TO CARE FOR YOU (v. 7)

7. Cast all your anxiety on him because he cares for you.

Remember that Peter is writing to people who are enduring a "painful trial" of persecution (1 Peter 4:12). They may be overwhelmed with care, but God is not. It is good to remember this when our own cares seem overwhelming (Psalm 55:22; Luke 12:22). The God of all history is the God who comforts Christians of every era (cf. 1 Thessalonians 3:2-4; 2 Thessalonians 1:4; 2 Peter 2:9; Revelation 3:10).

C. TRUST GOD AND RESIST THE DEVIL (vv. 8, 9)

8. Be self-controlled and alert. Your enemy the devil prowls around like a roaring lion looking for someone to devour.

Casting all our care on God does not mean we become careless. If you give *the devil* a chance, he, *like a roaring lion*, will *devour* you (cf. Psalm 22:13; Jeremiah 51:34). This calls for vigilance, alertness. Trust God, yes; but don't expect him to keep you safe when you recklessly deliver yourself right into the enemy's camp.

9. Resist him, standing firm in the faith, because you know that your brothers throughout the world are undergoing the same kind of sufferings.

The devil is not so terrible as some people think. He gains great power by enslaving weaklings who surrender to him. If you strongly *resist him*, he runs away (James 4:7). It is encouraging to know that *your brothers* and sisters all over *the world* are fighting and winning the same spiritual battle that you are.

D. TRUST GOD TO PERFECT YOU (v. 10)

10. And the God of all grace, who called you to his eternal glory in Christ, after you have suffered a little while, will himself restore you and make you strong, firm and steadfast.

Verses 6 and 7 call us to trust in *God,* but verses 8 and 9 emphasize our own responsibility. Then we come to verse 10, the verse of blessed assurance. His *grace* is his favor that we do not deserve, favor purchased by the death of Christ. If in our hearts we remain truly devoted to him, he graciously forgives our faults and failures.

The *eternal glory in Christ* into which he has *called* us surely shall come after we *have suffered a little while.* But we are not there yet. When those sufferings come we greet them with joy because we know they can make us better (Romans 5:3-5). In the meantime we fix our eyes on *the God of all grace* who prepares us for eternal glory.

CONCLUSION

We do set a good example most of the time, don't we? But did you, today or yesterday or last week, stumble into some small wrong? Even Jesus' dearest disciples did that. On the eve of the day of his death they lapsed into selfish wrangling (Luke 22:24). Jesus rebuked them with an object lesson for the ages. He, the Lord and Master, took a basin of water and took the place of a lowly slave as he washed their dirty feet (John 13:1-17).

When we came to the Lord, God washed away our sins and made us clean (Acts 22:16). Yet we walk in an unclean world and continue to dirty ourselves with small wrongs. Even so, God is still ready to wash us: "If we confess our sins, he is faithful and just and will forgive us our sins and purify us from all unrighteousness" (1 John 1:9). As God set an example of service to us, let us set an example as well.

Discovery Learning

This page contains an alternative lesson plan emphasizing learning activities. Classes desiring such student involvement will find these suggestions helpful. The next page is a reproducible activity page to further enhance discovery learning.

LEARNING GOALS

After participating in this lesson, each student will be able to:

1. Tell some ways Peter says a Christian can set a good example.

2. Explain why setting a good example is important for the sake of other believers and also unbelievers.

3. Spend time with a new Christian and give him or her guidance and encouragement.

INTO THE LESSON

To begin, move the learners into groups of four or five. Say, "This week's lesson is called, 'Set a Good Example.' To us get started, I would like each small group to prepare a twenty-second radio commercial. We all have heard radio commercials trying to encourage us to eat at a certain restaurant or to buy a certain product. What we don't hear are commercials that encourage us to be good examples for others or simply to do something that is good. Discuss in your group what it is you want to encourage. Then prepare your commercial to present to the class."

Allow six to eight minutes for each group to prepare the commercial. Then ask the groups to present their commercials. Say, "We've heard some very creative commercials encouraging us to set a good example. Our text today describes ways Christians can be an example for others. Turn to 1 Peter 2, and let's see how God encourages us to set a good example."

INTO THE WORD

Keep the same small groups for this activity. Ask a class member to stand and read the lesson text aloud. Then give each group a copy of the questions below. Say, "As we look carefully at what the lesson text says, answer each of the questions on this sheet. I will give you about ten minutes." Prepare the following questions on the handout.

1. What are some ways Peter says a Christian can set a good example? (*Abstain from sinful desires, 2:11; live good lives, do good deeds, 2:12; be clear minded, self-controlled, 4:7.*)

2. What attitudes should Christians have when they suffer for "doing good" (3:17)? (*Blessed, not afraid or frightened, 3:14.*)

3. In what sense does Peter want us to be prepared? (*"Always . . . to give an answer," 3:15.*)

4. How does "good behavior" influence evildoers who speak evil of you? (*"They may be ashamed of their slander," 3:16.*)

5. In light of the coming "end of all things," what does Peter urge Christians to do? (*"Be clear minded and self-controlled" 4:7.*)

6. How are Christians to use the gifts they receive from God? (*"To serve others" 4:10.*)

7. What is the ultimate purpose of the gift received by Christians? (*That "God . . . may be glorified through Jesus Christ," 4:11.*)

8. What warning does Peter give these Christians in light of the plea to "be self-controlled and alert," 5:8? (*The devil is "looking for someone to devour."*)

10. What positive benefits come to those who "suffered a while," 5:10? (*God will "restore you and make you strong."*)

INTO LIFE

Answer the questions with the class. Then bring the whole class together. Make a transparency from the reproducible activity, "Why Be Good?" from the next page, or make enough copies for each student to have one. Ask, "Why should Christians set a good example for believers, and why should they set a good example for unbelievers?" Write (or have the students write) in the proper column each suggested answer.

Prior to class, secure a list of the church's new Christians in the past year and photocopy the reproducible activity "Compassion Covenant" from the next page. (Make enough copies of these "covenant" sheets and the list of new members for each student to have one of each.)

Ask the following questions and write suggested answers on the board: "What are some ways to encourage a new Christian?" "What are some ways to guide a new Christian?" After several answers have been written, distribute the "covenant" sheets and the lists of new Christians. Say, "Select one new Christian to spend time with this week, providing both guidance and encouragement. Fill in the information on your 'covenant' and sign your name."

After giving a few minutes to complete the forms, make a prayer circle and ask for God's blessing on the covenants made today.

Why Be Good?

Make two lists of reasons why one should be good. Make one for how goodness encourages believers; make the other for how goodness influences the unbeliever.

BELIEVERS   UNBELIEVERS

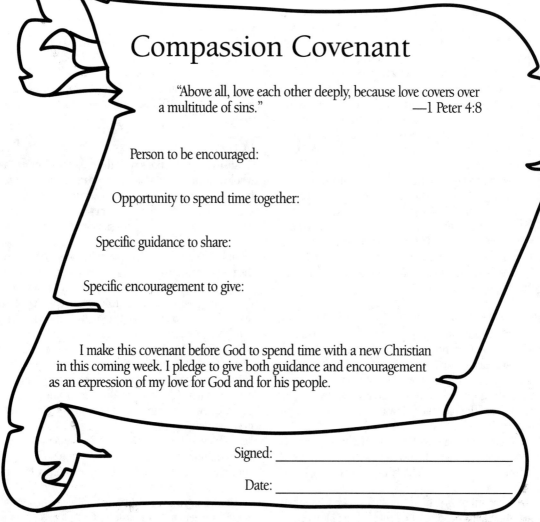

Compassion Covenant

"Above all, love each other deeply, because love covers over a multitude of sins."
—1 Peter 4:8

Person to be encouraged:

Opportunity to spend time together:

Specific guidance to share:

Specific encouragement to give:

I make this covenant before God to spend time with a new Christian in this coming week. I pledge to give both guidance and encouragement as an expression of my love for God and for his people.

Signed: _____

Date: _____

GROW IN FAITH

LESSON 7

WHY TEACH THIS LESSON?

Several years ago, a Bible-college professor left his U.S. classroom to take a short-term preaching and teaching trip to England. On one occasion he invited a couple to a Bible study that he would be teaching the following morning. The wife readily agreed, but the husband declined, saying, "I already know all that." Was this man being arrogant or was he merely naïve? Either way, the result was the same: a stagnant Christian of limited use to the kingdom of God.

We can shake our heads in wonder at this man's attitude, but it also serves as a valuable warning to your learners. A deadly and deadening sense of "spiritual self-satisfaction" can hit us at any stage of life, whether we are new Christians or hold a Ph.D. in theology. When your learners think they have mastered the Word of God, they no longer allow themselves to be mastered by the Word of God! Today's lesson will help your learners steer clear of this danger.

INTRODUCTION

Watching the children pour out of a third-grade classroom, I was surprised to see one student taller than I was, though I was a full-grown man. Later I asked the teacher, "Why is that big boy in third grade?"

She answered with a half-smile. "Because he's too big to sit in a first-grade seat where he belongs. He can't even read at first-grade level."

"What kind of a handicap does he have?"

"Who knows? His eyesight and hearing are normal. We've had them checked."

"What about his IQ?"

"He doesn't have one. With a psychiatrist as with a teacher, he has one answer to every question: 'I don't know.'"

"So he's just mentally incompetent?"

"I don't think so. He seems normal on the playground. He plays sports with the big boys—soccer, basketball, or softball, you name it."

"So it's only in the classroom that you'd call him a slow learner?"

"I don't call him a slow learner," the teacher snapped. "He's a no-learner!"

A. NO-LEARNERS IN THE CHURCH

Are there any no-learners in your church? The first-century church had some. A wise leader wrote, "Though by this time you ought to be teachers, you need someone to teach you the elementary truths of God's word all over again. You need milk, not solid food! Anyone who lives on milk, being still an infant, is not acquainted with the teaching about righteousness" (Hebrews 5:12, 13).

We all know some people like that in our twenty-first-century churches. They are not nitwits. They are well-informed and capable farmers, mechanics, and professional people. Such folks are eager to learn ever more about their trades and professions, but have no similar desire to grow in Christianity. They are saved! What more can anyone want? So they sit through sermons without listening and through Bible lessons without learning.

DEVOTIONAL READING:
EPHESIANS 3:14-21
BACKGROUND SCRIPTURE:
2 PETER 1
PRINTED TEXT:
2 PETER 1:3-15

LESSON AIMS

After participating in this lesson, each student will be able to:

1. Cite the characteristics of a mature Christian as described in today's text.

2. Identify aspects in his or her life that help encourage Christian growth.

3. Make arrangements with another student to hold each other accountable for working on a specific area of growth.

Oct
19

KEY VERSE

His divine power has given us everything we need for life and godliness through our knowledge of him who called us by his own glory and goodness.—2 Peter 1:3

The apostle Peter will not have such complacency. As we shall see in our text, he exhorts every Christian to become a better Christian. Paul likewise calls us to keep on improving "until we all . . . become mature, attaining to the whole measure of the fullness of Christ" (Ephesians 4:13). Until we all become like Jesus himself! What boundless room we all have for Christian growth!

B. LESSON BACKGROUND

Our text is from "Simon Peter, a servant and apostle of Jesus Christ" (2 Peter 1:1). It was originally sent "to those who . . . have received a faith as precious as ours" (1:1). That is, it was addressed to Christians like us. Exactly who they were and to which churches they belonged, we cannot say. They were aware of some of the apostle Paul's writings (3:15). Either they had received letters from Paul or Paul's letters to other churches had been shared with them. Apparently, however, they had not taken Paul's instructions to heart; some of Peter's readers were complacent, self-satisfied, and not eager to improve themselves and the church.

But was there ever a time when the church did not have self-satisfied members? Perhaps we can profit most from our text by considering today's lesson against the background of the church and Christians as we see them today. Then we can make today some of the improvements that Peter recommended two thousand years ago.

I. GOD'S GIFTS (2 PETER 1:3, 4)

Before speaking of what we need to do to grow in faith, Peter reminds us of what God already has done for us. Let us, then, first look at God's gifts that underlie and encourage the growth that he expects.

A. HIS POWER (v. 3)

3. His divine power has given us everything we need for life and godliness through our knowledge of him who called us by his own glory and goodness.

We are not alone in caring for ourselves and building the kind of character that Peter recommends. God has given us all the essential materials *we need for life and godliness.* For physical *life* we need food, clothing, shelter, and the like. These are rightly seen as God's gifts (Matthew 6:25-33). We suspect, however, that Peter is talking about more than physical life. This is the "eternal life," the "abundant life," that Jesus came to bring (John 3:16; 5:24; 10:10).

For *godliness* we need the guidance of God's own Word, and God has given us that, too. It is his Word that provides us the *knowledge of him who called us by his own glory and goodness.* This understanding doesn't come through personal visions, crystal balls, or horoscopes—it comes through the written Word. The more we study that Word, the more we come to realize how much he has given us in calling us to glory and goodness. When we think about this "glory and goodness," we must be careful to understand that this is referring to God's own "glory and goodness," and not ours! It is not until we come to recognize the glory and goodness of God that we hear and respond to his call.

Goodness here translates a Greek word that can mean almost any kind of goodness. It is used of the goodness of God, the goodness of people on earth, the goodness of a cow or a sheep, even the goodness of a table or chair. It is fitting, then, that human beings made in the image of God are called, not only to goodness, but also to godliness (also v. 6, below). God himself is the model for our goodness. We cannot hope or even wish to match his power and glory, but in our human relations we can aspire to God's own perfection (Matthew 5:48). Can we then be satisfied with anything less?

WHAT DO YOU THINK?

What can the church do to ensure its new members will receive knowledge "for life and godliness"?

[Romans 10:14-17 and Hebrews 4:2, 3 can help start your thinking.]

INGREDIENTS OF "THE GOOD LIFE"

Have you ever felt like all the "stuff" you have is more of a burden than a blessing? Actor Tim Robbins appeared on television some time ago, talking about "downsizing" his life. He said he was getting rid of stuff he didn't need, such as voice mail. When asked how people would contact him, he said, "They'll have to call me when I'm home." The audience cheered!

The late twentieth century brought us gadgets by the score that soon became "necessities" for many: computers, cell phones, and laptops, for example. We learned a new vocabulary: PDAs, CDs, DVDs, RAM, etc. High-powered executives—and even middle-school students!—found they couldn't function without a cell phone. But we also found that last year's computer wasn't fast enough and didn't have enough memory for all the new programs we wanted to use. Last year's cell phone was a bit bulky, so we "needed" a new, smaller one. Social philosophers have been warning us for decades that technology is not a savior; on the contrary, it can send life spinning out of control.

What a marvelous contrast is the text for today! The foundational provisions God makes for us, accompanied by his wonderful promises—these are what makes life good. Then, when we respond faithfully and begin to grow in the Christian graces mentioned in our text, that's when life *really* takes on meaning!   —C. R. B.

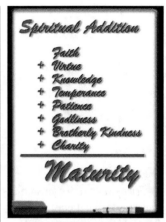

The visual for today's lesson provides a convenient summary of the qualities cited in verses 5-7.

B. HIS PROMISES (v. 4)

4. Through these he has given us his very great and precious promises, so that through them you may participate in the divine nature and escape the corruption in the world caused by evil desires.

God's greatest gifts to us are his *very great and precious promises*. According to those promises we participate in *the divine nature*, meaning that we become children of God (Galatians 3:26), growing more and more like Jesus (Ephesians 4:13). Quarrels, fighting, and other kinds of *corruption* come from our selfish *desires* for money, pleasure, power, or popularity. We read about that in our lesson for September 28 (James 4:1-4). In becoming God's children, we escape from such corruption. Our thinking is turned way from evil; we think on things that are good (Philippians 4:8).

II. GOD'S EXPECTATIONS (2 PETER 1:5-9)

God gives us all we need for life and godliness (v. 3); in so doing, he sets us free from worldly corruption and makes us his children (v. 4). We respond with gratitude, of course, and we show our gratitude by acting as God's children ought to act. That means we keep growing in all the good traits of Christian character.

A. THE MEANS (vv. 5-7)

5. For this very reason, make every effort to add to your faith goodness; and to goodness, knowledge;

We are to *make every effort* to try to be what God's children ought to be. We have *faith*, of course; we couldn't be Christians without it. To that we add *goodness*. As noted above in verse 3, that means every kind of goodness the children of God ought to have. But how can we add goodness to our character and our living unless we know what is good and what is bad? We get that kind of *knowledge* by reading the Bible. If we read several chapters of it every day, we shall not pass many days without seeing something that is good for us to do.

6. . . . and to knowledge, self-control; and to self-control, perseverance; and to perseverance, godliness;

Self-control is moderation. With that added to our personality, we keep a cool head in all situations and we control our behavior (cf. 2 Corinthians 12:20; Eph-

WHAT DO YOU THINK?

What can the church do to convince believers that they must put consistent effort into becoming mature spiritual Christians?

esians 4:25-32; Colossians 3:8; 1 Timothy 2:8). We keep our voice down as we reason with another, trying to win him or her to the same kind of goodness. *Perseverance* is not just waiting quietly and doing nothing. The same Greek word is sometimes translated "steadfastness." This is the quality of Christian character that keeps us doing and promoting what is right, but doing it with temperance and self-control, not with violence (James 5:7-11). *Godliness* is a lifestyle consistent with reverence for our awesome God, a lifestyle designed to please him (see 2 Peter 1:3, above). Indeed, knowledge of truth leads to godliness (cf. Titus 1:1).

7. . . . and to godliness, brotherly kindness; and to brotherly kindness, love.

Brotherly kindness is the affectionate mutual helpfulness seen in blood siblings at their best. Peter extends the idea to all Christianity (cf. 2 Corinthians 6:6; Galatians 5:22; Colossians 3:12). The crowning feature of this whole list is *love*. This is not romantic love—especially not the idealistic romance of novels and movies. This is love like that of God for the needy world (John 3:16). This is a heartfelt wish to do what is best for others, even at great cost to oneself.

B. THE ENDS (vv. 8, 9)

8. For if you possess these qualities in increasing measure, they will keep you from being ineffective and unproductive in your knowledge of our Lord Jesus Christ.

If we keep on adding knowledge to our faith, we shall come to greater *knowledge of our Lord Jesus Christ* and his will. But such knowledge in and of itself is worthless—it needs to lead us to fruitful service. As we continue to add the things listed in verses 5-9 above, we shall find more and more opportunities to help people who need help.

9. But if anyone does not have them, he is near-sighted and blind, and has forgotten that he has been cleansed from his past sins.

He that *does not have* these things is *blind* and unproductive in the Lord's work. Jesus had a lot to say about the dangers of spiritual blindness (Matthew 23:16-19). A person so afflicted cannot look ahead and catch a vision of God's glory to which he or she is called (1 Peter 1:3, above). Therefore he or she is not motivated by the hope of glory (Colossians 1:27). Neither can such a person look back and recall *that he has been cleansed from his past sins.* This person is therefore not motivated by gratitude for this cleansing and sees no reason to work for the Lord. Such a person is idle.

III. OUR REWARD (2 PETER 1:10, 11)

As we have just seen, the dangers of neglecting to grow in the Christian life are real and sobering. But Peter doesn't want merely to point out the negative. The positive aspects of Christian growth have magnificent eternal consequences!

A. CALLING AND ELECTION (v. 10)

10. Therefore, my brothers, be all the more eager to make your calling and election sure. For if you do these things, you will never fall,

Rather than being blind and idle like the person described in verse 9, every Christian is to make his or her *calling and election sure*. We do this by allowing God to work through us (Philippians 2:12, 13). It is God who saves us; but he does not do it against our will. We are not saved by any good works we do, but neither are we saved without doing any good works. God saves us by his grace and through our faith (Ephesians 2:8, 9), but our faith is dead unless it causes us to do something (James 2:17). So Peter urges us to add to our faith all the good things listed in verses 5-7. That is the way to make our salvation sure, *for if you do these things, you will never fall.*

B. WELCOME AND KINGDOM (v. 11)

11. . . . and you will receive a rich welcome into the eternal kingdom of our Lord and Savior Jesus Christ.

How can we be sure of being in Christ's *eternal kingdom?* In addition to having faith in King Jesus, we simply obey him, do his will, and serve him (John 14:15). Evidence of our allegiance is seen in all the things that Peter urges us to add to our faith in 2 Peter 1:5-7, above. When we have these in abundance, we are constant in our service to Christ (v. 8), and there can be no doubt about our citizenship in his kingdom.

IV. PETER'S PLEA (2 PETER 1:12-15)

Simon Peter never went to teacher's college (Acts 4:13), but he understood the importance of repetition in Christian education. He wants us to know Christian principles so well that we apply them automatically and come up with the right answers.

A. REPEATED REMINDER (v. 12)

12. So I will always remind you of these things, even though you know them and are firmly established in the truth you now have.

These things that Peter is teaching (vv. 5-7) were not new to first-century Christians, and they are not new to us. But they are so important to good Christian living (vv. 8, 9) and so important to citizenship in Heaven (vv. 10, 11) that Peter repeats them to people who already *know them.*

B. LIMITED TIME (vv. 13, 14)

13. I think it is right to refresh your memory as long as I live in the tent of this body,

A *tent* is a temporary structure (cf. Exodus 26). Peter's tent as he writes is his physical body. (Paul uses the same metaphor in 2 Corinthians 5:1.) Peter thinks it is proper to continue reminding his readers of what they already know as long as he is living in that body and is able to write. His purpose is not just to repeat well-known words; it is *to refresh* our *memory,* and to stir us up—to motivate every Christian to do what is taught in this text.

REMEMBER . . . AND REMEMBER

The year was 1944. Two students at a Christian college in Texas were engaged to be married. They were deeply in love, but their peers and professors discouraged the interracial relationship. Anne was a white American. Her fiance, Masaaki, was also an American but of Japanese descent. In those times in America anyone of Japanese ancestry was looked upon with great suspicion. Eventually the force of this prejudice drove them apart.

In the years to come each married someone else, raised a family, and was eventually widowed. But "first loves" have a way of being remembered. Now single again, Masaaki tracked Anne down using the Internet. Fifty-six years after they had parted, Masaaki and Anne married, with their families celebrating the event at their sides. Anne said of the phone call when she first heard Masaaki's voice again, "I knew instantly that he wanted me back. During all those years he was always in the back of my mind."

Peter says of the Lord, who should be the first love of our hearts and spirits, that he should ever be in the back of our minds, always directing our thoughts and behavior. We are to remember (and remember . . . and remember . . .) that we are the bride of Christ, whose love for us never dims or fades. And neither should our love for Him. —C. R. B.

DAILY BIBLE READINGS

Monday, Oct. 13—Trust God, Send Out Roots (Jeremiah 17:5-10)

Tuesday, Oct. 14—The Righteous Grow, Produce Fruit (Psalm 92:5-15)

Wednesday, Oct. 15—Be Rooted and Grounded in Christ (Ephesians 3:14-21)

Thursday, Oct. 16—Live in the Spirit (Romans 8:9-17)

Friday, Oct. 17—Support Your Faith With Goodness (2 Peter 1:1-7)

Saturday, Oct. 18—Eagerly Confirm Your Call (2 Peter 1:8-15)

Sunday, Oct. 19—Be Attentive to the Prophetic Message (2 Peter 1:16-21)

HOW TO SAY IT

Colossians. Kuh-LOSH-unz.
Corinthians. Kor-IN-thee-unz.
Ephesians. Ee-FEE-zhunz.
Masaaki. Mah-sah-AH-key.
Philippians. Fih-LIP-ee-unz.

14. . . . because I know that I will soon put it aside, as our Lord Jesus Christ has made clear to me.

Peter knows his time for teaching is short; he will not live much longer. Jesus himself had told him that. Peter undoubtedly recalls the warning in John 21:18, 19, and he means to make good use of the time he has left on earth. (Tradition has it that Peter was crucified in Rome.)

C. NEVER FORGET (v. 15)

15. And I will make every effort to see that after my departure you will always be able to remember these things.

Peter is writing about things that are vastly important to Christians living on earth (v. 8) for their eternal life in Heaven (vv. 10, 11). He intends to repeat *these things* so that his readers will not forget them after his death. Even today they are fresh in our memory. If we heed them well, they will guide us through our earthly life and ensure our entrance into the kingdom eternal (v. 11).

CONCLUSION

We introduced this lesson by taking note of slow learners and no-learners in the church. Most churches have some of them. These people are Christians, they say, and that is enough. They seem to have no desire to be moving upward toward "the whole measure of the fullness of Christ" (Ephesians 4:13). But there is another side of the picture.

A. LEARNERS, DOERS, AND REPEATERS

Mary Ann thinks her class of third graders is the best in the Sunday school. "These little people are so eager," she says. "They soak up facts and Bible stories like so many sponges. This is the learning-est class!" And we remember that Jesus said, "Unless you change and become like little children, you will never enter the kingdom of heaven" (Matthew 18:3).

Brandon thinks his class is the best in the Sunday school. His students are middle-aged, prime-of-life people. On Saturday they may visit the church to pick up litter, weed the flower beds, or mow the lawn. This is the class that sends a welcoming committee to greet newcomers in the neighborhood. Brandon says they have been learning for a long time, and now they are the doing-est class.

Nels teaches the old folks' class, and he thinks that is the best class of all. Seldom does he startle his students with anything they have not heard before, but they love to go over passages they learned long ago. When the teacher wants to call attention to a verse of Scripture, he quotes its opening words and pauses. Half a dozen voices in unison finish the verse. The old folks do take an interest in the few things they hear for the first time, but their greater delight is in recalling and repeating what they learned long ago. That does not mean the old folks are not doers. Those who are physically able are right there alongside the younger men and women whenever the church has ministries that need to be done.

B. SUMMARY

The children may be the fastest learners, and they are learning what Christians do as well as what Christians know. The middle-agers may be the greatest doers, and they are learning from their doing as well as from the Bible. The old folks grow stronger spiritually as they review their learning. If their doing is limited by failing strength, it is refined by growing wisdom. So in your church and my church the slow learners and no-learners are outnumbered by the learners, doers, and repeaters—God's work is being done as they grow in faith.

WHAT DO YOU THINK?

Peter was eager that the Christians be assured and convinced of the things he wrote about. He wanted to be sure they clung to them even after his death. How can churches or individual Christians develop a zeal and a faith that last beyond the influence of certain leaders?

PRAYER

Father in Heaven, thank you for holding before us the ideal toward which we grow: "the whole measure of the fullness of Christ." Thank you for the unfailing guidance of your Word; thank you for minds that can learn and plan; thank you for strength to do. In gratitude we promise our best efforts to learn your will and do it. In Jesus' name, amen.

THOUGHT TO REMEMBER

You're either growing in Christ or withering away—there is no standing still.

Discovery Learning

This page contains an alternative lesson plan emphasizing learning activities. Classes desiring such student involvement will find these suggestions helpful. The next page is a reproducible activity page to further enhance discovery learning.

LEARNING GOALS

After this lesson each student will be able to:

1. Cite the characteristics of a mature Christian as described in today's text.

2. Identify aspects in his or her life that help encourage Christian growth.

3. Make arrangements with another student to hold each other accountable for working on a specific area of growth.

INTO THE LESSON

Create the following word-find activity on a large poster board or an overhead transparency. Display it and say, "There are seven words of at least four letters hidden in this puzzle, spelled forward or backward, up or down, or diagonally. When you find a word, call it out and I'll circle it for all to see." (These words are hidden: *child, appetite, seed, grass, weed, hair, love*.)

```
F D S A G V U C M F O Z
R E P R R I A H E N T Y
W E A P P E T I T E U E
O S E J O L S L P Q V M
S F A C W E E D X O I S
T I D H A G N P L E B Z
```

Allow a few minutes for all the words to be found. Then say, "Now discuss with your neighbor what these words all have in common." Allow two minutes for discussion; then ask for suggestions from the class.

If the answer is not suggested by the class, tell them: "These are all things that grow." Say, "Today, we focus on something else that grows: our faith. Turn to 2 Peter 1:3-15, and let's see how God says our own faith can grow."

INTO THE WORD

Ask a class member to read the lesson text aloud to the class. For this question-and-answer activity, move the class into groups of three students each. Prior to class time, prepare the following questions on a work sheet and make enough copies so that each group has one.

1. What has God's divine power given us? (*Everything we need for life and godliness, 2 Peter 1:3.*)

2. What have God's precious promises to believers empowered them to be able to do? (*Participate in the divine nature; escape the corruption in the world, 2 Peter 1:4.*)

3. What did Peter say contributed to the world's corruption? (*Evil desires, 2 Peter 1:4.*)

4. What are the characteristics of a mature Christian for a believer who "gives all diligence"? (*Faith, goodness, knowledge, self-control, perseverance, godliness, brotherly kindness, love, 2 Peter 1:5-7.*)

5. What result does Peter promise for believers who have those characteristics in their lives? (*They will not be ineffective and unproductive, 2 Peter 1:8.*)

6. How does Peter describe believers who do not have these characteristics? (*Nearsighted, blind, forgotten about cleansing of personal sin, 2 Peter 1:9.*)

7. What promise does Peter give to those who "make your calling and election sure"? (*You will never fall, 2 Peter 1:10.*)

8. As long as Peter was alive, what did he say was necessary for him to do? (*Refresh their memory of these things, 2 Peter 1:12, 13.*)

Allow six to eight minutes for groups to work. As a whole class, review the answers.

INTO LIFE

Prior to class, make copies of the reproducible activity "Christian Maturity Indicator Scale" from the next page. Give one to each student now and say, "Peter teaches that faith grows. I want each of us to evaluate the strength of the eight characteristics of a mature Christian in our lives. Place a "dot" on the line from each at the point indicating the strength of that characteristic in your own life. Then draw a line from dot to dot." Allow time for reflection and for completing this self-analysis. Say, "Peter identifies qualities that help encourage Christian growth: promises of God, v. 4; diligence, v. 5; remembrance of cleansing, vv. 9, 13, 15. What in your life helps encourage Christian growth?" Write suggested answers on the board.

State: "Peter held these believers accountable by reminding them of God's promises." Make copies of the reproducible activity "The Accountability Factor" from the next page, and give one to each person, and say: "We must be held accountable. Select a classmate and make a commitment to contact each other during this week to encourage growth in one of your low-ranked characteristics. Complete two cards with the names and contact information of you and your partner; each of you keep one. Then, close the class time by praying for each other as you seek to grow in your personal faith."

Christian Maturity Indicator Scale

Self-Analysis Graph

Like Jesus
10
9
8
7
6
5
4
3
2
1
New Christian

Faith | Goodness | Knowledge | Self-Control | Perseverance | Godliness | Brotherly Kindness | Love

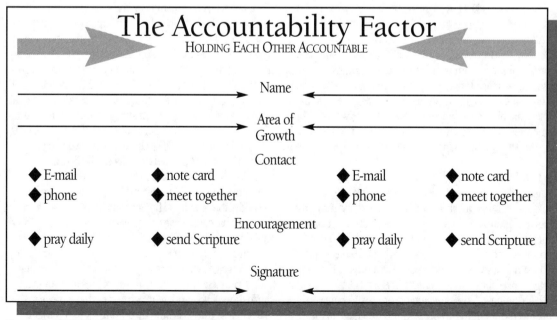

The Accountability Factor

HOLDING EACH OTHER ACCOUNTABLE

Name

Area of Growth

Contact

◆ E-mail   ◆ note card   ◆ E-mail   ◆ note card
◆ phone   ◆ meet together   ◆ phone   ◆ meet together

Encouragement

◆ pray daily   ◆ send Scripture   ◆ pray daily   ◆ send Scripture

Signature

TRUST GOD'S PROMISE

LESSON 8

WHY TEACH THIS LESSON?

The world of track-and-field sports has given us the phrase "track record." Merriam Webster's dictionary defines it as "a record of performance often taken as an indicator of likely future performance." Since this phrase has been around only since about 1952, the first-century New Testament writers wouldn't recognize it as such. They would, however, agree with the concept.

We trust God to keep his promises because of his track record. His record of performance is not merely "an indicator of likely future performance," but is an *absolute guarantee* of future performance! So, when earthly trials, physical ills, and spiritual doubts torment your learners, where will they look for solutions? Will they fall under the sway of non-Christian explanations and solutions? Or will they trust their futures to the God who has a track record going back thousands of years? Today's lesson makes the choice clear.

INTRODUCTION

A. TRUSTING JESUS

The Ampro Writers' Club invited an editor of Christian publications to discuss the kinds of writing used in those publications. Part of the discussion is printed below, with a writer called W and the editor called E.

W: Do you teach that Jesus is going to come back?

E: Yes, we do. He promised.

W: I'm afraid I can't go along with you on that. He's not coming back.

E: May I ask where you got that information?

W: From history. From science. From observation. From common sense. After all, it's been two thousand years. How long do you wait for a promise to be kept?

E: That depends on who made the promise. For Jesus' promise, we wait as many thousands of years as it takes. He is dependable.

B. LESSON BACKGROUND

Very plainly Jesus said he would come back. He said his coming would be announced by the failure of sun, moon, and stars. He said angels would gather Jesus' people from all over the world (Matthew 24:29-31). Jesus said also that he will separate those destined for a prepared kingdom from those destined for everlasting fire (25:31-46). If we believe Jesus, we had better give heed to his warning, "Therefore keep watch, because you do not know the day or the hour" (25:13).

But as Peter writes his second and final letter in the mid-60s A.D., it's now been about thirty-five years since Jesus made his promise to return. Some fear that Jesus already has returned and that somehow they have missed it. (See 2 Thessalonians 2:1-3.) Others are becoming skeptical that Jesus will *ever* return.

But Peter has the solution to their skepticism. In last week's text he was emphatic in telling his readers that he was repeating things they already knew. He said that he was going to keep on repeating them as long as he lived on earth so his readers would remember those repeated teachings long after he was dead (2 Peter 1:12-15).

DEVOTIONAL READING:
HEBREWS 10:19-25

BACKGROUND SCRIPTURE:
2 PETER 3

PRINTED TEXT:
2 PETER 3:3-18

LESSON AIMS

After participating in this lesson, each student will be able to:

1. Summarize Peter's teaching about the Lord's return.

2. Compare the scoffing of the first-century mockers with that of modern disbelievers.

3. Suggest a specific way to obey the command of 2 Peter 3:14.

Oct
26

KEY VERSES

So then, dear friends, since you are looking forward to this, make every effort to be found spotless, blameless and at peace with him. Bear in mind that our Lord's patience means salvation.
—2 Peter 3:14, 15

In the opening verses of chapter 3 he returns to that theme. He is stirring up his readers' minds with "reminders," making sure that they keep in mind the teaching of the inspired prophets and the apostles of Jesus (3:1, 2). In the beginning of this week's text he explains why it is so necessary to keep that true teaching in mind. Scoffers are coming to make fun of the truth—indeed, they already abound. Christians must be ready to respond to them with "wholesome thinking" (3:1).

I. ANTICIPATING THE SCOFFERS (2 PETER 3:3-7)

Like the first readers of this letter, we need to be prepared with the ancient truth taught by the prophets and apostles. Scoffers can cause a lot of damage if we're not alert to their activities and quick to respond. (See 1 Timothy 4:1-3; 2 Timothy 3:1-9; and Jude 17-19.) We begin by anticipating the scoffers and their arguments. As the old saying goes, "Forewarned is forearmed!"

A. THEIR ATTITUDE (vv. 3, 4)
3. First of all, you must understand that in the last days scoffers will come, scoffing and following their own evil desires.

The last days are all the days of the Christian era, all the time between Jesus' first coming to his second coming (Hebrews 1:2; 1 Peter 1:20; 1 John 2:18). This is the last era of the earth as we know it. *Scoffers* have been busy throughout most of this era, trying to turn God's people away from the truth. Their foundational problem is that they follow *their own evil desires* instead of following Jesus. They are concerned about their own profit, pleasure, and pride, and not about the kingdom of God and his righteousness (Matthew 6:33). It is not in their selfish interest to accept that history might come to an end at any time.

4. They will say, "Where is this 'coming' he promised? Ever since our fathers died, everything goes on as it has since the beginning of creation."

It's been about thirty-five years since Jesus made the promise of his return. "*Where is it?*" the scoffers ask. The *fathers* may mean the scoffers' own fathers—the first generation of Christians, the men who had come to Christ in the beginning days of the church. They had believed the promise that Jesus will come back; they had lived out their lives expecting to see him. But now they are dead. The scoffers say that it is silly for the next generation to continue believing a promise that has not been kept. And since Jesus has not kept his promise, they say it is pointless to be bound by his teaching. Why not be crooked in business if it is profitable? Why not commit adultery if it is fun? Why do anything for the poor and sick who cannot do anything in return?

The Bible promises that spectacular events will accompany Jesus' return (Luke 21:25-28). But *everything goes on as it has since the beginning of creation*. It must be time to abandon Christianity, the scoffers say, because the passing of time has proven it to be a failure.

WHAT DO YOU THINK?

Using James 1:19 as a starting point, what are some good techniques for Christians to use when witnessing to scoffers?

B. THEIR ERROR (vv. 5, 6)
5, 6. But they deliberately forget that long ago by God's word the heavens existed and the earth was formed out of water and by water. By these waters also the world of that time was deluged and destroyed.

There is nothing wrong with ignorance when it cannot be helped. Everyone is ignorant of some things. But willfully ignoring the truth one ought to be aware of is, in fact, a rejection of the truth. This is the sin of the scoffers: they *deliberately forget* the fact that it was *by God's word* that the *heavens* and *earth* came into being in the first place! This same word of God, as expanded by Jesus, is what promises an end to that old creation.

Further, it simply is not true that the ordinary course of nature has gone on since the beginning of creation. Long after the creation, the normal course of nature was interrupted by another spectacular event: the great flood of Noah's day. *The world of that time,* standing out of the water, was *deluged* with water, and most of humanity was *destroyed* in a judgment scarcely less spectacular than the one promised in Matthew 25:31-46 (see Genesis 6–8).

C. THE PROMISE (v. 7)

7. By the same word the present heavens and earth are reserved for fire, being kept for the day of judgment and destruction of ungodly men.

The present heavens and earth came into being by the word of God (v. 5). By the same word a flood destroyed most of the conscious living things of that world (Genesis 6:13). *By the same word* the creation we see is reserved unto fire. It will be burned up (v. 10), and the *ungodly* will perish.

D. B. COOPER AND JESUS

On November 24, 1971, D. B. Cooper boarded a plane in Portland, Oregon, showed a flight attendant what appeared to be a bomb in his carry-on luggage and demanded two hundred thousand dollars and four parachutes. When the plane landed at Seattle, Cooper was given the money and parachutes; he then directed the pilot to fly to Mexico. Shortly after takeoff he opened the rear door of the plane and jumped out, never to be seen again. No body was ever found. The only clue to his disappearance was found nine years later: a pack of twenty-dollar bills matching the serial numbers recorded by the FBI.

For nearly thirty years, a tavern in Ariel, Washington, has held a celebration on the anniversary of Cooper's escapade. Some people think of him as a folk hero; some probably consider the day simply an excuse for revelry.

It's been nearly two thousand years since Christ arose and promised to return. Every year we celebrate his resurrection and anticipate his second coming. Peter warned that skeptics would have fun at our expense, and it is so. What is the difference between Jesus and D. B. Cooper? At least two significant differences exist. First, Cooper risked the lives of others for his own profit; Christ gave his life so others could gain. Second, Cooper is almost certainly dead, but Jesus lives again. We can admire what Jesus did and trust the promise of what he is yet to do. —C. R. B.

II. REMEMBERING THE TRUTH (2 PETER 3:8-10)

Scoffers who ridiculed the idea of Christ's return also probably ridiculed the idea that the earth would be burned up. I knew a high-school teacher who mocked that prospect. "The earth was born in fire," he said. "It was burned to a cinder in its birth. It's fireproof." But nothing in this world is immune to God's fire.

A. EXPLANATION OF DELAY (vv. 8, 9)

8. But do not forget this one thing, dear friends: With the Lord a day is like a thousand years, and a thousand years are like a day.

Limited as we are by time, it is hard for us to grasp eternity. Eighty years is a long time to a person on earth, for it leaves him or her only a few more years to live. But when God lives *a thousand years,* he has as many years to live as he had when the thousand years began, for his life has neither beginning nor end (cf. Psalm 90:4).

9. The Lord is not slow in keeping his promise, as some understand slowness. He is patient with you, not wanting anyone to perish, but everyone to come to repentance.

By the word of God . . . the world that then was, being overflowed with water, perished.
—*2 Peter 3:5, 6*

Display this visual from the Adult Visuals packet as you discuss verses 5 and 6 of the text.

WHAT DO YOU THINK?

God's perspective of time is much different from ours. How important do you think that is? Why?

WHAT DO YOU THINK?

What do we learn about God's nature from the fact that he has not yet brought about the Day of Judgment?

WHAT DO YOU THINK?

What can every Christian do (or not do!) to be prepared for the second coming of Christ?

[Make sure you don't overlook Matthew 24:36; 25:13; 2 Thessalonians 3:12; 1 Peter 1:15, 16; 2 Peter 3:11-13; and Revelation 3:3 as you frame your answer.]

Distressed by the evil reported in halls of government, in places of business, in schools, on the street, and in homes, do you ever wonder why God hasn't destroyed this wicked world before now? Here is the answer: God is waiting for more people to repent. God's patience is an important biblical theme (Exodus 34:6; Romans 2:4; 9:22). And some are indeed repenting, but not nearly enough. Do you suppose God is satisfied with what we are doing to bring more people *to repentance?*

B. END OF DELAY (v. 10)

10. But the day of the Lord will come like a thief. The heavens will disappear with a roar; the elements will be destroyed by fire, and the earth and everything in it will be laid bare.

In this context *the day of the Lord* means the time of Jesus' second coming (v. 4). It is also the day of other tremendous events. *A thief* comes when he is not expected, and so will *the day of the Lord.* The New Testament describes Jesus' return "as a thief" in several places (see Matthew 24:42-44; Luke 12:39; 1 Thessalonians 5:2; Revelation 3:3; 16:15), so we must be ready.

The day of the Lord, however, will not also depart unseen and unheard as *a thief* does. On that day the people of earth "will see the Son of Man coming on the clouds of the sky, with power and great glory" (Matthew 24:30). God's people will see the angels bringing them together to meet their Savior (24:31). Every person in the world will hear himself or herself pronounced blessed or cursed (25:34, 41). It is a day on which *the Lord* will bring about the end of the world and the universe that we know (Joel 2:10; Mark 13:24-27; Revelation 20:11). *The heavens* that we admire on a clear night *will disappear with a roar.*

"A-MAZE-INGLY" COMPLICATED

Justin Taylor and Chris Taylor, recent college graduates, took out a small business loan, rented five acres of land just a few miles outside Memphis, Tennessee, bought some seed corn, and started Mid-South Maze. They became part of a franchise business that has built about one hundred mazes across America. The Taylors pay 6 percent of their profits to the parent company for the privilege of confusing patrons of their maze.

Their field was planted at about twice the density of a normal cornfield. When the plants were a foot tall, they cut the maze into it with a weed cutter. By the time the crop matured, one could not see through the closely planted rows of corn. The two miles of paths winding through the field were five feet wide, and had so many turns and dead ends that it typically took people an hour or so to find their way through it.

Complicated as these mazes can be, it is as nothing compared with what some Christians do with the prophecies surrounding the end of the world. It is "a-maze-ing" how complicated some preachers and teachers make the simple message of Scripture, trying to plot an intricate series of events leading up to the end and pinpoint the time at which it will come. Peter says the day will come unexpectedly, so our concern should not be when the day will come, but whether we will be prepared for it.

—C. R. B.

HOW TO SAY IT

Corinthians. Kor-IN-thee-unz.
Galatians. Guh-LAY-shunz.
Hebrews. HEE-brews.
Jeremiah. Jair-uh-MY-uh.
Philippians. Fih-LIP-ee-unz.
Thessalonians. THESS-uh-LO-nee-unz.

III. IMPLEMENTING THE TRUTH (2 PETER 3:11-18)

In modern culture the question "So what?" usually is a flippant one. Often it is intended to imply that nothing important will come from what has been said or done. But in this case, "So what?" is a serious and important question since the answer points to eternal truth. This truth assures us that Jesus will come back according to his promise. The events he predicted in Matthew 24 and 25 will come to pass: the gathering of his people and the judgment of all humanity. This future reality should cause us to live our lives in certain ways.

A. WHAT WE DO AND EXPECT (vv. 11-14)

11. Since everything will be destroyed in this way, what kind of people ought you to be? You ought to live holy and godly lives

Peter asks a rhetorical question, and the answer he expects is obvious. The way we *live* and act day by day should make it plain that we are God's *people, holy,* dedicated, set apart for his service. Living *godly lives* causes us to show reverence and awe before God, along with continual obedience to his teaching. "The world and its desires pass away, but the man who does the will of God lives forever" (1 John 2:17).

12. . . . as you look forward to the day of God and speed its coming. That day will bring about the destruction of the heavens by fire, and the elements will melt in the heat.

We know the ground where we stand is going to be burned up along with the rest of the earth and the universe, but that knowledge brings us no terror (cf. Revelation 6:12-17). Eagerly we *look forward to* that *day;* gladly we *speed its coming.* That great day is the climax of all history; it brings the realization of all our hopes. In this light we can pray, as John does in the next to the last verse of the Bible, "Amen. Come, Lord Jesus."

13. But in keeping with his promise we are looking forward to a new heaven and a new earth, the home of righteousness.

God's *promise* of *a new heaven and a new earth* is seen in Isaiah 65:17; 66:22. John saw the new creation in a vision (Revelation 21:1), and he gives a marvelous description of the New Jerusalem that he saw (21:2). Peter says nothing about the size or shape of the new heavens and earth, but he states the most important difference between them and the earth we know: the new heavens and earth are *the home of righteousness* (cf. Jeremiah 23:5-7; 33:16; Revelation 21:27).

14. So then, dear friends, since you are looking forward to this, make every effort to be found spotless, blameless and at peace with him.

Since we are to live in that new creation where righteousness lives, we are to take care to be righteous here and now. Just as Christ was *spotless* and *blameless* (see 1 Peter 1:19), so are we to be. It is his blood that makes us so. When we see that our daily lives are not quite spotless, we are disappointed but not dismayed. Our hope remains sure; we know that we are forgiven (1 John 1:9).

B. WHAT PAUL SAYS (vv. 15, 16)

15. Bear in mind that our Lord's patience means salvation, just as our dear brother Paul also wrote you with the wisdom that God gave him.

The Lord's long wait before coming provides an opportunity for more and more people to repent and be saved. This repeats what has been said in verse 9. Paul's letters offer similar information—see especially Romans 2:4.

16. He writes the same way in all his letters, speaking in them of these matters. His letters contain some things that are hard to understand, which ignorant and unstable people distort, as they do the other Scriptures, to their own destruction.

When Peter speaks of *the other Scriptures,* he is recognizing that Paul's *letters* have the authority of Scripture as well (cf. 1 Corinthians 14:37). Although Paul had to correct Peter on one occasion (Galatians 2:11-21), it was a correction of behavior and not of teaching. We never find any contradictions between these two apostles. Different as their writings are, there are no mistakes in either, for the Holy Spirit inspired both.

DAILY BIBLE READINGS

Monday, Oct. 20—*Hold Fast to Our Hope (Hebrews 10:19-25)*

Tuesday, Oct. 21—*God Is Faithful (1 Corinthians 1:4-9)*

Wednesday, Oct. 22—*In Christ, It Is "Yes" (2 Corinthians 1:18-22)*

Thursday, Oct. 23—*God's Word Shall Not Return Empty (Isaiah 55:8-12)*

Friday, Oct. 24—*Where Is the Promise? (2 Peter 3:1-7)*

Saturday, Oct. 25—*God Is Not Slow (2 Peter 3:8-13)*

Sunday, Oct. 26—*Regard God's Patience as Salvation (2 Peter 3:14-18)*

WHAT DO YOU THINK?

Which is the greater threat to the average Christian, a scoffer or a supposed believer who distorts the Word of God? Why?

[Passages such as Matthew 7:15; 2 Thessalonians 2:1-5; 2 Timothy 4:4, 5; and Titus 3:9-11 will be important to consider as you frame your answer.]

PRAYER

Forgive us, Father. We do confess the sins that spot our holiness and make us less than we want to be. And along with your gracious forgiveness that makes us clean, please give us wisdom, strength, and courage to keep ourselves clean today and tomorrow and all through the week. In Jesus' name, amen.

WHAT DO YOU THINK?

Why is it important for Christians to grow in grace as well as in knowledge?

[Be sure to consider 1 Corinthians 8:1 in your answer.]

THOUGHT TO REMEMBER

All of God's promises are trustworthy.
Are we?

However, Peter says Paul's writings contain *some things that are hard to understand,* and we would agree. Jesus spoke difficult things as well (John 6:60). That should not surprise us. It would be more surprising if we could easily understand all the deep things of God that are spoken and written by inspiration of his Spirit.

All of us need to be careful not to *distort* those difficult passages—twisting them into some meaning not intended by the writers. Scripture-twisting is a never-ending problem (see Jeremiah 23:36; Acts 20:30; 2 Corinthians 4:2; and Jude 4). The way to avoid such error is to seek truth and truth teachers all our lives (2 Thessalonians 2:10-13; 2 Timothy 2:15; 1 Peter 1:22; 2 Peter 1:12). Then we shall not stand condemned as *ignorant and unstable people* who twist Paul's writing and *the other Scriptures* as well.

C. WHAT WE AVOID (v. 17)

17. Therefore, dear friends, since you already know this, be on your guard so that you may not be carried away by the error of lawless men and fall from your secure position.

Jesus warned of shallow believers in Matthew 13:5. As Peter writes this letter, only about thirty-five years after Jesus returned to Heaven, already some people are losing confidence in his promise to come back. Two thousand years later, relatively few people are seriously guiding their lives today by the thought that he may return tomorrow.

But when Jesus does indeed return, he will find that countless people, including some so-called Christians, have been *carried away by the error of lawless men.* They will find themselves cursed rather than blessed in the judgment (Matthew 25:34, 41). That is what we want to avoid. So we hold ourselves in a dual readiness. We are ready to drop what we are doing and soar with joy to meet our Lord in the air (1 Thessalonians 4:17); and we are no less ready to go on with our customary life on earth, spotless and blameless (2 Peter 3:14)—and quick to admit it when we find we are not quite spotless (1 John 1:9).

D. WHAT WE DO, PART 2 (v. 18a)

18a. But grow in the grace and knowledge of our Lord and Savior Jesus Christ.

We *grow* in the *knowledge of* Jesus as we read about him in the Bible, as we walk with him day by day, and when we die to sin with him. This was Paul's own earnest desire (Philippians 3:10, 11). We *grow* in *grace* when we increase our service in various ways (e.g., 2 Corinthians 8:7) and continually recognize how gracious God has been to us. This is true Christian growth!

E. GLORY TO JESUS (v. 18b)

18b. To him be glory both now and forever! Amen.

We grow in grace and the knowledge of Jesus also for the *glory* of Jesus. All we do can never earn life everlasting. Jesus redeemed us with his death; in paying sin's price, he saved us by his grace, his mercy, his forgiveness. All praise, honor, and glory properly belong to him *now and forever. Amen!*

CONCLUSION

Let's conclude this lesson with a long look at ourselves in the light of the ideal set forth in verse 14 of our text. Is the life we are living really "spotless and blameless"? If a long look reveals a few spots in our way of life, let's apply the spot remover recommended in 1 John 1:9 (see next week's lesson). And let us do so with full trust in the one who always has kept his promises, and always will.

Discovery Learning

This page contains an alternative lesson plan emphasizing learning activities. Classes desiring such student involvement will find these suggestions helpful. The next page is a reproducible activity page to further enhance discovery learning.

LEARNING GOALS

After this lesson each student will be able to:

1. Summarize Peter's teaching about the Lord's return.

2. Compare the scoffing of the first-century mockers with that of modern disbelievers.

3. Suggest a specific way to obey the command of 2 Peter 3:14.

INTO THE LESSON

In preparation for this week's lesson, prepare the following statement-completion activity and make a copy for each student. The statement to introduce the lesson and to be completed is this: "When people break promises they have made to me, it affects both my own attitude and my perception of them. My attitude becomes _____, and I begin to think of them as _____."

Say, "Each of us has had the experience of someone breaking a promise made to us. Today we begin by reflecting on how broken promises affect both our attitudes and our perceptions of those who failed to keep their promises. Complete the statement by writing your thoughts and feelings about how broken promises affect you." Distribute the statement-completion sheet, and give a minute or two for class members to write their answers. Then ask class members to reveal their answers; write these on the board. (Take all the answers to the first part before discussing the second part.) Say, "Broken promises tend to discredit the trustworthiness of those who made the promises. Our text from 2 Peter 3 identifies those who believe God has broken His promise to us."

INTO THE WORD

Prior to class, prepare the following matching activity and make copies for all class members. Ask a class member to read aloud 2 Peter 3:3-18. Pass the activity sheet out to the class and say, "Read each phrase on the left side and select the best answer from those on the right. Write the letter of your selected answer in the space provided. An answer may be used more than once."

List the following phrases on the left side, each with a short blank line in front for writing the letter of the selected answer.

1. heavens will disappear, v. 10
2. earth reserved for fire, v. 7
3. come like a thief, v. 10
4. heavens by fire, v. 12
5. a new heaven and new earth, v. 13
6. world destroyed, v. 6
7. fall from a secure position, v. 17
8. holy and godly lives, v. 11
9. following their own evil desires, v. 3
10. spotless, blameless, and at peace, v. 14.

List the following answers on the right: A. Ignorant scoffers; B. His promise; C. Be on your guard; D. Make every effort; E. Day of God; F. Day of the Lord; G. Everything will be destroyed; H. Day of judgment and destruction. The answers are: 1-F; 2-H; 3-F; 4-E; 5-B; 6-A; 7-C; 8-G; 9-A; 10-D.

Move the students into groups of three and say, "As scoffers mocked the first-century believers, so the mockery continues. Compare the scoffing that Peter addressed with that of modern disbelievers." Use the reproducible activity "Scoffing Mockery: An Ageless Reality" from the next page. Make a copy for each small group. Give about seven minutes for the groups to write suggested answers. Then, ask for volunteers to share their answers with the class.

INTO LIFE

State: "Mockers truly are a present-day reality. But the Lord's patience is an opportunity for mockers to come to repentance. What does a clear understanding of the coming day of the Lord lead us to do?" *(Be holy and godly, v. 11; look forward to that day, v. 12; make every effort, v. 14; beware that we don't fall, v. 17; grow in grace and knowledge, v. 18).* Use the reproducible activity "Make Every Effort" from the next page. Give a copy of this action sheet to each student, and say, "The command in 2 Peter 3:14 is to, 'Make every effort to be found spotless, blameless and at peace with him,' when the Lord returns. What do you need to do to bring these realities about in your own life?" Indicate that the first has to do primarily with relationship to God; the second, relationship to others; the third, relationship to self. Encourage students to give serious thought and reflection and to write in the spaces provided what they intend to do. Close the class time with a prayer of dedication and commitment. Include the concepts of 2 Peter 3:14 in your prayer.

Scoffing Mockery: An Ageless Reality

Read 2 Peter 3:3-18 and compare the mocking our our day with that of Peter's day.

FIRST-CENTURY MOCKERS *How did the scoffers mock first-century believers?*	PRESENT-DAY DISBELIEVERS *In what ways do scoffers mock believers today?*

Make Every Effort (2 Peter 3:14)

Suggest specific ways and means you can employ to grow in the areas listed on the chart below.

SPOTLESS	To make my life "spotless," I need to . . .
BLAMELESS	To make my life "blameless," I need to . . .
AT PEACE	To make my life "at peace," I need to . . .

ENJOY FELLOWSHIP WITH GOD

LESSON 9

WHY TEACH THIS LESSON?

Consider the typical "fellowship dinner" that churches occasionally hold. A date is announced, a sign-up sheet is posted, and on the anticipated day people show up with their dishes to share for the common meal. As everything is being set up, and during the meal itself, people chat about everything under the sun: the weather, the performance of the local sports team, politics, how the grandkids are doing in school—the list is endless. But most of what passes for "fellowship" on such occasions is more accurately described as "socializing."

Perhaps the superficiality we see in church fellowship dinners is an indicator of the lack of depth in our relationship with God. He wants your learners to have a close, deep fellowship with him. Your learners get beyond the superficiality when they truly come to grips with what he has done to rescue them from sin. Today's lesson will help your learners move toward that deeper level that God desires.

INTRODUCTION

Deep in New Mexico's Carlsbad Caverns, a guide halted our tourist group on the trail and asked, "Would you like to see what total darkness looks like? Perhaps some of you have never seen darkness as complete as it is in here when the lights are out." There was a murmur of assent, and the guide went on: "See if you can find something to hang on to or lean against. I don't mean you can't stand alone, but it will be good to feel something solid closer than the soles of your feet."

My wife and I put our backs against a wall of solid rock. Others lined up beside us. Perhaps half of the tourists simply sat down in the middle of the trail. A few found a chair-high ledge of rock to sit on. Then the lights went out.

What came to my mind was a line from Exodus 10:21: "Darkness that can be felt." I imagined the darkness was a living thing, pushing us back against the cold stone. I shivered and pressed closer to the warmth of my wife. The eerie silence was as oppressive as the darkness. It was as if we were alone, cut off from the world, lost, helpless, and hopeless.

Then the lights came on. There was a flutter of talk and relieved laughter.

A. DARKNESS

Darkness is a symbol of ignorance, the ignorance from which we Christians have escaped because God has called us "out of darkness into his wonderful light" (1 Peter 2:9). We are children of God (John 1:12), and therefore children of light (1 Thessalonians 5:4, 5).

Darkness is a symbol of evil, the evil that had its hour of power when Jesus was arrested (Luke 22:53). As Jesus was dying, the world was darkened as evil seemed to be victorious (Matthew 27:45). But our Father in Heaven "has rescued us from the dominion of darkness and brought us into the kingdom of the

DEVOTIONAL READING:
EPHESIANS 5:1-10
BACKGROUND SCRIPTURE:
1 JOHN 1:1–3:10
PRINTED TEXT:
1 JOHN 1:5–2:6, 15-17, 29; 3:1

LESSON AIMS

After participating in this lesson, each student will be able to:

1. Tell the various ways John says that a Christian can develop a relationship with God.

2. Give examples of the things of the world that hinder our fellowship with the Lord.

3. Memorize 1 John 1:7 and ask God to help him or her to walk in the light.

Nov 2

KEY VERSE

If we walk in the light, as he is in the light, we have fellowship with one another, and the blood of Jesus, his Son, purifies us from all sin. —1 *John 1:7*

Son he loves" (Colossians 1:13). Therefore we "have nothing to do with the fruitless deeds of darkness, but rather expose them" (Ephesians 5:11).

Darkness is also a symbol of punishment (see Matthew 25:29, 30; Jude 6, 13). What a privilege and joy it is for Christians who have been turned "from darkness to light, and from the power of Satan to God" (Acts 26:18)!

B. LESSON BACKGROUND

For more about light and darkness, we turn to the first letter of John, written by one of the fishermen who became apostles of Jesus. None of the Twelve was closer to Jesus than was John. After Jerusalem was destroyed in A.D. 70, John lived in Ephesus, a city on the western coast of Asia Minor (modern Turkey). It was probably there that John wrote his first letter (epistle) between A.D. 80 and 90. More than half a century had passed since Jesus rose from the dead and ascended to Heaven. The church was being invaded by false teachers who valued human opinion more than divine revelation, much as some false teachers do today.

In response to such false teaching John began his letter with a strong declaration of his own personal acquaintance with Jesus and his own accurate knowledge of the Master's teaching (1 John 1:1-4). Then our text begins by presenting some of what John had learned from Jesus.

I. AVAILABLE LIGHT (1 JOHN 1:5-10)

False teachers were telling lies instead of truth, and some people were accepting the falsehoods. In other words, darkness was being promoted instead of light, and deceived people were turning away from the light to wander in darkness. The false teaching sounded so scholarly! How could the hearers know it was not true?

A. GOD IS LIGHT (v. 5)

5. This is the message we have heard from him and declare to you: God is light; in him there is no darkness at all.

John brought *the message* that he and the other apostles *heard* from Jesus himself. Jesus said that *God is light; in him there is no* trace of ignorance or evil. Since God's Son spoke God's word on earth, everyone ought to know that any contradiction of it was false.

B. WALKING IN THE LIGHT (vv. 6, 7)

6. If we claim to have fellowship with him yet walk in the darkness, we lie and do not live by the truth.

To *walk in the darkness* is to do wrong, to behave in evil ways. Anyone who does that makes it plain that he or she is not in *fellowship* with God, for God is light. Fellowship with him means walking in the light: that is, doing right. Some of the false teachers agree that God is altogether good; but they say everything material is evil, including the physical bodies of people. What those evil bodies do is not important, say the false teachers. They say their spirits are in fellowship with God, even while their bodies are doing wrong. John says that is a *lie*.

7. But if we walk in the light, as he is in the light, we have fellowship with one another, and the blood of Jesus, his Son, purifies us from all sin.

To *walk in the light, as he is in the light* is to do right according to the teaching we have from God. All of us who accept God's standards and live by them *have fellowship with one another* as well as with God. That does not mean we never do anything wrong, for we are not so wise or so strong as we would like to be. "We all stumble in many ways" (James 3:2). But Jesus died to atone for our sins. If we believe in him and accept his gift of grace, his blood *purifies us from all sin*.

WHAT DO YOU THINK?

Why is it important to have a healthy caution for the risk of having friendships with the children of spiritual darkness?

[Make sure you consider 1 Corinthians 15:33 and 2 Timothy 4:10 in your answer.]

WHAT DO YOU THINK?

How can Christians live in the midst of a sin-darkened world without becoming "of the darkness" themselves?

[You may find Matthew 13:22 and John 17:9, 15-17 useful in forming your answer.]

Brightening Up the Night

In less than a month, many people will be placing Christmas lights on their houses and in their yards. Lighting up the darkness of long winter evenings is a fitting symbol for our celebration of the coming of the One who is the "light of the world." But sometimes darkness tries to prevail in spite of us.

An eighty-five-year-old handicapped widow responded to a young man's plea for work by giving him forty-five dollars to buy some Christmas lights for her. She never saw him again. At her daughter's insistence, she reported the matter to the police. The young police officer who took the report couldn't get it out of his mind. A few days later, he and his wife and a fellow officer showed up at the widow's door with enough lights to light the eaves and bushes around her house and then proceeded to put the lights in place. When the widow offered to pay them for their efforts, they refused, because they wanted to do something to brighten what would have been a dreary season for her otherwise.

We don't know whether the officers were Christians, but they were acting as if they were! Their act of kindness was perfectly in keeping with John's instruction for us to walk in the light. When we demonstrate compassion for the unfortunate, we show that we are walking in the light of Christ, and in the process we help to brighten up a very dark world.

—C. R. B.

This stark image is a dramatic illustration of verse 7. Discuss the significance of the parents' leading the child to the light.

C. Don't Fool Yourself (vv. 8-10)

8. If we claim to be without sin, we deceive ourselves and the truth is not in us.

Some think they can have fellowship with God even while doing wrong (v. 6). They claim that they have no *sin* in their spirits even while their physical bodies are sinning. But they are only fooling themselves with that kind of thinking.

9. If we confess our sins, he is faithful and just and will forgive us our sins and purify us from all unrighteousness.

It is better to be honest, to *confess our sins* instead of trying to deny them with the nonsensical theory that the sins of our bodies are not our sins. Then God is ready to *forgive us our sins and purify us from all unrighteousness.*

10. If we claim we have not sinned, we make him out to be a liar and his word has no place in our lives.

It is bad enough to fool ourselves and say we are sinless (v. 8). It is worse to accuse God of lying. We do that *if we claim we have not sinned,* for he says all of us have sinned. He says it emphatically and repeatedly in his written Word (1 Kings 8:46; Psalm 14:3; Ecclesiastes 7:20; Isaiah 53:6; 64:6; Romans 3:23).

II. SIN AND CLEANSING (1 JOHN 2:1-6)

All of us are sinners (Romans 3:23), and "the wages of sin is death" (Romans 6:23). But not all sinners must accept what they have earned. Romans 6:23 adds, "The gift of God is eternal life in Christ Jesus our Lord." How can we escape the wages we have earned and receive the gift we have not earned?

A. Our Advocate (v. 1)

1. My dear children, I write this to you so that you will not sin. But if anybody does sin, we have one who speaks to the Father in our defense—Jesus Christ, the Righteous One.

John has been writing that all human beings are sinners, but he does not want that to be taken as an excuse for sinning. On the contrary, he is writing to help his readers keep from sinning any more. Still, he points out that our case is not hopeless even if we do sin. For, *we have one who speaks to the Father in our defense—Jesus Christ, the Righteous One.* In any courtroom a criminal needs an advocate, a lawyer who can argue his case better than he himself can. If guilt cannot

What Do You Think?

Do we confess our sins only to God? Why, or why not?

[James 5:16; Hebrews 8:1-6; and 1 Peter 2:5 can help start the discussion here.]

What Do You Think?

Is fear of death and Hell a legitimate motivation for deciding to follow Jesus? Why, or why not?

be denied, perhaps the advocate can point to mitigating circumstances or some other reason to treat this criminal with mercy. Jesus is our advocate in God's court of justice. He is righteous; he will not resort to lying or anything wrong to save us from punishment. He knows we have sinned, and God knows it, and we know it. Then why should God have mercy on us? See the next verse.

B. OUR PROPITIATION (v. 2)
2. He is the atoning sacrifice for our sins, and not only for ours but also for the sins of the whole world.

Jesus is *the atoning sacrifice* (or "propitiation" in older translations), the means of appeasing God's wrath. The punishment we deserve has been given to him, and so we can receive God's mercy. Furthermore, the sacrifice Jesus made is enough to atone for *the sins of the whole world;* but that does not mean all the sinners will receive mercy instead of justice. There are proud sinners who declare they will gain Heaven by their own merits or not at all. Unless they repent, it will be not at all. There are other sinners who deny that there is a God or a Savior, a Heaven or a Hell. Unless they repent, they will learn the truth too late.

C. KNOWING OUR ADVOCATE (vv. 3, 4)
3. We know that we have come to know him if we obey his commands.

Do we really *know* Jesus, our advocate, our atoning sacrifice, our Savior? There is an easy way to answer that question. If we ignore *his commands* and do as we please, that is proof that we do not know Christ. On the other hand, if we consistently shape our lives by his commandments, that is convincing evidence that we *know him.* This is true even if sometimes we are tricked into disobedience.
4. The man who says, "I know him," but does not do what he commands is a liar, and the truth is not in him.

With this powerful blow the writer clinches the truth he drove home in verse 3. What one does is more convincing than what one says.

D. PERFECTION OF LOVE (vv. 5, 6)
5. But if anyone obeys his word, God's love is truly made complete in him. This is how we know we are in him:

Keeping God's *word* is the same as keeping his commandments in verses 3 and 4. It is guiding one's life by God's directions. One who does that shows that his or her *love* for God is *made complete,* is mature, is what it ought to be. But the Greek word translated *made complete* can also mean "brought to its goal." With that in mind, some students take this verse to mean that God's love for us intends to bring us to obey God; and when we do obey God, his love for us is brought to its goal (cf. Psalm 119:11).
6. Whoever claims to live in him must walk as Jesus did.

The way we *walk* means the way we live, the way we conduct ourselves, the way we behave. Everyone who claims to be in Christ ought to live as Christ did. Of course that does not mean every Christian ought to walk on water and do other miracles as Jesus did. But every Christian ought to copy Jesus' attitudes and his actions that were not miraculous. Every Christian ought to be honest, kind, generous, helpful, considerate, courteous. If one does not act like Jesus, that shows that he really is not in Jesus; he is not a real Christian.

III. MORE ABOUT LOVE (1 JOHN 2:15-17, 29; 3:1)
Our lesson concludes with some important reflections on the objects of our love. One is very common, and one is not.

WHAT DO YOU THINK?

How is it possible for us to presume upon God's grace when we willingly decide to sin?

[Be sure to consider Hebrews 10:26, 27 and Romans 6 in your answer.]

A. Mistaken Love (vv. 15-17)

15. Do not love the world or anything in the world. If anyone loves the world, the love of the Father is not in him.

God loved *the world*—loved it so much that he gave his only begotten Son to die for it (John 3:16). We are God's people. How can John tell us not to *love the world* that God loves? That is a legitimate question, but it's not hard to find an answer, is it? With about a minute's thought we see that the word *world* in our text does not mean what the same word means in John 3:16.

John 3:16 is saying God loved the people of the world, loved them so much that he sent his Son to redeem them. God still loves the people of the world, and so do God's people. Missionaries sacrifice much to take the message of God's love and salvation to people who need it. The rest of God's people sacrifice a little to support the missionaries. That is good.

When John says, *Do not love the world,* he is not thinking of people, but the things that are *in the world,* such things as money and things money will buy. We ought to earn money enough to support ourselves (2 Thessalonians 3:11, 12) and our families (1 Timothy 5:8). But if anyone is so in love with money that he or she will lie or cheat or steal to get it, that is bad (1 Timothy 6:10). That greedy kind of love for things of the world can so fill a person's heart that there is no room for the love of God, as we see in the last part of verse 15.

16. For everything in the world—the cravings of sinful man, the lust of his eyes and the boasting of what he has and does—comes not from the Father but from the world.

Cravings are our desires. Our bodies desire the food they need, but they do not stop there. They desire more than they need. If we do not take control and stop eating when we have enough, we become fat. Some people actually train their bodies to lust for nicotine or alcohol or some illegal drug. Such a lust of the flesh is likely to overpower a person and make him or her a slave.

The *eyes* desire what looks good. If a person does not control that lust, he may drive a more expensive car than he can afford, or she may fill her closet with more lovely clothes than she can use in a lifetime. *Boasting* takes place when we desire better things than the neighbors have. If we do not keep those desires under control, our happiness will always be marred by envy.

The Father in Heaven gives us the desires for all we need to be at our best. All our desire for what is bad, and all our desire for too much of what is good, *comes not from the Father but from the world.* If we do not control those worldly desires, they will control us, and they will make us less than our best.

Persistent Desires

"Models for Millionaires" was the heading of an advertisement in a slick-paper, upscale metropolitan magazine. Along with the picture of an attractive, thirty-five-ish woman were these teasers: "Now there is a way to find a relationship with model quality, commitment-minded women who want a lifetime partner. . . . If you are ready to settle down with a 9 or 10, we need to talk. . . . This is a no nonsense way of bringing you the type of woman you deserve." In just a quarter-page of copy and photo, the advertiser managed to appeal to every one of the persistent desires John mentions in our text. First, the ad was for an "escort service"—there you have the lust of the flesh; second, the photo appealed to the lust of the eyes; and third, the phrase "the type of woman *you deserve*" was a direct appeal to the pride of life of the "millionaire gentlemen" (as well as the women who would like to date a millionaire).

But you don't have to be a millionaire looking for a beautiful "trophy" to find temptations in our world today. Even the most common of us is daily bombarded with appeals to our base desires or attempts to raise our legitimate desires to a

What Do You Think?

Considering Luke 12:34 as well, what does our reaction to our culture's consumerism say about our sincerity in regard to the biblical teaching about worldliness?

DAILY BIBLE READINGS

Monday, Oct. 27—*Imitate God, Live in Light (Ephesians 5:1-10)*

Tuesday, Oct. 28—*We Have Fellowship With God (1 John 1:1-5)*

Wednesday, Oct. 29—*Walk in the Light (1 John 1:6-10)*

Thursday, Oct. 30—*Walk as Christ Walked (1 John 2:1-6)*

Friday, Oct. 31—*Love Other Christians (1 John 2:7-11)*

Saturday, Nov. 1—*Do Not Love the World (John 2:12-17)*

Sunday, Nov. 2—*Abide in Christ (1 John 2:26–3:3)*

PRAYER

Father in Heaven, we can never say enough in praise of your perfect righteousness and your perfect love. Thank you for holding before us a faultless example, and thank you for sending Jesus to show us that faultless righteousness is possible even where we live. Again we must beg forgiveness for our recurrent unrighteousness, and again we must ask for wisdom and strength as we try daily to be more like you. In Jesus' name, amen.

THOUGHT TO REMEMBER

"Our fellowship is with the Father and with his Son, Jesus Christ" (1 John 1:3).

covetous level. But John puts life in its proper perspective: everything in this world and our desires for it will pass away. Only those who do God's will shall survive forever.

—C. R. B.

17. The world and its desires pass away, but the man who does the will of God lives forever.

This *world* is not forever. No worldly lust will outlast the world. But God is *forever*, and Heaven is forever, and we are forever if we do God's will. So let's be in training for eternity.

B. THE FATHER'S LOVE (2:29–3:1)

29. If you know that he is righteous, you know that everyone who does what is right has been born of him.

A person is not born again as a child of God by living right, but a life of doing *what is right* is convincing evidence that one has been *born of* God. A man can go through the motions of becoming a Christian just to please his wife. He can profess repentance without really repenting. He can mouth a confession of faith with no real faith in his heart. He can be baptized without really being born again. But it is hardly possible to live a life of righteousness like that of God without really being a child of God. Such a life, day after day and year after year, is the proof that a person has been born of God.

3:1. How great is the love the Father has lavished on us, that we should be called children of God! And that is what we are! The reason the world does not know us is that it did not know him.

God *called* the Christians his *children*. What kind of *love* do you think that meant he had given them? It must have been a very great, everlasting love. Certainly it was a love that the Christians valued highly. And surely it was a love that made them very important. But God's love gave them no importance in the eyes of the people around them. Most of those people were pagans. They worshiped many imaginary gods. They probably thought that the Christians' God was no better than one of theirs. Since they did not know God was important, they did not know his children were important. But the Christians knew. They knew God was the only real God, the Almighty. They knew his love set them apart from all the other people. They knew they were the most favored people on earth.

CONCLUSION

Some things never change. God is eternally the same; his righteousness is the same, and so is his love. In the course of centuries we have replaced the Christians to whom John wrote, but is that really a change?

Like the first-century Christians, we know God's righteousness is flawless, and we know ours is flawed. Like those Christians of long ago, we are trying to prove that we are God's children by matching our righteousness with His. But we have no referee, other than ourselves, to blow the whistle when we fall short.

So take a critical backward look. Examine what you have done in the week just past. Count the times when your righteousness has been less perfect than God's. If you find no such time, look again. But do not be dismayed if you find more flaws than you expected. "If we confess our sins, he is faithful and just and will forgive us our sins and purify us from all unrighteousness" (1 John 1:9).

Then take a look at the week that lies ahead. Plan not to repeat any of the fouls of last week. Perhaps you will not be as perfect as you plan to be, but you can make some progress. Thus you will "become mature, attaining to the whole measure of the fullness of Christ" (Ephesians 4:13).

Discovery Learning

This page contains an alternative lesson plan emphasizing learning activities. Classes desiring such student involvement will find these suggestions helpful. The next page is a reproducible activity page to further enhance discovery learning.

LEARNING GOALS

After participating in this lesson, each student will be able to:

1. Tell the various ways John says that a Christian can develop a relationship with God.

2. Give examples of the things of the world that hinder our fellowship with the Lord.

3. Memorize 1 John 1:7 and ask God to help him or her to walk in the light.

INTO THE LESSON

Prepare an opening activity worksheet called "At One With God," a statement completion based on 1 John 1:7. The statement, including the missing words (blanks), is as follows: "But if we _____ in the _____, as _____ is in the _____, we have _____ with one _____, and the _____ of _____, his _____, _____ us from all _____." (Make certain the spaces or lines are long enough for the words.) On the work sheet place the following missing words either above or below the statement: *blood, fellowship, sin, walk, he, light, another, Jesus, purifies, light, Son.*

Give each student a copy of the work sheet and say, "This week's lesson focuses on the topic, 'Enjoy Fellowship With God.' To begin looking at this subject, fill in the missing words of the sentence by selecting the correct word for each blank space from those provided. Each word is to be used only once. When you complete the sentence, look up so I'll know you are finished."

When you have determined that nearly all have completed this activity, ask for someone to volunteer to read the completed sentence. Make corrections, if needed. Say, "The apostle John gives us a number of ways we can develop our relationships with God. Turn to our lesson text in 1 John, and let's discover those ways."

INTO THE WORD

Ask someone to read 1 John 1:5–2:6, 15-17, 29–3:1 aloud. After the reading, ask the following questions:

1. What are the various ways John says we can develop our relationship with God? (*Possible answers: walk as Jesus did, 1 John 2:6; confess our sins, 1 John 1:9; do the will of God, 1 John 2:17; do what is right, 1 John 2:29.*)

2. What do you think John means when he uses the phrase, "walk in the darkness" (1 John 1:6)? (*To do wrong, to behave in evil ways.*)

3. John says in 1 John 2:16 that "the cravings of sinful man, the lust of his eyes and the boasting of what he has and does" hinder our fellowship with God. What are examples of things that hinder a Christian's relationship with God?

Move the class members into three groups of no more than five. (For classes larger than fifteen, make additional small groups and repeat assignments.) Label the groups A, B, and C. Say, "John gives us several verses that describe what we say (our talk), what we do (our walk), and even verses that combine what we say and do. Group A will look for those verses that describe what we say; Group B will look for those verses that describe what we do; and Group C will focus on those verses that describe both. You have ten minutes to (1) find the verses that apply to your group; (2) identify the talk, walk, or both and the natural result of such responses; and (3) indicate which are positive and which are negative."

Group A: 1 John 2:6 (positive); 1 John 1:8, 10 (negative). *Group B:* 1 John 1:9, 1 John 2:17, 29 (positive); 1 John 2:1, 15 (negative). *Group C:* 1 John 1:6, 1 John 2:4 (negative); 1 John 1:7, 1 John 2:5 (positive).

When the time is up, ask each group to report. After Group C's report, say, "John makes it clear that walking the talk is what is needed in each of our lives. We need to memorize 1 John 1:7." Divide the verse and the class into four groups and assign a phrase to each. Have the groups recite their phrases in order so that the total verse is rehearsed aloud. Shift the phrase to a different section and repeat the process until each has stated all four phrases: "But if we walk in the light, as he is in the light," "we have fellowship with one another," "and the blood of Jesus, his Son," "purifies us from all sin."

INTO LIFE

Use the reproducible activity "Songs of Light, Fellowship, and the Blood" from the next page. Give learners time silently to make a few entries to the lists. Then ask the groups to identify aloud songs they have entered. Each person should then have ten or more titles listed.

Direct the learners to follow the directive at the bottom of the activity sheet, selecting songs for their personal times of devotion during the coming week. If time allows, sing a few of the songs as a group. Then close with prayer expressing thanks for the light of Christ, the fellowship of the church, and the blood of Calvary.

Walk the Talk

In today's text John challenges disciples to live up to what they claim. Complete the chart below to see how behavior that does not match one's speech means trouble, but consistent behavior means blessing.

Verse	What I Say	What I Do	What That Means
1 John 1:6			
1 John 1:7			
1 John 2:4			
1 John 2:5			

Songs of Light, Fellowship, and the Blood

Make three lists of hymns and choruses related to the three key concepts of 1 John 1:7. See if you can identify at least seven.

Light	Fellowship	The Blood

Select and circle seven songs and choruses from this list that you will use with your personal Bible study and devotional times this week. Review and recite 1 John 1:7 before you use each song.

LOVE ONE ANOTHER

LESSON 10

WHY TEACH THIS LESSON?

Writer and poet Ralph Waldo Emerson (1803–1882) observed that "Love is our highest word, and the synonym of God." As a former minister, Emerson may have been thinking of 1 John 4:8 ("God is love") when he penned that thought.

Perhaps we moderns take 1 John 4:8 a bit too much for granted. To claim that "God is love" was actually a startling thing to say in the pagan culture of the apostle John's day. The Greeks and Romans had a whole assortment of imaginary gods, and these so-called gods were understood to be quite fickle. One day they might like you, the next day they might not. One day could be a day of blessing and the next a day of terror, depending on the gods' whims.

But none of those gods ever sent his Son to die to pay sin's price. Only a God who *is* love would do that. The more your learners come to grips with the magnitude of this love, the closer fellowship they will have with him. And the closer they get to him, the closer they bond to each other. Our lesson today helps your learners to do both.

INTRODUCTION

English-speaking people are fascinated with the word *love*, and we use it in a wide variety of contexts. We love our spouses and we love chocolate sundaes, but we love our spouses with all our hearts and love sundaes with our taste buds. We love our children and we love holidays, but those two loves are different things. We love our friends and, if we are Christians, we love our enemies; but even if both those loves are sincere, they do not feel exactly alike. So many shades of meaning for such a small word!

A. LOVE, THEN AND NOW

The English language actually has over a dozen "specialized" words for *love* when we need them. Words such as *adore, cherish* (verbs), *endearment*, and *friendship* (nouns) are examples. The same is true of the word *love* in the Bible. In our English translations some form of this word occurs in the New Testament over three hundred times, and love is a major theme in the writings of the apostle John. In today's lesson we sift through a small part of what he has to say about love.

B. LESSON BACKGROUND

In the background of last week's lesson we noted that the first century saw the rise of false teachers who valued human opinion more than divine revelation. These false teachers led many people away from God's truth. John wanted his readers to reject such mistaken leading and cling to the truth that he and the other apostles had heard from Jesus while he was teaching on earth.

Years before John wrote this letter, Paul warned Timothy against men whose teaching was perverted because their love was perverted. They loved themselves more than they loved their fellowman, and they loved pleasures more than they loved God. Therefore they became bad characters indeed (2 Timothy 3:1-5). In contrast, we now hear John urging Christians toward proper love.

DEVOTIONAL READING:
1 CORINTHIANS 13:1-13

BACKGROUND SCRIPTURE:
1 JOHN 3:11–4:21

PRINTED TEXT:
1 JOHN 3:11-16; 4:7-16

LESSON AIMS

After participating in this lesson, each student will be able to:

1. Tell the source, expression, and result of Christian love.

2. Compare God's love for us with our love for others.

3. Suggest one specific way to demonstrate godly love to someone this week.

Nov
9

KEY VERSE

Dear friends, since God so loved us, we also ought to love one another.   —1 John 4:11

LESSON 10 NOTES

I. LOVE FOR OTHERS (1 JOHN 3:11-16)

In the world around us we see evidence of mistaken love (1 John 2:15-17). John helps clarify our thinking about the proper objects of our love.

A. MESSAGE OF GOD (v. 11)

11. This is the message you heard from the beginning: We should love one another.

To *love one another* is a theme John introduced in 1 John 2:9-11. This theme was important *from the beginning,* during Jesus' earthly ministry (John 13:34, 35). It still bears repeating as John becomes the church's elder statesman in the latter years of the first century. A lack of brotherly love is evidently a problem in some parts of the church as time moves on (Galatians 5:15; James 4:1-3, 11, 12).

WHAT DO YOU THINK?

In confusing "doing" with "feeling," how do people misuse the word love?

B. EXAMPLE OF EVIL (vv. 12, 13)

12. Do not be like Cain, who belonged to the evil one and murdered his brother. And why did he murder him? Because his own actions were evil and his brother's were righteous.

Cain is an example of the extreme opposite of what a Christian ought to be (see Genesis 4:1-16). His problem was that he *belonged to the evil one,* the devil. As a result, he did wrong instead of right. That was the reason the Lord refused to accept his offering (Genesis 4:7; Hebrews 11:4). But instead of repenting, Cain went wild with jealousy and *murdered his brother* Abel.

So I am warned. If I feel inclined to hate a fellow Christian, is it possibly because he or she is more *righteous* than I am? Should I be cleaning up my own way of living instead of envying someone whose godly living wins for him or her some honor that is denied to me?

13. Do not be surprised, my brothers, if the world hates you.

The world has a lot of people who are doing wrong, and they hate you because you are doing right. Don't *be surprised* at that (cf. John 15:18–16:4), and don't worry about it. It is far better to do right and be hated by the world (Mark 13:13) than to do wrong and hate those who are doing right.

C. EVIDENCE OF LIFE (vv. 14, 15)

14. We know that we have passed from death to life, because we love our brothers. Anyone who does not love remains in death.

Before we became Christians we were dead in our sins (Ephesians 2:1). But when we became Christians we *passed from death to life*—eternal life! Our sins were forgiven; we were made alive (Ephesians 2:1-5). As children of God, we love God's other children, the other Christians. They have their faults as we have ours, but we love them because they are our brothers and sisters. This proves that *we have passed from death to life,* that we really are Christians. Likewise anyone who does not love fellow believers proves that he or she is still dead; such a person is not really a Christian even if his or her name is on the church roll.

15. Anyone who hates his brother is a murderer, and you know that no murderer has eternal life in him.

Anyone who hates a fellow Christian *is a murderer* at heart, even if he or she lacks the courage to kill. This verifies the last part of verse 14. Since the one who hates a fellow Christian does not have *eternal life in him,* such a person is not really a Christian. See Matthew 5:21, 22.

WHAT DO YOU THINK?

If I find that I have hateful feelings toward someone, what should I do? Do Matthew 5:21, 22 and 1 John 3:15 mean I am lost? Why or why not?

D. EXAMPLE OF LOVE (v. 16)

16. This is how we know what love is: Jesus Christ laid down his life for us. And we ought to lay down our lives for our brothers.

God's Son *laid down his life for us.* The Son's *love* is a model for us in that *we ought to lay down our lives for our brothers.* Of course we cannot (and need not) do this just as Jesus did: we cannot atone for others' sins by giving our lives. But the verse that follows (not in our text for today) makes it clear that God expects us to spend our time and resources in providing help for fellow Christians who need it. If we refuse to help, we demonstrate that we are lacking in love.

TWISTED VALUES

Juanita Baird told police she thought she had been shot by someone she knew. Little did she know how right she was! Nothing had been taken from her modest home in Houston, so it was clear that robbery was not the motive. As detectives pieced together the story, it became ever stranger.

For a least a year the plot had been hatching, and the principals in the story turned out to be Mrs. Baird's daughter and four teenage grandchildren. Those five family members paid sixty dollars to a fourteen-year-old girl to shoot the grandmother and her husband. Another fifteen dollars was paid to a thirteen-year-old male accomplice.

The reason for the attempted murder is just as surprising: the daughter and children were on welfare and received room and board in the Baird home under what they felt were overly-strict rules. But the shooting was precipitated by the fact that the Bairds refused to build a swimming pool or basketball court for the younger family members!

The incident tends to confirm statistics that indicate a person is more likely to be murdered by an acquaintance than by a stranger. What twisted values our society sometimes exhibits! Unlike the Baird family, however, the family of God lives by a different standard—one established by our Lord, who laid down his life for us. In addition to paying sin's price, this sets an example of love as the standard for our treatment of others.   —C. R. B.

II. GOD'S LOVE AND OURS (1 JOHN 4:7-11)

Children are expected to be like their parents. Even Jesus became a carpenter like his stepfather Joseph; and indeed, Jesus' Heavenly Father was the first and greatest of all carpenters, the maker of Heaven and earth (Genesis 1:1). As children of God, we shape ourselves to be like our Father in Heaven—not necessarily in the work of our hands, but certainly in the love of our hearts (Luke 6:35, 36).

A. SOURCE OF LOVE (vv. 7, 8)
7. Dear friends, let us love one another, for love comes from God. Everyone who loves has been born of God and knows God.

Although God's children are to love their enemies (Luke 6:27-29), this lesson is about loving *one another*—about loving our fellow Christians. *Love comes from God* (indeed, "God is love," v. 8), and all of God's children ought to be loving as he is loving. Such love in us is powerful evidence that we really are God's children.
8. Whoever does not love does not know God, because God is love.

Sadly, the opposite is true as well. Unloving people do not even *know* God. He is a stranger to them.

B. PROOF OF LOVE (vv. 9, 10)
9. This is how God showed his love among us: He sent his one and only Son into the world that we might live through him.

No Christian can doubt that God loves *his one and only Son,* Jesus. Yet God sent Jesus from Heaven to earth not only to live as a man among men, but also to be despised, rejected, persecuted, tortured, and killed! A loving God subjected

WHAT DO YOU THINK?

In what ways is it possible to love others as much as Jesus loves us? In what ways is it impossible?

[You may find Matthew 10:42 useful as you consider your answer.]

Display today's visual as you begin to discuss 1 John 3:16.

WHAT DO YOU THINK?

The lesson writer says God's love "is beyond measure, beyond understanding." How, then, can he say, "Thank God it is not beyond belief"? How can we believe what we cannot really grasp?

his beloved Son to all that in order *that we might live through him.* Then how great is God's love for us! It is beyond measure, beyond understanding. But thank God it is not beyond belief. It cannot be doubted, for God proved it by sacrificing his Son to pay sin's penalty for us (John 3:16, 17).

10. This is love: not that we loved God, but that he loved us and sent his Son as an atoning sacrifice for our sins.

We discussed the idea of *an atoning sacrifice* in lesson 9. *Love* in all its fullness, love in all its power, love in all its splendor is not seen in our puny love for God. Rather, it is seen in God's tremendous love for us. God demonstrated it by sending his Son to give his life in atonement for our sins.

GIVING UP A CHILD

There always have been unwanted children. The "abortion on demand" movement in Western society is a sufficient—if grisly—indication that the trend is alive and thriving. But even among women who do not abort their babies, unwanted children are still a significant social problem. All too frequently we hear of a newborn baby left at the door of a hospital or a church—or worse yet, in a trash dumpster in a back alley.

A few years ago the city of Hamburg, Germany, resurrected and updated an old approach to this perennial problem. Project *Findelbaby*—for "foundling"—offers desperate mothers a delivery slot where they can place their babies in a warm bed and then leave anonymously. A sensor makes attendants aware that a baby has been delivered to their care. Impetus for the project came from testimony at a murder trial where a woman admitted hiding three pregnancies and snuffing out the tender lives shortly after birth. Her husband had said he would kill her if she bore another child.

Such cases are tragedies for all concerned. How starkly they contrast to what God did in giving up his Son, not abandoning him to a foundling home, but giving him to a caring mother and father. They would raise him to love us enough to give his own life to save us. As John says, this is what love is all about!　　—C. R. B.

C. RESULT OF LOVE (v. 11)

11. Dear friends, since God so loved us, we also ought to love one another.

To despise a fellow Christian for whom God's Son died is unthinkable! This week, how can we be more helpful and loving to fellow Christians, those here at home as well as those on the other side of the world?

III. WE IN HIM, HE IN US (1 JOHN 4:12-16)

We do love one another, don't we? We cannot take pride in that, however, because our love seems tiny in comparison with God's immeasurable love for us. As we read the final verses of our text, we see that we are in God and he is in us. We can rejoice because we are so close to him; but we cannot boast, because the closeness is his doing, not ours. He redeemed us; he forgave us; he made us his children. Thank God!

WHAT DO YOU THINK?

What one characteristic, more than any other, identifies us as followers of Christ? Why?

[Make sure that you use John 13:35 to undergird your answer.]

A. OUR STATUS (vv. 12, 13)

12. No one has ever seen God; but if we love one another, God lives in us and his love is made complete in us.

In John 1:18 the apostle also stresses that *No one has ever seen God.* There, however, he adds that God's Son, "who is at the Father's side, has made him known." We can know God very well by learning about his Son, who walked the earth in the visible form of a man and spoke God's truth (John 6:46; 14:9). In a much smaller way, people who do not know Jesus form their idea of God from the way we, God's other children, imitate his love, for *God lives in us*. What a sobering thought!

God's *love is made complete in us* as *we love one another.* God's love completes its work when we copy his love and give help to one another in his name. In love God wants to give us help; he enables his loving people to give that help.

13. We know that we live in him and he in us, because he has given us of his Spirit.

John's observation that *we live in him and he in us* is a way of saying our relationship with God is close and complete (cf. 1 John 2:24; 4:15). When we imitate God's love and help one of his needy people, God *in us* is doing it. But if we were not *in him*, we would not imitate his love and do his work. It is a mutual indwelling, but we do not live together as equals. He is God, the Creator, the all-wise, the all-powerful. He lives in us as director and controller. In old-fashioned terms, he is our Lord and Master and we are his willing slaves. We live in him as devoted and obedient servants. Let us say, as Jesus said, "not my will, but yours be done" (Luke 22:42).

We know we dwell in God *because he has given us of his Spirit.* God is the one who "set his seal of ownership on us, and put his Spirit in our hearts as a deposit" (2 Corinthians 1:22). The Spirit indwells us as God's temple (1 Corinthians 3:16). We know also because we find ourselves abandoning our own wills to do God's will.

BECOMING ONE WITH THE STORY

The 1965 film *The Sound of Music* is one of the greatest movie hits of all time. One measure of its success is the fairly recent phenomenon known as the "Sing-along Sound of Music," which got its start in England and has been making the rounds of American cities on tour.

The fact that this is a "feel good" movie shows in the way people come to the sing-along version. They dress in costumes representing the various characters in the film. As the lyrics to the songs appear in subtitles on the screen, the audience sings heartily without self-consciousness. Voices range from good to bad, and everything in between. Caught up in the spirit of the film, the viewer-participants live out, for a few moments, the positive message portrayed on the screen. As one reviewer put it, "the teary-eyed woman to my right cradled her darling daughter in her lap as they earnestly sang along to 'Edelweiss.'" At the end of the film, "when love conquers all and hope waits on the horizon, my neighbor leaned over and kissed his wife."

Isn't this a picture of what John is calling us to? Today will we be so caught up in the spirit of what God has done for the world in Christ—the greatest "love story" of all time!—that we willingly and unself-consciously give ourselves over to living out God's story of selfless love, and letting that story live in us?   —C. R. B.

B. OUR TESTIMONY (v. 14)

14. And we have seen and testify that the Father has sent his Son to be the Savior of the world.

John and the other apostles actually had *seen* Jesus (1 John 1:1-3). They had been with him almost continually for three years. From his teaching and the teaching of the Holy Spirit they knew *the Father* had *sent his Son to be the Savior of the world.*

Over and over the apostles have given that testimony, have given it far and wide. We have not seen Jesus, and we are not inspired as the apostles were; but we can repeat the apostles' testimony as confidently as they gave it: God indeed did send his Son to be the Savior of the world.

DAILY BIBLE READINGS

Monday, Nov. 3—*Love Believes, Hopes, Endures (1 Corinthians 13:1-7)*

Tuesday, Nov. 4—*Love Never Ends (1 Corinthians 13:8-13)*

Wednesday, Nov. 5—*Lay Down Life for Another (1 John 3:11-17)*

Thursday, Nov. 6—*Love in Truth and Action (1 John 3: 18-24)*

Friday, Nov. 7—*Love Is From God (1 John 4:1-7)*

Saturday, Nov. 8—*God Is Love (1 John 4:8-12)*

Sunday, Nov. 9—*We Love Because God Loved Us (John 4:13-21)*

HOW TO SAY IT

agape (Greek). uh-GAH-pay.
Ephesians. Ee-FEE-zhunz.
Galatians. Guh-LAY-shunz.
Hebrews. HEE-brews.

C. OUR CONFESSION (vv. 15, 16)

15. If anyone acknowledges that Jesus is the Son of God, God lives in him and he in God.

One who says *that Jesus is the Son of God* agrees with the truth, and agrees also with countless Christians who have said the same thing before.

Of course, this agreement is more than merely saying so. If one really *acknowledges* that Jesus is the Son of God, then he or she lives a life in agreement with what the Son says. He or she loves, honors, and obeys Jesus even as Jesus loves, honors, and obeys his Father. Thus such a person makes it evident that *God lives in him and he in God.*

16. And so we know and rely on the love God has for us.

God is love. Whoever lives in love lives in God, and God in him.

If we *know* who Jesus is and have faith in him as our Savior, we *rely on* his promise. We are sure we have everlasting life. To Jesus we turn over all we are and all we have, sure that in him we shall be more than we could be without him.

We know that *God is love.* But we know that God is more than that. He is also light (1 John 1:5), Spirit (John 4:24), a consuming fire (Hebrews 12:29), our refuge and strength (Psalm 46:1), King of all the earth (Psalm 47:7), my help (Psalm 54:4), my fortress (Psalm 59:9), and my light and my salvation (Psalm 27:1). But in our text John is writing about God as love. Evidence of God's love is everywhere, from the sunshine and rain and bountiful harvest to the gift of his Son to rescue us from death and give us life everlasting. Every good thing that nourishes our life or brings us joy is evidence of God's love.

Love is intrinsic to God. Without his love, God would not be the God we know. Perhaps he would be a frightening monster like some of the imaginary gods of the pagans. And it is sobering to think what monsters we would be if we had no love either for God or for our fellow humans.

But God is love, and anyone who *lives in love lives in God.* We live in God, and he lives in us. There are comfort and security in these thoughts. Even our fear of God is not terror; it is reverence and awe that live alongside our love.

CONCLUSION

A. THE CHRISTIAN'S BADGE

To write the conclusion of this lesson, we have only to copy the title printed above it: "Love One Another." This is the badge that identifies us as Christians, for Jesus said, "By this all men will know that you are my disciples, if you love one another" (John 13:35). God's love for us is the model we follow in loving one another. The towering evidence of God's love was the sacrifice of his Son. So let us not turn thoughtlessly away when we see an opportunity for a great sacrifice for our brothers and sisters. Our Father's love is seen continually in daily bread, in the beauty of a sunset or a rose, in "every good and perfect gift" that makes us glad (James 1:17). Our love for one another is seen most often in tiny bits of kindness, courtesy, and help.

B. ONE MORE THOUGHT

We can hardly leave the subject of love without mentioning one thought that is not in this lesson, but is in the teaching of Jesus. He said, "Love your enemies" (Matthew 5:44). In this also we follow the example of our Father. It was a world of lost sinners that he "so loved . . . that he gave his one and only Son" (John 3:16), and sinners share his gifts of sunshine and rain (Matthew 5:45). "As we have opportunity, let us do good to all people, especially to those who belong to the family of believers" (Galatians 6:10).

PRAYER

Our Father in Heaven, how can we begin to thank you for your example of unfailing love? Forgive our failure to model your love, and so stir our minds and hearts that we shall not fail again. In Jesus' name, amen.

THOUGHT TO REMEMBER

God is love, and so are we.

Discovery Learning

This page contains an alternative lesson plan emphasizing learning activities. Classes desiring such student involvement will find these suggestions helpful. The next page is a reproducible activity page to further enhance discovery learning.

LEARNING GOALS

After participating in this lesson, each student will be able to:

1. Tell the source, expression, and result of Christian love.

2. Compare God's love for us with our love for others.

3. Suggest one specific way to demonstrate godly love to someone this week.

INTO THE LESSON

Prepare an agree/disagree work sheet activity entitled, "Love: Pinning It Down." Print the five statements below with a 1-7 scale next to each. Explain that the 7 indicates "strongly agree," and the 1 indicates "strongly disagree."

1. Love that is verbally expressed to others is genuine.

2. Love that is outwardly demonstrated toward others is genuine.

3. Only love that is both verbally expressed and outwardly demonstrated toward others is genuine.

4. Love that is expressed verbally to others can be insincere.

5. Love that is demonstrated outwardly to others can be insincere.

Make enough copies so each class member has one. To begin class, distribute the work sheets and say, "Our topic today is 'Love One Another.' To help us begin thinking, I've prepared an agree/disagree work sheet. Read each statement and circle the number that best represents your opinion: strongly agree, 7, to strongly disagree, 1." Allow a few minutes for the class to complete the work sheet. Then, go over each statement to see whether there are different levels of agreement or disagreement. Ask class members to tell their numbers and their reason(s). Say, "We've discussed a number of interesting positions. It's not as easy as you may have thought to pin down a set formula or expression. However, in our text today, the apostle John describes this concept of love and adds an essential component of genuineness. Turn to 1 John 3, and let's see whether we can identify that component."

INTO THE WORD

Ask a class member to read the whole lesson text aloud. Then ask each class member to review the passage of Scripture with a neighbor and try to identify the essential component of genuine love. After a few minutes, ask for suggested answers. *(The essential component is the aspect of personal sacrifice for others.)*

Ask the following questions to review the text.

1. What is the source of Christian love? *(God, 4:7.)*

2. What is the ultimate expression of Christian love? *(God's sending his Son into the world, 4:9.)*

3. What is the result of Christian love? *(God's love is made complete in us, 4:12.)*

4. Why is the Old Testament example of Cain presented in the lesson text? *(He failed to love his brother, was influenced by the evil one, and sinned, 3:12.)*

5. What does a failure to love others reveal about the person? *(He remains in death, 1 John 3:14; he is a murderer, 3:15; he does not know God, 4:8.)*

6. What conclusions can be drawn from the text about a person who does love others? *(He has passed from death to life, 3:14; he is born of God, he knows God, 4:7; God lives in him, and his love is made complete in him, 4:12.)*

7. From the lesson text, what is necessary for God to live in us? *(We need to love one another, 4:12; we have been given his Spirit, 4:13; we have acknowledged that Jesus is the Son of God, 4:15; we live in love, 4:16.)*

INTO LIFE

Say: "John has clearly described God's love for us in sending Jesus to lay down his life for us. We need to compare that kind of love with our love for others." Distribute copies of the reproducible activity "Measuring Our Love for Others" from the next page. Observe that God loves every person and every group infinitely—without showing favoritism. Then ask each learner to rate his or her own intensity of love for others. Say, "We know that we all need to do better at loving others. What practical ways can we demonstrate godly love?" As suggestions are given, write them on the board.

Direct attention to the "Demonstrative Love" activity of the reproducible page. Say: "Think about a specific person to whom you would like to demonstrate God's love this week, and write his or her name in. Next, think about some specific ways that you could demonstrate godly love to this person. Write those ways in also."

Encourage each person to carry this statement all week as a reminder to demonstrate God's love. Close the class time with a prayer of commitment to show love to someone this week.

Measuring Our Love for Others

Consider how much God has demonstrated his love to all and how much you have demonstrated God's love toward others. On the scale below circle the number that best represents the intensity of your love—from a "0," non-existent, to a "7," like Jesus—for each of the people or groups listed. Suggest a specific person to whom you need to do better at demonstrating love for the last item.

PEOPLE GOD WANTS ME TO LOVE	LEVEL AT WHICH I HAVE DEMONSTRATED LOVE FOR THESE PEOPLE							
FAMILY	0	1	2	3	4	5	6	7
FRIENDS	0	1	2	3	4	5	6	7
NEIGHBORS	0	1	2	3	4	5	6	7
WORK ASSOCIATES	0	1	2	3	4	5	6	7
HOMELESS PEOPLE	0	1	2	3	4	5	6	7
PRISONERS	0	1	2	3	4	5	6	7
_____	0	1	2	3	4	5	6	7

Demonstrative Love

> "Dear friends, since God so loved us, we also ought to love one another."
> —1 John 4:11

As a result of this lesson on "Love One Another," I make this commitment to demonstrate God's love this week to:

Knowing that 1 John 3:18 says, "Let us not love with words or tongue but with actions and in truth," I will demonstrate God's love by

I will do (or begin) this by this date: _____

Signed: _____

LIVE WITH CONFIDENCE

LESSON 11

WHY TEACH THIS LESSON?

A few years ago a chain of restaurants ran a national advertising campaign featuring the catchy slogan, "No rules, just right!" Hearing that got me to thinking. If I dined at one of those restaurants would I be able to walk out without paying since there are "no rules" that say I must do so? Could I go and eat some food off of other people's tables since there are "no rules" that forbid me from doing so? Would I get food poisoning there because "no rules" means that the kitchen workers are free to ignore health department regulations?

Obviously this restaurant chain does indeed operate by various sets of rules. Otherwise they couldn't stay in business! Christianity also has rules. They are God's rules, he expects us to obey them, and he provides us with the strength to do so. This set of rules is not the burdensome code of the Old Testament law (see Colossians 2:14). It is, rather, the New Testament commandments of Christ, which include the law of love. Today's lesson will strengthen your learners to live by that law with confidence. And what a glorious confidence it is!

INTRODUCTION

Some people think Pete is not very bright, but Pete thinks he is bright enough. He earns a living and lives alone in his own little house. He goes to church every Sunday and reads from the Bible every day. He likes best to read what Jesus did, and especially about the time Jesus walked on the water (John 6:16-21). Pete likes to imagine Jesus, tall and handsome, walking across the little lake outside the town where Pete lives.

One day Pete read that Jesus said, "Anyone who has faith in me will do what I have been doing. He will do even greater things than these, because I am going to the Father" (John 14:12). Didn't that mean Pete could walk on water, too? He hurried out to the lake and straight into it. In a minute he knew he could not walk on water.

Pete had some disappointments worse than that. Seeing a man with terminal cancer, he prayed that the man would be well. But the man died. How could that be? Didn't Jesus say, "If you believe, you will receive whatever you ask for in prayer" (Matthew 21:22)?

Pete always had thought the Bible was true in every detail, but now he had to wonder. Is it possible that the Bible is wrong sometimes? Is it possible that not all of Jesus' promises are kept? Pete had to do some heavy thinking about that. In the midst of his thoughts he chanced to notice 1 John 5:14: "If we ask anything according to his will, he hears us."

So Jesus' will makes a difference, and Jesus' will is the same as God's will. Of course it makes a difference! God didn't want Pete to walk on water. Thinking about it again, Pete knew it would be a pretty silly thing for him to do. God allowed that cancer patient to die because that was the only way he could get to Heaven. Being well in Heaven is much better than being well on earth.

Now Pete has a new purpose in his Bible reading. Daily he is looking for what God wants him to do. When he finds that, he does it. Some people still think

DEVOTIONAL READING:
ROMANS 5:1-11
BACKGROUND SCRIPTURE:
1 JOHN 5
PRINTED TEXT:
1 JOHN 5:1-15

LESSON AIMS

After participating in this lesson, each student will be able to:

1. Summarize the facts that we know about Jesus Christ from today's text.

2. Tell how faith in these facts helps us to live as confident Christians.

3. Write a statement of confident faith in Jesus as Lord and Savior.

Nov
16

KEY VERSE

This is the testimony: God has given us eternal life, and this life is in his Son.   —1 John 5:11

Pete is not very bright, but through the Word of God the Holy Spirit is teaching him something every day.

A. ARE WE BRIGHT ENOUGH?

Like Pete, most of us have made our peace with the fact that we don't always get what we pray for. We, too, have read Jesus' promise in Matthew 21:22 about receiving "whatever you ask for in prayer." But even as we read it, we know that the promise is not really as absolute as it seems.

First of all, we know that God will not do anything wrong, even if dozens of us are begging for it every day. God knows what is right and what is wrong much better than we do.

Second, our own experience confirms the saying that is repeated often among Christians: "God has three ways of answering our prayers. Sometimes he says 'Yes,' sometimes he says 'No,' and sometimes he says 'Wait.'" Our confidence in God is unshaken even when he says "No" because we know his "No" is for our greater benefit.

Third, we are bright enough to see that it's logically impossible for God to say "Yes" to all our prayers. Perhaps I am asking to have a sunny day for my picnic while you, at the same time, are asking for a heavy rain for your cornfield. Neither of us is going to find fault with God because my picnic is rained out or your cornfield is dry for another day or two.

B. LESSON BACKGROUND

Last week's lesson centered our attention on loving one another, but we gave a passing thought to the outreach of our love beyond the circle of our fellow Christians. Our love reaches out in two directions. First, it reaches upward to our heavenly Father, who loves us with a love that is close and personal even while it is transcendent and supernatural. Second, our love reaches out horizontally to people. This includes enemies who do not love us (Matthew 5:43-45; 22:37-39) as well as friends and family who do.

This week's lesson overlaps that of last week. Beginning with thoughts on love, it leads us on to think of faith and confidence. Let us be not slow to follow where it leads, for faith and confidence can give a heavenly serenity even in the midst of worldly troubles.

I. CHILDREN OF GOD (1 JOHN 5:1-5)

Our lesson title counsels us to "Live With Confidence," and that is excellent advice. Confidence frees us from anxiety and worry, makes us optimistic, and helps us do our best each day. But let us understand at the outset that John is not talking about self-confidence. He's actually talking about something much better than that: our confidence in the Son of God, Jesus (verses 13 and 14 of our text). We trust Jesus; we obey him; we expect his help, and we get it.

The word *confidence* appears near the end of our printed text. Near the beginning of our lesson we see the words *believes* and *faith*. Faith in Jesus includes believing in Jesus. This type of faith trusts him, depends on him, and does his will. It shapes our lives! So the words *confidence* and *faith* are related. In this lesson we do not want to get lost in word games, but we do want to understand the words we are reading.

HOW TO SAY IT
Corinthians. Kor-IN-thee-unz.
cryonics. cry-AHN-iks.
Galatians. Guh-LAY-shunz.
Hebrews. HEE-brews.

A. REQUIREMENTS (vv. 1-3)

1. Everyone who believes that Jesus is the Christ is born of God, and everyone who loves the father loves his child as well.

When we believe *that Jesus is the Christ,* he gives us the "right to become children of God" (John 1:12). Because of our belief, our faith, God brings us to rebirth (John 1:13; Galatians 3:26). Our bodies look as they did before, but our spirits are reborn (John 3:3-6). "If anyone is in Christ, he is a new creation; the old has gone, the new has come!" (2 Corinthians 5:17).

Since God brings about our rebirth, the new creatures we become are God's children. As proper children do, we love our Father, God; and we love all his other children, our fellow Christians. This repeats and reemphasizes the theme of last week's lesson, "Love One Another."

2, 3. This is how we know that we love the children of God: by loving God and carrying out his commands. This is love for God: to obey his commands. And his commands are not burdensome,

John's thinking is easier to understand when we begin at the end of this two-verse section and work backward through it. God's *commands are not burdensome*—obedience to them does not place a heavy burden on us. Jesus said, "My yoke is easy and my burden is light" (Matthew 11:30). It is our *love* for *God,* not a sense of obligation, that motivates us to *obey his commands* in our daily living. *By loving God and carrying out his commands,* of course, *we love the children of God.* That is one of God's clear commandments. Jesus taught on this theme often (see John 14:21, 23; 15:14; cf. 1 John 3:23).

B. RESULTS (vv. 4, 5)

4, 5. . . . for everyone born of God overcomes the world. This is the victory that has overcome the world, even our faith. Who is it that overcomes the world? Only he who believes that Jesus is the Son of God.

Someone who is *born of God* is any one of the children of God whom we have been reading about, any faithful Christian. Here *the world* refers to the godless world, the selfish world, the world that is constantly tempting a Christian to turn away from God for the sake of worldly profit and pleasure. Any faithful Christian resists the world's temptations and so overcomes *the world.* (In his Gospel, the apostle John speaks more of "the world" than the three other Gospel writers combined!)

It is *our faith,* our belief in Jesus, the Son of God that enables us to overcome. *The world* is insistent with offers of dishonest gain and wicked pleasure, but we have a better offer, an inheritance reserved in Heaven for us—"an inheritance that can never perish, spoil or fade" (1 Peter 1:4).

That eternal inheritance is better than anything the world can offer. And this is not the first time that John has spoken of "overcoming," either. Quoting Jesus many years earlier, John wrote, "In this world you will have trouble. But take heart! I have overcome the world" (John 16:33; see also 1 John 2:13, 14; 4:4). Neither will this be the last time John speaks on this subject. Looking toward our eternal salvation, John passes along this revelation: "To him who overcomes, I will give the right to eat from the tree of life, which is in the paradise of God" (Revelation 2:7), and "He who overcomes will not be hurt at all by the second death" (Revelation 2:11). Other great "overcoming" promises are found in Revelation 2:17, 26; 3:5, 12, 21; 21:7.

FAITH THAT OVERCOMES

Floyd Goodman, Jr. was trapped! While working at his job in a peanut warehouse, he fell into a silo containing tons of unshelled peanuts. As he sank into the peanuts he did two things: he refused to panic, and he prayed. He later said his prayer was, "Lord, help me. This is not the way I would like to go. Lord, I know

WHAT DO YOU THINK?

Is it possible to love God without loving his Son, Jesus Christ? Why, or why not?

[Consider John 14:6 in this discussion.]

WHAT DO YOU THINK?

Some people claim that belief in Christ requires a "leap in the dark." Starting with Luke 1:1-4, what conclusive evidence can you cite to refute that claim?

Daily Bible Readings

Monday, Nov. 10—We Walk by Faith (2 Corinthians 5:4-9)

Tuesday, Nov. 11—We Speak of What We Know (John 3:11-21)

Wednesday, Nov. 12—Hope Doesn't Disappoint (Romans 5:1-5)

Thursday, Nov. 13—God Proves His Love in Christ (Romans 5:6-11)

Friday, Nov. 14—Our Faith Conquers the World (1 John 5: 1-5)

Saturday, Nov. 15—A Testimony in Our Hearts (1 John 5: 6-12)

Sunday, Nov. 16—That You May Know (1 John 5:13-21)

that's not the way you want me to go." It took an hour and a half to rescue him. Later, at the hospital, he was found to be in good condition.

So, did Floyd Goodman's faith save him? It can't be proved scientifically, of course. Did being rescued prove he was right about "knowing" that wasn't the way God wanted him to die? Again, there is no way to prove it. To say "yes" to either question is an assertion of *our* faith, which, of course, is just as legitimate an assertion as saying "no" to the questions.

But this much we can say: Floyd Goodman's faith in the power of God to help him overcome the avalanche of peanuts that engulfed him gave him the power to focus on what he needed to do. Floyd prayed for help, and God answered, giving him the calmness of spirit to slow down his breathing, which raised considerably the likelihood of his survival. Perhaps that is one of the most practical results of faith: it enables us to approach the troubles of this world with a calm spirit, knowing that God will see us through.
—C. R. B.

II. WITNESSES TO TRUTH (1 JOHN 5:6-8)

We who believe that Jesus is the Son of God (v. 5) have good reasons for that belief. No doubt the first-century believers were as sure as we are. But there were false teachers who boldly said many false things about Jesus—about how he came to this world and about his true nature. So John wrote briefly about why we believe that Jesus is the Son of God.

A. Spirit, Water, and Blood, Part 1 (v. 6)

6. This is the one who came by water and blood—Jesus Christ. He did not come by water only, but by water and blood. And it is the Spirit who testifies, because the Spirit is the truth.

When *Jesus Christ* was about thirty years old, he was baptized in the Jordan River, and then he began his great work of teaching and preaching. So *by water,* that is, by his baptism, he came as the teacher of Israel. More than three years later he was crucified and shed his *blood* on Calvary. So by *blood,* that is, by his death, he came to be the Redeemer of believers. Jesus was fully human and fully God.

The Holy *Spirit* is the one *who testifies* to these facts (John 1:32-34). John and the other apostles give the testimony in human language, but the Holy Spirit inspires them. Jesus himself promised that the Holy Spirit would guide those apostles into all truth (John 16:13). The Spirit not only speaks truth, he *is the truth* (cf. John 14:17). He cannot be mistaken.

B. Spirit, Water, and Blood, Part 2 (vv. 7, 8)

7, 8. For there are three that testify: the Spirit, the water and the blood; and the three are in agreement.

It does seem strange to say *water* and *blood* are witnesses that *testify,* but the strangeness disappears when we realize that the word *water* means Jesus' baptism and the word *blood* means his death. At Jesus' baptism God himself spoke from Heaven, saying, "You are my Son, whom I love; with you I am well pleased" (Mark 1:11). You can't find better testimony than that.

While Jesus was on the cross, his enemies derided him by saying his death proved that he was not the Son of God (Matthew 27:39-43). How wrong they were! Jesus' manner and words on the cross, three hours of darkness before he died, an earthquake at his death—all these were so convincing that even pagan soldiers decided that Jesus really was the Son of God (Matthew 27:45-54). Any remaining doubts were dispelled by the resurrection (John 20:24-28).

What Do You Think?

If a fellow believer confessed that he felt guilty because he sometimes had doubts about Jesus, how would you counsel him?

III. DECLARATION OF LIFE (1 JOHN 5:9-15)

Our closing verses summarize our certainty about Jesus and the life he brings.

A. TESTIMONY AND RESULT (vv. 9-12)

9. We accept man's testimony, but God's testimony is greater because it is the testimony of God, which he has given about his Son.

We do indeed accept the *testimony* of men. In every court of law it is the basis of decisions (cf. John 8:17; 19:35). More than that, almost every day of our lives we accept what people tell us, making their statements the basis of decision and action.

God's testimony, however, *is greater* than the testimony of man, as much greater as God is greater than people on earth (cf. John 5:36). And it is God's own testimony that tells us Jesus is God's *Son.* The three witnesses of the Holy Spirit, the water (Jesus' baptism), and the blood (Jesus' death) give us God's own testimony. The apostles put in human language the testimony of the Holy Spirit, and the Spirit is God. The voice from Heaven at Jesus' baptism was God's own voice. The darkness and the earthquake gave power to the testimony of Jesus' death, and the darkness and the earthquake were God's own work. Thus in different ways God is telling us that Jesus is his Son. How can anyone doubt it?

10. Anyone who believes in the Son of God has this testimony in his heart. Anyone who does not believe God has made him out to be a liar, because he has not believed the testimony God has given about his Son.

If we accept God's *testimony* and *believe* that Jesus is God's *Son,* then we have God's testimony in ourselves. It is in our minds to guide us in everything we think or say or do; it is in our hearts to make us give glad obedience to every command of the Father or the Son. "The man who has accepted it has certified that God is truthful. For the one whom God has sent speaks the words of God" (John 3:33, 34; cf. 12:44-50).

There is no middle ground here: you either believe God's testimony *about his Son* or you don't. And if you don't, then you're calling God *a liar.*

11. And this is the testimony: God has given us eternal life, and this life is in his Son.

The *testimony* doesn't stop with the fact that Jesus is God's *Son.* The record goes on to proclaim the *eternal life* he brings. This doesn't mean "life forever" with all the problems, trials, temptations, and distresses that beset us now. It is life forever in Heaven! (See Revelation 22.)

12. He who has the Son has life; he who does not have the Son of God does not have life.

The line is clearly drawn. Despite modern ideas of "many paths to God," there really is only Jesus. "I am the way and the truth and the life. No one comes to the Father except through me" (John 14:6). This path is very narrow (Matthew 7:13, 14). Eternal life is for those redeemed by Jesus, and for no one else.

B. KNOWLEDGE AND CONFIDENCE (vv. 13-15)

13. I write these things to you who believe in the name of the Son of God so that you may know that you have eternal life.

This verse is the "purpose statement" for John's letter (cf. John 20:30, 31). No doubt John's readers already *know* that God is giving them *eternal life* because they *believe* in Jesus. But John wants to reinforce that knowledge, wants to fix the truth so firmly in their minds that they will never forget it.

As a result, John's readers will find encouragement in it when life on earth is troubled. We, no less than they, find encouragement in the same assurance. If

Display this poster as you discuss verse 11. You will find it in the Adult Visuals *packet.*

WHAT DO YOU THINK?

What assurance does John give you when he says, "God has given us eternal life"? (Note the verb tense suggests completed action—he "has given" it to us, not he "will give" it to us.)

PRAYER

Father in Heaven, we know your power and goodness and love are complete and faultless forever. Thank you for being dependable. In Jesus' name, amen.

this time is full of trouble, it is good to know that it is only the prelude to an untroubled eternity.

Since John is writing to people who already believe that Jesus is God's Son, the words *that you may know* can be taken to mean "keep on believing." John wants his readers of that time and our time to cling to that belief, to keep it in mind even when false teachers are denying it.

THE PROMISE OF IMMORTALITY

For a mere twenty-eight thousand dollars, you can be guaranteed immortality! Well, maybe "guaranteed" is putting it a bit strongly, but the *possibility* of immortality through having your body quick-frozen at death is at least suggested by the advertisements.

Robert C.W. Ettinger is credited with starting the cryonics movement in the mid-1960s with the publication of a book entitled *The Prospect of Immortality*. Soon after that book was published, the Immortalist Society was founded, and today it publishes *The Immortalist* magazine. The movement continues to play on humanity's fears of nonexistence. As one of the many cryonics organizations says on its web site, cryonics is "the only hope for the elderly or terminally ill, or for those who die suddenly. Cryonics—the only alternative to the despair of death and disease. A new technology of life potentially without limits."

The movement appeals to peoples' hopes—some would say their gullibility—by noting that many things are possible today that were once thought impossible. This is true, of course, but the Bible presents a profoundly different view of life everlasting. True eternal life is found, not in the genius of modern science—or, more realistically, in the prospect of a scientific process that may *never* be developed—but in identification with the Son of God, who alone is the source of life. He offers us abundant life both here and now, and in God's eternal future.   —C. R. B.

14, 15. This is the confidence we have in approaching God: that if we ask anything according to his will, he hears us. And if we know that he hears us—whatever we ask—we know that we have what we asked of him.

We do have this same *confidence*, don't we? We expect that God will do what *we ask* him to do. Without such confidence, we have no promise of a favorable answer. Jesus said, "Whatever you ask for in prayer, believe that you have received it, and it will be yours" (Mark 11:24). Speaking of one who prays for wisdom, James said, "When he asks, he must believe and not doubt" (James 1:6).

WHAT DO YOU THINK?

Why does prayer seem to work for some people some of the time, but not for all people all of the time?

[A few useful passages to challenge your thinking are Jeremiah 7:16; 11:14; 14:11, 12; Lamentations 3:8, 44; and 1 Peter 3:7.]

Even so, we try to be reasonable in our prayers and our expectations. We pray for daily bread according to Matthew 6:11, but we do not expect God to cook our dinner and put it on the table while we watch television in the living room! God does not promise to do what we ask unless it is *according to his will;* so if we do not get what we ask, perhaps we can amend our asking to match his will. And if we are not getting what we ask for, the fault is ours, not God's (James 4:2, 3).

CONCLUSION

How blessed it is to live a life of confidence! This is not confidence in our own abilities, our earning power, our stock portfolios, or the number of educational degrees we have. It's a confidence in the God of the universe, who is "on our side." We know God can do anything, and he will do what we ask,

    . . . if it is the right thing to do.

    . . . if we really believe he will do it.

    . . . if we do our part in accomplishing it.

So we trust God and concentrate on doing our part.

THOUGHT TO REMEMBER

"So do not throw away your confidence; it will be richly rewarded" (Hebrews 10:35).

Discovery Learning

This page contains an alternative lesson plan emphasizing learning activities. Classes desiring such student involvement will find these suggestions helpful. The next page is a reproducible activity page to further enhance discovery learning.

LEARNING GOALS

After participating in this lesson, each student will be able to:

1. Summarize the facts that we know about Jesus Christ from today's text.

2. Tell how faith in these facts helps us to live as confident Christians.

3. Write a statement of confident faith in Jesus as Lord and Savior.

INTO THE LESSON

Prepare an opening activity work sheet called, "Modest Metaphors." This work sheet should contain the following statements: "If confidence were a color, it would be _____ because. . . ." "If confidence were an animal, it would be a _____ because. . . ." "If confidence were an object, it would be a _____ because. . . ."

Give a work sheet to each student, and say, "Today our lesson is on confidence. To help us begin to think about this subject, I've prepared a few metaphors for you to complete. If confidence were a color, an animal, or an object, what would it be, and why? I'll give you three minutes to complete these sentences and then we can share them with the class." After several minutes, ask for some volunteers to reveal their answers on the color. Then ask for suggested answers to the animal and object that would describe confidence. Once you hear several, say, "Confidence is something we desire when we sense that we don't have it. The apostle John, in our lesson text, encourages us to live in confidence. Turn to 1 John 5:1-15, and let's read why we can have such confidence."

INTO THE WORD

Ask a class member to read the lesson text aloud. Move the class into groups of three and distribute copies of the reproducible activity "Confident Christian Faith" from the next page. There are two columns and eight rows in this worksheet. State: "Our confidence is tied directly to our faith. Read the verses in the left column. Then write in the space provided the impact belief has on our lives." *Possible answers include: (1a) born of God; (1b) loves God; (2) loves God's children; (3) keeps his commandments; (4) overcomes the world; (6-13) eternal life; (14) confident prayer; (15) answered prayer.* After about five minutes, ask for answers.

Move the class back together as one group and ask the following questions:

1. What does John mean by the terms *water* and *blood* in 1 John 5:6? (*Baptism by water and shed blood on the cross.*)

2. What facts do we learn from today's text about Jesus Christ? (*Son of God, v. 5; baptized, v. 6; shed his blood, v. 6*)

3. How does John say we know that we love our brothers and sisters in Christ? (*Love God and keep his commandments, v. 2*)

4. What does John mean by the phrase, "his commands are not burdensome"? (*Not a heavy burden, not very hard to obey.*)

5. What confidence can we have by John's use of the phrase "overcomes the world"? (*We can resist the temptations in the world.*)

6. What are the witnesses that bear record in Heaven and the witnesses that bear record in earth that Jesus is the Son of God? (*Heaven: Father, Word, Holy Spirit; earth: Spirit, water, blood, vv. 7, 8.*)

INTO LIFE

State: "Jesus helps us to live confident lives in this world. Consider some areas of your life where you have confidence or lack confidence."

Distribute copies of the reproducible activity "My Level of Confidence" from the next page. Give time for each to consider and mark his or her chart appropriately. Then ask, "What are the foundations for confidence?" Expect the basic response to relate to a history of demonstrated faithfulness, dependability. Point out that the root meaning of the word *confidence* has to do with maintaining fidelity, faithfulness. Ask, "Why is it completely appropriate for us to have confidence in Jesus?" If no one mentions the thoughts of these Scriptures, ask individuals to find and read them: Lamentations 3:22, 23; Hebrews 13:8; Revelation 22:13.

After sharing these areas of personal confidence or lack of it, move the class into a prayer circle. End the class with prayers of praises and thanksgiving for all that Jesus has done and will do for us. Incorporate petitions for freedom from the doubts, anxieties, and fears that debilitate us when we live without confidence in God. Then encourage the class to live with confidence in him this week.

Confident Christian Faith

Our confidence is tied directly to our faith. Read the verses in the left column. Then write in the space provided the impact belief has our lives.

The Impact of Belief on Our Lives (1 John 5:1-15)

1 John 5:1a

1 John 5:1b

1 John 5:2

1 John 5:3

1 John 5:4

1 John 5:6-13

1 John 5:14

1 John 5:15

My Level of Confidence

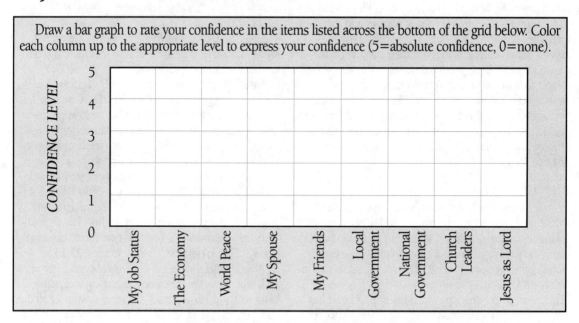

Draw a bar graph to rate your confidence in the items listed across the bottom of the grid below. Color each column up to the appropriate level to express your confidence (5=absolute confidence, 0=none).

CONFIDENCE LEVEL: 5, 4, 3, 2, 1, 0

Items: My Job Status, The Economy, World Peace, My Spouse, My Friends, Local Government, National Government, Church Leaders, Jesus as Lord

What criteria are you using to determine your level of confidence in each? What would need to happen to increase your level of confidence in each?

Faith Faces the World
Unit 4: Live With Purpose
(Lessons 12, 13)

REMAIN LOYAL

LESSON 12

WHY TEACH THIS LESSON?

Have you noticed that the concept of *loyalty* is almost nonexistent these days? In the 1950s a breadwinner expected to remain loyal to the same employer for an entire career. Today's young adults fully expect to change employers several times in their lives. Family loyalty has faded as well: marriages and traditional family units seem to have become much more "disposable" since the 1960s. The only sense of loyalty we are to have, say those who are wise in the ways of the world, is to be "true to ourselves"—whatever that means.

But God has a different idea. He expects loyalty to the truth, to our fellow believers, and in our faithfulness to him. These are nonnegotiable! And it's a good thing, too, because it is our loyalty to God and his expectations that keep us on the road to eternal life. Today's lesson will remind your learners that they have a choice to make. It is a choice that cannot be avoided, and it is the most important choice a Christian will ever be confronted with.

INTRODUCTION

A. THE BIG PICTURE

One of the helpers of a noted first-century evangelist gave up that kind of work because he "loved this world" (2 Timothy 4:10). In the twentieth century a young preacher's wife deserted her husband and took a job in her uncle's law firm because she thought the preacher "was never going to make any money." In the twenty-first century three families left a church because they wanted red carpet in the auditorium, and all the other members voted for green carpet.

At times we all fail to see the big picture. The church is Christ's body, and he is the head of it (Ephesians 1:22, 23; Colossians 1:18). In this picture only the head is perfect. The parts of the body all have their faults, but we put up with them because we have faults, too. There is no way to forsake Christ's body without forsaking its head as well. To be faithful and loyal to Christ (the head), and to the church (his body), and to the Bible (his Word) is our constant challenge.

B. LESSON BACKGROUND

After three lessons from 1 John, we turn to 2 John and 3 John for more instruction from that inspired apostle.

Second John is addressed to a Christian lady and her children, who are well loved by other Christians (2 John 1). Nothing is said about her husband, so we may suppose that she was a widow. Some think that he was still living, but was a pagan with no interest in Christianity. On the other hand, some think "the lady" to be figurative language for a local church, or possibly for the church universal, consisting of all the churches in the world. If that is what John had in mind, the lady's children would be the members of the church, or of all the churches. In either case, John's thoughts are helpful for Christians everywhere.

Third John is addressed to a good Christian man named Gaius. Here again we find teaching that is beneficial for all Christians as we read this man's mail. Let us see how those two letters encourage all of us to remain loyal.

DEVOTIONAL READING:
JOHN 15:1-11
BACKGROUND SCRIPTURE:
2 AND 3 JOHN
PRINTED TEXT:
2 JOHN 4-9; 3 JOHN 3-12

LESSON AIMS

After participating in this lesson, each student will be able to:

1. Describe the course of faithfulness and love for the truth that John commends in 2 and 3 John.

2. Name some current false teachings that cause doubt and confusion about who Jesus is.

3. Select one person who is faithful in his or her discipleship and express gratitude to that person.

KEY VERSE

Dear friend, do not imitate what is evil but what is good. Anyone who does what is good is from God. Anyone who does what is evil has not seen God. —3 John 11

Nov
23

I. OUR WALK (2 JOHN 4-6)

John frames our loyalty to Christ in terms of our Christian walk. He begins his thoughts with an example.

A. WALK OF TRUTH (v. 4)

4. It has given me great joy to find some of your children walking in the truth, just as the Father commanded us.

Walking in the truth means living in accordance with the Christian teaching given by the apostles as passed on by those who learned from them. *The Father* has *commanded us* to live in that way (cf. 1 John 3:23). John has encountered some of the lady's *children* who are doing that, and he is delighted.

To say that some things are true means that other things are not true. When we walk *in the truth*, we reject those things that are not true. All truth ultimately comes from God, whether he reveals it to us in his Word or allows us to discover it by some natural means. But John is speaking of spiritual truth—the truth that we have received from the Father. This is the truth that keeps us on the road to eternal life. We stray from that truth at our peril.

THE TEST OF LOYALTY

What is loyalty? Sometimes we talk about loyalty to a sports team. Fans of the New York Mets stuck with their baseball team for years through losing seasons before they finally won the World Series in 1969. But more often loyalty in sports is like that of Los Angeles Dodgers' pitcher Don Sutton when he was discussing free agency several years ago: "I'm not disloyal. I'm the most loyal person money can buy."

Politics has its own standards of loyalty also. Political pundits generally agree that Hubert Humphrey lost the presidential election to Richard Nixon in 1968 because, as Vice President, Humphrey had acquiesced to Lyndon Johnson's Vietnam war policy. Humphrey later explained his actions by saying, "Where you stand often depends on where you sit."

However, the apostle John's standard of loyalty is expressed differently: walk in the truth and live out the Lord's commandments regardless of the consequences. Economic, social, or political outcomes are not to be a part of the equation. This is difficult for us to do, isn't it? But no more so than for first-century Christians who also faced the possibility of persecution because of their stand for the truth. The call to discipleship is still the same today: walk in the truth and keep God's commandments.   —C. R. B.

B. WALK OF LOVE (vv. 5, 6)

5. And now, dear lady, I am not writing you a new command but one we have had from the beginning. I ask that we love one another.

In previous lessons we have noted more than once that both Peter and John vigorously repeated teaching that already was well known. Peter gave special emphasis to his repeating (2 Peter 1:12-15). Now we read John's urgent request to the lady, and it does not concern anything new. It is a plea for remembering and continuing in that which *we have had from the beginning.* He asks *that we love one another.*

6. And this is love: that we walk in obedience to his commands. As you have heard from the beginning, his command is that you walk in love.

Easily we understand that our love for God is shown by keeping *his commands* (John 14:15, 24; 15:10). But now we are reading of our *love* for one another, and it is a bit surprising to read that loving people consists of keeping God's commandments. See how this is confirmed by Romans 13:8-10, where Paul points

WHAT DO YOU THINK?

Every teacher in the church wants his or her learners to be "walking in the truth." What does a teacher need to do to ensure that this happens?

Psalm 119:11 and 2 Timothy 3:16, 17 can be starting points for your discussion.

out that all of God's commandments about human relations are summed up in one commandment, "Love your neighbor as yourself." The *command* to love one another is one that we *have heard from the beginning* of our acquaintance with Christian teaching. Now, as always, we should *walk in love*. That is, we should be obeying that commandment continually in our daily living.

II. OUR ENEMY (2 JOHN 7-9)

From our lessons in 1 John we recall that John was writing fifty-some years after Jesus ended his life as a man on earth. Many people had come along to contradict the truths taught by Christian teachers (1 John 2:18). Men, proud of their intellect, thought their own opinions to be more dependable than God's own revelation (cf. 1 Corinthians 2:13; Colossians 2:8). Now we come to one more warning against false teachers and one more call for Christians to remain loyal to the truth.

A. AVOIDING DECEIVERS (vv. 7, 8)

7. Many deceivers, who do not acknowledge Jesus Christ as coming in the flesh, have gone out into the world. Any such person is the deceiver and the antichrist.

Christians take care to be loyal to the truth because *many deceivers . . . have gone out into the world* and are teaching falsehood. Some are even in the church itself (2 Peter 2:1), and some have come into the church and left—taking others with them as they go. The falsehood at issue in this verse is that they *do not acknowledge Jesus Christ as coming in the flesh*. This could mean that the deceivers deny that Jesus had been a human being, born in a body of flesh. It could also mean that they deny that Jesus, the man in the flesh, was the *Christ* (the Messiah), the eternal Word described in John 1:1-5. Anyone who denies either *is the deceiver and the antichrist*. (Contrast Martha's godly confession in John 11:27.)

LIES—NO MATTER HOW THEY ARE TOLD!

Have you heard about the program that has been in your computer for months taking pictures of you unawares and sending them out over the Internet? Or the map put out by the Fuji company that deletes Israel from the Middle East? Or the poisoned envelopes at the ATM machine? Or the HIV-infected hypodermic needles attached to the underside of gas pump handles? Or the . . . well, you get the idea!

All of the above are hoaxes! They can be checked out at http://hoaxbusters.ciac.org or similar Web sites. Something about us humans makes us fall for lies, whether fraudulent moneymaking schemes or chain letters or almost-plausible stories that trigger our fears and fantasies.

Falling for falsehoods is an age-old human trait; only the technology seems to have changed! John warns us strictly against those who deny the testimony of the eyewitnesses that Jesus, the man, was God's Son. It doesn't matter how (or by how many) the message is spread. It is still a lie.   —C. R. B.

8. Watch out that you do not lose what you have worked for, but that you may be rewarded fully.

John expresses a fear somewhat similar to that of Paul: "I fear for you, that somehow I have wasted my efforts on you" (Galatians 4:11). A full reward in eternity is our goal (cf. Matthew 5:12; 1 Corinthians 3:8; Revelation 11:18; 22:12). That is the reason John charges his readers to *watch out* for themselves—in other words, "Be careful!"

All that they *have worked for*—meaning Christian faith, Christian action, and full reward in Heaven—will be lost by Christians who let themselves be deceived by false teachers who spread lies about Jesus. If you're not strong enough to resist what these deceivers have to say, then just stay away from them!

Visual for lessons 6 and 12. This poster illustrates a practical way to "Remain Loyal" to the Lord. Display it as you begin the lesson.

WHAT DO YOU THINK?

What are some specific things believers can do to heed John's warning here?

B. AVOIDING DECEIT (v. 9)

9. Anyone who runs ahead and does not continue in the teaching of Christ does not have God; whoever continues in the teaching has both the Father and the Son.

The deceivers mentioned in verse 8 are spreading deceit—wrong teaching. Any person who does not stay with correct teaching, but leaves it for the false teaching of liars, abandons God as well. On the other hand, any person who remains loyal to the true *teaching of Christ* remains loyal both to God *the Father* and to Jesus his *Son.* Paul has a lot to say about the importance of sound doctrine in his pastoral letters (see 1 Timothy 1:3, 10; 4:16; 6:3; 2 Timothy 4:3; Titus 1:9; 2:1).

III. OUR FAITHFULNESS (3 JOHN 3-8)

As we turn from 2 John to 3 John, we consider specific Christian action; and before we finish the lesson we shall be reading also of specific un-Christian action.

This short letter is addressed to a certain man named Gaius (v. 1). The New Testament mentions several men of that name, but there is no way to know whether this Gaius was the same as any of them. All we really know about him is learned from the letter now before us.

A. FAITHFUL TO TRUTH (vv. 3, 4)

3. It gave me great joy to have some brothers come and tell about your faithfulness to the truth and how you continue to walk in the truth.

Without any wild flights of imagination we can be sure that *some brothers,* some fellow Christians, have seen Gaius and have told John that *the truth* is in him. As we saw in our brief study from 2 John, what the apostle calls *the truth* is the gospel and other Christian teaching that he and other teachers have been spreading for half a century. Gaius holds all that teaching in his mind and cherishes it in his heart. He is shaping his life by true Christian teaching. He is doing what that teaching indicates he ought to do.

4. I have no greater joy than to hear that my children are walking in the truth.

John is now an old man, perhaps the only apostle of Jesus still living on earth. He has devoted his life to teaching, and most of his pupils are younger than he. Undoubtedly John has seen many of his spiritual *children* fall away from the *truth* (cf. 2 Timothy 4:10). How sad this must be! Even so, John focuses on the *joy* he has over those who *continue to walk in the truth.*

B. FAITHFUL IN HOSPITALITY (vv. 5-8)

5. Dear friend, you are faithful in what you are doing for the brothers, even though they are strangers to you.

Gaius has done something good for *the brothers,* and John commends him. Without further information it seems reasonable to suppose Gaius had extended them hospitality, giving them food and lodging while they were in his town. Most Bible students agree that the *strangers* are Christians who had been unknown to Gaius. Probably they carried a letter of introduction from John or some other trusted person so Gaius could know they really were fellow Christians. One way we walk "in the truth" (v. 4) is by extending hospitality (see Romans 12:13; 1 Timothy 3:2; 5:10; Hebrews 13:2; and 1 Peter 4:9). We are not to give the same kind of help to false teachers. In fact, we are specifically prohibited from doing so (2 John 10, 11).

6. They have told the church about your love. You will do well to send them on their way in a manner worthy of God.

DAILY BIBLE READINGS

Monday, Nov. 17—I Press On (Philippians 3:10-15)

Tuesday, Nov. 18—Hold Fast (Philippians 3:16-21)

Wednesday, Nov. 19—Abide in Christ (John 15:1-7)

Thursday, Nov. 20—Walk in Truth (2 John 1-6)

Friday, Nov. 21—Be on Guard, Don't Lose Out (2 John 7-12)

Saturday, Nov. 22—Be Faithful to the Truth (3 John 1-8)

Sunday, Nov. 23—Imitate What Is Good (3 John 9-15)

When traveling Christians return to their own city and their home church, they tell the whole congregation how helpful Gaius has been. He is simply demonstrating *love* on a personal level.

The latter part of verse 6 recommends another way of helping our fellow Christians. After supplying food and lodging while they are in town, it is good *to send them on their way* with silver in their pockets for purchasing food and lodging in other towns where there will be no Christians to provide for them (cf. John 13:20; Galatians 4:14, 15). The next verse helps us understand why this is appropriate.

7. It was for the sake of the Name that they went out, receiving no help from the pagans.

Traveling *for the sake of the Name* means that these Christians are traveling evangelists, teachers, and missionaries. They move about to spread the gospel and plant churches in places where there are none. They are traveling to strengthen and encourage existing churches by winning new converts for them and by repeating the Christian teaching that Peter was eager to reinforce (2 Peter 1:12-16). As these Christians travel about in their ministries, they are *receiving no help from the pagans*—they are not asking or receiving any pay from the Gentiles to whom they offer the gospel.

The apostle Paul followed that same policy. Traveling evangelists could accept contributions from Christians in established churches (2 Corinthians 9:12-14; Philippians 4:15-18), and Paul would earn much of his living by secular work (Acts 18:1-4). He would offer the gospel "free of charge" to the sinners who needed it (1 Corinthians 9:18). The fact that these Christians are "receiving no help from the pagans" may have something to say about the various "fund raisers" that churches engage in today.

8. We ought therefore to show hospitality to such men so that we may work together for the truth.

Because the traveling Christians are taking nothing from the unbelievers, other Christians ought to welcome these fellow believers and help them by supplying room and board without charge. Thus Christians will be helpers to travelers who are working *together for the truth,* helping to spread it far and wide. Many years previously, John himself was on "the receiving end" of such hospitality (Mark 6:7-10).

IV. OUR EXAMPLES (3 JOHN 9-12)

Past lessons reminded us of false teachers who constantly opposed those loyal to Christ and the truth. After giving us a thumbnail sketch of the good work of Gaius, our text brings us a glimpse of the evil work of one of the false teachers. That is followed by another good example.

A. A BAD EXAMPLE (vv. 9, 10)

9. I wrote to the church, but Diotrephes, who loves to be first, will have nothing to do with us.

No doubt *the church* to which John wrote is the one where Gaius is a member. And no doubt John wrote a letter of instruction and advice such as Paul wrote to churches in Rome, Corinth, and elsewhere. Then we read no more about John's letter to that church, and the adversative conjunction *but* indicates that what follows is somehow in opposition to that letter.

The problem seems to be centered on a certain *Diotrephes*. We recognize his attitude of loving *to be first* as existing yet today. He wants to be Number One among the church members. He wants to be in charge. He wants to run the show. Consequently, he resents any advice from John.

HOW TO SAY IT

Corinth. KOR-inth.
Corinthians. Kor-IN-thee-unz.
Demetrius. De-MEE-tree-us.
Diotrephes. Die-OT-rih-feez.
Ephesians. Ee-FEE-zhunz.
Gaius. GAY-us.
Galatians. Guh-LAY-shunz.
Philippians. Fih-LIP-ee-unz.

WHAT DO YOU THINK?

Why does Christian hospitality seem to be a dying ministry today?

WHAT DO YOU THINK?

How can we develop new leaders in the church while at the same time helping keep those emerging leaders from the sin of loving "to be first"?

PRAYER

Our Father in Heaven, how good it is to know that you have verified the great Christian truths by the miracles of your Son, and by his resurrection and ascension. Today we pledge our loyalty to your Son and the truth you have given us; and we look to you for wisdom, strength, and courage to remain loyal. In Jesus' name, amen.

As Diotrephes sees it, John is butting in. As a matter of fact, the Holy Spirit is guiding John into all truth (John 16:13). What John is saying or writing is God's Word, so this apostle properly has authority over churches and Christians everywhere.

But Diotrephes wants to be the top authority in his church. We can imagine that Diotrephes intercepted John's letter, and most of the church members knew nothing about it. If the letter had been read in the congregation, Gaius would have known it; it would not be necessary for John to tell him he had written it.

10. So if I come, I will call attention to what he is doing, gossiping maliciously about us. Not satisfied with that, he refuses to welcome the brothers. He also stops those who want to do so and puts them out of the church.

Here we have a list of four wrongs of which Diotrephes is guilty. First, by *gossiping maliciously* he is complaining about John and others who speak God's truth. Gossip is condemned in Romans 1:29; 2 Corinthians 12:20; and 1 Timothy 5:13. Second, he is not welcoming loyal teachers such as those Gaius welcomed and helped. Third, he is forbidding other church members to welcome such loyal teachers. These two violate the Christian obligation to extend hospitality (Romans 12:13; 1 Peter 4:9). Fourth, he casts *out of the church* any church member who defies him.

Diotrephes is someone who thinks of himself more highly than he ought to think (Romans 12:3). If by himself he can expel members of the church—perhaps even Gaius himself—then this is indeed a church run by one man. If John could visit that church, he would *call attention to* Diotrephes's evil deeds to denounce them.

B. A Good Example (vv. 11, 12)

11, 12. Dear friend, do not imitate what is evil but what is good. Anyone who does what is good is from God. Anyone who does what is evil has not seen God. Demetrius is well spoken of by everyone—and even by the truth itself. We also speak well of him, and you know that our testimony is true.

If Diotrephes (v. 10) personifies *what is evil*, then *Demetrius* personifies *what is good*. It's one thing to give general advice to embrace good and avoid evil. Some folks, however, can benefit from concrete examples. Perhaps Gaius is one of those, and that is the reason John seems to be saying to him, "Imitate *this* guy and not *that* guy!"

As Gaius is urged to remain loyal to God and his truth, so are we—even if the whole congregation is led away to falsehood and wrongdoing. One who keeps on doing *good* is one of God's people; one who does wrong is not.

WHAT DO YOU THINK?

What are some sources of evil that people imitate? How do we resist imitating what we see in those sources?

[Use Psalm 101:3; Proverbs 23:17; 24:1, 2; and 3 John 11 to help answer the second question.]

CONCLUSION

Our lesson title invites us to remain loyal, to be faithful, to be dependable, to take a firm stand. Gaius, John, and Demetrius were loyal to God, to Christ, and to the truth that the Holy Spirit spoke by the mouths of the apostles and prophets. This is the kind of loyalty for us!

Diotrephes, on the other hand, was loyal to himself and his selfish ambition. Undoubtedly he had made some kind of confession of Christ, but what good was it?

"The world" has made no confession of Christ at all. The world still offers us the deceivers of 2 John 7. Since they "do not acknowledge Jesus Christ as coming in the flesh," they are loyal to their lies. Make no mistake: our spiritual health depends on where our loyalties lie!

THOUGHT TO REMEMBER

Before we were loyal to God, he was loyal to us.

Discovery Learning

This page contains an alternative lesson plan emphasizing learning activities. Classes
desiring such student involvement will find these suggestions helpful. The next page
is a reproducible activity page to further enhance discovery learning.

LEARNING GOALS

After participating in this lesson, each student will be able to:

1. Describe the course of faithfulness and love for the truth that John commends in 2 and 3 John.

2. Name some current false teachings that cause doubt and confusion about who Jesus is.

3. Select one person who is faithful in his or her discipleship and express gratitude to that person.

INTO THE LESSON

Prior to this week's lesson, prepare a half-page worksheet titled "Acrostic Antonym Puzzle." The puzzle is to look something like this:

ACROSTIC ANTONYM PUZZLE

PART A:

_ _ _ _ _	war
_ _ _	sorrow
_ _ _ _	hate
_ _ _	hot
_ _ _ _	energetic
_ _ _	sad
_ _ _ _ _ _ _	finish

PART B: _ _ _ _ _ _ _

Give a copy of the puzzle to each class member. Say, "Today, we begin with an 'acrostic antonym puzzle.' The missing words are antonyms of the clue words. After filling in the words in Part A, select the letters underlined and unscramble them into a word. Write that word in part B. You have five minutes."

Go over the correct answers (*peace, joy, love, cold, lazy, happy, initiate*) and the unscrambled word: *loyalty*. Say, "One can be loyal to a spouse, a job or company, and even to a product. Our text talks about loyalty to Christ. Let's turn to 2 and 3 John and see what John says about loyalty."

INTO THE WORD

Ask one class member to read 2 John 4-9 and another to read 3 John 3-12 aloud. Then move the class into groups of four, and ask each group to answer the following question: "What does John indicate are characteristics of faithfulness?" (*Answers: walking in truth,*

2 John 4; loving one another, 2 John 5; walking after his commandments, walking in love, 2 John 6; showing hospitality, 3 John 7, 8; following what is good, 3 John 11.) After several minutes, ask for answers.

Say, "Faithfulness is also demonstrated by not being deceived by false teachers, as 3 John 7, 8 says. To help remove some confusion about what three religious groups teach about Jesus, I've asked _____ (give names) to serve on a panel. Will you come to the front now and tell us what these groups teach about Jesus?"

In preparation for this, select three members from the class to serve as a panel on "Mormonism, Islam, and Jehovah's Witnesses: False Teaching About Jesus." Panelists will need more than a week to research the assigned religion's teaching on the identity and role of Jesus. Have each panelist make a three-minute presentation on what the religion teaches about Jesus; then allow a few minutes for questions. Distribute copies of the reproducible activity sheet "False Teaching About Jesus" (page 112), and encourage learners to record information on that.

Say, "These groups sometimes lead Christians astray. And sometimes they are led astray like Diotrephes in 3 John 10. What were his four errors?" (*Spoke maliciously against John, refused to welcome the brothers, stopped those that did receive them, and put them out of the church.*)

INTO LIFE

Point out the example of Demetrius, a faithful believer with a good report (v. 12). Say, "There are many loyal Christians like Demetrius today. Name some members of our congregation whose loyalty you admire." As individuals are suggested, write their names for all to see.

Distribute copies of the reproducible activity "Thankfulness for Faithfulness" from the next page. (Copy this on certificate-quality paper.) Say, "Today, we want to honor some of the people in our congregation who have remained loyal, who have demonstrated faithfulness. On this certificate, write the name of a person you want to thank. For the next few minutes, express your gratitude to this person by describing the specific areas in which the person has demonstrated loyalty to Christ."

Give the class about five minutes to complete this activity. Encourage the learners to hand deliver these certificates to the ones selected.

Close with a prayer of thanksgiving.

False Teaching About Jesus

Fill in the following as classmates report on the three groups (or from your independent study).

	IDENTITY: Who Is Jesus?	ROLE: What Did Jesus Do?
Mormonism		
Islam		
Jehovah's Witnesses		

Thankfulness for Faithfulness

Name of Faithful Christian: _____

"It gave me great joy to have some brothers come and tell about your faithfulness to the truth and how you continue to walk in the truth" (3 John 3).

In recognition of your faithful discipleship to the Lord and your commitment to walk in the truth of his Word, you are awarded this certificate of "thankfulness for faithfulness." In particular, I want to thank you for

(Signature)_____

(Date) _____

Unit 4: Live With Purpose
(Lessons 12, 13)

MAINTAIN STEADFAST FAITH

LESSON 13

WHY TEACH THIS LESSON?

Guy Fawkes, Benedict Arnold, Vidkun Quisling, Ethel and Julius Rosenberg, Alger Hiss, Robert Philip Hanssen, Aldrich Ames, Judas Iscariot—perhaps you recognize those names as some of the most notorious traitors in history. Traitors betray their own country, team, or friends to others. How difficult it can be to discover and oppose an enemy who lurks in your very midst, an enemy whom you thought to be on your side!

But traitors have been with us always, and probably will be until Jesus returns. As we shall see in today's lesson, the first-century church struggled to deal with the dangerous situation such people created. The most important part of the solution was to protect the spiritual well being of those who might be influenced by the traitors to the faith. Hopefully, your learners will never have to deal with a situation such as Jude did. But if a similar situation does arise, today's lesson will make sure that your learners are ready.

INTRODUCTION

Jesus is the Prince of Peace (Isaiah 9:6). He blesses the peacemakers (Matthew 5:9). The apostle Paul desires "If it is possible, as far as it depends on you, live at peace with everyone" (Romans 12:18). On the other hand, Jesus himself said that he "did not come to bring peace, but a sword" (Matthew 10:34). The text of this week's lesson urges Christians to "fight the good fight of the faith" (see also 1 Timothy 6:12). So, which way is it? Shall we fight, or shall we make peace?

A. WAR AND PEACE

An extended family moved to our town: an elderly couple with two grown sons, each of whom had a wife and family of his own. The three men came to town to work in a department store that had recently been purchased and added to a chain of such stores. The adults and older children quickly became members of the local church, and the six adults took their places in two adult Sunday school classes, where they happily joined in the discussions.

These newcomers liked Jesus' teaching and meant to follow it, they said. But they were impatient with what they called "Christian myths." They were full of questions. "What difference does it make whether Jesus was born of a virgin or not? If he was, does that make his teaching any truer?" "Who cares whether Jesus did miracles or not? If he did, does that add value to what he said?" "Did Jesus really rise from the dead and take his body to Heaven with him, or did he just die and go to Heaven as we do? In either case, his teaching is good for us to follow." "Can't we follow him without pretending he is a demigod?"

Long-time members of both adult classes were firmly convinced that what the Bible says is true, and they were quick to say so. So lively debates arose.

Two thousand years ago, Jude addressed a similar (but more dangerous) situation. His short letter is "To those who have been called, who are loved by God the Father and kept by Jesus Christ" (Jude 1). Our lesson is about what he had to say to "them"—and to us.

DEVOTIONAL READING:
GALATIANS 6:1-10
BACKGROUND SCRIPTURE:
JUDE
PRINTED TEXT:
JUDE 3, 4, 8-13, 16-23

LESSON AIMS

After participating in this lesson, each student will be able to:

1. Tell what it is to contend for the faith and why it is so important to do so.

2. Cite some contemporary issue that is, or may become, the source of a challenge to one's faith, similar to the challenge described by Jude.

3. Suggest some specific manner of dealing with that challenge.

KEY VERSE

Keep yourselves in God's love as you wait for the mercy of our Lord Jesus Christ to bring you to eternal life. Be merciful to those who doubt.
—Jude 21, 22

Nov
30

LESSON 13 NOTES

B. LESSON BACKGROUND

Jude describes himself as "a servant of Jesus Christ and a brother of James" (Jude 1). This James wrote the book that bears his name, from which we took our lessons in September. Paul calls James "the Lord's brother" (Galatians 1:19). So we see that both James and Jude were sons of Joseph and Mary, and half-brothers of Jesus (see Matthew 13:55, where "Jude" is spelled "Judas"). Neither James nor Jude was a disciple of Jesus before his resurrection (John 7:5).

Jude's letter is addressed to faithful Christians without specifying any place. This is the reason it is included among the "general" epistles. It is not dated either, and many scholars say merely that it was written in the latter half of the first century. Its message, as we shall see, is timeless.

I. ALARM (JUDE 3, 4)

Jude wishes peace, mercy, and love for his readers (Jude 2). He does not pause to praise the beauty and glory of peace, however, nor to cite Jesus' blessing for peacemakers (Matthew 5:9). Instead he issues an unabashed call for contenders and warriors—not fighters with swords and spears, but contenders with ideas, words, and character. Remember the armor of God that Paul recommends in Ephesians 6:10-18.

A. CONTEND FOR THE FAITH (v. 3)

3. Dear friends, although I was very eager to write to you about the salvation we share, I felt I had to write and urge you to contend for the faith that was once for all entrusted to the saints.

The shared *salvation* is given to Jude and all faithful Christians. No doubt Jude could *write* lengthy books about that salvation; but as he thinks about it, he sees that there is one thing he *had to write*: his readers must *contend for the faith*. That applies to his readers in the first century and to those in the twenty-first.

In our New Testament, *faith* normally means belief and trust in Jesus. Here, however, *the faith* refers to the body of Christian doctrine to be believed—all that was taught by the apostles and passed on by faithful teachers. This includes both the "milk" and "meat" beliefs of Christianity (Hebrews 5:12-14). That body of doctrine was *once for all entrusted to the saints*, or all Christians (cf. Acts 2:42; Romans 6:17). Having received this faith, Christians must be on the alert, ready and able to defend it against all the attacks made by false teachers.

B. ENEMIES OF THE FAITH (v. 4)

4. For certain men whose condemnation was written about long ago have secretly slipped in among you. They are godless men, who change the grace of our God into a license for immorality and deny Jesus Christ our only Sovereign and Lord.

Jude speaks of *certain men* who are not real Christians since they do not hold to the faith once delivered to the saints. They *slipped in* before the other members became aware that they were not real Christians. Jesus warned of wolves who "come to you in sheep's clothing" (Matthew 7:15). How difficult it can be to recognize such dangerous people! But rest assured that God has known about them from eternity past—their *condemnation was written about long ago*.

These phony Christians are *godless men;* they prove it by changing *the grace of our God into a license for immorality*. God's *grace* is his favor, the mercy by which he forgives our sins. The *godless men* think, or pretend to think, that grace gives us license to keep on sinning in whatever evil way our *worldly desires* may suggest, and still count on God to forgive us. Even worse than misinterpreting the promise of forgiveness, the *godless men* put their own opinions above God's

HOW TO SAY IT

Balaam. BAY-lum.

Corinthians. Kor-IN-thee-unz.

Deuteronomy. Due-ter-AHN-uh-me.

epistles. ee-PIS-uls.

Gomorrah. Guh-MORE-uh.

Jude. Jood.

Korah. KO-rah.

Meribah. MEHR-ih-buh.

Sodom. SOD-um.

Thessalonians. THESS-uh-LO-nee-unz.

Word, thus denying *Jesus Christ our only Sovereign and Lord*. These men may fool themselves into thinking they're following Christ. But if their teaching doesn't match his, then they have replaced him with something false. That's idolatry!

II. INFORMATION (JUDE 8-13, 16)

Verse 4 introduces some phony Christians and announces their condemnation. Jude has more to say about them, but first he pauses to give some examples of people and angels who were condemned and punished. This he does in verses 5-7, which are omitted from our printed text. With such examples on the record, everyone ought to know unbelief and disobedience will be punished. But these pretended Christians ignore the warning and continue in their wrong ways.

A. CHARACTER OF THE ENEMIES, PART 1 (vv. 8-10)

8. In the very same way, these dreamers pollute their own bodies, reject authority and slander celestial beings.

The phrase *"in the very same way"* ties the sins of the ungodly men of verse 4 with the sexual perversion of Sodom and Gomorrah in verse 7 (cf. 2 Peter 2:6). The types of perverse activities such *dreamers* involve themselves in to *pollute their own bodies* we try not to imagine! When they *reject authority and slander celestial beings,* they prove they have no respect for leaders who ought to be respected. Some students believe the *celestial beings* here are angels. If so, then these godless men have no respect for God's servants in Heaven or on earth.

9. But even the archangel Michael, when he was disputing with the devil about the body of Moses, did not dare to bring a slanderous accusation against him, but said, "The Lord rebuke you!"

The archangel Michael is probably the one who spoke with Daniel many centuries earlier (Daniel 10:13, 21; 12:1). Michael's struggles against *the devil* are ongoing (see Revelation 12:7). The dispute between the two *about the body of Moses* is not recorded in any other Scripture. But it is generally supposed that Michael was God's agent in the burial of *Moses* (Deuteronomy 34:5, 6), and that the devil claimed that Moses' body was his because of Moses' sin at the water of Meribah (Numbers 20:12, 13).

The point Jude is making is that a holy angel did not use insulting language even when he was disputing with the most evil of all beings, the devil himself (2 Peter 2:11). How much less should we use such language against our fellow human beings who are created in God's image!

10. Yet these men speak abusively against whatever they do not understand; and what things they do understand by instinct, like unreasoning animals—these are the very things that destroy them.

Unlike the angel Michael, the phony Christians freely use insulting talk whether they know what they are talking about or *not*. There are some things they do indeed *understand by instinct, like unreasoning animals* do: hunger and thirst, sexual desire, and power (cf. Mark 10:42-45). By such things these phonies *destroy* themselves. For the sake of selfish desires they give up truth and decency.

SPEAKING EVIL

Nearly everyone agrees that there has been a coarsening of Western culture in the last fifty years or so. Rudeness and disrespect, from "road rage" and abuse of elderly family members to simple lack of courtesy in everyday interactions, have all been documented. Television and movies now often use formerly forbidden profanities. In fact, such expressions are so common as to have lost their shock value.

WHAT DO YOU THINK?

How can Christians prepare themselves to recognize and refute false teaching?

[John 4:23, 24 and 2 Timothy 3:14-17 serve as launching points for your answer.]

WHAT DO YOU THINK?

How should we confront those calling themselves Christians who believe and teach doctrinal errors? How do we "contend" without being "contentious"?

[Passages such as Acts 18:24-26; 1 Corinthians 5; Ephesians 4:15; and Titus 1:10, 11; 3:10, 11 can be important in framing your answer.]

DAILY BIBLE READINGS

Monday, Nov. 24—The Steadfast Are Kept in Peace (Isaiah 26:1-6)

Tuesday, Nov. 25—O Lord, We Wait for You (Isaiah 26:7-13)

Wednesday, Nov. 26—The Righteous Have Steady Hearts (Psalm 112:1-8)

Thursday, Nov. 27—Keep My Word (Revelation 3:7-13)

Friday, Nov. 28—Don't Give Up in Doing Right (Galatians 6:1-10)

Saturday, Nov. 29—Contend for the Faith (Jude 1-13)

Sunday, Nov. 30—Build Up Your Faith (Jude 16-25)

A newspaper reporter recently questioned college students about why there is so much foul language at college athletic events. One said, "It's a lot of fun. . . . Foul language debases my self-image, but I use it anyway out of habit." Another does it because he wants to "encourage" his team. He added that it probably isn't appropriate because "there are little kids there. But I don't feel bad."

Jude tells us that disrespect for others—especially leaders—is just one of many attitudes that impugn our character and have a destructive effect on the life of the church and society. As Christians we ought to provide an example that is strongly contrary to the way the cultural winds are blowing.   —C. R. B.

B. SIMILARITIES TO THE PAST (v. 11)

11. Woe to them! They have taken the way of Cain; they have rushed for profit into Balaam's error; they have been destroyed in Korah's rebellion.

Out of envy, *Cain* killed his brother Abel (Genesis 4:3-8; 1 John 3:12). For a fee, *Balaam* tried to call down a curse on Israel (Numbers 22–24; 2 Peter 2:15, 16; Revelation 2:14). In a lust for power, *Korah* staged a rebellion against Moses (Numbers 16:1-33). The phony Christians will all come to *woe*, as did Cain, Balaam, and Korah.

C. CHARACTER OF THE ENEMIES, PART 2 (vv. 12, 13, 16)

12a. These men are blemishes at your love feasts, eating with you without the slightest qualm—shepherds who feed only themselves.

In first-century churches the Sunday meetings featured *love feasts* that we might call fellowship dinners. After such a meal they would observe the Lord's Supper.

The phony Christians mar the beauty and joy of these occasions because their love is only for themselves and members of their clique. They sit together and share their food with no one else. They do this without fear of spoiling the fellowship this custom is meant to cultivate. This is why they are *blemishes* (cf. 2 Peter 2:13). Or perhaps *without the slightest qualm* means not having any reverence for the sacredness of the occasion (cf. 1 Corinthians 11:20, 21).

12b, 13. They are clouds without rain, blown along by the wind; autumn trees, without fruit and uprooted—twice dead. They are wild waves of the sea, foaming up their shame; wandering stars, for whom blackest darkness has been reserved forever.

Now Jude uses some metaphors to add to what he says in verse 12a. As *clouds* that bring no rain, and as *trees* that are both fruitless and *uprooted*, the phonies are unproductive and useless (cf. Luke 13:6-9). Further, as *wild waves of the sea* they make a lot of noise but do not get any useful work done (cf. 2 Peter 2:17).

The Greek word for *wandering* provides the root for our English word *planet*. People in ancient times had no concept of what planets were. But when they looked up into the night sky, they could see that almost all the heavenly points of light kept their place night after night. However, a few of those points of light— which today we know as the planets Venus, Mars, Jupiter, and Saturn—shifted positions nightly. As *wandering* stars they are unreliable reference points. Any mariner setting the course of his ship by them is in danger!

16. These men are grumblers and faultfinders; they follow their own evil desires; they boast about themselves and flatter others for their own advantage.

Can't you hear these phonies grumbling and whining when they don't get their way? This sounds quite different from the "wild" waves mentioned in verse 13, and we are reminded that "problem people" do not all sound alike. And perhaps all of them change their tune from time to time, now whining in frustration,

WHAT DO YOU THINK?

True Christians can be recognized by their productive lives (Matthew 7:15-20). What "fruit" can rightly be expected in the lives of genuine followers of Christ?

[A good place to start in answering this question is Galatians 5:22, 23.]

now raging in anger, now flattering other people in order to take *advantage* of them (cf. Romans 16:18; 1 Thessalonians 2:5; 2 Peter 2:18).

III. ADVICE (JUDE 17-23)

Jude does not suggest that we spend time denouncing the enemies as he has been doing. There is certainly a time and place for that (see Titus 3:10), but Jude wants to stress something else.

A. REMEMBER THE WARNINGS (vv. 17-19)

17. But, dear friends, remember what the apostles of our Lord Jesus Christ foretold.

Our faith is based on the testimony of *the apostles* who saw what *Jesus* did and heard what he taught. Of the four gospel writers, Matthew and John were apostles; their books are the testimonies of eyewitnesses. We do not know how much Mark knew of Jesus personally, but there is ancient testimony that Mark recorded what the apostle Peter taught. Luke came to Jerusalem years after Jesus was gone. As a careful historian he interviewed many eyewitnesses and separated verified truth from fiction (Luke 1:1-4). He was also a companion of the apostle Paul. We can depend on the writings of these men (cf. John 20:30, 31).

18. They said to you, "In the last times there will be scoffers who will follow their own ungodly desires."

The apostles plainly foretold the coming of unbelievers who would make fun of the miracles mentioned above (e.g., 2 Peter 3:3, 4). Such *scoffers* are not so much interested in God's truth as in *their own ungodly* lusts.

19. These are the men who divide you, who follow mere natural instincts and do not have the Spirit.

The mockers *divide* the Christians by convincing some of them that the miracle stories cannot be true. In their sensuality the mockers put the testimony of their own senses above the testimony of the apostles. The mockers never saw a miracle, so they suppose no one else ever saw one.

But the apostles did see miracles. In addition, they had the Holy Spirit to guide them so they would make no mistake in the record (John 16:13). Since the mockers *do not have the Spirit*, they can and do make mistakes.

B. KEEP THE FAITH (vv. 20, 21)

20. But you, dear friends, build yourselves up in your most holy faith and pray in the Holy Spirit.

As in verse 3, *faith* here is substantive. It means "the body of Christian doctrine to be believed." We become stronger and more assured in what we believe by reviewing the evidence presented in Scripture and by recognizing the enemies of the faith for who they are. To *pray in the Holy Spirit* is to speak our prayers according to the wishes of the Holy Spirit, who lives in us (1 Corinthians 3:16).

21. Keep yourselves in God's love as you wait for the mercy of our Lord Jesus Christ to bring you to eternal life.

Keeping ourselves *in God's love* means honoring God's will as he reveals it to us in the Bible. We do that by waiting for and expecting *the mercy of our Lord Jesus Christ to bring* us to *eternal life*. When we have a proper understanding of eternal life, our current, earthly life stays in perspective (2 Corinthians 4:18).

C. SAVE THE DOUBTERS (vv. 22, 23)

22. Be merciful to those who doubt;

There are differences in translation here because of uncertainty in the original Greek text. Some versions have something like, "Have compassion on some who

WHAT DO YOU THINK?

What character flaws might betray a professing Christian as a person of shallow, superficial faith? How dangerous are these flaws?

[Galatians 5:19-21 can start your thinking on this one.]

Make a Difference

Display this poster from the Adult Visuals packet as you discuss verse 22.

WHAT DO YOU THINK?

What are some ways we can have compassion on weak Christians who are listening to enemies of the faith? How do good listening skills play a part?

PRAYER

How good it is to have a clear record of the truth taught by Jesus and his apostles! Thank you, Father, for the security we find in our faith based on that truth. Keep us from unseemly pride, and make us humble helpers of fellow Christians in need of help. In Jesus' name, amen.

THOUGHT TO REMEMBER

Maintain steadfast faith—your own and that of your Christian brothers and sisters.

are in doubt." This points to weak Christians who have listened to enemies of the faith and are beginning to have doubts. We do not denounce them or regard those who are wavering as enemies. Rather, we are *merciful* to them. We reason with them gently, lovingly—reviewing the evidence for the truth and trying to build them up in the most holy faith.

23. . . . *snatch others from the fire and save them; to others show mercy, mixed with fear—hating even the clothing stained by corrupted flesh.*

The *others* are those who have gone further in their doubting, who have almost joined the enemy. With them we reason more vigorously, perhaps even pointing out the eternal *fire* that lies at the end of the road they are taking. We reason *with fear* of losing them—or does Jude mean we reason *with fear* that we ourselves may be contaminated by our contact with those far gone in doubt? If the *flesh* of anyone's body is filthy, the garment in contact with that flesh is likely to become *stained* or soiled. So in our contact with one far advanced in doubt we must be sure not to become contaminated ourselves by that doubt. But if we succeed in bringing doubters back to the true faith, it is like snatching them out of *the fire.*

THE POWER OF ENCOURAGING WORDS

The early days of World War II were dark ones for Great Britain. Hitler's armies had swept across Europe with no more than short-lived resistance. Then came the blitz of London, when night after night the German *Luftwaffe* fire-bombed the city. But rather than waste his words with condemnation of the Nazis, Prime Minister Winston Churchill "mobilized the English language and sent it into battle," as John F. Kennedy said.

With British and French forces reeling from the German conquest of France, Churchill said on June 4, 1940, "We shall defend our Island, whatever the cost may be. We shall fight on the beaches, we shall fight on the landing grounds, we shall fight in the fields and in the streets, we shall fight in the hills; we shall never surrender." Two weeks later he added, "Let us therefore brace ourselves to our duties, and so bear ourselves that, if the British Empire and its Commonwealth last for a thousand years, men will still say, 'This was their finest hour.'"

The words of Jude reflect this same spirit: although he had harsh words for those who were doing evil, he chose a different approach in advising Christians on what their course of action should be. To them he offered strong words of encouragement, strengthening their faith so that they could reach out to the lost and save them from their painful destiny. Never underestimate the power of encouraging words!
—C. R. B.

CONCLUSION

We need to remember that Jude advises us first to strengthen ourselves and our own faith, then to help others do the same for themselves and their faith. This calls for a word of caution.

No doubt enemies of the faith have infiltrated churches of our time as they did churches of the first century. If we set ourselves to find them and expose them, we face a triple danger to ourselves.

First, we may make false accusations, for fellow believers who need to strengthen their faith may be at heart as loyal as we are. Second, we may become as divisive as the enemies are (v. 19).

Third, we may become too critical, too judgmental, too disagreeable in lacking discernment between issues of doctrine and opinion. For those who need help in strengthening themselves in our most holy faith, Jude advises us to be helpers, not detectives and prosecutors.

Discovery Learning

This page contains an alternative lesson plan emphasizing learning activities. Classes desiring such student involvement will find these suggestions helpful. The next page is a reproducible activity page to further enhance discovery learning.

LEARNING GOALS

After participating in this lesson, each student will be able to:

1. Tell what it is to contend for the faith and why it is so important to do so.

2. Cite some contemporary issue that is, or may become, the source of a challenge to one's faith, similar to the challenge described by Jude.

3. Suggest some specific manner of dealing with that challenge.

INTO THE LESSON

Prepare a handout with two parts; title it "Greatest Challenge." The first part lists three individuals—a parent, an athlete, and Jesus—and asks the students to describe the greatest challenge ever faced by each of these. Leave plenty of space between these identifications for class members to write. Part two asks the students for a two-word definition or description of *challenge*.

Give each student a work sheet, and say, "This morning I want us to think about the topic of *challenge*. On this work sheet, write what you think is the greatest challenge a parent, an athlete, and Jesus ever faced. Then, after describing those challenges, write a two-word definition or description of *challenge* in part two. I'll give you three minutes to complete this."

Encourage class members to reveal their answers. Possible answers to part two: *great opportunity, difficult situation, personal struggle,* or *serious threat.* Say, "The word *challenge* can be looked at either as a positive or a negative concept. Today, our lesson text focuses on the serious threat that challenges Christians in their struggle to 'maintain steadfast faith.' Turn to the book of Jude, and let's read about the challenge of contending for the faith."

INTO THE WORD

Ask a student to read the whole lesson text aloud. State: "As you hear, there were some 'Fakes Among the Family' who had crept in unawares. In pronouncing woe upon them, Jude uses several Old Testament illustrations. To help us understand those illustrations, I want you to complete this work sheet in small groups." Move the class into groups of four students each. Give each a copy of the reproducible activity "Fakes Among the Family" from the next page. This chart contains four

rows and three columns. Assign some groups to start with Cain, some with Balaam, and some with Korah so that all three will be given full attention and completed. Allow ten minutes.

When time is up, ask the groups to report their answers to The Point and The Application. Then move the groups back into one group for the following questions:

1. What does Jude mean when he exhorts Christians to "contend for the faith" (v. 3)? (*Be alert, ready, and able to defend the faith against all attacks of false teachers.*)

2. Why is it important for Christians to contend for the faith? (*To avoid being pulled away from Christ; to provide a stronger witness of the trustworthiness of the gospel.*)

3. How did ungodly men treat God and His grace (v. 4)? (*They denied God and Jesus and turned grace into license for immorality.*)

4. What is meant by the phrase "reject authority" (v. 8)? (*They don't respect leaders in the church and in the world.*)

5. What is the point of the illustration about Michael and the devil (v. 9)? (*Michael did not use abusive language when disputing with the devil; neither should we when talking with any person.*)

6. Describe the character of the intruders (v. 16) and the type of response Jude instructs Christians to make (vv. 20-23). (*They murmur, find fault, follow their evil desires, boast, and flatter others selfishly. We pray, build ourselves up in the faith, show compassion, try to save them.*)

INTO LIFE

State: "As in the days of Jude, there are challenges to one's faith today. What contemporary issues do you see as a challenge to Christian's faith?" Write suggested issues on the board for all to see. (*Expect such entries as multiculturalism, postmodernism, anti-conservatism, rampant immorality, relativism, and others.*) Distribute copies of the reproducible activity "Challenging the Challenge!" from the next page, and have learners use that to record their answers. Ask each to identify and circle an issue that creates a personal challenge to him or her. Ask each then to write that challenge on the sheet, along with a specific response in the section called, "My Challenging Response."

After two minutes, close the class time in prayer asking God to help each one maintain steadfast faith in a world and culture that lives in whimsy and skepticism.

Fakes Among the Family

Read the Scriptures identified with each of the following Old Testament "Fakes in the Family." Use the chart below to explain Jude's reference to each one (Jude 11).

OLD TESTAMENT EXAMPLE	THE POINT	THE APPLICATION
CAIN Genesis 4:3-8 1 John 3:12		
BALAAM Numbers 22-24		
KORAH Numbers 16:1-33		

Challenging the Challenge!

Identify what is to you a major challenge to Christian purity and discipline in the contemporary world. Write that under "The Challenge" below. Then consider how you can confront that challenge. List some specific actions you can perform or organizations with whom you can partner. Write your ideas under "My Challenging Response."

THE CHALLENGE:

MY CHALLENGING RESPONSE:

Winter Quarter, 2003–2004

Special Features

		Page
Variety, the Spice of Life	John W. Wade	122
A Child Is Given/Lessons From Life (Map Feature)		125
Special Children (Chart Feature)		126

Lessons

A Child Is Given

December	7	Samuel: Dedicated to God	1 Samuel 1:20, 24-28; 2:1-8a	127
	14	John: Forerunner of Jesus	Luke 1:67-80	135
	21	Jesus: God With Us	Matthew 1:18-25	143
	28	Jesus: Growing in God's Favor	Luke 2:40-52	151

Lessons From Life

Unit 1: Job: Integrity in Times of Testing

January	4	Integrity in the Midst of Suffering	Job 2:1-10	159
	11	Integrity in Seeking God	Job 9:32-35; 13:20-24; 19:25-27; 23:10-12	167
	18	Integrity in Everyday Life	Job 27:2-5; 31:5-15, 24-28	175
	25	Integrity in God's Presence	Job 38:1-7; 40:6-9; 42:1-6	183

Unit 2: Wisdom for the Times of Our Lives

February	1	A Time for All Things	Ecclesiastes 3:1-15	191
	8	A Time to Remember	Ecclesiastes 11:7–12:8	199
	15	A Time for Love	Song of Solomon 2:8-13; 7:10-12; 8:6, 7	207
	22	A Time for Courage	Esther 3:1-6; 4:7-16	215
	29	A Time to Celebrate	Esther 8:3-8; 9:17-23	223

About These Lessons

Our two sets of lessons for the quarter could be called "Expecting and Reflecting." The first set tells of births that changed history. Let us expect them to change us as well! The second set challenges us to stop and reflect about life in various ways. May our service improve as we do!

Dec 7

Dec 14

Dec 21

Dec 28

Jan 4

Jan 11

Jan 18

Jan 25

Feb 1

Feb 8

Feb 15

Feb 22

Feb 29

Variety, the Spice of Life

by John W. Wade

If variety is indeed the spice of life, and if you enjoy spices, you will enjoy the lessons of this quarter. They include lessons from both the Old and New Testaments, involving familiar Scriptures and Scriptures that we rarely study in the Uniform Lesson Series. This great variety we find in the Bible is one reason for its universal appeal. If one is willing to search, he or she is certain to find something to meet every human need.

The theme for the first four lessons is "A Child Is Given." Since the lessons begin in December, one's first thought would be that they deal with the traditional Christmas story about the birth of Christ. But that supposition would be only half true, for the first two lessons deal with the births of Samuel and John the Baptist, while the last two deal with Jesus' birth and growth.

Lesson 1 provides us information about the events that surrounded the birth of Samuel. Elkanah had two wives, a not uncommon practice in that day. One wife, Peninnah, had borne him several children, while the other wife, Hannah, was barren. Since children were considered a precious blessing, Hannah became the object of scorn and ridicule. On one of her visits to the tabernacle, she prayed earnestly that God would grant her a son. So desperate was she for a son that she promised to dedicate him to God if her prayer were heard. God heard her prayer and granted her a son, whom she named Samuel. When Samuel was weaned, she was true to her promise and brought him to the tabernacle where she left him to be reared by the elderly priest, Eli.

Lesson 2 also tells of a barren woman, Elizabeth, whose husband, Zechariah, was a priest. On one occasion when he was serving in the temple, the angel Gabriel appeared to him, telling him that he would have a son. But he doubted the divine messenger and was left dumb, unable to speak until after the birth of his son, John. Much of the lesson text deals with the prophecy that the aged priest uttered concerning his son.

Lesson 3 relates a portion of the Christmas story that we never grow tired of hearing. At the heart of the lesson is the virginal conception of Jesus by the Holy Spirit. This created a delicate situation that Joseph sought to avoid by putting Mary aside quietly without making a public scandal of it. But before he could take this action, Joseph was confronted in a dream by an angel of the Lord, who assured him that he need not hesitate to take Mary as his wife. What was happening was a fulfillment of a prophecy that a virgin would conceive and bear a child.

The closing verses of the second chapter of Luke is the basis for *Lesson 4*: "Jesus: Growing in God's Favor." We read about Jesus' visit to Jerusalem as he accompanied his parents there to observe the feast of Passover. This is the only account we have about the life of Jesus from the time his parents returned to Nazareth and the beginning of his ministry. Christians have often wondered what those growing-up years were like. To satisfy this curiosity, various apocryphal stories of those years have been circulated. Of course, many of them are quite fanciful and even silly. We have every reason to believe that Jesus was an obedient son, obeying his parents and not burdening them with the worries that most parents have to deal with—with the exception of the incident related in this lesson. Here he behaved like, well, a typical twelve-year-old, driven by curiosity about the inner activities of the temple. But even in this activity, which so upset Mary and Joseph, he was obeying his heavenly Father.

The next unit of this quarter, beginning in January, is titled "Job: Integrity in Times of Testing." It consists of four lessons dealing with the life of this great man of faith.

Lesson 5 introduces us to Job and the problem of human suffering that he struggles to deal with for the remainder of the book. The traditional orthodox view was that suffering came as the result of sin, either the sin of the sufferer or the sin of someone else. But in Job's experience this theory did not square with the facts in the situation. Job was a good man—a very good man, by normal human standards—and yet he suffered. Of course, what he didn't realize at the time was that he was caught in a struggle between God and Satan. The first chapter of Job tells how he lost his possessions and his children. The second chapter, the basis for this lesson, relates the terrible physical suffering he underwent. Only his wife was left, and she certainly wasn't any help to him in this situation.

Lesson 6 uses four short texts scattered from chapter 9 to chapter 23 to give us glimpses of the struggle Job was going through. He pleads for God to give him a chance to prove his innocence. The fact that God had not answered his plea leaves him bewildered. Yet, in the midst of his pain and emotional struggle, he still does not lose his faith in God. "I know that my Redeemer lives," he cries out, "and that in the end he will stand upon the earth" (Job 19:25). This statement alone makes the study of the book of Job worthwhile.

In the midst of all his suffering, Job is visited by three of his friends, Eliphaz, Bildad, and Zophar. But with friends like these, he didn't need enemies! They only added to his burden. In *Lesson 7,* "Integrity in Everyday Life," Job responds to his friends' challenges. He maintains his integrity by refusing to admit that he was guilty of any of the sins his friends accused him of.

The final lesson in this unit, *Lesson 8,* gives us the conclusion of Job's agonizing struggle. In the depths of his trial, Job comes dangerously close to challenging God's wisdom. God answers him out of a whirlwind, asking Job a series of questions that demonstrate Job's ignorance and finiteness. Job is completely humbled, affirming "my ears had heard of you but now my eyes have seen you" (Job 42:5). This experience led him to abhor himself and repent in dust and ashes.

The book of Job is one of the great pieces of literature that comes to us from the ancient world. The fact that it is part of the Holy Bible makes it imperative to study.

The next unit, "Wisdom for the Times of Our Lives," allows us to explore some other precious gems from the Old Testament. *Lesson 9* is based on the book of Ecclesiastes, and the issues it deals with sound as contemporary as this morning's newspaper. Many believe the author was King Solomon, and he had it all. But in the end, "Meaningless! Meaningless! Everything is meaningless!" is his conclusion. Yet in this lesson he passes along some of the wisdom he had accumulated through his life. His theme is "timeliness." There is an appropriate time for all of our activities. If we could just get this one lesson from this study, it would be worth the effort we spend on it.

Lesson 10, "A Time to Remember," is an appropriate follow-up on the previous lesson from Ecclesiastes. Much of the content of this book is rather cynical. While it stresses the importance of doing everything at an appropriate time, its emphasis upon things in this world does not give the reader much of a glimpse of the more important things beyond. The message of this lesson is especially important for young people: "Remember your Creator in the days of your youth." Young people often want to "sow their wild oats" while they are young, expecting to survive and later settle down to become responsible citizens. Unfortunately, it doesn't always work that way. We all have seen young people who have become

JANUARY

FEBRUARY

caught up in sex and drugs with devastating results. They don't live long enough to reach maturity! Remembering God in one's youth not only protects a person from the ravages of these evils, but gives a person many more years to serve the Lord.

Lesson 11 is quite unusual. In the long history of the Uniform Lesson Series, only a couple of times has the Song of Solomon been used for a lesson. The reason is quite obvious: the book speaks quite frankly about the physical aspects of love. In past years sexual matters were rarely spoken about in public, much less studied in a Sunday school lesson. Yet this book is in the Bible, and that makes it worthy of study. But further, God made us physical beings, and he expects us to deal with sexual matters in an honest and wholesome manner.

The final two lessons of the quarter are based on the book of Esther. *Lesson 12* has all the drama of a Hollywood production. Esther, an orphan girl, brought up by her uncle or cousin, Mordecai, becomes queen to Xerxes, king of the Persian Empire. The villain, Haman, hates Mordecai and plots to take him out by having all the Jews in the empire killed. The king, ignorant of what was behind the plot, goes along with it. Then Esther, encouraged by Mordecai, courageously puts her life on the line to save her people. Her courage certainly serves as a model for us today. In the end Haman is hanged because of his treacherous plot, and Mordecai takes his place as the king's counselor.

Lesson 13 closes the quarter by telling how the Jews were able to escape the trap set for them by Haman. Their victory becomes the occasion for their feasting and rejoicing. The feast of Purim, one of the minor festivals in the Jewish calendar, is based on this incident.

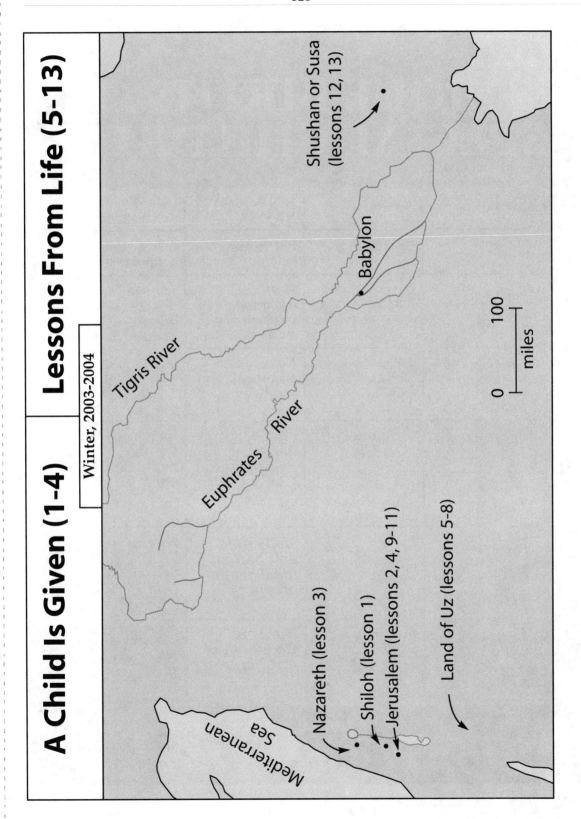

A Child Is Given (1-4)

Lessons From Life (5-13)

Winter, 2003-2004

Mediterranean Sea

Nazareth (lesson 3)

Shiloh (lesson 1)

Jerusalem (lessons 2, 4, 9-11)

Land of Uz (lessons 5-8)

Tigris River

Euphrates River

Babylon

Shushan or Susa (lessons 12, 13)

0   100
miles

UNIQUE BIRTHS OF SPECIAL CHILDREN

Child	Text(s)	How the Child Is Special	Life Accomplishment
Cain	Genesis 4:1	First human child	Cursed as the first murderer
Isaac	Genesis 18:1-15; 21:1-7	Mother old and barren; prophesied by an angel	Fathered Jacob, the father of Israel
Samson	Judges 13:2-24	Mother barren; announced by an angel	Championed Israel against the Philistines; died in shame
Samuel (Lesson 1)	*1 Samuel 1:1-20*	*Mother barren; dedicated to God's service*	*As judge, prophet, and priest, anointed the first kings of Israel*
John the Baptist (Lesson 2)	*Luke 1:5-25, 57-66*	*Mother old and barren; fulfillment of prophecy*	*Forerunner of the Messiah; herald of God's kingdom*
Jesus (Lesson 3,4)	*Matthew 1:18-25; Luke 1:26-35; 2:1-7*	*Father is God; born of a virgin*	*Messiah and Savior of all believers*

SAMUEL:
DEDICATED TO GOD

WHY TEACH THIS LESSON?

A certain Christian couple was in favor of sending workers into the mission field. On numerous occasions many in the church heard them talk about the importance of overseas mission work. Their sincerity was tested, however, when one of their own children left for the mission field! How hard it was to watch that young adult move so far from home. But the parents' support remained strong.

Parents today cannot really "dedicate" a child to any particular life path as we see Hannah doing for young Samuel in today's text. The reason is simple: the child will make his or her own decision in that regard when the time comes. Even so, we all have an obligation to affirm others in the unique paths of service to which God has called them, even if it means that we have to experience some discomfort in "letting go" of those loved ones. Today, your learners will find encouragement and guidance in an ancient example of this "letting go."

INTRODUCTION

A. THE SHIRT OFF HIS BACK

In 1994, Alex Dovales was drifting toward Miami on a rickety boat with twenty-seven other Cubans. Two years later, Dovales saw fourteen exhausted, penniless Cuban rafters wash ashore on Key Largo and said, "I felt like I had just arrived here myself." The twenty-five-year-old dishwasher, who cleared $197 per week, walked home and gathered all the presents from under his Christmas tree. He gave shirts and other clothing to the new arrivals. "They were wet and cold," explained Henry Paez, Dovales's roommate. "Alex took off his shirt and gave it to them."

The Old Testament book of 1 Samuel begins with an example of even greater selflessness. At this time of the year when we express our love and generosity in the giving of gifts, it is appropriate that we look to an example of one who gave out of her worship to the Lord. Hannah's dedication of her son, Samuel, to the service of the Lord is an act of devotion that still challenges believers today.

B. LESSON BACKGROUND

"The period of the judges" lasted roughly three hundred and fifty years, from about 1406 to 1050 B.C. Samuel's prophetic ministry began during the latter part of those deplorable years; this was a time when Israel had no king (Judges 18:1; 19:1). This was also a time when moral conditions among the people were chaotic as "everyone did as he saw fit" (Judges 21:25). Just before Samuel is born, a man named Eli holds a judgeship that ultimately lasts some forty years. But Eli's judgeship is a spiritual failure, largely because he allowed his sons to pervert worship at the tabernacle and to engage in blatant sexual immorality (1 Samuel 2:12-17, 22; 3:13, 14).

DEVOTIONAL READING:
1 SAMUEL 1:9-18

BACKGROUND SCRIPTURE:
1 SAMUEL 1:1–2:10; LUKE 1:46-55

PRINTED TEXT:
1 SAMUEL 1:20, 24-28; 2:1-8a

LESSON AIMS

After participating in this lesson, each student will be able to:

1. Tell how Hannah's devotion to God is seen in her prayerful request to the Lord for a son and in her faithfulness in carrying out her vow after the birth of Samuel.

2. State the importance of keeping spiritual commitments, no matter how difficult.

3. Suggest a specific commitment that he or she will fulfill in keeping with Hannah's example of faithfulness.

KEY VERSES

"I prayed for this child, and the Lord has granted me what I asked of him. So now I give him to the Lord. For his whole life he will be given over to the Lord." And he worshiped the Lord there.
—1 Samuel 1:27, 28

LESSON 1 NOTES

So God determined that new leadership was needed at the tabernacle. The birth of Samuel was God's answer to Israel's need. Samuel was to be God's leader who would bring Israel back to spiritual health. Things had to change!

In his transitional role, Samuel is sometimes referred to as "the last of the judges" (cf. 1 Samuel 7:6, 15-17) and "the first of the prophets" (cf. 1 Samuel 3:20; Acts 3:24; 13:20). One of Samuel's most important tasks would be to assist the people of Israel in their desire for a king (1 Samuel 8:4-22) even though Samuel did not think that was such a good idea (8:6). Samuel would be the prophet to anoint Israel's first king, Saul (10:1), and second king, David (16:13).

But the story of Samuel's ministry begins with godly parents. Hannah and Elkanah, Samuel's mother and father, were worshipers of the living God. When Hannah came to worship the Lord at the tabernacle in Shiloh (about twenty miles north of Jerusalem), she carried intense longings for a child. She understood, as so many modern believers do, that the deepest needs in life can find their answer only in the Lord of the universe. She trusted that the one true God would show his generosity to her, and she found him to be ready to answer her prayers.

I. HANNAH'S PROMISE (1 SAMUEL 1:20, 24-28)

The opening verses of 1 Samuel introduce us to Samuel's parents. Elkanah is described as "a certain man" in 1:1, a phrase that gives no indication that he is of any rank or position. Apparently he is a common man. He is married to Hannah and they live in a town in the hill country of Ephraim. This is in the northern part of the spine of mountains that runs through Palestine.

In addition to Hannah, who is childless, there is another wife named Peninnah. The two are rivals because Peninnah has borne children (1:2) and often uses this fact to embarrass Hannah (1:6, 7; cf. Genesis 16:1-6). In the bitterness of her soul Hannah carries her request for a child to the Lord during one of the family pilgrimages to the tabernacle for a feast day (1 Samuel 1:9, 10). As with other notable women of the Bible who faced the challenge of barrenness (Genesis 11:30; 25:21; 29:31; Judges 13:2), Hannah depends on the mercy of the Creator of life for this plea to be answered.

A. THE LORD HEARS HANNAH'S PRAYER (v. 20)

20. So in the course of time Hannah conceived and gave birth to a son. She named him Samuel, saying, "Because I asked the LORD for him."

Verse 19 tells us that the Lord is moved to answer Hannah's prayer uttered at the tabernacle. After that prayer, she and her family return home and sometime later God's gift to Hannah becomes obvious. Verse 19 and the words *in the course of time* indicate that the natural processes of conception and childbirth applied in the case of Hannah (contrast Luke 1:26-38). This would imply that Hannah goes home from Shiloh not knowing for sure how God will work out an answer to her prayer, even though Eli the priest had offered comforting words (1 Samuel 1:17).

When Hannah receives her precious gift from the Lord, she names him in such a way as to announce it to the world. The name *Samuel* contains within it the idea of the "name of God," and permits Hannah's play on words that this name is appropriate because she had *asked* for Samuel from God.

INFERTILITY

When James and Carol Herget went to Jamaica in 1949, they went to do what most missionaries do: preach and teach. When they found that they would be childless, they adopted a little boy—then a second, a third, a fourth, and a fifth. When they took in the sixth child, they learned that a private home could not take

WHAT DO YOU THINK?

What are some indicators in 1 Samuel 1 that a common faith strengthened the relationship of Elkanah and Hannah? How did this relationship help them in some of the tough decisions they had to face?

WHAT DO YOU THINK?

What can we learn about the nature of God as he answers Hannah's prayer? What does he expect from those who benefit from his care? What could we expect to be the result of misusing God's gifts?

WHAT DO YOU THINK?

Parents will readily acknowledge that the arrival of a child— especially the first—produces marked changes in their lives. How are the changes experienced by Hannah and Elkanah similar to or different from your own experiences or the experiences of parents you know?

in more than six children. So they started the Jamaica Christian Boys Home. Over the years, fifty-eight orphaned boys found a home there.

After twenty-nine years in Jamaica the Hergets went to the more challenging field of Haiti. They used what they had learned in Jamaica to found Christianville, where today fifteen hundred students receive an education and two meals a day. They added a church, medical and dental clinics, and a nutrition center. When James died, Carol founded Village of Hope, where today more than four hundred children receive an education and two meals a day.

It is possible—in fact it is likely—that none of this would have happened had the Hergets not been childless. God used Hannah's situation in a marvelous way; he used the Hergets' situation also in a marvelous, but different, way. The Hergets' disappointment became his appointment. God always can use people to fulfill his plan, no matter what their situation. Today, are you wallowing in self-pity because of some circumstance, or are you looking for God's plan within that circumstance?—R. C. S.

B. HANNAH FULFILLS HER VOW (vv. 24-27)

24. After he was weaned, she took the boy with her, young as he was, along with a three-year-old bull, an ephah of flour and a skin of wine, and brought him to the house of the LORD at Shiloh.

An infant's weaning period is three years, according to the non-Biblical account found in 2 Maccabees 7:27. No doubt Hannah treasures these short years with the son she has devoted to the Lord.

When the time comes for little Samuel to be taken to the tabernacle, we see no hesitation on Hannah's part. She makes the journey to *Shiloh* with the necessary sacrifice, a three-year-old bull. You may have a footnote in your Bible that gives the alternate translation "with three bulls." If the family is traveling with three bulls, the first may be for a special burnt offering, while the other two can serve as Elkanah's yearly sacrifice to the Lord (Numbers 8:8; 1 Samuel 1:3). If the phrase describes just one bull that is three years old, then they are sacrificing a bull in its prime. The *flour* and *wine* may serve as sustenance for the journey.

The note that *the boy* is *young* dramatizes the sacrifice to which Hannah has committed herself, as well as the unusual decision that permits a young child to be given into the custody of the tabernacle service. Hannah fulfills her promise to the Lord even though it undoubtedly is painful to let go. In both the Old and New Testaments (unlike so often today), vows are not taken lightly (Judges 11:30-40; Proverbs 20:25; Ecclesiastes 5:4-6; Matthew 14:6-10; Acts 18:18).

25. When they had slaughtered the bull, they brought the boy to Eli.

Presenting the young *boy* to the tabernacle at this age is out of the ordinary: a Levite's son is usually not presented for such service until he has reached an age of about twenty-five. He would then continue in office until retiring at age fifty (Numbers 8:23-26). Samuel is beginning his life-long service some twenty-two years ahead of schedule!

26. . . . and she said to him, "As surely as you live, my lord, I am the woman who stood here beside you praying to the LORD.

Hannah reminds the high priest Eli of the incident a few short years earlier when she *stood* before the tabernacle in prayer asking for a child (see 1 Samuel 1:11-18). The phrase *as surely as you live* is a common oath formula (see 1 Samuel 17:55; 20:3; 25:26; 2 Samuel 11:11; 14:19).

Hannah's purpose in using this oath is to guarantee to Eli that whether or not his memory can effectively recall the incident in which she prayed for a child, she is speaking the truth about the matter. By the New Testament era, the religious leaders had perverted the practice of oath-taking (see Matthew 23:16-22). Oaths should be unnecessary for those who are always to speak the truth anyway

HOW TO SAY IT

Eli. EE-lye.
Elkanah. EL-kuh-nuh or El-KAY-nuh.
Ephraim. EE-fray-im.
Hannah. HAN-uh.
Maccabees. MACK-uh-bees.
Peninnah. Peh-NIN-uh.
Shiloh. SHY-low.
Zechariah. ZEK-uh-RYE-uh.

VISUALS FOR THESE LESSONS

The visual pictured in each lesson (e.g., page 131) is a small reproduction of a large, full-color poster included in the Adult Visuals *packet for the Winter Quarter. The packet is available from your supplier. Order No. 292.*

(Matthew 5:33-37; James 5:12). Even so, the apostle Paul continued to take oaths in matters of extreme importance (see 2 Corinthians 11:31; Galatians 1:20).

27. "I prayed for this child, and the LORD has granted me what I asked of him.

Hannah intends that Eli understand that her prayer before the tabernacle was an authentic prayer (instead of drunkenness, as he concluded in 1 Samuel 1:14), and that the Lord had been gracious in answering that prayer. Her words to Eli are spoken so as to correspond with his own words to her in 1:17.

C. SAMUEL IS DEDICATED TO THE LORD (v. 28)

28. "So now I give him to the LORD. For his whole life he will be given over to the LORD." And he worshiped the LORD there.

Hannah now expresses her intentions regarding the destiny of young Samuel: she will leave him at the tabernacle as her way of giving back to the Lord who blessed her. His role will be to serve in the tabernacle as one of the assistants (see 2:11). But Hannah will not allow Samuel to escape her thoughts. Each year she will produce clothing for him, and she will deliver these items when she travels with her husband to Shiloh for annual worship (2:19). Nevertheless, Samuel will stay behind when the time comes for Hannah and her husband to return home.

The word *he* in the statement *he worshiped the LORD there* most likely refers to Samuel rather than Eli or Elkanah, since the immediate context addresses the ministry of young Samuel. Perhaps the statement conveys how Hannah's son quickly takes up his role in a very serious way (cf. 2:18). Hannah's unselfish dedication of her son begins to produce immediate results.

LETTING GO

A lady said that when she was young there was in her family a vase that was a cherished heirloom. It had been handed down through the family. It occupied a place of honor in the living room. One day she broke it. Her mother came running. But there was no anger in the mother's eyes. "Are you hurt?" she asked as she picked up the child. Recalling that event the lady said, "That day I discovered that *I* was the family treasure."

Samuel must have known that he was the family treasure. He must have become aware at some time in his life that it had not been easy for his parents to keep his mother's vow and give him wholly to the Lord's service. Today's parents might not find it easy to see their adult children go off to the mission field—taking the grandchildren with them!—for years at a time. Unwed mothers do not find it easy to give up their children to adoptive parents who can provide a better home. But when people put God's plans ahead of their personal desires, great things can happen.

In today's lesson a father and mother make the greatest possible sacrifice when they give Samuel to the Lord to grow up in the tabernacle. But their unselfish act was good for all concerned: for the family, for the child, and for the people of God. As a result, Samuel's godly influence reverberates through time and history. And it all began when two loving and faithful parents decided to honor a vow to God. What sacrifice is God asking you to make for him today?   —R. C. S.

II. HANNAH'S SONG OF PRAISE (1 SAMUEL 2:1-8a)

At such a moment Hannah expresses joy and adoration to the Lord as recorded in the verses that follow. We may compare her song with that of Mary after the birth of Jesus (Luke 1:46-55) and with the song of Zechariah at the birth of John the Baptist (Luke 1:67-79). See also the words of Moses and Miriam in Exodus 15:1-18, 21, the song of Moses in Deuteronomy 32:1-43, Deborah's song in Judges 5, and David's song in 2 Samuel 22. These show how Old Testament worshipers expressed their gratitude in joyful praise.

A. HANNAH REJOICES (v. 1)

1. Then Hannah prayed and said: "My heart rejoices in the LORD;
*   in the LORD my horn is lifted high.*
My mouth boasts over my enemies,
*   for I delight in your deliverance.*

Hannah directs her praises to *the Lord* by expressing the joy of knowing him as a God of *deliverance*. Some commentators suggest that these words may be a quotation of a hymn that Hannah had learned at the tabernacle in Shiloh.

Whether Hannah learned these verses from someone else or wrote them herself, they are a richly descriptive tribute to the God who hears the prayers of the humble worshiper. She begins by proclaiming her gratitude for the Lord who brings us victory over our *enemies*, who are powerless when God moves to protect his people.

When Hannah refers to herself in this prayer, she speaks of her *heart*, her *horn*, and her *mouth* as the human instruments from which she offers praise. "Horn" is a poetic description of her "strength" (cf. 1 Samuel 2:10), since horned animals often raise their horns high in the air to prepare for battle and self-protection (as in Deuteronomy 33:17; Psalm 92:10). Hannah proclaims the Lord to be her *deliverance* from defeat and humiliation.

Many men and women today understand the agony faced by Hannah. But these verses remind believers that the Lord is the source of victory for those who trust in him.

B. GOD IS EXALTED (v. 2)

2. "There is no one holy like the Lord;
*   there is no one besides you;*
*   there is no Rock like our God.*

In her praise Hannah carefully describes a God who deserves our worship exclusively. Hers is a world dominated by the pagan worship of innumerable gods and goddesses. Hannah's expression of the unique holiness and power of the Lord puts her firmly on the side of Old Testament teaching about God (Exodus 15:11; Psalm 99:3, 5, 9; Isaiah 5:16). She affirms that only the Lord deserves this praise. Referring to God as a *rock* is one of the most recognized ways of describing his protection for believers (see Genesis 49:24; Deuteronomy 32:4; Psalms 18:2, 31, 46; 95:1; Isaiah 17:10). When we sing "Rock of Ages cleft for me, let me hide myself in Thee," we also praise God as the rock of our protection.

C. GOD IS SOVEREIGN (vv. 3-8a)

3. "Do not keep talking so proudly
*   or let your mouth speak such arrogance,*
for the LORD is a God who knows,
*   and by him deeds are weighed.*

In contrast to her praise for the Lord of our protection, Hannah now prays warnings upon those who take pride in their own strength. To what extent her prayer refers to the arrogant talk she has heard from her rival, Peninnah, cannot be determined (1 Samuel 1:6). But Hannah's prayer takes aim at those who believe that their own strength and knowledge are sufficient. All human pride is useless (see Psalms 31:18; 138:6; Proverbs 16:18; Isaiah 5:15, 16).

4. "The bows of the warriors are broken,
*   but those who stumbled are armed with strength.*

Hannah now begins a series of contrasts that extend through verse 7. *Bows* are weapons of war often used by the powerful military forces that have dominated

UNIQUE BIRTHS OF SPECIAL CHILDREN

Child	Text(s)	How the Child is Special	Life Accomplishment
Cain	Genesis 4:1	First human child	Cursed as the first murderer
Isaac	Genesis 18:1-15; 21:1-7	Mother old and barren; prophesied by an angel	Fathered Jacob, the father of Israel
Samson	Judges 13:2-24	Mother barren; announced by an angel	Championed Israel against the Philistines; died in shame
Samuel (Lesson 1)	1 Samuel 1:1-20	Mother barren; dedicated to God's service	As judge, prophet, and priest, anointed the first kings of Israel
John the Baptist (Lesson 2)	Luke 1:5-25, 57-66	Mother old and barren; fulfillment of prophecy	Forerunner of the Messiah; herald of God's kingdom
Jesus (Lesson 3,4)	Matthew 1:18-25; Luke 1:26-35; 2:1-7	Father is God; born of a virgin	Messiah and Savior of all believers

Use this visual to illustrate how God chose people for his service from their earliest years.

DAILY BIBLE READINGS

Monday, Dec. 1—Hannah Prays for a Son (1 Samuel 1:1-11)

Tuesday, Dec. 2—God Answers Hannah's Prayer (1 Samuel 1:12-20)

Wednesday, Dec. 3—Hannah Presents Samuel to God (1 Samuel 1:21-28)

Thursday, Dec. 4—Hannah Praises God (1 Samuel 2:1-5)

Friday, Dec. 5—The Lord Raises Up the Poor (1 Samuel 2:6-10)

Saturday, Dec. 6—Mary's Song of Praise (Luke 1:46-50)

Sunday, Dec. 7—He Has Helped His Servant Israel (Luke 1:51-55)

the earth. *Broken* bows, however, are useless for obtaining military victory. Thus God's power can humble the most powerful armed forces, while giving victory to those people who seem to stumble in weakness.

5. *"Those who were full hire themselves out for food,*
    but those who were hungry hunger no more.
She who was barren has borne seven children,
    but she who has had many sons pines away.

Two more contrasts describe the great reversals brought about by the Lord who protects the humble servant. The person who is *full* and well-fed becomes destitute to the point of needing to earn more money just to eat (e.g., 1 Samuel 2:36), while those without adequate food ultimately are supplied with plenty (2 Kings 7:3-8). Those, like Hannah, who have no children are given *children* by this God who cares for lowly people; on the other hand, *many sons* will be no guarantee of strength and security (cf. Jeremiah 15:7).

6. *"The LORD brings death and makes alive;*
    he brings down to the grave and raises up.

Hannah's praise also extends to the Lord's power over life and *death*. In her own case the Lord had acted to make *alive* by bringing life to her childless womb. Meanwhile God's judgment can extinguish life for those who oppose him, as ultimately occurs with Eli and his sons (1 Samuel 4:12-18; cf. 1 Kings 2:27).

7. *"The Lord sends poverty and wealth;*
    he humbles and he exalts.

This God, says Hannah, is powerful enough to determine and even reverse the fortunes of anyone. Perhaps Hannah is remembering the account of Joseph (Genesis 37, 39–50).

8a. *"He raises the poor from the dust*
    and lifts the needy from the ash heap;
he seats them with princes
    and has them inherit a throne of honor."

The Lord can humble those who are rich and proud in this life, while lifting the poor person. He can lift a humble man like Saul as he hides among the luggage (1 Samuel 10:22) to be king over Israel; but God also brings about his downfall (1 Samuel 15:26-28; 31:1-6). Hannah's praise reflects adoration for the way that God extends mercy to those battered by the discouragements of this life.

So Hannah not only brings her son to dedicate him for the Lord's service, but also to open her heart to praise him in vibrant worship. She is no reluctant promise-keeper. Hannah's praise shows that she fulfills her vow with gladness in her heart. She knows that she has been blessed with the gift of this child, and she considers it a privilege to be able to commit him to the Lord's service.

We could only hope and pray that such a spirit would be found within us when it comes time to fulfill promises that we have made to our God! Mothers and fathers who consider the example of Hannah will stand in awe of her devotion to give so much. But every believer who reflects on Hannah's single-minded dedication in carrying out fearlessly a bold and costly promise made in her hour of desperation will realize that in her actions lies an example for the church.

CONCLUSION

When Hannah dedicated Samuel to God's service, she unknowingly presented to Israel a powerful force for reform of the nation. She did it without knowing how God would use this future prophet to draw an entire people back to him. She did it without knowing that Samuel would be the first prophet to foretell the days of Christ (Acts 3:24). What courage! What faith!

PRAYER

Lord, we pray today that you will take our lives and let them be wholly consecrated to you. May we withhold nothing today that we have promised to give to you. In Jesus' name, amen.

THOUGHT TO REMEMBER

Trust God to know "the bigger picture."

Discovery Learning

This page contains an alternative lesson plan emphasizing learning activities. Classes desiring such student involvement will find these suggestions helpful. The next page is a reproducible activity page to further enhance discovery learning.

LEARNING GOALS

After participating in this lesson, each student will be able to:

1. Tell how Hannah's devotion to God is seen in her prayerful request to the Lord for a son and in her faithfulness in carrying out her vow after the birth of Samuel.

2. State the importance of keeping spiritual commitments, no matter how difficult.

3. Suggest some specific commitment that he or she will fulfill in keeping with Hannah's example of faithfulness.

INTO THE LESSON

As class members enter the classroom, have the following acrostic on vertical display: GOD ANSWERS PRAYER. Give each a copy of the reproducible activity "God Answers Prayer" from the next page.

As the class begins say, "I want you to think about how God answers prayer requests." Then ask class members to move into groups of three to five and have them answer these questions:

1. What specific needs (or desires) have you ever prayed to have met by God?

2. What ultimatums (such as time frame or conditions) have you given God?

3. Why is diligence and fervor necessary for a healthy and fruitful prayer life?

Affirm, "God does answer all prayers, and it is important to be aware of his answer and how it fits into his big picture. Today we see Hannah as a picture of effective praying and responding to God's answer." Convey that prayer is an interactive process that often mirrors our relationship with our friends. Point out that most of us never demand from friends what we do of God.

INTO THE WORD

Ask the class members when, where, why, and how they pray. Note that we spend hours daily planning how to better ourselves at work, working out at the gym, watching TV, or spending time with children, but only minutes a day in prayer. Ask the class, "How do environmental factors (such as location and time of day) influence your interaction with your children? Then state, "If these factors influence other aspects of our lives, then why would they not influence our spiritual lives? To be successful in anything, one must plan, prepare, and exe-

cute efficiently and consistently. What can you do to provide more fervor to your prayer life?"

To integrate the above activity with the Scriptural text, consider presenting a mini-lecture on 1 Samuel 1:21–2:8a. Have the class turn to 1 Samuel 1 and 2 to follow along.

Along with the topics covered in the interactive phase of the lesson, emphasize prayer and the resultant blessings that sometimes come with sacrifices.

Say, "When the time came for Samuel to be taken to the tabernacle, there was no hesitation on Hannah's part. She journeyed to Shiloh with the necessary sacrifice. Hannah fulfilled her promise to the Lord even though it was painful." Move the class back to small groups to discuss, "What can we learn about prayer from Hannah?" The reproducible activity "Hannah's Prayer" from the next page may be useful in this activity.

Make sure your class includes such principles as the following: (1) do not let circumstances preclude possibility—see 1:5; (2) do not let the doubts of others stifle hope in yourself—see 1:6; (3) acknowledge blessing in the midst of pain—see 1:8; (4) be willing to show to God the depth of emotion you feel—1:10; (5) though you cannot deal face-to-face with God, feel free to promise him a response and do it—see 1:11, 28.

Examine other elements of Hannah's story for similar prayer principles. You may want to state these principles to your class orally and ask them to identify verses which reveal the truth in Hannah's life, or you may give each group a printed list and ask them to agree on how each truth is represented in Hannah's story.

INTO LIFE

State: "Some people have called prayer 'a powerful tool,' but this is a misnomer. To think of prayer as a tool assumes we have control and the right to direct it as necessary. Instead, prayer is an attitude and act of communication—an interaction with a friend, our Father and Creator. It is a source of inspiration, guidance, and empowerment." Say: "As we conclude today, let's reflect on how we need to change our own prayer attitude and act to demonstrate the faith of Hannah."

After a few minutes of silent thinking, have all make a personal list they need to change, in two columns: ATTITUDES and ACTS. Suggest they keep their lists in an easily observable location for the next week or longer.

God Answers Prayer

Write a word(s) that relates to the theme for each of the letters in the acrostic. Examples are given to get you started. Write notes you believe necessary and helpful to the right of each.

G _____

O _____

D Dependably   Every prayer is answered . . . if we simply can notice.

A _____

N _____

S _____

W Wisely   He knows what is best when we do not.

E _____

R _____

S _____

P _____

R _____

A _____

Y _____

E _____

R _____

Hannah's Prayer

Draw symbols of what you have learned regarding Hannah's prayer.

JOHN: FORERUNNER OF JESUS

LESSON 2

WHY TEACH THIS LESSON?

Most of us live "low profile" lives. We work at typical jobs, we live in adequate houses, and we can walk down the street without being accosted by thousands of screaming fans or detractors. I don't know about you, but I praise God for such a life! Before we are tempted to envy the very few who live "high profile" lives, we would all do well to consider what their fame really costs them personally.

Even so, God expects us to walk the path he has laid out for us, be it low or high profile, whatever the cost. John the Baptist was one who faithfully followed God's leading to a high profile calling. His job was not typical, his housing was inadequate, and he had many public supporters and detractors. But he recognized the importance of God's plan and accepted his own part in it—a part that eventually led to martyrdom. Today's lesson will help your learners appreciate the unfolding of God's plan and will motivate them to seek their own part in it as well.

INTRODUCTION

A. THE RESCUE MISSION

On March 5, 1994, a man armed with a bomb and a gun entered the Salt Lake City library and took hostages. A deputy sheriff, who was dressed in street clothes and who just happened to be in the building at the time, saw what was happening and voluntarily joined the group as the gunman herded them into a room. The deputy sheriff then waited. When time and circumstance were right, he made his move and shot the gunman to death. The hostages escaped unharmed.

A human parallel such as this can remind us—in a very small, inadequate way—of what God did to deliver us from the power of sin and the devil. The Gospels teach that God dressed himself in "street clothes" and entered our world to bring about this rescue. But his was no spur-of-the-moment plan! He did not come unprepared, nor did he come as many expected. Today's lesson demonstrates how carefully God prepared the way for that rescue operation.

B. LESSON BACKGROUND

Luke the physician was a missionary companion of the apostle Paul (Colossians 4:14; 2 Timothy 4:11; Philemon 24). He was not one of the twelve apostles and perhaps had no direct contact with either John the Baptist or Jesus during their ministries. But Luke had investigated carefully the facts about the "things that have been fulfilled among us" (Luke 1:1). The Holy Spirit chose just the right person to document the facts of the birth and ministry of John the Baptist.

After introducing the purpose of his gospel (Luke 1:1-4), Luke begins his narrative with the heavenly announcements of the coming births of both John (1:5-25) and Jesus (1:26-38), the details of those births (1:57-66; 2:1-38), and the poetic, worshipful praise of both Mary and Zechariah (1:46-55, 67-79). Luke describes

DEVOTIONAL READING:
ISAIAH 40:3-11
BACKGROUND SCRIPTURE:
LUKE 1:5-80
PRINTED TEXT:
LUKE 1:67-80

LESSON AIMS

After participating in this lesson, each student will be able to:

1. Tell how Zechariah saw that John's birth initiated the fulfillment of messianic prophecy.

2. List the various reasons for Zechariah's joy and praise to God.

3. Express praise and thanksgiving to God for the salvation that is ours through Jesus Christ.

KEY VERSE

And you, my child, will be called a prophet of the Most High; for you will go on before the Lord to prepare the way for him.   —Luke 1:76

WHAT DO YOU THINK?

Zechariah, a highly educated and well-trained priest, was taken by complete surprise by the angel's message. What does Zechariah's experience teach us about God and ourselves?

Zechariah and Elizabeth as upright in their worship of the Lord, but Elizabeth was barren and they were praying for a son (Luke 1:5-7, 13). During his ministry in the temple as a priest, Zechariah saw an angel, who announced that Elizabeth would deliver a son. Because Zechariah had a difficult time believing this, the angel gave him a sign by striking him mute.

Nevertheless, Elizabeth became pregnant in her advanced age. Zechariah, for his part, was unable to speak until the birth of his son, John the Baptist. When Zechariah finally spoke, his first words were a kind of hymn of praise including a prophetic announcement about his son. Zechariah's prophecy is often called the "Benedictus" after the word *blessed* in the Latin translation.

The prophecy falls into two main parts: Zechariah's praise for the deliverance that would come from the Messiah (1:68-75), and Zechariah's celebration of John's birth and prophecy about John's future ministry in relation to that of Jesus (1:76-79). Luke's description of Zechariah and Elizabeth presents certain parallels to Hannah and Elkanah in 1 Samuel 1 (see last week's lesson).

I. PRAISE FOR DELIVERANCE (LUKE 1:67-75)

After John is born, Zechariah is again able to speak (1:57-64). The neighbors want to know, "What then is this child going to be?" (1:66). Zechariah responds with a prophecy that reveals some of God's plan of salvation.

A. FILLED WITH THE HOLY SPIRIT (vv. 67, 68)

67, 68. His father Zechariah was filled with the Holy Spirit and prophesied:
　"Praise be to the Lord, the God of Israel,
　　because he has come and has redeemed his people.

As Elizabeth is *filled with* the Spirit in Luke 1:41, so now is *Zechariah.* In this way Zechariah is enabled to speak, as did the prophets of the Old Testament, the truth that God wants revealed (e.g., Jeremiah 2:1; Ezekiel 28:1; Hosea 1:2). The God whom Zechariah praises is called *the God of Israel* because Zechariah knows very well that this God is the One who called that nation to usher in the Messiah. The terms *Israel* and *people* are parallel here, as Zechariah defines Israel as the people who belong to him in a special way for a special purpose (see also v. 77). Zechariah's praise is directed toward the God who has taken action on behalf of his people—a nation that he chose from all the nations of the earth.

Zechariah identifies two actions by God. First, God *has come* to his people with a remedy for their need (cf. Matthew 25:36, 43; James 1:27). Later in the ministry of Jesus some will repeat this idea when they see the power of Jesus' miracles and perceive that God has come to be with his people (Luke 7:16).

The second action is redemption. This concept extends back to the exodus in which God freed the Hebrew slaves from Egyptian bondage and then required the redemption of the firstborn (Exodus 12:1–13:16). Jesus' disciples will come to expect ultimate redemption to come through Jesus himself (see Luke 24:21).

WHAT DO YOU THINK?

When Zechariah again was able to speak, he began immediately to praise God. How are Zechariah's reasons for praise similar to reasons why we should give praise today?

B. GOD'S FAITHFULNESS TO DAVID (vv. 69-71)

69. "He has raised up a horn of salvation for us
　in the house of his servant David

The messianic emphasis of Zechariah's praise becomes clear as he praises God because he is fulfilling his ancient promise to King *David* (2 Samuel 7:11-16). Even though the promise takes almost ten centuries to reach this fulfillment, the Lord has remembered the deliverance he promised to David's royal dynasty.

The *horn of salvation* is a figure of speech from the world of animal husbandry. See the discussion in last week's lesson concerning Hannah's prayer, page 131.

Here the reference must be to Jesus and not to John, because Jesus is the One who traces his ancestry back through King David. See also Psalm 132:17.

70. " . . . *(as he said through his holy prophets of long ago),*

The *holy prophets* refer to those whom God allowed to foresee, many hundreds of years earlier, the future ministry of the Messiah. The first of these ancient prophets was Samuel (Acts 3:24), as we saw last week.

Examples of prophecies of Christ are found in Isaiah 42, 49, and 53. Those who will listen carefully to the teachings of the apostles will see how such prophecies describe a Messiah who comes to restore Israel's spiritual awareness of God's will, and that this Messiah has to suffer and die in this cause (see Acts 2:22-37).

71. " . . . *salvation from our enemies*
    and from the hand of all who hate us—

In this context Zechariah uses the term *salvation* to speak of political deliverance from *enemies* that may want to threaten the nation with intimidation or war (compare Psalm 2; 97:10; Acts 4:25-28). God has rescued his people in the past and will do so again! Verse 77 of Zechariah's praise blends spiritual themes of deliverance with this political one, and Zechariah is happy to praise the God of Israel for both blessings.

One of the failures of the church in industrialized nations today is that its members do not thank the Lord for the peace their nations have enjoyed. Unfortunately, the focus of many of those church members seems to be on political matters, being unduly concerned with candidates and governmental policies. We frequently neglect the admonition of Scripture to pray for "kings and all those in authority" so that each believer may lead "peaceful and quiet lives in all godliness and holiness" (1 Timothy 2:2).

C. GOD'S FAITHFULNESS TO ABRAHAM (vv. 72-75)

72, 73. " . . . *to show mercy to our fathers*
    and to remember his holy covenant,
    the oath he swore to our father Abraham:

Zechariah's praise of God's faithfulness to David took us back to a time some one thousand years before Christ. Now Zechariah takes us back almost twice that far for another example of God's faithfulness. The *holy covenant* to which Zechariah refers is the promise God made to *Abraham* in Genesis 12:1-3; 17:2; and 22:16-18. God swore an oath that he would bless Abraham and make his descendants a mighty nation as numerous as the stars in the sky or the sand on the seashore. He also promised that through this nation all people on earth would be blessed.

Zechariah praises the Lord God of Israel because Zechariah has lived to see this promise of God unfolding before his very eyes! (Compare Simeon's praise in Luke 2:28-32.) Indeed, when we reach these two verses, we have come to the central point in Zechariah's praise. The poetic structure emphasizes the terms *covenant* and *oath*. As Zechariah portrays the arrival of John the Baptist (just born) and Jesus Christ (yet to be born), these events are not the basis for some new and unexpected religion that pops up without warning. Zechariah sees the births of Jesus, the Messiah, and his forerunner, John the Baptist, as the goal toward which the Old Testament faith was pointing from the beginning. God has taken great care to develop his plan for the salvation of his people.

PROMISES, PROMISES

Every time he got an offer for a new credit card, he accepted it. And every time he bought something, he charged it. His credit card debt soared. He promised to

How To Say It
Amos. AY-mus.
Benedictus. BEN-eh-**DIK**-tus.
Cornelius. Cor-NEEL-yus.
Elkanah. EL-kuh-nuh *or* El-KAY-nuh.
Ezekiel. Ee-ZEEK-ee-ul *or* Ee-ZEEK-yul.
Hosea. Ho-ZAY-uh.
Isaiah. Eye-ZAY-uh.
Jeremiah. Jair-uh-MY-uh.
Malachi. MAL-uh-kye.
messianic. mess-ee-AN-ick.
Simeon. SIM-ee-un.
Zechariah. ZEK-uh-RYE-uh.

pay but he never did. He dismissed it by saying, "I'm the most promising young man in town. I promise to pay for this and I promise to pay for that."

The promises of people may not always be kept, but God's always are. He is in this sense "more promising" than we are. His promises are greater and his promises are sure to be kept. That's why when we sing that old song "Standing on the Promises," we note the last words of the refrain: we're "standing on the promises of God." Those are the only promises on which we can truly stand.

The promises of people often fail. You cannot stand on them. Some people never intend to keep their promises in the first place. Some intend to keep them but are prevented by circumstances beyond their control.

But God intends to keep his promises, and he has the resources necessary to do so. Sometimes we dismiss the assurances that come from people and say cynically, "Promises! Promises!" But no one can dismiss God's promises with such cynicism.

Today's lesson shows that it does not matter how old a promise is. God will keep it. You can see it in the Bible. You can see it in life. He may delay the keeping of the promise. He may keep it in a way we do not expect. But we may be certain God's promises will be kept.

—R. C. S.

74, 75. ". . . to rescue us from the hand of our enemies,
and to enable us to serve him without fear
in holiness and righteousness before him all our days.

God's action does not imply that God's people now can be idle. If the Lord has granted his people deliverance from their *enemies,* then those people have a responsibility to *serve* before the Lord. The negative expression of this duty is the opportunity to serve *without fear.* The positive expression of this duty is service *in holiness and righteousness* (cf. Malachi 3:3).

Thus Zechariah correctly summarizes God's will for all believers (see Ephesians 4:24). When believers join their worship together on Sunday, they should also join in their commitment to live by standards that far surpass those of an ungodly culture that is passing away. Singing praises to the God of all holiness includes pledging ourselves to living holy lives before him (cf. Hebrews 12:14).

II. PREDICTION OF MINISTRY (LUKE 1:76-80)

Zechariah turns now from praising the Lord to prophesying through the Spirit what the ministry of both John and Jesus will mean.

A. PREPARING THE WAY (v. 76)

76. "And you, my child, will be called a prophet of the Most High;
for you will go on before the Lord to prepare the way for him.

Without being carried away with pride in his own son, Zechariah provides a sketch of what John's ministry will accomplish. His role will be a preparatory one. His mission will be *to prepare* for the coming of One greater than himself.

This preparation will be as one who arrives ahead of a traveling dignitary to make arrangements for that dignitary's visit to the town. Implied in this ministry is the kind of prophetic work Israel knew from earlier times when prophets like Hosea, Amos, Isaiah, and Jeremiah took up their own prophetic ministries. John will speak for the Lord by addressing the need of Israel to return to God. Such a picture is consistent with the announcement of the angel regarding John's birth, saying that John will "go on before the Lord, in the spirit and power of Elijah" (v. 17) and will bring the people of Israel "back to the Lord their God" (v. 16).

About seven centuries earlier Isaiah had predicted that there would come a certain "voice of one calling: 'In the desert prepare the way for the Lord, make straight in the wilderness a highway for our God'" (Isaiah 40:3; cf. Luke 3:4).

WHAT DO YOU THINK?

In Luke 1:74, Zechariah reminds the people that the deliverance promised to the Israelites comes with an expectation of service. What are some expectations that come as we begin our relationship with the One who has saved us from our sins? How do these change our lives?

[Passages such as Matthew 28:19, 20; John 4:24; Romans 6:4; 12:7; Galatians 6:10; and 1 Peter 1:15, 16 can jump start your thinking.]

Thou, child, shalt be called the prophet of the Highest: for thou shalt go before the face of the Lord to prepare his ways.
— Luke 1:76

Use this artwork of Zechariah's praise song to illustrate today's Key Verse.

(This famous passage is also part of Handel's *Messiah,* which you may be privileged to hear this Christmas season.) Malachi 3:1 had foretold, "See, I will send my messenger, who will prepare the way before me" (see also Malachi 4:5; Matthew 17:10-13). Zechariah affirms that these prophecies present a description of John's ministry before the coming of the Messiah, Jesus Christ.

A SENSE OF BEING CALLED BY GOD

John was a man very well aware of his calling to be the prophet who would prepare the way for the Messiah. Not everyone grows up with a sense of calling like that, though some do. Rowan LeCompte is one. When he was fourteen, he visited the yet unfinished National Cathedral in Washington, D.C. Looking at the great edifice inspired him to work in stained glass. Eventually his dream came true and he designed more than forty-five stained glass windows for that magnificent structure.

A young man went to preach his first sermon in a little country church. After he had stumbled through it a man said, "Son, I believe that you are called to preach." Encouraged by those words, he kept trying and recently completed sixty years of preaching. Through more than half a century he was sustained by the confidence that God had called him to preach.

Some are not as fortunate in receiving a clear "call." They never seem to be sure what God has in mind for them to do or what the purpose of their lives is to be. Whatever calling they have is vague and indistinct. It may be that they will not know until they get to Heaven. Perhaps only then will they understand the part they played in God's plan. Often when people escape a serious accident or survive a serious illness they say, "I think God left me here for a purpose." Even if that purpose is never made quite clear, we serve God the best we can and leave the rest to him. As an old song says, "We'll understand it better by and by."   —R. C. S.

B. PREACHING REPENTANCE (vv. 77, 78)

77, 78. " . . . *to give his people the knowledge of salvation*
    through the forgiveness of their sins,
because of the tender mercy of our God,
    by which the rising sun will come to us from heaven.

At this point Zechariah's emphasis on salvation turns from the political theme (see v. 71, above) to the spiritual one. The phrase *knowledge of salvation* expresses the need for God's people not just to know "about" salvation, but to know it through experiencing it. This salvation will permit God's people to escape *their sins. Forgiveness* of sins will characterize the message of John's ministry (cf. Luke 3:1-3).

After Jesus' resurrection from the dead, he commissions his apostles to preach forgiveness of sins to the whole world (Luke 24:47). Peter continues this theme in his Pentecost sermon when he instructs the crowd to repent and be baptized "for the forgiveness of your sins" (Acts 2:38). Peter also proclaims the forgiveness of sins to Cornelius as the Gospel extends to the Gentiles (Acts 10:43; see also Acts 13:38-48; 26:16-18).

The rising son is a figure of speech for Jesus himself, the One whom John heralds. As that rising sun, Jesus is the light who dawns on both Jew and Gentile (Isaiah 9:1, 2; 42:6; 49:6; 60:1-3; Matthew 4:16; Luke 2:32). The earlier reference that the Lord "has come" to them (Luke 1:68) gave us a vivid picture of God's personal attention to bringing about his program of salvation and redemption; now the figure of a rising sun communicates the bright hope of forgiveness that is granted from the Heavenly Father to a world stumbling in darkness.

In this connection Zechariah speaks of *the tender mercy of our God.* Without this mercy there would be no forgiveness of sins. Zechariah's magnificent words remind us that God's motivation for sending the Messiah and the forgiveness of

DAILY BIBLE READINGS

Monday, Dec. 8—*Prepare the Way of the Lord (Isaiah 40: 3-11)*

Tuesday, Dec. 9—*An Angel Appears to Zechariah (Luke 1: 5-11)*

Wednesday, Dec. 10—*The Promise of a Son (Luke 1:12-17)*

Thursday, Dec. 11—*Elizabeth Conceives (Luke 1:18-25)*

Friday, Dec. 12—*John Is Born (Luke 1:57-66)*

Saturday, Dec. 13—*Zechariah Prophesies (Luke 1:67-75)*

Sunday, Dec. 14—*John Will Be God's Prophet (Luke 1:76-80)*

WHAT DO YOU THINK?

For various reasons many first-century Israelites were hesitant to accept the "knowledge of salvation" from the lips of Jesus and John the Baptist. What are some roadblocks we should be prepared to overcome today as we spread the gospel to a skeptical world?

PRAYER

Lord of my salvation, may I offer as much praise today as Zechariah offered, though he saw only the beginning of your plan of redemption, and I have seen much more. May this make me humble and obedient. In Jesus' name, amen.

sins that came through his ministry is the mercy of God's own heart. No better reason can be named for coming before the Lord in worship than to honor the merciful God who is moved to send to sinners a remedy for their sin. Here is the "God so loved the world" of Zechariah's prophecy. As believers sing the beloved carols of Christmas at this time of year, how appropriate that we raise our voices in praise to the merciful God who wants us to have this deliverance!

C. SHOWING THE PATH (v. 79)

79. " . . . *to shine on those living in darkness*
    and in the shadow of death,
    to guide our feet into the path of peace."

The rising sun shines *on those* surrounded by *darkness* and brings guidance for their *feet* so that they do not fall to their destruction. The imagery is especially striking for those who live in the time of Zechariah. With no streetlights, no automobile headlamps, and no flashlights for moving around at night, the darkness can seem overwhelming. This is especially true on nights when the sky is covered with clouds. The image of a town or village sitting in darkness, where walking along the paths can literally be fatal, is the picture presented by Zechariah's words. See verse 78 above for the Old Testament roots of this imagery.

Zechariah, however, is not thinking of the mortal danger in falling over a cliff while walking in the dark. He predicts that the coming Christ will shine such a light on those who believe that their feet will be guided *into the path of peace.* The theme of the peace brought by Christ is also the theme of the angels' song to the shepherds on the night of Jesus' birth (Luke 2:14). This peace describes the new relationship between people and God (Romans 5:1). It is a peace that consists of a new status with God as those pardoned from sin. How important, then, John's preparatory ministry will be!

D. GROWING IN SPIRIT (v. 80)

80. *And the child grew and became strong in spirit; and he lived in the desert until he appeared publicly to Israel.*

Even in his youth, John's development toward the destiny predicted for him is apparent. Becoming *strong in spirit* may refer either to John's determined willingness to conform to God's will, or it may describe the presence of the Holy Spirit in his young life. John's absence from the relative comforts of city life in Judea prepares him for the introduction of his ministry in Luke 3:2. See also the parallel statements about the early growth of Jesus in Luke 2:40 and 2:52.

WHAT DO YOU THINK?

We can only imagine the sense of obligation that Zechariah and Elizabeth must have felt as they assumed their parental duties for young John, the forerunner of the Messiah. In what ways have all Christian parents been given a similar responsibility?

When the time does come for John the Baptist to start his ministry, he begins preaching in the area of the Jordan River. He becomes the voice of one "calling in the desert" (Luke 3:4; cf. Isaiah 40:3). When crowds come, he charges them to turn their hearts to God in repentance and be baptized (Luke 3:7-18). We hear echoes of the tribute to the Messiah paid by John's father, Zechariah, when John says, "I baptize you with water. But one more powerful than I will come. . . . He will baptize you with the Holy spirit and with fire" (Luke 3:16).

CONCLUSION

Though the story is old to us, Zechariah offers the praise of a believer whose heart has been moved by the freshness of seeing God's plan unfold. Believers today will be blessed by this Christmas season all the more if we can capture for ourselves the sense of surprise and thankfulness in Zechariah's reflections on God's decision to act by sending the Christ into the world. Zechariah's reflections on his son John's obedience can motivate our own obedience as well.

THOUGHT TO REMEMBER

God had a plan for Zechariah, Elizabeth, and John—and God has a plan for you!

Discovery Learning

This page contains an alternative lesson plan emphasizing learning activities. Classes desiring such student involvement will find these suggestions helpful. The next page is a reproducible activity page to further enhance discovery learning.

LEARNING GOALS

After participating in this lesson, each student will be able to:

1. Tell how Zechariah saw that John's birth initiated the fulfillment of Messianic prophecy.

2. List the various reasons for Zechariah's joy and praise to God.

3. Express praise and thanksgiving to God for the salvation that is ours through Jesus Christ.

INTO THE LESSON

Last week, we saw the power of prayer through the story of Hannah and Samuel. Today, we study how the Lord guides the lives of the righteous as seen in the story of Zechariah and his son, John the Baptist (Luke 1:67-80). We see the great joy involved in being in the will of God and understanding the joy of redemption.

Display in large letters the word *JOY*. Have the letter *O* lined internally as it were into jigsaw puzzle pieces. Ask your class, "What puts the 'O!' in joy? That is, what are the components of joy?" As classmembers suggest ideas, write them onto various "puzzle pieces." Expect such concepts to be mentioned as *happiness, delight, jubilation, deep emotion, contentment*. At the end ask the class to look for all of these components in today's text and context of Luke 1.

Mary's Song in Luke 1 and Zechariah's in today's text are both songs of joy. Copy and distribute the reproducible activity "Compare . . . Contrast" from the next page. Establish groups of three or four to work on filling in the boxes. After a time, ask the groups tell others what they have found.

Keep the class members in their small groups. Ask each group to develop a word picture of the concept just discussed. Tell them to cut out words from magazines and newspapers you have provided that might deal with the "Big Idea." They can paste these on a sheet of newsprint in such a way that they create a shape representing today's subject.

INTO THE WORD

Direct the class to today's text, Luke 1:67-80, and affirm to them, "Zechariah had every reason to rejoice, for he could see in his newly born son the fulfillment of a host of God's promises to Israel." Show the following list of Old Testament Scripture references and ask the class to find them and write each one in at an appropriate point in Zechariah's song (suggestions are given in parentheses): Genesis 12:2, 3 (see v. 73); 2 Samuel 22:3 (v. 69); Ezra 7:27 (v. 68); Job 38:12 (v. 78); Psalm 83:10 (v. 76a); Psalm 136:24 (v. 71); Psalm 144:10 (v. 69); Isaiah 9:2 (v. 79); Haggai 2:9 (v. 79); Malachi 3:1 (v. 76b).

Note verse 67 of the text at the end of this matching exercise: Zechariah is prophesying on the basis of being filled with the Holy Spirit, even as writers of the Old Testament were. God fulfills his promises. Note that this, in itself, is a reason for rejoicing and a deep sense of joy.

Point out again that both Mary's exclamation of verses 46-55 and Zechariah's in verses 67-79 are often labeled *Song*. Emphasize the joy each felt in being part of God's plan. Each was asked to give a son to God's will. Say, "Reflect on your commitment to and relationship with God and evaluate your ability to handle such difficult requests and expectations from the Lord."

INTO LIFE

Those of your learners who have children can understand the sacrifice both Zechariah and Mary displayed by allowing God's will to be done. Ask the class, "How were Zechariah and Mary able to do this?" Emphasize that each was filled with the Holy Spirit, allowing each one to see the larger picture and how a seemingly difficult experience was actually a blessing. As with last week's lesson, God continues to reemphasize our need to be open to his will in his time.

Say to your class, "Like Zechariah, let's write a brief song of praise to God using special event(s) in our own spiritual journey and relationship." Tell the group you are going to call out a phrase or affirmation from Zechariah's song, and that after each you would like someone to personalize it. For example, you say, "We have 'salvation from our enemies,'" and someone says, "My enemy death is nothing to be feared." Or, "You, my child, will . . . give his people the knowledge of salvation," and someone responds, "Thank you, God, for (name), who taught me about salvation." After working through other parts of the text, recommend that all do a personal journal this week on the truths of Zechariah's prophetic declaration.

Option. The reproducible activity "Songwriting" from the next page may be used to help your learners to personalize the truths of today's text.

Compare . . . Contrast

Look at both Zechariah's song (Luke 1:67-80) and Mary's song (Luke 1:46-55). Note their comparable elements in column one. Note their differences in column two.

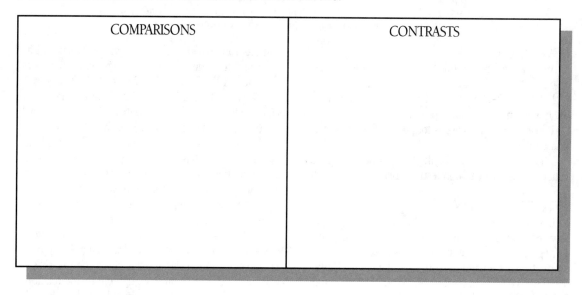

COMPARISONS	CONTRASTS

Songwriting

Zechariah's praise is often referred to as a "song." (Compare the "songs" of Mary and Elizabeth earlier in Luke's Gospel.) You can create a song of praise to God as well. Using Luke 1:46-55, Luke 1:67-80, or similar passages as a backdrop, write some new words to the tune of a familiar song.

JESUS: GOD WITH US

LESSON 3

DEVOTIONAL READING:
JOHN 14:6-14

BACKGROUND SCRIPTURE:
MATTHEW 1:18-25

PRINTED TEXT:
MATTHEW 1:18-25

Dec
21

WHY TEACH THIS LESSON?

Could there possibly be anything worse in life than to hear God say, "I am against you"? Unfortunately, God finds it necessary to use this phrase numerous times in the Bible. (See, for example, Jeremiah 21:13; Ezekiel 13:8; and Nahum 2:13.) When God utters those words, judgment and wrath always follow.

But on the other hand, there is nothing better than to hear God say, "I am with you"! This phrase also occurs numerous times in the Bible. (See, for example, Isaiah 41:10; Jeremiah 30:11; and Matthew 28:20.) As we shall see today, "God with us" is the vital part of the Christmas message. Many of your learners undoubtedly feel distressed by the secular pressures and family expectations that come with the Christmas season. Today's lesson will help them cut through all those distractions to recall what is really important: God is indeed with us!

INTRODUCTION

A. WHEN TRUST IS MISPLACED

At ten minutes to midnight on June 1, 1999, the passengers on a flight to Little Rock, Arkansas, discovered that they had misplaced their trust. They came to this realization as the aircraft in which they were traveling careened off the end of the runway while landing in bad weather, causing eleven fatalities.

In the aftermath one question just wouldn't seem to go away: why did such a highly experienced flight crew exercise such bad judgment in attempting to land during a severe thunderstorm? The captain himself could not answer the question since he died in the crash. Nothing about his record as an airline pilot suggested him to be untrustworthy in either flying skills or judgment.

But our fellow humans can and will let us down from time to time, occasionally with deadly results. Curiously, many people who will continue to trust fallible airline pilots, air traffic controllers, etc., for their earthly destinies will hesitate when offered the chance to trust the infallible God for their eternity!

Although today's lesson features the birth of Jesus, we cannot help but notice the actions of Mary and Joseph, who were challenged to trust God in ways they never would have dreamed about. We not only celebrate this week the most important birth in history, we also keep our eyes on the faith that carried Mary and Joseph through the difficulties of their predicament. Their ability to trust in God's guidance will serve us well as we attempt to navigate through the thunderstorms of life ourselves.

B. LESSON BACKGROUND

Even before Jesus' birth was announced, there was speculation everywhere in first-century Palestine about the coming Messiah—much of it misguided. Some Jews expected two different Messiahs, one a teacher and one a warrior. On more than one occasion pretenders incited Jewish enthusiasts to believe that the Messiah had come and it was time to march on the Romans (compare Acts 5:35-38).

But Matthew establishes that Jesus is no pretender. It is Jesus alone who has the credentials to sit on David's throne as the messianic promises foretold, and

LESSON AIMS

After participating in this lesson, each student will be able to:

1. Cite several ways in which Mary and Joseph demonstrated faith in trusting and obeying God.

2. Tell how believers can show trust in God as they make decisions about difficult life situations.

3. Make a commitment to take a risk in being obedient to the Lord.

KEY VERSE

"The virgin will be with child and will give birth to a son, and they will call him Immanuel"—which means, "God with us."
—Matthew 1:23

LESSON 3 NOTES

his ministry will proclaim the pure Word of God as would be expected of One truly sent from above.

After presenting a genealogy that establishes Jesus' credentials through the royal line of David, Matthew turns to the details of the birth of Jesus. The drama of the story is unfolded in such a way as to show clearly how the Lord God acted in this event to bring Jesus into the world and protect him from the forces of evil that stood against him.

I. JOSEPH'S DILEMMA (MATTHEW 1:18, 19)
A. MARY'S PREGNANCY (v. 18)
18. This is how the birth of Jesus Christ came about: His mother Mary was pledged to be married to Joseph, but before they came together, she was found to be with child through the Holy Spirit.

Matthew's Gospel, unlike that of John, does not reflect on the preexistence of Christ in the presence of God before the beginning of the world (see John 1:1, 2). Instead, Matthew begins his account with an earthly genealogy of Jesus and a sketch of his *birth* in Bethlehem. Yet this is not a "natural" conception and birth—far from it! Matthew hints at this in 1:16 when he notes that Joseph is "the husband of Mary, of whom was born Jesus"; a typical genealogical statement might have said that Joseph was the father of Jesus.

That Joseph and Mary did not engage in sexual relations prior to Jesus' birth is clear. But at this point in the story no one but Mary herself knows the true source of her pregnancy (Luke 1:26-38). It is difficult to imagine the trauma that the statement *before they came together, she was found to be with child* implies for her life in her culture. Not only will she face stern disapproval from her family and neighbors, she also must have many questions about what is happening and how her role will play itself out.

Yet both the Gospels of Matthew and Luke indicate that Mary and Joseph meet their uncertainties with an unquestioning faith in God. Both set examples that remind modern believers that participating in the will of God does not always mean we will see clearly how God will use us for his purposes. Those whom God uses in his service must be willing to trust him for the unexpected twists and turns that will come our way as a result. Anyone who insists that the Lord draw straight pathways to follow, where every step is fully illuminated and every objective is explained fully, cannot be used effectively in his service.

B. JOSEPH'S DECISION (v. 19)
19. Because Joseph her husband was a righteous man and did not want to expose her to public disgrace, he had in mind to divorce her quietly.

The fact that Joseph is *a righteous man* implies that he is concerned to meet the situation of Mary's pregnancy in accordance with his sense of duty before God. He realizes that he is unable to take Mary as his wife under the conditions of her pregnancy, since from his perspective she must have committed adultery with another man. He knows the regulations in Deuteronomy 22:23-27 require a death sentence for Mary. Even though Roman occupation of Israel prevents the Jews from exercising the death penalty, Joseph can still publicly humiliate Mary as an adulteress.

Instead, Joseph can present Mary with a bill of *divorce* in the presence of a few witnesses in accordance with Deuteronomy 24:1-4, since an engagement is as legally binding as a marriage. He chooses this more private course of action to meet his obligations before the law, while at the same time sparing Mary the *public disgrace*.

HOW TO SAY IT

Ahaz. AY-haz.
Bethlehem. BETH-lih-hem.
Deuteronomy. Due-ter-AHN-uh-me.
Gentile. JEN-tile.
Herod. HAIR-ud.
Immanuel. Ih-MAN-you-el.
Isaiah. Eye-ZAY-uh.
Jerusalem. Juh-ROO-suh-lem.
Joshua. JOSH-yew-uh.
Messiah. Meh-SIGH-uh.
messianic. mess-ee-AN-ick.
Zechariah. ZEK-uh-RYE-uh.

So Joseph must react to a situation about which he has neither been warned nor prepared. His sense of obedience to God motivates him to respond to Mary's pregnancy in the most appropriate way he can think of. His knowledge of God's law and his desire to "do the right thing" by Mary serve as his guiding lights. But we can only guess at the turmoil that such events create within him. Nevertheless, Joseph's reaction allows us to gain some insight into how faith in our all-knowing God can be useful for times such as these.

II. GOD'S DIRECTION (MATTHEW 1:20-23)

A. THE DREAM (v. 20)

20. But after he had considered this, an angel of the Lord appeared to him in a dream and said, "Joseph son of David, do not be afraid to take Mary home as your wife, because what is conceived in her is from the Holy Spirit.

Joseph is now permitted to see events from God's perspective. Joseph's experience corresponds to examples from the Old Testament in which angelic messengers reveal the will of God to his servants (e.g., Genesis 31:11).

The description of Joseph as *son of David* connects him to the preceding genealogy. This reinforces the theme of the royal ancestry of Jesus. But the main purpose in the message from the angel is to direct Joseph's course of action. Thus the angel commands him to *take Mary home* with him as his *wife*, offering the explanation that her pregnancy is the result of the work of the *Holy Spirit* rather than the adultery that Joseph has assumed.

The command not to *be afraid* could be a reference to Joseph's concern that he would be breaking God's law to marry a woman who had become pregnant out of wedlock. It is also possible that the fear has reference to the social pressures that will result from going ahead with the marriage.

B. THE PROMISE (v. 21)

21. "She will give birth to a son, and you are to give him the name Jesus, because he will save his people from their sins."

The message of the angel provides further details to Joseph about this birth, using terminology familiar in birth announcements in the Old Testament (see Genesis 16:11; 17:19; 1 Kings 13:2). The Greek name *Jesus* is a form of the Hebrew name "Joshua," which carries the idea that "the Lord is salvation" or "the Lord saves." This implies that the role of this *son* of Israel will be one of bringing the nation deliverance from the Day of Judgment. This sense of the name *Jesus* seems to be drawn from Psalm 130:8, which predicts that the Lord God "will redeem Israel from all their sins."

Of course no details about how Jesus will accomplish this are revealed to Joseph. But the rest of Matthew's Gospel will present astonishing facts about how the Messiah must redeem Israel by sacrificing his own life as a ransom (20:28) to save his people from their sins. Jewish expectations frequently promote the idea that the Messiah would free Israel from Roman tyranny and also purify his people. However, the notion that the Messiah would die a criminal's death is too much to accept for most of the Jewish faithful. The idea of the Messiah as a "suffering servant" (cf. Isaiah 53) seems unreal to them.

The full meaning of the phrase *his people* will unfold throughout Matthew's Gospel. These people are those who belong to the Messiah, whether they are from a Jewish or Gentile background; and being a Jew by birth will not mean being counted automatically as among the saved (Matthew 3:9, 10; 8:11, 12). Christians today can give thanks for the fact that Jesus' arms of mercy include people of many ethnic and national backgrounds!

WHAT DO YOU THINK?

The Jews had heard others claim to be the Messiah or that there might even be two Messiahs. If you were in Joseph's shoes, what signs would have convinced you that this Child indeed was going to be the very One promised to "save his people from their sins"?

DAILY BIBLE READINGS

Monday, Dec. 15—Believe in God, Believe in Christ (John 14: 1-5)

Tuesday, Dec. 16—Know Christ, Know the Father (John 14:6-10)

Wednesday, Dec. 17—I Am in the Father (John 14:11-15)

Thursday, Dec. 18—Christ in God, We in Christ (John 14: 16-20)

Friday, Dec. 19—Isaiah Prophesies Immanuel (Isaiah 7:10-17)

Saturday, Dec. 20—Jesus Is Born (Luke 2:1-7)

Sunday, Dec. 21—Prophecy Fulfilled (Matthew 1:18-25)

WHAT'S IN A NAME?

Through a character in one of his plays William Shakespeare posed the question, "What's in a name?" (*Romeo and Juliet,* Act II, Scene 2). Most of the names we give to our children have meanings, but we rarely pay much attention to those meanings. We do not think of the fact that *Anna* means "grace" or that *David* means "beloved." We are not conscious of the fact that *Timothy* means "honoring God."

Unfortunately, we also do not always think about the meaning of the name *Jesus.* Certainly, people who use it in profanity do not think of its meaning. Neither do those who drop the name casually. But God thought it important enough to make doubly certain that that was the name given to our Lord. It is significant that the name *Jesus* means Savior. Of course, he would have been our Savior no matter what his name. But surely it was for our benefit that God chose the name *Jesus.*

But we must also wonder if it did not have an effect on Jesus himself! If your name is *Joy,* do you feel a need to be cheerful? If your name is *Faith,* does it affect your conduct? In Hebrew culture the giving of a name was always regarded as highly significant. If you are called a *Christian,* does it affect your life in some positive way—a way that others can see this Christmas season?   —R. C. S.

C. THE PROPHECY (vv. 22, 23)

22. *All this took place to fulfill what the Lord had said through the prophet:*

The terms *fulfill* and *fulfilled* are very important in Matthew's Gospel. They appear numerous times to describe how Old Testament predictions are reaching fruition (e.g., Matthew 2:15, 17, 23). Matthew's theme of fulfillment makes it clear that the gospel message has its roots in Old Testament events and promises.

23. *"The virgin will be with child and will give birth to a son, and they will call him Immanuel"—which means, "God with us."*

This prophetic quotation—more than seven hundred years old!—comes from Isaiah 7:14. The original context is the prophecy spoken by Isaiah to King Ahaz of Judah when he was threatened with attack. To defeat this attack, King Ahaz was considering asking for Assyrian help when the Lord commanded him (through Isaiah) to put his trust in the Lord instead. Isaiah offered King Ahaz a sign that would confirm that God would keep his promise that Jerusalem would go unharmed if the king would depend on the Lord. When King Ahaz refused to ask for a sign, Isaiah gave him one anyway, saying, *"The virgin will be with child and will give birth to a son, and will call him Immanuel"* (Isaiah 7:14).

Naturally we may ask just how the prediction of the birth of a child to a virgin would have represented a sign to King Ahaz over seven hundred years earlier! We can answer this question by realizing that prophecies in the Old Testament can be understood either as "predictions that persuade people immediately" (as in Exodus 4:8, 9), or as sweeping statements to serve as "future confirmations" of something (as in Exodus 3:12).

In the case of King Ahaz the prophecy of Isaiah 7:14 fits the second of these two, since Ahaz will be long dead by the time Jesus is born. Isaiah in his day sees destruction coming not just to Ahaz in particular, but also for "the house of David" in general (Isaiah 7:2, 13), resulting in the loss of the throne. Long after King David's dynasty has ended, it will be Jesus, born to a virgin and born of David's line, who comes to carry the government of God's people upon his shoulders (Isaiah 9:6). Jesus is the one for whom the nation waits. He is the "confirmation" of the truth of Isaiah's words.

Those who faithfully await the arrival of the Messiah will gladly *call him Immanuel . . . God with us.* What better blessing could one ask for than to know that

WHAT DO YOU THINK?

The prophecy from Isaiah 7:14 reveals God's patience in developing his plan over hundreds of years, even with a rebellious people. In what ways has God been patient with you?

God wants to dwell with his people? (See also Isaiah 60:18-20; Revelation 21:3.) Jesus made all of this possible for believers when he left his eternal glory to put on flesh and come to earth to die for our sins. He promises to include his people in a great banquet at the end of time when again he will be with us in glory (Revelation 19:6-9).

III. JOSEPH'S OBEDIENCE (MATTHEW 1:24, 25)

A. He Takes Mary as His Wife (v. 24)

24. When Joseph woke up, he did what the angel of the Lord had commanded him and took Mary home as his wife.

Joseph's response to *the angel of the Lord* is immediate. As soon as he wakes up, Joseph moves with obedience to the Lord's command. The message that has been revealed convinces him that taking Mary to be *his wife* is exactly the Lord's will.

Here we see the beginning of a pattern of quick responses to the Lord's direction in the accounts of Jesus' birth. Later, in Matthew 2:12, the wise men quickly obey the divine instructions not to return the way they came because of Herod's intentions. When Joseph later receives a warning of Herod's plan to murder the baby Jesus, he quickly obeys the message that he should take the infant and travel to Egypt (2:14). See also Matthew 2:21 and Luke 2:15, 16.

Throughout all of these incidents we see God's providential hand protecting this unique baby from those who oppose the program of salvation that has been announced from the Lord. Matthew's account as a whole also shows us the kind of believers, both Jewish and Gentile, whom God uses in the work of his kingdom. Joseph's example of trusting God when called upon to make risky decisions challenges us: how do we exercise our own faith when life throws unexpected curveballs?

Though Joseph cannot see with unhindered vision all that God has in store for him in the birth of Jesus, he nevertheless answers each challenge with faithfulness. He does this by applying his understanding of God's will as revealed both in the Scriptures and in the dream, as well as his recognition of God's sovereignty over the events that confront him.

As Joseph moves through the surprising news of Mary's pregnancy and his own sense of what must be done, he does so with an ear tuned to how the Lord might next direct him. The dramatic message in the night convinces him that he must act upon this new insight into Mary's pregnancy and take her as his wife. Once that information is disclosed to him, his faith moves him again to act with decisiveness. We can compare Joseph's decisiveness with the hesitation and doubt of the highly educated priest Zechariah in Luke 1:18.

Each one of us faces moments in which our confidence in the Lord's plan for our lives will be tested. Today we cannot expect God to reveal his specific will for us in dreams (see Hebrews 1:1, 2). Rather, we will have to make decisions on the basis of our faith and our general knowledge of God's expectations of us as expressed in the pages of Scripture.

At times we will need to act with confidence that our best tool is our trust in God's ability to move us in the right direction. As with Joseph, we may find out during the unfolding drama that a change in course is necessary. When those times come, will we trust God to guide us through these adjustments? Of first importance is that we keep our hearts open for his direction.

B. He Names the Baby "Jesus" (v. 25)

25. But he had no union with her until she gave birth to a son. And he gave him the name Jesus.

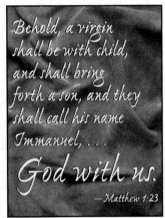

Use this poster to draw attention to today's Key Verse.

What Do You Think?

Joseph responded immediately to the angel's instructions. Is Joseph's reaction a model for us today? Why, or why not?

What Do You Think?

Suppose Joseph and Mary had hesitated by asking God "why?" What kind of response could they have received? And what kind of answer can we expect when we ask "why?"

Joseph takes on his role of family patriarch in naming *Jesus* by his God-given name, and making him his own son in the legal sense. The naming occurs at Jesus' circumcision, eight days after his birth. Some profound things happen at that time (see Luke 2:21-38).

Had no union with her is Matthew's way of making it clear that the conception of this unique baby was not the result of any marital consummation between the parents. Joseph respects the initiative of God in the life of his spouse so much that even after their marriage is ceremonially inaugurated he delays the normal marital relationship with Mary. Thus Joseph brings Mary into his house, but continues to treat her sexually as if the relationship were in the premarital engagement phase until after the time of Jesus' birth.

The word *until* is significant because it indicates a change that takes place after the birth of Jesus—the picture is that of Joseph and Mary in a normal married relationship, which includes a sexual relationship as God intends. Later Matthew will supply information about Joseph and Mary's other children, half-brothers and half-sisters to Jesus (Matthew 12:46). Matthew also includes the names of some of these—James, Joseph, Simon, and Judas (13:55). There is no support in the Bible for the concept of the "perpetual virginity" of Mary as some today mistakenly believe.

TAKING THE CHRIST CHILD HOME

An American Indian pueblo in the western United States has an interesting custom. After the midnight service on Christmas Eve, one family takes the doll from the manger home with them. They keep the Christ child in their home for the twelve days of Christmas—until January 6. It is considered a great honor to be the family chosen to do this. What a thought! They take the Christ child home with them!

Joseph and Mary took the Christ child home with them. In a sense every family attending church on Christmas Eve can take the Christ child home with them—and they should! If we are wise, we will not only take the Child home with us, but we will keep him there throughout the year. Although we may lack the symbolism of the doll the Americans Indians use, ultimately we do not really need that symbolism. It is in our hearts we will take him home, and he will remain in our hearts as well as our house.

Anyone who has brought home a baby knows that that moment changes everything. It did for Mary and Joseph as it does for every family. Spiritually, taking the Christ child home with us also "changes everything"—in the home and in the heart, for now and for eternity.

—R. C. S.

CONCLUSION

The birth of Jesus came about in a most extraordinary way! But the parents of Jesus were ordinary people whose faith served them well in extraordinary circumstances. They were obviously not expecting to meet such challenges during those days when the happy couple planned together for sharing a lifetime of marriage. But their faith in the Lord was firm from the very start. As a result, their decisions could be made in a context of obedience to God's will as that will became progressively obvious to them.

Modern believers also face challenges as we make decisions about important issues. Mary and Joseph teach us to trust in the Lord to guide us even as we wonder what is coming next. What is really around the next corner—no one knows! But whatever it is the Lord has in store for us, we can submit ourselves to him. We realize that our God "knows what he is doing." Often we will live to see how it all makes sense in light of God's bigger plans.

WHAT DO YOU THINK?

Joseph's role in the drama of the coming of the Messiah required heroic decisions but garnered few accolades. What important lessons can we learn from Joseph in this regard?

PRAYER

All-knowing God, we ask forgiveness where our own blindness has prevented us from meeting new challenges with faith and obedience. Lead us through the surprises of life, and please pardon us where we fail to trust you. Empower us to meet those future challenges that await us. In the name of your Son who saves his people from their sins, amen.

THOUGHT TO REMEMBER

He will always show us "why"—if not in this life, then in the next.

Discovery Learning

This page contains an alternative lesson plan emphasizing learning activities. Classes desiring such student involvement will find these suggestions helpful. The next page is a reproducible activity page to further enhance discovery learning.

LEARNING GOALS

After this lesson each student will be able to:

1. Cite several ways in which Mary and Joseph demonstrated faith in trusting and obeying God.

2. Tell how believers can show trust in God as they make decisions about difficult life situations.

3. Make a commitment to take a risk in being obedient to the Lord.

INTO THE LESSON

This is Christmas Sunday. Begin by brainstorming the question, "What do you consider to be the operative word for the season?" Encourage everyone to contribute whatever he or she thinks without feeling that the ideas are going to be evaluated. Have someone take notes.

You may get secular responses like *Santa*, *presents*, or *family*, as well as religious responses such as *Christ's birth*. For continuity with the previous weeks, emphasize the concept of faith. Say, "Isn't faith what truly sets us apart as Christians in the Christmas season?" Take a quick oral survey of how many members have lost faith in schools, the government, businesses, or another organization. No doubt you will get a wide show of hands. Ask, "How does this lack of faith affect your interaction with these groups?" Ask also, "How does faith in the Bible account of Jesus' birth make Christmas more meaningful?"

Distribute copies of the reproducible activity "Banner of Faith" from the next page. Fill that "banner" in as a group. Then ask, "How many of you have had a prayer request go seemingly unanswered? How has that affected your faith in God? It would not be unusual for it to affect your belief, at least slightly. In such tests, one solidly grounded in faith is able to differentiate himself or herself from others who are not."

INTO THE WORD

Select and recruit three of your best oral readers and assign them these three "Christmas texts" respectively to read to the class as you begin: John 1:1-5, 14-18; Luke 1:26-38, 2:1-7; Matthew 1:18-25.

Provide each class member with writing materials. Ask the class to go through Matthew 1:18-25 and conduct his or her own Personal Checklist. Each one is to write down answers to the question: "What do these verses tell me about Mary, about Joseph, and about God?" Ask each class member to list everything he or she can find in about five minutes in three separate columns. Encourage each to star items that speak to him or her personally in current circumstances.

Ask learners to match the behaviors of Mary and Joseph to what God reveals and what they obviously believe about him. For example, when God reveals Mary's "mysterious" pregnancy, in her believing she affirms that God is able to set aside his universal controlling laws. When Joseph plans to do the right and gracious thing toward Mary, God suggests he do something even more righteously daring: marry her. He did.

Ask, "Are you ready and willing to do the same? What if God asked you to sacrifice your way of life to follow his will? Would you wait for *another* sign that would provide a loophole?" After discussion ask, "How did Mary's faith and Joseph's enable them to overcome their fears? What makes you different from Mary and Joseph?"

Distribute copies of the following personal evaluation and decision activity labeled "Faith and Obedience":

(1) I believe God has spoken to me; so I will . . . .

(2) I believe God has the power to do things I cannot imagine; therefore, I will . . . .

(3) I believe Jesus is the virgin born child of Mary and Son of God; therefore, I will . . . .

(4) I believe that Jesus has honored the meaning of his name (Savior); therefore, I will . . . .

INTO LIFE

To introduce this section state: "As a year draws to a close, we often make resolutions we hope to keep: to become slimmer, spend more time with our kids, improve our walk with the Lord. What we really need to do is learn how to let go. God has a plan for personal success, and he has revealed it. Only through faith can we experience joy and achieve the goals God has for us.

Suggest that rather than a list of "New Year's Resolutions," each class member prepare a list of "New Life Responses," honoring the faith and submission of Mary and Joseph. (Or have them complete the reproducible activity "Depending on God" from the next page.)

If you have access to a badge maker, prepare a badge for each, carrying the letters NYR and the universal prohibition vertical slash. Pin one on each learner, and tell all to use it as a conversation starter with family, friends, and work associates on the true meaning of Christmas and New Year's: faith and obedience.

Banner of Faith

Make a banner describing faith with words or phrases.

Faith is . . .

Depending on God

List five responsibilities you will face this week, either at home, on the job, or in the church. In these areas of responsibility, how will depending on God make a difference?

1.

2.

3.

4.

5.

A Child Is Given
(Lessons 1-4)

JESUS:
GROWING IN GOD'S FAVOR

WHY TEACH THIS LESSON?

Modern educational systems are quite taken with the concept of measuring intellectual achievement. The American system, for example, has become an alphabet soup of SAT, GMAT, GRE, and IQ scores. Those with letters such as B.A., M.S., and Ph.D. behind their names are seen as "educated." And every child certainly knows the difference between an "A" and an "F" on a report card.

Now if only spiritual growth could be measured this easily! Part of the problem is that many consider intellectual and physical growth to be more important than maturing spiritually, so measuring the latter is a low priority. But God thinks differently, as today's key verse indicates. If it was important for the youthful Jesus to grow spiritually, should it not be important for us as well? Today's lesson will remind your students that spiritual maturity is a lifelong process. For those who are spiritually stagnant, the example of twelve-year-old Jesus can be a great motivator to get started—or get started again.

INTRODUCTION

A. THE YOUTH OF TODAY

Josh McDowell continues to challenge today's youth as he has done for more than thirty years. But in a 1997 interview with the *Dallas Morning News* he said that what he has seen happening to kids over the past several years disturbs him very much.

His chief concern is that young people do not believe in absolute truth. They may believe that God exists, but they don't connect that belief to the fact that there is a set of unchanging universal values established by that God. The modern notion of "tolerance" undermines young Christians' faith. And when a person accepts everything, he or she loses the ability to discern right from wrong.

The result is that instead of having morality we just have different opinions. Since much of today's theology and world outlook are based on emotional hurt rather than rational thought, children twelve or thirteen years of age are making life decisions and adult choices with adolescent emotions.

Sadly, Josh McDowell is right. The result is that many of our young people are virtually lost to the church today. He goes on to say that Christian parents must do more than teach the Bible to their children. They must practice what they preach. If they don't, their teens will be lost to a society that questions everything.

Luke's Gospel describes a young person who had a different outlook on life from that of many of today's youth. His was a mind drawn very early to the Lord and the things of the Lord. Luke chooses one incident in the life of young Jesus to illustrate a point about the sense of duty to God that characterized Jesus from his youth. This account teaches us of the value of bringing to bear every noble spiritual influence upon all the young people we can reach for the gospel.

DEVOTIONAL READING:
JOHN 5:19-24

BACKGROUND SCRIPTURE:
LUKE 2:40-52

PRINTED TEXT:
LUKE 2:40-52

Dec
28

LESSON AIMS

After participating in this lesson, each student will be able to:

1. List the details provided in today's text concerning the early years of Jesus' life, including his sense of his unique role as the Son of God.

2. Tell how the growth of Jesus in his knowledge of God and his interest in spiritual things reminds us of how essential it is for children to acquire a devotion for God at a young age.

3. Express a commitment to participate in helping area young people come to love the Lord.

KEY VERSE

And Jesus grew in wisdom and stature, and in favor with God and men.   —Luke 2:52

B. LESSON BACKGROUND

Luke 2:40-52 is part of a longer unit within the early narrative of Luke's Gospel, a unit that encompasses all of chapter 2. The focus in this larger unit is Jesus' birth and early life. Throughout the passage Luke highlights events that show how Joseph and Mary conduct themselves before and after that birth.

Just after the birth, Luke shows us a picture of parents who are careful "to do for him what the custom of the Law required" (Luke 2:27; cf. Exodus 13:2, 12, 13, 15; Leviticus 12:3). Luke points out that the family of the young Jesus was serious in keeping the Passover in Jerusalem (Luke 2:41), and even though the law of Moses did not require women to go, Mary's presence will be carefully noted. This follows after the example of Hannah in 1 Samuel 1:7 and 2:19. Even Jesus' presence in Jerusalem as a young boy will be described as "according to the custom" (Luke 2:42).

Luke notes this care again at the end of this earlier episode in the temple when commenting that Mary and Joseph "had done everything required by the Law of the Lord" (Luke 2:39). This emphasis finds expression in today's lesson text. Modern believers thus get a glimpse into the spiritual life of this dedicated family—a family where the oldest son happens to be the Son of God!

I. TO THE FEAST (LUKE 2:40-42)

A. JESUS GROWS UP (v. 40)

40. And the child grew and became strong; he was filled with wisdom, and the grace of God was upon him.

Like bookends, Luke 2:40 and 2:52 enclose the narrative about the journey of Jesus' family to Jerusalem for the Passover feast. In addition, verse 40 provides us with a transition from the previous account of Jesus' dedication in the temple as a baby to the present episode twelve years later.

A brief note about the growth of *the child* Jesus—both spiritual and physical— begins Luke's account of this particular family journey to Jerusalem. Luke stresses that Jesus is *filled with wisdom, and the grace of God was upon him.* The mention of wisdom prepares us to understand the incident that follows.

WHAT DO YOU THINK?

The text notes of Jesus that "the grace of God was upon him." In what ways has God extended his grace to you?

Parents who lovingly chart the growth of their children in terms of height, weight, strength, athletic ability, academic progress, and social life are making a mistake if they do not also seek to encourage their children's spiritual development as well. From the young Jesus, to the young Timothy, to the young John and Charles Wesley, to the young Alexander Campbell, to the young Dwight Moody—these examples remind us that parents can bring a great influence to bear upon their children in spiritual matters. Modern parents must take every opportunity to shape the clay of their children's lives while it is still soft and pliable. (See Deuteronomy 4:9; 6:6, 7; 11:18, 19.)

WHAT DO YOU THINK?

How rare it is today to hear a child labeled as "wise"! What "markers of wisdom" would we have to see today to use "wise" to describe a twenty-first century child? How does an adult's view of wisdom differ from a teenager's view of wisdom?

B. JESUS OBSERVES THE PASSOVER (vv. 41, 42)

41. Every year his parents went to Jerusalem for the Feast of the Passover.

Deuteronomy 16:16 establishes that "three times a year all your men must appear before the Lord your God at the place he will choose." That passage then goes on to list the three major Jewish celebrations of Unleavened Bread (Passover), Weeks (Pentecost), and Tabernacles (Booths) as those "three times."

The Feast of Unleavened Bread lasts one week and occurs immediately after the *Passover* celebration; these two together (which, practically speaking, form one celebration) commemorate the deliverance of the Hebrew slaves from their bondage in Egypt. That deliverance included the powerful hand of the Lord that spared the firstborn of Israel (Exodus 12; Numbers 28:16, 17).

The Jewish historian Josephus implies that Jews were scattered so far from *Jerusalem* by the first century A.D. that many were fortunate to travel to that great city once in a lifetime. It is providential that Mary and Joseph live only seventy miles or so from Jerusalem.

Even so, this is not an easy trip for them to make in an age before automobiles. The fact that Mary and Joseph make this pilgrimage *every year* reveals to us their sense of duty to God. This sense of duty must be evident also to their young son and anyone who witnesses their annual trek out of Galilee and back home again. By mentioning this pattern, Luke gives us a snippet of family life in the home of Jesus. Are we surprised at God's choice of earthly parents for him?

42. When he was twelve years old, they went up to the Feast, according to the custom.

This is the point where Luke makes clear the specific age of Jesus. At the age of *twelve* Jesus is nearing a point in life where Jewish boys are expected to become aware of their duties before the Lord. Jewish literature outside the Bible states that the age of thirteen is the point at which Jewish boys become obligated to the law of Moses. But the following episode will illustrate that Jesus has advanced far beyond what is expected of other Jewish boys.

II. ON THE ROAD (LUKE 2:43-45)

A. PARENTS UNAWARE (vv. 43, 44)

43. After the Feast was over, while his parents were returning home, the boy Jesus stayed behind in Jerusalem, but they were unaware of it.

Galileans traveling to Jerusalem at feast times journey in large groups, perhaps as an extended family or clan. At his age, Jesus may be permitted to choose with whom he will travel. Under these circumstances, Mary and Joseph perhaps assume that Jesus is traveling with other members of the caravan—cousins, uncles and aunts, or neighbors from Galilee.

Nothing is said about whether Jesus remains *behind in Jerusalem* deliberately or simply gets "lost in the shuffle." In either case, he puts the time to good use while he is there, as we shall see.

44. Thinking he was in their company, they traveled on for a day. Then they began looking for him among their relatives and friends.

A day's journey means that Joseph and Mary may have walked fifteen or twenty miles of the sixty-mile journey before realizing that young Jesus is missing. This probably corresponds to the end of a day's travel when the parents look for Jesus among the other relatives before making camp for the night.

Today we might think of parents who missed seeing their twelve-year-old child for eight to ten hours as negligent in their duties. But some of our assumptions are based on modern news stories about young people being abducted and brutally treated. Even the fictional adventures of Tom Sawyer in today's context make us wonder about whether Jesus' caretakers were negligent for letting him roam so far and wide. But although travelers always face some degree of risk on this kind of journey (cf. 2 Corinthians 11:26), traveling in a large *company* reduces this risk significantly. Mary and Joseph trust those with whom they travel to be caretakers toward all of the younger people on the journey.

B. PARENTS FRANTIC (v. 45)

45. When they did not find him, they went back to Jerusalem to look for him.

It is easy to imagine the fear that Mary and Joseph feel upon discovering that their son is missing. They probably didn't get much sleep that night before turning *back* again! Jesus' absence could mean that something terrible has happened.

WHAT DO YOU THINK?

Jesus' parents were diligent about observing the Passover. How can we make sure that observances of tradition today are not merely empty routine?

HOW TO SAY IT
Corinthians. Kor-IN-thee-unz.
Deuteronomy. Due-ter-AHN-uh-me.
Galilee. GAL-uh-lee.
Jerusalem. Juh-ROO-suh-lem.
Josephus. Jo-SEE-fus.
Nazareth. NAZ-uh-reth.
Philippians. Fih-LIP-ee-unz.

DAILY BIBLE READINGS

Monday, Dec. 22—A Branch Will Grow (Isaiah 11:1-5)

Tuesday, Dec. 23—This Is My Son, My Chosen! (Luke 9: 28-36)

Wednesday, Dec. 24—Here Is My Servant (Matthew 12: 15-21)

Thursday, Dec. 25—I Am Well Pleased (Matthew 3:13-17)

Friday, Dec. 26—The Father Loves the Son (John 5:19-24)

Saturday, Dec. 27—Jesus Grew With God's Favor (Luke 2:40-44)

Sunday, Dec. 28—Jesus in His Father's House (Luke 2:45-52)

As they set out at daybreak, they are undoubtedly scanning the road on both sides with each step, fearing that they might come upon their son's lifeless body. Perhaps they fuss and blame each other along the way, exchanging mournful "if onlys." Perhaps they make promises to each other as they walk along, saying that "something like this will never happen again."

Even wonderful parents can have regrets. It is always possible to say that "more could have been done" to care for any particular youngster. But doubtless Joseph and Mary also know that every parent has limitations regarding what can be predicted about the events of life. If parents could have the kind of foresight that compares with their hindsight, parenting would be much easier indeed!

III. IN THE TEMPLE (LUKE 2:46-50)

A. JESUS ASTONISHES THE SCHOLARS (vv. 46, 47)

46. After three days they found him in the temple courts, sitting among the teachers, listening to them and asking them questions.

The *three days* can be understood to include the day's journey away from Jerusalem of verse 44, the day it takes to travel back again, and one more day in Jerusalem locating Jesus. Looking for someone in a Passover crowd is a daunting task, since Jerusalem's "normal" population of between sixty and one hundred twenty thousand can swell five-fold during this time.

But one wonders whether Joseph and Mary may have a notion about where to look for Jesus, and thus perhaps they head straight for *the temple*. Even if they suspected that he would be there, it will be no small project to locate him. The temple's complex of courts covers more than twenty-five acres!

Jewish literature indicates that during special feast days priests might come out from the temple sanctuary (where no "ordinary" worshiper can go) to mingle with the people in the various courts on the temple grounds and teach about the law. Perhaps it is in such a gathering that young Jesus stands listening to the teachers and *asking them questions*. We can barely tolerate not knowing what questions Jesus may be asking, but Luke is silent about this.

What is important to Luke is a portrait of a young Jesus completely captivated by God's truth. Even after being separated from his parents for days, his concentration is on those matters of God's will that believers find precious.

47. Everyone who heard him was amazed at his understanding and his answers.

The spiritual maturity that Jesus displays amazes the crowd. It is not just that Jesus is able to ask deep questions (2:46), but that he also provides *answers* to questions—answers that reveal deep *understanding*. His knowledge and devotion to the Lord reflect a maturity beyond his twelve years. This certainly will not be the last time in Luke's Gospel that Jesus causes astonishment (see 4:22, 32, 36; 5:26; 9:43; 11:14).

THE AMAZING CHRIST

Before television became common, there was a popular radio program called *Quiz Kids* in the 1940s. Children under the age of sixteen would be asked to answer questions that most adults would find difficult. The program had a wide audience. People were amazed that children could have so much information.

Yet amazement with children did not start in the 1940s. The teachers in the temple long ago were startled at the knowledge and wisdom of Jesus. So are we. We have the added benefit of observing his whole life, not just a few hours. We share the wonder of Charles H. Gabriel (1856–1932) who wrote, "I stand amazed in the presence of Jesus the Nazarene." Our amazement grows with each passing year. John Newton (1725–1807), the great preacher who wrote the song "Amazing Grace," once said, "I wonder that I do not wonder more!"

But some have lost their sense of wonder. They have "heard it all" and heard it so often that they no longer feel the full impact of the story of Christ. We need to sit again with those teachers in Jerusalem, with the disciples by the sea, and with the multitude on the mountain. We need to sit there long enough to recapture our amazement at the Christ who understood us so well, who loved us so much, and who saved us so freely.

Ultimately, there is nothing in the environment of Jesus that fully explains his wisdom. There is nothing in his ancestry to explain it. There is nothing in his life experience to explain it completely. The only truly satisfactory explanation is the one the Bible offers: he was the Divine Son of God. Those who do not stand amazed in his presence have closed their eyes to his genius.   —R. C. S.

B. JESUS PUZZLES HIS PARENTS (vv. 48-50)

48. When his parents saw him, they were astonished. His mother said to him, "Son, why have you treated us like this? Your father and I have been anxiously searching for you."

Luke permits us a glimpse of the emotions experienced by Joseph and Mary when they finally find their *son*. Their first reaction is amazement, which may be connected with the preceding scene (Luke 2:47) that astonished so many others in the crowd that day. Joseph and Mary, along with the others in their party, marvel as they witness their son as he sits with the teachers of Israel and communicates an impressive understanding of the Word of God.

But after their sense of amazement has settled a bit, they become aware again of the terrible sense of desperation they have felt in wondering what has happened to young Jesus. Mary is the one who takes the initiative in speaking to Jesus about this. She communicates the natural emotions of parents who have faced traumatic doubts about the safety of a child. It would be interesting to speculate why Joseph lets Mary do the talking!

49. "Why were you searching for me?" he asked. "Didn't you know I had to be in my Father's house?"

In reply to the question from his mother, Jesus gives an answer that encapsulates his mission as the Son of God. Within this answer we notice that Jesus refers to the Lord God as his Father. This implies that Jesus is Son of God in a way that describes no one else. We also can wonder if by "my Father's house" Jesus intends to make a contrast with Mary's reference to "your father" in Luke 2:48.

50. But they did not understand what he was saying to them.

The words of Jesus present riddles to Joseph and Mary that they cannot solve. Why does their boy believe that he has to be in the temple? What does he mean by speaking of the Lord God Almighty as his Father? How could their own teachings at home have given him the depth of understanding about the Lord that is evident in those conversations with the temple teachers? True, Mary and Joseph had been presented with certain facts about Jesus' birth and future ministry at the time of Jesus' conception (see Luke 1:30-33). Even so, it is obvious here that they have not been able to grasp the entire picture.

They should not be too ashamed. How could any parent understand completely what such a comment means? This same refrain will be heard more than once during the ministry of Jesus. Over and over those who witness his miracles and hear his words will be asking themselves what Jesus means by what he does or says (see Luke 4:22; 9:45; 18:34).

In all of these scenes, Luke will draw a sharp contrast between the wisdom of Jesus Christ and the slowness of those around him. What we see before us and in Luke 2:40, 47, 52 is an opening emphasis on the wisdom of Jesus.

WHAT DO YOU THINK?

Instead of answering his parents directly, Jesus asked a question—suggesting a deeper meaning without becoming condescending or disrespectful. How can we use this technique in our interactions with fellow believers as well as with unbelievers?

WHAT DO YOU THINK?

Some people today have had to choose between pleasing their Heavenly Father and their earthly families. When have you seen people make the right choice in this regard, and when have you seen them make the wrong choice?

[Use passages such as Mark 3:21; 10:29, 30; and Luke 14:26 to undergird your discussion.]

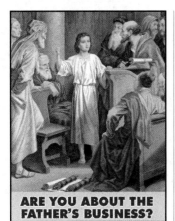

ARE YOU ABOUT THE FATHER'S BUSINESS?

Use this illustration to challenge your learners to be about "their Father's business" (KJV).

IV. TOWARD HOME (LUKE 2:51, 52)

A. JESUS' OBEDIENCE (v. 51)

51. Then he went down to Nazareth with them and was obedient to them. But his mother treasured all these things in her heart.

The previous verses by themselves may leave the impression that Jesus is a defiant child. But Luke's comment here about Jesus' obedience to his parents cancels that possibility. Thus Jesus lives through his teenage years as a young man who shows respect toward his parents. He is a lad who demonstrates his godly life before the whole village of *Nazareth*, a town of only several hundred people. Sadly, these very people will be ones to show the least faith in years to come (see Matthew 13:53-58).

B. JESUS' GROWTH (v. 52)

52. And Jesus grew in wisdom and stature, and in favor with God and men.

Luke's brief and simple statement about Jesus' boyhood years carries none of the sensationalism of the invented, non-Biblical accounts of Jesus' life that come along a few years later. Instead, Luke fully represents the human nature of Jesus in this summary, as if to say that he experiences all the normal stages of human growth—whether physical, mental, or spiritual.

Although Christ came to earth "fully God," he voluntarily put on the limitations of human flesh (Philippians 2:7). Thus his increase *in wisdom* speaks to the growth in his "fleshly side." His growth *in favor with God and men* tells us that this growth is evident to all—that he is blessed by God and accepted by people around him (cf. Proverbs 3:4). See again Luke's previous statement in Luke 2:40.

"MY, HOW YOU'VE GROWN!"

When going to visit grandmother after a long absence, every child knows exactly what she is going to say: "My, how you've grown!" And in many cases the child will be ushered to the kitchen where there are marks on the door frame. The child will stand up straight, back against the frame, and a new mark will be made. Both child and grandmother will be so proud to see how much the child has grown in stature.

The growth of the young Jesus was not just physical, but also in "wisdom" and "in favor with God and men." How sad it is if today a child's growth in stature is not matched by spiritual growth! How much sadder still if the child grows smaller spiritually while growing taller physically! Modern science teaches us that a child's physical stature is controlled by the pituitary gland and hereditary influences; thus there is little if anything we can do to make a child grow taller in stature (cf. Matthew 6:27). But we can do much to help a child grow in favor with God and people.

As adults we know we cannot govern our height. (As for our girth—that's another story!) But each of us definitely has the power to change our spiritual stature. Whether for children or adults, we want to be sure that spiritual growth is never taken for granted—that each of us "stands taller" each year. If God showed us the marks that chart our spiritual growth, would we be embarrassed to discover that we have not grown at all? Or that we have in fact shrunken in size?   —R. C. S.

CONCLUSION

This incident from the boyhood of Jesus is all that the Gospels offer us regarding this stage in Jesus' life. It is obvious that the Gospel writers were selective in their choice of material! Yet this episode well demonstrates the remarkable nature of Jesus' early development and his awareness of his identity and mission. All this was nurtured when his godly parents created for him the best spiritual environment possible.

Discovery Learning

This page contains an alternative lesson plan emphasizing learning activities. Classes desiring such student involvement will find these suggestions helpful. The next page is a reproducible activity page to further enhance discovery learning.

LEARNING AIMS

After participating in this lesson, each student will be able to:

1. List the details in today's text concerning the early years of Jesus' life, including Jesus' sense of his unique role as the Son of God.

2. Tell how the growth of Jesus in knowledge of God and interest in spiritual things reminds us of how essential it is for children to acquire a devotion for God at a young age.

3. Express a commitment to participate in helping young people to come to love the Lord.

INTO THE LESSON

As we begin this section of Scripture, we get a glimpse of Jesus' youth. Assign pairs to discuss the following questions briefly:

1. Remember being someplace as a child when your parents didn't know where you were. Where were you and what were the consequences when you were reunited?

2. Recall an occasion wherein you were the only youth in the midst of an adult conversation, yet being free to participate in the conversation? What was being discussed? How did you fare?

INTO THE WORD

Assign small groups and give each group some magazines and a sheet of poster board. Begin this activity by saying, "Read Luke 2:40-52. Then make a montage with pictures, words, or ads to describe each trait (as revealed in the text) that expresses the kind of child Jesus was.

After a time of discussion, allow each to share one of the traits identified. Continue until every trait has been identified and explained as to the kind of child Jesus was. Write these where all can see them.

As an alternative way of looking at Jesus' characteristics, play a wordgame with your class. Have the following words on individual cards: *submissive, purposive, exceptional, child, inquisitive, astonishing, "lost."* Either have members of the class volunteer to give the stimulus clues or do it yourself. Do it in the order of words given. For example, for *submissive,* the clue could be, "One who yields to the will of another is being _____" For *purposive,* the clue could be, "Rather than living life aimlessly, without a goal, it is better to be _____" When all seven words are identified, attach the seven cards to the wall or board one atop the other. When all are displayed, ask the class to note the word spelled by the first letters: *special.* Ask, "How is Jesus a special child and how is he not?" and "How is Mary and Joseph's rearing of Jesus a pattern for successful growth?"

Following the character traits discussion, ask these questions to the class:

(1) How does Jesus address his mission? (2) What benefit was it for Mary to keep all of this "in her heart"? (3) Describe the confidence Joseph and Mary placed in Jesus. Once they found him, what was their attitude? (4) Explain whether Jesus was performing the role of teacher or student in the temple. (5) Why was it important for Jesus to obey his parents? (See Exodus 20:12.) (6) How are Jesus' next eighteen years summarized?

If time permits, discuss why Luke included—at the Spirit's direction—this particular episode of Jesus' life.

INTO LIFE

Whatever the age of your class members, the following discussion and decisions should prove to be valuable. The "Train a Child" and "Commitment to Children" sections of the reproducible page that follows can be useful in the following activities.

Ask, "What did Mary and Joseph do right in helping Jesus to grow 'in wisdom and stature, and in favor with God and men'?" Such matters as their great carefulness for his physical safety as an infant, their willingness to obey God's direction in all matters—including leaving home and family, making the annual pilgrimage to Jerusalem for the Passover, trusting Jesus to be responsible—their willingness to confront Jesus when they thought he had done wrong, even though they knew his divine nature, Mary's regular consideration (treasuring these things in her heart) of who he is in dealing with him.

Designate three groups to discuss and recommend answers to the following questions: What can we as a class (or individually) do (1) to support the spiritual nurture of the children in our congregation? (2) to support parents in their godly rearing of their children? (3) to encourage the teachers who work in our children's ministry? Once the groups report and recommend, consider having the class select two or three projects to accomplish within the coming calendar year. Suggest that each member select a personal project as well.

Train a Child

Proverbs 22:6 expresses a clear and simple principle of childrearing: "Train a child in the way he should go, and when he is old he will not turn from it." Use Mary and Joseph's model to list three principles of good child nurture. Write them on the "index card" below.

Three Principles of Childrearing (From the Example of Mary and Joseph)

1.

2.

3.

A Commitment to Children

What are some practices you (and your class) can institute to show full support for the children in your congregation's ministry and the children within your family?

THINGS TO DO FOR THE CHILDREN	THINGS TO DO FOR THEIR PARENTS	THINGS TO DO FOR THEIR TEACHERS

INTEGRITY IN THE MIDST OF SUFFERING

LESSON 5

WHY TEACH THIS LESSON?

When I was a boy, my father once showed me a machine that could test the strength of metal. The machine did its work by pulling on a piece of metal until that piece broke in two. The integrity of that metal was tested by putting it under tremendous strain.

Our own integrity is also tested by strain. Maintaining integrity is easy when things are going smoothly. But when pressure and suffering come, the results are often unpredictable. Some will "sell out" for very little (e.g., Genesis 25:27-34). Others will endure great hardship and not compromise in the slightest. Job was such a one. He was able to maintain his integrity because he had prepared himself to do so. Your learners need to realize that the time to work on their character and integrity issues is *not* when "the pressure is on." Ungodly compromise is likely if they do! Rather, the time to work on integrity is now, and that's our topic for today.

INTRODUCTION

A. THE TEST NO ONE WANTS TO TAKE

How do you feel about taking tests? Some people enjoy tests, seeing them as an opportunity to prove their proficiency or expertise. Others agonize over approaching tests to the point of suffering paralysis or panic. Most of us fall somewhere between those two extremes.

There is one test, however, that we are certain no one wants to take. It is "The Job Test." Even though James 1:2, 3 tells us to consider testing a joyful experience, and even though James 5:11 holds Job up as a model, most Christians look at Job and hope they are never tested in such an intensely unpleasant way.

But what would happen if Christians today faced real persecution? What if you lost what Job lost? It is difficult to even think about what Job experienced. Yet, there are lessons for us to learn from Job's experience. As you read and learn, question the depth of your faith and trust in God. Are you ready to be tested?

B. LESSON BACKGROUND

The book of Job is layered with mysteries. There are more unanswered questions about Job than any book of the Bible (except perhaps Revelation). In most instances we know the authors, the approximate time frame, and the recipients of Bible books. Those facts influence our interpretation. With Job we are unenlightened about so many things!

We are certain, however, that Job was not a fictitious character (see Ezekiel 14:14, 20; James 5:11). He lived in "the land of Uz" (Job 1:1), which was in the territory of the Edomites, south of Palestine (Lamentations 4:21). Job was wealthy—perhaps the wealthiest man of his time (Job 1:3). Job was the head of a large family (1:2). Job was a man whose reverence for God caused him to lead a

DEVOTIONAL READING:
ROMANS 8:18-25
BACKGROUND SCRIPTURE:
JOB 1:1–2:10
PRINTED TEXT:
JOB 2:1-10

Jan
4

LESSON AIMS

After participating in this lesson, each student will be able to:

1. Summarize the trials of Job and how he responded to them with integrity.

2. Indicate ways that Christians can hold on to hope during times of testing.

3. Express a commitment to respond to trials with the same integrity shown by Job.

KEY VERSE

[Job] replied, . . . "Shall we accept good from God, and not trouble?"

In all this, Job did not sin in what he said.　　—Job 2:10

righteous life (1:1). Job lived sometime in the age of the patriarchs, between 1000 and 2000 B.C. There is no evidence that Job was aware of the Old Testament law.

The book of Job is one of the most profound writings in history. Many people today who could not readily differentiate between the Old and New Testaments could, nevertheless, tell you what the book of Job is about. Its position as a literary classic can compromise its spiritual message, however. Job is about suffering, patience, faith, and trust. It is also about the righteousness and sovereignty of God.

In order to appreciate fully this week's lesson text, you must read Job 1 as background. There you learn about Job's character, position, and family (1:1-6). After that, a scene from Heaven is presented (1:7-12). Satan (whose name means "adversary") appears before God. God asks Satan if he has noticed the faithfulness of Job (1:8). Satan accuses God of offering such protection and prosperity to Job that he has no reason to be unfaithful (1:9, 10). Satan proposes that God strike Job down—then Job will curse God (1:11). Note that Satan proposed that God do this evil to Job. God refused, but gave Satan permission to test him (1:12). God's only restriction at this point was that Job not be harmed physically (1:12).

So Satan went to do his dirty work. A succession of messengers came, telling Job of the loss of livestock and servants (1:13-17). Then, in what was surely the most devastating moment of his life, Job was told that a windstorm had demolished the house in which his children were gathered. All were dead (1:18, 19).

Despite Satan's dastardly deeds, Job remained faithful. He worshiped, blessed God, and refused to blame God (1:20, 21). In the midst of the unimaginable emotional anguish, Job did not sin (1:22). These events set the stage for this week's lesson and the three that follow in this unit of study.

I. GOD'S AFFIRMATION (JOB 2:1-3)
A. SATAN'S APPEARANCE (vv. 1, 2)
1. On another day the angels came to present themselves before the LORD, and Satan also came with them to present himself before him.

We are not told how much time elapses between the end of Job 1 and the beginning of Job 2. It may have been a relatively brief time, or it may have been years. Satan's scheme has not worked, but he is not ready to give up on Job.

Satan is mentioned by name fewer than twenty times in the Old Testament. Most of those instances are in the book of Job. Here Satan is presented in a scene from Heaven, as in 1:6. *The angels came to present themselves before the Lord.* They apparently are required to come before God to give account of their activities.

We should remember that Satan is a fallen angel, a created being, who did not hold to the truth (John 8:44). Isaiah 14:12-14 and Ezekiel 28:12-15 clearly refer to earthly kings, but may also refer to Satan as the one who incited the evil actions of those kings.

IS SATAN PRESENT EVERYWHERE?
A retired preacher went to serve a little country church. There, in Sunday school, he was asked a question no one had ever asked him before. "Is Satan, like God, present everywhere? Or is omnipresence an attribute only of God and not of the devil?" Not only had he never been asked that before, he said he had never even contemplated such a question. So he delayed answering until he could give some thought to it.

He happened to be on the campus of a Bible college so he asked one professor, "Is Satan present everywhere?" The professor answered, "He's present everywhere I've been!" That was a good answer, but another professor gave him an equally good answer. When asked, "Is Satan present everywhere?" the second professor simply replied, "The doctrine of Satan is not fully developed in the Bible."

Use this time line to help your learners keep "the big picture" in mind.

While the second professor's answer is more definitive, the first's may be more practical. We must *always* guard against temptation by assuming that Satan is constantly nearby. We never know when we will be attacked by our spiritual enemy. But judging from the book of Job, we may be certain that our experience is part of a larger drama, and that our struggle with sin and suffering is a part of a much larger struggle (cf. Revelation 12:7).   —R. C. S.

2. And the LORD said to Satan, "Where have you come from?"
Satan answered the LORD, "From roaming through the earth and going back and forth in it."

The Lord repeats his question from 1:6. God, of course, already knows where Satan has been and what he has been doing. But God's question is designed to start a conversation. In the New Testament era Satan's activities are more restricted (see Matthew 12:29; Luke 10:18; 11:21, 22; Revelation 20:1-3), but he is still quite dangerous (e.g., 1 Thessalonians 2:18; 1 Peter 5:8; Revelation 2:13). Popular culture puts Satan in a red suit with horns and a trident. But he is far more subtle and devious than that (see 2 Corinthians 11:14). Satan is not omnipotent ("all powerful") like God, but we dare not underestimate his ability to deceive.

B. GOD'S ACKNOWLEDGMENT (v. 3)

3. Then the LORD said to Satan, "Have you considered my servant Job? There is no one on earth like him; he is blameless and upright, a man who fears God and shuns evil. And he still maintains his integrity, though you incited me against him to ruin him without any reason."

As in 1:8, God asks *Satan* if he has taken note of *Job*. It almost seems as if God is daring Satan to confront him about this man. In the time that has passed between these two appearances it is obvious that Job's integrity has not waned. Can you imagine God mentioning your name to Satan? (Compare Luke 22:31.) Are you a person of such spiritual integrity that God could point to you as a model of righteousness?

Notice that it is God's turn to make an accusation against Satan by reminding him that his (Satan's) accusation about Job (1:9, 10) is proven false. Job does not honor God just to receive God's blessing. Job's reverence for God is not a *quid pro quo* ("something for something") arrangement. That had been Satan's original accusation. Now God reminds the evil one that the facts as they have unfolded prove otherwise!

Why do you honor God? Is it because you think you will be blessed if you do? Is your faith a matter of "fire insurance," just making sure you do not go to Hell? It is easy to love and honor God when all is going well and you are "on top of the mountain." What about when all is not well and you are in "the valley"?

II. SATAN'S ACCUSATION (JOB 2:4-6)

A. "NOT TOUGH ENOUGH" (vv. 4, 5)

4. "Skin for skin!" Satan replied. "A man will give all he has for his own life.

One can almost sense the venom in Satan's response to God. The phrase *Skin for skin* is difficult to interpret. It may be a well-known proverb of the time. *Satan* may be complaining to God, "I've only taken off one layer of skin, so the test so far hasn't been fair!"

We can understand Satan's intent from the context: God has not permitted Satan to be tough enough on Job. Satan is accusing God of knowing that the limit for any *man* is his very *life*—that point at which he surely will curse God—but God has not allowed Satan to push Job to that limit.

WHAT DO YOU THINK?

How do we apply to our lives the things we discover about God and Satan in the early verses of Job 2?

WHAT DO YOU THINK?

Job was a person of integrity. If you were to look for someone of integrity today, what markers would you use to verify that you had identified such a person?

HOW TO SAY IT

Corinthians. Kor-IN-thee-unz.

Edomites. EE-dum-ites.

Ephesians. Ee-FEE-zhunz.

Ezekiel. Ee-ZEEK-ee-ul or Ee-
    ZEEK-yul.

Hebrews. HEE-brews.

Isaiah. Eye-ZAY-uh.

Jeremiah. Jair-uh-MY-uh.

Lamentations. Lam-en-TAY-
    shunz.

omnipotent. ahm-NIH-poh-tent.

omnipresence. AHM-nih-PREZ-
    ence.

quid pro quo. kwid-pro-kwoh.

Thessalonians. THESS-uh-LO-
    nee-unz.

5. "But stretch out your hand and strike his flesh and bones, and he will surely curse you to your face."

Satan again tries to get God to afflict Job. Although Job has suffered great emotional stress and personal loss, he has not yet suffered physically, since his own his flesh and bones have not been affected. Is God afraid to do this? Could it be that God knows that physical pain will be Job's breaking point? Satan's method changes, but not his goal. His goal is still to get Job to *curse* God and thus destroy their relationship.

This is Satan's goal even today. He works on Christians to get them to give up on God. He knows God will not give up on us, so the breaking of the bond between us has to be our doing. C. S. Lewis's classic book *The Screwtape Letters* provides marvelous insight into the deviousness of Satan. We must be aware of his schemes (2 Corinthians 2:11), and we must not let him succeed (Ephesians 6:11)!

GOD UNDERSTANDS US BETTER THAN SATAN DOES

The man was highly successful and highly respected in his profession. So it was a shock when his son was arrested and put in jail. Then the father suffered a stroke at an age when a stroke would not have been expected. Paralyzed on one side, unable to continue in his profession, he was unable to care for his own basic needs.

This brilliant and successful man sat all day long in front of his window, completely dependent on others. His minister remarked that it must be hard to deal with a stroke like that. "Oh," the man said, "this is easy compared with knowing that my son is in prison! That's much harder to face."

Every parent can understand that anguish. But you will notice that Satan "didn't quite get it." He thought that illness, pain, and physical suffering would be worse for Job than what he already had endured. But it was not. When Job's children died, Satan already had played his highest card; he already had done his worst. God knew Job as Satan did not.

It should comfort us to know that God understands us much better than Satan does. That is why God is able to help us and to strengthen us when we face either temptations or trials. There is a wonderful declaration in 1 John 4:4: "Greater is he that is in you, than he that is in the world." Not only is God greater, he is smarter. He knows us because he made us. We always will be better off to accept his directions for life and to reject Satan's!   —R. C. S.

B. GOD'S RESPONSE (v. 6)
6. The LORD said to Satan, "Very well, then, he is in your hands; but you must spare his life."

God's confidence in Job is astonishing. God will not bring evil upon Job, but he will permit *Satan* to escalate the level of Job's suffering.

Why does Satan think that afflicting Job physically will matter any more than the previous tragedies and losses? Perhaps Satan reasons that as long as Job is healthy, he knows he can replace what he once had. He can father more children. He can rebuild his financial empire. Satan's scheme goes beyond afflicting Job's health. He wants to disable Job completely and thus rob him of hope. Satan will work in every possible way to rob us of hope as well.

Think about how important hope is. Most people can endure a great deal if they think there is light at the end of the tunnel. Satan, the "prince of darkness," will do all he can to obliterate that light! People who live without hope will eventually give up on everything, including life itself.

The writer of the New Testament book of Hebrews calls our hope in God an "anchor of the soul" (Hebrews 6:19). Such hope helps us hang on through difficult times. There is a beautiful passage about hope in Lamentations. Jeremiah lost hope, but then his hope was renewed when he remembered the compassion and faithfulness of God (Lamentations 3:1-24).

Satan is a liar and a deceiver. He will try to rob you of hope. Do not let him succeed! Remember Job and Jeremiah. Renew your hope by remembering the character of God. He is loving. He is faithful. He keeps all his promises. Our ultimate hope is in him and him alone!

III. JOB'S INFIRMITY (JOB 2:7, 8)

A. PHYSICAL (v. 7)

7. So Satan went out from the presence of the LORD and afflicted Job with painful sores from the soles of his feet to the top of his head.

We now come to a section of Job that is graphic and painful to read. Most of us have suffered with some kind of physical malady. We, however, live in an age of powerful medications and painkillers. As you read these verses, remember that Job does not have a pharmacy just down the street.

Devious as he is, *Satan* chooses as his method of torture an affliction that God himself promises (through Moses) to those who disobey; see Deuteronomy 28:35. Boils are extremely *painful* to the touch. Any pressure on them is excruciating. Imagine having them everywhere, even on your feet! Whether sitting, lying, or standing, there is no relief.

We are not given a precise diagnosis of Job's condition. We can, however, describe some of the symptoms. He lost weight (Job 19:20). He has a constant fever, and his skin has turned black (30:30). His pain is constant (30:17, 27). Poor Job—he even has bad breath (19:17)!

His appearance is so disfigured that his friends will not even recognize him when they first see him (2:12). Long bouts of physical pain can change a person's appearance. The toll on the body is reflected in the face.

Perhaps you have despaired because of physical pain. We speak of people who have high or low thresholds of pain. Some people deal with pain better than others. Most of us, however, have some means of lessening the pain. We may take medications or treatments, or we may even have surgery. For most people there is hope of the pain being decreased or completely relieved. Job, it seems, is without hope. Nothing will help. Death looms (10:20-22; 17:1).

B. SPIRITUAL (v. 8)

8. Then Job took a piece of broken pottery and scraped himself with it as he sat among the ashes.

Job's only means of temporary relief from the interminable pain and itching of the boils is scraping himself with the rough edge of *a piece of broken pottery.* We must note, however, where Job has chosen to suffer. He does not remain at home where he might have had some measure of comfort. He is outside sitting *among the ashes!*

In many ancient cultures, sitting in dust and ashes is a sign of mourning and/or repentance (Jonah 3:6; Esther 4:3). Job eventually makes it clear that sitting in ashes is an act of repentance for him (Job 42:6). That, of course, is at the end of the book, after God has chastised him.

When we first find Job sitting in the ashes, however, we may ask what he is repenting of. Has not God said of Job that he is "blameless and upright" (1:8; 2:3)? Is Job repenting at first, or does he repent in chapter 42 only after God humbles him in chapters 38 and 39? Throughout most of the book Job contends that he has not sinned. Is Job sitting in ashes at this point merely to mourn the deaths of his children? This is a question we cannot answer.

DAILY BIBLE READINGS

Monday, Dec. 29—Compare Present Suffering With Future Glory (Romans 8:18-23)

Tuesday, Dec. 30—All Things Work Together for Good (Romans 8:24-28)

Wednesday, Dec. 31—God Is for Us (Romans 8:29-33)

Thursday, Jan. 1—Nothing Can Separate From Christ's Love (Romans 8:34-39)

Friday, Jan. 2—Job Was Upright (Job 1:1-5)

Saturday, Jan. 3—Job Kept Integrity in Suffering (Job 1:13-22)

Sunday, Jan. 4—Job Would Not Curse God (Job 2:1-10)

We can safely conclude, however, that Job is a man in spiritual turmoil. He is confused. Most people of Job's time directly connect their actions with God's blessings or his wrath in a "cause and effect" way (cf. John 9:1, 2). That, in essence, is the argument of Job's so-called friends. Job must have done something terribly wrong to incur such a ferocious outpouring of God's wrath. Are they right? Is Job right? Confusion rules the day!

IV. JOB'S INTEGRITY (JOB 2:9, 10)

A. QUESTIONED (v. 9)

9. His wife said to him, "Are you still holding on to your integrity? Curse God and die!"

Someone has lamented Job's situation by noting that all he had left was a nagging *wife!* But remember that Job's wife, too, has lost children and financial security. Perhaps she thinks that some sin of her husband is responsible. In any case, she cannot understand why Job does not just give up. Perhaps if Job would *curse God*, he would be struck dead. At least then he would be out of his misery!

Some have seen a parallel between Eve and Job's wife. Both presented temptation to their husbands. Job's wife, however, was responding to the despair in her life. She lashed out at her husband and at God. She is like many who are willing to quit before the game is over.. Job's *integrity* means something to him. It apparently has little meaning to her.

B. CONFIRMED (v. 10)

10. He replied, "You are talking like a foolish woman. Shall we accept good from God, and not trouble?"

In all this, Job did not sin in what he said.

Job rebukes his wife with stinging words. Her words are *foolish*. Job's question about receiving both *good* and *trouble* from God still rings in the human heart. The word translated *trouble* is quite often translated *evil* as well. With that in mind, we should note that there are two kinds of evil: physical evil and moral evil. God does not inflict moral evil upon us (see James 1:13), and that is not what Job is talking about here. It is Satan who is responsible for offering us the moral evils that we at times so willingly embrace.

But God does cause and permit trouble and pain (which we could call "physical evil") to come into our lives. That seems to be what Job has in mind here. Sometimes God allows such evil to come about as a natural consequence of our own sin. Sometimes God sends these consequences specifically and intentionally (e.g., the plagues in Exodus 7–11). All pain and suffering can serve God's divine purposes in some way. Pain and trouble can cause us to understand our frailty and our need for God (cf. 2 Corinthians 12:7-10).

The "bottom line" here is that Job's integrity is confirmed. He refuses to curse God. He will not give up. He has faith in the ultimate goodness of God. Even when he does not understand God's ways, he acknowledges God's sovereignty and righteousness.

CONCLUSION

When life gets tough, what do you do? When the road of life gets rocky, are you tempted to take a detour? Job's integrity and trust in the face of adversity provide a powerful example for us. Remember that God knows our limits, and that he will not permit us to be tested beyond what we are able to bear (1 Corinthians 10:13). Satan loves quitters! God, on the other hand, loves those who hold on. Job did not understand everything about God, but he knew not to let go of God.

WHAT DO YOU THINK?

Why do some Christians continue to be positive while living in deplorable conditions while others seem to crumble at small inconveniences?

WHAT DO YOU THINK?

Satan loves to create confusion and wrong thinking, as we see in the attitude of Job's wife. How does Satan still use this technique today?

WHAT DO YOU THINK?

How could the caustic remark by Job's wife have been especially damaging to his emotions?

PRAYER

Father, help us hold on to you! When we are weak and struggling, help us remember Job. Reinvigorate our faith. Increase our trust. Remind us that you are always with us, even in the midst of our struggles and pain. Help us rely on the Holy Spirit's power. In Jesus' name, amen.

THOUGHT TO REMEMBER

Without God, what else is there?

Discovery Learning

This page contains an alternative lesson plan emphasizing learning activities. Classes desiring such student involvement will find these suggestions helpful. The next page is a reproducible activity page to further enhance discovery learning.

LEARNING GOALS

After this lesson each student will be able to:

1. Summarize the trials of Job and how he responded to them with integrity.

2. Indicate ways that Christians can hold on to hope during times of testing.

3. Express a commitment to respond to trials with the same integrity shown by Job.

INTO THE LESSON

During the week, ask three class members to share a brief account of a painful experience from their lives. If you can and the individuals are able to talk of it, invite someone who has lost a child, someone who has experienced great financial loss, and someone who has dealt with debilitating health. Begin class by asking them to share what they have suffered.

Ask questions such as, "Why does God want us to know of Job's intense suffering? Can we learn about suffering from reading about Job, or do we have to experience suffering firsthand?"

Say, "Job not only suffered, but he did so with integrity." Ask why this is important to God and also to us.

INTO THE WORD

Ask for seven volunteers to stand in the front of the class to hold a statement regarding Job's travails. All these will need to do is read aloud their statements when you direct. Have each of the following seven events on separate sheets:

1. Sabeans attack, take Job's oxen and donkeys, and kill the servants in charge.

2. Fire from heaven kills Job's sheep and the servants tending to them.

3. Chaldeans steal Job's camels and kill the attendant servants.

4. A strong wind destroys the house where Job's children are and kills them all.

5. Job is afflicted with sores (boils) from head to foot.

6. Job's wife challenges him to curse God and die.

7. Job's friends arrive to grieve with him (and challenge his morality and ethics).

Shuffle these so members stand randomly across the front. Have them read their statements left to right as they face the class. Once the random reading is accomplished, ask seated classmembers to look at chapters 1 and 2 of Job and tell cardholders, one at a time, to move and where to move to get these events in correct chronological order. When they have finished, have the statements reread; comment on the cumulative effect of Job's woes.

A related activity, "Woe Is Me," involving listing Job's woes is on the reproducible activity page that follows.

Next, have ten 8 1/2 by 11 sheets with the words from Job 1:22 on one side and the letters (and exclamation mark) of the word *INTEGRITY!* respectively on the reverse. The sheets will have these obverse/reverse pairings: *Job-I; did-N; not-T; sin-E; by-G; charging-R; God-I; with-T; wrongdoing-Y;* (blank)-! As you Plasti-Tak™ each sheet—words showing—onto the wall, have the class join you in saying the word on each. After all ten are up, have the class read the whole in unison.

Then tell that you have letters on the backs of these sheets, and ask the class to guess. As a correct letter is guessed, turn the sheet over. When someone knows and says the word *INTEGRITY,* turn all the letters over. Save the exclamation mark until someone comments on the "leftover" sheet. At that point, turn it over and comment, "Job demonstrated integrity with an exclamation mark!"

Establish groups of three to five people. Give each group this same written statement: "Look for the 'Secrets of Hope in Difficult Times' as seen in Job's life and reactions to great stress and distress." Give each group a different example on their assignment sheet; for example, "Be in the right relationship with God before bad things occur" (see 1:1); "Begin each day early with a time of worship to God" (see 1:5); "Be such a good example of righteousness that even Satan notices" (see 1:9); "Realize that God sends rain (and storms) on the just and the unjust" (see 2:10); "Recognize and reject bad advice" (see 2:9, 10); "Count on your friends to comfort; hope that they will" (see 2:11-13). After a time, ask for the principles they have concluded. Write them for all to see.

INTO LIFE

Give each learner a copy of the reproducible activity "Like Job" from the next page. Make certain the class members understand the four elements listed on the activity in relationship to Job's life and losses. Ask students to initial each line as they consider the implications for their own daily lives.

Woe Is Me

If anyone ever had a justifiable reason to exclaim, "Woe is me!" it was Job. Consider the devastating events the devil brought to bear on Job, with God's permission. Make a list of Job's woes as described in the following texts:

Job 1:13-15—

Job 1:16—

Job 1:17—

Job 1:18, 19—

Job 2:7, 8—

Job 2:9—

Job 2:11-13; chapters 4 and following—

Like Job

All of the godly want to emulate Job's faith: "Though he slay me, yet will I hope in him" (Job 13:15). Though Job had anguish over family, fortune, physical well being, and friends, he could still bless the Lord. If you agree with the prayer of each line of the following, put your initials to the right of each.

God give me grace to honor you

    in all family problems;   _____

    in financial difficulty;   _____

    in personal illness and weakness;   _____

    in social conflict.   _____

INTEGRITY IN SEEKING GOD

LESSON 6

WHY TEACH THIS LESSON?

All of us go through times of sorrow in this fallen world. While it's likely that none of us has suffered to the degree that Job suffered, sometimes we almost begin to believe that we have. Serious—even terminal—illness may strike on the heels of financial difficulties. Added to that may be concern for another family member who is also experiencing distressing circumstances. We may feel that we are approaching the limit of what we can bear.

When that happens, it's natural to ask God, "why?" But when we seek God in such times, it's important to keep our motives pure. Do we ask "why?" because we just want to complain and argue? Or are we really seeking to put our difficulties into God's hands so that he can take them and make something beautiful?

Maybe some of your students are experiencing near Job-like difficulties today. If they aren't, they probably will at some future time. In today's lesson, Job will give you and them some help in how to cope with such a situation. He will show us how to seek God with integrity, even in the midst of our pain.

INTRODUCTION

A. "WAIT 'TIL WE GET TO COURT"

One of my sons-in-law is a police officer in a large city. He has many interesting stories about his encounters with people who are breaking the law. When he was a rookie, he would often spend his days in a patrol car stopping speeders. Because of his youthful appearance, many would try to intimidate him by promising to show up in court to present their cases. They would often say, "Wait 'til we get to court!" In very few cases did those folks actually appear to plead their cases. In this week's lesson we will find just the opposite in a man who desperately seeks the opportunity to appear before God and plead his case.

B. LESSON BACKGROUND

Job was a figure of some note in his corner of the world (Job 1:3). Upon hearing of his unfortunate situation, three men who knew him decided to attempt to console him (2:11). Job's physical condition alarmed his friends. They sat with him for a week before even beginning to speak (2:13). Finally Job spoke, pouring out his anguish in great torrents of despair (chapter 3). Job was overcome. He said he wished that he had never been born (3:3), or that he had died at birth (3:11). Job cried out that the thing he dreaded most in life had happened (3:25). He had no consolation—no peace (3:26).

At this point Job's friends began to speak. This starts a cycle of back-and-forth discussions. Eliphaz and Bildad, two of Job's friends, address him three times. Another friend by the name of Zophar addresses Job twice. Each of their arguments is countered by Job.

This week's lesson records Job's responses to four discourses from his friends. Two of the discourses are from Bildad, one is from Zophar, and one is from Eliphaz. We know virtually nothing of these men. They are not characters who appear in any other Biblical texts. They obviously cared about Job. They obviously

DEVOTIONAL READING:
PSALM 26

BACKGROUND SCRIPTURE:
JOB 9:21-35; 13:1-27; 19:2-29; 23:2-17

PRINTED TEXT:
JOB 9:32-35; 13:20-24; 19:25-27; 23:10-12

Jan
11

LESSON AIMS

After participating in this lesson, each student will be able to:

1. Tell what Job said he wanted from God in the midst of his suffering.

2. Compare Job's need for a mediator with the need that is fulfilled by Jesus as our Mediator.

3. Praise God that we have Jesus Christ to make intercession for us.

KEY VERSE

"But I desire to speak to the Almighty and to argue my case with God."   —Job 13:3

LESSON 6 NOTES

thought they could help. Their "help," however, only deepened Job's despair and heightened his frustration (16:2).

I. DESIRE TO PLEAD A CASE (JOB 9:32-35)

As we come to Job 9, we find that Bildad has just accused Job of charging God with injustice (8:3). Bildad also contends that Job's children have lost their lives for their sins (8:4). This is fuel on the fire of Job's anguish. In this moment of great despair his friend essentially says, "Your kids got what they deserved." Bildad insists that Job can right himself with God by becoming pure and blameless (8:6). This, of course, implies that Job has been otherwise. Now Job responds.

A. THWARTED BY GOD'S NATURE (v. 32)

32. "He is not a man like me that I might answer him,
**   that we might confront each other in court.**

Job already has argued against Bildad's theory that he (Job) has not been pure and blameless (see 9:21). The problem, as Job sees it, is that he cannot appear before God to present his case. There are many problems. The first is that God is not like a human judge. *He is not a man* who sits at a bench and dispenses justice. Job is distressed because he cannot find a courtroom in which to appear! Job understands that God is not confined to flesh and bone. Job knows that he and God are not equals. Job might have said, "If only God were a man so I could talk to him face-to-face!"

B. THWARTED BY LACK OF AN INTERCESSOR (vv. 33, 34)

33. "If only there were someone to arbitrate between us,
**   to lay his hand upon us both,**

Job is not only frustrated by his inability to meet God face-to-face, he also is frustrated that there is no one to act as a judicial middleman. Job desires an arbitrator to act as an intercessor or "go-between" to help solve a dispute between two parties (cf. Deuteronomy 5:5; Galatians 3:20).

Job wants someone who can see his side of the story. Although unspoken, the idea of a mediator or arbitrator (some versions say "umpire") appeals to Job because such a go-between also can explain what has happened to Job from God's point of view. But Job understands that no such mediator exists. The thought of someone placing his *hand upon* God and explaining his ways is, of course, ludicrous. Even so, that is Job's fervent hope (see also Job 16:19-21).

The great blessing of the Christian life is in knowing that the Mediator whom Job longs for has made himself known. Jesus Christ is that Mediator (1 Timothy 2:5). Jesus is perfectly capable of representing us to the Father because Jesus is fully God (John 1:1; 10:30; 14:9-11).

Jesus is also uniquely qualified to be our High Priest because his sacrifice accomplished what the sacrifice of animals could not. His blood did not merely forestall God's judgment. His blood actually has the power to remove the stain of sin from the human soul (Hebrews 9:11-14).

We realize that no one stands before God as blameless. All people are sinners (Romans 3:23). No one meets God's standard of perfect righteousness. Thus, our view of our intercessor is different from that of Job. We do not need one who will present a call for justice on our behalf. Justice is precisely what we do not want! If justice were meted out to us, we would have no hope. Our Mediator is one who pleads our case as those who have been justified by his sacrifice on our behalf. His blood has covered our sin. His death paid the penalty that God's righteousness demanded. Praise God for such a powerful and loving Mediator!

WHAT DO YOU THINK?

Job wanted to declare his case to the Judge of the universe. How is Christ similar to and different from a lawyer who presents a case before a judge on another's behalf?

34. "... someone to remove God's rod from me,
so that his terror would frighten me no more.

Job's frustration bubbles over into a cry of fear and dread. If there were an intercessor, he could explain Job's innocence. Surely then God would then quit punishing Job! But there is no such mediator or arbitrator. Does Job think God is continuing to punish him because he is unaware of Job's innocence? Whatever the case, Job is tired of living in fear.

From the beginning of time people have associated divine blessings and curses with their behavior. In last week's lesson, we noted John 9:1, 2 in this regard. Ancient people see things such as droughts or fires as divine punishment for evil. If one reads the entire book of Job, it seems that Job's friends are trying to persuade him that some evil in his life has brought about his suffering. Jesus opposed this kind of thinking in Luke 13:1-5.

We should also remember that while there are indeed built-in consequences for many sins, not everyone who sins will automatically suffer those consequences. Some people smoke and never get cancer. Indeed, Bible writers noticed that evil people seemed to prosper while decent people suffered (cf. Ecclesiastes 8:14; Jeremiah 12:1; Malachi 3:14, 15). This is all part of living in a fallen world where God has allowed free will.

The Bible does speak of God's correction or chastisement (Psalm 89:32; 94:12; Proverbs 3:11, 12; Lamentations 3:1). God's punishment can be an act of loving discipline (Revelation 3:19). Parents know that correcting children is not always easy, but is a necessary part of their upbringing. Repeating Proverbs 3:11, the writer of Hebrews 12:5 reminds us that we are not to take the Lord's discipline lightly. God is not anxious to punish us. He is not "quick with the whip." His discipline and correction are for our benefit (Hebrews 12:6-11). It is to keep us from further damage and eternal harm.

But remember: Job is not being punished. However, Job thinks that that is what is happening. His incorrect assumption adds to his misery and frustration. Do we ever fall into this same trap?

LIVING IN FEAR

There is a section along the North Carolina coast called *Cape Fear.* There are several explanations offered for this unusual name. Some say the name was given because early settlers feared attack by Native American Indians. Some say that they feared the pirates who once roamed that coast. Others say it was a more generalized fear, that the broad estuary of the river left them vulnerable to invasion.

Today the only thing you have to fear is the traffic in Wilmington or sunburn on Wrightsville Beach! Perhaps the best explanation is that it was not originally named *Cape Fear* at all—that it was actually named *Cape Fair* and some mapmaker misread it.

Certainly it is true that those who decide to live in fear will do so no matter how fair the circumstances. Of course, we need a healthy respect for danger. Living without fear does not demand that we forget to be prudent and careful. But it does mean that we should never let fear dominate out lives. To fear God means that we respect him and show him reverence.

Some say that Abraham Lincoln's Bible naturally fell open to Psalm 34, suggesting that he may often have turned there. Psalm 34:4 states, "I sought the Lord, and he answered me; he delivered me from all my fears." Of course, our love is never perfect, but God's love *is* perfect. A loving God does not want us to live in fear.   —R. C. S.

C. THWARTED BY REALITY (V. 35)

35. "Then I would speak up without fear of him,
but as it now stands with me, I cannot."

HOW TO SAY IT

Bildad. BILL-dad.
Corinthians. Kor-IN-thee-unz.
Deuteronomy. Due-ter-AHN-uh-me.
Ecclesiastes. Ik-LEEZ-ee-AS-teez.
Eliphaz. EL-ih-faz.
Galatians. Guh-LAY-shunz.
Hebrews. HEE-brews.
Isaiah. Eye-ZAY-uh.
Jeremiah. Jair-uh-MY-uh.
Lamentations. Lam-en-TAY-shunz.
Malachi. MAL-uh-kye.
Zophar. ZO-far.

WHAT DO YOU THINK?

Like Job, some people spend much time living in a theoretical world of "But what if . . ." or "If only. . . ." How do we help people move on to more productive thinking?

WHAT DO YOU THINK?

Job's clumsy friends essentially said, "You got what you deserved." How do we sort out the punishment caused by sin, the testings that come because of Satanic attack, and sufferings from random occurrences? Why should we even try?

Job has a bad case of the "if onlys." If only there were an intercessor! If only he were not so afraid! If only he could appear before God! If only he could *speak* to God face-to-face (cf. Exodus 33:11)!

Job knows, however, that these are pipe dreams. As much as he might wish these things to be true, they are not so. It seems, at least at this point, that it does not occur to Job that he can cry out to God and be heard. Job incorrectly assumes that God is punishing him and is, therefore, unwilling to listen to him.

Incorrect assumptions about God still separate many people from him. That is why knowing and understanding the Bible is so important. When we study God's Word, we have knowledge, not assumptions. How spiritually priceless!

II. DESIRE TO PRESERVE A STANDING (JOB 13:20-24)

In Job 12 and 13 we find Job responding to Zophar. Zophar has been rather harsh with Job. Like the others, Zophar seemed to believe that if Job is suffering, he must have sinned. Zophar seemed to think Job has sinned so grievously that he is not being punished enough (11:6). He wondered why Job would think God should ignore his wickedness (11:11). He accused Job of being vain (11:12). He counseled Job to confess and repent of his wickedness (11:12-14). Job's reply to this nonsense begins with sarcasm (12:2) and moves to issues of Job's fears.

A. JOB'S FEAR OF FEAR (vv. 20, 21)

20. *"Only grant me these two things, O God,*
    and then I will not hide from you.

Living in fear is stressful, and Job wants to *hide from* God (cf. Job 6:4). If God will *grant* just *two things,* then Job will come out of hiding and present himself to God. We will see what two things Job requests in the following verses.

21. *"Withdraw your hand far from me,*
    and stop frightening me with your terrors.

The first of two things Job wants God to do is simply to leave him alone. Fear does strange things to people. Job is afraid of continuing to live in such fear of God that he feels the need to hide (v. 20). President Roosevelt rallied the U.S. with his declaration, "The only thing we have to fear is fear itself." First John 4:18 says that fear is cast out by perfect love. Christians should have an appropriate respect for God, but not a paralyzing fear. Experiencing God's love removes fear.

B. JOB'S FEAR OF SILENCE (v. 22)

22. *"Then summon me and I will answer,*
    or let me speak, and you reply.

Job's second request is communication. He wants the opportunity to talk to God. If God will call, Job will *answer* and clear the record. Job fears silence!

C. JOB'S FEAR OF IGNORANCE (vv. 23, 24)

23. *"How many wrongs and sins have I committed?*
    Show me my offense and my sin.

Job argues that if God would just tell him what he has done wrong, he could make it right. Job desires a list with categories, dates, and places. Most of us do not have Job's problem. We are all too familiar with our *sins!*

24. *"Why do you hide your face*
    and consider me your enemy?"

Job also fears that he has lost his standing with God. Job wants God to know that he is not his *enemy!* Even though he does not know the nature of his sin, whatever it might be it is not rebellion against God. And Job has not become God's enemy in response to his (Job's) travails. Job wants to preserve his standing before God. He does not want that standing diminished by fear, silence, or ignorance.

III. DESIRE TO PRESERVE A LEGACY (JOB 19:25-27)

In Job 18 we find Job responding to a second discourse from Bildad. Bildad saw Job's rebuttals as refusals to acknowledge that he has been caught in his sins (18:8-10). Bildad has also referred to a man's legacy (18:17). In chapter 19 we see that Job is certainly one who does not want his legacy tarnished!

A. JOB BELIEVES IN HIS REDEEMER (v. 25)

25. *"I know that my Redeemer lives,*
    and that in the end he will stand upon the earth.

Some speculate that Job thinks he may die, and he wants to reaffirm his ultimate trust in God. No matter what has happened, Job's faith in God remains unshaken. Job believes God ultimately will vindicate him.

Have events in your life shaken your confidence in God? Do you believe Romans 8:28? Is your faith as solid as that of Job? What will your own spiritual legacy be?

A SOURCE OF COMFORT

When former British Prime Minister Winston Churchill died, he was not buried in Westminster Abbey as might have been expected. Certainly he was important enough to have been buried there with others who greatly influenced the nation. But he chose in advance to be buried in the little village cemetery at Bladon, near his birthplace and where his family members were buried.

One enters the cemetery through a covered archway called a *lych-gate*. The gateway is covered as a place for funeral processions to wait until the minister can come out of the church and lead the way. As one leaves the cemetery and passes again under the lych-gate, a quotation from the Bible is visible, engraved across the top of the arch. It is a verse in the *King James Version* from this lesson: "I KNOW THAT MY REDEEMER LIVETH."

What a comfort to any Christian family leaving the grave of one they loved! What a comfort to us! It is remarkable that Job had this confidence long before the promises of Jesus in John 14, long before Jesus himself rose from the dead. If Job could believe it, with the limited information he had, surely we can believe it all the more.

To know that our Redeemer lives is the basis for our confidence that we, too, shall survive the grave. It is not surprising that this grand text has found its way into sacred music and sermons. It is a glorious affirmation that gives us comfort when we grieve and gives us hope when we contemplate our own deaths.   —R. C. S.

B. JOB BELIEVES IN LIFE AFTER DEATH (v. 26)

26. *"And after my skin has been destroyed,*
    yet in my flesh I will see God;

In the Old Testament there are just a few affirmations of life after death, and this is one of them. Job not only believes in such life, he even indicates a belief in a bodily resurrection (cf. Isaiah 26:19; Daniel 12:2). The New Testament clearly establishes the promise of this resurrection (Acts 24:15; Romans 8:23; 1 Corinthians 15:12-55; etc.). Job's legacy is that of a man who believes God can do anything, including making the dead live again.

C. JOB BELIEVES HIS LONGING WILL BE FULFILLED (v. 27)

27. *" . . . I myself will see him*
    with my own eyes—I, and not another.
    How my heart yearns within me!"

DAILY BIBLE READINGS

Monday, Jan. 5—Vindicate Me, O Lord (Psalm 26:1-7)

Tuesday, Jan. 6—I Walk in My Integrity (Psalm 26:8-12)

Wednesday, Jan. 7—In Trouble I Call on You (Psalm 86:1-7)

Thursday, Jan. 8—Job Wishes to Speak to God (Job 9:32-35)

Friday, Jan. 9—Let Me Speak, and You Reply (Job 13:20-24)

Saturday, Jan. 10—I Know That My Redeemer Lives (Job 19:23-28)

Sunday, Jan. 11—He Knows the Way I Take (Job 23:8-12)

PRAYER

Father, increase our faith! Help us endure even when we do not understand. Help us remember your grace. When we are tempted to complain about the unfairness life, remind us of the unfairness of Jesus' sufferings. May we trust you more. In Jesus' name, amen.

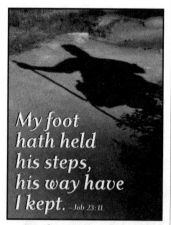

My foot hath held his steps, his way have I kept. —Job 23:11

Job is convinced that he will one day *see* God face-to-face. That meeting will fulfill the longing of Job's heart. Job understands that he may not get to have that meeting with God right away, but he believes that God truly knows his heart. God will not condemn him unjustly. Most of all, Job simply yearns to see God. He wants people to remember that yearning.

IV. DESIRE TO BE ACKNOWLEDGED (JOB 23:10-12)

In chapter 22 we find Job confronting the arguments of Eliphaz. Eliphaz has accused Job of social injustice, of exploiting the poor (22:6-9). He also seems to accuse Job of treasuring his gold and silver more than he treasures God (22:23-26).

A. GOOD AS GOLD (v. 10)

10. *"But he knows the way that I take;*
    when he has tested me, I will come forth as gold.

Job turns Eliphaz's accusation on its ear. Job does not treasure precious earthly metal, but he wants to be seen as a treasured asset in God's eyes. Job knows that God treasures faith. Job may not understand why he is suffering, but he believes that God will, in the end, acknowledge his ultimate faithfulness.

B. ON THE STRAIGHT AND NARROW (v. 11)

11. *"My feet have closely followed his steps;*
    I have kept to his way without turning aside.

The Bible often uses road, path, or *way* metaphors for the godly life (e.g., Psalm 16:11; 119:105). Job knows that he has stayed on the right path. His footsteps have not wavered. He has not taken any detours from God.

Jesus speaks of two paths in Matthew 7:13, 14. One leads to life. The other leads to destruction. Have you chosen the path that leads to life?

C. RECOGNIZING THE SOURCE OF LIFE (v. 12)

12. *"I have not departed from the commands of his lips;*
    I have treasured the words of his mouth more than my daily bread."

Job continues to profess his innocence. He also acknowledges his complete dependence upon God. God's instruction is as necessary for Job's spiritual life as *daily bread* is for his physical life.

In turn, Job wants God to acknowledge his faith—a faith that is completely dependent on God. Job is no longer acknowledged as wealthy and influential. He is no longer acknowledged as the father of a large family. But he clings to the hope of being acknowledged as God's faithful servant. This is one of the reasons the accusations of his friends wound him so grievously.

God will later tell Moses, "Man does not live on bread alone but on every word that comes from the mouth of the Lord" (Deuteronomy 8:3). Jesus will repeat much the same thing (Matthew 4:4). Job understood this truth centuries before!

CONCLUSION

Most people have heard the saying, "There is a right way and a wrong way to do everything." Job, as far as he is able, seeks God the right way. Job overwhelmingly upholds God as just, although we notice just a couple of places where Job begins to question that justice (see Job 19:7 and, for next week, 27:2). These can be explained as Job grasping for straws in the midst of his enormous pain. God will correct Job's slip-ups in his response (40:8), but overall God will praise Job for speaking "of me what is right" (42:7). Even though Job complained to God, he did it with integrity.

Discovery Learning

This page contains an alternative lesson plan emphasizing learning activities. Classes desiring such student involvement will find these suggestions helpful. The next page is a reproducible activity page to further enhance discovery learning.

LEARNING GOALS

After this lesson each student will be able to:

1. Tell what Job said he wanted from God in the midst of his suffering.

2. Compare Job's need for a mediator with the need that is fulfilled by Jesus as our mediator.

3. Praise God that we have Jesus Christ to make intercession for us.

INTO THE LESSON

Before class get a large sheet of newsprint and felt-tip pens. Cut the newsprint into fairly narrow length-wise sections to create a narrow strips of paper like banners.

Assign class members to groups of three to five. Distribute banner paper and pens to each group. Distribute copies of the reproducible activity "Close to God" from the next page, and ask learners to fill in their answers and discuss them within the groups. Afterwards, allow three minutes for the group members to jot down ideas on their banners and decorate them in any way they wish. Then have each group tell some of their ideas or experiences. Display each banner. (Students can write on the "banner" on the reproducible activity if you are unable to secure larger banners as described above.)

Then say, "In spite of all the negatives Job experienced, he never gave up; he always felt close to God. What a testimony!"

INTO THE WORD

State: "The Scriptures in this lesson contain some of the most significant thoughts Job had regarding seeking the Lord." Distribute copies of the reproducible activity "Making the text Mine" from the next page. Divide the class into four groups and ask each group to paraphrase one of the texts on the activity sheet. Each group is to write descriptive conclusions of Job's feelings, what Job says about his friends, and what he asks from God.

Upon completion of each group's paraphrase, allow each to share its completed section; then discuss their findings with the entire class. In the discussion, make sure the groups have included the following ideas:

Job 9: Job wished he could come to trial with God, so that he could prove his innocence. *Job 13:* Job begged God to withdraw his terrifying hand and explain his sin or give him an opportunity to plead his innocence. *Job 19:* Job affirmed that his Redeemer lives, with confidence that one day he would experience that truth (a clear Old Testament affirmation of life after death.) *Job 23:* Job reaffirmed that his testing would prove him to be faithful.

Say to the class, "It has been said that 'The person who acts as his own lawyer has a fool for a client.' In a real sense, Job was in the difficult place of having to represent himself legally before God. (And any such representation has a built-in foolishness!) How is the Christian advantaged by having Christ to represent him or her before God?" Assign the following Scriptures to be read aloud. After each is read, ask, "What do you hear from this that gives us an advantage over Job and for which we need to praise God?" Scriptures: Matthew 3:16, 17; John 15:13-16; John 17:24; Hebrews 4:14-16; 1 Peter 3:21b, 22; 1 John 2:1, 2.

INTO LIFE

This activity will help each student relate Job's confession of faith in Job 19:25 to his or her own life situation. Write these instructions and show them:

Discuss this question: "Can you say with Job, 'I know my Redeemer lives'?"

Sing as a group the hymn, "Redeemed," especially verse three. Consider the meaning of the word *Redeemer*, and name an attitude or habit you want Christ to redeem you from right now.

Discuss the following: "If Job, from his perspective, could know with assurance that his Redeemer was alive, what is keeping you from the same assurance that your Redeemer can free you?"

Ask groups who did the paraphrase activity to discuss these issues. Provide every class member with paper or a 3 x 5 card for those who need them. Ask each one in the class to rephrase the paraphrase to show what his or her love for God has caused him or her to do.

Then ask each group to pray for the power of Christ to cover the current situations in their lives. Tell them you will lead them in directed prayer by using phrases from Hebrews 7:25-28. As you read the following phrases one at a time, pause to allow brief prayers of thanksgiving: (1) Jesus "is able to save completely"; (2) Our high priest is "holy, blameless, pure, set apart from sinners, exalted above the heavens"; (3) He "does not need to offer sacrifices day after day . . . He sacrificed for their sins once for all, when he offered himself"; (4) Some advocates "are weak" but he "has been made perfect forever."

Close to God

Think about the following questions:

When do you feel the closest to God?

☐ When praying? ☐ When worshiping? ☐ When in church?

☐ When listening to music? ☐ When deeply hurt? ☐ Outdoors in nature?

Why do you think that is?

Make a banner, jotting down ideas, words, or pictures that come to mind.

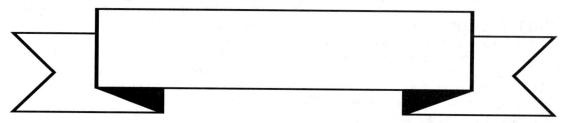

Making the Text Mine

If the teacher assigns groups to develop paraphrases of the following texts, get the gist of each response when it is given. If no groups are used, write your own paraphrase for each.

GROUP 1:   Job 9:32-35

GROUP 2:   Job 13:20-24

GROUP 3:   Job 19:25-27

GROUP 4:   Job 23:10-12

INTEGRITY IN EVERYDAY LIFE

LESSON 7

WHY TEACH THIS LESSON?

TV producers are always looking for a new "angle" to attract and hold an audience. "Reality TV" was one such angle that really took off a few years ago, especially the *Survivor* series. People flocked to their TVs to watch with fascination the secret infighting and backstabbing that occurred as people set aside all pretense of morals and ethics to gain cash prizes. In a ten-second advertisement I saw for one of these shows, a contestant frankly admitted that, "It looks like I'm going to have to throw my ethics out the window."

Job, by contrast, was a man whose integrity was not for sale under any circumstances. God himself proclaimed that there was no one else on earth like this man (Job 1:8). Can there be any higher praise than this? Perhaps Satan will not challenge any of us to the degree that he challenged Job. But challenges to our character are certain to come nonetheless. When we maintain our integrity in everyday life, we maintain our Christian witness as well. Today's lesson lets us see how.

INTRODUCTION

A. "WHATEVER YOU WANT TO HEAR"

The proliferation of television cable channels has brought some great old movies to the small screen. Some of the cops-and-robbers movies have scenes in them that are very similar to one another. A suspect is brought into the police station for interrogation. The suspect is put under bright lights and given "the third degree." The policemen blow cigarette smoke in the suspect's face as they play "good cop, bad cop."

Finally, exhausted and desperate, the suspect blurts out, "Whatever you want to hear, I'll say it!" The movie plot then usually hinges on the truth or falsehood of the suspect's confession. Another very dramatic scene may play out in the courtroom when the suspect recants his confession and accuses his interrogators of coercion.

Job's friends were definitely guilty of coercion. They did not use bright lights and cigarette smoke to weaken Job's resolve, but their constant accusations take a toll. Can Job remain steadfast in pleading his innocence? Will Job maintain his integrity in the midst of such vile assaults on his character?

B. LESSON BACKGROUND

The text for this week's lesson records portions of Job's final discourse to his three friends. After "The words of Job are ended" in Job 31:40, Job will not speak again until he addresses the Lord in chapter 42 (included in next week's lesson). Job has heard three discourses from Eliphaz, three discourses from Bildad, and two discourses from Zophar. These discourses, filled with accusation and acrimony, could have worn Job down. A lesser man might have simply thrown up his hands and said, "Okay. Okay. Whatever you say. I'm guilty." Not Job!

Job responded to Bildad's last discourse (Job 25) with a resounding acknowledgment of God's power (Job 26). Job's faith is intact. Job will not, however, capitulate to his friends' requests for confessions of guilt.

DEVOTIONAL READING:
PSALM 15
BACKGROUND SCRIPTURE:
JOB 27:1-6; 31
PRINTED TEXT:
JOB 27:2-5; 31:5-15, 24-28

LEARNING AIMS

After participating in this lesson, each student will be able to:

1. Summarize Job's arguments that he has been falsely accused.

2. Explain how truth is the best defense against false accusations.

3. Give a specific example of how a person overcame accusations with the truth.

Jan
18

KEY VERSE

"As long as I have life within me, the breath of God in my nostrils, my lips will not speak wickedness, and my tongue will utter no deceit." —Job 27:3, 4

LESSON 7 NOTES

I. THE TESTED MAN (JOB 27:2-5)

A. SPEAKING FROM PAIN (vv. 2-4)

2. "As surely as God lives, who has denied me justice,
    the Almighty, who has made me taste bitterness of soul,

Job now has endured three cycles of conversation with Eliphaz, Bildad, and Zophar—Job's "miserable comforters" (16:2). The oath "As surely as God lives," familiar in Eastern custom, is seen as an invitation for God to strike the speaker dead if he does not tell the truth. This is a desperate measure to persuade Job's accusers of the veracity of his denials. He's "had it" with them! They apparently get the message because after this response we hear no more from those three.

Job does not feel that he has been given his "day in court." He has been denied the appropriate opportunity for just judgment. He will not accuse God of some fault in finding him guilty.

Job does, however, call out to God and decry his lack of opportunity to defend himself. God is the one whom Job believes has *denied* him *justice* (cf. 19:7).

Job does not deny that he is suffering and bitter. He cries out to know why he is suffering. He mistakenly attributes his suffering solely to God. It apparently does not occur to him that Satan could be involved.

People still react as Job did. When something bad happens, they immediately question God. Why do people never give proper credit to Satan? He is the maker of mischief and sower of sorrow in people's souls.

3. "... as long as I have life within me,
    the breath of God in my nostrils,

Job's resolve is expressed in these words. Even to his last *breath* he will remain steadfast in his denials. Job understands that God is his Creator (e.g., Job 26:7-14). It is God who has breathed into man and given life (Genesis 2:7; Job 12:10). Even though Job does not understand why God is permitting such evil to come to him, Job will acknowledge God as the one who created and sustained his *life*.

4. "... my lips will not speak wickedness,
    and my tongue will utter no deceit."

Job has not and will not lie! The irony of Job's situation is that in order to please his friends, he would have to tell lies. He would have to become what they falsely accuse him of being.

There are many ways for a person's speech to become wicked. The New Testament warns about the many evils of the tongue (James 3:1-12). Are you ever guilty of slander, gossip, or *deceit*? Is God honored in your language? Is it sometimes tempting to combat lies told about us by lying about the teller of those lies? Job staunchly refuses to commit evil by speaking that which is not true.

TELLING THE TRUTH

Not so long ago a very prominent American official admitted to lying under oath. Someone wrote to a newsmagazine defending him and said, "Let's be honest. Everybody lies." What an obviously self-contradictory statement!

The first half of the statement we can all agree with. We should be honest. We do not always have to be brutally frank, however—that could be hurtful. But we do have to be honest.

The second statement in the quotation is, of course, wrong. It is simply not true that everybody lies. It used to be said of an honest man, "His word is his bond." It meant that he did not have to swear to tell the truth—he always told the truth. He did not have to pledge a sum of money to guarantee that what he said was the truth.

We can depend on the truthfulness of Jesus who "committed no sin, and no deceit was found in his mouth" (1 Peter 2:22). We can depend on the truthfulness of his apostles. The world needs to be able to depend on the truthfulness of believers.

WHAT DO YOU THINK?

Insurance companies refer to natural disasters as "acts of God" in their insurance policies. Is this fair to God? Why, or why not?

"All the while my breath is in me, and the spirit of God is in my nostrils; my lips will not speak wickedness, nor my tongue utter deceit." —Job 27:3, 4

This illustration of verses 3 and 4 will challenge your learners to consider their own loyalties.

We do it to be like Christ. We do it because we know the destiny of all liars (Revelation 21:8). We do it because we know that "The Lord detests lying lips" (Proverbs 12:22). If Job in his day could keep his tongue from deceit, surely we who have both the example of Christ and the power of the Holy Spirit can do it, too.   —R. C. S.

B. Admitting No Wrong (v. 5)
5. *"I will never admit you are in the right;*
      till I die, I will not deny my integrity."

The *you* in this verse is plural as Job addresses all three friends. They have not succeeded. Job will not *admit* that they are accurate in their portrayals of his character. They want Job to be contrite. Instead, he is stubborn. The more they accuse Job, the more he digs in his heels. He will "stick to his story" until he dies!

Some people admire Job's resolve, but question his pragmatism. Job can end the whole thing by saying, "Yeah, you guys are right!" Then they can leave the dump, go to Job's house for some pie and coffee, and Job can send them back home. At least he then will relieve himself of the suffering of listening to their harping. To do so, however, would compromise his *integrity*. Job is not that kind of fellow. Truth means more to him than convenience. Can that be said of you?

II. THE TEFLON MAN (JOB 31:5-15, 24-28)
A. "Hypocrisy" Won't Stick (vv. 5-8)
5, 6. *"If I have walked in falsehood*
      or my foot has hurried after deceit—
   let God weigh me in honest scales
      and he will know that I am blameless—

Job's refusal to admit any wrongdoing leaves him vulnerable to accusations of hypocrisy. How can anyone be so perfect? A character in Shakespeare's play *Hamlet* was suspicious of another who "doth protest too much." Often the more guilt a person bears, the louder he or she proclaims innocence. We know this is not the case with Job, however, because of what God says about him in Job 1:8.

So Job still defends his integrity with every attack. His "walk" with the Lord is true, and he again pleads for the opportunity to prove that he is genuine in thought and action. Many goods today are preweighed on electronic scales. But in ancient times balance *scales* were part of everyday life. Several passages note the Lord's view of honest scales, plus his own actions in weighing motives and value (see Psalm 62:9; Proverbs 11:1; 16:2; 20:23; 21:2; Isaiah 40:12). Job earlier alluded to balance scales in describing the depth of his agony (Job 6:2, 3).

Job wants the opportunity to vindicate himself by having God *weigh* him in an accurate scale to determine the genuineness of his life. He is not a hypocrite. His integrity is not an act!

7. *"... if my steps have turned from the path,*
      if my heart has been led by my eyes,
      or if my hands have been defiled,

Even under intense cross-examination, Job has not "changed his story." He has walked the straight and narrow. He has not let his *heart* be *led* by his *eyes* (cf. Job 31:1). His friends have spoken abstractly about God's punishment of evildoers, but they can't point specifically to any area where Job's hands are sullied by the filth of corruption (6:24, 30). Job's moral résumé is pretty impressive!

Most of us know that we could not say what Job said. We have not always walked God's path. We may have been on God's path at one time, but we found lots of detours. Most of us have been enticed by things we have seen, and we have let our desires run ahead of our discretion and dedication to God. Most of

What Do You Think?

Look at how Job "dug in his heels" in the face of an onslaught! If you had to face such a situation, how would you find the words and the strength to hold to the truth, even if you were "a minority of one"?

What Do You Think?

Job was willing to be weighed "in honest scales" so God would know of his integrity. Would you be willing to have your integrity tested in this way? Why, or why not?

us have "dirty *hands*." The businessperson who sings loudly in church on Sunday and cuts under-the-table deals on Monday cannot make Job's claim. That businessperson is the poster child for hypocrisy. Job is ready to have all his actions weighed in whatever perfect balance scales God has.

8. "... then may others eat what I have sown,
and may my crops be uprooted."

In being willing to let another *eat what* he has *sown,* Job is ready to pay a heavy penalty if he is guilty of any of the offenses of verse 7. He offers what is equivalent to giving away a year's salary. Job, however, knows that he has nothing to worry about. He is not guilty of the offenses. He could make such an offer because he knows nothing is at risk. His conscience is clear.

Job's offer reminds us of a similar offer by a man who met Jesus. Zacchaeus was a wealthy tax collector who lived in Jericho (Luke 19:1, 2). Zacchaeus's life changed that day he met Jesus. Expressing his commitment in terms most familiar to him, Zacchaeus told Jesus that if he had cheated anyone, he would repay that person fourfold (Luke 19:8), in addition to offering half his goods to the poor. Was Zacchaeus guilty of cheating people and trying to make that right by his offer? Or was Zacchaeus like Job—confident that he was guiltless? Scholars debate the issue. The important point in both cases is that the offer was made. In Job's case, the offer is made because he knows that he can stand the scrutiny.

Try as they may, Job's friends cannot make the charge of hypocrisy stick. Job calls on God as his witness (Job 31:4). Job knows that God knows his heart. There is no pretense to Job. He does not fear examination. Hypocrites fear that someone will find out about the "other side" of their lives. Not so, Job!

B. "Adultery" Won't Stick (vv. 9-12)
9. "If my heart has been enticed by a woman,
or if I have lurked at my neighbor's door,

Job's friends do not make a specific accusation regarding his sexual purity. But since sexual temptation is so strong for men, Job may be addressing the matter just to "cover all the bases." For whatever reason, Job makes it clear that he is not guilty of sexual sin (again, see 31:1). He has not lurked at his *neighbor's door* to get a peek at his neighbor's wife or perhaps to find a woman alone in the house.

10. "... then may my wife grind another man's grain,
and may other men sleep with her.

Job's offer seems almost perverse. If he has been guilty of sexual sin, then he offers his wife in both the domestic sense (grinding *grain*) and the sexual sense (*sleep with her*). This may seem callous, but remember—Job knows that no charge can stand against him. Even though his wife offered him no comfort (2:9), he is not contemplating getting rid of her! He is not looking for another woman. This reveals the seriousness of Job's convictions and commitments.

11. "For that would have been shameful,
a sin to be judged.

To be guilty of sexual *sin,* especially the taking of another man's wife, is abominable. Most cultures of ancient times considered marriage to be sacred (unlike today). The breaking of the marriage bond through adultery is damaging to the individuals involved and to society as a whole (like today). One of the strongest threads in the fabric of any culture is the stability of the family unit. Jesus redefined adultery—moving beyond the act to include the desire of the heart as well (Matthew 5:27, 28). If Job is guilty of adultery, why has he not been judged?

12. "It is a fire that burns to Destruction;
it would have uprooted my harvest.

What Do You Think?

Job knew where the boundaries of sexual purity were. How have these lines been blurred today, and why should we care?

Job understands the insidious power of sexual temptation, even though it is very unlikely that he has access to Solomon's teaching in Proverbs 6:23–7:27. The word translated *Destruction* is the Hebrew word *Abaddon*. It refers to the world of the dead (Job 26:6; 28:22; Proverbs 27:20). Sexual sin is a killer! AIDS has made this true in the physical sense. It has always been true in the spiritual sense.

Job realizes the far-reaching effects of sexual sin. Were he guilty, even his prosperity will be forfeit. How many times have we seen such a scenario unfold before us? A man gets involved in an affair and before long he has lost his wife, his children, his job, his house, and eventually his life savings. Most seriously, that man also loses his relationship with God (cf. 1 Corinthians 6:12-20).

The charge of adultery will not stick to Job. It is not merely that he has not been caught in sexual sin. He has, in fact, not committed sexual sin.

C. "INJUSTICE" WON'T STICK (vv. 13-15)

13. "If I have denied justice to my menservants and maidservants
    when they had a grievance against me,

Job's blameless behavior extends to the treatment of his servants. He has treated them justly, even when they had grievances against him personally.

Job apparently understands the important dynamic of social justice with those who are (in society's eyes) in an inferior position in life. While a grievous sin like adultery may have been readily noticed, the treatment of servants is of little social concern in Job's day. Despite that, Job knows that he has dealt with his servants justly; he also makes his claim knowing that three of his servants are still alive to contradict him if he is lying (Job 1:15-17).

14. ". . . what will I do when God confronts me?
    What will I answer when called to account?

Job understands that he is accountable to *God* for his treatment of others. This is not merely a matter between humans. God watches and knows how people in authority treat those in "lesser stations." Part of Job's motivation in treating others correctly is his realization of accountability to God. The apostle Paul addresses the same issue in Ephesians 6:9. See also James 5:1-6.

15. "Did not he who made me in the womb make them?
    Did not the same one form us both within our mothers?"

Job shows remarkable humility. He understands that class positions in society are inventions of man, not God. God is the Author of all life, regardless of earthly position. All humanity is precious to God! Jesus provided a powerful reminder of this truth in Matthew 25:31-46. We should be very careful how we treat people who may be in a so-called "lesser station" in life.

Despite his prominence as one of the great men of his time (Job 1:3), Job does not mistreat those who are less fortunate. Job's servants even have remarked about his generosity to them (Job 31:31). The charge of injustice will not stick!

D. "IDOLATRY" WON'T STICK (vv. 24-28)

24. "If I have put my trust in gold
    or said to pure gold, 'You are my security,'

Even though Job was very wealthy before his tragedy, he knew better than to make *gold* the center of his life. This directly refutes an accusation made by Eliphaz (Job 22:23-25).

GOLD OR GOD?

The words "under God" appear in America's Pledge of Allegiance. The words "In God We Trust" appear on American coins. There have been "on again, off again" efforts in recent years to remove those words. (Political pundits say the issue

HOW TO SAY IT

*Abaddon (Hebrew). Uh-BAD-
   dun.*
Bildad. BILL-dad.
Corinthians. Kor-IN-thee-unz.
*Deuteronomy. Due-ter-AHN-uh-
   me.*
Eliphaz. EL-ih-faz.
Ephesians. Ee-FEE-zhunz.
Isaiah. Eye-ZAY-uh.
Zacchaeus. Zack-KEY-us.
Zophar. ZO-far.

DAILY BIBLE READINGS

Monday, Jan. 12—My Eyes Are Turned Toward You (Psalm 141:1-8)

Tuesday, Jan. 13—I Direct My Steps (Psalm 119:121-128)

Wednesday, Jan. 14—The Righteous Walk Blamelessly (Psalm 15:1-5)

Thursday, Jan. 15—Job Declares His Integrity (Job 27: 2-6)

Friday, Jan. 16—Let God Know My Integrity (Job 31:3-8)

Saturday, Jan. 17—Job Defends Himself (Job 31:13-23)

Sunday, Jan. 18—Job Declares His Loyalty to God (Job 31:24-28)

Father, help us treasure our integrity—not as a cornerstone of self-righteousness, but as our means of showing you that we are truly devoted to living as you want us to live. When people falsely accuse us and knowingly lie about us, help us remember the example of Job.

Help us remember that your Word tells us to repay evil with good. Empower us to maintain our integrity in every situation. Strengthen us through the Holy Spirit's power within us. In Jesus' name we pray, amen.

WHAT DO YOU THINK?

In an attempt to prove his innocence, Job provides several benchmark examples. Why are some of these important markers of righteousness even today?

[Passages such as Job 31:5-15, 26, 27; Luke 20:47; Galatians 5:20; 1 Timothy 4:2; and James 2:11 can stimulate your thinking.]

THOUGHT TO REMEMBER

We are to combat falsehood and ignorance with grace and truth.

"has no traction"!) But even with the words remaining, some have remarked that the sentiment is not accurate. Perhaps not, but they speak to America's ideals, goals, and hopes.

Others have said that if we were totally accurate we would replace "In God We Trust" on the coins with "In Gold We Trust." Let the word *gold* stand for materialism, wealth, and property, and you will probably agree that those living in prosperous societies trust more in gold than in God.

Job, however, did not. We must all look at ourselves honestly and ask, "Can I say what Job said? Would people who know me best agree that my trust is in God and not in gold?" The proof is in our actions and attitudes. Which gets us more riled up—politicians trying to delete references to God, or politicians messing with our various government-sponsored "entitlements"?

Those of us who live in the United States know that we live in a very materialistic society. How we respond to that materialism will communicate volumes to our children and grandchildren. What we must consciously communicate to them is that we know that ultimate security comes only from God, not from gold.   —R. C. S.

25. ". . . if I have rejoiced over my great wealth,
    the fortune my hands had gained,

Job does not seem to have been the kind of man who paraded his *wealth* or sought to impress others with his possessions. He had been extremely wealthy, but he is not foolish enough to think that that *wealth* was of his own doing (cf. Luke 12:13-21).

26, 27. ". . . if I have regarded the sun in its radiance
    or the moon moving in splendor,
so that my heart was secretly enticed
    and my hand offered them a kiss of homage,

Job also denies another form of idolatry: he is not a worshiper of any of the heavenly bodies. Many in the ancient world worship the *sun*, the *moon*, and other things they see in the sky (Jeremiah 7:18; 44:15-25; Ezekiel 8:16; Acts 7:43). However, the Old Testament law is quite specific in forbidding the worship of such things (Deuteronomy 4:19; 17:3). Job may have raised his hands to acknowledge and worship God, but he has never raised his hands in worship of the sun or moon.

28. ". . . then these also would be sins to be judged,
    for I would have been unfaithful to God on high."

Job fully grasps the gravity of idolatry. Even if Job is unaware of the Old Testament law forbidding idolatry (Exodus 20:3-5), there is a natural instinct within him that rules it out (Romans 1:19, 20).

Idolatry is a word often relegated to ancient times. We think of people bowing down to images of wood, stone, or metal. We should remember that idolatry takes many forms. Anything or anyone taking precedence over God in our lives becomes an idol to us. May we be like Job! As the charge of idolatry will not stick against him, may the same be said of us.

CONCLUSION

What pressure Job was under! His tragedies, his unanswered questions, and his friends' accusations could have driven him to irrational, and even evil, retaliations. He could have given up and decided that living a righteous life was simply not worth the effort. He could have become a different man, emboldened to sin by the seeming lack of reward for doing good.

He did not do any of that. Perhaps he felt his integrity was all he had left. For him, that was enough. Would the same be true for you?

Discovery Learning

This page contains an alternative lesson plan emphasizing learning activities. Classes desiring such student involvement will find these suggestions helpful. The next page is a reproducible activity page to further enhance discovery learning.

LEARNING GOALS

After participating in this lesson, each student will be able to:

1. Summarize Job's arguments that he has been falsely accused.

2. Explain how truth is the best defense against false accusations.

3. Give a specific example of how a person overcomes accusations with the truth.

INTO THE LESSON

Put these two words on display, with several blank underlines between them: INNOCENT and GUILTY. Tell the class, "I want you to do the old word game of changing one word to another by changing one letter per line to form an intervening word. Who has the first suggestion?" Someone very quickly will notice that these two words do not have the same number of letters and cannot be thus altered. When someone notes this, say, "You're right! The only way this could be done is if one ignores the rules of the game; that is, only if one cheats." Comment further that that's exactly what would have to happen for Job to be declared guilty. Truth affirms his claim of innocence; no one can change innocent to guilty.

As an alternative, have class members express words and phrases relating to the words, "NOT GUILTY" in an acrostic. Provide poster board or newsprint and a felt pen for putting a word to each letter vertically that relates to innocence. Tell them you'll "give them a bonus point" if they can relate their words to Job's story and the book of Job. Sample choices: *godly* for *G*, *undeserved* for *U*.

INTO THE WORD

Invite a judge or lawyer to be present. Allow this legal professional to make a short address on the term Job continuously repeated: "Not Guilty."

Say, "Today, we are going to be judged by 'judge and jury.' Forgetting all the good things you have done, in a court of law what would be the most impressive thing you could tell the judge you have not done?"

Have each class member open the Bible to Job 31. Job had previously challenged God to meet him and either present His case or let Job speak (Job 13:20-24). Now he plays out his role as the accused, even though there is no evidence that God is paying any attention. He will take his solemn oath—his hand on the Bible so to speak— and protest his innocence.

Divide the class into groups of three to five; ask them to examine the entire text of Job 31 or assign the groups the following verses: 5-8; 9-12; 13-15; 24-28 to identify the supposed accusations and Job's responses to each. Give each group a sheet of paper or transparency with two headings: *Accusation* and *Plea*. Direct them to compile the list. (*Students should come up with the following accusations: vanity, deceit, adultery, prejudice and partiality, greed and avarice, idolatry. To each charge, Job's plea is, "Not guilty!"*)

As the groups complete their time together, ask each to report its findings on their transparency or simply orally and share with the rest of the class. Note, "Though Job is accused of a variety of serious offenses toward God, to each he could say, 'Not guilty!'"

As an option, you may choose to use the reproducible activity "Briefly Speaking" to explore these same texts. The activity is on the next page. The next activity, "How Do You Plead?" would make a good follow-up activity to this one.

INTO LIFE

Lead everyone in meditating on Job 27:3, 4. Begin the activity by asking all to bow their heads in a spirit of meditation and reverence, as you lead them through some questions and implications of the text.

Read aloud verse 3: "As long as I have life within me, the breath of God in my nostrils;" and then ask these questions, pausing after each: "What does this phrase mean in terms of my personal life? How do I feel about God knowing my way? What is one specific 'way' in my life I am assured he knows about me right now? Are there any areas in my life I would rather he didn't know about?"

Move to verse 4: "My lips will not speak wickedness, and my tongue will utter no deceit." Share these questions for reflection: "What did Job mean in this verse? In what area in my life is God 'trying' me? What is he wanting to accomplish through this? Will I always be on trial before God? Who decides whether or not I'll come forth with integrity in my everyday life? How can I apply Job's principle of fighting accusations with truth? At home? At work? In every relationship?"

Briefly Speaking

A reader may tire of the many words Job and his friends use to state their positions. Read each of the following Scriptures and determine the key idea—the irreducible minimum statement!

Job 31:5-8

Job 31:9-12

Job 31:13-15

Job 31:24-28

How Do You Plead?

For each of the following sins Job pleaded, "Not Guilty!" How would you have to plead for each?

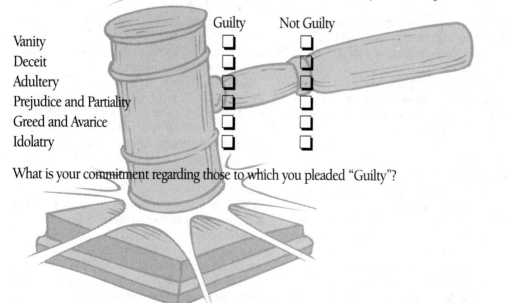

	Guilty	Not Guilty
Vanity	☐	☐
Deceit	☐	☐
Adultery	☐	☐
Prejudice and Partiality	☐	☐
Greed and Avarice	☐	☐
Idolatry	☐	☐

What is your commitment regarding those to which you pleaded "Guilty"?

Lessons From Life

Unit 1: Job: Integrity in Times of Testing
(Lessons 5-8)

INTEGRITY IN GOD'S PRESENCE

LESSON 8

WHY TEACH THIS LESSON?

A savvy co-worker enlightened me with a bit of wisdom one day when he advised, "Don't ask the question if you can't stand the answer!" Often when we ask a question, we expect a certain response, don't we? Oh sure, we may ask with a neutral tone in our voice as if *any* reasonable answer will satisfy us. But frequently if the answer we get doesn't serve to advance our own agenda, we get irritated! This can be true whether we are asking of another person or of God.

But God can see through all hidden agendas and wrong motives. Nothing can be kept secret from him. He knows whether we ask out of integrity or not. Job knew this, too. Had Job lived in New Testament times, perhaps he would have been the one to write, "When you ask, you do not receive, because you ask with wrong motives" (James 4:3a). Through this lesson your learners will begin to recognize that right motives and integrity help us to mature in our faith.

INTRODUCTION

A. "I JUST EARNED MY MASTER'S DEGREE"

I once attended a seminar sponsored by a local university. Eighteen people gathered in a room to spend the day discussing the subject of adult education. A young lady breezed into the room about thirty minutes after the first paper had been read. She immediately injected herself into the discussion, even though she had heard only the last couple of minutes of the paper that had been presented. She continued to make comments throughout the discussion, even though it was apparent to everyone that she knew virtually nothing about the subject of the paper. To put it bluntly, she was unbearably obnoxious!

Finally, the moderator asked the young woman why she felt it necessary to comment on everything that was said. The young lady responded, "Well, I just earned my master's degree, and I thought I might help enlighten everyone." The moderator peered over the top of her glasses at the young woman and said, "Young lady, everyone in this room—except you—has a *doctorate* in some field of education." The young woman did not make any other comments that morning, and she did not return to the seminar after the lunch break.

In this week's lesson we will see know-it-all Job get his comeuppance. He had asked for a hearing before God—and he got it! Things did not, however, turn out quite the way Job expected.

B. LESSON BACKGROUND

In last week's lesson we learned of Job's responses to the accusations of his three friends. In the chapter preceding this week's lesson texts, another character had presented himself, a man named Elihu (Job 32–37). Elihu's speech forms a potent preamble to God's response to Job. Elihu reminded Job of God's ultimate

DEVOTIONAL READING:
ISAIAH 6:1-8
BACKGROUND SCRIPTURE:
JOB 38–42
PRINTED TEXT:
JOB 38:1-7; 40:6-9; 42:1-6

LESSON AIMS

After participating in this lesson, each student will be able to:

1. Summarize God's answer to Job, and tell how Job responded.

2. Tell why it was necessary for Job to recognize his own unworthiness and God's sovereign control.

3. Make a statement of submission to God's sovereignty.

Jan
25

KEY VERSE

My ears had heard of you but now my eyes have seen you.
—Job 42:5

justice (Job 34). He reminded Job that he should speak to God humbly, carefully addressing his Creator (Job 35). He argued that Job should acknowledge God's sovereignty (Job 36). He called on Job to express his ultimate trust in God, regardless of his understanding of God's ways (Job 37). We have no record of any response from Job. The next voice we hear is that of God himself (Job 38).

I. SOVEREIGN POWER (JOB 38:1-7)

God spoke to Job in the midst of a mighty windstorm. The storm would descend upon Job and his companions with an intense fury, and out of that fury Job would hear God speaking to him. Job gets what he requested. God is there, but God will speak while Job listens.

A. PREPARING FOR THE TEST, PART 1 (vv. 1-3)

1. Then the LORD answered Job out of the storm. He said:

Elihu's speech ended with a reminder that people fear (or revere) God because of his splendor, majesty, power, and justice (Job 37:22-24). Then God speaks. Job has wanted God to answer him (31:35). Now God is doing just what Job wants, but his voice does not come to Job in the midst of a moment of quiet contemplation. God's voice rises above the howling gale of a terrible *storm*. We might compare how God speaks here with how he speaks in passages such as Exodus 19:16-19; 1 Kings 19:9-12; and Ezekiel 1.

2. "Who is this that darkens my counsel
    with words without knowledge?"

What an opening question! Imagine the scene: you are in the middle of a maelstrom, and suddenly you hear the voice of God. And God's voice is not comforting you—he is asking you why you are such a smart aleck.

In his presumption Job thinks he has God all figured out! The bad things that have happened came about because God did not have enough information. Job wants to talk to God to tell him what he does not know. Job wants to argue.

As we consider Job's words, however, we recall that he "did not sin by charging God with wrongdoing" (1:22), and that "Job did not sin in what he said" (2:10). The *words without knowledge* that God points out likely include Job's complaint—out of his very great pain!—that God has not heard his cry, thereby denying him justice (19:6, 7; 27:2). Even so, when all is said and done it is Job (and not Eliphaz, Bildad, and Zophar) who has spoken of God "what is right" (42:7, 8). Whenever we question God's justice today we, too, speak foolish "words without knowledge."

3. "Brace yourself like a man;
    I will question you,
    and you shall answer me."

God tells Job to get ready for a battle. This is not to be a physical wrestling match as in Genesis 32:22-28, but Job will know that he has been in a battle when God is through questioning him.

Is Job prepared for this mental test (cf. 1 Peter 1:13)? Will he be able to defend himself on the charge of presumption? God is going to be a demanding Teacher—and Job had better be ready with good answers.

B. TAKING THE TEST, PART 1 (vv. 4-7)

4. "Where were you when I laid the earth's foundation?
    Tell me, if you understand.

God now begins a series of more than seventy questions to Job. The first question alone reminds Job of his proper place.

"Where were you when I laid the earth's foundation?"

Job 38:4 NIV

This magnificent "space shot" will remind your learners of their relationship to the Creator.

LOOKING FOR ANSWERS

William Temple (1881–1944) said that God minus the world would still equal God, but that the world minus God would equal nothing. If we eliminate God from our thinking, then there are too many questions without answers and too many puzzles without solutions. Certainly believers do not have all the answers, but they have better answers than those who do not believe.

Just the thought of a universe without God is depressing: a universe empty, lonely, friendless, and without purpose. But believers can look out into the vastness of space and know that we are not alone; we are not orphans. We are children. Like all children we keep asking questions. And like all children, we receive answers to some of them, but not to all of them. A child does not need to know all the answers, and we do not need to know all the answers. We have a Heavenly Father who does know all the answers, and we are to be content with that.

It is not wrong to ask questions. Job, Moses, and John the Baptist are among the many in the Bible who asked questions. But they asked them out of a heart of faith. Some think faith never asks questions, but they are wrong. Some think faith has all the answers, but they are wrong. Faith asks questions, accepts God's answers when they are given, and rests serenely when God withholds answers. The old song is right: "We'll understand it better by and by."   —R. C. S.

5. *"Who marked off its dimensions? Surely you know!*
   Who stretched a measuring line across it?

Picture a man using a *measuring* tape. He can hold one end and read the measurements, but he needs someone else holding the other end of the tape at the proper place. Did God need such a helper? If he did, was Job that helper? Given all the scientific knowledge we have today about the scope and dimensions of the universe, how much more humbled should we be by these questions than Job!

6. *"On what were its footings set,*
   or who laid its cornerstone—

God asks Job an intriguing question: to what is the earth fastened? Job has indicated an elementary understanding of the fact that the earth is suspended in space (Job 26:7). So God's question to Job about the earth's foundations is, of course, figurative.

God is using the analogy of the earth as a building. Was Job present when earth's *cornerstone* was laid? Does Job even begin to comprehend *who laid* that cornerstone? In 38:31 God will use some of Job's own words from 9:9 to make a similar point about stars. "Come on, Job. Do you know?"

7. *"... while the morning stars sang together*
   and all the angels shouted for joy?"

Stars could refer to the literal points of light in the sky as they declared God's glory by their very existence (cf. Psalm 19:1). It is also possible that *morning stars* refer figuratively to *the angels*. In many translations both Isaiah 14:12 and Revelation 22:16 use "morning star" to refer to living beings, so the exact usage here is hard to determine. In either case, Job was not there to hail God's creative powers as the morning stars were. Can Job possibly know how all these events occurred?

II. SOVEREIGN JUSTICE (JOB 40:6-9)

Throughout chapters 38 and 39, God continues to question Job regarding his knowledge—or lack of knowledge—of the elementary workings of the systems of the earth and its creatures. Now God switches themes as he begins to question Job about his accusations (Job 40:1, 2). It seems that Job is beginning to get the picture because he does not try to answer. He knows this is a time to keep his mouth shut (Job 40:3-5). Job's silence does not, however, silence God.

WHAT DO YOU THINK?

The best teachers help their students grow in both understanding and character. How did God's "test questions" help Job develop in both areas as a student of the Almighty?

A. PREPARING FOR THE TEST, PART 2 (vv. 6, 7)

6. Then the LORD spoke to Job out of the storm:

Amazingly, *the storm* has not abated. Poor Job—he finally gets to talk to God, but he has to do so in the midst of a tornado!

Job has admitted that he is "unworthy" (Job 40:4). Perhaps he thinks that will put a stop to God's onslaught. It does not. God continues to make his points.

7. "Brace yourself like a man;
   I will question you,
   and you shall answer me.

God repeats his warning from 38:3. Job's admission of his unworthiness is not sufficient. God has not declared himself the winner of this battle of wits. He has scored enough points to win, but Job still has lessons to learn, and God is still willing to serve as Job's teacher. So he again warns Job to prepare for battle.

B. TAKING THE TEST, PART 2 (vv. 8, 9)

8. "Would you discredit my justice?
   Would you condemn me to justify yourself?

Job is now faced with a far more serious charge. God's questions have made it clear to Job that he is ignorant of his ways. Now, however, God directly confronts Job with Job's allegations of injustice in Job 19:6, 7 and 27:2.

WHAT DO YOU THINK?

When tragedy strikes, many today question the justice of God as Job did (Job 19:6, 7). How can Job 40:6-14 help us in rough times?

We find many people today who are very willing to accuse God of injustice. They ask why God causes (or allows) disasters like floods, earthquakes, and hurricanes. They ask why children die in the midst of wars. They, like Job, need to learn that we do not have the right to question God's justice. The prophet Habakkuk learned this lesson when God told him, in a nice way, "shut up!" (Habakkuk 2:20). God's sovereign *justice* prevails in his appointed time and fashion.

God asks another penetrating question: must God be wrong in order for Job to prove himself right? Job has spoken against God, although the depths of Job's pain make his "crossing the line" somewhat understandable. As noted before, in the end it is Job who has spoken right of God, and not his friends (Job 42:7, 8).

9. "Do you have an arm like God's,
   and can your voice thunder like his?"

God reminds Job of his limitations. In his moment of greatest strength, Job could not accomplish what God can do in his moment of greatest weakness!

WHAT DO YOU THINK?

While speaking to Job, God reveals clues about his nature. What are some of these and why are they important?

My fifteen-year-old son will begin learning how to drive a car in a few months. Like most boys his age, he already thinks he knows how. He thinks it perfectly appropriate to criticize my driving occasionally. That's when I ask him how he gained such expertise. I do not instruct him in playing the trombone (which he does very well) or in diving off the high dive (which he also does very well). When it comes to driving, however, I am the resident expert. Job has to be reminded that God is the one who is sovereign—the Resident Expert in all things!

III. SHAME AND SORROW (JOB 42:1-6)

We now hear Job speak. He has been inundated with questions he cannot answer. He has admitted that he is unworthy. Will God's questions lead Job to the proper conclusion? Will Job finally see the "big picture"?

A. GOD'S SOVEREIGNTY (vv. 1, 2)

1. Then Job replied to the LORD:

Job's longing for the opportunity to speak with God has been fulfilled. He has listened to God's litany of rhetorical questions. Job has spoken much about God. Now he will speak to God.

2. *"I know that you can do all things;*
   no plan of yours can be thwarted.

In his previous response to God, Job had admitted quickly that he was unworthy of the opportunity to speak with God. Then Job decided that the wisest course of action was to remain silent (Job 40:3-5). Silence, however, does not mean that Job has given up his contention that he has been dealt with unjustly. Job's admission simply may indicate that he knows he is overmatched. Job already had indicated that he knew he could not successfully argue with God (9:14). Job may be willing to be silent because he knows he cannot win such a debate. This does not rule out the possibility, however, that Job still thinks he is right!

Job has acknowledged God's sovereignty all along, so the admission *I know that you can do all things* is nothing new. Job realizes now, however, that his insistence to have his case heard in God's court is foolish since God knows all thoughts anyway. The sovereign God who can do all things is the one who has been fully aware of Job's situation all along.

B. JOB'S IGNORANCE (v. 3)

3. *"You asked, 'Who is this that obscures my counsel without knowledge?'*
   Surely I spoke of things I did not understand,
   things too wonderful for me to know.

Job seems to be crawling out from beneath his layers of self-defense as he uses the same words God has spoken against him (38:2). Job is saying, in essence, "Yes, God—you have me pegged." Job's attitude goes from that of a Mister Know-It-All to one of humble admission. This is the kind of transformation that we could all use from time to time!

Realizing the limits of your knowledge and wisdom can be very liberating. It seems so with Job. He moves beyond his pride and finds the joy of honesty. He realizes that he has pondered on matters far beyond his intellectual capacity. He finally concludes that the ways of God are beyond his comprehension. He does not have God figured out, after all. And that is okay! It is not Job's responsibility to define God's path. That is a valuable lesson for all of us to learn. There is a limit to how much we can analyze God. Above all, he is there to be adored!

A BIBLICAL DRAMA

For many years Orlin Corey of Kentucky's Georgetown College has produced an outdoor drama entitled *The Book of Job*. Presented each summer at Pine Mountain State Resort Park near Pineville, Kentucky, the drama has received national attention because of Corey's unique "stained glass" makeup and costume design. It is regarded as a major event in American theater history.

Of course, the book is a natural for the stage. It *is* a drama. Just as the Bible contains poetry, history, and biography, so it contains drama. And just as Corey's theater production is unique, so the book and its message are unique.

The opening verses of the final chapter sum up this book and its message. G. K. Chesterton (1874–1936) said, "Great literature has always been allegorical. The *Iliad* is only great because all life is a battle. The *Odyssey* because all life is a journey, the Book of Job because all life is a riddle."

As believers we know the outcome of the battle, the end of the journey, the solution to the riddle. But "knowing the outcome" and "learning the lesson" are two different things! We must learn, as Job did, to be humble before God. God is wiser than we are. God is more powerful than we are. It is worth reading through the whole book of Job to learn that. Nothing will serve believers better in facing life than a genuine humility. One of the world's greatest dramas can teach us one of God's best lessons.
                                                                    —R. C. S.

HOW TO SAY IT

Abednego. Uh-BED-nee-go.
Bildad. BILL-dad.
Elihu. Ih-LYE-hew.
Eliphaz. EL-ih-faz.
Meshach. ME-shack.
Nebuchadnezzar. NEB-yuh-kud-
  NEZ-er.
Shadrach. SHAY-drack or
  SHAD-rack.
Zophar. ZO-far.

DAILY BIBLE READINGS

Monday, Jan. 19—My Soul Thirsts for God (Psalm 42:1-6)

Tuesday, Jan. 20—John's Vision of Christ (Revelation 1: 12-18)

Wednesday, Jan. 21—Isaiah's Vision of God (Isaiah 6: 1-8)

Thursday, Jan. 22—The Lord Speaks to Job (Job 38:1-7)

Friday, Jan. 23—God Calls for Job's Response (Job 40:1-5)

Saturday, Jan. 24—God Questions Job (Job 40:6-14)

Sunday, Jan. 25—Job Is Humbled by Seeing God (Job 42:1-6)

C. GOD'S IDENTITY (vv. 4, 5)

4. "You said, 'Listen now, and I will speak;
I will question you,
and you shall answer me.'

Again, Job quotes the Lord's words back to him (38:3). God has instructed Job to listen, and Job has indeed heard. Job is beginning to understand God's true nature.

5. "My ears had heard of you
but now my eyes have seen you.

Previously, Job had known about God. Now he is actually getting to know God. Many people know about God. They, like Job, think they have God all figured out. They can quote Bible verses and recite church doctrine. But they have no personal relationship with God. How sad to know facts but not the Father! (See John 14:8, 9.)

D. JOB'S REPENTANCE (v. 6)

6. "Therefore I despise myself
and repent in dust and ashes."

Job's new, correct view of God has changed his view of himself. This verse records a turning point of Job's life. His efforts at self-vindication cease. He stops looking at himself in his own mirror and starts looking at himself in God's mirror.

Job's experience in the presence of God reminds us of the experience of Isaiah. When Isaiah saw God, he also was overcome with a sense of his own unworthiness (Isaiah 6:5). As is the custom in that part of the world, Job's repentance is expressed visually by covering himself with *dust and ashes*. He previously had covered himself in ashes to express sadness due to his suffering (Job 2:8). Now he covers himself in dust and ashes to express repentance. His arrogance has been an affront to God. His accusations have been false. His sense of God has been too low, his sense of self too high.

Spiritual arrogance is a destructive force in many churches today. God's Word instructs us to be humble (Matthew 18:4; Romans 12:3; James 4:10; 1 Peter 5:5). The humility God desires is exemplified in the life of Jesus. How many of us are truly like him in that respect?

Job's integrity was his banner. He thought it unquestionable. He finally comes to the point of true integrity when he is willing to tell the truth about himself. He does not know everything. He does not have God figured out! He insisted on seeing God through a distorted lens, a lens that "must" be right. When Job finally talks to God, he is ashamed of himself. He is sorry not only for what he has done, but also for what he has been!

CONCLUSION

Many people think the book of Job is about suffering or patience. Those themes are part of the book, but more important is faith. What was the essence of Job's faith? Did he understand that God has the right to declare without explanation? God's sovereignty authorizes declaration, not explanation!

When Shadrach, Meshach, and Abednego refused to worship the image of Nebuchadnezzar, they were thrown into a fiery furnace. They believed God would deliver them from that fate, but their faith is expressed in this declaration: "but even if he does not . . . we will not serve your gods or worship the image of gold you have set up" (Daniel 3:18). Even if God decided not to deliver them, it made no difference. The essence of faith is trusting God even when you do not understand what he is doing. Job finally learned that valuable lesson. How about you?

WHAT DO YOU THINK?

In being able to speak directly with God, Job experienced something very rare indeed! Would you want to have a direct conversation with God? Why, or why not?

PRAYER

Father, we thank you for being who you are. Help us learn to trust you more. May we remember Job when we are tempted to question your ways or your timing. Help us to follow the Spirit's leading in our lives when the way is not clear. In Jesus' name, amen.

WHAT DO YOU THINK?

Which lesson is more important to learn from the book of Job: how to respond to adversity or the need to repent? Why?

THOUGHT TO REMEMBER

"Though he slay me, yet will I hope in him" (Job 13:15).

Discovery Learning

This page contains an alternative lesson plan emphasizing learning activities. Classes desiring such student involvement will find these suggestions helpful. The next page is a reproducible activity page to further enhance discovery learning.

LEARNING GOALS

After this lesson each student will be able to:

1. Summarize God's answer to Job, and tell how Job responded.

2. Tell why it was necessary for Job to recognize his own unworthiness and God's sovereignty.

3. Express submission to God's sovereignty.

INTO THE LESSON

Option 1: Ask students to share a "foot-in-the-mouth" experience, a time when they spoke too soon, spoke out of ignorance, or made a humorous verbal blunder. Make the transition to Bible study by saying: "Job made a foot-in-the-mouth blunder demonstrating spiritual arrogance."

Option 2: Explain that God has spoken to people through a variety of unusual and unique media and in various environments. Write on a chalkboard or marker board the following open-ended sentences and ask students to respond. A similar activity is included in the student workbook, *NIV® Bible Student.*

1. "Some of the environments or media through which God spoke to people in the Old Testament include. . . ." *Examples: burning bush (Moses), still small voice (Elijah), whirlwind (Ezekiel), voice in the night (Samuel).*

2. "Some of the media or environments through which God spoke to people in the New Testament include. . . ." *Examples: dreams (magi, Joseph), angel (Mary), light from Heaven (Saul), vision (John).* Make a transition to Bible study by saying, "God used another powerful medium to speak to Job—a tornado, a *storm* in the text."

INTO THE WORD

Give a brief lecture on Lesson Background (pages 183, 184). Use a visual you have prepared with the heading "Elihu Reminded Job" through the entire study. Under the heading write the following reminders: Chapter 34: God's ultimate justice; Chapter 35: Speak humbly to the Creator; Chapter 36: Acknowledge God's sovereignty; Chapter 37: Trust God, regardless of your understanding.

Below these chapter notes write a new heading, "God's Message to Job." Explain that we will discover God's answer to Job, which has a powerful lesson for us. Read Job 38:1-7. Ask groups to paraphrase verses 2 and 3. After allowing a few to be shared, tell the class that Job had a problem with pride, so God is addressing his spiritual arrogance. Ask two people to read aloud

God's questions (vv. 4, 5), giving attention to intonation and emphasis that God may have used. Then ask for an interpretation of God's meaning in verses 5 and 7. Finally, ask, "What is God's message to us in this passage?" Add to the chart, "Chapter 38," and note the student answers to, "What is God's message to us?"

Ask a student to read Job 40:6-9, a text that continues God's peppering Job with tough questions. Ask, "What serious charge is God making to Job here?" Explain the background for this charge. Ask, "What is God's message to Job and to us?" On the visual write, "Chapter 40," and list the student responses to the last question.

Read Job 42:1-6, Job's response to God's tough questions. Distribute copies of the reproducible activity "Changes of Heart and Attitude" from the next page. After giving time for learners to respond to the elements in that activity, discuss the answers as a whole class. Then return to the chart and add, "Chapter 42—Job's reply." List each of the following categories numbered below as you ask and discuss, "What did Job learn about (1) God's sovereignty? (vv. 1, 2); (2) his own wisdom? (v. 3); (3) knowing God? (vv. 4, 5)." Note the student responses to these questions on the visual. Use the lesson commentary to summarize Job's comments in verse 6.

INTO LIFE

Testimonials: Remind the class that today's message to Job jolted him out of spiritual arrogance and changed his attitude. Ask the class how their attitudes have been affected by God's revelation about his relationship to us. What probed their hearts and changed their values?

Prayer Circles: Hang four signs in the corners of the room. One is to read "Spiritual Arrogance (I thought I had God pegged!)." Another: "Pride (Not enough humility)." A third: "God's Injustice—failing to accept God's way." The fourth: "Unrelated and Unspoken Needs." As you hang the signs, explain that one may highlight a need or shortcoming class members have discovered in their own lives. Tell them to move to a sign appropriate to their needs, assuring them they will not have to reveal their need specifically. Each group will ask individuals to pray for the needs of that group. Close by singing the chorus of "I Surrender All."

Distribute copies of the reproducible activity "C to See" from the next page. Encourage each person to clip the "coupon" and to carry it this week.

Changes of Heart and Attitude

After being peppered with probing questions, Job discovered his spiritual arrogance and pride. However, Job learned his lesson. He responded to God by saying, "I despise myself and repent in dust and ashes" (42:6). Job's new glimpse of God changed his view of himself.

How do you react to God using this method of peppering over seventy questions to Job as a way to "set him straight"? Why did God do this?

What similarities or contrasts do you see in Job's attitudes (before his repentance) and your own views of God?

Describe a time when your own spiritual arrogance may have surfaced in your life.

Read the epilogue to Job's book (42:7-17). What comfort and assurance do you receive from this blessing of Job?

C to "See . . ."

The text below echoes God's teaching to Job and to us . . . that we must submit to God's infinite knowledge and wisdom.

Copy or clip this coupon. Carry it with you all week, reading and memorizing it.

See a wonderful view of God's sovereignty!

> "For my thoughts are not your thoughts,
>   Neither are your ways my ways," declares the Lord.
> "As the heavens are higher than the earth,
>   So are my ways higher than your ways
>   And my thoughts than your thoughts."
>
> —Isaiah 55:8, 9

Lessons From Life

A TIME FOR ALL THINGS

LESSON 9

WHY TEACH THIS LESSON?

A well-known Christian leader was dying of cancer. The man was advanced in years, and the disease had reached the point where doctors could do nothing else. As death loomed, a friend stopped by the hospital room to inform him that many in the church were praying fervently for his recovery. "Tell them to stop immediately!" the dying man exclaimed. "We all die, and it's obvious that this is my time." Would that we could all accept the seasons of life with such wisdom!

When we accept with grace the fact that there are seasons of life, we can fulfill God's will for us at every stage. Growing in such wisdom is our topic for today.

INTRODUCTION

A. THROUGH A GLASS

Glass is one of God's most remarkable gifts to mankind. Glass has been known and used for hundreds of years, but only in the past century or so have we become aware of its great versatility. We use it for windows, of course, and we also use it to package our food and beverages. We use it to insulate our houses, to make roofing materials, and to make fabrics to decorate our houses.

One of the most important uses of glass is in the field of optics. Perhaps you're reading this text through eyeglasses that sharpen your blurring vision. In the microscope and telescope we have fashioned glass into powerful lenses that open vistas beyond the range of even the sharpest eyes.

In a way, the microscope and the telescope symbolize two ways to look at life. The writer of Ecclesiastes uses the microscope to analyze life "up close" in its frustrating twists and turns. This gives us a sobering and sometimes pessimistic view of life. But the Scriptures also give us a telescopic view of life, allowing us to see beyond the confines of time and to catch a bit of God's purposes in eternity.

B. LESSON BACKGROUND

The book of Ecclesiastes is not often studied in our churches and Sunday schools. As a result, we have missed many of the valuable lessons it has to teach us. In some ways it presents a rather pessimistic and even cynical view of life. Yet these very elements make it most worthy of study, for many of the views expressed in this book are as prevalent today as they were when Ecclesiastes was written three thousand years ago.

The Hebrew title of the book, *Qohelet*, is not clearly understood by modern scholars. The title we use today comes from the Greek translation *ekklesiastes*, which means "assemblyman," leading to translations of it as "Teacher" or "Preacher" (Ecclesiastes 1:1, 2; 12:8). The writer of the book identifies himself as "the Teacher, son of David, king in Jerusalem" (1:1). This naturally leads us to believe that this king was Solomon. The tenor of the book certainly seems to fit the lifestyle of King Solomon, who started his reign so well but who enjoyed too many things too soon. As the years passed, he looked back on all his activities and began to feel the sense of emptiness expressed in verse 2 of the first chapter: "Utterly meaningless! Everything is meaningless!"

DEVOTIONAL READING:
PSALM 1
BACKGROUND SCRIPTURE:
ECCLESIASTES 3
PRINTED TEXT:
ECCLESIASTES 3:1-15

LESSON AIMS

After participating in this lesson, each student will be able to:

1. Point out the contrasts that exist in the normal routines of life.

2. Express the comfort that comes from knowing that God is in control, even in the extremes of life.

3. Give a testimony of God's grace that sustained him or her through one of life's "extreme" periods.

Feb
1

KEY VERSE

There is a time for everything, and a season for every activity under heaven. —Ecclesiastes 3:1

I. DISCUSSION ABOUT TIME (ECCLESIASTES 3:1-8)

A. IN NATURE (vv. 1, 2)

1. There is a time for everything,
   and a season for every activity under heaven:

This verse introduces a series of contrasts of things that may be observed in nature and in a variety of human activities. The seasons are not limited to the four seasons of the year, but apply to a whole range of activities that people are engaged in or observe.

2. . . . a time to be born and a time to die,
   a time to plant and a time to uproot,

The first in this series of contrasts pairs the beginning of life with the end of life. Every person has experienced birth and, barring the return of the Lord, will experience death. Modern medicine has made it possible for premature babies to survive. Medicine is able to extend life expectancy, yet all of us will still experience the birth-death cycle.

All the other activities the writer uses fall between these two events. The first is a recognition that there is *a time to plant.* Those living in an agricultural economy are keenly aware of this, and that planting time is not the same for all crops.

There is also *a time to uproot* those crops. Annual crops must be harvested or plowed under. Even trees that are set out have a definite life span depending upon the species, and in the cycle of life must eventually be cut down and disposed of.

Further, there is a time to plant and uproot in a nonagricultural sense (see Jeremiah 1:10; 4:3; Matthew 13:24-30). Knowing just when those times come requires spiritual wisdom—a wisdom God expects us to develop.

A TIME TO DIE

Solomon was right: there is a time to die. There is a time when our bodies wear out. A faithful Christian with terminal cancer commented, "I'm ready to go. I know the Lord is waiting for me, and I'm so tired." This man was able to speak with calm assurance about his death because he had lived a faith-filled life. He was prepared and ready to die.

There is a time when we are alone. A 103-year-old Christian was only half joking when she said, "I need to hurry up and die or all of my friends in Heaven will think I went the other way." This woman had outlived her husband, her friends, her peers, and even her children. She was prepared and ready to be reunited with them.

There is a time when we no longer can serve, except perhaps through our prayers. A frail Christian in her eighties asked her young minister, "Why won't the Lord let me go to sleep and not wake up? I'm ready to die. I can't get out. I can't write letters. I can't hear people on the phone. I want to go home." There may be ways to serve we have not considered, but this woman was prepared and ready for death's release.

The acceptance of death is not the same as a reason to put innocent people *to* death; we do not have that right. But anticipating death is Biblical. The apostle Paul wrote, "I am already being poured out like a drink offering, and the time has come for my departure. I have fought the good fight, I have finished the race, I have kept the faith. Now there is in store for me the crown of righteousness, which the Lord, the righteous Judge, will award to me on that day" (2 Timothy 4:6-8). Paul was prepared and ready to die.

The only time not to die is when you are unprepared to stand before the Lord. How are your preparations coming?   —J. D. J.

This montage of life-event images will reinforce today's Key Verse.

B. IN BEHAVIOR (vv. 3, 4)

3. . . . a time to kill and a time to heal,
    a time to tear down and a time to build,

Some commentators think the *time to kill* refers to war, but war is specifically mentioned in verse 8. This verse may refer to executions, as the Old Testament law specified. (See Genesis 9:6; Exodus 19:13; cf. Acts 25:11.)

A time to heal may have in mind the normal process through which one may experience the healing of a wound or the recovery from a serious illness. Or it might also extend to the healing of emotional wounds one has suffered or the repairing of broken relations between individuals.

To tear down and *to build* describe the process of destruction and construction. We today are familiar with urban renewal or highway construction where the old must be broken up and removed before the new and better can take its place. Those living in Solomon's day would have been quite aware of this process because of his many building projects.

4. . . . a time to weep and a time to laugh,
    a time to mourn and a time to dance,

A person may *weep* for joy, but here the reference clearly is to weeping in sorrow (cf. Romans 12:15; James 4:9). Weeping occurs at the time of death or some other serious tragedy. Laughing and rejoicing normally occur when a child is born, when some important victory is gained, or during some other festive occasion.

The ancient Israelite people do not hesitate to display their emotions. Mourning over a death, for instance, often follows definite rituals that include hiring professional mourners as seen in Jesus' day (Mark 5:38-41). Dancing is often a part of a wedding ceremony. It can also be an act of religious devotion, as in the case of David when the ark of the covenant was returned to Jerusalem (2 Samuel 6:14).

C. IN BUSINESS (vv. 5, 6)

5. . . . a time to scatter stones and a time to gather them,
    a time to embrace and a time to refrain,

The most likely explanation for scattering *stones* refers to the practice of clearing a field prior to planting a crop or setting out vines. The land in ancient Israel is quite stony and much labor is required to prepare it for crops. The stones are gathered together and are used in the construction of houses, walls, or terraces. This process has to be done in a timely fashion, because obviously one cannot build walls until stone is first gathered.

6. . . . a time to search and a time to give up,
    a time to keep and a time to throw away.

The first part of this verse seems to apply to many situations beyond one's control, while the second part seems to apply to conditions under which one consciously makes decisions. Success usually requires hard work, but we all know that outside factors can intervene. A farmer or a businessperson realizes that occasionally there are bad times, and these must be accepted. In our day we have experienced the wild gyrations of the stock market during the roaring 1990s when some made huge fortunes, and then during more recent years when these fortunes evaporated.

A couple may acquire a lot of things such as clothing, tools, mementos, and books that they eventually no longer use and merely clutter their closets. Then in retirement they move to smaller quarters and are faced with the painful task of disposing of all these accumulated things. Probably Solomon never had to make such decisions—he just built a bigger palace!

DAILY BIBLE READINGS

   Monday, Jan. 26—*God's Promise of Seasons* (Genesis 8:15-22)

   Tuesday, Jan. 27—*Human Time as Nothing to God* (Psalm 90:1-6)

   Wednesday, Jan. 28—*Teach Us to Count Our Days* (Psalm 90:7-12)

   Thursday, Jan. 29—*Prosper the Work of Our Hands* (Psalm 90:13-17)

   Friday, Jan. 30—*The Righteous Prosper, the Wicked Perish* (Psalm 1:1-6)

   Saturday, Jan. 31—*A Season for Everything* (Ecclesiastes 3:1-8)

   Sunday, Feb. 1—*God's Gift of Work* (Ecclesiastes 3:9-15)

WHAT DO YOU THINK?

Was there ever a time when you had to break off a friendship because it was the right thing to do? If so, explain why.

[To expand the discussion, include the instructions found in Proverbs 1:10-19; 2:12-22; 6:23-29; 24:1, 2; 1 Corinthians 5; 2 Corinthians 6:14; and Titus 3:10.]

WHAT DO YOU THINK?

Ecclesiastes 3 is among of the most well-known pieces of literature in the Old Testament. In what ways have you seen its wisdom used—or misused?

WHAT DO YOU THINK?

Ecclesiastes 3:8 speaks of proper times for love, hate, war, and peace. How do we recognize when times have changed, requiring that we shift our attitudes and our actions?

[Add insight to your discussion by considering Matthew 5:38-44; Romans 12:9; 13:3-5; and Revelation 2:6.]

WHAT DO YOU THINK?

How should Ecclesiastes 3:9, 10 influence our work ethic today, if at all?

[See also Ecclesiastes 3:22; Proverbs 14:23; 21:25; Matthew 6:19-21; and 2 Thessalonians 3:10.]

D. IN SOCIETY (vv. 7, 8)

7. . . . a time to tear and a time to mend,
a time to be silent and a time to speak,

The immediate reference may be to the rending of one's garment as an act of mourning (cf. Esther 4:1), but it certainly has wider applications. It can involve the tearing of a garment into smaller patches to be used to mend another garment. It could even apply to personal relationships (cf. Joel 2:13). Most of us on occasion have had to sever relationships with long-time friends, painful though this may be. For example, a recovering alcoholic sometimes has to give up his old drinking buddies if he is to recover from his addiction.

Many of us have a problem of knowing when *to be silent* (cf. Psalm 4:4; Amos 5:13). We sometimes speak harshly and in anger, intending to bring pain to others. At other times, even with good intentions, our words are hurtful. But in many situations "silence is golden"! (See Psalm 39:1.) Even so, there also are times to speak up (cf. Esther 4:12-14; Matthew 28:19, 20). Knowing which is which is an issue of spiritual maturity.

8. . . . a time to love and a time to hate,
a time for war and a time for peace.

Drawing upon Old Testament law, Jewish teachers taught that there are times and situations when one is obligated *to hate* an enemy. Jesus challenged this concept in Matthew 5:43, 44. Even so, we are still to hate evil (Romans 12:9; Revelation 2:6).

Unfortunately, most of us are all too familiar with *war*. As the nineteenth century came to a close, many believed that the twentieth century would usher in an era of worldwide peace—some expected Utopia! After all, humanity had become "enlightened." Instead, the twentieth century turned out to be the bloodiest hundred-year period in history. World Wars I and II were fought by the most "educated" countries on earth. Numerous smaller conflicts and "ethnic cleansings" added to the death and misery.

As horrible as war is, there are times when it is preferable to an unjust *peace*. For example, if the Western allies had not adopted a policy of appeasement against Hitler in the 1930s, the Holocaust that murdered millions of innocent people might have been avoided. The events of September 11, 2001, remind us that terrible evil is still at work in our world in the twenty-first century.

II. FROM TIME TO ETERNITY (ECCLESIASTES 3:9-15)

A. GOD ALLOWS SUFFERING (vv. 9, 10)

9. What does the worker gain from his toil?

Some see in this verse an expression of the writer's despair. Since God is in complete control, there is nothing we can do to change the situation. Such a viewpoint can only lead to utter pessimism—why work, since there is no benefit in it? This possibility serves as a lead-in to the next verse.

10. I have seen the burden God has laid on men.

The burden is the labor mentioned in the previous verse. As a result of humanity's fall, God pronounced a curse upon the ground (Genesis 3:18, 19). Although we have found ways to avoid the full burden of this curse, it still remains heavy upon the human race. We may escape the most tiring physical labor, but we often substitute for it the more demanding mental labor.

Even though we are still under this curse, God has given us the spiritual and mental resources that will allow us to find pleasure and satisfaction in our work. This allows us to escape the pessimism that comes from viewing verse 9 in isolation, as the following verse shows.

DIVINE IRRITATION

A man picks up a Pinctada mollusk lying in a shallow ocean bay. He pries open the shell and cuts into the mollusk's inner flesh to insert a tiny object. He closes the shell and lays the mollusk back in the water. Inside, the creature secretes crystalline calcium carbonate to heal its wound. This mucous surrounds the tiny object lodged in the mollusk's skin. Month after month, layers of this nacre form around the tiny object and harden. After three years, a man picks up the oyster, pries open the shell, and removes a beautiful pearl.

Pearls grow only after an oyster is injured. But this injury must be precisely placed. If a mollusk is too young, or if the man handling it is not careful, the oyster will die. If the insertion is made improperly, a misshapen lump will develop or no pearl will grow. Experienced pearl growers know just how to irritate an oyster to produce beauty.

God knows just how to disturb people, too (cf. Hebrews 12:11). The Lord irritated Moses and produced a great leader. God bothered Isaiah and Jeremiah and developed courageous prophets. The Lord goaded Saul of Tarsus and produced an amazing apostle.

You may feel the Lord has laid an unwanted burden on your back, and you may be right. But as with the mollusk, only when God gets "under your skin" can he make something beautiful in his time. Endure irritations with patience for the Lord. Let God work in your life.   —J. D. J.

B. GOD'S WORKS ARE BEYOND UNDERSTANDING (v. 11)

11. He has made everything beautiful in its time. He has also set eternity in the hearts of men; yet they cannot fathom what God has done from beginning to end.

God has created a *beautiful* universe, hasn't he? In the process of creating the universe, God *also* set *eternity* in people's *hearts*. Although we live under the burden of God's curse, he has planted in our hearts a glimpse of that eternity.

This inspires our hope that he has something better in store for us, and drives pessimism away. Yet this bit of eternity that we carry in our bosoms is but a hint of God's infinite wisdom since no one can *fathom what God has done from beginning to end.*

C. WE CAN ENJOY GOD'S GIFTS (vv. 12, 13)

12. I know that there is nothing better for men than to be happy and do good while they live.

While we're living with eternity in mind (v. 11), *there is nothing better* for us than *to be happy and do good*. Real joy and satisfaction come when we are actively involved in reaching out to help those who are in physical, emotional, or spiritual need. The testimony of the saints through the centuries gives ample proof of this. **13. That everyone may eat and drink, and find satisfaction in all his toil—this is the gift of God.**

Even though sin has brought upon the human race the curse of burdensome labor, God has also given us the insights to see labor as a gift from him. Too often we try to avoid work by passing it on to someone else or looking for a government handout. But in so doing we deny ourselves the real joy that God wants us to have when we work. Food and *drink* always taste better when you've really earned it!

D. GOD IS ETERNAL, BEYOND TIME (vv. 14, 15)

14. I know that everything God does will endure forever; nothing can be added to it and nothing taken from it. God does it so that men will revere him.

In the halls of Heaven there is no need of clocks or calendars. But human beings on planet Earth are confined by the boundaries set by time. As a result, we

WHAT DO YOU THINK?

What are some things we find in life that are valuable and give us pleasure? How is the Christian's perspective on such things different from a non-Christian's?

HOW TO SAY IT

Ecclesiastes or ekklesiastes
   (Greek). Ik-LEEZ-ee-AS-teez.
Jeremiah. Jair-uh-MY-uh.
Jerusalem. Juh-ROO-suh-lem.
Qohelet (Hebrew). Koe-HEL-it.
Solomon. SOL-o-mun.

PRAYER

Almighty God, although we live in a world that is wracked with decay and destruction, let us not fall into the throes of gloom and despair. Give us the vision to see beyond all these things. Remind us again that a day is coming in which you will set all things right. In Jesus' name, amen.

pay close attention to clocks and calendars, and there is no way that we can break out of these constraints in this world. God has granted us freedom on earth, but that freedom is always limited to a short bit of time and to a very small space. We can neither add to nor take away from his absolute sovereignty in this regard.

As a result we should *revere him.* We should understand this as the reverential awe that we experience as we come to realize that he is a righteous God who has made ample provisions for our physical needs. He is also a loving God who will deal with us with justice tempered by grace.

15. *Whatever is has already been,*
    and what will be has been before;
    and God will call the past to account.

The old saying, "History repeats itself" is true. Many things that are happening now, particularly sinful things, have happened *before.* They undoubtedly will happen again. But in requiring whatever *has already been,* God calls all of history to account.

CONCLUSION

A. "CHANGE AND DECAY"

By our contemporary experiences, the decades before America's Civil War in the nineteenth century may seem like a relatively stable period in history. Yet when Henry F. Lyte wrote "Abide With Me" in 1847, he expressed a much different sentiment: "Change and decay in all around I see." How much more appropriate those words seem in our own times! The twentieth century was torn by wars, crime, oppressive governments, and violent ideologies. In more recent times we have witnessed the upsurge of terrorism that amounts to a strange, worldwide war. Are there any solid foundations left?

The study of history leads us to realize that times always have been unstable and threatening. The few brief periods of peace this old world has enjoyed seem only to be a prelude to greater violence. If this view seems pessimistic, then so be it; but that is the view we find expressed by the writer of Ecclesiastes.

If we look only at the things immediately around us, we are very likely to fall into dark despair. Indeed, we often run into people who are in these desperate straits. In spite of the fact that we enjoy the greatest prosperity the world has ever known and in spite of the fact that we have more things to cater to our comfort and pleasure, our suicide rates remain frighteningly high—a clear sign of despair.

B. "THOU WHO CHANGEST NOT"

But Henry Lyte had an answer for all the change and decay he saw in the culture of his day. He appealed to God, "O Thou who changest not." Like the writer of Ecclesiastes, he knew that there was a God ruling over the universe who was present, always had been present, and would be present regardless of whatever else might change. How reassuring it is to know that amid all the confusion and chaos we see, God stands immovable.

But there is more. Our God is not some distant monarch who has no concern for us and doesn't even know that we exist. Rather, he is a loving Father. We do not see this viewpoint very clearly expressed in Ecclesiastes. But when we turn to the New Testament we learn that our God is a warm, personal God. He is the God who hears and answers our prayers.

Henry Lyte recognized this in the ending words of each stanza: "Abide with me." He had every reason to be assured that God would hear his plea. Indeed, God already answered that plea through his Son, Jesus.

THOUGHT TO REMEMBER

"The Lord is my rock, my fortress and my deliverer" (Psalm 18:2).

Discovery Learning

This page contains an alternative lesson plan emphasizing learning activities. Classes desiring such student involvement will find these suggestions helpful. The next page is a reproducible activity page to further enhance discovery learning.

LEARNING GOALS

After participating in this lesson, each student will be able to:

1. Point out the contrasts that exist in the normal routines of life.

2. Express the comfort that comes from knowing that God is in control, even in the extremes of life.

3. Give a testimony of God's grace that sustained him or her through one of life's extreme periods.

INTO THE LESSON

Choose one of the following activities to introduce this lesson.

Option 1. As class members arrive, give each a sheet of paper with a bold heading reading "I wish I had more time for. . . ." Ask students to write appropriate answers. After a few minutes allow students to share their answers. Make the transition to Bible study by noting that time is a quantity to be managed. What we do and when we do it are important in time management. State, "One book of the Old Testament has a strong philosophical flavor; it has principles about time that can be helpful to us. However, it also teaches that some events and happenings in life are simply in God's control."

Option 2. Prepare a large poster with a heading printed in bold letters, "A Discussion About Time." Ask the class this question: "If you could choose to discuss anything you wish about the concept of *time,* what would you choose?" Write their responses. Make the transition to Bible study by saying, "Time is an extremely important issue. There are many things we would like to talk about under this heading. One of the books of the Old Testament has a strong philosophical flavor, addresses this issue of time, and gives clues to God's control and grace in life's events."

INTO THE WORD

Give a brief lecture about the author and purpose of this book. The Lesson Background will be helpful. Also you may wish to consult a Bible survey book or a commentary introduction to the book of Ecclesiastes.

Distribute copies of an activity sheet described below to groups of four to six. Each group will be working on identical tasks. (This activity is also included in the student book activity pages.) You may give each group a photocopy of the lesson commentary on verses 1-9.

The activity sheet should have three columns: "Time," "The Concept," and "The Application." The rows below the first column should be IN NATURE (3:1, 2), IN BEHAVIOR (3:3, 4), IN BUSINESS (3:5, 6), and IN SOCIETY (3:7, 8). Include space for writing below each line.

Ask the groups to discuss and summarize the concept of each Scripture, noting what God wants us to learn for life under "The Application" column. After they complete the task, ask groups to share their applications from the four passages.

Read verses 9-15. Ask the following discussion questions (included in the student book's "Discovery Learning" section):

1. Are verses 9, 10 a statement of despair (see 2:17-26), or would you read this passage as a writer's device simply to stimulate thinking about the significance of toil? Why?

2. What is this passage saying about the relationship of work to life's joys and satisfactions? Why do you agree or disagree?

3. What does verse 15 say about God's concept of time? What does God want us to understand?

INTO LIFE

Option 1. Allow the same groups that worked together earlier to do the following. Explain that we can apply these Scriptural concepts about time and life tasks everyday. We can zero in on things we must face and do during specific times of our lives. Ask each group to write a new version of this Scripture (vv. 1-8) appropriate for one of the following people groups. Assign one people group to each activity group: college student, parents of young children, husband and wife (age forty), career mid-level manager, elderly couple, terminally ill woman. Allow each group to read their version to the entire class.

Option 2. Testimonial time. Remind the class of the variety of life's tasks that face us at different times. Sometimes those challenges are very difficult. Ask people to share times when life has been difficult, yet where they have seen God's sustaining power at work.

Option 3. Distribute copies of the reproducible activity page that follows. Use the activity "Giving Thanks for the Times in My Life" to encourage personal application. "A Season for Saying So" will prompt a loving move toward another.

Giving Thanks for the Times in My Life

Ecclesiastes 3:2-8 probably brings images to your mind that come from your life experiences. Let's focus on those experiences that have blessed you. As you read these selected lines from Ecclesiastes, note a blessing (event, person, or thing) that comes to your mind for which you are grateful.

A TIME TO . . .

THANKSGIVING FOR . . .

A time to be born and a time to die

A time to plant and a time to uproot

A time to kill and a time to heal

A time to tear down and a time to build

A time to mourn and a time to dance

A time to keep and a time to throw away

A time to love and a time to hate

A time for war and a time for peace

A Season for Saying So

Perhaps it is time for you to tell someone you appreciate the time and place that one has occupied in your life. Complete, clip, and mail the box below. Better yet, rewrite and complete the message on a personally selected card or sheet of stationery and mail that.

Dear _____,

    Our Sunday school class study of Ecclesiastes reminded me of how grateful I am for your place in my life. I wanted to tell you I am thankful for the blessing God has given me in you. I am so thankful for . . .

                                                  Thankful for you,

_____

Lessons From Life
Unit 2: Wisdom for the Times of Our Lives
(Lessons 9-13)

A TIME TO REMEMBER

LESSON 10

WHY TEACH THIS LESSON?

Think of all the stuff you have to help you remember things: photographs, to-do lists, knickknacks—the possibilities are almost endless. Some people take great comfort in surrounding themselves with lots of these mementos and reminders. To other people such things are mere clutter, and they have little use for them.

The Bible takes a balanced viewpoint on what we are to spend time trying to remember. On the one hand Paul tells us of his own efforts at "forgetting what is behind" (Philippians 3:13). On the other hand today's lesson encourages us to "Remember your Creator in the days of your youth" (Ecclesiastes 12:1). Even if our youth is long gone, what more important being is there to remember and meditate on than God himself? Today's lesson is one to be, well, remembered!

INTRODUCTION

A. READY, AIM—!

Few things are more awe inspiring than watching and hearing a battleship fire a broadside. With an earsplitting roar the huge sixteen-inch guns belch flame and smoke, hurling hundreds of pounds of steel and high explosives toward a target hidden beyond the horizon.

But if the shells are to hit their target, several involved calculations must be made. The range of the target must be determined either by sight or by radar. The powder charge must be accurately measured. The speeds of both the firing ship and the target must be taken into account. Allowance must be made for pitch and roll. Even temperature and humidity are important. When we think about all these factors, we are amazed that naval gunners ever succeed. They succeed by excluding every other concern to concentrate on hitting the target.

Life is like this in some ways. When we pick out our "targets"—our life goals— we must concentrate upon them intensely. While Christians may have many short-term goals, our ultimate goal is Heaven. Often we miss many of our goals because we never really aimed at them. How tragic the life that wanders aimlessly about without any real goals! Sometimes we miss our goals because we do not take into consideration all the factors involved—our abilities, opportunities, and preparation. Occasionally we must aim at a target that is out of sight, obscured by time and circumstances. Like the gunner, we must use our radar—our Christian faith—that allows us to aim at the target even when we cannot see it.

Ready, aim—AIM!

B. LESSON BACKGROUND

Have you ever found yourself wishing that you could go back and relive your youth? Most of us have dreamed wistfully of those younger years at one time or another, especially when time begins to take its inevitable toll on our bodies. But most of us also have some reservations about going back. We would want to take with us the wisdom that years of experience have given us. That experience would help us avoid many of the foolish mistakes we made, mistakes that brought pain to others and to ourselves.

DEVOTIONAL READING:
PSALM 143:1-8
BACKGROUND SCRIPTURE:
ECCLESIASTES 11, 12
PRINTED TEXT:
ECCLESIASTES 11:7–12:8

LESSON AIMS

After participating in this lesson, each student will be able to:

1. Give reasons why it is better to remember the Creator in the days of youth rather than in old age.

2. Describe ways the church can do a better job of reaching out to young people.

3. Identify a young person and work for him or her to become a follower of Jesus Christ, or to grow in that relationship.

Feb
8

KEY VERSE

Remember your Creator in the days of your youth, before the days of trouble come.
—Ecclesiastes 12:1

LESSON 10 NOTES

Today we will sense "the Teacher" (Solomon) going through that experience. He knew, of course, that he couldn't go back. But at least he could share some of his wisdom so that others could avoid some of the mistakes he had made. In these few verses he spells out the life cycle that all of us must travel—birth, childhood, adolescence, adulthood, old age, and death—if the Lord gives us enough years. He gives us a few general principles about attitudes concerning life rather than a list of specific moral teachings. As we study the book of Ecclesiastes, we can learn some valuable lessons from one who has "been there and done that."

I. ADVICE TO YOUTH (ECCLESIASTES 11:7-10)

A. LIFE IN PERSPECTIVE (vv. 7, 8)

7. Light is sweet,
    and it pleases the eyes to see the sun.

WHAT DO YOU THINK?

What are some things that make life enjoyable no matter what our age? How are those things sometimes abused?

We may take *light* in its most obvious sense of physical light, especially the light of the sun. But the writer often uses figurative language that involves much more. He may very well have in mind here the whole sweep of life, and so light refers to the events and experiences that illuminate our time on earth.

We feel sorrow for those who lack eyesight, because it is one of the most wonderful blessings God has given us. Our eyes allow us to do many things, including experiencing sweeping vistas of beauty. Light is indeed *sweet*, as it allows us to enjoy and use our eyesight even with glasses or after laser surgery. We who have our eyesight can scarcely imagine what it would be like to be blind.

8. However many years a man may live,
    let him enjoy them all.
But let him remember the days of darkness,
    for they will be many.
    Everything to come is meaningless.

Even as we enjoy life as it unfolds, we are given a solemn reminder to keep things in perspective. The *days of darkness* are old age (cf. Ecclesiastes 12:2, below). Those of us who have yet to experience the challenges of old age can nevertheless see its effects all around. The nursing homes and long-term care facilities are not populated with young people! Younger adults today face the delicate problem of taking the car keys away from their elderly parents who no longer should be driving—a problem that didn't exist in Solomon's day.

This verse closes with the pessimistic warning that *everything to come is meaningless*. Perhaps it is best to think of this as a ploy to get our attention about how we ought to prepare ourselves for earthly life rather than a realistic appraisal of what life really is from an eternal perspective. Or perhaps this is indeed a realistic appraisal for the ungodly as they go through the seasons of life. Certainly life is not vanity (empty and meaningless) for a Christian.

B. LIFE IN THE SHADOW OF JUDGMENT (vv. 9, 10)

9. Be happy, young man, while you are young,
    and let your heart give you joy in the days of your youth.
Follow the ways of your heart
    and whatever your eyes see,
but know that for all these things
    God will bring you to judgment.

WHAT DO YOU THINK?

Jeremiah 17:9 tells us that "the heart is deceitful above all things." Yet Solomon says in Ecclesiastes 11:9 to "follow the ways of your heart." How do we reconcile the two?

"The Teacher" (Solomon) continues to stress the importance of enjoying life, especially in one's youth. His suggestion that young people *follow the ways* of their hearts sounds quite contemporary on the surface—"whatever works for you." How frightening! Certainly Christian parents would not give this advice to their children. To give such advice to a teenager who is trying to cope with raging hormones and a desire to fit in with other teenagers is likely to be disastrous.

But Solomon is quick to establish boundaries for his advice in noting that *for all these things God will bring you to judgment.* This is a solemn warning that those who follow their own desires to the point of ignoring God's standards must face God's judgment, either here or hereafter. (See Ecclesiastes 3:17.)

10. So then, banish anxiety from your heart
    and cast off the troubles of your body,
    for youth and vigor are meaningless.

The Hebrew word for *anxiety* also occurs in Ecclesiastes 1:18, where it is translated "sorrow," and 2:23, where it is translated "grief." Sorrow and grief over the results of our actions can create anxiety. In our own times anxiety has become an epidemic, and people spend millions on counseling and medications to cope.

This verse points the way to avoiding this sorrow in advising us to *cast off the troubles of your body.* When we avoid the evil that causes trouble, we treat the actual cause of much anxiety, and not just the symptoms (cf. 1 Peter 2:11).

The years of *youth* can seem to be *meaningless* because they are "fleeting," which is another way to translate this word. For teenagers eager to attain adult status, these years seem to drag. But to those who have reached maturity or beyond, those youthful years were all too brief.

II. FRUSTRATION OF AGING (ECCLESIASTES 12:1-8)

A. COMING STORMS (vv. 1, 2)

1. Remember your Creator
    in the days of your youth,
  before the days of trouble come
    and the years approach when you will say,
    "I find no pleasure in them"—

Deathbed confessions may, in some cases, be legitimate. But how much better it is when one makes a commitment to the *Creator* in his or her *youth!* There are at least two good reasons why this is so. First, children and adolescents are less "set in their ways"; it is much easier for them to make that decision than for an adult whose life patterns have become increasingly rigid. Second, the younger that one is when joining the Lord's army, the more time he or she has to be involved in Christian ministry and enjoy the blessings that result from a lifetime of service.

Before the days of trouble come gives the reason for remembering God in our youth. Those evil days are the later years in life with their infirmities and pain. They seem especially evil to young people who rarely suffer such disabilities.

The writer himself has *no pleasure* in those closing years of life. Today, however, many have learned to cope with the problems of aging, and, freed from the pressures of jobs and rearing a family, they find a peace that earlier they could not enjoy.

IN THE DAYS OF YOUTH

A few years ago Barna Research discovered that people are most likely to come to Christ in their preteen years. Perhaps Solomon knew that faith commitments come easier in the earlier years when he wrote, "Remember your Creator in the days of your youth" (Ecclesiastes 12:1). We must not overlook the importance of leading young people to the Lord!

Yet conversion at a young age has its dangers. Children can commit their lives to Christ without a clear understanding of what this commitment involves (cf. Matthew 13:6). Parents naturally fret about this. Is age seven too young to walk down the aisle and make a formal faith commitment? How about age ten? Children

---

WHAT DO YOU THINK?

Truly we live in the shadow of God's judgment. Why is it difficult to communicate this message to our culture?

WHAT DO YOU THINK?

The Scripture describes God in several ways. Why do you think Solomon chose to use the title "Creator" in his challenge to youth?

[Although Solomon didn't have them, passages such as 2 Corinthians 5:17; Galatians 6:15; and Colossians 1:16 are important for us today.]

WHAT DO YOU THINK?

Imagine that you are writing an advice column for youth. What will you caution them to avoid?

HOW TO SAY IT

cistern. SIS-turn.
Deuteronomy. Due-ter-AHN-uh-me.
Ecclesiastes. Ik-LEEZ-ee-AS-teez.
larynx. LAIR-inks.
Solomon. SOL-o-mun.

who are pushed too hard may become resentful and fall away from Christ later—in effect, they can become "inoculated" against faith.

Nevertheless, children need to be encouraged to devote themselves to the Lord. Their hearts are open, they are eager to learn, and, even before they become teenagers, they are capable of making decisions they will follow their entire lives.

You can help by volunteering in the children's ministry or youth ministry in your church. You can help by inviting neighborhood children to Bible study classes or other programs for them. You can help by praying for the young people in your congregation. And you can help by financially supporting your church's children's ministries and youth ministries. The days of youth can produce lifelong servants for the Lord, and you can help.   —J. D. J.

2. . . . *before the sun and the light*
        and the moon and the stars grow dark,
        and the clouds return after the rain;
This verse and several that follow deal with some of the problems that the aging must face. The meanings of the figurative language used to describe some of these problems are not always clear, and not everyone agrees about the correct references. Yet there is no question that the writer is describing conditions that accompany advancing years.

B. DECLINING HEALTH (vv. 3, 4)
3. . . . *when the keepers of the house tremble,*
        and the strong men stoop,
    when the grinders cease because they are few,
        and those looking through the windows grow dim;
"The Teacher" (Solomon) describes the physical decline that accompanies advancing years in terms of the parts of a house. *The keepers of the house* probably refers to the hands and arms. They protect the house and care for it. As a person grows older, the hands and arms *tremble*, a common problem of older people suffering from various neurological afflictions or general physical weaknesses. *The strong men* who *stoop* may refer to the legs and back that become bent by age.

The grinders are, of course, the teeth. Older people in primitive societies are often toothless or nearly so. Today most older people living in cultures with advanced dentistry either have their own teeth or have dentures that work very well.

The windows of this figurative house are the eyes. There are not many people who escape the problem of failing eyesight. Moses was one of the few who avoided this weakness (see Deuteronomy 34:7).

4. . . . *when the doors to the street are closed*
        and the sound of grinding fades;
    when men rise up at the sound of birds,
        but all their songs grow faint;
Interpreting the symbolism in this verse is more difficult. One possible interpretation for *the doors* is as a reference to the ears. Ears can be thought of as doorways "into" a person in terms of being able to conduct a conversation. Physical problems may contribute to one's inability to converse, but older folks are often shut out of conversations because of poor hearing.

Helen Keller (1880–1968), perhaps the most well-known deaf and blind person of the twentieth century, is purported to have said that she would prefer to have the sense of hearing over eyesight, if given a choice. This was because lack of eyesight cuts us off from things, but lack of hearing cuts us off from other people. Modern culture has an advantage in this area with the marvel of hearing aids (although most of us know someone who is too stubborn to use one!). But mod-

DAILY BIBLE READINGS

Monday, Feb. 2—I Have Beheld Your Power and Glory (Psalm 63:1-8)

Tuesday, Feb. 3—I Consider the Days of Old (Psalm 77:4-10)

Wednesday, Feb. 4—I Will Remember Your Wonders (Psalm 77:11-15)

Thursday, Feb. 5—I Think About All Your Deeds (Psalm 143:1-8)

Friday, Feb. 6—God's Work Is a Mystery (Ecclesiastes 11:1-5)

Saturday, Feb. 7—Youth Is Fleeting (Ecclesiastes 11:6-10)

Sunday, Feb. 8—Remember Your Creator (Ecclesiastes 12: 1-8) ern culture also has a disadvantage of being very "noisy" (machinery, loud music, etc.), thus contributing to hearing loss.

The sound of the grinding fades probably refers to loss of teeth. With old age and loss of teeth come the inability to chew anything but mostly soft foods. The loss of teeth causes the cheeks to become sunken, making it more difficult to open the mouth. Again, modern dentistry can solve this problem, helping people avoid the look that once characterized many older people.

There are various interpretations to the statement *when men rise up at the sound of birds*. It may refer to the fact that many elderly people are light sleepers and are readily aroused by the early morning call of birds, even with a loss of hearing. A few suggest that it refers to the possibility that an older person's voice can become high pitched and chirpy like that of a bird.

The phrase *all their songs grow faint* poses similar problems of interpretation. This may refer to the larynx and vocal cords, as they become enfeebled by age. Another possibility is that elderly people who have become hard of hearing no longer can take pleasure in the beauty of a woman's singing voice.

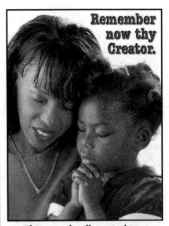

This visual will remind your learners of the responsibility they have to lead youth to God.

C. GROWING FEARS (v. 5)

5. . . . when men are afraid of heights
     and of dangers in the streets;
   when the almond tree blossoms
     and the grasshopper drags himself along
     and desire no longer is stirred.
   Then man goes to his eternal home
     and mourners go about the streets.

To be *afraid of heights* may refer to the problems that older people have in climbing stairs or hills. Weak of limb and short of breath, they can find even a small ascent to be threatening. *The almond tree* in Palestine blooms in mid-winter, perhaps pointing to the "winter" of a person's life—but with the important difference that there is no spring to follow. In the same way insects such as the *grasshopper* move very slowly when the weather is cold. This also is a picture of old age. It is at such a time that *desire no longer is stirred* as interest in food and sex begin to fade away.

The last part of this verse looks to the end of life. The *mourners*, then, are professionals who have been hired to participate in the funeral ceremonies that surround a death.

D. LOOMING DEATH (vv. 6, 7)

6. Remember him—before the silver cord is severed,
     or the golden bowl is broken;
   before the pitcher is shattered at the spring,
     or the wheel broken at the well,

The figures used in this verse all describe death. *The silver cord* suspends a lamp, *the golden bowl*. When the cord breaks, the lamp drops to the floor and the light is extinguished. Water is drawn from wells using clay vessels. Occasionally a pitcher would be dropped, shattering it and ending its useful existence.

The wheel refers to a device used to draw water from a deep *well*. When the wheel breaks, no more water can be drawn.

7. . . . and the dust returns to the ground it came from,
     and the spirit returns to God who gave it.

God formed humanity from *the dust* of the earth (Genesis 2:7; 3:19). In death the body returns to the earth from whence it came, a quite dismal prospect.

PRAYER

Gracious Father, may this lesson remind us that this life is fleeting, that from a worldly point of view it is vanity. Give us the wisdom to look beyond the emptiness of life to see the opportunities for service you have for us and the hope we have for eternal life through Jesus Christ, through whom we pray, amen.

But happily the verse does not end there because *the spirit returns to God who gave it.* Here is one of the rare references to life after death in the Old Testament. "The Teacher" (Solomon) ultimately concludes that people do indeed have an advantage over the animals (cf. Ecclesiastes 3:18-21).

WORN HEADSTONES

When was the last time you walked through a cemetery? We don't usually frequent such places. Even visiting www.findagrave.com on the Internet seems a little "creepy"! We generally visit cemeteries only for funerals or on Memorial Day.

But in graveyards there is wisdom for the seasons of our lives. One gravestone warns, "As you are now, so once was I. As I am now, so you must be, so prepare for death and follow me." My infant sister's gravestone says, "Asleep in Jesus," reassuring us that even though she is "absent from the body," she is "present with the Lord" (2 Corinthians 5:8).

Cemeteries remind us that we will return to dust no matter who we are. Cemeteries also remind us that we have value. We do not put markers in our gardens for deceased plants. Few make it a practice to honor their deceased pets with gravestones. Only humans regularly receive this honor in death. Perhaps it was God who put the drive to do this within us because we are made in His image. Even when people are gone, we erect these markers in the hope that they not be forgotten.

But headstones become worn with age. This reminds us that the relentless passage of time eventually wipes away our memories from planet Earth. Many gravestones that are one hundred years old or more are hardly legible. Only God remembers the people buried in such places.

You will die unless Jesus comes first. Yet you are valued because you bear God's image. Eventually, others will forget you, but you always will be precious to God. Devote yourself to Him now so that He will devote Himself to you for eternity.—J. D. J.

E. CLOSING LAMENT (v. 8)

8. "Meaningless! Meaningless!" says the Teacher.
    "Everything is meaningless!"

With these words *the Teacher* (Solomon) returns to the theme with which he began the book of Ecclesiastes: *Meaningless! Meaningless!* (1:2). This is certainly an appropriate conclusion to his discussion of physical life. Everything we accomplish on the earth eventually is left to others (2:18).

But life does not end at the grave. As Longfellow reminds us, "Dust thou art, to dust returnest, Was not spoken of the soul" (from "A Psalm of Life"). Thanks be to God for our resurrected Lord, through whom we have the hope of life eternal!

CONCLUSION

Rather than the *days* of youth, it may be more appropriate to speak of the *daze* of youth. Young people today are subjected to such a wide variety of threats and temptations that there is little wonder that many of them have distorted views of reality.

This puts a heavy responsibility on parents to provide guidance. Unfortunately, many parents cannot or will not provide this guidance. Thus a growing responsibility falls upon churches to fill this void.

This lesson ought to motivate your church to take a careful look at what it is doing for its young people. Many churches today have youth ministers, and a few visionary churches have hired children's ministers for pre-teens. That's good!

But just hiring extra church staff can give church members the false sense of security that "we've got those bases covered." That's bad! Reaching our pre-adults for Christ takes more—it takes you. There is no higher calling than to help a young person develop a walk of Christian faith. What role will you play?

THOUGHT TO REMEMBER

"For you have been my hope, O Sovereign Lord, my confidence since my youth" (Psalm 71:5).

Discovery Learning

This page contains an alternative lesson plan emphasizing learning activities. Classes desiring such student involvement will find these suggestions helpful. The next page is a reproducible activity page to further enhance discovery learning.

LEARNING GOALS

After participating in this lesson, each student will be able to:

1. Give reasons why it is better to remember the Creator in youth rather than in old age.

2. Describe ways the church can do a better job of reaching out to young people.

3. Identify a young person in the church and pray that he or she become a follower of Jesus Christ or grow in that relationship.

INTO THE LESSON

Option 1. Say, "We are going to play the 'What if' game." Display a poster that reads: "What if I could relive my high school or college years?" Continue, "Most of us probably would not actually want to relive those years; however, if we could change something about those years, what would we change? What would we do better? What would get more emphasis?" Allow each person to tell one other person what he or she would change.

Remind the class that the Bible values the years of youth. God knows the value of formative years and how those years will affect later life.

Option 2. Find a large dartboard with a series of circles for a target and attach numerous balloons to it. Label the board "Goals of Youth." Ask the class members to cite what appears to be the center of focus for high school students today. Use a marker to label the balloons with their answers. Cite a few examples: a car, sex, drugs, good grades, volunteering, worshiping God, starting a career, graduation, friends, popularity, Christian dates and relationships, computer gaming. When someone mentions a spiritual goal such as "serve or worship God," write that on the balloon in the center of the target.

Say, "Many things are tugging for the attention of youth in today's world. Unfortunately, some youth really don't have goals of significance. However, God's love for youth and for the lives they are beginning is demonstrated in today's text. He offers a very clear target for youth." To conclude this activity, break the balloon in the center of the target.

INTO THE WORD

Put the class into groups of four or five. Give each group one of the following assignments:

Task 1. Give groups with this assignment a copy of the lesson commentary on Ecclesiastes 11:7–12:1. Also give them a worksheet with the heading and instructions: "Task Force 1: Discovering Lessons for Young People! Read Ecclesiastes 11:7–12:1 and discover God's lessons for youth. Write your discoveries on this sheet. Assign someone to be ready to report your discoveries."

Task 2. Give groups with this assignment a copy of the lesson commentary on Ecclesiastes 12:1-8. Also give them a worksheet with the heading and instructions: "Task Force 2: Interpreting Lessons for Aging! Read Ecclesiastes 12:1-8 and discover God's lessons for aging. Write your discoveries on this sheet. Assign someone to be ready to report your discoveries."

After groups complete the assignments, ask the spokesperson from each to move to a group that did not study the same text. That person will read the text and tell the answers that his or her task force found; thus, class members teach each other.

After this activity, make a few comments about the significance of 12:8. See the lesson commentary for helpful information.

INTO LIFE

Remind the class that the church has an opportunity and responsibility to encourage spiritual growth in youth. Ask them to brainstorm ways the church can do this effectively by building an acrostic using the letters of the words "*Days of Youth.*" Copy and distribute this activity from the reproducible page that follows.

Then, challenge the class to become encouragers to at least one teenager. Bring a list of high school youth and their addresses to the class; ask each person to select the name of one in the congregation. Class members should not select the same person. For the remaining three weeks in the month, class members should send an anonymous weekly note of encouragement, appreciation, and promises of prayer for the young person chosen. No gifts should be given. Notes and cards—including a promise to pray for the teen, admiration of spiritual qualities or personal traits, prayers you have offered—should be sent to the young person's home address. (Men should select boys and women select girls; husband and wife pairs can select either.)

Class members may reveal their names to their "secret pal" in their third and last note or in person.

Days of Our Youth

One of the opportunities of the local church is to encourage and help our youth to grow in their relationships to the Lord. Use each of the letters in "Days of Youth" to form words or phrases that note ways we can help youth develop a healthy relationship with the Lord. The letters of the acrostic may begin, end, or merely be included in the words or phrases you choose. (An example has been included to stimulate thought.)

D

A

Y

S

AFFIRMATI**O**N

F

Y

O

U

T

H

And Days of Silver Cords

Solomon writes "Remember him (your Creator) before the silver cord is severed." It is good for people of all ages to reflect periodically and evaluate relationships with the Lord. Use the questions below to help you.

1. Have you accepted Jesus as the Savior from your sins? If not, would you like to do so? Who in your class or congregation can help you understand and submit to God's redemptive plan?

2. How satisfied are you with your prayer and devotional life? Very satisfied? Somewhat satisfied? Somewhat dissatisfied? Very dissatisfied? How would you like to improve it?

3. Is there an area of your life that you have not yet given to Christ? If so, do you wish to change? If needed, from whom could you find help or establish accountability in this process?

Lessons From Life

Unit 2: Wisdom for the Times of Our Lives
(Lessons 9-13)

A TIME FOR LOVE

LESSON 11

WHY TEACH THIS LESSON?

Many Bible college and seminary campuses have rules against "PDA"—public display of affection. Such rules recognize that there is a proper place for adults to show romantic affection for one another, and the school cafeteria is not it!

Rules against PDA do not denigrate physical affection—in fact, quite the opposite. God is the one who created attraction between the sexes in the first place (cf. Hebrews 13:4). But this is a viewpoint that Hollywood does not endorse. Its movies, TV shows, and commercials overpower us with images of sexual involvement without marital commitment. Today's lesson will help your learners counteract those depictions. There is indeed "a time for love." Our Creator has decreed it!

INTRODUCTION

A. "HOW DO I LOVE THEE?"

Elizabeth Barrett (1806–1861) was born into a well-to-do family and received a good education. As a child she began to write poetry that attracted attention. This brought her into contact with many of the literary luminaries of her day. But her poor health almost completely eliminated any chance she had of getting married. To compound the problem, her father, who ruled his family with an iron hand, forbade his children to marry.

Then Elizabeth met Robert Browning, a rising young poet, six years her junior. The two carried on a secret correspondence and eventually fell in love. But when Browning proposed to her, she turned him down, insisting that she didn't want to burden him with a sickly wife who could never have a normal life. Browning persisted, however, and they were secretly married. Her father was furious when he learned of it, and as a result the Brownings spent most of their married life in Italy, a life together that proved extremely happy.

In her *Sonnets From the Portuguese* Elizabeth poured out her love for her husband:

How do I love thee? Let me count the ways,
I love thee to the depth and breadth and height
My soul can reach, when feeling out of sight
For the ends of Being and ideal Grace.
I love thee to the level of everyday's
Most quiet need, by sun and candle-light,
I love thee freely, as men strive for Right;
I love thee purely, as they turn from Praise.
I love thee with the passion put to use
In my old griefs, and with my childhood's faith,
I love thee with a love I seemed to lose
With my lost saints,—I love thee with the breath,
Smiles, tears, of all my life!—and, if God choose,
I shall but love thee better after death.

We all know how much modern culture has emphasized sex. This has cheapened the physical aspects of love to the point that many cannot appreciate the type of love that overcomes barriers and grows richer through the years!

DEVOTIONAL READING:
JEREMIAH 31:1-5
BACKGROUND SCRIPTURE:
SONG OF SOLOMON 2:8-13; 7:10-12; 8:6, 7
PRINTED TEXT:
SONG OF SOLOMON 2:8-13; 7:10-12; 8:6, 7

LESSON AIMS

After participating in this lesson, students will be able to:

1. Describe the affection portrayed between the beloved and the bride in the Song of Solomon.

2. Contrast the view of marital love in the text with contemporary sexual standards.

3. Commit themselves to renewed sexual and relational purity and faithfulness.

Feb
15

KEY VERSE

Place me like a seal over your heart, like a seal on your arm; for love is as strong as death, its jealousy unyielding as the grave.
—Song of Solomon 8:6

B. LESSON BACKGROUND

The Song of Solomon (or Song of Songs, or Canticles, as it is sometimes called) is controversial. Both Jewish and Christian commentators, put off by its erotic content, have often interpreted it in very figurative ways.

Some Jews see in the book a picture of God's love for his people expressed in physical terms. Some Christians similarly see in it Christ's love for the church. At times, both Jews and Christians have looked upon physical love as evil, permissible only for procreation. It was thus more acceptable to explain the obvious references to the physical aspects of love in figurative terms.

Perhaps the only good thing that has come out of the so-called sexual revolution of the past fifty years is that we can talk more freely and without embarrassment about sexual matters. Thus we can now begin to see the book as it was originally written—a beautiful and wholesome expression of the love between a man and a woman within the bonds of marriage.

Even within this viewpoint, however, scholars see this book in different ways. Many take it to be a collection of love songs to be sung at weddings, often by professional musicians. Others see in this book a drama being played out in which there are three characters: King Solomon, the maiden, and her lover, who is a shepherd. According to this view, Solomon seeks to win the maiden, but she remains loyal to her true love. This view has some appeal, but the evidence is not all that clear.

Regardless of the approach one takes to the Song of Solomon, we can appreciate its poetic beauty and the many delightful glimpses it gives us of love and courtship. This book also reminds us that foundational human relations between men and women have not changed radically across the centuries.

I. THE BELOVED'S APPROACH (SONG OF SOLOMON 2:8-13)

A. JOYFUL ANTICIPATION (v. 8)

8. Listen! My lover!
   Look! Here he comes,
leaping across the mountains,
   bounding over the hills.

We are not sure of the name of the young woman who is the heroine of this book. Some believe it was "Shulammite" (6:13), but this word probably designates her hometown. She seems to be recalling an earlier meeting with her *lover.* She eagerly awaits his arrival. As he approaches, he is not moving at a leisurely pace!

BEHOLD, HE IS COMING

Many animals actively court their potential mates. Pacific tree frogs sing solos. Peacocks display spectacular plumage. Female moths produce perfume to attract a mate. Male wolf spiders give their "dates" a gift of food wrapped in silk. Emphid flies spin balloons out of spider silk to give to their potential mates. Many animals go through elaborate courtships before they come together as mates.

Humans behave in similar fashion. Men and women dress up in "spectacular plumage." They put on cologne and perfume. People take their dates out to eat. Couples sing special songs together. We may bring each other wrapped gifts.

On a more intimate level, a person will hang on every word of a potential mate. We make time to spend together. We share our innermost thoughts and feelings. Through these experiences, we attract each other, we find a kindred soul, and we join our lives together.

Unfortunately, courtship often declines after marriage begins. Husbands and wives stop hanging on each other's words. They stop buying gifts or dressing up.

DAILY BIBLE READINGS

Monday, Feb. 9—*I Love You, O Lord (Psalm 18:1-6)*

Tuesday, Feb. 10—*A Commandment to Love God (Deuteronomy 6:4-9)*

Wednesday, Feb. 11—*Love Others as Christ Loves Us (John 15:8-12)*

Thursday, Feb. 12—*No Greater Love (John 15:13-17)*

Friday, Feb. 13—*God's Everlasting Love (Jeremiah 31: 1-5)*

Saturday, Feb. 14—*A Song of Love (Song of Solomon 2: 8-13)*

Sunday, Feb. 15—*Love Is Strong as Death (Song of Solomon 7:10-12; 8:6, 7)*

They take each other for granted. Mates neglect to make time for each other once their beloved has already come "leaping upon the mountains" for them.

The apostle Paul has godly advice for both husbands and wives in Ephesians 5:22-33. Husband, will you love your wife enough to continue courting her? Wife, will you love your husband enough to continue responding to him? What will each of you do this week to keep your courtship alive?   —J. D. J.

B. TIMID APPROACH (v. 9)
9. My lover is like a gazelle or a young stag.
  Look! There he stands behind our wall,
gazing through the windows,
  peering through the lattice.

Although the lover hurries to meet the object of his affection, he becomes shy as he approaches. As she watches his behavior, she compares him with *a gazelle or a young stag*. The gazelle is a small deer or antelope. It is noted for its agility. *A young stag* is a male deer or similar animal. However, we cannot precisely identify what this species is. They are considered extinct in Palestine today.

These animals are extremely shy, and this seems to be the idea the young woman wishes to express. Her lover conceals himself behind a wall, perhaps in the garden. But he is visible when he peers through the latticework of an opening. There doesn't seem to be any particular reason for the lover's shy behavior, except that lovers sometimes display such courtship rituals. Perhaps he is not quite sure that he has her approval for his efforts to woo her.

C. APPEALING INVITATION (vv. 10-13)
10, 11. My lover spoke and said to me,
  "Arise, my darling,
  my beautiful one, and come with me.
  See! The winter is past;
  the rains are over and gone.

The young woman recognizes the presence of her *lover*. As a result he overcomes his shyness and speaks, inviting her to join him outside the house.

The winter is past and the coming of spring has awakened nature, making his invitation an attractive one. Spring in Palestine is a beautiful time of the year. Most of the rainfall comes during the fall and winter. The rains end in the spring and the temperature becomes most pleasant.
12. Flowers appear on the earth;
  the season of singing has come,
  the cooing of doves
  is heard in our land.

The wild *flowers* are awakened from their slumber by the previous rains, and the hills become lovely blankets of color. It is a time made for courting, far better than the chilly, rainy days of winter.

Many commentators believe that *the season of singing* refers to the singing of the workers as they go about their spring work.

The cooing of doves refers to the plaintive cooing of the turtledove. A type of wild pigeon, the turtledove is normally a migratory bird in Palestine. However, some may remain to nest there, and their songs fill the warm spring air.
13. The fig tree forms its early fruit;
  the blossoming vines spread their fragrance.
  Arise, come, my darling;
  my beautiful one, come with me.

WHAT DO YOU THINK?

What suggestions would you offer to a young married couple about how to "keep the flame alive"? How would your suggestions differ from what secular culture seems to think is important in this regard?

Figs are grown throughout ancient Israel. They can be dried and preserved, thus forming a stable part of the diet the year around (e.g., 1 Samuel 25:18; 30:11, 12). Many fig trees blossom and set fruit before they put out leaves. When the fig trees begin to set fruit, it is a good sign that spring is near at hand. Occasionally a late freeze will destroy the early fruit, but the tree will produce new fruit later.

Grapes were widely grown by the Canaanites long before the Israelites took possession of the land. For example, the spies returned from Canaan with one cluster of grapes so large that it had to be carried on a pole between two men (Numbers 13:23). The grapes blossom in the early spring. The blossoms of many varieties give off a pleasant aroma, adding to the delight of the early spring days.

All these signs of the passing of winter and the arrival of spring offer the perfect opportunity for a courtship invitation. So the beloved suggests that the maiden join him in enjoying this pleasant environment. He has already extended the invitation earlier, but apparently she has coyly ignored it or rejected it. So a second invitation is necessary.

II. THE BRIDE'S COMMITMENT (SONG OF SOLOMON 7:10-12)

A. THE BRIDE'S SURRENDER (v. 10)

10. I belong to my lover,
    and his desire is for me.

In the verses immediately preceding this verse we read an erotic description of some of the physical aspects of love, which some attribute to Solomon. Some students believe this verse portrays the young woman's rejection of the king's advances and her faithfulness to her shepherd *lover*.

However, this passage might portray her acceptance of Solomon's descriptive words acclaiming his love for her. This verse echoes 6:3: "I am my lover's and my lover is mine," indicating a surrender of each to the other. Mutual surrender is at the heart of marital bliss.

B. THE BRIDE'S SENTIMENT (vv. 11, 12)

11, 12. Come, my lover, let us go to the countryside,
    let us spend the night in the villages.
Let us go early to the vineyards
    to see if the vines have budded,
if their blossoms have opened,
    and if the pomegranates are in bloom—
    there I will give you my love.

Perhaps feeling threatened and hemmed in by the city, the maiden invites her *lover* to go with her *to the countryside*. There in the open countryside and the villages that dot the rural areas she feels they will have an opportunity to enjoy their affection for one another. This is a joy that the busy, noisy city conspires to deny.

They find pleasure as they wander through the *vineyards*, checking the buds that begin to turn green and will soon burst forth as leaves. This may be a symbol of their love that grows and develops with the passage of time. The buds are soon followed by the *blossoms* and then the tender grape.

Pomegranates bud in early spring, and their blossoms are orange-red in color. The fruit is about the size of an orange, and in the ancient world is considered a symbol of fertility and eternal life. Perhaps this is the reason that Solomon had pomegranates carved into beams in the temple (1 Kings 7:18, 20, 42). Along with grapes and figs, it is one of the most widely cultivated fruits in the ancient Near East.

WHAT DO YOU THINK?

Could it be that the location and time the two lovers met seemed ideal only because of their strong emotions? Explain how a loving relationship can affect our perceptions.

WHAT DO YOU THINK?

The text seems to indicate that this couple was completely devoted to one another. How does modern culture belittle the idea of exclusive devotion?

WHAT DO YOU THINK?

What kinds of circumstances can distract us from growing in our marital relationships? How does our text assist us in refreshing our marriages?

III. THE BOND OF LOVE (SONG OF SOLOMON 8:6, 7)

A. LOVE IS STRONG (v. 6)

6. Place me like a seal over your heart,
like a seal on your arm;
for love is as strong as death,
its jealousy unyielding as the grave.
It burns like blazing fire,
like a mighty flame.

"*Set me as a seal upon thine heart.*"
—— Song of Solomon 8:6.

Use this image to reinforce the first part of today's Key Verse.

In ancient times it was a common practice to authenticate a document with a seal pressed into moist clay or soft wax, rather than with a signature as today (cf. 1 Kings 21:8; Esther 8:8; Job 38:14). The beloved alludes to this practice as a guarantee of the steadfastness of their *love* (cf. 2 Corinthians 1:22; Ephesians 1:13).

The young woman asserts that her love is just as *strong* as *death* and cannot for long be resisted. Death never releases its prey once it has been seized, and love is just as relentless.

The point of the statement that *jealousy* is *unyielding as the grave* is that the woman's love is exclusive and will not tolerate rivals. Jealousy is an incredibly powerful emotion. The Bible speaks of God as a jealous God; this is not jealousy in a petty or selfish sense, but the type that demands undivided loyalty of his followers (Exodus 20:5). Loyalty is what the young woman has in mind.

Jealousy is sometimes spoken of as a *flame* that burns relentlessly (cf. Deuteronomy 4:24; 6:15; Zephaniah 3:8). When jealousy is petty and selfish, it can be a consuming *fire* that destroys all the parties involved. We can hope that the beloved does not have such an attitude, but only a thin line separates this kind of jealousy from the type of jealousy that God has for his children.

WHAT DO YOU THINK?

The text speaks of a "seal" upon the heart. What are some things we use today as "marriage seals"? Why are they important?

B. LOVE IS UNQUENCHABLE (v. 7)

7. Many waters cannot quench love,
rivers cannot wash it away
If one were to give
all the wealth of his house for love,
it would be utterly scorned.

The young woman's *love* cannot be extinguished by water. It is as if one were to try to extinguish a river of hot lava with a garden hose. In this dramatic figure she reaffirms her devotion to her husband.

Even if a man would give all the substance of his house for love, it would be rejected or *scorned*. This is an interesting statement in view of the fact that Solomon was the richest king Israel ever had. If the woman is saying to him that her love cannot be purchased, she is modeling true love! In Christian marriage ceremonies couples are asked to commit themselves to one another through health and sickness, in wealth and poverty. This affirms that love has its basis in something other than material possessions.

LOVE'S POWER

Love is so powerful! When a person is in danger of losing his life, he does not think of his boss, his neighbor, or his accountant. He thinks of his loved ones. Love has the power to cause a person to change careers and to forego wealth.

One who discovered this was Edward VIII, King of England, who ascended to the throne on January 21, 1936. Less than a year later he announced, "I have found it impossible to carry the heavy burden of responsibility and to discharge my duties as king as I would wish to do without the help and support of the woman I love."

HOW TO SAY IT

Canticles. KAN-tih-kels.
Deuteronomy. Due-ter-AHN-uh-me.
pomegranate. POM-ih-gran-it.
Solomon. SOL-o-mun.
Shulammite. SHOO-lum-mite.
Zephaniah. Zef-uh-NYE-uh.

The woman King Edward referred to was twice divorced, and British law prohibited the monarch from marrying a divorced person. Therefore, Edward voluntarily gave up his crown and went into lifelong exile in order to marry Wallis Simpson.

Love is so powerful! King Edward was willing to give up prestige, popularity, and "perks" for the one he loved. What are you willing to give up for those you love—a TV show, a nap, an evening in your garage, time on the computer? Show your loved ones you value them by giving your time, interest, and energy to them. When your life is done, you will be glad you did. For the greatest thing in life is love.   —J. D. J.

CONCLUSION

A. THE SEXUAL REVOLUTION

After World War II an assault began on the traditional standards of sexual morality, standards that were Biblically based and widely accepted. These standards were ridiculed as "prudish," "old-fashioned," "Puritanical," or "Victorian." We were told that more relaxed sexual standards would free us from old fears and superstitions. The open rejection of traditional standards on TV and in the movies has made adultery look attractive, desirable, and fun.

We now have had five decades of this new "freedom." Enough data is in to allow us see the appalling results. In the early 1960s the divorce rate began to rise. Today, for every two new marriages in the U.S. there is about one divorce. Many children caught between warring parents never fully recover from the trauma.

As the disdain for the institution of marriage grew, the number of births to unwed mothers skyrocketed. Along with an absence of shame came poverty as single mothers tried to hold families together without a husband in the picture. Live-in boyfriends just don't provide the income or the stability to build a solid home. Sexual "freedom" actually has become a kind of slavery.

But sadly there is more. Sexual promiscuity has caused a substantial increase in the number of cases of sexually transmitted diseases. At one time many believed that antibiotics would eliminate them. But growing sexual promiscuity and the increased resistance of these diseases to treatment has dimmed this hope.

But the worst was yet to come. A little over two decades ago, AIDS burst upon the scene. In Africa this terrible disease now decimates the population. Millions of dollars have been spent seeking a cure. But at best researchers have succeeded only in prolonging the lives of those who are HIV positive or have full-blown AIDS—and this only in nations that have access to the medications.

B. THE CHRISTIAN RESPONSE

The home is the solid foundation for any stable society. Six thousand years of human history prove it. An active campaign to bolster the home must include Biblical teaching about sexual purity and true love. We must never compromise this message. This is a message we must teach in our youth classes because all too often their bodies are growing up more rapidly than their moral values.

Yet it is not enough just to teach. Leaders of the church must demonstrate by their own lives that following God's standards for love and marriage brings life-long happiness and emotional security. We must do this despite the presence of high-profile examples of infidelity and the general acceptance of immoral behaviors and lifestyles.

This could be a good time to discuss with your class what your church is doing in this area. If your church is doing very little, your class can become a force to stimulate action. One does not have to be a prophet of gloom and doom to realize that the hour is late and the threat is serious. A church that is willing to take an active role in building stronger Christian homes is a church that will grow.

Discovery Learning

This page contains an alternative lesson plan emphasizing learning activities. Classes desiring such student involvement will find these suggestions helpful. The next page is a reproducible activity page to further enhance discovery learning.

LEARNING GOALS

After participating in this lesson, students will be able to:

1. Describe the affection portrayed between the beloved and the bride in the Song of Solomon.

2. Contrast the view of marital love in the text with contemporary sexual standards.

3. Commit themselves to renewed sexual and relational purity and faithfulness.

INTO THE LESSON

Early in the week, telephone married couples from the class and invite each to bring a picture of themselves from their dating days or from their honeymoon. Both persons should be in the photograph. Assure the couple they will get the picture back. As students arrive, ask them to attach the photos to a poster or bulletin board.

Give students time to enjoy the photos. Tell them the class will talk about these later in the session. Also give each one a small adhesive colorful circle or dot. Ask the students to apply the colored circle near the statement that they believe is most accurate on a poster that reads: "God's purpose for including a sensual love letter (Song of Solomon) in the Bible is . . .

(a) "God thought it would spice up his Bible;

(b) "It is symbolic of God's love for his people;

(c) "It is a collection of love songs sung at weddings;

(d) "It is intended to affirm the beauty of sexual and human love."

After all stickers have been placed, use the commentary's Lesson Background to prepare and deliver a brief lecture on the purpose of the book.

INTO THE WORD

Distribute an activity guide to groups of four or five. Assign one of the activities to each group. The guide should have the heading, "A Model for Love and Sex." Include the following instructions:

Activity 1: Read 2:8-13. Rewrite this scene, placing it in a contemporary setting of dating and courtship.

Activity 2: Read 7:10-12. Earlier verses in this chapter include an erotic declaration of physical love by the man or lover. Our text is the woman's response and commitment. (a) What is the key phrase in her response? ("*I am my beloved's.*") Why is this statement significant in husband and wife relationships?

(b) What does this text imply about the woman's role in the dance of love and sexual behavior?

(c) Paraphrase this text, putting it into contemporary words and setting.

Activity 3: Copy and distribute the reproducible activity page that follows. Allow time for the students to answer the questions on the activity page. (If time is short, divide the class into three groups and assign one question to each group.) Then review the questions together and discuss the issues raised.

INTO LIFE

Write on a display board: "So what?" Tell the class we want this text song to speak to believers in the year 2004. Ask the following questions: (a) What lessons about love and sex do you find in this love letter we've read today? (b) What disturbing variances from this beautiful snapshot of male and female relationships do you see in some contemporary views of love and sex? What dangers lie in some of those views? List these answers on the visual in two columns.

Point to the snapshots brought by married couples. Ask, "What potential problems endangering healthy sexual intimacy face couples today?" Then ask what messages this lesson has for single adults today. What values are implied?

Distribute the following commitment guide. One side should have the heading "Married Couples." The other side should have "Single Adults." (Tell them to check all that apply.) The side for married adults should read "As a married adult, (a) I will be physically and emotionally faithful to my spouse from this day forward; (b) Within a week I will find one way (card, love letter, intimate conversation, or other) to express my love and commitment to my spouse and lover; (c) I will discuss a time with my spouse when we can retreat from life's hubbub for at least two days just to be together."

The side for singles should read "Understanding the wonderful joy and intimacy God offers in marriage and to support these values, I will . . . (a) Respect God's boundaries about sexuality by controlling my desires and refrain from sexual intimacy unless I marry; (b) Respect and honor marriage by rejoicing in other people's successful marriage relationships; (c) Respect and honor single adulthood by demonstrating faithfulness to my God and serving in his church."

My Lover's Desire

In today's text there are many lovers' metaphors that deserve a personal look. Three from Song of Solomon 8:6 are listed below. After reading them, note your feelings about the questions listed.

LOVE IS AS STRONG AS DEATH
How is human love as strong as death? What is love's strength?

ITS JEALOUSY IS UNYIELDING AS THE GRAVE
Why would the lover in this text say jealousy is unyielding as the grave? What are some of the benefits and the dangers of jealousy?

LOVE BURNS LIKE BLAZING FIRE
Many love songs have used the theme or word *fire* as an expression of love's passion. Name just a few of these songs. Why is the figure an appropriate one?

Lessons From Life

Unit 2: Wisdom for the Times of Our Lives
(Lessons 9-13)

A TIME FOR COURAGE

LESSON 12

WHY TEACH THIS LESSON?

"I'd rather be a live coward than a dead hero!" "He who fights and runs away lives to fight another day." "There are old soldiers and there are bold soldiers, but there are no old, bold soldiers." Any of those adages sound familiar? Hopefully you've never used one of them to justify a lack of courage in your Christian walk! All three of those little dictums have the same philosophy behind them: my own earthly life—my personal self-interest—is more important than anything else.

But Christians know that this simply isn't true. Many of God's people in the pages of Scripture model courage for us at the risk (or cost) of their own lives. Mordecai and Queen Esther are just two. They risked their lives to do the right thing—and saved their own lives and many others in the process. Legend has it that all the faithful apostles except John died the deaths of martyrs. But whether we keep or lose our lives, God expects us to step out with courage when it is time to bring him glory. That's the lesson we need for today and every day.

INTRODUCTION

A. WHEN GOD PICKS UP THE PEN

On October 8, 1871, a great fire began to sweep across the city of Chicago. As the fire burned day after day, homes, factories, and businesses were consumed. Thousands were left homeless and destitute. In the midst of the confusion an old Quaker, whose home and business had been burned, seemed not the least perturbed. Someone said to him, "Don't you realize what this means? We're finished! This is the last chapter for us!" The old man smiled as he replied, "God begins to write anew when men lay down the pen."

Through the machinations of evil Haman, King Xerxes had signed a decree that meant death to the Jews in his domain. Wicked men were writing the last chapter for the Jews. But godly Mordecai was not quite ready to accept this. When he challenged Esther with these words, "Who knows but that you have come to royal position for such a time as this?" he was in effect saying, "It is now time for God to begin to write."

B. LESSON BACKGROUND

Xerxes, who ruled the Persian Empire from 486 to 465 B.C., is also known as Ahasuerus. Xerxes is the name the Greeks gave to him. The book of Esther opens by mentioning a feast that took place in the third year of his reign (Esther 1:3). At this time more than fifty years have elapsed since the first wave of Jewish exiles had returned to their homeland in Judah (2 Chronicles 36:22, 23), but the time of Ezra and Nehemiah is still some twenty-five years in the future.

Some believe that the king's feast is an occasion to rally his leaders for an attack on Greece. (This attack, which took place in 480–479 B.C., resulted in a Greek victory.) This feast proved to be an occasion of unrestrained drunkenness (Esther 1:5-8). When Queen Vashti was ordered to appear before the revelers, she refused (1:10-12). This refusal came at the cost of her position! The plot of the story that follows is both involved and intriguing.

DEVOTIONAL READING:
PSALM 27:1-8
BACKGROUND SCRIPTURE:
ESTHER 3, 4
PRINTED TEXT:
ESTHER 3:1-6; 4:7-16

LESSON AIMS

After participating in this lesson, each student will be able to:

1. Tell how the Jews in Esther's day were threatened, and how Esther was persuaded to take action to avert the danger.

2. Compare the challenge to Esther's faith with some challenge he or she is facing.

3. State how he or she will confront a specific challenge to personal faith in the coming week.

Feb
22

KEY VERSE

"I will go to the king, even though it is against the law. And if I perish, I perish."
—Esther 4:16

LESSON 12 NOTES

I. HAMAN (ESTHER 3:1-6)

As the search for a new queen begins, we are introduced to "fair and beautiful" Esther; she is an orphan who was reared by a close relative named Mordecai (Esther 2:7). As the result of a long and involved beauty contest, Esther becomes the new queen (2:8-18). During this whole process Esther keeps her Jewish heritage a secret (2:10, 20). Next, the evil Haman enters the picture.

A. HONOR AND REFUSAL (vv. 1-4)

1. After these events, King Xerxes honored Haman son of Hammedatha, the Agagite, elevating him and giving him a seat of honor higher than that of all the other nobles.

Haman is an *Agagite*, which may indicate his lineage from King Agag of the Amalekites (see 1 Samuel 15:7-33). We are not told why Haman is elevated to a position that is *higher than that of all the other nobles.* No doubt Haman is a man of some ability. But as the story unfolds, it will also be obvious that he is a clever operator—someone who takes every opportunity to advance his own career.

2, 3. All the royal officials at the king's gate knelt down and paid honor to Haman, for the king had commanded this concerning him. But Mordecai would not kneel down or pay him honor.

Then the royal officials at the king's gate asked Mordecai, "Why do you disobey the king's command?"

In Oriental courts it is a common practice for *royal officials* to bow or prostrate themselves before their superiors. We wonder, then, why *the king* has to issue a special order that *Haman* be honored this way. Perhaps Haman has been elevated over other officers that he had served formerly, and thus needs the king's command in order to receive the new treatment that is "due" him.

But Mordecai refuses to bow before Haman. Is Mordecai just being stubborn, or is something deeper involved? Perhaps he is inspired by the prophet Daniel's behavior more than fifty years previously (Daniel 6).

4. Day after day they spoke to him but he refused to comply. Therefore they told Haman about it to see whether Mordecai's behavior would be tolerated, for he had told them he was a Jew.

It does not take long for *Mordecai's behavior* to attract the attention of his companions. Perhaps out of concern for Mordecai's well-being, they speak to him about his actions. But Mordecai *refused to comply.* We can almost hear them pleading with him daily!

There are times when we need to listen to the advice of others; but there are other times when we must take our stand and refuse to go along with the crowd. For Mordecai this is one of those times.

To bow down out of respect for an earthly king or superior is not wrong if it's merely a sign of respect or honor (Genesis 27:29; 2 Samuel 14:4; 1 Chronicles 21:21). But as a devout *Jew* Mordecai knows there is a line he must not cross. Perhaps *Haman* sees all this bowing as worship. Or perhaps Mordecai's refusal stems from his knowledge that Haman is descended from an ancient enemy of the Jews (again, 1 Samuel 15:7-33).

In either case, Mordecai refuses to heed the advice of his companions. Perhaps they do not understand his Jewish beliefs, or they may harbor antagonism toward Jews. In any event, they reported Mordecai's actions to Haman.

B. ANGER AND PLOT (vv. 5, 6)

5. When Haman saw that Mordecai would not kneel down or pay him honor, he was enraged.

WHAT DO YOU THINK?

First Peter 2:17 requires that we show proper respect to those in authority. But Mordecai refused to honor Haman. How do we know which example or precept to follow?

[Use Ephesians 6:2; 1 Timothy 5:17; and 1 Peter 2:17 to start your thinking.]

Haman makes a point to observe Mordecai's behavior. When he sees that *Mordecai* is not bowing and scraping before him, he is furious. Like many people who feel inferior or inadequate, he vents his feelings against those who raise any question about his authority.

RIGHTEOUS REBELLION

At the end of 1941, Lieutenant Damon Gause fought in the hopeless battle for the Philippines. When the Japanese overran Bataan, Gause was captured. He made a dash for freedom and swam to Corregidor Island. When the Japanese took Corregidor, Gause swam back to Bataan and hid in the mountains. Eventually, with the help of courageous Filipinos, Gause and another American sailed over three thousand miles to Australia in a twenty-foot skiff.

Lieutenant Gause could have given up hope on Bataan, on Corregidor, or any number of times thereafter. After he reached Australia and was flown back to the United States, Gause could have retired from the fighting. But Lieutenant (later Major) Gause rejoined the war until he died in a training accident in England.

Wars are terrible, but sometimes a just war is better than an unjust peace. Had Gause and thousands of men like him been unwilling to fight, who knows how we might all be living today!

And sometimes we have to fight alone, at least in the beginning. When Martin Luther nailed his ninety-five theses to the Wittenberg church door in 1517, he stood alone. Luther fought against wrongs he saw in the church. Eventually, he was excommunicated. But he stood up for what was right according to Scripture.

Mordecai stood up, both literally and figuratively, for what was right. He would not stoop to Haman despite this powerful man's wrath. You may not be challenged to bend your body to a human, but you will be challenged to bend your will to Satan. Sometimes you have to stand up for what is right. "Therefore put on the full armor of God, so that when the day of evil comes, you may be able to stand your ground, and after you have done everything, to stand" (Ephesians 6:13). —J. D. J.

6. Yet having learned who Mordecai's people were, he scorned the idea of killing only Mordecai. Instead Haman looked for a way to destroy all Mordecai's people, the Jews, throughout the whole kingdom of Xerxes.

Haman's immediate thought is to seize *Mordecai* and have him imprisoned or executed. But when he learns that Mordecai is a Jew, all of Mordecai's *people* became a target of his rage.

II. MORDECAI (ESTHER 4:7-9)

Haman sets the plan in motion "in the twelfth year of King Xerxes," or about 474 B.C. (Esther 3:7). Esther has been queen for five years (2:16) by the time Haman goes to the king with the charge that "a certain people" do not keep the king's laws and that it would be in the king's best interest to eliminate them (3:8, 9).

Xerxes goes along with the proposal. The appropriate documents were drawn up and dispatched to the far reaches of his empire (3:12-15), with the massacre scheduled to be carried out on a set day. It is to include "all the Jews—young and old, women and little children" (3:13). The king apparently does not know that his decree is a death sentence for his own wife as well!

When Mordecai hears the news, he goes into mourning. He tears his clothes and puts on sackcloth and ashes (4:1). There is similar mourning by Jews across the empire (4:3). When Esther learns of Mordecai's distress, she sends him new clothes so that he can enter the king's court. But he refuses to accept them (4:4). Then she sends "Hathach, one of the king's eunuchs" to inquire of Mordecai what is troubling him (4:5).

WHAT DO YOU THINK?

How are the causes and results of Haman's anger similar to effects of anger you've observed in people?

DAILY BIBLE READINGS

　　*Monday, Feb. 16—Council
Sees Disciples' Boldness (Acts
4:13-22)*

　　*Tuesday, Feb. 17—A Prayer
for Boldness (Acts 4:23-31)*

　　*Wednesday, Feb. 18—Whom
Shall I Fear? (Psalm 27:1-8)*

　　*Thursday, Feb. 19—Morde-
cai Will Not Bow (Esther 3:1-6)*

　　*Friday, Feb. 20—Mordecai
Grieves for His People (Esther
4:1-5)*

　　*Saturday, Feb. 21—Esther,
Called Upon to Show Courage
(Esther 4:6-11)*

　　*Sunday, Feb. 22—Esther
Prepares to Plead the Cause
(Esther 4:12-17)*

A. MESSAGE SENT (vv. 7, 8)

7. Mordecai told him everything that had happened to him, including the exact amount of money Haman had promised to pay into the royal treasury for the destruction of the Jews.

Mordecai gives Hathach all the bad news, mentioning *the exact amount of money* Haman has *promised to pay* the king to allow the Jews to be slaughtered. There is nothing at this point to suggest that Hathach or anyone else in the king's court knows that Esther is Jewish.

It may seem surprising to us that Esther knows nothing about Haman's plot to kill her people. But we need to keep in mind that the harem of an Oriental potentate is virtually isolated from the world of politics and from most other activities as well.

8. He also gave him a copy of the text of the edict for their annihilation, which had been published in Susa, to show to Esther and explain it to her, and he told him to urge her to go into the king's presence to beg for mercy and plead with him for her people.

Since Mordecai is not allowed to enter the harem compound, he has to rely upon a third party. This person is Hathach, who as a eunuch helps keep watch over the harem.

To carry out his task, Hathach has some specific things to do. His first task is to take *a copy of the text of the edict* and *show* it to *Esther.* The decree has been issued in *Susa,* which is the winter capital of the Persian Empire. This city is located about two hundred miles east of Babylon (cf. Nehemiah 1:1; Daniel 8:2). Then Hathach is to *explain it to her.* Finally, he is to *urge* Esther to go before the king to plead on behalf of *her people.*

B. MESSAGE RECEIVED (v. 9)

9. Hathach went back and reported to Esther what Mordecai had said.

Hathach faithfully carries out his part of the plan. Now, as we say, "the ball is in Esther's court." She can, of course, ignore Mordecai's request. At first glance this would seem to be the safest course. But to ignore his request might not actually be all that safe. There is always the possibility that her heritage would eventually be revealed, a fact that Mordecai mentions to her (4:13, below). But more important than doing the *safe* thing is doing the *right* thing.

III. ESTHER (ESTHER 4:10-16)

Esther had been obedient as a child (2:10). This is a character trait that proves to be of great significance for what follows.

A. ESTHER'S PROBLEM (vv. 10-12)

10, 11. Then she instructed him to say to Mordecai, "All the king's officials and the people of the royal provinces know that for any man or woman who approaches the king in the inner court without being summoned the king has but one law: that he be put to death. The only exception to this is for the king to extend the gold scepter to him and spare his life. But thirty days have passed since I was called to go to the king."

Even if Esther chooses to do as Mordecai asks, she has a big problem. Anyone who approaches the king *in the inner court* without being called faces the death penalty. This seems like a very severe law, but Oriental rulers are surrounded with all kinds of intrigue and plots against their lives (cf. 2 Kings 12:19-21; 15:10, 25, 30; 21:23). Under such conditions this severe rule seems to be a reasonable precaution. Indeed, we see one assassination plot already has

A Time for Courage

Use this artwork to stress the need for courage in the service of God in all situations.

been foiled in Esther 2:19-23. (The king's precautions do not prevent his murder in 465 B.C., however.)

There is one exception to the death penalty of the king: if the person seeking an audience finds favor in his sight, *the king will extend his gold scepter* and the law will be suspended. But Esther has another problem. She has not been called into the presence of the king for *thirty days.* Such a lengthy period of time may make Esther wonder if she has fallen out of favor with the king.

12. When Esther's words were reported to Mordecai,

Does Esther hope that her situation will relieve her of further responsibility in the matter? Or does she hope that the king will call her on his own? Of course, if she waits until he calls it could be too late. Or does she hope that *Mordecai* will come up with another plan that has a better chance of succeeding?

B. MORDECAI'S CHALLENGE (vv. 13, 14)

13. . . . he sent back this answer: "Do not think that because you are in the king's house you alone of all the Jews will escape.

Most of us try to avoid situations where we have to make hard decisions, but sometimes in life they are unavoidable. Mordecai reminds Esther that she cannot hope to find safety in the *king's* palace. Hathach already knows that she is Jewish and sooner or later others will find out, sealing her fate along with that of her people.

14. "For if you remain silent at this time, relief and deliverance for the Jews will arise from another place, but you and your father's family will perish. And who knows but that you have come to royal position for such a time as this?"

Mordecai's plan seems like the best idea at the time. But even if Esther does not cooperate, he firmly believes that God will deliver his people in some other way. He knows enough history to understand that in times past God had delivered his people in various ways and can do so again.

Although God works through people in his plan for human redemption, he is not limited to one person or a small group of people to carry out that plan. This is true for your own life situation as well. There are things that God "wants done" where you live. Will he work through you or will he have to find someone else?

C. ESTHER'S RESPONSE (vv. 15, 16)

15, 16. Then Esther sent this reply to Mordecai: "Go, gather together all the Jews who are in Susa, and fast for me. Do not eat or drink for three days, night or day. I and my maids will fast as you do. When this is done, I will go to the king, even though it is against the law. And if I perish, I perish."

Esther is determined not to "go it alone" once she has made her decision. Knowing that *all the Jews* of *Susa* are joining her in a three-day *fast* will provide moral support. Although prayer is not specifically mentioned, we can be certain that those fasting hours were filled with numerous requests offered up to God for deliverance (cf. 9:31). Once she has made her decision Esther faces the consequences with an unwavering resolve: *if I perish, I perish.*

PRAYER PARTNERS

"Irene has been taken to the hospital. She may have had a stroke. Please pray she will recover." Our prayer chain was on the line to each other and to God. Urgent requests start the prayer chain. Members pause to pray and then dial the next link in the chain. In this way we can call more than twenty-five households to prayer within an hour.

WHAT DO YOU THINK?

Esther was called upon to make a choice: obey the legal expectations of the king or attempt to make a plea for her people. Why was the one she chose the more noble—the "greater good"?

WHAT DO YOU THINK?

"Who knows but that you have come to royal position for such a time as this?" is a question that confronts all of us. What has God called you to do through the special circumstances of your own life?

WHAT DO YOU THINK?

Esther made certain preparations before she presented herself to the king with her request. How could this be an example for us? What are the dangers in spending too much or too little time preparing?

HOW TO SAY IT

Agagite. AY-guh-gite.

Ahasuerus. Uh-haz-you-EE-rus.

Amalekites. AM-uh-leh-kites or Uh-MAL-ih-kites.

Corregidor. Ko-REE-guh-door.

Ezra. EZ-ruh.

Haman. HAY-mun.

Hammedatha. Ham-med-DAY-thuh.

Hathach. HAY-thak.

Mordecai. MOR-dih-kye.

Nehemiah. NEE-huh-MY-uh.

Persian. PER-zhun.

Susa. SOO-suh.

Vashti. VASH-tie.

Wittenberg. VIT-ten-burg.

Xerxes. ZERK-seez.

THOUGHT TO REMEMBER

Know the times, live your convictions.

Around a candle in a darkened room, four young men kneel. They begin with confession—owning up to sins in their actions and attitudes. They move to requests for God's help in their lives. Finally, they intercede for friends they know to be in need. This prayer time together is the highlight of their week. It refreshes them and restores their sense of purpose for Christ.

In place of plates heaped with food sat cups of apple juice. Instead of a pitch-in dinner, the missions ministry invited people to a time of fasting at a prayer banquet. One by one, missionaries and their needs were lifted to God. Those who gathered recognized that their prayers were reaching all around the world. And they gave thanks for the opportunity to "ask the Lord of the harvest, therefore, to send out workers into his harvest field" (Matthew 9:38).

Esther asked all the Jews of Susa to fast with her for three days; no doubt they also prayed. Prayer chains, prayer partners, or special prayer events continue to call us to God. If your church has a prayer group, join it. Prayer groups help us make time for prayer. Invite a friend or two to pray with you. "For where two or three come together in my name, there am I with them" (Matthew 18:20). Sincere prayer helps God's kingdom to come and God's will to be done on earth as it is in Heaven.　　　　　　　　　　　　　　—J. D. J.

CONCLUSION

A. "FOR SUCH A TIME AS THIS"

Esther is the only book in the Bible that does not mention God. Yet imbedded in Mordecai's challenge to Esther is a profound biblical truth, a truth based upon the belief that God is active in human lives. Mordecai believed that God had been preparing Esther all of her life for this major crisis. That she grew into a beautiful young woman who was chosen to become the queen to the powerful Persian king was no accident of history! She came to be in a crucial position at just the right time because God had planned it that way.

This reminds us of a somewhat similar situation centuries earlier when Joseph confronted his brothers in Egypt. Previously, they had sold Joseph into slavery. In a fit of jealousy they had taken action to rid themselves of him.

But when the brothers were finally reunited years later, Joseph was a ruler in Egypt. He had access to food during a time of severe famine. Joseph was thus able to save his family from starvation. Joseph saw God's hand at work and did not seek revenge. Instead, he said, "Now, do not be distressed and do not be angry with yourselves for selling me here, because it was to save lives that God sent me ahead of you" (Genesis 45:5).

We may not always be where God wants us to be. We are, after all, free to rebel against him and his purpose for us. But one of the joys of a Christian life is looking back at crucial points and seeing how God has providentially used us.

B. A TIME OF DECISION

Most of us live out our lives in quiet routine, free of heroic choices such as Esther had to make to save her people. And yet God calls each of us to decisions that are spiritually heroic, even though they will never make the front page of the newspapers.

The most important decision we ever make, obviously, is to become a Christian. But there are many other important decisions as well. Will we be regular in our church attendance (Hebrews 10:25)? Will we resist the lure of illegal drugs? Will we avoid becoming involved in sexual immorality? The list could go on. The decision we make in each one of these situations can involve great courage. But our decisions will go a long way toward determining our eternal destiny—and, perhaps, the destinies of others.

Discovery Learning

This page contains an alternative lesson plan emphasizing learning activities. Classes desiring such student involvement will find these suggestions helpful. The next page is a reproducible activity page to further enhance discovery learning.

LEARNING GOALS

After this lesson each student will be able to:

1. Tell how the Jews in Esther's day were threatened and how Esther was persuaded to take action to avert the danger.

2. Compare the challenge to Esther's faith with some challenge he or she is facing.

3. State how he or she will confront a specific challenge to personal faith in the coming week.

INTO THE LESSON

Option 1. Give each class member a three-by-five index card. Ask each to write on the card one of the challenges he or she faces in maintaining or developing a relationship with the Lord or with another person—a personal habit, a desire, an individual, a relationship, a task to do. No one will be asked to share this information.

They are to put the cards away until needed. Make the transition to Bible study by telling the class, "Sometimes we need a model or an example to show us how to face life's challenges. Today we begin a two-lesson study of one of the Old Testament's greatest heroines, who may give us encouragement to face what we need to face and to make heroic decisions."

Option 2: Ask the class to name individuals who significantly influenced the course of history—and how they did it. List these on a poster or marker board. Make the transition to Bible study by saying, "We will look at one of history's greatest heroines. A woman who changed Jewish history and gives us a great model for facing life's tough moments has an entire Bible book dedicated to recording her experience: Esther."

INTO THE WORD

Option 1. Copy and distribute the reproducible activity "Definitive Decisions" from the next page. Give time for the students to complete the activity; then discuss the lessons they learned.

Option 2. Give each student a copy of the worksheet described below. Allow learners to read through the text and complete the worksheet.

The worksheet will have two sections. The first section heading is "Leading Characters in Esther's Drama." Under the heading have three columns. The headings for the columns are "Character or Place," "Position or Role," and "Activity or Event." Under the first heading include the names Xerxes, Haman, Mordecai, Hathach, Esther, and Susa. Leave space for class members to write answers in the second and third columns.

In the second column ask the groups or class to identify the position or role each character (or place) plays. In the third column students are to jot brief notes about what each person did (or what happened in a place). When the groups are reporting (or during the class discussion), ask the following questions or make comments: Haman—"Why did Haman have such power and influence with the king?" "What were Haman's character flaws as seen in this drama?"; Mordecai—"What other Old Testament hero faced a similar challenge?" *(Daniel)*; Hathach—"Few people have ever heard of Hathach; fewer still have any idea how important he was in this plan. How was he important, and what were his tasks?"; Susa—Simply tell the class the significance of this place; Esther—"What was the tension in the decision Esther had to make?" "What makes her decision heroic?"; Xerxes—Explain the significance of the golden scepter.

The second worksheet heading should read "The Story Line of Esther's Drama." The story of Esther is complicated, so this activity will help sort out the events leading to Esther's decision. On this section they should note in simple sentences the story's events as they occur.

INTO LIFE

Remind the class that most of us live lives of quiet routine, never having to make such a heroic choice as Esther. However, we do make decisions heroic in the sense that they benefit other people or our own character. Distribute copies of the reproducible activity "A Memo to Me" from the next page. Give examples, such as making a decision that no matter what sexual temptation comes, one will be faithful to a spouse.

If you did *Option 1* of the "Into the Lesson," remind the students of what they identified on their cards. If you did not, ask them to think about what challenges them most in their walk with the Lord. Stress that life's challenges often require personal heroic decisions, requiring personal sacrifice for the benefit of someone else. Ask them to identify the "heroic" parts of their challenges and write it on the "memo." Encourage each person to take a step in meeting this life challenge during the coming week.

Definitive Decisions

All of the people named below made important decisions that influenced the lives of others. We can learn from each of them and from the outcomes of their actions. After reading the story, jot a few notes citing lessons you learned (or hope to learn) from these characters.

Haman, lessons about pride:

Haman, lessons about prejudice and hatred:

Hathach, lessons about service:

Mordecai, lessons about faithfulness to God:

Esther, lessons about heroic decisions:

A Memo to Me

Life may not hold for you the kind of heroic decision Esther was forced to make. However, in the challenges of life, we are often called upon to make heroic decisions that call for sacrifice on behalf of another person or persons. If possible, identify a challenge to your relationship with another person or with God. Write yourself a memo identifying a step to take to meet that challenge. See, you can make heroic decisions!

MEMO

To: _____ (Your name)

From: Me

re: A Heroic Decision

A TIME TO CELEBRATE

LESSON 13

WHY TEACH THIS LESSON?

In the early morning hours of October 16, 1946, the infamous Julius Streicher was one of ten Nazi war criminals being sent to the gallows. When asked if he had any last words Streicher exclaimed, "Purim Fest 1946!" Streicher had devoted much of his evil effort in Hitler's regime to destroying innocent people of Jewish descent. As he faced his own execution, Streicher apparently saw himself in the role of Haman (Esther 7) who found the tables turned against him more than twenty-four centuries previously—resulting in a celebration known as *Purim*.

The fact that a thug such as Streicher would have this level of familiarity with one of the "minor" Jewish feasts is amazing! This fact can also be a little embarrassing to Christians who have carried their Bibles for years and don't know what *Purim* signifies. Today's lesson corrects that embarrassment. But more than that, this lesson reminds us that our religious celebrations can and should serve a higher purpose—God's purpose—as they help to build our faith. Our celebrations look to God's acts in the past as guarantees of his faithfulness in the future.

INTRODUCTION

A. HOLIDAYS

Festivals and holidays are an important part in the life of Christianity. They help give us an identity and bind us together. For example, Christians around the world observe many holidays, but the most important are Christmas and Easter. This is rightly so, for they mark the two most significant events in the life of our Lord—his birth and his resurrection.

Festivals and holidays are important to nations as well. Citizens of the United States observe July 4 as an important date in their history—the signing of the Declaration of Independence in 1776. France observes Bastille Day on July 14, marking an important event that occurred in the French Revolution in 1789.

Other holidays are not considered to be "major" celebrations, although they may commemorate important events. How much attention is given to such observances varies widely. For example, many in Britain and parts of the Commonwealth observe Guy Fawkes Day on November 5; Fawkes was a conspirator who attempted (and failed) to blow up the king and Parliament in the infamous Gunpowder Plot of 1605. Columbus Day in the United States, however, often passes without much notice.

Likewise, the ancient Jews had what we could call both "major" and "minor" feasts and celebrations. The major feasts, such as Passover and Pentecost, are well known to most Christians today. But along the way—particularly after the exile—the ancient Jews added other festivals. One of these was Purim, which celebrated their deliverance from the efforts of Haman to exterminate them. Our two lessons from the Book of Esther show us the origins of this feast.

B. LESSON BACKGROUND

The book of Esther reads like a thriller that Hollywood would dream up—except it isn't fiction, it is history. In last week's lesson we saw Haman's hatred of

---

DEVOTIONAL READING:
PSALM 98

BACKGROUND SCRIPTURE:
ESTHER 8, 9

PRINTED TEXT:
ESTHER 8:3-8; 9:17-23

LESSON AIMS

After participating in this lesson, each student will be able to:

1. Summarize the events that led to the beginning of the Jewish festival of Purim.

2. Discuss the importance of celebrating special events in his or her Christian life to help strengthen faith.

3. Plan a church or family celebration to commemorate a specific milestone or victory.

KEY VERSE

For the Jews it was a time of happiness and joy, gladness and honor.
—Esther 8:16

Feb
29

Mordecai. This hatred led Haman to seek revenge, so he secured a decree from King Xerxes (also known as Ahasuerus) to exterminate all Jews in the Persian Empire. Then Mordecai prevailed upon Esther to intervene.

In the text not included in either of our two lessons, Esther makes her appeal at a banquet she hosts for the king and Haman (Esther 7). Before that banquet, however, Haman had ordered a huge gallows to be built upon which to execute the Jew Mordecai (Esther 5:14). Yet at about the same time, and without Haman's knowledge, the king decided to honor Mordecai for foiling an assassination plot earlier (2:19-23; 6:1-3).

The supreme irony came when the king asked Haman (who had just arrived to request the death of Mordecai) how to reward "the man the king delights to honor" (6:6a). Haman, thinking that he himself was the one to be rewarded, replied that such a man should be dressed in the finest clothes and be paraded through the streets, mounted on a fine horse led by a leading citizen (6:6b-9). Imagine Haman's chagrin when he learned that Mordecai was the one to be honored and that he (Haman) was the one to lead the horse!

During the banquet that followed, Esther told the king about the plight of her people (7:1-6). In another great irony the king ordered Haman hanged on the gallows that Haman had built for Mordecai (7:9, 10). The closing chapters of the book tell how the king issued a new order allowing the Jews to defend themselves against their enemies. The time of their deliverance came to be celebrated with feasting and rejoicing from that day forward.

I. THE JEWS RESCUED (ESTHER 8:3-8)

As we join the narrative, Haman has just been executed (7:10). Further, the king has given Haman's estate to Esther that same day (8:1), and Mordecai receives the honor that previously belonged to Haman (8:2). Even so, Esther realizes that there is work yet to do.

A. PLEA OFFERED (v. 3)

3. Esther again pleaded with the king, falling at his feet and weeping. She begged him to put an end to the evil plan of Haman the Agagite, which he had devised against the Jews.

One would suppose that Mordecai could revoke the decree that called for the death of his people. We might think this because of the fact that he now possesses the king's signet ring that Haman had used to issue that decree in the first place (3:10-12; 8:2). But such is not the case. Among the Medes and Persians a decree once issued cannot be withdrawn. It is set in stone. (See Daniel 6:8, 12, 15.)

Esther's plea was one filled with genuine emotion. When is it proper to vent our emotions, and when should we control (or suppress) them?

For this reason Esther once more has to step forward to save her people. Emboldened by her earlier success, she approaches *the king* a second time. This time she falls prostrate before him *with tears* to plead for protection against the scheme Haman has devised to destroy her people.

B. PLEA HONORED (v. 4)

4. Then the king extended the gold scepter to Esther and she arose and stood before him.

Esther must realize that she is in the good graces of *the king*, and her judgment is correct. He extends his *scepter* again (cf. Esther 5:2), indicating that he understands her plea and is willing to take some action in regard to it. Thus she arises and stands *before him*. The problem now is how to revoke a law that cannot be revoked!

C. WISH STATED (vv. 5, 6)

5. *"If it pleases the king," she said, "and if he regards me with favor and thinks it the right thing to do, and if he is pleased with me, let an order be written overruling the dispatches that Haman son of Hammedatha, the Agagite, devised and wrote to destroy the Jews in all the king's provinces.*

Like a lawyer pleading a case, Esther carefully lays out her argument point by point. Her first appeal is a personal one: *if he regards me with favor.* Of course, she has clear evidence that she has found favor in the king's sight. But a reminder won't hurt.

The phrase *and thinks it is the right thing to do* is Esther's appeal to the king's sense of justice. Unfortunately, justice is not an absolute thing among human beings. Without the Word of God to control our thinking, one person's justice is another person's crime. For example, certain Muslim radicals today believe that murdering a non-Muslim (an "infidel") is a righteous act. Most of us are horrified by such a concept of justice.

On the other hand, Esther understands the concept of self-defense when she appeals to the king's sense of right and wrong. Like most ancient rulers, he is at times brutal and heavy-handed. But he comes through as reasonably decent when compared with others of his time.

In requesting that the king overrule *the dispatches* devised by Haman, Esther places the blame for the evil decree on Haman rather than on *the king.* All rulers, even those today, rely on those who work under them to provide the information needed to make decisions. This is especially true in a kingdom as vast as the ancient Persian Empire, where communications were not as swift and as readily available as they are today. Obviously, no ruler can be wise enough to understand every issue in every village in every province. Rulers need advisors for this.

So King Xerxes had trusted Haman completely. Consequently, when the schemer presented the king with a decree to destroy the Jews, the king had "bought off on it" with the understanding that it would be beneficial to his empire. Little did he realize that the decree was rooted in Haman's personal desire to get revenge against Mordecai for a personal slight.

6. *For how can I bear to see disaster fall on my people? How can I bear to see the destruction of my family?"*

At the time he had approved the death decree, the king had no idea that Esther was Jewish. Now, of course, he realizes the impact that it is certain to have on her. We can feel sorrow when we read of thousands of people in a foreign land being massacred; but we will feel it much more strongly if the victims are friends and relatives.

NATIVE MISSIONARIES

In the heat and squalor of one of the poorest spots on earth, a "native missionary" ministers for Christ. He works with people who have very little education and even less money. He battles daily with superstition, unsanitary conditions, violence, and abject poverty. It is hard work, but he continues to serve.

This missionary does not have to stay where he is. With his earned Master's degrees he could be serving in affluent North America, where he studied. He could live in an upscale home and drive an expensive car. He could work with college-trained church members and a well-paid staff. But like many others, this man chose to leave these advantages behind. He chose to go home, back to his native land to serve his people.

Every year men and women from all over the globe come to North America to train for ministry. When they arrive, they often enter a new world. Wealth, convenience, safe drinking water, electricity every day, smooth roads, and easy access to

WHAT DO YOU THINK?

In addition to the fact that Esther was his wife, in what ways had Esther earned the king's approval prior to presenting her "case"? How is this important to family relationships today?

HOW TO SAY IT

Agagite. AY-guh-gite.
Ahasuerus. Uh-haz-you-EE-rus.
Assyrian. Uh-SEAR-e-un.
Haman. HAY-mun.
Hammedatha. Ham-med-DAY-thuh.
Herodotus. Heh-ROD-uh-tus.
Josephus. Jo-SEE-fus.
Maccabees. MACK-uh-bees.
Medes. Meeds.
Mordecai. MOR-dih-kye.
Persians. PER-zhunz.
Purim. PEW-rim.
Susa. SOO-suh.
Xerxes. ZERK-seez.

health care surround them. Luxuries we take for granted leave these Christians wide-eyed with wonder. Like Esther in the king's palace, it is easy to forget about their heritage. It is very easy to find a reason to stay. Many do.

But many also echo the words of Esther: "How can I bear to see disaster fall on my people? How can I bear to see the destruction of my family?" So they go home as "native missionaries" to bring the message of eternal life.

Encourage such folks whenever you can! Ask about international students at a Bible college or a campus ministry near you. Support their education. Welcome them into your home. Pray for them. Warn them of the dangers of the affluent culture to which they temporarily belong. Caution them with the example of Demas (2 Timothy 4:10). In short, be a Mordecai! Perhaps God has "raised you up" to do just that.   —J. D. J.

D. DECREE ISSUED (vv. 7, 8)

7. King Xerxes replied to Queen Esther and to Mordecai the Jew, "Because Haman attacked the Jews, I have given his estate to Esther, and they have hanged him on the gallows.

Xerxes realizes that he has been tricked by *Haman,* so he takes steps to rectify the problem. He begins his response by reminding both *Esther* and *Mordecai* about Haman's fate. Although the king's swift action against Haman has settled that part of the problem, the evil decree still stands.

8. "Now write another decree in the king's name in behalf of the Jews as seems best to you, and seal it with the king's signet ring—for no document written in the king's name and sealed with his ring can be revoked."

Once the king understands the situation, he wastes no time in providing a remedy. He turns to Mordecai and gives him the authority to *write* a *decree* as he sees fit. The king places his trust in Mordecai to do the right thing. The king's trust in Haman had been misplaced. Now the king seems certain that Mordecai can be trusted. He has good reason for this conclusion because it was Mordecai who earlier had reported the conspiracy against the king, quite possibly saving the king's life (Esther 2:19-23).

Although the first decree cannot be rescinded by any man, its effects can be nullified by another decree granting the Jews the right to defend themselves if attacked. Mordecai is the one to write this second decree. It will circulate under the authority of the king, bearing his seal. In matters of state the king's word is final—it may not *be revoked.* He doesn't have to worry about legislatures or courts overriding it as is the usual process in a democracy.

II. THE FEAST OF PURIM ESTABLISHED (ESTHER 9:17-23)

In the verses between 8:8 and 9:17 we learn that Mordecai loses no time in using the king's authority to carry out his plan to save his people. The first thing he does is to call in scribes to make copies of the new decree that will be dispatched to the remote corners of the Persian Empire. The empire consists of one hundred twenty-seven provinces, stretching from India to Ethiopia. Many languages are spoken throughout the empire. The scribes thus not only copy the decree, they also translate it into the language appropriate to each province (8:9).

Once the translations are made and sealed, Mordecai dispatches them to the far reaches of the realm. The Persians have one of the best postal systems in the ancient world, and they quickly and efficiently deliver their messages (8:10, 14). The Greek historian Herodotus (485–425 B.C.) described this postal service in these words: "Neither snow nor rain nor heat nor gloom of night stays these couriers from the swift completion of their appointed rounds." (This statement is inscribed

WHAT DO YOU THINK?

Mordecai's character must have marked him as a different kind of advisor than Haman. What were some of Mordecai's strengths that evoked a high level of trust by the king? How can we emulate these today?

today on the New York City General Post Office building.) Getting the message out swiftly is essential, because the Jews need time to prepare for their defense.

Many may be willing to attack Jews who are defenseless, but most will have second thoughts about challenging those who are armed and organized. Some, however, do attack the Jews out in the provinces, and thousands of the attackers are killed (Esther 9:5, 16). In Susa, the capital city, the Jews kill about eight hundred over two days (9:12-15).

A. DAY OF CELEBRATION (vv. 17-19)

17. This happened on the thirteenth day of the month of Adar, and on the fourteenth they rested and made it a day of feasting and joy.

These bloody conflicts occur mainly on two days—the *thirteenth* and *fourteenth* day of *Adar* (this month corresponds to late February or early March). The time that had been set for the destruction of the Jews becomes, instead, days of salvation for them—a time of rejoicing and *feasting*. The plan by which the enemies of the Jews hoped to destroy them becomes an event that binds them closer together across the empire.

18, 19. The Jews in Susa, however, had assembled on the thirteenth and fourteenth, and then on the fifteenth they rested and made it a day of feasting and joy. That is why rural Jews—those living in villages—observe the fourteenth of the month of Adar as a day of joy and feasting, a day for giving presents to each other.

The *Jews* in different parts of the empire have different experiences in defending themselves. As a result, they apparently do not all observe this special event on the same day. How Mordecai handles this difference is the subject of the next verse.

B. LETTER TO THE JEWS (vv. 20, 21)

20, 21. Mordecai recorded these events, and he sent letters to all the Jews throughout the provinces of King Xerxes, near and far, to have them celebrate annually the fourteenth and fifteenth days of the month of Adar

It would seem that there is some disagreement about when the feast should be observed—some want to celebrate on *the fourteenth* and some want to celebrate on the *fifteenth*. Because of his work in saving *the Jews* from Haman's scheme, *Mordecai* has become the recognized leader of the Jewish people wherever they may live in the empire. Thus he is the one who settles the issue: instead of celebrating on a single day, the Jews will have two days to celebrate. This is a wise decision because it easily includes both points of view—and no one will object to having an extra day for celebration!

C. FROM SORROW TO JOY (vv. 22, 23)

22, 23. . . . as the time when the Jews got relief from their enemies, and as the month when their sorrow was turned into joy and their mourning into a day of celebration. He wrote them to observe the days as days of feasting and joy and giving presents of food to one another and gifts to the poor.

So the Jews agreed to continue the celebration they had begun, doing what Mordecai had written to them.

This joyous festival becomes known as "Purim." This term comes from the Assyrian word *pur,* which means "lots." It indicates that in some way Haman cast lots to eliminate the Jews (Esther 3:7; 9:24; cf. John 19:24; Acts 1:26).

Second Maccabees 15:36, which describes some events that happen about one hundred and sixty years before Christ, calls it "Mordecai's Day." The Jewish historian Josephus also mentions this festival. But this festival is not mentioned

Use this time line to help your learners keep "the big picture" in mind.

WHAT DO YOU THINK?

Mordecai made everyone happy by his compromise to hold the celebration over two days' time instead of one. When is compromise a good idea, and when is it not? Explain.

WHAT DO YOU THINK?

What was an occasion that for you "turned . . . from sorrow to joy, and from mourning into a good day"? Why did it happen, and what was it about such an occasion that helped you grow spiritually and strengthen your faith?

DAILY BIBLE READINGS

Monday, Feb. 23—The Lord Sets the Prisoners Free (Psalm 146:1-9)

Tuesday, Feb. 24—A Song of Praise Is Fitting (Psalm 147:1-5)

Wednesday, Feb. 25—Sing to God With Thanksgiving (Psalm 147:6-11)

Thursday, Feb. 26—Praise Your God, O Zion! (Psalm 147: 12-20)

Friday, Feb. 27—God Has Brought Victory (Psalm 98:1-9)

Saturday, Feb. 28—Esther Saves the Jews (Esther 8:1-8)

Sunday, Feb. 29—The Jews Celebrate Their Deliverance (Esther 9:18-23)

PRAYER

All-loving God, we thank you that across the centuries you have given guidance and protection to your people, leaving memorials to remind them of your goodness. Give us the faith we need to see that in our day you have not left us but are ever present to lead and protect. In the name of our Savior we pray, amen.

THOUGHT TO REMEMBER

Whenever you celebrate, don't forget why!

in the New Testament, perhaps because it is not one of the major Jewish feasts, and, being celebrated only locally, is not a factor in the ministry of Jesus.

GIFTS TO THE POOR

Every November a volunteer army rises up to provide Thanksgiving dinners for the needy. Businesses offer food and equipment. Warehouses reserve space for supplies. Donations flow from individuals throughout the community. Public schools open their cafeterias to cook and serve the meals. And hundreds of workers stay up through the night to roast turkeys, peel potatoes, bake pies, and mix dressing.

You may have something similar in your community. At Thanksgiving, Christmas, or other occasions throughout the year, people volunteer time, effort, and resources to provide such "gifts to the poor." This is a way to celebrate God's goodness.

The apostle Paul wrote, "You will be made rich in every way so that you can be generous on every occasion, and through us your generosity will result in thanksgiving to God. This service that you perform is not only supplying the needs of God's people but is also overflowing in many expressions of thanks to God" (2 Corinthians 9:11, 12). When we help people in need in the name of Christ, we bring joy to them. We also provide a reason for them to give thanks to God.

As Mordecai urged the Jews in Persia, so we can help the poor on our own "days of feasting." God's own Son saved us from wrath and destruction, so how can we not help the poor celebrate right alongside us? The Jews were to treat the poor among them as God had treated them—with grace.

This remains a wonderful way to celebrate God's goodness to us. What can you do to celebrate by serving? Do you have a special day or a special achievement coming up? Mark this milestone with the joy of helping someone in need. Then your celebration will honor both God and humanity. —J. D. J.

CONCLUSION

Memories are a vital part of our personalities. In fact, we are largely defined by our memories. All of us have hundreds of memories, some painful, some pleasant, that have shaped us into the kind of people we are and the kind of people we will be. Psychologists tell us that a person may be scarred permanently by the memories of a violent or discouraging childhood.

Many of us have had the painful experience of visiting an old friend who is in the advanced stages of Alzheimer's disease. Her memory is gone. She no longer knows who she is. Her life is lived out in a gathering gloom.

Families can suffer a similar fate. Parents and their children share many common memories. But then grandchildren and great-grandchildren lose these "memory ties" that bind them together. Over the years they drift apart. The common values they once cherished gradually erode and disappear.

Institutions can suffer a similar fate. They lose sight of their original purpose. They eventually dissipate their energies, becoming involved in activities that are quite foreign to their original "reason for being." The church has not completely escaped this trap. (See Galatians 1:6; Revelation 2:4.)

God, knowing our tendency to forget, has left us some important "memorial markers." Those markers he allowed the ancient Jews to have eventually gave way to those he established for the church. Baptisms remind us of his sacrifice for us (Romans 6:1-11). The Lord's Supper reminds us of his body, broken for our sins, and his blood, poured out for us. Each time we participate, our minds are stirred again to remember his sacrifice for us (1 Corinthians 11:23-25).

God gave (or allowed) the ancient Hebrews various feasts and holy days to remind them of his providential care for them. So also he has given us these memorials lest we forget.

Discovery Learning

This page contains an alternative lesson plan emphasizing learning activities. Classes desiring such student involvement will find these suggestions helpful. The next page is a reproducible activity page to further enhance discovery learning.

LEARNING GOALS

After this lesson students will be able to:

1. Summarize the events that led to the beginning of the Jewish festival of Purim.

2. Discuss the importance of celebrating special events in their Christian lives to help strengthen faith.

3. Plan a church or family celebration to commemorate a specific milestone or victory.

INTO THE LESSON

Have a class member give a brief report on the Jewish feast of Purim, which originated in Esther's bravery. The focus should be the reason for the celebration, when Jews celebrate, and how they have celebrated down through the centuries since Esther.

Your reporter will need resources. Early in the week give this individual a photocopy of the lesson commentary on 9:22, 23. Also give the reporter a Bible dictionary with the pages marked that tells about this feast. You might suggest that your reporter call a local rabbi and conduct a brief telephone interview. Of course, the Internet is also a valuable tool for such research.

After the presentation say, "Holidays are an important part of every religion and nation." Ask the class to name the major national and Christian holidays, and list these for later use.

INTO THE WORD

Activity 1: Begin with a brief lecture on the Lesson Background, summarizing last week's study. Make a visual of the story line from last week's lesson to summarize Esther's story up to the time she made her dramatic decision.

Activity 2: Call three class members during the week and ask them to do a brief dramatization of Esther 8:1b-8. The characters will be Xerxes, Esther, and Mordecai. Ask them to meet about fifteen to twenty minutes before class and rehearse, putting the text into contemporary words. Simple props may include a crown, ring, a cane or umbrella for a scepter, and large nametags to wear around the neck.

Following the drama, read the printed text and ask the following discussion questions:

(1) Remember that to enter the king's throne room without an invitation meant death—unless the king offered his scepter as an expression of pardon. Esther did not wait for the king to offer his scepter before she made her appeal. Why did she jump right in before the king could decide whether or not to make the offer?

(2) The challenge was how to revoke a law that could not be revoked. The king's word was irrevocable law. What was Esther's plan?

Activity 3: Ask someone to read the remainder of Esther 8 to the class. Ask three class members to be a "listening team," ready to summarize a small portion of the text. Ask one to note especially where the edict went. A second is to summarize the edict. A third will report the reactions of the Jews and other nationalities.

Activity 4: Tell the class that the next portion of the text records the first celebration of the feast of Purim. Then read Esther 9:17-23. Highlight a few of the remarks made by your reporter in the lesson introduction.

INTO LIFE

As you point to your list of national and religious holidays, ask the class to identify the values of holidays. Write their remarks on another poster. Answers may include the values of teaching history, ethics, God's will or purpose, building family relationships, or others.

Form groups of three to five, and give each a large piece of poster board and a marker. Each group is to brainstorm how to make the celebration of a particular holiday effective and meaningful for families or individuals, especially how we can teach God's values and priorities. Assign each group one of the holidays listed in the Into the Lesson activity. Allow each group time to compile its suggestions and then to report its suggestions with its poster on display.

Conclude the class by asking members to complete a commitment card. The card will have three statements:

1. The next holiday/celebration in my family or life is. . . .

2. The value and opportunities that this holiday presents include. . . .

3. I will use this holiday to teach, or remind us of, Christ's values and priorities.

Signed _____

Option: The reproducible activity page that follows offers options for applying this lesson to life. The "Looking Back" activity will allow a bit of introspection. The "Looking Ahead" activity will encourage learners to plan for extending the truths of today's lessons into life. Consider using these in class or encouraging personal use.

Looking Back

If you are like most people, you have done some courageous—and some not-so-courageous—things in your life. Think back to the first eighteen to twenty years of your life. In the rearview mirror below, jot a note about an occasion when you showed a bit of courage in your faith. Also note one of the moments when you were more cowardly in your actions.

Looking Ahead

Now is the time to plan a courageous act and testimony. Think of a friend or family member who is not living up to his or her commitment to the Lord. Jot a few notes about what that person needs to hear on the "note pad" to the right. Plan for a time to act courageously, and tenderly speak to that person about his or her need.

Spring Quarter, 2004

Special Features

		Page
In the Stream of History	Ronald L. Nickelson	232
The City of Jerusalem (map feature)		235
Jesus' Victory Over Death		236

Lessons

Jesus Fulfills His Mission

Unit 1: Road to the Cross

March	7	Love and Betrayal	*Matthew 26:3-15, 20-25*	237
	14	Loaf and Cup	*Luke 22:7-23*	245
	21	Prayer and Arrest	*Matthew 26:36-50*	253
	28	Trial and Sentence	*Mark 14:53, 55-64; 15:1, 2, 12-15*	261

Unit 2: Victory Through Death

| April | 4 | Jesus' Crucifixion | *John 19:16b-24, 26-30* | 269 |
| | 11 | The Empty Tomb | *Matthew 28:1-15* | 277 |

Living Expectantly

Unit 1: Preparing for the Lord's Return

	18	Faithful in His Service	*1 Thessalonians 1:2-10; 3:6-10*	285
	25	Ready for His Return	*1 Thessalonians 4:13-18; 5:2-11*	293
May	2	Reflecting His Glory	*2 Thessalonians 1:3, 4, 11, 12; 2:13–3:4*	301

Unit 2: Visions of Hope

	9	Worshiping the Lamb	*Revelation 5:1-10*	309
	16	Receiving God's Salvation	*Revelation 7:1-3, 9, 10, 13-17*	317
	23	Enduring With the Saints	*Revelation 14:6-13*	325
	30	Dwelling With God	*Revelation 21:1-7, 22-27*	333

About These Lessons

Our Christian faith is anchored in the fact that Jesus' death and resurrection secure our eternity. Historical reality and "future history" work together to tell us how to live today. Past, present, and future—it's all here!

Mar 7

Mar 14

Mar 21

Mar 28

Apr 4

Apr 11

Apr 18

Apr 25

May 2

May 9

May 16

May 23

May 30

In the Stream of History

by Ronald L. Nickelson

The problem with most people," one observer lamented, "is that they live their lives as if history began on the day they were born."

The sad result of such an outlook is what we might call tunnel-vision living. Without a larger sense of history, people tend to see only their immediate situations, living only for the present moment. History becomes irrelevant because, after all, "that was then; this is now."

But the Bible assures us that history is indeed important. The birth, death, and resurrection of Jesus Christ were events that occurred at specific times and places. Each has its own meaning as determined by God. All other points along God's time line of salvation-history either lead up to the occurrence of these events, or build upon them as established facts.

And what a stream of history this is! From our twenty-first century vantage point we have the privilege of marveling at how God has brought about his plans over thousands of years. Fulfilled prophecy proves Christianity to be the only true religion. Fulfilled prophecy is the firm basis upon which Christians stand in the here-and-now as we look confidently toward future fulfillment. How tragic it is to see people live their lives day by day with no sense of God's movement in history!

The lessons of this quarter invite us to stand in this stream of history and look both ways. We will begin by looking two thousand years into the past. There in the gospel accounts we will see Jesus fulfill the sobering requirements of God's plan for our eternal salvation.

As our lessons move forward, our gaze ultimately will shift to "future history"—to the time (if we can use that term) when we are in our eternal home. That eternal home (Heaven) will be for those who have repented because they recognize what the God of all history has done for us in history through Jesus Christ.

MARCH

JESUS FULFILLS HIS MISSION

UNIT 1: ROAD TO THE CROSS

Lesson 1: Love and Betrayal. Our first lesson opens to us the final week of Jesus' earthly ministry as depicted in Matthew's Gospel. As we see people react to Jesus with the extremes of love and hatred, we realize that it is unlikely that anyone involved in this drama (other than Jesus himself) understood what roles they were playing in the grand sweep of history. The two thousand years of hindsight that we have on the lives of these people should give us pause: do we live out our own lives for Christ with a sense of how our behavior may affect others many years—even centuries—hence?

Lesson 2: Loaf and Cup. This lesson from Luke's Gospel could also be titled "In the Eye of the Hurricane," since this is a period of calm in the midst of Jesus' hectic final week. The tumult of the triumphal entry and temple confrontation are past at this point, while arrest and crucifixion are yet future. It is within these few hours that Jesus shifts the course of history in an entirely new direction: Lord's Supper observances have begun, and Passover celebrations are to be no more. Whenever we participate in the Lord's Supper, do we have the sense of history that we need to understand the importance of this shift?

Lesson 3: Prayer and Arrest. The calm that is in the eye of the hurricane is about to come to an end as we move back to Matthew's Gospel. In his hour of crisis, Jesus is all alone. His disciples are nearby in a physical sense, but in an emotional or supportive sense they are very much absent. The reason is simple: they don't understand the critical importance of this brief moment in history. Do we?

Lesson 4: Trial and Sentence. This lesson from Mark shows us Jesus on trial before people who are caught up in their personal agendas and sense of self-importance. These individuals include members of the Jewish Sanhedrin plus the Roman Governor Pontius Pilate. Their arrogance and "situation ethics" blind them to the sobering roles they are playing in history. They don't have a clue!

Even so, history is still moving inexorably toward its conclusion. On that great, final day when God concludes history, these leaders will find the roles reversed: they will be the ones standing for judgment before the one whom they judged unjustly. When that day comes, where will *we* be standing?

UNIT 2: VICTORY THROUGH DEATH

Lesson 5: Jesus' Crucifixion. The Gospel of John portrays the reality of Jesus' death for us. At his crucifixion, Jesus' friends and disciples asked themselves, "How could this possibly be happening?" At the same time, Jesus' enemies gloated, "We have finally stopped him!" But in the final analysis it was only Jesus himself who had the correct sense of history. It was only Jesus who had a true sense of the importance of what was really happening.

APRIL

The truth was that Jesus' death was neither tragic accident nor the triumph of an earthly foe. Rather, it was Jesus' voluntary, intentional payment of sin's price. Do we have the right view of history to understand this today?

Lesson 6: The Empty Tomb. Jesus' triumph over death was disbelieved by both friend and foe, and Matthew's Gospel shows us a small part of these reactions. Even though the initial disbelief of the disciples quickly gave way to amazement, their reactions revealed misconceptions. They had been taught personally by the Lord for more than three years, and they still did not understand. With the completed Bible in our hands, God has given us the capability of interpreting this vital historical event correctly. Have we?

LIVING EXPECTANTLY

UNIT 1: PREPARING FOR THE LORD'S RETURN

Lesson 7: Faithful in His Service. With the writing of 1 Thessalonians, time has moved forward some twenty years from the crucifixion and resurrection. The Thessalonians have demonstrated through their faith and service a proper understanding of those historical facts. With all the additional information we have today through completed revelation, will we understand as well as the Thessalonians did?

Lesson 8: Ready for His Return. What an interesting blend of past, present, and future we see in this lesson! Jesus died and rose again (past), and he is coming again (future). These past and future events affect how we are to live in the present, as Paul stresses in his counsel to the Thessalonians. Will we accept Paul's instructions to them as our marching orders as well?

Lesson 9: Reflecting His Glory. Having firmly established the importance of both past and future events regarding the Christ, we are ready in this lesson from 2 Thessalonians to view Paul's focus on the present. History, which has revealed the power, glory, and goodness of God, *must* shape how we live our lives day by day. Do people see us living out our calling by his power?

MAY

Unit 2: Visions of Hope

Lesson 10: Worshiping the Lamb. With the final four lessons in this quarter our attention shifts decisively to future history as depicted in the book of Revelation. The events we will read about can indeed be called "future history" because the probability that they will happen is 100 percent. The certainty of these blessed promises should cause us to worship. Does it?

Lesson 11: Receiving God's Salvation, and **Lesson 12: Enduring With the Saints.** Every Christian suffers. Some suffer more than others. Some Christians suffer even to the point of martyrdom, yet they remain steadfast in their faith. How do they do it? There is only one way: they focus on the eternal reward that awaits them. Are you one of these?

Lesson 13: Dwelling With God. The first act of history was creation itself (Genesis 1:1). The climactic acts that bring down the curtain on history will be the return of Christ, final judgment, and the unveiling of the new creation. But the new creation (with its new Jerusalem) is only for those who have renounced the depravity and decay of the old creation and who have Jesus Christ as their Savior. Are you one of these?

This quarter's lessons are just what we need to keep a perspective on past and future history. And what a breathtaking stream of history we stand in! What a marvelous future awaits us!

Even so, many today are so blinded by the allures and distractions of this world that they cannot (or will not) see that eternal destruction is their sobering destiny. We reach these people for Christ by sharing with them what Christ did for us some two thousand years ago. But telling the story isn't enough. We must live it as well.

The City of Jerusalem

Calvary

Garden Tomb

to Bethany 2 miles

Pilate's Praetorium

Mount of Olives

Garden of Gethsemane

Temple Area

Palace of Herod

House of Caiaphas

Upper Room

Kidron Valley

This map shows a possible location for many of the significant places in the final week of Jesus' life, some of which are included in lessons 1-6 of the current study.

Jesus' Victory Over DEATH— Jesus' Death Gives Us LIFE

Lesson	Theme
1	Prepared for Death; Betrayed to Death
2	Remembering His Death
3	Facing Death
4	Sentenced to Death
5	Death by Crucifixion
6	Death Conquered
7	Life in the Lord
8	Raised to Life
9	The Glorified Life
10	A Book of Life
11	Life With God
12	Life After Death
13	Eternal Life

Jesus Fulfills His Mission
Unit 1: Road to the Cross
(Lessons 1-4)

LOVE AND BETRAYAL

WHY TEACH THIS LESSON?

The Roman historian Suetonius tells of events of March 15, 44 B.C., when Julius Caesar was assassinated. Recognizing his friend Marcus Junius Brutus as one of the conspirators, Caesar cries out "Et tu, Brute?" which means "And you, too, Brutus?"

The subject of "love and betrayal" is neither new nor rare. It is the stuff of novels, songs, and theater. It is a theme that has found its way into the titles and subtitles of dozens of books. It is even the title of a 1989 movie. People seem to be fascinated with subject matter that seems to be self-contradictory, as this one is.

But screenwriters, novelists, and historians have yet to outdo the level of drama we will see in today's lesson. Just imagine it: the Son of God betrayed by one of his twelve disciples, one whom Jesus had taught personally for three years! Today's lesson serves, among other things, as a warning to modern disciples lest we, too, end up rejecting and betraying Jesus, thus trampling "the Son of God under foot" (Hebrews 10:29).

INTRODUCTION

Are you basically a "meat-and-taters" person, the consummate "I'll try anything once" connoisseur, or something in between? People differ in tastes, but the differences from person to person run much deeper in importance than that.

A. DIVERSITY

As humans we share much in common, yet no one questions our diversity of thought patterns and behavioral styles. Some researchers conclude that people can be categorized broadly in terms of how they approach a task. One person just wants to get the job done as quickly as possible. Another wants to do the job while interacting with people. One person wants to do the job in a way that keeps the peace. Yet another wants to do the job correctly above all else. Each will take a different approach to the same job.

Similarly, with our diversities of race, religion, education, socioeconomic standing, gender, worldviews, and personal agendas, it should not surprise us to see different people react in various ways to the same person or situation. In today's lesson we observe people reacting in four different ways to Jesus. The Jewish leaders, a loving woman, the apostles as a group, and Judas in particular all display differing responses to the Lord.

B. LESSON BACKGROUND

The final week of Jesus' ministry left the world changed forever. Jesus' normal base of operation when in Judea was Bethany, a village about two miles southeast of Jerusalem (see Matthew 21:17; Mark 11:1-11). His dear friends Mary, Martha, and Lazarus lived there (John 11:1, 2), as well as Simon the leper (see below).

Our text today picks up after Jesus has spent some intense days in Jerusalem. After a triumphal entry, Jesus had driven money changers out of the temple, had verbally jousted with the enemies who wanted to trap him, had denounced their

DEVOTIONAL READING:
PSALM 55:12-22
BACKGROUND SCRIPTURE:
MATTHEW 26
PRINTED TEXT:
MATTHEW 26:3-15, 20-25

LESSON AIMS

After participating in this lesson, each student will be able to:

1. List the ways, both good and bad, that people reacted to Jesus in today's text.

2. Tell how the same reactions are expressed today.

3. Suggest one concrete way that the believer can imitate Mary's example of showing extravagant love for Christ.

KEY VERSES

And while they were eating, he said, "I tell you the truth, one of you will betray me."

They were very sad and began to say to him one after the other, "Surely not I, Lord?"

—Matthew 26:21, 22

hypocrisy, had warned his disciples of the coming destruction of Jerusalem, had challenged them to be prepared for the final judgment, and had reminded them once again that he would be betrayed and crucified (Matthew 21:1–26:2). And the week was far from over!

I. PREMEDITATED TREACHERY (MATTHEW 26:3-5)

First we consider the reaction of the Jewish leaders. They have opposed Jesus for most of his ministry, but now events take a particularly ominous turn.

A. LEADERS MEET (v. 3)

3. Then the chief priests and the elders of the people assembled in the palace of the high priest, whose name was Caiaphas,

This assembly constitutes an informal gathering of the Sanhedrin, Israel's "supreme court." This is an unscheduled meeting to carry out a sinful, misguided agenda. Yet Jesus himself had just predicted his death in Matthew 26:1, 2! Jesus' death ultimately is in his own hands, and not in the hands of *the chief priests and the elders of the people* (Matthew 26:53, 54; John 10:18).

B. LEADERS PLOT (vv. 4, 5)

4. . . . and they plotted to arrest Jesus in some sly way and kill him.

Only one item appears on the agenda. In consultation, they plot to take Jesus into custody as an enemy of the state. And their treachery is evident. Rather than arresting Jesus boldly and openly, they opt to do it in a *sly way*.

Jesus' *arrest*, however, is only the first step toward their real objective: they want to *kill him*. Without his death their plan will be incomplete. An informal meeting to plot the execution of a man who has not yet been tried or convicted violates Jewish law (John 7:51). Yet the presumed spiritual leaders of Israel have fallen into such corruption that they are willing to set aside the law to have Jesus eliminated.

DARK NIGHTS AND DARK DEEDS

During Russia's Bolshevik revolution, Czar Nicholas II and the royal family were taken captive. Their captors transferred them to a private residence in the town of Ekaterinburg. Shortly after midnight on July 17, 1918, the family was awakened and taken to a basement room on the pretext that it was for their protection.

Soon a team of assassins burst into the room and killed the family. Still under the cover of night, conspirators took their bodies by truck to an abandoned mine pit and burned them. Acid was poured on the remains to cover the atrocity. A legend grew up around the event to the effect that Princess Anastasia had been spared and remained alive until late in the twentieth century.

Compare this story with the events surrounding Jesus' arrest and crucifixion. The Jewish leaders also chose the cover of night as they prepared to secure Jesus' death. Darkness enabled them to keep their evil deeds from the common people. As for the survival of Anastasia—whose name, ironically, means "resurrection"—this legend was an act of grasping at the proverbial straw of hope during the dark night of Communism's reign over Russia. Jesus' resurrection, on the other hand, was attested by hundreds of eyewitnesses (1 Corinthians 15:6). Our hope is real!

But the point of our text is that evil people choose darkness (both physical and spiritual) to cover the darkness of their hearts and deeds. They still do so in the twenty-first century. Praise God for the light we have that defeats that darkness (John 1:5).

—C. R. B.

5. "But not during the Feast," they said, "or there may be a riot among the people."

WHAT DO YOU THINK?

Events leading to the crucifixion of Jesus brought out character defects in the Jewish leaders, in Pontius Pilate, and even in Jesus' own disciples. How do we recognize and overcome such flaws in our own lives? How might having an "accountability partner" help?

[Passages such as 2 Corinthians 13:5; James 1:5, 22; and 1 John 1:9 may stimulate your thought.]

VISUALS FOR THESE LESSONS

The visual pictured in each lesson (e.g., page 241) is a small reproduction of a large, full-color poster included in the Adult Visuals packet for the Spring Quarter. The packet is available from your supplier. Order No. 392.

Jesus' popularity with the masses poses a real threat to the power of the Jewish leaders (John 11:48). To arrest Jesus openly could spawn *a riot* among the sympathetic populace. The "normal" population of Jerusalem is probably somewhere between sixty thousand and one hundred twenty thousand. This figure may temporarily swell fivefold during the Passover!

Overcrowding during such a *Feast* day means that tempers sometimes run short. The populace is already worked up over Jesus' triumphal entry and teaching. A riot over having Jesus falsely arrested can result in Roman intervention, jeopardizing the Jewish leaders' standing with Rome. To keep the peace and maintain their own political clout, the Jewish leaders seek an opportune time to seize Jesus.

II. PRECIOUS GIFT (MATTHEW 26:6-13)

Next we contrast the hatred the religious elite have for Jesus with the extravagant love of a woman whose story has endured through the ages.

A. GIFT GIVEN (vv. 6, 7)

6. While Jesus was in Bethany in the home of a man known as Simon the Leper,

Bethany is about two miles southeast of Jerusalem. *Simon*, a man apparently healed by Jesus, opens his home to friends to prepare a meal in the Lord's honor. Mary, Martha, and Lazarus are there as well as Jesus' disciples (Mark 14:3; John 12:2, 3).

John 12:1, 12 specifically place this event before the triumphal entry, and thus earlier than what we have just read in Matthew 26:3-5. This means that Matthew places this event where he does in his text in order to achieve a certain dramatic effect. When we compare the reason the Jewish leaders are assembled in Matthew 26:3-5 with the reason for the assembly at Simon's house, the contrast is startling indeed!

7. . . . a woman came to him with an alabaster jar of very expensive perfume, which she poured on his head as he was reclining at the table.

John informs us that it is Mary, the sister of Lazarus and Martha, who is the *woman* who anoints Jesus' *head* with precious ointment or *perfume* (John 12:3). It is customary to anoint the heads of important guests, but this act is extraordinary in more than one respect. The *alabaster jar* probably is a cherished family heirloom. The precious ointment is worth a great deal of money (John 12:5).

Mary not only pours the perfume on Jesus' head while he is having supper, she also anoints his feet, wiping them with her hair (John 12:3). Generally it is considered immodest for a woman to loosen her hair in mixed company, but Mary defies a prevailing cultural norm in expressing her devotion. She is willing to give up a family treasure and her own reputation among those who value tradition over truth in order to show her love to the Lord.

B. GIFT CRITICIZED (vv. 8, 9)

8, 9. When the disciples saw this, they were indignant. "Why this waste?" they asked. "This perfume could have been sold at a high price and the money given to the poor."

Judas is the spokesman who raises concerns about the proper use of the *perfume* (John 12:4, 5). His motives are based in personal greed (John 12:6). But he couches the argument in such a way that *the disciples* are easily swayed to his point of view. Judas's counter-proposal sounds spiritual to the rest of the disciples. None of them really seems to understand where these events are leading (Matthew 16:21-28; 26:40, 43, 45).

HOW TO SAY IT

Anastasia. An-ah-STAY-shuh.
Bethany. BETH-uh-nee.
Bolshevik. BOLL-shuh-vick.
Caesar. SEE-zur.
Caiaphas. KAY-uh-fus or KYE-uh-fus.
Deuteronomy. Due-ter-AHN-uh-me.
Ekaterinburg. Eh-KAH-ter-in-berg.
Isaiah. Eye-ZAY-uh.
Jerusalem. Juh-ROO-suh-lem.
Judas Iscariot. JOO-dus Iss-CARE-e-ut.
Messiah. Meh-SIGH-uh.
Sanhedrin. SAN-huh-drun or San-HEED-run.
Suetonius. Soo-TOE-nee-us.
Zechariah. ZEK-uh-RYE-uh.

WHAT DO YOU THINK?

Mary defied prevailing cultural norms to demonstrate her devotion to the Lord. What are some cultural norms we must defy today? How do we do this properly?

[Acts 5:29 and 1 Peter 3:15, 16 will be important to consider in this discussion.]

WHAT DO YOU THINK?

Suppose you were to do something out of good motives but, unlike Mary, your actions turned out to be misguided despite your good intentions. How would you handle the criticism that may follow?

C. GIFT HONORED (vv. 10-13)
10. Aware of this, Jesus said to them, "Why are you bothering this woman? She has done a beautiful thing to me.

Before Jesus responds, Mary must feel as if "no good deed goes unpunished." She has honored the Lord in a profound way, but one that still probably falls short of the Lord's worth in her own eyes. The disciples should be applauding rather than criticizing the selfless and generous nature of her love.

11. "The poor you will always have with you, but you will not always have me.

Many of Jesus' teachings contain a "startle factor" that grabs attention. This is one of them. On the surface it would appear that Jesus is minimizing the concern we are to have for *the poor.* But actually he is reaffirming Deuteronomy 15:11. Jesus' recognition that the poor *will always* be among us indirectly acknowledges our need to minister to them. That will not change until the Lord returns.

We should also recognize that some service opportunities are timeless, while others are narrowly time bound. When the window of opportunity to serve in the time-bound cases is shut, it is permanently lost. When Jesus says that they *will not always have* him with them, he reveals that the opportunity for his followers to honor him in the final tragic hours of his earthly ministry is severely limited. On the stage of history, Mary seizes the opportunity of a lifetime.

12. "When she poured this perfume on my body, she did it to prepare me for burial.

As Mary anoints Jesus with the ointment, does she realize that she is doing it *for* his *burial?* We cannot be certain that Mary does indeed realize this, but Jesus himself certainly sees the deeper meaning. This incident provides the Master with yet another opportunity to teach.

13. "I tell you the truth, wherever this gospel is preached throughout the world, what she has done will also be told, in memory of her."

Jesus makes a bold prediction that history confirms. Though she wants nothing more than the privilege of honoring her Lord, Jesus guarantees that Mary herself would receive a memorial. The very fact that we study this story today establishes the truthfulness of Jesus' prediction. Like Mary, we also can seize those unique moments in which we demonstrate that we "would rather have Jesus than silver or gold."

WHAT DO YOU THINK?

Jesus said that Mary's act of devotion would be remembered throughout time. For what will you be remembered? Why do you think so?

III. PERSONAL BETRAYAL (MATTHEW 26:14, 15, 20-25)
How much the disciples "get the idea" at this point we don't really know. The one definite exception is Judas. The lure of cold hard cash leads him down the path of ultimate infamy.

A. BETRAYER'S CONTRACT (vv. 14, 15)
14. Then one of the Twelve—the one called Judas Iscariot—went to the chief priests

Judas's previous greed and theft are indications that he has already turned away from the Master in an appreciable way. However, going *to the chief priests* to deal with Jesus constitutes a total rejection of the Lord. This is treason!

15. . . . and asked, "What are you willing to give me if I hand him over to you?" So they counted out for him thirty silver coins.

As an insider, Judas has exact knowledge of the whereabouts and movements of Jesus. Consequently, he knows where and when the authorities can arrest him secretly, without fear of a riot. Jesus came to earth to deliver Judas from sin to eternal life; Judas goes to the chief priests to deliver him from life unto death.

As a result, the Jewish leaders "put out a contract" on Jesus' life. The *thirty silver coins* is no more than what the Old Testament requires as compensation for the death of a slave (Exodus 21:32). What a low value Judas and the Jewish leaders placed on the life of the King of the universe! (See also Zechariah 11:12.)

We do not know if Judas has motives other than greed. Speculation abounds as to what could make such a close companion of Jesus turn so drastically. Possibly Judas has become disillusioned because Jesus isn't quite the type of Messiah that Judas expects. Maybe Jesus' stinging rebuke in Matthew 26:10-13 has pushed Judas over the edge. All we know for sure is that a heart once drawn to accept the call to apostleship now sets into motion the wheels of ultimate betrayal.

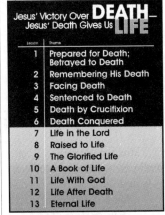

Visual for lesson 1. *Leave this chart posted to highlight the Death and Life emphases of this quarter.*

CONSPIRACY THEORIES AND A REAL CONSPIRACY

Some people simply insist on getting things all wrong. One example is *The Horrifying Fraud,* the English title of a best-selling French-language book written by Thierry Meyssan and published early in 2002. Meyssan is a conspiracy-theorist who conjured up this scenario for what "really" happened on September 11, 2001: the terrorist attacks were carried out by U.S. government officials for economic and military reasons to allow America to attack Afghanistan and Iraq; the story we all got from the news media was a "loony fable"; no plane really struck the Pentagon—the explosion was triggered on the ground; the planes that struck the World Trade Center were flown by remote control and guided by navigational beacons in the towers.

This bizarre nonsense devalues the lives of all who died in those attacks. It also demonstrates that the author has much in common with Judas and those Jews whose conspiracy to kill Jesus devalued the life of the Son of God.

There is another similarity: just as Thierry Meyssan was unable to see the reality of "9-11," neither Judas nor the Jewish leaders could accept the truth about the real nature of Jesus' mission. It simply didn't fit their own ideas of who they thought the Messiah "should" be. As a result, they constructed a terribly misguided version of reality. How many today continue to construct untruths about Jesus because the truth he confronts them with is too uncomfortable? —C. R. B.

B. BETRAYER'S CHARADE (vv. 20-22)

20. When evening came, Jesus was reclining at the table with the Twelve.

The scene now shifts to the *evening* of Jesus' final Passover observance with his disciples. Judas already has agreed to the contract on Jesus' life, but none of the disciples know that. Therefore, when the *evening came* for them to share the Passover, it is easy for Judas to take his place as one of *the Twelve* with his plan undetected.

21. And while they were eating, he said, "I tell you the truth, one of you will betray me."

After Peter's confession of Jesus as the Son of God, the Lord had begun to reveal that he would be rejected by the Jewish leaders, suffer, and be killed (Matthew 16:21; Luke 9:22). This is the first time, however, that they have heard him say *one of* them would *betray* him.

22. They were very sad and began to say to him one after the other, "Surely not I, Lord?"

Jesus' comments hit the group with maximum force. They are extremely distressed, exceedingly sorrowful. They never dreamed that the cancer of betrayal could infiltrate their group. Judas conducts his charade so flawlessly that no one suspects him.

Out of emotional anguish and with personal urgency each asks, *Surely not I, Lord?* Each man trusts the others, so the only place to look is inward. Each one wonders if some fatal character flaw will be exposed to his own shame and

WHAT DO YOU THINK?

To their credit, each of the disciples asked, "Surely not I, Lord?" and not "Is it him?" How can we develop a pure, godly attitude that resists pointing fingers?

[Make sure your class considers Matthew 6:33 and John 21:20-23 in this discussion.]

DAILY BIBLE READINGS

Monday, Mar. 1—The Psalmist Mourns a Friend's Betrayal (Psalm 55:12-17)

Tuesday, Mar. 2—A Friend Violates a Covenant (Psalm 55: 18-22)

Wednesday, Mar. 3—Zeal for Your House (Psalm 69:6-14)

Thursday, Mar. 4—A Woman Pours Ointment on Jesus (Matthew 26:1-13)

Friday, Mar. 5—Judas Agrees to Betray Jesus (Matthew 26:14-19)

Saturday, Mar. 6—Jesus Announces Upcoming Betrayal (Matthew 26:20-25)

Sunday, Mar. 7—Peter Promises Not to Desert Jesus (Matthew 26:31-35)

PRAYER

Dear Father, we marvel at how the Lord Jesus still loved in the face of hatred, his disciples' lack of discernment, and the betrayal of one so close. Give us grace to be extravagant in loving you, for you are worth everything we have to give. In Jesus' name, amen.

THOUGHT TO REMEMBER

Let the extravagance of our love for him reflect the extravagance of his love for us.

disgrace. And all the while Judas acts as if he is as distressed as the others in the room.

C. BETRAYER'S EXPOSURE (vv. 23-25)

23. Jesus replied, "The one who has dipped his hand into the bowl with me will betray me.

Jesus' answer at this point is still somewhat general. The one who has dipped his hand with me in the dish could refer to anyone in the room, for all of them are sharing in that activity during the evening meal. By saying the same will betray me, Jesus reemphasizes that the betrayal will indeed come from within their group.

24. "The Son of Man will go just as it is written about him. But woe to that man who betrays the Son of Man! It would be better for him if he had not been born."

Jesus acknowledges his willing intent to fulfill God's plan as it has been written of him in the Old Testament (cf. Isaiah 53). He never dodges the work of giving his life to pay sin's price for our eternal salvation.

But Jesus sternly warns that his betrayer will not be allowed to dodge the consequences of his rebellion either. In the terrible judgment he will face, Judas will not be able to argue, "Well, I wasn't warned." (See also Acts 1:15-20.)

25. Then Judas, the one who would betray him, said, "Surely not I, Rabbi?" Jesus answered, "Yes, it is you."

Judas maintains his charade of loyalty to the very end. Knowing full well that he is the one, he still asks Surely not I, Rabbi? In true prophetic fashion Jesus throws off the cover to reveal Judas's wicked betrayal. If Judas thinks he has successfully hidden his evil work, he finds out what he should have known all along: nothing can be hidden from the Lord.

But the Lord's reply falls on deaf ears. Although Jesus makes it clear to Judas that he knows about the nefarious plan, Judas will betray him anyway.

CONCLUSION

Love and betrayal step to center stage in today's lesson text. But they do not stand there alone. Hatred and lack of discernment make their appearances as well.

The hatred of the Jewish leaders for Jesus demonstrates the depths of corruption to which people in power can sink. The very people who should have accepted the message were the ones who resisted it by all means possible. The same is true today.

The extravagant love of Mary for Jesus challenges us to love him just as completely. If she had to break a conventional norm to anoint Jesus' feet, or if she needed to let go of a family treasure to satisfy her longing to serve Christ, she just did it. May we do the same.

The disciples allowed themselves to get caught up in what seemed like a pious position, only to discover their own lack of discernment. How important it is that we evaluate all sides of an issue and then reach a conclusion with spiritual insight! To do otherwise causes us unintentionally to devalue our Lord.

And then there is Judas. How tragic that a man who had been invited into such close fellowship with the Son of God could turn so completely! While we take great pleasure in our relationship with Christ, we should never take it for granted. What will we do when we find ourselves in situations where we ask, "Will it be I who betrays the Lord?" Instead of running toward Christ's enemies, let us decide right now that in every circumstance, regardless of the cost, we will run full speed to the Lord of glory!

Discovery Learning

*This page contains an alternative lesson plan emphasizing learning activities. Classes
desiring such student involvement will find these suggestions helpful. The next page
is a reproducible activity page to further enhance discovery learning.*

LEARNING GOALS

After participating in this lesson, each student will be able to:

1. List the ways, both good and bad, that people reacted to Jesus in today's text.

2. Tell how the same reactions are expressed today.

3. Suggest one concrete way that the believer can imitate Mary's example of showing extravagant love for Christ.

INTO THE LESSON

To begin thinking about how individuals respond differently to different things, hold a Popularity Poll. As you mention things, events, or people, ask class members to indicate how much they like or dislike each. Begin with selections that will create friendly feuds: foods (pizza, chocolate, etc.), activities (bowling, skydiving, etc.), favorite sports teams (Green Bay Packers, New York Yankees, etc.), or style of music (classical, bluegrass, etc.). Move to people, beginning with political figures. Maybe even let the class cheer or boo as each name is mentioned (if this will not disrupt neighboring classes).

As you take the vote, ask for reasons why students like or dislike each one. Use this to introduce the idea that as one looks at the next event in the life of Jesus, he or she will find differences of opinion about Jesus, ranging from extravagant love to intense hatred. The attitudes are generally not stated directly, but demonstrated by actions. Describe how the individuals in the lesson would answer the opinion poll about Jesus. (If you would like to get your class members thinking about the lesson, consider sending the list home with them the week before, or send an e-mail for them to complete and bring to class.) This same pattern is repeated in future lessons as well, as every aspect of Jesus' life and ministry drew widely varying responses from people.

INTO THE WORD

Examine the four different responses to Jesus discussed in this lesson. Use the reproducible activity "What Do You Think of Jesus?" from the next page or place the following headings on columns on a board: *Person or Group, Scripture, Response to Jesus,* and *Contemporary Example.* The last column will list individuals or groups who demonstrate the same response to Jesus today. Under the *Person or Group* heading review their specific actions, and summarize the attitudes reflected. *(Jewish leaders were antagonistic, planning to kill Jesus, Matthew 26:3-5; Mary demonstrated extravagant love, willing to publicly show her love, in costly, humbling, even potentially embarrassing ways, Matthew 26:6, 7; John 12:3-5; the apostles, including Judas, were indignant at first, seeing this act of worship as extreme waste, Matthew 26:8, 9.)* Come back to the *Judas* line later, as Judas responded very differently from the other apostles to Jesus' words. Complete that line as noted below.

Jesus provided his personal commentary on the extravagant actions of the woman described in this story: he explains that her acts came from a heart overflowing with love, prompting her to express her love for the Savior publicly (Matthew 26:10-14). He also notes that her actions will be recounted by future generations when the gospel is told, leaving a living legacy to this special tribute. Go back at this point and complete the *Response to Jesus* column, contrasting Judas with the other apostles. The other apostles seemed to get the point. There is no further record of their arguing this way, and they are identified as followers of Jesus later in the Gospels and other places in the New Testament. Judas, however, shows that he would not accept the teaching of Jesus; instead he approaches the chief priests and offers to betray Jesus for thirty pieces of silver (Matthew 26:14-16). Discuss the difference between those who first respond wrongly but then listen and change, versus those who become hardened in their resistance to Jesus.

INTO LIFE

Finish the last column, *Contemporary Example.* As a class, list people or groups today that demonstrate the same response to Jesus as each of the four you have been examining. Discuss what these attitudes look like today *(antagonistic; loving extravagantly; misguided but teachable; or greedy and selfishly resistant).* Judas and Mary have become famous for their actions, leaving a legacy we still remember. If Jesus provided commentary, as he did regarding Mary, what would you want him to say was the significance of your life? What steps will you take this week to build such a pattern in your life and to prepare yourself for unique events that might be the lasting moment remembered about you?

What Do You Think of Jesus?

In a study of Jesus from the Gospels, it is helpful to examine the various responses of those who encountered him. The responses range from intense, murderous hatred to extravagant, sacrificial love. Fill in the following chart based on today's study. The Scripture texts in the second column will be helpful.

As you note examples in the news and neighborhood, fill in the "Contemporary Examples" column.

Person or Group	Scripture(s)	Response to Jesus	Contemporary Example
Jewish Leaders	Matthew 26:3-5		
Mary	Matthew 26:6, 7 John 12:3-5		
Apostles (in general)	Matthew 26:8, 9		
Judas (in particular)	Matthew 26:14-16		

Unforgettable

Jesus said that Mary's actions would be remembered everywhere the gospel is proclaimed (Matthew 26:13). Among the Christians you know, whose faith is demonstrated most unforgettably? What actions or habits make this person so unforgettable as a person of faith?

What can you do this week to imitate the faith (in action) of this person?

What can you do to express your appreciation for his or her good example?

Jesus Fulfills His Mission

Unit 1: Road to the Cross
(Lessons 1-4)

LOAF AND CUP

LESSON 2

WHY TEACH THIS LESSON?

I think that God must delight in hiding himself behind small things. Look at a beautiful flower, and what do you see? The flower only, or the creative power of God who stands behind it?

And what about the loaf and cup of our Communion service? These are such simple things, really! A small bit of unleavened bread, a sip of fruit of the vine—that's it. Or is it? In fact, there is an eternally important reality that stands behind these modest elements: the death of the Son of God for the sins of the world. When your learners participate in the Lord's Supper, they can either simply "go through the motions," or they can use each occasion to remember anew the profound reality for which those elements stand. This lesson will help them make the right choice.

INTRODUCTION

A. PRICELESS TIMES

A major credit card company capitalized on how important special times are. In its TV ad everything was priced, except one—tickets to the game, sixty dollars; game program, ten dollars; hot dogs and drinks, fifteen dollars; autographed baseball, forty dollars; an evening with your son, priceless!

There are indeed times that have infinite meaning. A chaplain once told me that the greatest fear of a child facing death is that Mom or Dad might not be there. With Mom or Dad there, a child can face the most threatening time confidently. Times together are priceless.

Jesus had looked forward to one of those priceless times with his disciples. In the face of terrible danger he longed to be with the men in whom he had invested so much of himself. He also longed for one final time to provide instruction and guidance.

B. LESSON BACKGROUND

God commanded the Jewish people to observe the Passover feast in memory of their dramatic deliverance from bondage in Egypt (Exodus 12:1-32). As a result, Passover became a national spiritual holiday that called on God's people to remember their birth as a nation. God had commanded it to be celebrated in Jerusalem on the fourteenth day of the first month (Leviticus 23:5). This was the month of "Nisan" (formerly called "Abib") in the Hebrew calendar, which is late March and early April. It was an event that the spiritually minded anticipated with enthusiasm.

Jesus knew that his whole life pointed to a final Passover that would be the most eventful of all. This particular Passover would not be merely an act of faithful observance, but one of ultimate obedience. He would be preparing himself to fulfill his mission as the perfect Passover Lamb (John 1:29; 1 Corinthians 5:7; Revelation 5:12; 13:8) in giving his life in sacrifice for the sins of humanity. One last Passover with his closest friends would mark the beginning of a new Lord's Supper that galvanizes Christian worship to this day.

DEVOTIONAL READING:
JOHN 13:1-15
BACKGROUND SCRIPTURE:
LUKE 22:7-30
PRINTED TEXT:
LUKE 22:7-23

LESSON AIMS

After participating in this lesson, each student will be able to:

1. Summarize the events of Jesus' last supper with his disciples and the institution of the Lord's Supper.

2. Articulate the significance of the emblems of the Lord's Supper.

3. Recommit himself or herself to faithfulness to the Lord Jesus Christ and his church.

KEY VERSES

"This is my body given for you; do this in remembrance of me."

In the same way, after the supper he took the cup, saying, "This cup is the new covenant in my blood, which is poured out for you." —Luke 22:19, 20

I. SUPPER PREPARATION (LUKE 22:7-13)

A. THE DISCIPLES' QUESTION (vv. 7-9)

7. Then came the day of Unleavened Bread on which the Passover lamb had to be sacrificed.

Technically, the feasts of *Unleavened Bread* and *Passover* are separate festivals, with Passover occurring on the fourteenth of Nisan, and the Feast of Unleavened Bread running from the fifteenth to the twenty-first (Leviticus 23:5, 6; Numbers 28:16, 17). Because these celebrations occur back-to-back, the Jews naturally think of them as one (e.g., 2 Chronicles 35:17).

When *the day* to begin the celebration comes, there is much to be done. Families need to secure *the Passover lamb* that is to be killed. Part of the process involves sending a representative to the priests to have it slaughtered in the temple that afternoon, then returning with the meat that will feed the entire family that night. In addition to the lamb, many other preparations will have to be made (see v. 13, below).

8. Jesus sent Peter and John, saying, "Go and make preparations for us to eat the Passover."

The disciples have asked Jesus where he wants them to prepare *the Passover* meal (Mark 14:12). Jesus knows that Judas is looking for a time and place to report his whereabouts to the authorities, but Jesus undoubtedly doesn't want his Passover celebration interrupted (we shall see why later). So he delegates the work of securing a place to *Peter and John*, two leading men among his disciples he knows he can trust.

9. "Where do you want us to prepare for it?" they asked.

Sometimes the opportunity to show one's true colors comes through a willingness to take care of the details. Peter and John express their desire to do just that. Moreover, their devotion to the Lord and sensitivity to his desires cause them to seek his leading even in the small things. "We should always ask the Lord of all, to lead in everything, big and small!"

B. THE LORD'S DIRECTIONS (vv. 10-12)

10. He replied, "As you enter the city, a man carrying a jar of water will meet you. Follow him to the house that he enters,

Jesus' deity reveals itself again as he gives the disciples a sign. *A man carrying a jar of water* will certainly stand out, even in a large crowd. Women, not men, almost always carry such jars. Even more telling is the fact that Jerusalem is flooded with visitors at Passover. That the disciples will meet this man at an exact place and time in such a crowd points to Jesus' divine guidance. Thus Jesus gives Peter and John what they need to know, without providing Judas an exact address where he can report the Lord's whereabouts to the Jewish authorities.

11. "... and say to the owner of the house, 'The Teacher asks: Where is the guest room, where I may eat the Passover with my disciples?'

Jesus apparently has made previous arrangements with *the owner of the house* for the use of the *guest* chamber, where Jesus can *eat the Passover with* his *disciples*. In speaking to this owner, the disciples are to use certain words—*the Teacher asks*—to indicate to him that they come from Jesus.

12. "He will show you a large upper room, all furnished. Make preparations there."

At the mere mention of the Teacher, this nameless follower will be ready to assist the disciples. Many of us today will never serve in positions of great prominence like the apostles, but we can be ready to support those who do with our willing cooperation.

WHAT DO YOU THINK?

We see in the disciples a willingness to take care of details. Why is this still important, even in an age of advanced technology? How is technology sometimes used as a substitute for true preparation?

WHAT DO YOU THINK?

The house owner was expected to make his guest chamber available to the Teacher. Beside monetary gifts, what can we offer the Lord to demonstrate our devotion to his cause?

The fact that this man's house has an upper room large enough to accommodate thirteen men indicates that the owner probably is well-to-do. We are encouraged to note how this wealthy man shares the use of his possessions with the Lord. We should never assume that riches in and of themselves will corrupt the human heart. When the wealthy make Jesus the Lord of life, they display humble generosity and unselfish sharing of their possessions for godly purposes.

THE IMPORTANT THING

The land called Israel has not known much peace since the modern nation was founded in 1948. Occasionally, the land has been peaceful enough for tourists to travel there safely. In such times, a typical tour of Jerusalem includes a visit to "the Upper Room." If the tour guide were honest, he would inform the tourists in his charge that the room was only "similar to" the one we read about in our text today, since the room Jesus used ceased to exist long ago.

The upper room the visitors see is like most other "holy" sites on the modern tour: it is either an uncertain location, is at an archeological level above the original site, or is obscured completely by a structure built upon it many centuries later.

The upper room in which Jesus kept the Passover with his disciples was like other sites in his ministry: each is significant, not in itself, but in the fact that a very important act of God took place in that location. That particular upper room was no more holy than any other upper room in the city of Jerusalem that evening.

What was significant is what Jesus did there: he established the table of the Lord as a memorial to the offering of his life on the following day. We honor him more by our participation in the Lord's Supper each time it is served than by any number of pilgrimages to Jerusalem.   —C. R. B.

C. JUST AS HE SAID (v. 13)

13. They left and found things just as Jesus had told them. So they prepared the Passover.

Are we surprised that Peter and John find everything *just as Jesus had* said to *them*? More personally, are we surprised to find things in life as Jesus has told us they will be, including his gracious provision for us?

Even with Jesus' promise, however, the disciples have their own work to do. The room they find is "furnished" (v. 12), but this probably refers only to the presence of a low table surrounded by pallets for reclining. The furnishings do not include food, which the disciples will have to provide.

To make ready the food for the Passover will involve preparing or purchasing several things: the Passover lamb, which would take some time to kill and roast; unleavened bread—meaning bread made with no yeast—to remind them of the haste of the departure from Egypt; a bowl of salt water to remind them of the Red Sea; bitter herbs as a reminder of their bitter experience as slaves; a paste or sauce made of a mixture of fruit and nuts; and fruit of the vine to drink. All this preparation has to be finished on the fourteenth of Nisan within the space of just a few hours (see Exodus 12:6; Numbers 9:3; Deuteronomy 16:6).

II. SUPPER FELLOWSHIP (LUKE 22:14-18)

A. JESUS' DESIRE (vv. 14, 15)

14. When the hour came, Jesus and his apostles reclined at the table.

The hour occurs at sunset. When that time arrives, Jesus sits down, reclining with his friends. Couches (for reclining while eating) line perhaps three sides of the table. At the most important time in his life Jesus surrounds himself with the people with whom he has shared so many memorable experiences.

DAILY BIBLE READINGS

Monday, Mar. 8—Disciples Prepare the Passover Meal (Luke 22:7-13)

Tuesday, Mar. 9—Jesus Eats With Disciples (Luke 22:14-18)

Wednesday, Mar. 10—Do This in Remembrance of Me (Luke 22:19-23)

Thursday, Mar. 11—Jesus Washes the Disciples' Feet (John 13:1-5)

Friday, Mar. 12—Peter Protests (John 13:6-10)

Saturday, Mar. 13—Jesus Sets an Example (John 13:11-15)

Sunday, Mar. 14—Jesus Teaches About Greatness (Luke 22:24-30)

HOW TO SAY IT

Abib. A-*bib.*

Deuteronomy. Due-ter-AHN-uh-me.

Jerusalem. Juh-ROO-suh-lem.

Judas. JOO-dus.

Leviticus. Leh-VIT-ih-kus.

Nisan. NYE-san.

This occasion also gives Jesus valuable last-minute opportunities for continued training of his disciples. This is something he takes seriously to the end—even while dying (e.g., John 19:25-27).

15. And he said to them, "I have eagerly desired to eat this Passover with you before I suffer.

Jesus' strong yearning to share this meal with them is apparent in the emphatic language *I have eagerly desired.* Jesus knows he soon will suffer agony at the hands of his enemies, and *this Passover* prefigures his own death as the perfect lamb of God (John 1:29).

The Jewish people have long anticipated a "new exodus" in which God will deliver them from their political oppression (cf. Acts 1:6). They are looking forward to a new, messianic Moses. What God provides instead is the perfect sacrificial Lamb. The Lamb will die in their place, paying the price that God's wrath demands for sin, thereby granting deliverance from eternal condemnation (Romans 3:21-26; 5:9). With so much at stake, Jesus longs for fellowship with his chosen few.

B. JESUS' PREDICTION (vv. 16-18)

16. "For I tell you, I will not eat it again until it finds fulfillment in the kingdom of God."

Jesus predicts that this will be the last Passover they will eat together, while also indicating that in some way there will be "a next time" (cf. Matthew 8:11; Revelation 19:9). Today we celebrate the Lord's Supper "until he comes" (1 Corinthians 11:26). It is when that great event occurs that the kingdom of God will be fulfilled in its ultimate sense.

17. After taking the cup, he gave thanks and said, "Take this and divide it among you.

The Passover celebration normally follows a set order. After the opening prayer comes the first of four cups of fruit of the vine and a dish of bitter herbs and sauce. The Passover story is recited, Psalm 113 is sung, and the second cup introduced.

Grace is then offered and the participants eat the main course of roast lamb and unleavened bread. Next comes another prayer followed by the third cup, called "the cup of blessing." After singing Psalms 114–118 (cf. Matthew 26:30), participants drink the fourth cup.

We can't be certain exactly which of the four cups Jesus takes at this point in the narrative, but it is probably "the cup of blessing." When Jesus gives thanks and instructs the disciples to *divide it among* themselves, he is providing them with a lifelong reminder to strengthen their faith (see v. 20, below).

18. "For I tell you I will not drink again of the fruit of the vine until the kingdom of God comes."

By declaring this to be the last time he would share *the fruit of the vine,* Jesus offers a solemn farewell to the Old Testament Passover ceremony. The Passover celebration is temporary and now gives way to something better. Jesus' death on the cross will make that old covenant obsolete (Hebrews 8:6-13). After Jesus' resurrection and ascension the church will find the living Christ, not in the old Passover feast, but in the new Lord's Supper (1 Corinthians 11:23-26). See also comments on verse 16, above.

III. SUPPER INSTITUTION (LUKE 22:19, 20)

A. JESUS REMEMBERED (v. 19)

19. And he took bread, gave thanks and broke it, and gave it to them, saying, "This is my body given for you; do this in remembrance of me."

WHAT DO YOU THINK?

The disciples must have been startled when Jesus' Passover words were not what they were used to hearing. What changes in the normal worship routine make you uncomfortable? Which do you accept? Why?

The Passover meal is nearly complete. With the old covenant within hours of passing away, Jesus is inaugurating the supper that will symbolize the new covenant. Receiving the *bread* of Communion calls for prayers of *thanks* yet today as we remember what Christ has done for us.

As Jesus breaks the bread and gives it to the disciples, he does all he can to communicate its spiritual and symbolic import. With Jesus physically present, the bread is symbolic for his *body*. The bread of Communion will be a tangible symbol of that fact and a concrete *remembrance* of the death of Christ for our sins from this time forward. His body will not be taken against his will; rather, it is given freely for our salvation.

B. NEW COVENANT RATIFIED (v. 20)
20. In the same way, after the supper he took the cup, saying, "This cup is the new covenant in my blood, which is poured out for you.

The *cup* Jesus returns to after supper is packed with so much significance! A *covenant* refers to a formal, solemn, and binding agreement. Here the agreement has the force of a will, which can be ratified only at death, or as Jesus said, by the shedding of his *blood* (see Hebrews 9:14-26).

This reminds us of the prophecy of the Lord's suffering "servant" who *poured out* "his life unto death" and "bore the sin of many" (Isaiah 53:12). The horrible prospect of a violent, lingering, unjust death cannot stop Jesus from dying in our place. Through the power of his blood we discover the forgiveness of sins (Romans 3:25; 5:9; Ephesians 1:7; Colossians 1:20; Hebrews 9:22; 13:20; 1 Peter 1:18, 19; 1 John 1:7; Revelation 1:5; 5:9). The result is that we can relate to God on the basis of the new covenant of grace revealed in the New Testament.

IV. SUPPER WARNING (LUKE 22:21-23)
A. GENERAL WARNING (v. 21)
21. "But the hand of him who is going to betray me is with mine on the table.

Luke reminds us of the prelude to Jesus' betrayal. The unthinkable is that *the hand of him who is going to betray* Jesus is reclining with his *on the* same *table*. Ancients would have considered this extreme treachery. They view hospitality and the sharing of table fellowship as creating a close bond. To betray such a bond is scandalous indeed! See Psalm 41:9.

B. SPECIFIC WARNING (v. 22)
22. "The Son of Man will go as it has been decreed, but woe to that man who betrays him."

God's sovereign plan had determined that *the Son of Man* must go to face unjust trial, persecution, and crucifixion. The preaching of the first-century church recognized God's foreknowledge and predetermined plan that led to Jesus' betrayal (Acts 2:23). It was important to let the world know that the events of Jesus' death, burial, and resurrection are not mere coincidence or freak accidents of history.

Even so, God's plan never overrode Judas's free will. He betrayed the Lord by choosing freely his sinful path. In a final effort to turn him around, Jesus warned Judas of the woe to come—God's extreme displeasure and hellish penalty that Judas would suffer (Acts 1:25). But Judas refused to listen.

C. GROUP INVENTORY (v. 23)
23. They began to question among themselves which of them it might be who would do this.

Visual for lesson 2. *Use this elegant yet sobering imagery to reinforce today's Key Verses.*

WHAT DO YOU THINK?

What do you find most significant about the observance of the Lord's Supper? Why?

[Whatever particular details your learners bring up, look for the Scriptural basis.]

PRAYER

Father, we praise your holy name for the love you have shown us in your Son Jesus Christ. When he poured out his blood for our forgiveness, he also poured on us his love. Lord, we ask you to form in us an unending desire to fellowship weekly with you and your people during the Supper that you have given us. For this divine Communion with you, your Son, your Spirit, and your people, we give thanks! In Jesus' name, amen.

On this same evening the disciples bicker over who is the greatest, and who will get the chief seats in God's kingdom (Luke 22:24). Here they find themselves doing the opposite—wondering who is the worst among them. But even as Judas carries out his sinful charade, nothing in his behavior makes them suspect him over anyone else (John 13:27-29). This thing thus results in both history's greatest injustice and the gateway to our eternal life.

COULD I POSSIBLY DO SUCH A THING?

Out of the horrors of the terrorist attacks on September 11, 2001, came many tales of heroic action. For example, several passengers on a flight to San Francisco learned that terrorists had crashed three other planes into the World Trade Center towers and the Pentagon. Their plane had also been hijacked and turned back east. With terrorists at the controls, there was no doubt that they faced a similar fate.

However, the brave souls on that flight did not consider a few more minutes of life for themselves to be more precious than the lives of those who would surely be killed when their plane crashed into the White House or Capitol. So they overpowered the terrorists, forcing the plane to crash in a field in western Pennsylvania.

The heroes on board that plane have been memorialized in many ways. One of them was Tom Burnett. After a street was named for him in the town where he lived, his widow said, "Twenty years from now, children will know a wonderful story of an American hero is connected with that name."

Whether the act we are contemplating is noble, as this one was, or like the despicable act Judas would soon be committing, the question of the other disciples is one worth asking: could I possibly do such a thing? Do I have the moral courage to avoid evil actions? Would I do good in spite of the cost? Is there anything in my character that would tempt me to deny my Lord by word or deed? Those who follow us will surely know the answer! —C. R. B.

CONCLUSION

Some parents, in wanting their children to have the very best, fail to give them what is truly priceless. How can you put a price tag on love expressed, encouragement offered, instruction supplied, faith modeled, and time given? The most important things seldom have a price attached to them.

Jesus opted to give us something more valuable than money. It was something upon which the core of our souls can feast, regardless of life's circumstances. The psalmist anticipated a memorial feast wherein both rich and poor would satisfy their souls (Psalm 22:26-29).

When Jesus instituted the Lord's Supper as a regular observance in worship, he gave us exactly what we need. In Communion we remember his sacrificial death. In that moment we also rely on him to help us fulfill our destiny as witnesses of his love and great salvation.

We marvel that the Lord designed this event in which he invites us corporately into his presence. The Guest of honor wants the honor of our presence. What a great reminder of how many ways he loves us!

Moreover, the bread that represents his broken body and the cup that signifies his blood call us to cherish our participation in a new covenant. The old covenant, for all of its strengths, could never have broken the stranglehold of sin nor delivered us from eternal judgment. The loaf and cup remind us that we are the recipients of grace through a death that satisfied God's wrath. This in turn motivates us to greater service for Jesus Christ.

For centuries millions have discovered the power and importance of this loaf and cup. The only price we can put on this priceless spiritual feast is the one that Jesus himself paid in dying for our salvation.

WHAT DO YOU THINK?

If you could plan a special Communion service, what would you include? Why? What is the significance of your proposed changes?

THOUGHT TO REMEMBER

Participate faithfully in the loaf and cup, priceless reminders of Christ's sacrificial love.

Discovery Learning

This page contains an alternative lesson plan emphasizing learning activities. Classes desiring such student involvement will find these suggestions helpful. The next page is a reproducible activity page to further enhance discovery learning.

LEARNING GOALS

After this lesson each student will be able to:

1. Summarize the events of Jesus' last supper with his disciples and the institution of the Lord's Supper.

2. Articulate the significance of the emblems of the Lord's Supper.

3. Recommit himself or herself to faithfulness to the Lord Jesus Christ and his church.

INTO THE LESSON

Ask class members to complete the reproducible activity "Photo Album Memories" from the next page and tell about experiences that taught them significant, life-changing lessons (illness, job change, war experience, mission trip). Ask, "What lessons learned from the experience still influence you? What do you do to help remember those lessons?"

Discuss traditions class members and their families have. Are there certain ways they celebrate particular holidays or have reunions? What are the benefits of such traditions? Say, "Today we will explore a tradition at the heart of the Christian family experience, one instituted and explained by Christ himself."

INTO THE WORD

Watch a short clip from a video* that recounts the first Passover in Exodus 11:1–12:36. (This could be taken from the classic movie, *The Ten Commandments*, or from the more recent animated film, *Prince of Egypt*). Use this to prompt your class members to look more closely at Scripture and examine the story. After viewing the clip, discuss how the events were portrayed. In what ways did it recount the biblical story accurately? In what ways is it inaccurate? How are details not in the Bible dealt with in the video clip? Is the tone created by the film appropriate?

Compare the key elements of the Passover as observed in the Old Testament and the meaning of the Lord's Supper in the New Testament. Consider these questions: What did it commemorate? (*Being spared from death and receiving freedom from bondage in Egypt/the introduction of the new covenant, where Jesus,* the Passover Lamb, is sacrificed to spare us from eternal death and free us from bondage in sin.*) What was the significance of the bread? (*Unleavened bread, as well as eating while dressed ready to travel, reminded them of leaving Egypt in haste, while the bread in the last supper represents Jesus' body, broken for sinners.*) What was the significance of the blood? (*In the old covenant, blood from the sacrificed lamb was sprinkled on the doorpost to remind of God's protection from death when they sacrificed in the way God prescribed. In the new covenant, it represents the blood of Jesus, offered as payment for our sin.*)

Ask, "How much did the apostles get the point of the lesson?" Consider the things they talked about during the meal: who would betray Jesus (Luke 22:23); who was the greatest (Luke 22:24-27). Notice the focus on themselves rather than on Jesus' teaching about himself. Then ask, "What can be done to avoid this self-centered attitude and remain open to what God wants us to learn? What situations make you, as a learner, most impressionable? When are you most ready to listen to someone give you direction? What are areas where you miss (or resist) God's message to you because your focus is on other things?"

INTO LIFE

In 1 Corinthians 11:17-34, Paul gave us a key to understanding and assessing our practice of this memorial to Jesus Christ. It involves all aspects of our lives: past, present, and future. Past—Does the commemoration focus on the work of Jesus and remind us of what he has done to make payment for our sin? Present—Does our observance demonstrate the common bond and resulting love we share because of our commitment to Jesus Christ? Read chapter 11 and highlight the ways lack of love and fellowship with each other actually desecrated the observance (allowing others to go hungry, being drunk, participating individually and ignoring others and the corporate experience). Future—Does the observance remind us that this is a temporary command, to be fulfilled only "until he comes" (1 Corinthians 11:26)?

Have the learners fill in the "God's Family Album" section of the reproducible page, and discuss ways you can keep these aspects current and fresh in your heart and life, so that you are prepared for the Lord's Supper the next time and each time you observe it together with fellow believers.

*For information about licensing the use of copyrighted videos contact Christian Video Licensing International. Phone: (888) 771-2854; Internet: www.cvli.org.

Photo Album Memories

Imagine that the following boxes are the backs of photos from your family album—photos of life events that you consider among the best. Jot a note on each, giving the date, the event, and the names of people in the photo.

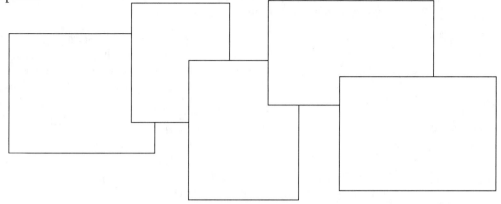

What common threads run through these events? How do you and your family keep the memories alive?

God's Family Album

If God were maintaining a family album—and in a certain sense he has in the Bible and in his omniscience—certainly some of the most poignant images would be from the occasion of his Son instituting his Supper of remembrance and the humiliation and death of his Son on the cross. Over the image of grapes and grain below, write a list of some of the "images" you want to call to mind the next time you are participating in the Lord's Supper.

PRAYER AND ARREST

LESSON 3

WHY TEACH THIS LESSON?

In modern, industrialized cultures, people by and large are unaccustomed to extended periods of solitude and silence. The TV, in many households, is turned on first thing in the morning and stays on all day long, providing a continuous low drone of background noise. If we were to ask someone who lives this way, "When was the last time you had an hour of complete silence and solitude?" we might be met with a blank, uncomprehending stare!

Yet Jesus was someone who eagerly sought solitude (cf. Mark 1:35). He renewed and strengthened himself in prayer during such times. This is true nowhere more than in the Garden of Gethsemane on the night he was betrayed. As we consider all the events, intrigue, and injustice that swirl around Jesus that lead up to his crucifixion, let us not overlook the lesson he teaches us about prayer in this hour of agony. It will be a lesson to strengthen us our entire lives.

INTRODUCTION

A. BIG PRAYERS BEFORE BIG ACTIONS

It can be foolish to act before praying, but there is also a time to change your prayer into action. When Moses and the Israelites were pinned against the shore of the Red Sea with the Egyptian army rapidly approaching, that was a big problem. God asked Moses, "Why are you crying out to me? Tell the Israelites to move on" (Exodus 14:15). Moses had already prayed. Now it was time to act.

After Jesus' resurrection, Peter and John were brought before the Jewish authorities and sternly warned not to preach in Jesus' name (Acts 4:18). The church faced the prospect of persecution if they did. How could they maintain courage and boldness with the threat of punishment hanging over their heads? That was a big problem. Yet those in the early church knew that they must offer big prayers when facing big problems. After praying, the church went into action (Acts 4:31).

When Jesus went to Gethsemane, he faced the biggest problem any human ever would. The impending reality of betrayal, unjust conviction, savage beating, and brutal crucifixion would be enough to make even the bravest cower in fear. In addition, Jesus would carry the sins of the whole world, tasting the full fury of God's wrath. But Jesus knew that if he brought big prayers to the biggest problem of all, he would have the ultimate victory.

B. LESSON BACKGROUND

At the conclusion of their final Passover meal together, after the institution of the Lord's Supper, Jesus and his disciples sang a hymn together (Matthew 26:30; Mark 14:26). Then they made their way to Gethsemane, a garden just outside of Jerusalem on the western slope of the Mount of Olives. Most likely this was the usual place of retreat for Jesus and the disciples following the Passover each year.

As we saw last week, Jesus had not allowed Judas to know the exact address of their last Passover meal together because of the need for uninterrupted time with his disciples. Judas, however, had full knowledge of the usual post-Passover

DEVOTIONAL READING:
JOHN 12:27-36

BACKGROUND SCRIPTURE:
MATTHEW 26:36-50

PRINTED TEXT:
MATTHEW 26:36-50

Mar
21

LESSON AIMS

After participating in this lesson, each student will be able to:

1. Tell of Jesus' experiences in Gethsemane, both in his prayers and in his betrayal and arrest.

2. Suggest some times of temptation during which disciples may be called on to imitate their Master's resolve.

3. State a plan of action to make prayer a consistent and effective weapon against temptation.

KEY VERSE

[Jesus] fell with his face to the ground and prayed, "My Father, if it is possible, may this cup be taken from me. Yet not as I will, but as you will."

—Matthew 26:39

LESSON 3 NOTES

meeting place that Jesus liked to use (John 18:1, 2). It was just a matter of time until the betrayer, intent on his evil plot, showed up with an armed guard to take Jesus into custody. Jesus refused to face the most challenging few hours in human history without intensely seeking his heavenly Father's help.

I. THE PASSIONATE PRAYER (MATTHEW 26:36-44)

A. NEED FOR PRAYER (vv. 36-38)

36. Then Jesus went with his disciples to a place called Gethsemane, and he said to them, "Sit here while I go over there and pray."

Gethsemane means "oil press," which tells us what this hillside area is used for. Here Jesus brings the entire band of disciples, minus one. The human side of Jesus shines through this moment, as he desires the companionship of his closest friends. He does not want to go through this agony alone.

Even so, there is also a need for solitude and space, allowing him the freedom to wrestle in private prayer. Thus Jesus has the disciples *sit* at the entrance of the garden while he goes to *pray* yonder.

WHAT DO YOU THINK?

Jesus wanted his closest friends nearby even as he took time alone with his Father. When has the presence of brothers and sisters in Christ been most helpful to you, and why?

"HELLO? IS ANYONE THERE?"

For nearly forty years, a telephone booth sat in the middle of California's Mojave National Preserve—fourteen miles from the nearest paved road—for the benefit of an occasional miner who needed to contact the "outside world." In 1997, a desert wanderer found the booth and put a story about it on the Internet.

People who read his story started calling the number. Most of the time no one answered. However, occasionally someone would monitor the phone. Rick Karr, a Texan, was one such person. He said, "The Holy Spirit told me to go out there and answer the`phone."

Karr spent thirty-two days there and answered more than five hundred calls from all over the world. Why call? Why answer? One caller said, "Someone answers, a person you have absolutely no connection with. You exchange names and talk about the weather. What a thrill!" In other words, lonely people were reaching out for a "friend" to talk to. (The phone was removed in March 2000, because all the traffic was destroying the environment.)

Compare this foolishness to Jesus' experience in the Garden of Gethsemane. That garden was also a deserted place—especially at night—when Jesus went there. But he went with friends, not searching for them. He was seeking to make a connection, but he wasn't in doubt. He talked frequently with the Father, and so he could always expect "someone to answer when he called." Perhaps our prayer lives could profit from such regularity.   —C. R. B.

37. He took Peter and the two sons of Zebedee along with him, and he began to be sorrowful and troubled.

Undoubtedly, Jesus has a powerful relationship with the crowds. Deeper still is his relationship with the Twelve. His deepest relationship is with *Peter and the two sons of Zebedee,* namely James and John. These three are the only ones allowed to witness Jesus' raising of Jairus's daughter from the dead (Mark 5:35-42). Jesus selects these three to accompany him on the mountain of transfiguration (Matthew 17:1-13). Now he desires their companionship in this hour of extreme distress.

Jesus' distress is captured in the words *sorrowful and troubled.* Overwhelming sadness and deep anguish flood his heart and mind as he begins to focus on what lies ahead.

38. Then he said to them, "My soul is overwhelmed with sorrow to the point of death. Stay here and keep watch with me."

"Yet not as I will, but as you will."
—*Matthew 26:39, NIV*

Visual for lesson 3. *This captivating artwork makes vivid the Key Verse of this lesson.*

Communication is a key to any relationship and situation. Some make the mistake of assuming that those around them should know what they are feeling or what to do in a difficult time. Jesus does not make that mistake. He tells the disciples clearly and specifically how he is feeling and what his expectations are for them.

Moreover, Jesus tells his disciples exactly how they can be of comfort when he says *stay here.* Jesus plans to move on ahead of them just far enough to get some comfortable space, and he wants them to wait nearby.

Yet he is not asking them to be passive as they wait. He calls them to stay awake, to be alert, and to *watch with* him. He asks them to take note of his passion, feel his pain, and offer prayers for their own trials and temptations that are just around the corner (Luke 22:40). As they observe him wrestling with the weight of the world, he expects them to be ready to offer help and consolation. His agonizing in prayer will at one point cause him to sweat drops like blood (Luke 22:44).

Even without the benefit of hearing Jesus' voice inflection or seeing his body language, we can sense the urgency of his appeal to his friends. His anguish penetrates to the deepest part of his being, and he needs their comfort. Jesus' words are very similar to parts of Psalms 42 and 43.

B. SUBJECT OF PRAYER (v. 39)
39. Going a little farther, he fell with his face to the ground and prayed, "My Father, if it is possible, may this cup be taken from me. Yet not as I will, but as you will."

A little farther is about a stone's throw according to Luke 22:41. There is no one acceptable position for prayer, but the position we take can speak volumes about the depth of our emotion. Jesus does indeed go to his knees (again, Luke 22:41), but that's just the start of falling prostrate—on *his face*—as he throws his total being into this prayer.

Jesus begins his prayer as he taught the disciples to begin theirs in Matthew 6:9: *My Father.* The closeness Jesus has known with God the Father from before the foundation of the world now serves as the rock on which he leans.

The *cup* Jesus fears is a figure of speech for the terrible ordeal he is about to experience at the hands of sinful people. But even worse than that, this cup stands for the wrath of the Father that Jesus will bear as he dies to pay sin's terrible price. "Cup" frequently stands for God's wrath in the Old Testament (see Psalm 75:7, 8; Jeremiah 25:15, 16; Ezekiel 23:31-34).

Given the pain and suffering of the cross that lies just ahead—physically and especially spiritually—it is natural for Jesus to look for an alternative that will allow the cup to *be taken from* him. Could there possibly be a "Plan B"?

Of course, there is no "Plan B." Jesus' prayer helps prepare him to set aside his own will and self-interest to do as God wills. To accomplish the eternal plan for saving humanity remains Jesus' uncompromised priority. Although he seeks to find a way other than the cross, nevertheless he decides that nothing can keep him from obeying God, loving us, and completing his mission. There are no shortcuts, as Satan had tried to offer him at least twice before (Matthew 4:1-11; 16:21-23).

IS THERE ANY WAY OUT OF THIS?
Most of us have been in situations that seemed to be so difficult that we could see no clear or satisfying way to deal with our circumstances. This brings to mind a fable about an old, decrepit mule that fell into a well. The farmer decided the well was too shallow, and was also a danger to passersby. Further, the mule was too old

HOW TO SAY IT

Ephesian. Ee-FEE-zhun.

Ezekiel. Ee-ZEEK-ee-ul or Ee-ZEEK-yul.

Gethsemane. Geth-SEM-uh-nee.

Jeremiah. Jair-uh-MY-uh.

Jerusalem. Juh-ROO-suh-lem.

Judas. JOO-dus.

Mojave. Mow-HAH-vee

Rabbi. RAB-eye.

Zebedee. ZEB-eh-dee.

WHAT DO YOU THINK?

What difference would it have made if the disciples had stayed awake and prayed with Jesus before the arrest?

to be any good, so the farmer called in his neighbors and said, "Help me fill in this well and bury my mule at the same time."

The mule panicked as the first shovelful of dirt hit his back, but he quickly noticed that the dirt was falling off his back and down into the bottom of the well. So he accepted the pain from the clods and occasional rock that hit him, and kept on stepping on the dirt as it dropped to the bottom. It wasn't too long before the well was filled and the mule stepped right out onto level ground. He did what he had to do!

Jesus' prayer to be able to avoid what he knew to be ahead of him was a very human prayer. Over an extended period of time that night Jesus prayed for release. But also each time he stated his commitment to God's will.

Sometimes we simply have to do what we know must be done and trust God for the outcome. He is faithful and will grant eternal deliverance for those who trust him. As the poet Robert Frost has said, "The best way out is always through."

—C. R. B.

C. EXHORTATION TO PRAYER (vv. 40, 41)

40. Then he returned to his disciples and found them sleeping. "Could you men not keep watch with me for one hour?" he asked Peter.

Although Jesus speaks directly to Peter, the phrase *you men* is plural in the Greek, so the message is for all three disciples (v. 37, above). This is neither the first nor last disappointment Jesus experiences with the *disciples* during this trying time.

Even so, Jesus does not get angry, ranting and raving over their failure. He knows that people get sleepy after a heavy meal, and that the disciples really don't have much of a clue as to what is about to happen.

41. "Watch and pray so that you will not fall into temptation. The spirit is willing, but the body is weak."

The disciples had already proven that they were susceptible to *temptation*. Previously that evening they had bickered over who was the greatest (Luke 22:24), and Judas has already set the wheels of betrayal into motion.

The next few hours and days will be fraught with opportunities to fall into even more temptation. These temptations could lead them into momentary setbacks (such as Peter's denial of Christ), or irreversible rejections of Christ (like Judas's). It is crucial that the disciples seek God's strength for such dangerous times. Thus the need to watch and pray.

In the midst of his own agony, Jesus shows amazing concern for others. Jesus refuses to play the blame game, questioning the intentions or genuineness of his disciples. In spite of all their shortcomings, he knows their hearts are in the right place. Therefore, he offers his personal vote of confidence and his compassion by saying that *the spirit* indeed *is willing.* He knows they are spiritually minded men who want to do the right thing. This is one occasion when the disciples do not do the good they know they should do (see Romans 7:15). Jesus understands.

The very fact that *the body is weak* is the very reason the disciples need to heed Jesus' exhortation to watch and pray. Exhausted or not, there are times to rise above human weakness to tap into God's strength. This is one of those times.

D. TENACITY IN PRAYER (vv. 42-44)

42. He went away a second time and prayed, "My Father, if it is not possible for this cup to be taken away unless I drink it, may your will be done."

Except for matters of style, there is no addition or subtraction in the content of Jesus' *second* prayer. The issues and concerns have not changed. He knows his strength for the crisis at hand can come only from the *Father.* The reality of impending ultimate suffering causes an earthquake in his soul that finds him contemplating some other way to save the world. However, if the only way to achieve God's eternal purpose for us is for Jesus to drink the *cup* of suffering and death, then *drink it* he will!

43. When he came back, he again found them sleeping, because their eyes were heavy.

Jesus had hoped that these three would muster the strength to watch and pray, but sadly this is not to be. Yet once again the Lord proves his own empathy and restraint. In this critical hour he could have "blown a fuse" or "gone off" at them in anger because of their apparent lack of concern. Although he had hoped for more, he understands their weakness.

44. So he left them and went away once more and prayed the third time, saying the same thing.

Jesus' example in prayer during the biggest crisis of his life can save us from misconceptions in our own prayer lives. First of all, we should realize that repeating a prayer does not automatically place it in the category of vain or meaningless repetition that we see condemned in Matthew 6:7. That passage refers to pointless and mindless babble such as the pagan world used in praying to their imaginary gods; likewise, when we memorize certain formulas and repeat them without thinking, our prayers are meaningless.

Also, some mistakenly draw the conclusion that if we have faith, we should pray about something only once, trust God with its outcome, and leave it at that. To do otherwise is a lack of faith, they claim. But here Jesus demonstrates the error in that thinking. He prays about the *same* urgent matter over and over. No one can accuse Jesus of lacking faith! Satan wants Jesus to convince himself that he can find God's "Plan B." Jesus fights off the temptation to avoid God's one-and-only plan by using the same prayer of surrender over and over.

When an issue is heartfelt, we can pray about it in many different ways as we rely on our need for God's help. Our prayers may be short and repetitious (as Jesus' prayer here is); our prayers may last "all night" (Luke 6:12); and they may be persistent (Luke 18:1-8).

II. THE AWFUL ARREST (MATTHEW 26:45-50)

A. JESUS COMPLIES (vv. 45, 46)

45. Then he returned to the disciples and said to them, "Are you still sleeping and resting? Look, the hour is near, and the Son of Man is betrayed into the hands of sinners.

As Jesus completes his third cycle of prayer, his disciples are again asleep. His words can be construed as a sad question: *"Are you still sleeping and resting?* The opportunity to join me in the prayer battle has passed you by." In any case, they have missed an important chance to pray, and Jesus knows that *the hour* for *the Son of Man* to be *betrayed* has come. It is now time to change prayer into action.

46. "Rise, let us go! Here comes my betrayer!"

Whether he hears them coming, sees the torches in the distance, or senses divinely that the enemies are on their way, Jesus implores his disciples to *Rise, let us go.* The word *go* in the overall context does not suggest resignation or retreat, but a courageous advance to meet the enemy.

Jesus knows that the one leading the approaching band is the one who will betray him. Judas, called to follow, seeks to force events down a path of his own choosing. This one, who could have been sent into the world with a message of hope, now sends his Master on a journey of death. A man who was once known as Jesus' friend now wears for eternity the label *betrayer.*

WHAT DO YOU THINK?

Jesus gained ultimate victory by yielding to the arrest. How does that encourage us when we face difficult, seemingly no-win circumstances?

PRAYER

Dear Father, we thank you from the bottom of our hearts for Jesus' unwavering commitment to you! His inexhaustible love for us leaves us stunned and amazed. Lord, help us to overcome the weakness of the flesh and to be responsive always to your will. Shield us from ever committing an act of betrayal against you.

Father, also teach us to rely on prayer as Jesus did. Teach us to act as well. We surrender our lives to your leading, and we thank you for the blessings that result. In Jesus' name, amen.

THOUGHT TO REMEMBER

Surrender your all to God in prayer. Then act.

B. JUDAS BETRAYS (vv. 47-49)

47. While he was still speaking, Judas, one of the Twelve, arrived. With him was a large crowd armed with swords and clubs, sent from the chief priests and the elders of the people.

Betrayal, under any circumstance, is bad business. For it to come from *one of the Twelve* takes our breath away! From the standpoint of the *chief priests* and *elders of the people*, this is the moment they have been looking for: the opportunity to arrest Jesus in secret, far from the unpredictable mobs that might come to his defense.

They take no chances, arriving with an armed detachment of the Roman guard (John 18:3, 12). If there is to be resistance from this messianic revolutionary named Jesus, they are prepared for it. Such action, however, shows that the Jewish leaders, to the very end, understand neither Jesus nor the nature of his mission.

48. Now the betrayer had arranged a signal with them: "The one I kiss is the man; arrest him."

Recognizing people in the dark is difficult. This is especially true in an age before electric lights. There is no photography either, so few would know what Jesus looks like even in broad daylight. Thus the need for a prearranged sign—a *kiss*. In ancient culture, as in some cultures today, the kiss is a traditional form of greeting.

49. Going at once to Jesus, Judas said, "Greetings, Rabbi!" and kissed him.

Upon arrival, *Judas* wastes no time. His unassuming *"Greetings, Rabbi!"* is filled with treachery as he kisses *Jesus*. The term *kissed* is the same as that used of the Father's reaction to the prodigal son (Luke 15:20), and that of the Ephesian elders at Paul's farewell (Acts 20:37). Judas gushes over Jesus in a sickening, ostentatious display.

C. THE GUARD ARRESTS (v. 50)

50. Jesus replied, "Friend, do what you came for." Then the men stepped forward, seized Jesus and arrested him.

Jesus takes the high road by addressing Judas as *Friend*, and this is the point where the authorities step in. When they lay hands on Jesus, they set in motion a chain of events that will never be paralleled in the annals of history.

CONCLUSION

Over the years I have talked to several people whose greatest fear is that some day, through a bizarre set of circumstances, they will be falsely accused of a crime they did not commit and find themselves in prison, or even on "death row." What a nightmare!

That nightmare became a reality for Jesus. Even so, his unwarranted arrest was a part of the predetermined plan of God. There was no escape, short of disobeying the Father. But Jesus would be obedient to the end.

We marvel at Jesus' determination to "stay the course," to teach his followers to the end, to treat the most heinous betrayal with civility, to love mankind so extravagantly, and to obey the heavenly Father regardless of the cost.

Where can we find such power to obey? Where Jesus did! The fact that he threw himself so completely into his prayer is a witness to us. But turning to God in prayer—the kind of prayer where he wrestled repeatedly over the same issue, and where he totally surrendered to God's will—he found the power to overcome even the worst nightmare and the most painful reality.

But Jesus also found the power to act when the time for prayer had passed. This heroic example shines brightly for us as well, even two thousand years later!

Discovery Learning

*This page contains an alternative lesson plan emphasizing learning activities. Classes
desiring such student involvement will find these suggestions helpful. The next page
is a reproducible activity page to further enhance discovery learning.*

LEARNING GOALS

After participating in this lesson, each student will be able to:

1. Tell of Jesus' experiences in Gethsemane, both in his prayers and in his betrayal and arrest.

2. Suggest some times of temptation during which disciples may be called on to imitate their Master's resolve.

3. State a plan of action to make prayer a consistent and effective weapon against temptation.

INTO THE LESSON

Make a list of difficult situations caused by other people (for example, a co-worker lies on your personnel evaluation or a neighbor's dog keeps digging in your flower bed). Ask class members to rank them in order of difficulty to handle. Make suggestions of how not to handle the situation, then ideas for how to respond appropriately. State, "We will see a pattern for how to respond to such situations by examining how Jesus dealt with the most difficult situations."

INTO THE WORD

Jesus was "overwhelmed with sorrow" (Matthew 26:38). Ask the class to list reasons why. (*He had confronted the bickering of the disciples over who was the greatest; he knew he was about to face Judas's betrayal, false arrest and imprisonment, Peter's denial, beatings, the disciples' abandonment, crucifixion, and enduring the punishment for sin; see 2 Corinthians 5:21; 1 Peter 2:24.*)

Have the class fill in the reproducible activity "Facing Hard Times" from the next page and discuss what a "normal" response might be. (*Possibilities include seeking revenge, fleeing, fighting back, blaming others to save self, etc.*) Consider Jesus' response as a pattern for us.

Prayer—Immediately following the last supper Jesus left for Gethsemane to pray. Have the class compare this prayer with other New Testament passages regarding prayer (see Acts 4:23-30; 1 Timothy 2:1-3; 1 Peter 3:10-12) or explain how to respond when facing persecution (see Philippians 1:19-26; James 5:7-11; 1 Peter 3:8-16, 4:12-16). Discuss what these passages tell us about responding to suffering. (*Some possible answers: standing for Jesus and doing what is right, recognizing the value in suffering, seeking strength to endure and the ability to stand for Christ rather than focusing on eliminating the persecution.*)

Support from friends—Jesus brought the apostles with him, and kept Peter, James, and John near. We think of strength as the ability to stand alone and be independent. At Jesus' hour of greatest need he showed that it is natural to need people and request their support. He explained not only his need but also the way he wanted his followers to help. (*To wait, watch, and be ready to offer help, comfort, and consolation.*) Discuss: "What ways do we most often fail others in need? What could we do to assist when others face spiritual battles?"

Repeated prayer—Read Matthew 6:7, 8 and Luke 18:1-8. Ask the learners how to reconcile these passages. (*God answers prayer that comes honestly from a hurting heart seeking him, but he does not respond to prayer that we believe will be answered simply because of repetition—i.e., "babbling."*) What in the prayers of Jesus on this night help us differentiate repetitive prayers to avoid ("babbling like pagans") and repeated prayers that are encouraged? (*As Jesus repeated the same request, he demonstrated the appropriateness of echoing our requests to the Father when done in a right spirit; cf. Matthew 26:39, 43.*)

Surrender to the Father's will—This is not the first time Jesus has been confronted with a challenge to avoid the Father's plan and remove himself from difficulty. When tempted to avoid hunger, he chose to submit to the Father (see Matthew 4:3, 4). Now in his darkest hour, about to face the punishment for our sin, he again submits himself to the will of the Father.

Persevere through trials—In spite of the intense agony of this experience, Jesus faithfully fulfilled the will of the Father. This obedience was necessary to secure our salvation (Romans 5:18, 19; Hebrews 10:5-10).

INTO LIFE

Use the reproducible activity "A Hard Time for Me" from the next page, and ask the class to tell about some of the difficult situations they are facing. Determine how others can pray for them and other ways to provide encouragement and support throughout the week.

Ask church leaders or the missions committee for specific difficult situations some missionaries are facing, and commit yourselves to pray for them to have endurance and faithfulness. Send a card from the class, letting the missionaries know of your continued commitment.

Facing Hard Times

When Jesus came face to face with his imminent arrest and crucifixion, he demonstrated a successful five-step approach to his situation. Examine today's text and fill in the following table of godly procedure for dealing with life's difficult events.

JESUS' WAY	THE OPPOSITE WAY (without consideration of God)	MY WAY (how I typically react)
Pray		
Call for Support from One's Friends		
Persist in Prayer		
Surrender to the Father's Will		
Persevere		

A Hard Time for Me

Identify one difficult experience you know you will be facing in the near future.

What will be the nature of your specific prayer?

What individuals will you call on for their presence and support?

How will you word your persistent prayer, without "babbling like pagans" (Matthew 6:7)?

What will you need to concede before you submit to the will of God in the matter?

With what words will you affirm your commitment to persist in godliness and faith in the trying matter?

TRIAL AND SENTENCE

LESSON 4

WHY TEACH THIS LESSON?

In his 1974 book *The Roots of American Order,* Russell Kirk points out that the United States was founded under the influence of certain great historical cities. Two of these cities were ancient Jerusalem (for religion) and Rome (for the rule of law). There is much truth in this observation! But for all the strengths those cities brought to the table, there are also weaknesses. Today's lesson shows us Jerusalem and Rome at their worst as self-interest defaces both pure religion and the rule of law in the case of Jesus.

Yet God has a way of making beautiful that which is ugly. In this lesson we will see the quiet dignity of one who is carried along by an unjust sequence of events —events that he has the power to stop, but chooses not to. His godly dignity inspires our own. His refusal to use divine power to stop the proceedings results in our eternal salvation. It is now time to hear this story "again, for the first time."

INTRODUCTION

A. THE CASE OF RICHARD JEWELL

At about 1:20 A.M. on July 27, 1996, a bomb exploded in an Atlanta park during a celebration for the Olympic games. The explosion killed one woman and injured many other bystanders. The casualties likely would have been much worse but for the swift action of security guard Richard Jewell, who discovered the suspicious-looking green backpack and alerted the authorities. Jewell and the other authorities were in the process of evacuating the park when the bomb exploded.

Initially, Richard Jewell was hailed as a hero. But a few days later several media outlets named him as the primary suspect in the bombing itself. Their information was based on leaks from the FBI.

Several months later the FBI formally cleared Jewell of any wrongdoing. He indeed was a hero, he indeed had helped to save many lives, and he was innocent of every accusation. But great damage had already been done. Jewell lost his job, was abandoned by many of his friends, became burdened by huge debts, and found his reputation in ruins.

We would like to think that false accusations and judicial error—including those of "the court of public opinion"—are the stuff of repressive regimes. Some people and some judicial systems are flawed in spite of good intentions. Some are flawed, however, because of self-interest, character defects, and "political realities."

B. LESSON BACKGROUND

Untrue accusations, unjust imprisonment, and unfair punishment make up the story of our lesson today. Jesus is on trial for his life. It has been only a few hours since he sat at the table with his disciples, sharing with them the Passover. He has just been brought from the garden where he had been praying. God had answered Jesus' prayer to remove the cup from him; the answer was "No," and it was delivered by a mob led by Judas Iscariot.

DEVOTIONAL READING:
JOHN 10:22-30
BACKGROUND SCRIPTURE:
MARK 14, 15
PRINTED TEXT:
MARK 14:53, 55-64; 15:1, 2, 12-15

Mar
28

LESSON AIMS

After participating in this lesson, each student will be able to:

1. Summarize the events of Jesus' trials and condemnation.

2. Tell how God's will was carried out through the noble acts of Jesus and in spite of the contemptible acts of the Sanhedrin and Pilate.

3. Express a commitment to working in harmony with the purposes of God.

KEY VERSE

Again the high priest asked him, "Are you the Christ, the Son of the Blessed One?"

"I am," said Jesus.

—Mark 14:61, 62

In our text today we see Jesus standing in two different courts. The first is a religious tribunal. The Sanhedrin, which was the ruling council of religious leaders, had a strong interest in preserving its own power and influence (John 11:47, 48). In the council's eyes, this rabble-rouser Jesus was gathering support from the people and had to be removed.

The other court is a political tribunal with a similar set of interests. Pontius Pilate, the Roman governor in Jerusalem, wanted to maintain his position. To do that he had to keep the peace.

Each of these tribunals needed the other. The Sanhedrin could not legally execute a prisoner (John 18:31). Only the Romans could do that. But Pilate did not have the support of the people he governed. His success in governing depended on the support of the Sanhedrin. Thus, their common self-interest focused on one innocent figure: Jesus.

I. JESUS BEFORE THE SANHEDRIN (MARK 14:53, 55-64)

A. CONDEMNED BY LIES (vv. 53, 55-61a)

53. They took Jesus to the high priest, and all the chief priests, elders and teachers of the law came together.

Our text picks up the story immediately after Jesus' arrest in the Garden of Gethsemane. Of interest is the fact that the religious leaders are already assembled. This demonstrates that Jesus' arrest is not simply a whim motivated by opportunity, but rather is a well-planned and executed plot.

According to Matthew 26:57, this *high priest* is Caiaphas, the son-in-law of another high priest by the name of Annas. Little is known of Caiaphas other than his role in Jesus' crucifixion. Apparently he is greatly influenced by his father-in-law, for John 18:13 tells us that Annas takes the lead in questioning Jesus (cf. Acts 4:6).

John also tells us, "Now Caiaphas was he, which gave counsel to the Jews, that it was expedient that one man should die for the people" (John 18:14). The counsel of Caiaphas is especially significant because, as John explains, it was a prophetic utterance in keeping with Caiaphas's role as high priest (11:51, 52).

Caiaphas undoubtedly understood his words to mean that *Jesus* should die rather than continue to cause trouble for the authorities. God, however, puts His own "spin" on the message of the high priest. Caiaphas is right: one man is to die for the people. But Caiaphas is far more right than he knows, for Jesus is to die not only for the Jewish people of His time, but for all people at all times who call upon the name of the Lord.

55. The chief priests and the whole Sanhedrin were looking for evidence against Jesus so that they could put him to death, but they did not find any.

It appears that this assembly of religious leaders has reached its conclusion even before hearing any testimony. They are *looking for evidence* that will support their verdict that he deserves to die.

56. Many testified falsely against him, but their statements did not agree.

We can only imagine the frustration of those religious leaders who seek an airtight legal case against Jesus. Even within this sham procedure they cannot get enough testimony to convict him. Deuteronomy 17:6 requires more than one witness for the death penalty. If these leaders cannot get more than one witness to testify to a capital offense in their own hearing, then they will not be able to bring their case before the Roman authorities.

57-59. Then some stood up and gave this false testimony against him: "We heard him say, 'I will destroy this man-made temple and in three days will build another, not made by man.'" Yet even then their testimony did not agree.

According to John 2:19 this *testimony* is partly accurate. Speaking against the *temple* is a capital offense (see Jeremiah 26:1-19). But according to John 2:21, "the temple [Jesus] had spoken of was his body." Obviously these witnesses have no idea what exactly Jesus had been talking about. And once again the witnesses are unable to coordinate their testimony. Whether they differ in their interpretation of Jesus' intent or in the wording of his statement, their testimony is regarded as unreliable even in this biased court.

60. Then the high priest stood up before them and asked Jesus, "Are you not going to answer? What is this testimony that these men are bringing against you?"

We sense a bit of desperation that *the high priest* is feeling at this point. His witnesses have failed to convince anyone—even those who came into the trial with their minds already made up! They are preaching to the choir and the choir is not persuaded. The modern prohibition against self-incrimination that does not require a person to testify against himself or herself does not apply, however. So the high priest hopes that the accused will say something useful.

61a. But Jesus remained silent and gave no answer.

Jesus' lack of reaction is quite surprising to those of us who are used to "standing up for our rights." The prophet Isaiah describes the coming Messiah "as a sheep before her shearers is *silent*, so he did not open his mouth" (Isaiah 53:7). This is fulfilled prophecy.

We can look at this trial before the religious authorities from two perspectives. First, we can focus on the tragedy of an innocent man being framed for crimes he did not commit. This view looks at Jesus as victim, carried along by forces beyond his control to a fate he did not choose.

But rather than seeing Jesus as a passive victim of oppressive justice, we should see Jesus as being fully in control of the situation. He is not silent before the false accusations because of fear or because of a hope that he may be able to escape the fate his accusers plan for him. He is silent before the false accusers because he wants everyone to know exactly who he is: the Christ, the Son of the Living God. It is Jesus' silence that draws the high priest's question to bring this out (next verse).

B. CONVICTED BY TRUTH (vv. 61b-64)

61b. Again the high priest asked him, "Are you the Christ, the Son of the Blessed One?"

Suddenly the dynamic of the trial changes. Up to this point, Jesus has been asked to respond to untruths and half-truths. False witnesses have borne inconsistent testimony, failing to convince even those who desperately want to see Jesus convicted. But continued silence after the question *Are you the Christ, the Son of the Blessed One?* could be taken as a denial. It is time to affirm the truth.

62. "I am," said Jesus. "And you will see the Son of Man sitting at the right hand of the Mighty One and coming on the clouds of heaven."

We could say that Jesus at this point has "thrown down the gauntlet" to history. Clearly this passage indicates that he believes himself to be God's Son, the predicted Messiah. See Daniel 7:13.

63. The high priest tore his clothes. "Why do we need any more witnesses?" he asked.

The reaction of *the high priest* proves that he understands exactly what Jesus is claiming. What all of his *witnesses* have failed to do Jesus himself does with one statement. The tearing of clothes is a reaction intended to show the intensity of emotions (cf. 2 Kings 18:37; Acts 14:14).

64. "You have heard the blasphemy. What do you think?"

They all condemned him as worthy of death.

WHAT DO YOU THINK?

The witnesses twisted Jesus' words, either intentionally or unintentionally, regarding the temple. How should we respond when someone twists our words to make a false accusation?

[Be sure to consider 1 Peter 2:21-23; 3:16, 17 in your discussion.]

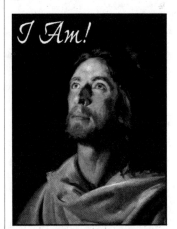

I Am!

Visual for lesson 4. *Display this powerful image to reinforce Jesus' answer to the high priest in verse 62.*

WHAT DO YOU THINK?

Suppose a coworker says to you, "Jesus was a great teacher, but that's all. He never even claimed to be any more than that. His disciples made up that stuff about his being the Son of God after his death." How would you respond?

WHAT DO YOU THINK?

The charge of using God's name in an improper way (blasphemy) could bring the death penalty in the first century. In what ways today do we not take the name of God as seriously as we ought? How can we do better?

DAILY BIBLE READINGS

Monday, Mar. 22—Jesus Is Arrested, Disciples Desert (Mark 14:46-52)

Tuesday, Mar. 23—Jesus Is Taken to the High Priest (Mark 14:53-59)

Wednesday, Mar. 24—Jesus Declares He Is the Messiah (Mark 14:60-65)

Thursday, Mar. 25—The Father and I Are One (John 10:22-30)

Friday, Mar. 26—Jesus Goes Before Pilate (Mark 15:1-5)

Saturday, Mar. 27—The Crowd Wants Barabbas Released (Mark 15:6-10)

Sunday, Mar. 28—The Crowd Shouts for Jesus' Death (Mark 15:11-15)

Blasphemy involves almost any speech that defames God. According to Leviticus 24:16, the punishment for blasphemy is *death* (cf. John 5:18; 10:33). In the minds of the religious leaders, Jesus' "defamation" is that a mere man would equate himself in any way with God.

AN INNOCENT'S DEATH; AN OUTPOURING OF MERCY

On January 13, 2000, eleven-year-old Merita Shabiu disappeared from her village in Kosovo. She had been abducted, assaulted, murdered, and then buried in a snowbank by a U.S. Army staff sergeant who was part of the peacekeeping force in that country. Her body was discovered by other Americans after the Army private who had helped bury the body admitted the truth about what had happened.

The private's truthful, but belated, witness was an important component in bringing the criminal to justice. (He's now serving a life term without parole.) The response of the perpetrator's fellow soldiers in some measure atoned for the evil deeds. Many of them attended Merita's funeral; an Army Reserve doctor took ten soldiers on a two-hour mission to the Shabiu home, where they apologized for the crime. The doctor helped the family design a grave marker, then paid for it. American troops collected four thousand dollars to be used for humanitarian purposes in Merita's name among the citizens of Kosovo. The worst action by an American also brought out the best in other Americans.

In a sense, we see a similar sequence in the first century. The one who betrayed Jesus, those who presented false testimony, the leaders who "set up" Jesus' crucifixion—they all represented the worst in human nature. But the unjust execution that resulted set in motion an amazing chain of events that brought an outpouring of mercy upon the human race: the possibility of eternal salvation from sin. What a God we serve!   —C. R. B.

II. JESUS BEFORE PILATE (MARK 15:1, 2, 12-15)

A. JESUS' BOLD CONFESSION (vv. 1, 2)

1. *Very early in the morning, the chief priests, with the elders, the teachers of the law and the whole Sanhedrin, reached a decision. They bound Jesus, led him away and handed him over to Pilate.*

The religious leaders have accomplished the first part of their goal in getting Jesus to "confess." In their minds he is clearly guilty of blasphemy. No longer do they need the unreliable witnesses who tried to profit from perjury. Now they themselves are the witnesses. In their presence Jesus has claimed to be the Son of God.

The next scene of Jesus' legal drama moves from the residence of Caiaphas (Mark 14:54) to the presence of the local Roman governor (or, more exactly, "prefect") named Pontius *Pilate*. Although the Jewish religious leaders can enforce religious law and punish offenders, they are not allowed to execute anyone. The Roman authorities have to authorize any executions. Thus, the religious leaders need Pilate in order to carry out their plans.

Pilate is an intriguing character for the religious leaders to be relying upon. Descriptions of him by the Jewish historian Josephus and the Greek-speaking Jew Philo are quite unflattering. They portray him as greedy, cruel, and willing to do almost anything to remain in power. Luke 13:1 refers to an incident where Pilate mingled the blood of certain Galileans with their own sacrifices, but no further details are recorded by history. Pilate is no friend of the Jews!

2. *"Are you the king of the Jews?" asked Pilate.*

"Yes, it is as you say," Jesus replied.

In some ways this is the high point of this entire passage. Pilate's plainspoken question *Are you the king of the Jews?* evokes a response that is equally plain.

There is no doubt in the mind of Pilate or anyone else hearing it that *Jesus* is indeed claiming to be some kind of king, although Jesus is quick to explain the spiritual nature of this kingdom in John 18:36.

When confronted with Jesus' answer, each of us must ask ourselves this question: Was Jesus telling the truth or not? Our answer affects where we spend eternity. It also determines how we live our earthly lives in anticipation of eternity. If Jesus is my King, how does that affect the way that I treat my neighbor? If Jesus is my King, how does that affect the way I talk about my coworker? If Jesus is my King, can anyone tell that I am subject to him?

B. Pilate's Cowardly Concession (vv. 12-15)

12. *"What shall I do, then, with the one you call the king of the Jews?" Pilate asked them.*

We know from the other Gospel accounts that *Pilate* believes Jesus to be innocent of any crime deserving death (Luke 23:4; John 18:38). But Pilate is unwilling to upset the community. He has established a tradition of releasing a prisoner each year as a sort of "Passover gift" to the people, so he assumes that the crowds will insist upon Jesus' release rather than someone else's. Pilate knows that it is from envy that the chief priests have arrested Jesus in the first place (Mark 15:10).

13. *"Crucify him!" they shouted.*

This cry of the crowd, inspired by the religious leaders (Mark 15:11), is shocking for at least four reasons. The first is, of course, the innocence of Jesus. Clamoring for the death penalty for someone who has stood for peace and humility, who has healed the sick and raised the dead, is an unspeakable horror.

The second reason this is so shocking is the swiftness with which the tide of public opinion has turned against Jesus. Less than a week earlier the crowds had hailed his coming. Now they call for his execution. The support that had seemed so unshakable only days before has turned into something quite different. The crowds now prefer the political rebel Barabbas (v. 15, below).

Third, we are startled to see the crowd's bloodthirsty desire to inflict the terrible cruelty of death by crucifixion. Victims of crucifixion die slowly of suffocation, shock, exposure, and infection while enduring excruciating pain for hours (and perhaps days) on end. Eagerly desiring such a death for anyone—let alone a fellow Jew—staggers the imagination.

Finally, the cry of the crowd is shocking because not only is crucifixion a cruel death, it is an accursed death (Galatians 3:13; cf. Deuteronomy 21:22, 23). The crowd not only wants Jesus dead, they also want his death to send a message to all Jews: this man is accursed by God!

Respect for the Word of God

What is the best-selling book in history? The Bible? You're right! Think of its effect on Western culture: inspiration for countless works of art, for great writers such as William Shakespeare and C. S. Lewis, and for freedom movements such as the American Revolution and the abolition of slavery. The English language is indebted to the Bible for some choice idioms: "the salt of the earth" and "Woe is me!" are just two.

But, ironically, the Bible may well be less read than many other books. The Barna Research Group does frequent scientific polls on things religious. This group has discovered, for example, that two-thirds of Americans don't read the Bible regularly and don't know the names of the four Gospels. It seems that acknowledgment of the Bible as the Word of God does not radically affect how people actually live!

How to Say It

Barabbas. Buh-RAB-us.
Caiaphas. KAY-uh-fus or KYE-uh-fus.
Deuteronomy. Due-ter-AHN-uh-me.
Gethsemane. Geth-SEM-uh-nee.
Josephus. Jo-SEE-fus.
Judas Iscariot. JOO-dus Iss-CARE-e-ut.
Kosovo. KOH-so-voh or Koh-SO-voh.
Leviticus. Leh-VIT-ih-kus.
Merita Shabiu. Meh-REE-tah Shah-BEE-ooh.
Messiah. Meh-SIGH-uh.
Philo. FIE-low.
Pontius Pilate. PON-shus or PON-ti-us PIE-lut.
Sanhedrin. SAN-huh-drun or San-HEED-run.

All of this should not surprise us, since the Word of God who came in the flesh (John 1:14) met with similar treatment. One day the crowds were hailing Jesus; a short time later they were calling for his death. But as we denounce their fickleness, we may also be passing judgment on ourselves. To what extent do we also give lip service to the Word of God—either the Word living or the Word written—but do not match it with our lives?

—C. R. B.

14, 15. "Why? What crime has he committed?" asked Pilate.
But they shouted all the louder, "Crucify him!"
Wanting to satisfy the crowd, Pilate released Barabbas to them. He had Jesus flogged, and handed him over to be crucified.

So we see the convergence of motivated self-interests. The religious officials want to get rid of a troublemaker who has a knack for stepping on toes and attracting followers. Pilate wants to keep the peace and maintain his position. In between these two parties stands one expendable man.

But we should not think of Jesus as a helpless victim. He is the one figure in this entire drama who is not motivated by his own interests. Rather, Jesus is the one who voluntarily "humbled himself and became obedient to death—even death on a cross" (Philippians 2:8). When he did, he took our place. This is the very heart of the Christian message!

CONCLUSION

Were we part of this drama, where would we have stood? Would we have pursued motives of profit and power? Would we have been swept up in the emotion of the crowd? We move toward an answer when we examine honestly "what motivates us"—is it God's interest, or our own?

The way we treat others is a direct reflection of our motives. Ask yourself, "Have I ever spoken badly of a coworker, seeking to lift myself up at her expense?" "Have I ever fudged the figures on my expense report or my taxes?" "Have I ever had some 'roast preacher' for lunch?" "Have I ever failed to speak up for what I knew was right because I feared what others might say?" Dig deeply enough, and each of us will find a piece of Caiaphas and of Pilate within our own hearts.

Yet we do not have to continue making the same mistakes they made. God's grace is great enough for anyone—whether high priest, Roman governor, or assembly line worker. Repentance and baptism lead us into God's forgiveness (Acts 2:38). Within his grace we can realign our priorities so that our interests coincide with God's purposes.

But those stuck in self-interest need to be warned: people cannot frustrate the designs of God. Caiaphas thought he was acting to remove a troublemaker. Pilate thought he was acting to appease the people. Both were acting for personal reasons to achieve personal goals.

But the end result was something far beyond either party's comprehension. God used their self-interests to achieve his ultimate goal: the eternal salvation of all who would accept it. Just as in the Old Testament, where God used the swords of pagans and the hubris of a Pharaoh to achieve his ends, so in the New Testament God uses the personal goals of a corrupt priest and a contemptible politician to achieve the ultimate of all goals. Joseph recognized the power of God to do such things. After having been sold into slavery and then rising to power in Egypt, he said to his brothers, "You intended to harm me, but God intended it for good to accomplish what is now being done, the saving of many lives" (Genesis 50:20).

WHAT DO YOU THINK?

Pilate sentenced Jesus to death, knowing his innocence. Why are people sometimes unwilling to stand up for what they believe? Where does the courage to do so come from?

PRAYER

Lord, we pray that our interests would be your interests. We pray that you would use us as your tools, your hands, your feet. We recognize that your will can be fulfilled in spite of us as easily as it can be fulfilled through us. We confess that far too often we are guilty of acting out of our own self-interests rather than seeking your interests. Forgive us for going our own way, and draw us into your plans so that we become willing participants in unfolding your will on earth as it is in Heaven. In Jesus' name, amen.

THOUGHT TO REMEMBER

God will achieve his purposes either through you or in spite of you. It's your choice!

Discovery Learning

This page contains an alternative lesson plan emphasizing learning activities. Classes desiring such student involvement will find these suggestions helpful. The next page is a reproducible activity page to further enhance discovery learning.

LEARNING GOALS

After this lesson, each student will be able to:

1. Summarize the events of Jesus' trials and sentence to death.

2. Tell how God's will was carried out through the noble acts of Jesus and in spite of the contemptible acts of the Sanhedrin and Pilate.

3. Express a commitment to working in harmony with the purposes of God.

INTO THE LESSON

Find and jot down a few of the more bizarre headlines that you see on tabloids. Read these to the class one at a time, and ask whether the learners believe the stories to be true or false. Then have them pretend to be editors of a first-century Jerusalem tabloid. Mention an event from Jesus' life, and have them write a headline they would give the story. Let class members work with partners or in teams. Stories you might use include raising a child from the dead, bringing Lazarus back to life after he was in the grave four days, or Jesus' teaching that the meek will inherit the earth. Finish with Jesus' teaching that he is the promised Messiah and his claim to be king of the Jews. Have several headlines read aloud. Ask, "How might people in Jesus' day have responded to these headlines? Why?" Today's lesson will examine the responses different people made to the claims of Jesus when he was on earth.

INTO THE WORD

Review how the story in today's text affirms that Jesus was completely innocent of any crime. The Jewish tribunal needed evidence for the Roman court to justify the sentence against Jesus. They were unable to find two witnesses who could agree in their testimony against Jesus, even when lying (Mark 14:56). This group could not muster enough evidence even for them to consider it credible (Mark 14:56, 59).

Use the reproducible activity "Questions, Claims, and Controversies" from the next page to introduce the two critical questions answered by Jesus. The religious leaders asked, "Are you the Christ, the Son of the Blessed One?" (Mark 14:61). The political leader with responsibility to ensure justice asked, "Are you the king of the Jews?" (Mark 15:2). If Jesus' claims are true, they demand a response of submissive worship and obedience. Consider together the responses of the different characters in this story to Jesus. Discuss how each person or group responded to Jesus and what motivated him or them.

The religious leaders: How did the religious leaders respond to Jesus? (*They looked for evidence that would allow them to kill Jesus; Mark 14:55.*) Why did the leaders hate Jesus so much? (*He had a growing following, had attacked and embarrassed them publicly, had disrupted their market in the temple, etc.*) What motivated them to act this way? (*They were protecting their own power and influence; even Pilate recognized they were motivated by envy; see Mark 15:10.*)

Pilate: How did Pilate respond to Jesus? (*He did not release Jesus and ultimately had him scourged and sentenced to be crucified; Mark 15:15.*) What motivated Pilate to respond this way? (*He was more concerned about satisfying people and keeping peace than about justice; Mark 15:15.*)

The crowds: How did the crowds respond to Jesus? (*We need to ask: "Which day of the week?" Less than a week earlier, the crowds in Jerusalem had shouted, "Hosanna; Blessed is he who comes in the name of the Lord"; Mark 11:9. Now, at the urging of the chief priests, this crowd was shouting, "Crucify him"; Mark 15:14.*)

Note that their response was influential in prompting Pilate to release Barabbas and have Jesus flogged and sentenced to be crucified (Mark 15:15). What motivated the crowds to respond this way? (*While the Scriptures do not clearly answer this question, we learn how easily people can be influenced by others and circumstances, and know that here some chose to follow the religious leaders instead of Jesus.*) Sadly, there is no record of anyone in the crowd standing up for the innocence of Jesus. It seems his closest followers had all deserted him. Even though the injustice was evident, no one was willing to risk speaking on his behalf.

INTO LIFE

Jesus has answered two critical questions in the affirmative: he is the Christ, and he is the King. Ask, "How does your life show that you believe his answers to be true? If other people were reading the story of your life, what would they say is your response to Jesus? Consider the answers from work, play, and home. What changes need to be made for others to see you responding affirmatively to these claims of Jesus?"

Questions, Claims, and Controversy

Two critical questions are asked in today's texts. Find and write those two questions here:

CRITICAL QUESTION #1 (see Mark 14:61)

CRITICAL QUESTION #2 (see Mark 15:2)

Jesus makes a significant claim to answer each of these questions. Find and write his responses here:

SIGNIFICANT CLAIM #1 (see Mark 14:62)

SIGNIFICANT CLAIM #2 (see Mark 15:2)

From the day the questions were asked and the answers given, people have believed and refused to believe the answers. What controversies arise from within the following groups, paralleling the reactions of the groups present at Jesus' trial and sentencing?

RELIGIOUS LEADERS (see Mark 14:55)	GOVERNMENT LEADERS (see Mark 15:15)	CROWDS OF ORDINARY PEOPLE (see Mark 15:14; cf. 11:1-10)

What others think and affirm is important, but the critical question is always, "What do I believe?" Affirm your own reaction to Jesus' claims to be both Christ and King.

JESUS' CRUCIFIXION

LESSON 5

WHY TEACH THIS LESSON?

The Eighth Amendment of the United States Constitution forbids "cruel and unusual punishments." The constitutions of other modern countries, including those of Canada and the United Kingdom, have similar prohibitions. Ancient cultures, however, seemed to have had precisely the opposite viewpoint. "The crueler and the more unusual, the better" was the apparent philosophy.

Few punishments were more dehumanizing than Roman crucifixion. This was death by one of the slowest, most agonizing means possible—designed for all to see, for all to fear. And yet it was a death that the Son of God voluntarily submitted himself to. It was his submission and agony that made possible our escape from the eternal punishment of Hell. This lesson is a sobering reminder that the Son of God was willing to die in our place.

INTRODUCTION

A. "I SURRENDER ALL"

All to Jesus I surrender,
    All to Him I freely give;
I will ever love and trust Him,
    In His presence daily live.
I surrender all,
    I surrender all.
All to Thee, my blessed Savior,
    I surrender all.
            —Judson W. Van DeVenter (1855–1939)

The decade of the 1890s was a heady time in America. Ellis Island was open to immigration, new inventions such as telephones and movies were making inroads, and the importance of the automobile ("horseless carriage") was asserting itself. It was in the midst of all this prosperity and promise that Van DeVenter wrote, "I Surrender All" in 1896. Could it be that he recognized a danger that we have yet to see?

Those of us who have grown up in the church, especially churches with a more traditional worship style, probably have known and sung this hymn for decades. But what exactly is it that we have surrendered to Jesus in the midst of our prosperity? Can you make a list right now of five things you have surrendered—meaning sacrificed or given up—so that you will not be distracted from following Jesus?

Unfortunately, most of us are much better at singing about surrender than we are at practicing it. Too often we content ourselves with fairly minor sacrifices: I will surrender watching the sporting event on TV to attend the church potluck; I will give up my old clothes for the missions project; I will use a week of vacation to work at church camp.

But are these really the sorts of sacrifice that Paul had in mind when he said to "offer your bodies as living sacrifices, holy and pleasing to God—this is your

DEVOTIONAL READING:
JOHN 10:11-18
BACKGROUND SCRIPTURE:
JOHN 19:16b-42
PRINTED TEXT:
JOHN 19:16b-24, 26-30

Apr
4

LESSON AIMS

After participating in this lesson, students will be able to:

1. Recount the details of Jesus' crucifixion as described in John's Gospel.

2. Discuss reasons why it was necessary for Jesus to die on the cross.

3. Pledge to live in a sacrificial manner to serve the one who died for them.

KEY VERSES

So the soldiers took charge of Jesus. Carrying his own cross, he went out to the place of the Skull (which in Aramaic is called Golgotha). Here they crucified him.
            —John 19:16b-18a

spiritual act of worship" (Romans 12:1)? What exactly can we sacrifice that truly honors Jesus—things that recognize the commitment he made to us while dying on the cross?

B. LESSON BACKGROUND

Crucifixion was an incredibly brutal, painful, and dehumanizing way to die. Roman crucifixion typically was reserved for non-Roman political and military enemies of the state and for those guilty of various heinous crimes. Runaway slaves were also subject to the cross.

As we peer at the scene before us on Golgotha, we see several related activities going on simultaneously. In the center our attention is drawn to Jesus, nailed to the cross—enduring the scorn of his contemporaries, the sins of humanity, and the wrath of his Father.

Near the cross are various clusters of bystanders. A group of soldiers is kneeling, engaged in a game of chance to divide Jesus' clothes. Another cluster is mostly women, friends of Jesus who came to mourn and to give him whatever support they had to offer. Still another group, whose numbers fluctuate with the passing hours, is there to gawk and deride. Farther away, we notice the religious officials and Pilate once again meeting, this time arguing over the wording of the sign above Jesus' head.

Those who acknowledge Jesus as the Messiah cannot help but hear the echoes of Isaiah 53 throughout Jesus' crucifixion. The outline for today's lesson takes its main points from Isaiah's prophecy. But the promise for all of us is also found in the prophet's words: "But he was pierced for our transgressions, . . . the punishment that brought us peace was upon him, and by his wounds we are healed" (Isaiah 53:5). In today's lesson we see Jesus surrender his very life—for us.

I. DESPISED AND REJECTED (JOHN 19:16b-24)

A. THE MAN CRUCIFIED (vv. 16b-18)

16b. So the soldiers took charge of Jesus.

Pilate is finished with Jesus. He has washed his hands of the matter—literally (Matthew 27:24). Although he found Jesus to be innocent, Pilate chooses to please the mob and condemn Jesus to die. He turns Jesus over to the Roman *soldiers*, who will be in *charge* of the crucifixion (cf. John 19:23, below).

17. Carrying his own cross, he went out to the place of the Skull (which in Aramaic is called Golgotha).

John's description of the actual crucifixion is brief and to the point. He omits many details that the other Gospel writers include. Much of the detail in the other accounts focuses on Christ's suffering. Although John also discusses Christ's suffering at points, this Gospel writer seems very intent to stress the overall plan of the Father and the Son's obedience within that plan.

Golgotha is an Aramaic (or Hebrew) word that John translates for his readers as *the place of the Skull.* The Latin word *calvaria* also means "skull," and this is where we get our well-known word *Calvary.* Perhaps this place gains its name from the skulls of executed criminals that could be found there. Or perhaps something about the terrain has the appearance of a skull. No one knows for sure. In any case, the place is likely very near a major road, as the Romans want their crucifixions to serve as public deterrents to sedition.

18. Here they crucified him, and with him two others—one on each side and Jesus in the middle.

Critics of Christianity sometimes accuse Jesus of manipulating events to appear to be fulfilling prophecy. In a way, that actually is not such bad theology:

Visual for lesson 5. *Use this stark visual of nails and rough wood to reinforce the sobering reality of today's Key Verses.*

Christians also believe that God is orchestrating events to align with the prophecies he has given!

But certainly some prophetic fulfillments are beyond mere human ability to coordinate. This is one of them. Hundreds of years previously the prophet Isaiah foretold that the Messiah would be "numbered with the transgressors" (Isaiah 53:12). If Jesus were merely a man, he could have had no way of making sure that others would be crucified alongside him.

B. THE MEN CRUCIFYING (vv. 19-24)

19. Pilate had a notice prepared and fastened to the cross. It read: JESUS OF NAZARETH, THE KING OF THE JEWS.

What an intriguing inscription! Before the Romans execute a prisoner, they prepare a sign detailing the person's crimes. That sign precedes the prisoner to the place of execution, informing everyone of the reason for the punishment. The sign is nailed above the criminal's head to reinforce the nature of the crimes.

In this case, no truer sign was ever posted! Jesus is indeed being crucified for who he claimed to be rather than for anything he did.

20. Many of the Jews read this sign, for the place where Jesus was crucified was near the city, and the sign was written in Aramaic, Latin and Greek.

Following Roman practice, Pilate makes sure that everyone knows what the "crime" of Jesus is. The sign is worded in the three major languages of the area so that anyone who can read will know why this man is being killed. But more than that, Pilate wants to humiliate the Jewish leaders who have manipulated him, as the next two verses show.

21. The chief priests of the Jews protested to Pilate, "Do not write 'The King of the Jews,' but that this man claimed to be king of the Jews."

This is not a small point that *the chief priests* make. There is quite a difference between someone who actually is *the King of the Jews* and someone who merely claims to be the King of the Jews. The religious leaders want Jesus dead, after all, because of statements like that. Pilate is now giving the world the very message that Jesus' death is supposed to silence.

WHAT'S IN A NAME?

Have you ever heard the argument over how the Baby Ruth® candy bar got its name? One story has it that the name came from Babe Ruth, the famous home-run hitter. The bar was first marketed in 1921, and as Babe Ruth's fame increased, he began signing his autograph on Baby Ruth® wrappers. The Curtiss Candy Company (maker of the confection) claimed it was named for "Baby Ruth," the daughter of U.S. President Grover Cleveland.

Eventually, Babe Ruth asked the Curtiss Company to pay him royalties, since he was helping to sell their product. The company declined, so Ruth gave his permission to another company to use his name, and they produced the Babe Ruth Home Run Bar. The whole issue went to court, and the Curtiss Company won the lawsuit.

If the American legal system had existed in Jesus' time, the Jewish leaders would undoubtedly have taken Pilate to court for putting the title "King of the Jews" on Jesus' cross. They may have claimed this was "trademark infringement" on something that belonged only to God. They certainly had already convicted Jesus in court on equating himself with God!

But Jesus' execution wasn't enough. These leaders also sought to strip Jesus of the wording on a piece of wood that sarcastically revealed his true identity—even as soldiers were stripping him of his most basic worldly possessions. Many who reject Jesus today do so by denying that Jesus is King. They also attempt to deny others their right to claim him as their King. The more things change . . . ! —C. R. B.

WHAT DO YOU THINK?

Combining our text with Matthew 27:44 and Luke 23:39-43, we learn that one of the thieves had a change of heart after first taunting Jesus. Why this change? How can we influence people to have a similar change of heart?

WHAT DO YOU THINK?

Some writers and speakers go into great detail to describe crucifixions. They paint gruesome word pictures that evoke tears and gasps from their audiences. The Bible, however, is quite brief in this regard. Why? How do we give details that are necessary for faith without manipulating people's emotions?

22. Pilate answered, "What I have written, I have written."

With this answer Pilate takes his revenge on the religious leaders who have manipulated him. Pilate's sign mocks Jesus, but it mocks the Jewish leaders even more! Pilate sees through their pretended allegiance to Caesar (John 19:15), and now declares the dying Jesus to be their king. But in so doing, Pilate also unknowingly speaks the truth: the crucified one is indeed the King of the Jews!

23. When the soldiers crucified Jesus, they took his clothes, dividing them into four shares, one for each of them, with the undergarment remaining. This garment was seamless, woven in one piece from top to bottom.

A squad of four *soldiers* usually attends Roman crucifixions (cf. Acts 12:4). They handle the details of the execution, prevent any escape or rescue attempt, and keep the mobs away from the condemned.

An apparent side benefit for soldiers conducting an execution is being able to claim at least some of the possessions of the condemned. To keep things "fair," these soldiers divide this clothing into *four* roughly equal parts. We can assume that Jesus' clothes are fairly plain and common for his time. Only item among several has enough value to create conflict among the soldiers.

24. "Let's not tear it," they said to one another. "Let's decide by lot who will get it." This happened that the scripture might be fulfilled which said,

> *"They divided my garments among them*
> *and cast lots for my clothing."*

So this is what the soldiers did.

Psalm 22:18 is the backdrop for this verse. Those who are crucified must give up some or perhaps all of their personal possessions to their executioners. Dignity dies when the beaten prisoner is marched through the crowds. Emotions explode as the condemned dies slowly in the presence of loved ones and enemies.

Nothing can be held back, nothing can remain hidden, nothing can stay personal. Crucifixion robs its victims of everything they have accumulated during life—finally stealing life itself. John uses Psalm 22:18 to show fulfillment of God's plan in a very sobering way.

II. A MAN OF SORROWS (JOHN 19:26, 27)

A. CONCERN FOR A MOTHER (v. 26)

26. When Jesus saw his mother there, and the disciple whom he loved standing nearby, he said to his mother, "Dear woman, here is your son,"

We can only imagine the intensity of emotions contained in this brief exchange between three people who love each other deeply. In the fog of pain, blood, and sweat, Jesus' eyes are clear enough to see *his mother* and John, one of his dearest disciples (cf. John 13:23; 20:2). They are standing together, part of a group that Luke describes as "a large number of people followed him, including women who mourned and wailed for him" (Luke 23:27). Years earlier Simon had warned Mary, "A sword will pierce your own soul too" (Luke 2:35). No doubt those words echoed in her heart long after witnessing Jesus' crucifixion.

Jesus captures in this moment the essence of being part of this world while being part of the kingdom of God. Who could fault him if, while consumed by his own pain and suffering, he would pay no attention to his surroundings? Yet not only does he see those around him, Jesus reaches out to them and makes sure that his mother will be taken care of (next verse). As the oldest child, it would have fallen to Jesus to care for his mother after the death of Joseph. Although Jesus has siblings (Matthew 12:46; John 2:12), they apparently are not part of the gallery (and might not even be in Jerusalem at the time).

WHAT DO YOU THINK?

We cringe at the callous behavior of the soldiers, gambling for Jesus' clothes while he hung dying above them. How is the same cold-hearted spirit displayed today? What similar guilt do Christians share?

WHAT DO YOU THINK?

Jesus was concerned for others in the midst of his own pain. Have you known people who could demonstrate concern even when experiencing hardship? What gives people that kind of outward focus? How can we duplicate it?

B. COMMITMENT OF A DISCIPLE (v. 27)

27. . . . and to the disciple, "Here is your mother." From that time on, this disciple took her into his home.

All of the disciples had fled when Jesus was arrested—but at least one has returned. John now stands with Mary and others who lament Jesus' pending death. Even as Jesus is dying, he faces the burden of caring for his *mother* as she ages.

Neither John nor Mary have yet reached fullness in their Christian faith (see John 20:8, 9), and this is undoubtedly their darkest hour. Yet it is in this very hour that John proves he still can accept instructions from his Lord. We can assume that John cared for Mary as well as any son would care for his own mother.

ACQUAINTED WITH GRIEF

On April 9, 2002, the British people laid to rest the remains of the "Queen Mum," mother of Queen Elizabeth. The Queen Mum's experiences over her life of one hundred one years were proof that wealth, power, and acclaim do not protect people from grief. Refusing the safety of exile, she stood with her husband, George VI, encouraging the British people during the long nights of bombardment in World War II. Her husband died in 1952, and she buried her daughter Margaret just two months before her own death.

We can only guess at the grief she endured in watching her grandchildren mock the dignity of the royal family by their disastrous personal lives. Yet, in spite of the sins of her descendants, she carried to her grave a sense of dignity and an openness to her people that made her a beloved figure.

Jesus, of course, was alone in the incalculable burden of grief that he carried over lost humanity. But he also endured sorrow for the frailties of his "descendants"—people he had created. These included family members who would not recognize him and disciples who doubted, denied, and even betrayed him. Even so, his compassionate life, courageous death, and miraculous resurrection have made him loved by billions of people from every nation and tongue. Devotion to all earthly leaders pales by comparison.   —C. R. B.

III. POURED OUT . . . UNTO DEATH (JOHN 19:28-30)

A. HUMAN THIRST (vv. 28, 29)

28. Later, knowing that all was now completed, and so that the Scripture would be fulfilled, Jesus said, "I am thirsty."

Crucifixion provides many physical reasons for Jesus' thirst. Blood loss, exposure to the hot sun, pain, and labored breathing can individually parch one's throat. Taken together, these mean that Jesus suffers terribly from dehydration.

The fulfillment of *Scripture* that is in view is Psalm 69:21. See also the use of Psalm 69 in John 2:17; 15:25.

29. A jar of wine vinegar was there, so they soaked a sponge in it, put the sponge on a stalk of the hyssop plant, and lifted it to Jesus' lips.

This wine vinegar is probably the inexpensive drink favored by the soldiers themselves. Jesus earlier had refused a wine mixture that would have dulled his pain (Mark 15:23); he chose, instead, to drink the full cup of agony from his Father.

Now thirst compels the Lord to request and accept the offer of drink (cf. Mark 15:36). If the solders intend to prolong Jesus' agony by slaking his thirst, then theirs is not an offer of compassion but one of additional torture.

B. DIVINE QUENCHING (v. 30)

30. When he had received the drink, Jesus said, "It is finished." With that, he bowed his head and gave up his spirit.

DAILY BIBLE READINGS

Monday, Mar. 29—Isaiah's Prophecy of the Suffering Servant (Isaiah 53:1-6)

Tuesday, Mar. 30—He Bore the Sins of Many (Isaiah 53:7-12)

Wednesday, Mar. 31—Jesus Is Crucified (John 19:16-20)

Thursday, Apr. 1—The King of the Jews (John 19:21-25a)

Friday, Apr. 2—It Is Finished (John 19:25b-30)

Saturday, Apr. 3—The Spear Pierces His Side (John 19:31-37)

Sunday, Apr. 4—Joseph and Nicodemus Take Jesus' Body (John 19:38-42)

HOW TO SAY IT

Aramaic. AIR-uh-MAY-ik.

calvaria (Latin). kal-vuh-REE-uh.

Golgotha. GAHL-guh-thuh.

Isaiah. Eye-ZAY-uh.

Messiah. Meh-SIGH-uh.

Nazareth. NAZ-uh-reth.

Pilate. PIE-lut.

WHAT DO YOU THINK?

Right to the end Jesus had his mission in mind. How can we have such a sense of mission, of knowing that our lives are fulfilling a great purpose for the Lord?

[You will find Matthew 28:19, 20; 1 Corinthians 15:58; and 2 Timothy 4:7 to be helpful in your discussion.]

PRAYER

Father, we stand in awe at the price Jesus paid for us. But we also stand in sorrow as we think of the lost. Change our hearts so that we will pay any price to reach them with your love. You paid the highest price for us—may we share your values. In Jesus' name, amen.

THOUGHT TO REMEMBER

Jesus has done his part. Have we?

The relief the vinegar cannot provide, death does. Relief is not to be found in this world. But from Jesus' words to the thief next to him we know that he was looking forward to being in Paradise that very day (Luke 23:43). Burning with a fever that could not be cooled, parched with a thirst that could not be quenched, Jesus finally finds refreshment at the table set for him in that place.

As cruel as this entire experience is, Jesus' suffering is comparatively brief. Those condemned to death by crucifixion often remain alive for two or even three days. The physical agony experienced by Jesus for several hours could easily have gone on for a much longer period of time. Mark 15:44 tell us that Pilate was surprised that Jesus was already dead.

Even so, Jesus' suffering is long and severe enough to fulfill the Father's plan. We see this fulfillment when Jesus says It is finished. This is the victory cry of one whose work is complete—it is not the cry of defeat. Jesus had spoken previously of the work he came to carry out (John 17:4), but the disciples hadn't understood it. And they still don't understand. It will be only after the crucifixion and resurrection that understanding will come.

The Gospel descriptions help us understand, too, the depths of the terrible price Jesus took upon himself to pay in dying for our sins. There is the obvious physical price—the torture and agonizing death of an innocent man. Much worse, however, is the spiritual torture of bearing our sins (Hebrews 9:28). This is the greater part of the punishment—a punishment that rightly belongs to us!

And Jesus did indeed suffer on our behalf. It was our sins that nailed Jesus to the cross. It was our sins that caused him such agony. He sacrificed himself to pay the penalty for our failures. "Since the children have flesh and blood, he too shared in their humanity so that by his death he might destroy him who holds the power of death—that is, the devil—and free those who all their lives were held in slavery by their fear of death" (Hebrews 2:14, 15).

Jesus sacrificed himself so that we could be reconciled to God. He took upon himself the sins of the world, accepting the punishment (death) due to each of us, so that we may have eternal life (Romans 3:21-26).

CONCLUSION

In a phrase, "dying for change" is exactly what Jesus did. He died for a change in us. He died that our relationship with God could change. Before Jesus' death, humanity was alienated from God. After his crucifixion, alienation changed into the possibility of reconciliation. Before his death, humanity was under a death sentence. After his crucifixion, the certainty of our death changed into the possibility of eternal life. The price that the holiness and justice of God demanded to be paid was indeed paid (Romans 3:25; 1 John 4:10).

"Dying for change" also describes much of the world. Think of your friends, your family members, your coworkers—think of the waitress in your favorite restaurant, the checker at the grocery store, the cop on patrol, the executive in her office. All are dying for change—and without a change they will die eternally.

Jesus sacrificed himself so that they could be saved. But how will they hear? How will they know? That is up to us. What will we sacrifice to bring them the message of the cross? Will we risk personal rejection and humiliation by talking to them? Will we risk careers, ambitions, even our very lives to reach the lost? A disgraced figure hanging on a cross hopes that we will take those risks.

But those aren't the only risks we are asked to take. Will we give sacrificially to fund missions and new church plants? A dying man watches soldiers gamble over the scraps of cloth he once wore and he prays that we will not focus on the goods of this world in such a way. Will we?

Discovery Learning

This page contains an alternative lesson plan emphasizing learning activities. Classes desiring such student involvement will find these suggestions helpful. The next page is a reproducible activity page to further enhance discovery learning.

LEARNING GOALS

After this lesson students will be able to:

1. Recount the details of Jesus' crucifixion as described in John's Gospel.

2. Discuss reasons why it was necessary for Jesus to die on the cross.

3. Pledge to live in a sacrificial manner to serve the one who died for them.

INTO THE LESSON

Begin by considering the costs involved in different activities. Write the name of an activity on the board, and let the class list and add up the costs, including costs other than money. Choose activities that interest several in your class. (*For example: taking a camping trip. Costs include equipment, vehicle travel, lot permits, food, bugs, sleeping on hard ground, cold or hot, wet from rain*). Note that there are costs involved with everything; discuss what it means to have "hidden costs."

Option: Use the reproducible activity "Should I Buy It?" on the next page.

Then say, "We all attempt to calculate what something costs, and then decide whether it is worth that expenditure of finances, time, and effort, as well as the sacrifice from other parts of our lives. Today we look at what it cost Jesus to secure salvation for us and then ask what price we should be willing to pay as a follower of Jesus."

INTO THE WORD

Many films and videos reenact the life of Jesus. Watch clips from one or two to see how they depict his time of suffering. (See page 251 for information on the use of copyrighted film clips.) Discuss the following: In what ways is the clip accurate? What is missing? Does each create a tone and atmosphere that captures the essence of these events in a realistic, memorable way? What new questions are raised? What does it teach you that you had not considered before? What forgotten truths does it remind you of?

Have four students read aloud the passages describing the suffering of Jesus (Matthew 27:27-37; Mark 15:16-26; Luke 23:26-43; John 19:16-30). Ask people what images stand out most to them. Pray, thanking God for the sacrifice made by his Son, Jesus. Consider incorporating the reproducible activity "Should God Buy Us Back?" from the next page.

Select several hymns or favorite songs you sing that speak of the suffering and death of Jesus. Distribute hymnals with pages of those songs marked, or provide copies of the words from contemporary songs (songs in the public domain or for which your church has obtained permission). The following songs are a sample of what is available: "At the Cross," "Alas! And Did My Savior Bleed?" "And Can It Be?" "Behold the Lamb," "Calvary Covers It All," "Hallelujah, What a Savior," "When I Survey the Wondrous Cross," "There is a Redeemer." (Many more will be listed in the topical section of your hymnal's index or by those who lead worship in your church.)

Divide the class into small groups. Provide each group with the words to two songs, and ask the members to analyze the words: What aspect of Christ's suffering do those songs emphasize? Is it an accurate portrayal? Overall, how does music help in highlighting and emphasizing the things that Scripture emphasizes? What part can music play in encouraging from us an appropriate response to Jesus' suffering?

Observe that John records the inscription that Pilate had attached to the cross: "Jesus of Nazareth, the King of the Jews" (John 19:19). It was posted in three different languages so that all would know the crimes. The chief priests asked Pilate to change the inscription, but he would not. While such a sign was a common means for posting the crime of the person being crucified, the inscription reflects the truth that Jesus was crucified for who he was rather than anything he did. Discuss why Jesus would suffer these things. (*He died for our sins, Isaiah 53:5, 6 and 1 Peter 2:24; he is the good shepherd who laid down his life for us, John 10:11.*) We have considered the great price paid or the "cost" to Jesus. Jesus fully knew what he was facing (no "hidden" costs) and still paid the price as he willingly let himself be the sacrifice for our sins (Hebrews 2:14, 15). Discuss ways to remind each other on a daily basis this week about the great sacrifice Jesus made to save us from our sin.

INTO LIFE

Ask students to list five things it "costs" a person to follow Jesus. Say, "In each of these areas, what sacrifices have you made to be his follower? Are there ways you know you should intensify your commitment or increase your personal sacrifice? What holds you back from that commitment?"

Should I Buy It?

In the box to the right, describe or draw something you would really like to have that you do not have.

Answer all these questions about your dream item:

☐ How often will I use or enjoy it?

☐ Who else will benefit from my having it?

☐ Where will I store it?

☐ How long will it likely last?

☐ Why do I want it?

☐ How much will it cost to acquire it?

☐ Is it worth the cost; that is, will having it demonstrate good stewardship?

In the boxes to the left above, number the seven questions in the order in which they are determining factors for you: 1, most important; 7, least important. After you have done so, decide whether there is a better, more godly order. If so, what would that be?

Should God Buy Us Back?

In the box to the left, sketch or attach a picture of yourself. How would God answer these questions?

☐ How much will I enjoy having this person? Of what use will this person be?

☐ How will others benefit from my having him/her?

☐ Where will I keep him/her?

☐ How long will he/she last?

☐ Why do I want to redeem him/her?

☐ How much will he/she cost?

☐ Do I consider this person worth the cost? Why?

Remind yourself why Jesus paid this extreme price. Read the following verses: Isaiah 53:5, 6; John 10:11; 1 Peter 2:24; Hebrews 2:14, 15.

How Much Will I Pay?

J. B. Phillips paraphrases Romans 12:1 to become this challenge for us: "With eyes wide open to the mercies of God . . . as an act of intelligent worship . . . give him your bodies, as a living sacrifice, consecrated to him and acceptable to him."

What sacrifices have you made for being his? How can you increase your personal sacrifice? What holds you back from paying the price as a living sacrifice?

Unit 2: Victory Through Death
(Lessons 5, 6)

THE EMPTY TOMB

LESSON 6

WHY TEACH THIS LESSON?

Companies traditionally have stressed all the features—all the "bells and whistles"—of their products to entice buyers. One interesting trend in the opposite direction in recent years has been the approach taken by those who market bottled water. They like to stress what their product *doesn't* contain! One company claims, for example, that its bottled water is so pure that "we promise nothing."

Christianity makes a similar claim: Jesus' tomb was (and is) empty! On that great resurrection morning there was nothing in that tomb except grave clothes (John 20:5-7). That particular "nothing" is our great hope for eternity. As Jesus' tomb was empty, so shall our own graves be (1 Corinthians 15:12-26). This is the lesson your learners need in order to keep all of life in perspective. This is the lesson that teaches us how Christianity is able to defeat the claims of all other religions.

INTRODUCTION

A. POSITIVE NEGATIVES

Sometimes the best news is the news of what is not there. "Your tests show there is no cancer"; "We found no signs of an intruder"; "The flood waters will not affect your property"; "Your daughter was not in the house when it caught fire." The American idiom that something is "found missing" sums up this type of news. The absence of the terrible can be quite wonderful!

B. LESSON BACKGROUND

The best news ever of something "found missing" was the body of Jesus. The women went to the place of Jesus' interment expecting to find a corpse. Instead, they found an angel and an empty tomb. They found Jesus' body missing!

Two wealthy and influential followers took possession of Jesus' body after his crucifixion (Matthew 27:57-60; John 19:38-42). As an executed "criminal," Jesus' body likely would simply have been thrown into a pit with those of the other two convicts, or according to Roman custom just left on the crosses to rot.

However, the Jewish religious leaders approached Pilate with a request. It was the day of Preparation—the day before a special Sabbath, in this case, the Passover Sabbath—and the religious leaders did not want dead bodies left out during this special time (John 19:31). Therefore, they asked Pilate's permission to have all of the bodies removed from the crosses and disposed of. Joseph of Arimathea and Nicodemus, members of the Sanhedrin (Luke 23:50; John 3:1; 19:38, 39), took Jesus' body and hastily prepared it for burial before sundown, the beginning of the Jewish Sabbath.

The two men anointed the body with a great quantity of spices (John 19:39), but their preparations had to be done quickly because of the coming sunset. With some exceptions, Jewish days were typically reckoned from sunset to sunset. Needing to be home before sundown, they had hurriedly placed Jesus' body in a nearby tomb owned by Joseph (Matthew 27:60).

DEVOTIONAL READING:
LUKE 24:1-12
BACKGROUND SCRIPTURE:
MATTHEW 28:1-15
PRINTED TEXT:
MATTHEW 28:1-15

LESSON AIMS

After participating in this lesson, each student will be able to:

Apr
11

1. List the aspects of Matthew's resurrection account that support the reality of the resurrection.

2. Explain why a literal bodily resurrection of Jesus is believable and, in fact, vital.

3. State at least one benefit he or she enjoys because Jesus rose from the dead.

KEY VERSES

The angel said to the women, "Do not be afraid, for I know that you are looking for Jesus, who was crucified. He is not here; he has risen, just as he said. Come and see the place where he lay."
—Matthew 28:5, 6

LESSON 6 NOTES

I. QUEST AND DECLARATION (MATTHEW 28:1-7)

A. ANGEL'S ANNOUNCEMENT (vv. 1-3)

1. After the Sabbath, at dawn on the first day of the week, Mary Magdalene and the other Mary went to look at the tomb.

Burial preparations typically are done by family members or close friends. Undoubtedly *Mary Magdalene and the other Mary* want to add their own resources to those provided by Joseph and Nicodemus. All four Gospels agree that the women came to the tomb in the earliest hours of the morning of *the first day of the week*.

There are several women named Mary mentioned in the New Testament, and we find two of them here. The word *Magdalene* simply means "from Magdala," a fishing village on the southwest shore of the Sea of Galilee. Luke 8:2 tells us that this Mary was one "from whom seven demons had come out"—demons cast out by Jesus. She is privileged to be the first to learn of Jesus' resurrection.

Matthew 27:56 helps us discover that "the other Mary" is "the mother of James and Joses." She may also be "the wife of Clopas" (John 19:25), but this is not certain. What is certain is that these two Marys know exactly where Jesus had been buried (see Mark 15:47).

2. There was a violent earthquake, for an angel of the Lord came down from heaven and, going to the tomb, rolled back the stone and sat on it.

Only Matthew mentions this *earthquake* in addition to the earlier one that accompanied Jesus' death (Matthew 27:51, 54). Quite possibly these are more significant to the Jewish writer Matthew than to the Gentile writers Mark and Luke, as earthquakes were sometimes associated with appearances of God on the earth in the Old Testament (e.g., 1 Kings 19:11-13; Isaiah 29:6).

Typically the tombs of wealthy men (like Joseph of Arimathea) are small caves hewn out of rock.s A large, circular *stone* is placed in front of the opening in an inclined groove. This makes the stone fairly easy to roll into place but extremely difficult to move away. Mark 16:4 describes this stone as being "very large." Normal circumstances would require several men working with levers to move it.

But these are not normal circumstances, and the stone is moved easily by divine action. An important point to note is that the tomb is already empty when the angel arrives. The stone is not moved to let Jesus out—the stone is moved to let the women in!

3. His appearance was like lightning, and his clothes were white as snow.

According to Mark 16:5, the angel, or messenger from God, looks like "a young man." Apparently some kind of light emanates from his face, and his clothing is unnaturally *white*. Given the dustiness of the Judean environment, purely white clothing is undoubtedly an unusual sight —unusual enough to be noted by three of the four Gospel writers (cf. Acts 1:10). Luke tells us that there were two angels, but it is common for writers to focus on only one figure when more than one are actually present.

B. GUARDS' REACTION (v. 4)

4. The guards were so afraid of him that they shook and became like dead men.

The guards are frightened out of their senses. The shock of the angel's appearance sends them into a *dead* faint. Perhaps we would react the same way!

The chief priests had requested guards from Pilate for the purpose of keeping the disciples from stealing the body (Matthew 27:62-66). Most likely these are Roman guards that serve as part of the temple police, a cadre of soldiers who maintain order in the temple. They serve the wishes of the religious officials at the permission of Pilate. This would explain why the members of this team of

---

WHAT DO YOU THINK?

How would you respond to a coworker who says, "Why worry about whether Jesus rose from the dead? If his life makes you a better person, that's what's important."

[Find information to help answer this question in 1 Corinthians 15.]

guards report back to the chief priests initially, and not to Pilate (Matthew 28:11-15, below).

C. WOMEN'S REJOICING (vv. 5-7)

5. The angel said to the women, "Do not be afraid, for I know that you are looking for Jesus, who was crucified.

The sudden appearance of the angel had caused the guards to pass out. His presence also puts fear into the hearts of the women. Angels tend to have this effect on humans; often an angel's first words to a person are *Do not be afraid* (cf. Daniel 10:12; Luke 1:13, 30; 2:10).

The angel knows why these *women* have come: they are looking for the body of *Jesus*. What is just as true, but unspoken, is the fact that the women are not looking for or expecting a risen Christ.

WHAT A MIXTURE OF EMOTIONS!

For seventy-seven hours in July, 2002, fear held the town of Quecreek, Pennsylvania, in its grasp: nine coal miners were trapped two hundred forty feet below ground in a flooded mine shaft. They managed to find an air pocket, but then had to wait and wonder in cold, wet, depressing darkness.

Workers above drilled an airshaft, and the miners' hopes rose. Hope was strengthened again as they heard the rescue shaft being bored toward them. But then despair came as the noise stopped for eighteen hours—the drill bit had broken, halting the rescue effort. The men vowed to live or die together and wrote out their wills, putting them into a lunch box.

But drilling resumed, and when the new drill broke through, despair turned to hope. Then, as the miners were brought to the surface one by one, hope turned to joy for the miners, their families, their rescuers, and literally an entire nation that had been watching on TV.

On the morning Jesus arose from where he had been entombed, there was a similar mixture of fear, despair, and joy. The guards were "frightened to death"—as the saying goes—by the sight of the angel. The women's own fear was mixed with despair that someone had stolen his body. But that despair would soon give way to joy when they heard that Jesus was alive. How blessed we are: because of their testimony we have no cause for fear or despair, only unmitigated joy!   —C. R. B.

6. He is not here; he has risen, just as he said. Come and see the place where he lay.

Jesus had predicted his resurrection on more than one occasion (see Mark 8:31, 32; 9:31; 10:32-34). Even the enemies of Jesus knew about this prediction (again, Matthew 27:63). The angel reminds the women of Jesus' own words, then invites them to *see* some (but not yet all) of the proof for themselves. The tomb is empty—the cave that had never been used as a tomb before is no longer being used as one now.

7. Then go quickly and tell his disciples: 'He has risen from the dead and is going ahead of you into Galilee. There you will see him.' Now I have told you."

Matthew 26:32 records Jesus' prediction at the last supper that he would "go ahead of you into Galilee" after his resurrection. Jesus will indeed meet them there (Matthew 28:16; John 21), but some important events in and around Jerusalem will intervene first (John 20:19-31).

II. APPEARANCE AND CONSPIRACY (MATTHEW 28:8-15)

A. JESUS' APPEARANCE (vv. 8-10)

8. So the women hurried away from the tomb, afraid yet filled with joy, and ran to tell his disciples.

"Fear not . . ." the tomb is empty!
— from Matthew 28:5

Visual for lesson 6. *This exciting visual will remind your learners of the good news of the Easter season.*

HOW TO SAY IT

Arimathea. AIR-uh-muh-THEE-uh.

Cleophas. KLEE-o-fus.

Colossians. Kuh-LOSH-unz.

Corinthians. Kor-IN-thee-unz.

Joses. JO-sez.

Magdalene. MAG-duh-leen or Mag-duh-LEE-nee.

Nicodemus. NICK-uh-DEE-mus.

Pilate. PIE-lut.

Sanhedrin. SAN-huh-drun or San-HEED-run.

Thessalonians. THESS-uh-LO-nee-unz.

Completely overwhelmed by the angel's news, *the women* begin running to meet the *disciples*. It takes little imagination to understand their mix of emotions. *Joy* and fear are natural reactions for such news! The appearance of the angel alone engendered fear; combined with the news the angel bears, these women have a front-row seat for the greatest demonstration of God's power since the creation. For them and for all of humanity, this is the most important demonstration of God's grace ever.

ACCEPTING A NEW ROLE

"Rosie the Riveter" was a determined-looking woman who wore a work shirt rolled up above her elbows and a kerchief tied about her head. She was flexing her biceps and saying, "We can do it!" Of course, Rosie was a fictional character who appeared on posters across America during World War II, encouraging women to work in the factories building machines and munitions while American men were on the battle lines fighting for freedom.

Rosie symbolized a strange new role that women of that time were unaccustomed to playing—factory workers who were asked to do everything men had previously done in the manufacturing processes. Without the women "manning" the factories, the men in the armed forces would not have had the materiel necessary to win the war. When the war was over many of the women enjoyed the irony of being asked to tell the returning soldiers how to do the jobs they were coming back to!

It is highly unlikely that the women who came to the tomb on the morning of Jesus' resurrection were expecting the unaccustomed role that would soon be thrust upon them. Nevertheless, when the angel charged them with the task of announcing the resurrection to the rest of Jesus' disciples, they rose to the occasion and became the first heralds of the greatest news ever told! Are you prepared to accept whatever role God calls you to fill?   —C. R. B.

9. Suddenly Jesus met them. "Greetings," he said. They came to him, clasped his feet and worshiped him.

As the women are running to tell the disciples, suddenly *Jesus* himself appears to *them*. What shock they must feel upon hearing Jesus' simple greeting! Jesus has just risen from the dead, the women have just talked to an angel, and Jesus starts this conversation by saying, in essence, "Hello!"

Now it all begins to come together for the women. Recognizing Jesus for who he is, they fall at *his feet* and worship *him*. What more appropriate reaction can there be? No doubts remain in their mind about him: truly he is the Christ, the Son of the Living God.

10. Then Jesus said to them, "Do not be afraid. Go and tell my brothers to go to Galilee; there they will see me."

No one can have a close encounter with the power of God and not *be afraid*. When one encounters the living God, creator of heaven and earth, ruler of the entire universe, it is a terrifying experience. Moses met regularly with God, as friends might meet. After those meetings Moses' face shone, likely in a way similar to that of the angel's face in our account. The result was that the Israelites wanted Moses to wear a veil to hide his face, for they were terrified of the power of their own God (Exodus 34:28-35).

When we harmonize the accounts of the four Gospels, it seems likely that the disciples did not believe the women's story. John tells us that he and Peter went to the tomb to check it out and found it empty as Mary Magdalene had told them. But even then they did not have the answers. Thomas is faulted for his refusal to believe until he can *see* the risen Christ with his own eyes, but all of the apostles acted in a similar manner. And although the women were told (both by

WHAT DO YOU THINK?

If it is true that "no one can have a close encounter with the power of God and not be afraid," then how ought we to demonstrate that reality in our lives?

[Make sure you consider 2 Peter 3:11 in your answer.]

the angel and by the Lord himself) to send the disciples *to Galilee,* it will eventually take a personal appearance by the Lord to the disciples to get them moving in the right direction.

The fear felt by the disciples gives us greater confidence in the reality of the resurrection. Consider that in just the few weeks between Passover and Pentecost the disciples make a transition from cowering in locked rooms (John 20:19) to preaching fearlessly and openly in Jerusalem (Acts 2:14-41). Only the confidence given by the risen Savior can explain this dramatic turnaround.

B. GUARDS' REPORT (v. 11)

11. *While the women were on their way, some of the guards went into the city and reported to the chief priests everything that had happened.*

We have already discussed who *the guards* were and why they were posted at the tomb (see v. 4, above). We cannot know exactly what some of them say *to the chief priests.* But when these soldiers report all the things that were done, they undoubtedly include the earthquake, the angel, and the empty tomb. The guards probably did not see the risen Lord; we should not assume that these were non-Christian witnesses to the resurrection.

C. PRIESTS' PLAN (vv. 12-15)

12. *When the chief priests had met with the elders and devised a plan, they gave the soldiers a large sum of money,*

This report by the guards creates a great deal of consternation among the religious leaders. They quickly gather together to cook up another plan. This plan involves bribing *the soldiers.*

The fact that it takes *a large* amount *of money* to pull this *plan* off indicates the stakes involved. The priests want this matter dealt with decisively. The story of an angel appearing would throw great doubt upon their role in Jesus' crucifixion. The *chief priests* and *elders* had declared during the crucifixion, "He's the King of Israel! Let him come down now from the cross, and we will believe in him" (Matthew 27:42). Now is their chance to realize the truth and make good on this pledge.

Truth, however, is not important to these leaders. What matters is the expediency of keeping the peace and keeping their own positions of power and influence. They prayed for a Messiah, then rejected Jesus because he was not the kind of Messiah they wanted or were expecting. They could not believe because they thought they knew what to expect from God.

But how often do we ourselves see the hand of God at work and refuse to believe it? We are not so different from those religious leaders at times. We pray for the healing of those in the hospital, then credit the doctors when the healing occurs. We pray for newcomers for our church, then credit our fine preaching or beautiful singing for packing them in. We pray for a new job, then credit our excellent résumé or fine interviewing skills for landing the position. We pray for rain, then complain when showers ruin our picnic.

We all need to be careful about putting God into a box of our own design. Solomon said, "But will God really dwell on earth? The heavens, even the highest heaven, cannot contain you. How much less this temple I have built!" (1 Kings 8:27). If Solomon's temple could not contain God, what makes us think that the "temples of expectations" that we erect will be any more successful?

13, 14. . . . *telling them, "You are to say, 'His disciples came during the night and stole him away while we were asleep.' If this report gets to the governor, we will satisfy him and keep you out of trouble."*

DAILY BIBLE READINGS

Monday, Apr. 5—I Am the Resurrection (John 11:20-27)

Tuesday, Apr. 6—The Stone Is Rolled Away (Luke 24:1-5)

Wednesday, Apr. 7—The Women Remembered Jesus' Words (Luke 24:6-12)

Thursday, Apr. 8—Jesus Has Been Raised (Matthew 28:1-6)

Friday, Apr. 9—Go Quickly and Tell (Matthew 28:7-15)

Saturday, Apr. 10—Jesus Stood Among the Disciples (John 20:19-23)

Sunday, Apr. 11—Death No Longer Has Dominion (Romans 6:4-11)

WHAT DO YOU THINK?

The Jewish leaders are amazing! They have evidence of a supernatural event, and their plan is to cover it up. How could they harden their hearts in the face of such evidence? How can we reach people like this today?

WHAT DO YOU THINK?

What lies are commonly reported in our own day? How can we convince people of the truth in these areas?

WHAT DO YOU THINK?

The chief priests seemed to have understood Jesus' predictions of resurrection better than the disciples did. How could that be? How can modern disciples avoid the type of blindness that infected the first-century disciples?

PRAYER

Lord, thank you for taking our sins on the cross. And thank you again for giving us new life—eternal life. We rely on your power that raised Jesus from the dead, and we trust in you, the God and Father of our Lord Jesus Christ. In Jesus' name, amen.

THOUGHT TO REMEMBER

Christ's resurrection guarantees ours!

Roman soldiers who are derelict in their duty can be executed (cf. Acts 12:18, 19). Members of the temple police are under the control of the Sanhedrin, however. With the right "connections," they may be able to escape such harsh punishment. The guards want to avoid this punishment just as much as the religious leaders want to maintain their own positions. So all agree on an "explanation" that *his disciples came by night, and stole him away while* the guards slept.

Obviously there is no fingerprint evidence, no crime-scene investigators, no video surveillance to contradict this lie. But even without such modern investigative techniques, this is a curious lie to tell and is easily exposed. If the guards were asleep, how would they really have known what happened? If one of the soldiers had been awake and saw the disciples, why didn't he awaken the rest of the group? The obvious weaknesses in this fabrication reflect both the haste in which it is created and the desperation felt by the religious leaders.

Furthermore, we can hardly imagine the disciples being able to muster the courage to steal Jesus' body. The disciples had fled when Jesus was arrested, Peter had denied he even knew Jesus, and perhaps only John was present at his execution. We see no evidence that the Eleven play any part in his burial, and they do not accompany the women on their trip to the tomb. Even after Jesus' resurrection they kept "the doors locked for fear of the Jews" (John 20:19).

In passing we should note that the chief priests seem to have paid more attention to Jesus' words than did his own disciples, for the Jewish leaders recalled that Jesus had said, "After three days I will rise again" (Matthew 27:63). The women and the Eleven did not comprehend this, for it was not until after the resurrection that they understood Jesus' promises.

15. So the soldiers took the money and did as they were instructed. And this story has been widely circulated among the Jews to this very day.

Matthew's Gospel is most likely written for a Jewish audience. Therefore it is quite natural that he would address a *story* that was circulating *among the Jews*. Rather than going into any great detail, Matthew simply reports what actually happens—Christ arises from the dead—and reports that *the soldiers* have to be bribed to tell their fabricated story.

CONCLUSION

Around the time of Easter every year, various magazines and talk shows focus on the person of Jesus. I listened in dismay to one radio program in March, 2002, where three scholars (two of whom claimed to be Christian) agreed that it did not really matter if Jesus rose from the dead. To them if the "spirit" of Christ (meaning his character and his attributes) lives in our hearts, a physical resurrection is unnecessary.

Yet Jesus invited the disciples to touch and confirm the reality of his living, physical, resurrected body (Luke 24:37-39; John 20:27). The apostle Paul makes it clear that the resurrection of Christ stands at the heart of Christian doctrine. He goes so far as to pin our entire faith on the truth of the resurrection: "And if Christ has not been raised, our preaching is useless and so is your faith" (1 Corinthians 15:14).

Regardless of what false teachers today might say, it matters greatly whether Christ rose from the dead. If he is still in the grave, then we are still in our sins. Paul associates the resurrection with our justification (Romans 4:24, 25), with our baptism (Romans 6:4; Colossians 2:12), and with our own expectation of resurrection and eternal life (1 Thessalonians 4:14). Christ's resurrection is the centerpiece of Christianity. We can have confidence in Matthew and the other Gospel writers when they tell us what they saw: Jesus Christ is risen indeed!

Discovery Learning

This page contains an alternative lesson plan emphasizing learning activities. Classes desiring such student involvement will find these suggestions helpful. The next page is a reproducible activity page to further enhance discovery learning.

LEARNING GOALS

After this lesson each student will be able to:

1. List the aspects of Matthew's resurrection account that support the reality of the resurrection.

2. Explain why a literal bodily resurrection of Jesus is believable and, in fact, vital.

3. State at least one benefit he or she enjoys because Jesus rose from the dead.

INTO THE LESSON

Ask the learners how families and churches annually celebrate Jesus' resurrection. Are there special services? Certain songs? Do families have special traditions? Are certain foods eaten at the Sunday dinner? Do these traditions place the focus appropriately? What traditions have class members observed that they believe best help people remember and celebrate the resurrection?

INTO THE WORD

Provide the following information as background: Jesus had clearly predicted his resurrection (Matthew 20:19; Mark 8:31; 10:34; Luke 18:33). The chief priests seemed to have understood him, for they cited his predictions as the reason to provide a guard for the tomb (Matthew 27:62-66). They simply rejected his teaching, calling him a "deceiver" and suggesting that his followers might try to steal the body. The disciples still did not understand this, even when they were confronted with the empty tomb (John 20:9).

Use the reproducible activity from the next page as you lead the class to consider the different responses from people as they were confronted by the empty tomb. Read each of the following passages and describe the reactions of each to this news. The Women—Matthew 28:8. *(They were afraid, yet filled with joy.)* The Disciples— John 20:3-9, 24-29. *(Disbelief, confusion, awakening belief, and doubt, that disappeared only after meeting with the risen Christ.)* The Chief Priests—Matthew 28:11-14. *(They rejected the possibility of the resurrection, deceitfully devised a cover story to mislead others, and bribed the soldiers to lie.)* The Guards—Matthew 28:15. *(Accepted bribe money to keep quiet, possibly out of fear for their own lives because they had failed in their duty, at least from their perspective.)*

Discuss what evidence you would present to members of each of these groups to confirm that Jesus truly had risen from the dead.

At times adults study the Bible looking so intently for details and new information that they overlook the power and simplicity of the biblical story. The following activity can rehearse the simple story, as well as give ideas to parents for sharing the story with their families. Gather as many of the following objects as you can: a silver coin, a thorny branch (rose stem), a large spike, a strip of linen/cotton cloth, a round flat rock, a jar of spices, an empty/full Dawn™ bottle, a plastic or paper snowflake, a small angel figurine, a map of Galilee, a watch, a large play money bill, and a small sealed but empty box. Either display all the objects at one time, or show one at a time, and ask the class to identify the item's relationship to the resurrection events as presented by Matthew and the other Gospel writers.

INTO LIFE

Challenge each to share this story with at least one person this week, maybe by telling about the activity done in class. Parents could find and use a selection of the objects, and go through the story as a family by showing one each night at bedtime, reading the corresponding Scripture, discussing what happened, and expressing their thanks to God for these events.

Finish class by praying together. Explain the traditional Christian greeting in which one says, "He is risen!" and the class responds in unison by saying, "He is risen indeed!" Instruct them that as you pray, whenever you say, "He is risen," that they should affirm their belief in this truth by saying together the response, "He is risen indeed!" Then pray aloud, looking at the past, the present, and the future. (Past—gratitude for the truth of the story that Jesus died in our place, paid the penalty for our sins, and then rose victoriously from the dead. Present—we serve a Savior who lives, and he currently serves as our high priest, interceding for us and opening the way for us to come into the Father's presence in prayer, Hebrews 4:14-16. Future—the resurrection of Jesus is the foundation of our hope that life goes beyond the grave, the dead in Christ will rise, and we can look forward to the return of Jesus and an eternity with him; 1 Corinthians 15:12-26; 1 Thessalonians 4:13-18.) As you conclude each section of your prayer, echo the phrase, "He is risen!" with " He is risen indeed!" Remind all that this fact is our hope, and hope is the true difference between believers and non-believers!

Resurrection Reactions

Jesus had clearly predicted his resurrection (Matthew 20:19; Mark 8:31; 10:34; Luke 18:33). The chief priests seemed to have understood him, for they cited his predictions as the reason to provide a guard for the tomb (Matthew 27:62-66). The disciples, on the other hand, still seemed to be confused about this element of Jesus' teaching (see John 20:9).

Read the Scripture(s) by each individual or group below, and then write what each might have said. Use the dialogue balloons.

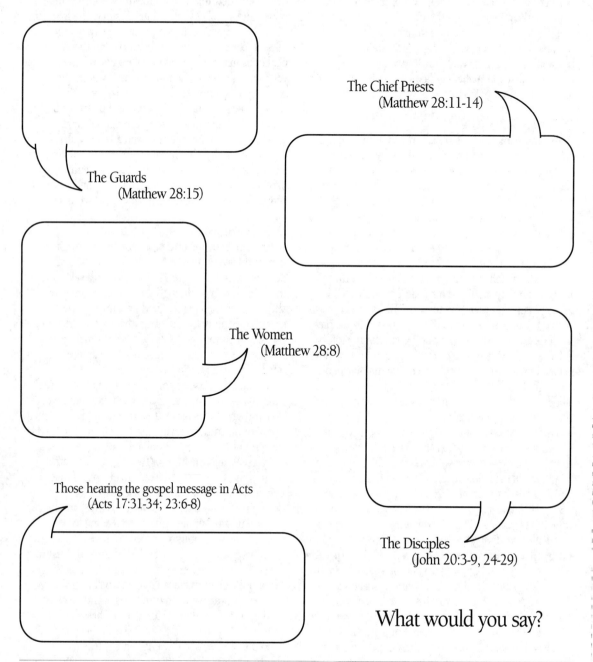

The Chief Priests
(Matthew 28:11-14)

The Guards
(Matthew 28:15)

The Women
(Matthew 28:8)

Those hearing the gospel message in Acts
(Acts 17:31-34; 23:6-8)

The Disciples
(John 20:3-9, 24-29)

What would you say?

Living Expectantly

Unit 1: Preparing for the Lord's Return
(Lessons 7-9)

FAITHFUL IN HIS SERVICE

LESSON 7

WHY TEACH THIS LESSON?

Lesson 3 of this quarter sketched for us a picture of loneliness, isolation, and solitude; today's lesson returns us to that theme. The Thessalonian Christians—who were little more than "babes in Christ"—had been left alone when the apostle Paul had to make a hasty departure. In their isolation, what were they to do?

Christians today may ask themselves the same question. A Christian may find himself or herself to be a "minority of one" in a secular workplace that is saturated with vulgarity and unseemly office politics. A teenager who wants to be baptized may have ungodly parents who refuse permission. Today's lesson will help us all to bear up and advance the kingdom of God as it reminds us that with the Holy Spirit in our hearts and the Word of God in our hands we are never truly alone in our struggles.

INTRODUCTION

A. FEELING ABANDONED

My mother told me that she would be back in just a few minutes. I was to wait quietly by the shopping carts while she went to the service desk to correct a cashier's mistake. She walked around to the other side of a cubicle and out of sight of her five-year-old son.

I knew my mother's instructions: wait quietly. I also knew that she would never abandon me. Certainly she was not away from me more than the few minutes that she promised. But those minutes felt like hours to a child who could not see his mother. I began to cry.

Soon a clerk came along and brought my mother to me. As I saw her reappear I realized that my fears were unfounded. I had never been left alone.

B. LESSON BACKGROUND

Before receiving 1 Thessalonians, the readers probably felt like they had been left alone. They had faced the hardships of rejection by friends and family who did not accept their new faith (cf. 1 Thessalonians 2:14). Some may have faced economic hardships when those suspicious of the new religion took their business elsewhere. Government officials also may have questioned their loyalty to the local gods or the emperor.

Adding to the distress was the fact that the founder of the new Thessalonian church, the apostle Paul, had been forced to leave town suddenly (Acts 17:5-10). Paul's hasty departure under cover of darkness undoubtedly made some people wonder whether he was just another fast-talking, fast-moving religious con man —a figure just as common in the Roman Empire as in this age of cable television.

Paul devotes much of the first three chapters of 1 Thessalonians to assuring those Christians that neither God nor he had abandoned them. He urges them to look beyond the negative circumstances to see the signs of God's presence with them. Their faithfulness to the gospel has been matched at every step by God's power at work in their lives. In the end, Christ's return will show that God has been in control at every step and that he has been faithful to his faithful people.

DEVOTIONAL READING:
1 THESSALONIANS 2:13-20

BACKGROUND SCRIPTURE:
1 THESSALONIANS 1-3

PRINTED TEXT:
1 THESSALONIANS 1:2-10; 3:6-10

LESSON AIMS

After participating in this lesson, each student will be able to:

1. Summarize Paul's commendation of the Thessalonian Christians for their active, faithful service despite difficulties.

Apr 18

2. Tell how faithfulness in serving God leads to victory over one's own difficulties and encourages others to be faithful as well.

3. Identify one specific way in which to serve actively and faithfully despite difficulties.

KEY VERSES

We always thank God for all of you, mentioning you in our prayers. We continually remember before our God and Father your work produced by faith, your labor prompted by love, and your endurance inspired by hope in our Lord Jesus Christ.
—1 Thessalonians 1:2, 3

LESSON 7 NOTES

I. ACTIVE FAITH (1 THESSALONIANS 1:2-10)

Paul's letters, like many other letters written in his day, generally begin with a statement of thanksgiving to the deity for blessings received. The deity to Paul is, of course, the one true God. In 1 Thessalonians 1, Paul uses this thanksgiving to announce a major message of his letter: the authenticity of the Thessalonians' faith is linked to the spread of the gospel. The gospel has not only spread *to* the Thessalonians, but *from* them.

A. PAUL'S PRAYER (vv. 2, 3)

2. We always thank God for all of you, mentioning you in our prayers.

Paul begins many of his letters by mentioning his *prayers* of thanks for the people to whom he writes. Whatever else Paul has to say to the Thessalonians, prayer comes first! And the word *we* shows us that he is not alone in his prayers —Silas and Timothy are with him in prayer (1:1). Prayer is at the center of Paul's life.

3. We continually remember before our God and Father your work produced by faith, your labor prompted by love, and your endurance inspired by hope in our Lord Jesus Christ.

Paul now explains exactly what he gives thanks for. Christians are accustomed to thinking of *faith*, *hope*, and *love* because of 1 Corinthians 13:13. However, this trio appears in many other passages as well. (See Romans 5:1-5; Galatians 5:5, 6; Ephesians 4:2-5; Colossians 1:4, 5; 1 Thessalonians 5:8; Hebrews 6:10-12; and 1 Peter 1:21, 22.)

Paul is giving thanks for more than just "armchair virtue." Faith, love, and hope provoke constant activity, like Paul's constant prayer. Elsewhere Paul sharply distinguishes faith and works to stress that salvation is not earned by what we do, but is given freely by God to those with faith in Christ. Here he stresses the other side of the faith equation: real faith always produces real works (cf. Ephesians 2:8-10; James 2:26).

Labor of love builds on the *work* of faith. Paul has in mind the way that Christians, prompted by God's love, put love into action by sacrificing time, energy, and money for others. Genuine love is more than saying, "You were always on my mind." Like genuine faith, it produces action.

In the New Testament, hope is more than just an optimistic wish for the future, as in "I hope that the weather gets better soon." Rather, hope expresses a confident expectation about the future, based on trust in God's promises. Paul connects hope to patience, meaning steadfastness or *endurance* (2 Thessalonians 1:4). Our confidence that God always delivers his people makes any problem something that we can endure.

SUPER MOVERS

The coastline near the Cape Hatteras lighthouse had been battered by the sea relentlessly. The survival of the lighthouse was threatened, so it was moved in 1999 to a safer site some twenty-nine hundred feet inland. For Jerry Matyiko, president of Expert House Movers in Sharptown, Maryland, moving the multi-million-pound tower was just another day's work (sort of). On July 9, 1999, he and his workers completed the move that took just twenty-three days.

Matyiko's company is one of just six such "super movers" worldwide. Another moved Howard Hughes's "Spruce Goose," one of the largest airplanes ever built, by barge to McMinnville, Oregon, from Long Beach, California. Yet another company moved a two-hundred-ton autoclave—twenty feet in diameter and nearly as long as a football field—eight hundred miles from an aircraft factory in Los Angeles to a military base in Ogden, Utah.

WHAT DO YOU THINK?

Paul constantly prayed for his new converts. Why is it important that we do the same? What methods can we use?

WHAT DO YOU THINK?

Discuss some specific ways that we can move from "armchair virtue" to real virtue. What "works" will show our faith, and what "labors" will show our love?

These "super movers" share a common faith in their very specialized equipment, love for their work, and an abundance of patience. In a sense, their job is an example of what we Christians are called to be: super movers! With faith in the moral and spiritual "equipment" God has given us—with love for our task of being God's reconciling agents to the world, patient assurance in God's calling, and reliance on prayer—we count ourselves to be "super movers" to accomplish, through his power, the movement of his will in human affairs (Matthew 17:20). May it be so until the Lord returns! —C. R. B.

B. THESSALONIANS' STATUS (vv. 4, 5)

4. For we know, brothers loved by God, that he has chosen you,

As he gives thanks for their faithfulness, Paul assures his readers that, by receiving the gospel, they have genuinely become God's people. Not only are they now Paul's *brothers*, they are beloved. They are the objects of God's favor, like Old Testament Israel (e.g., Psalms 60:5; 108:6).

Election or being *chosen* by God, for its part, is a concept that has incited much doctrinal controversy! When placed alongside other Scriptures such as Acts 10:43 and Ephesians 1:4, 5, our best interpretation is that all who respond with genuine faith to the gospel and its plan of salvation are the chosen people of God. God's "elect" do not believe because they were chosen; rather, they are chosen because they believe. God has foreknown our belief from eternity past. That's how he can decide in advance who will be in Heaven, and who won't.

5. . . . because our gospel came to you not simply with words, but also with power, with the Holy Spirit and with deep conviction. You know how we lived among you for your sake.

Paul now summarizes the evidence that the Thessalonian Christians are among God's chosen. They could easily have believed a false religious message. Their world was full of competing religions and philosophies, and not all of them could be true. But Paul reminds the Thessalonians that, by believing the gospel, they received something else: the *power* that comes only from God's *Spirit*.

Perhaps Paul also is referring to miracles that he performed in Thessalonica when he mentions power. Although Acts 17:1-10 does not speak of any miracles in Thessalonica, Paul's ministry is commonly marked by visible demonstrations of God's power (Romans 15:18, 19). Those miracles were not ends in themselves. Rather, they are visible signs of something even greater: the eternal salvation that God was working invisibly through the gospel of Christ.

The same *Holy Spirit* who enabled Paul to do these acts of power now is living in the Thessalonian Christians. Although they should not necessarily expect to do miracles as the apostle did, the same Holy Spirit power works in them to make their lives consistent with the gospel. When Christians look carefully, they will see the same evidence of the Spirit's power that Paul had: living the new life that God intended, the life that produces the fruit of the Spirit (Galatians 5:22, 23).

The fact that Paul's preaching has come to the Thessalonians in much assurance is probably his way of speaking of his own deep conviction. Paul is not the kind of preacher who is all *words* and no deeds. He has shown himself to be utterly sincere and completely sold out for Jesus, and the Thessalonians can remember that. Paul's genuineness is another source of confidence that the gospel is for real.

C. THESSALONIANS' ACTIONS (vv. 6-10)

6. You became imitators of us and of the Lord; in spite of severe suffering, you welcomed the message with the joy given by the Holy Spirit.

Your work of faith, and labor of love, and patience of hope

1 Thessalonians 1:3

Visual for lesson 7. *Use this series of images of Christians at work to illustrate today's Key Verses.*

Now Paul stresses how his readers are living out the gospel and fulfilling God's purpose in the world. Since he imitates Christ, Paul often urges Christians to imitate him (1 Corinthians 4:15, 16; 11:1; Ephesians 5:1; Philippians 3:17; 1 Thessalonians 2:14; 2 Thessalonians 3:7-9). Here he is especially stressing that the Thessalonian Christians have imitated him in accepting hardships that have come because of their faith.

The core of the gospel is Jesus' willing death on the cross in submission to God. Jesus' followers will face hardships that call for similar faithfulness (John 15:20). If we understand the cross, we realize that following Jesus will mean accepting hardship, daily carrying our own crosses (Luke 9:23, 24).

That life would sound bleak except for the important fact that despite *suffering*, the *Holy Spirit* brings *joy* to the Christian. If we can keep our eyes on the ultimate prize of eternal life, we, too, shall have this joy despite all temporary hardship.

7. And so you became a model to all the believers in Macedonia and Achaia.

As Paul has been *a model* of Christlikeness to the Thessalonians, so now they have become the same to others. *Macedonia* is the region of northern Greece in which Thessalonica is found. *Achaia* is the region of Greece just to the south of Macedonia that includes the important cities of Athens and Corinth. It is as if Paul is saying that the Thessalonians were known far and wide, in their own state and in the adjoining one. This really means something when we consider the rudimentary methods of communication available at the time.

IMITATING THE MASTER

While grade school kids played with yo-yos and teenagers were trying the Hula Hoop® in the 1950s, their parents were "painting by the numbers." It was a time when President Eisenhower and Winston Churchill were being celebrated as amateur painters. So in America, where the culture says anyone can aspire to greatness, why not imitate the President and the Prime Minister?

Not everyone has an eye for color, composition, and form, so painting by numbers was a help to many would-be artists. Strangely enough, the idea for this genre of pop art came from the great Leonardo da Vinci! He had left numbered sections of his paintings for his assistants to fill in. Centuries later, Dan Robbins and Max Klein of the Palmer Show Card Paint Company hit upon the idea that could make anyone an artist. So for the purchase price of two dollars and fifty cents, you, too, could imagine yourself to be assistant to one of the great Masters! Today, some of those 1950s paintings are on display in a museum (a nineteenth-century townhouse in Brooklyn) devoted to the genre.

Paul told the Thessalonian Christians they were doing the right thing in imitating him and Christ. In so doing, they were also providing others with an example of how to live. It is a principle that still works today: when we follow Christ, we make it easier for others to make their lives into works of art.   —C. R. B.

8. The Lord's message rang out from you not only in Macedonia and Achaia— your faith in God has become known everywhere. Therefore we do not need to say anything about it,

Now Paul draws the circle even more widely. The Thessalonian Christians may feel like a small, insignificant group of persecuted people, but from God's perspective they are powerful examples of what he wants us to be doing.

9. . . . for they themselves report what kind of reception you gave us. They tell how you turned to God from idols to serve the living and true God,

Paul now helps the Thessalonians understand the wider significance of their conversion to Christ. He does this by expressing his amazement that *they themselves*—meaning the inhabitants of places mentioned in verses 7, 8—are speak-

---

WHAT DO YOU THINK?

Paul notes how a seemingly insignificant people became powerful examples of faith to others. How have you been influenced by such people? How have you passed this influence on to others?

ing of the *reception* Paul enjoyed when he preached to the Thessalonians. The Thessalonians had received his message with enthusiastic faith that brought obvious change to their lives.

In turning to Jesus Christ, the Thessalonians renounced false gods to serve the *true God*. The Thessalonians' world is filled with idolatry. Every region has its own, local god. Even trade guilds and businesses have patron deities that they worship. Most people in Paul's day believe that if worshiping one god is good, then worshiping several is better.

The Scriptures, however, teach otherwise. There is only one true God. The pagan world is in rebellion against him. That rebellion is most obvious in the worship of *idols*. But the true God promises that ultimately he will make himself known to all the nations (Isaiah 2:2-4; 42:6; Micah 4:1-3; Zechariah 8:20-23).

This means that the Thessalonians' conversion is not just important to them personally. Through the spread of the gospel God is genuinely doing what he promised: he is making himself known to the nations in the end time. The Thessalonians may feel insignificant, but they are at the very center of God's work.

10. . . . and to wait for his Son from heaven, whom he raised from the dead—Jesus, who rescues us from the coming wrath.

Coming to know the true God means knowing him through *his Son*. The Thessalonians are not just converts to Judaism, as some in the Greco-Roman world had been. They now believe that the God of Israel has fulfilled his promises through *Jesus*, who entered into human history as a man, suffered death, and rose *from the dead*.

Jesus has indeed fulfilled God's promises. But as long as sin continues in the world, God's purpose is not complete. The gospel is turning the world around, but that turning will be complete only when Christ returns. Paul reminds these suffering Christians that they still look forward to God's final victory.

So where is Jesus now? Paul says that he will come *from heaven*. This means that right now Jesus is in the position of universal authority. Though he cannot be seen, Jesus rules over all the world from his heavenly position. His return will make his rule final, complete, and visible to all.

When he comes, Jesus will rescue the people of God from God's *wrath*. God's wrath can seem difficult to square with his love. How can God love the world and still have wrath? Sometimes we confuse the inconsistent, selfish anger that we see in humans with the holy wrath of God. If he is holy and just, he must abhor and punish sin. Otherwise, there would be no hope for justice in our unjust world. But how can God still love sinners and show mercy? The cross supplies the answer. In Jesus' death, God took on himself the punishment for our sin. In this way Jesus rescues his people from the wrath to come.

This has been God's purpose from the beginning: to reverse the effects of sin in the world, to crush the head of the tempter (Genesis 3:15). So by believing and faithfully living out the gospel, Christians share in the fulfillment of God's promises, even in hard times.

II. GROWING FAITH (1 THESSALONIANS 3:6-10)

In the verses between 1 Thessalonians 1:10 and 3:6 Paul recounts his labors among the Thessalonians and summarizes the circumstances that have kept him from returning. He stresses the example of his own faithfulness, the reality of hardship for God's people, and God's ongoing work in the midst of that hardship.

Recent events help Paul make his point. Concerned for the welfare of the Thessalonian church, Paul sent Timothy to visit those Christians. Timothy has now returned to Paul with an encouraging report (Acts 18:5).

HOW TO SAY IT

Achaia. Uh-KAY-uh.
Athens. ATH-unz.
Colossians. Kuh-LOSH-unz.
Corinth. KOR-inth.
Corinthians. Kor-IN-thee-unz.
Ephesians. Ee-FEE-zhunz.
Galatians. Guh-LAY-shunz.
Leonardo da Vinci. Lee-uh-NARD-oh duh VIN-chee.
Macedonia. Mass-eh-DOE-nee-uh.
Matyiko. Mah-TIE-eh-koh.
Silas. SIGH-luss.
Thessalonians. THESS-uh-LO-nee-unz.
Thessalonica. THESS-uh-lo-NYE-kuh (TH as in THIN).
Zechariah. ZEK-uh-RYE-uh.

DAILY BIBLE READINGS

Monday, Apr. 12—Paul Remembers Thessalonians' Faith (1 Thessalonians 1:1-5)

Tuesday, Apr. 13—You Have Become an Example (1 Thessalonians 1:6-10)

Wednesday, Apr. 14—Paul's Coming Was Not in Vain (1 Thessalonians 2:1-8)

Thursday, Apr. 15—You Received God's Word (1 Thessalonians 2:9-13)

Friday, Apr. 16—You Have Suffered for Christ (1 Thessalonians 2:14-20)

Saturday, Apr. 17—Timothy Sent by Paul to Encourage (1 Thessalonians 3:1-5)

Sunday, Apr. 18—Timothy Brings Back Good News (1 Thessalonians 3:6-13)

A. TIMOTHY'S REPORT (v. 6)

6. But Timothy has just now come to us from you and has brought good news about your faith and love. He has told us that you always have pleasant memories of us and that you long to see us, just as we also long to see you.

Timothy's report is specific: the Thessalonians continue in the *faith and love* that Paul commended in 1 Thessalonians 1:3. This is indeed *good news!*

As an example of that love, Paul mentions that the Thessalonians continue to remember him fondly. Despite his hasty departure from their city, the Thessalonians continue to regard Paul as God's ambassador. In fact, they look forward to renewing their fellowship when they are reunited, as Paul does also. Those who have experienced Jesus' love—love that binds people together despite differences and distances—can understand that the love of which Paul speaks comes only from the work of God himself.

B. PAUL'S ENCOURAGEMENT (vv. 7-9)

7. Therefore, brothers, in all our distress and persecution we were encouraged about you because of your faith.

Previously Paul had been concerned about the Thessalonians. He felt the burden of separation from them as much as they did from him. Elsewhere Paul speaks of the burden that he felt for all the churches (2 Corinthians 11:28), a burden of concern for their growth and welfare. Timothy's visit had *encouraged* the Thessalonians, and now Timothy's report encourages Paul.

8. For now we really live, since you are standing firm in the Lord.

Paul's language here seems extreme, but in fact it is very reasonable. His burden of concern is like death to him, so receiving a good report about the Thessalonians is like new life. Now that he knows of their faithfulness, he counts his joy as an example of the new life that Christians have (2 Corinthians 4:10-18). That joy will grow as the his readers continue steadfastly in faithfulness.

9. How can we thank God enough for you in return for all the joy we have in the presence of our God because of you?

God's grace is always so great that his people can never repay it. Paul reflects on that truth now as he thinks of his *joy* because of the Thessalonians' faithfulness. The people of God know that the greatest joy is seeing God at work in his people. For Paul this joy is almost like the joy of Heaven!

C. PAUL'S LONGING (v. 10)

10. Night and day we pray most earnestly that we may see you again and supply what is lacking in your faith.

Christians naturally feel a "holy restlessness" to be reunited when separated from their spiritual family. The great reunion is in Heaven, of course, but God gives us a foretaste of that reunion whenever we gather as his people.

Although the Thessalonians have been faithful, they have not "arrived." True Christians are always growing Christians, and Paul wants to contribute to the Thessalonians' growth—to perfect their faith. Do you think you have "arrived" in your Christian life, or do you admit that you have growing to do as well?

CONCLUSION

In a world where sin seems to hold sway, God's people can feel lonely and discouraged. But the eye of faith sees more than just outward appearances. It sees God's work going forward in the lives of God's people. It sees past disappointments, and recognizes the victories. It looks forward to the final victory. Seeing those things, it yields a life of faithful service: faith, love, and hope put into action.

Discovery Learning

This page contains an alternative lesson plan emphasizing learning activities. Classes desiring such student involvement will find these suggestions helpful. The next page is a reproducible activity page to further enhance discovery learning.

LEARNING GOALS

After participating in this lesson, each student will be able to:

1. Summarize Paul's commendation of the Thessalonian Christians for their active, faithful service despite difficulties.

2. Tell how faithfulness in serving God leads to victory over one's own difficulties and encourages others to be faithful as well.

3. Identify one specific way in which he or she will serve actively and faithfully despite difficulties.

INTO THE LESSON

Choice One: Neighbor Nudge. Ask class members to turn to a persons next to them and describe difficulties that prevent them from serving Christ actively and faithfully. Encourage them to give actual situations. What kinds of situations discourage them? What fears hinder them from serving actively and faithfully?

Allow about five minutes for this activity. After about two minutes, say, "If your partner has not started to share yet, wrap it up quickly and let him or her begin."

Call for three volunteers to share their difficulties with the entire class. After they share, make the transition to the lesson by saying, "All of us have difficulties that discourage us from serving Christ actively and faithfully. Let's keep these problems in mind as we look at today's text and watch for answers to our difficulties." (This activity is also included in the student book.)

Choice Two: Brainstorm. Ask the class to compile a list of difficulties that hinder Christians today from actively and faithfully serving Christ. Encourage the creation of as long a list as possible. Ask people to call out difficulties quickly. Ask members not to comment on or evaluate items during the listing process. Make a list so that the entire class can see it. Use an overhead projector, marker board, or piece of paper taped to the wall.

After you have a long list, read one entry at a time. Ask class members to raise their hands when you read a topic that is especially difficult for them. Put stars in front of the difficulties that elicit many hands.

Make the transition to the lesson by saying, "All of us have difficulties that discourage us from serving Christ actively and faithfully. Let's keep these problems in mind as we look at today's text and watch for answers to our difficulties."

INTO THE WORD

Choice One: Marginal Markings. Have someone read aloud 1 Thessalonians 1:2-10; 3:6-10. Then distribute copies of the reproducible activity page that follows. Ask learners to put marks in the margin of the texts on the activity sheet, placing one of these symbols by each verse:

C—Something for which Paul commended the Thessalonians.

?—I have a question about what this verse means.

E—This verse has encouragement for me and others.

Then ask which verses were marked with question marks; take time to talk about answers to those questions. Discuss the verses that received the other marks.

Choice Two: Praise List. Ask each class member to make a list of the things for which Paul commended the Thessalonians. For example, he commended them for their work of faith, labor prompted by love and endurance inspired by hope in 1 Thessalonians 1:3. He says they had imitated him and the Lord (v. 6). He said they had been models of service in the face of difficulties (v. 7). Learners should be able to find something in almost every verse. (This activity is also included in the student book.)

INTO LIFE

Choice One: Prayer of Thanks. Ask your class members to write a prayer for a young Christian based on how Paul prayed for the Thessalonians. Or they might paraphrase today's text and make it a prayer. For example, "Dear God, I am always thanking you for Charles, mentioning him by name in all my prayers. I thank you for his work produced by faith, his labor prompted by love, and his endurance inspired by hope in our Lord Jesus Christ."

Choice Two: Hymn Study. Many songs and hymns encourage believers to be faithful in the face of difficulties. Ask each learner to study a hymn or song and compare it with the encouragement Paul gives in today's text. For example, "His Eye Is on the Sparrow" (by Civilla D. Martin) says the believer can sing because he or she is happy. This is like 1 Thessalonians 1:6, where Paul says we can have joy given by the Holy Spirit in spite of severe suffering. Or verse 2 from "God Will Take Care of You" (also by Civilla D. Martin) says, "Beneath his wings of love abide." This parallels 1 Thessalonians 1:4, where Paul says we are loved by God.

Marginal Markings

Put one of the following symbols beside each verse:
C   Something for which Paul commended the Thessalonians.
?   A question about what this verse means.
E   A verse with a source of encouragement

1 THESSALONIANS 1:2-10

2 We always thank God for all of you, mentioning you in our prayers.

3 We continually remember before our God and Father your work produced by faith, your labor prompted by love, and your endurance inspired by hope in our Lord Jesus Christ.

4 For we know, brothers loved by God, that he has chosen you,

5 because our gospel came to you not simply with words, but also with power, with the Holy Spirit and with deep conviction. You know how we lived among you for your sake.

6 You became imitators of us and of the Lord; in spite of severe suffering, you welcomed the message with the joy given by the Holy Spirit.

7 And so you became a model to all the believers in Macedonia and Achaia.

8 The Lord's message rang out from you not only in Macedonia and Achaia—your faith in God has become known everywhere. Therefore we do not need to say anything about it,

9 for they themselves report what kind of reception you gave us. They tell how you turned to God from idols to serve the living and true God,

10 and to wait for his Son from heaven, whom he raised from the dead—Jesus, who rescues us from the coming wrath.

1 THESSALONIANS 3:6-10

6 But Timothy has just now come to us from you and has brought good news about your faith and love. He has told us that you always have pleasant memories of us and that you long to see us, just as we also long to see you.

7 Therefore, brothers, in all our distress and persecution we were encouraged about you because of your faith.

8 For now we really live, since you are standing firm in the Lord.

9 How can we thank God enough for you in return for all the joy we have in the presence of our God because of you?

10 Night and day we pray most earnestly that we may see you again and supply what is lacking in your faith.

READY FOR HIS RETURN

LESSON 8

WHY TEACH THIS LESSON?

Several years ago, I found myself caught in the middle of someone else's family reunion. I was sitting near a gate inside an airport, minding my own business. A plane had just landed, and when the door to the jetway opened, people from the plane and people in the terminal rushed to greet each other. The arrangement of the seating in that waiting area was such that I found myself right at the center of the action! I had a front-row seat to witness the joy of the reunion.

But it wasn't my reunion, so the joy was not mine personally. That will not be the case when Christ returns. At that great event, our shared joy with millions we have never met will truly be our reunion.

In the meantime we must learn how to live in such a way as to be ready for that event. That is the purpose of today's lesson.

INTRODUCTION

A. TWO VIEWS OF DEATH

Cemeteries tell stories. In some cultures, people were buried with important objects from their lives. In America of a bygone era, gravestones often listed the relatives and accomplishments of the deceased. Today the practices may be different, but the messages persist. To one gravestone mourners attach a deck of cards, a bottle of whiskey, and a pack of cigarettes—mementos of a life of hopeless indulgence. Beside it stands another marker with the simple inscription, "In hope of the resurrection of the dead."

How we look at death determines how we look at life. If death is the end of our existence, then at best life is, as one writer put it, "the unpleasant interruption of nothingness."

But the Bible teaches something different. God is faithful to his people even in death. Death for the Christian is not the end. It means being with Christ in an even greater way than we have been in this life. And at Christ's return, all of his people, those who have died and those who are still alive, will be reunited. The sting of death is gone!

B. LESSON BACKGROUND

Acts 17:1-10 tells us that Paul was forced to leave Thessalonica because of persecution. As a result he did not have the time to instruct the church thoroughly in the gospel's implications. It appears that after Paul left, some in the church were troubled by the ongoing reality of death. Perhaps the death of some member of the church prompted a crisis of faith for those who remained. What would happen to a Christian who died? How would God fulfill his promises to a person if that person were no longer alive?

Likewise, it appears that the Thessalonian Christians struggled to understand Christ's return. Those who knew the Old Testament understood its promise of a Messiah. Christians understood that Jesus is that Messiah. But the idea that the Messiah would ascend to Heaven and return a second time was new. What did this mean for his people on earth? What could it mean for those who had died?

DEVOTIONAL READING:
1 THESSALONIANS 5:12-24

BACKGROUND SCRIPTURE:
1 THESSALONIANS 4, 5

PRINTED TEXT:
1 THESSALONIANS 4:13-18; 5:2-11

LESSON AIMS

After participating in this lesson, each student will be able to:

1. Tell what Paul said about Christ's return and how Christians ought to live in anticipation of it.

2. Explain how hope in Christ's return brings comfort, even when loved ones die before that event.

Apr
25

3. Evaluate his or her feelings about the Lord's return and express them verbally or artistically.

KEY VERSE

For God did not appoint us to suffer wrath but to receive salvation through our Lord Jesus Christ. —1 Thessalonians 5:9

These are the kinds of questions that Paul addresses in this passage. Properly understood, the promise of the Lord's return radically changes our idea of life and death.

I. REUNION AT CHRIST'S RETURN (1 THESSALONIANS 4:13-18)

The foundation of the New Testament's teaching on Christ's return is God's faithfulness. As things stand, sin and evil are still rampant in the world. Will God abandon his people to this situation? God answers this question with an unqualified no. When Jesus returns, he will bring the final defeat of evil. He will reverse the effects of sin, including death. All of his people, living and dead, will be reunited with him and will remain with him forever.

A. ASSURANCE OF GOD'S PROMISE (vv. 13, 14)

13. Brothers, we do not want you to be ignorant about those who fall asleep, or to grieve like the rest of men, who have no hope.

In Paul's day it is common to refer to death politely as sleep (cf. John 11:11-14; Acts 7:60; 13:36). This figure of speech is suggested by the similarity in appearance between sleeping people and dead bodies. It does not imply that the dead have no consciousness beyond the grave, what some call "soul sleep." Paul will make that clear in verse 14 and in other passages (2 Corinthians 5:1-10; Philippians 1:20-23).

Paul's remark about grief must be carefully understood. He does not criticize the Thessalonian Christians for the natural sadness that they feel over the death of fellow Christians (cf. Philippians 2:27). Rather, their grief is not to be like that of the pagans, *who have no hope* of ever seeing their deceased loved ones again. A Christian's grief is tempered by the assurance that God will reunite them.

14. We believe that Jesus died and rose again and so we believe that God will bring with Jesus those who have fallen asleep in him.

The foundation of this hope is Jesus' own resurrection. By raising *Jesus* from the dead, *God* began to fulfill his promise to raise his people from the dead as well (Isaiah 26:16-19). Jesus' resurrection therefore can be seen as guarantee that God will complete his promise by raising all his people (1 Corinthians 15:20-23).

Furthermore, Paul says, Christ's resurrection means the defeat of death. It gives us the assurance that he will bring the dead in Christ with him when he returns. Christians who die are with Christ in Heaven and will continue to be with him when he returns.

WHAT DO YOU THINK?

What inspirational sayings or epitaphs have you read in cemeteries? What would you want on your tombstone as a testimony to your faith? Explain.

WHAT DO YOU THINK?

If Christians have such a wonderful after-death hope, why is it most of us don't want to die? And why do we so often cry at funerals? How do we balance grief with hope?

REUNIONS

Every year since 1947, the "Doolittle Raiders" have met to remember their comrades who died in an April, 1942, air raid on Japan that was America's first hopeful news since Pearl Harbor. Lieutenant Colonel Jimmy Doolittle had led sixteen B-25 bombers in a response ordered by President Roosevelt to show America's resolve to win a war it didn't want to fight.

A carrier take-off in B-25s had never been done in battle; it was impossible to land them back on the carrier. The pilots hoped they could fly on to China, but they suspected they might not make it that far. Jacob DeShazer was one of the crew members who had to bail out over Japan.

DeShazer later said that as interrogation, torture, and the executions of his comrades were causing him to lose hope, his captors gave him a Bible. He relates how the Bible's message of salvation caused him to "feel free and ready to die or to do whatever God wants me to do." His hope in Christ carried him through more than three years in prison camp. After the war was over, he soon returned to Japan as a missionary to share the hope he had experienced!

The number who attend the annual gatherings of these aged comrades-in-arms is shrinking every year. But DeShazer knows a greater reunion is ahead of him. That is the kind of hope Paul was trying to get us to experience—a hope that is assured in its outcome because of our faith in Christ.   —C. R. B.

B. PARTICULARS OF CHRIST'S RETURN (vv. 15-17a)

15. According to the Lord's own word, we tell you that we who are still alive, who are left till the coming of the Lord, will certainly not precede those who have fallen asleep.

Paul now begins to describe what Jesus' return will entail. His purpose here is not just to satisfy curiosity or to stimulate speculation. Rather, he aims to supply those details that will make a meaningful difference in the lives of his readers.

He begins by indicating that those who are *alive* when Christ returns will have no advantage over those who have died. This is probably not so much a statement of the chronology of events (which would matter little) as it is of the quality of events. Both the living and the dead in Christ will participate fully in the joy of his return.

16. For the Lord himself will come down from heaven, with a loud command, with the voice of the archangel and with the trumpet call of God, and the dead in Christ will rise first.

Shouts and *trumpet* blasts—what a celebration at Christ's return as *the voice of a mighty archangel* proclaims the victory! Christ's victory will be complete with the unfolding of this great event, and no one will be able to mistake it.

Again assuring his readers that all Christ's people will participate fully in his return, Paul stresses that the dead in Christ shall *rise first*. They will not miss out.

Of course, Paul had just spoken of Christ bringing the dead with him. So in what sense will they then *rise*? Many believe that the spirits of the faithful live without bodies in the presence of Christ until his return; at that time, their spirits come with Christ to take possession of their new bodies—bodies fit for the life of eternity. Others believe the dead have "spiritual bodies" until the time of Christ's return; at that time those bodies will be glorified in various degrees.

17a. After that, we who are still alive and are left will be caught up together with them in the clouds to meet the Lord in the air.

What a magnificent "reunion" this will be! *Caught up* implies a sudden, dramatic action. (The Latin translation here is *rapere* and is the basis for the expression "rapture.") *Clouds* sometimes appear in Scripture to depict the powerful presence of God (Exodus 13:21; Daniel 7:13; Acts 1:9). Meeting together in the clouds and *the air* suggests that God will gather people in the midst of his glorious presence, sharing in his victory.

A LONG-AWAITED RETURN

In a ceremony at the U.S. Customs House in July, 2001, fifteen million dollars' worth of artwork by Rembrandt and Dürer were returned to representatives of Germany's Bremen museum. The masterpieces had hung there for a century before being hidden during World War II. At the end of the war, Soviet troops took them as booty. The KGB then sent them to a museum in Azerbaijan.

Later, the art works were again stolen. Years passed, and somehow the paintings and drawings were smuggled into America. A former Olympic wrestler from Japan teamed up with a counterpart from Azerbaijan, and together they tried to sell the art to raise money for a kidney transplant. Finally, authorities tracked the art to a Brooklyn apartment in 1997. There it was recovered and the perpetrators arrested.

This string of incidents reminds us that when something of great value has been missing for a long time, there is still hope for its return. God's most valuable gift to

WHAT DO YOU THINK?

Many Christians seem to think the study of the end times is pointless. They say, "The subject is too hard," or, "God will work things out whether I understand them or not." How would you convince such a one that at least a basic understanding of the Bible's teaching on end times is necessary?

So shall we ever be with the Lord.
—1 Thessalonians 4:17

Visual for lesson 8. *Use this powerful visual to remind your learners that the "sunset" of earthly life will give way to the "sunrise" of eternal life.*

WHAT DO YOU THINK?

Does the unrelenting stream of Christian books and movies about "the end times" help or hinder our efforts to prepare people for the Lord's return?

WHAT DO YOU THINK?

Suppose someone came into your Sunday school class and claimed to have knowledge that Jesus would return on July 18 in the year 3198. What would be the danger in having such knowledge, even if it were true?

humanity—the one Person who has been the subject of more artistic works than any other in history—has been "missing" for twenty centuries. But Jesus left his followers with the promise that he would return. Paul informs us of some details of his return, but more importantly, Paul assures us of the fact of Jesus' return. We serve a God who keeps his word!   —C. R. B.

C. RESULTS OF GOD'S FAITHFULNESS (vv. 17b, 18)

17b. And so we will be with the Lord forever.

Paul now draws out the key implication of his description: God will not abandon his people. At Christ's return, God will reunite all his people fully in his presence. They will never be separated from him or from each other.

This teaching is not just a vague "whispering hope" that gives mild comfort. God's purpose in creation is to make for himself a people who will belong to him, living in fellowship with him and with each other for eternity. God will see his people through to that goal!

18. Therefore encourage each other with these words.

The passage has now turned full circle. Having begun with the objective that the readers not grieve hopelessly (v. 13), Paul now urges that they use this teaching to *encourage* and comfort one another. That encouragement and comfort will come from the assurance that death does not mean final separation from the fellow Christians whom we love, or any separation from the Lord who loves us.

What a comfort it is to serve such a God! As long as we do not drift away of our own accord (Hebrews 2:1-3), nothing can separate us from his love, not even death itself (Romans 8:38, 39). In the end, he will gather the multitude of his people (Revelation 21:3-4). He is with us "till we meet again . . . at Jesus' feet."

II. LIFE UNTIL CHRIST'S RETURN (1 THESSALONIANS 5:2-11)

The New Testament's teaching about Jesus' return revolves around two poles. One is that Jesus could return at any time. The other is that his return may take longer than his people expect or hope. Both of these ideas appear in the passage before us. Together, they urge Christians to live with expectancy and endurance.

A. EXPECTING THE UNEXPECTED (vv. 2, 3)

2. For you know very well that the day of the Lord will come like a thief in the night.

Paul has just stated that he has no need to teach the Thessalonians about "times and dates" (5:1). By this he does not mean that they know the time of the Lord's return or can figure it out (cf. Matthew 24:36). Paul's whole discussion insists that the time of Jesus' return is unknown. Rather, he is stressing that they should be able to understand that the times and dates call for alertness, a sense of urgency, and a readiness to remain faithful through difficulties.

Jesus himself compared his return with the coming of *a thief in the night* (Matthew 24:43; Luke 12:39; see also 2 Peter 3:10; Revelation 3:3; 16:15). Two observations should be made about this statement. First, his arrival will occur at a time that is unexpected. Some have understood the "thief" to arrive and depart secretly (as in the so-called "secret rapture"), but this is not the point of these texts.

Second, Jesus comes as a "thief" only for those who are unprepared. Jesus' return is a disaster only for those who do not believe in him and do not await him expectantly. Believers, ready for his return at any time, welcome him because he brings blessing. In Jesus' return, Christians have everything to look forward to and nothing to fear.

Paul refers to Jesus' return as *the day of the Lord.* This is an Old Testament expression that was used to refer to any action of God that brought great blessing or judgment (see Isaiah 13:6-16; Joel 1:15; Amos 5:18-20). Any such action can be "the day of the Lord," but the Scriptures anticipate a final "day"—God's final act of blessing and judgment. Jesus' return means God's final victory, the ultimate fulfillment of his purpose for creation.

3. While people are saying, "Peace and safety," destruction will come on them suddenly, as labor pains on a pregnant woman, and they will not escape.

Here we see the grave mistake of unbelievers who do not expect the day of the Lord. For them life seems to have *peace.* However, Paul teaches that real peace is available only through Christ (Romans 5:1; 1 Thessalonians 1:1; 5:23). So instead of *safety,* unbelievers face *destruction*—the complete ruin of their confidence and comfort—when Jesus returns.

Like *labor pains,* this event will happen suddenly and without the possibility of *escape.* In keeping with the context, we should not conclude that one can calculate in advance the approximate time of Jesus' return as an expectant mother can calculate the approximate time of her delivery. The comparison of Jesus' return to labor pains implies only that it is sudden and inescapable.

B. LIVING IN THE LIGHT (vv. 4-8)

4. But you, brothers, are not in darkness so that this day should surprise you like a thief.

Now Paul says openly what he has been implying. The fearful aspects of Jesus' return exist only for unbelievers. For believers, Jesus comes not as an unexpected *thief* who brings disaster, but as an expected deliverer bringing salvation.

Paul will now develop another aspect of his comparison. For unbelievers, Jesus comes as a thief in the night. Yet Christians are not people of the night but of the day. The contrast between a life in the *darkness* and a life in the light will make clear what it means to expect Jesus' return at any time.

5. You are all sons of the light and sons of the day. We do not belong to the night or to the darkness.

The Bible commonly associates *light* with God. God's first words in Scripture are "Let there be light" (Genesis 1:3). God's truth is often compared with light (Psalm 27:1; Proverbs 4:18, 19; Isaiah 9:2; Matthew 5:14; 1 John 2:8). In a figurative usage in the Bible, to be *sons* of something means to be characterized by that thing. So Christians are to be characterized by the light of God's truth.

The life of *darkness,* on the other hand, is a life centered on satisfying the self. In contrast to such a self-centered life, the gospel teaches a life of self-control and of being submissive to the will of God. The cross of Christ is one pillar of this new life: in the cross we see the horror of sin and the wonder of God's love. Another pillar is Jesus' return: he comes to bless his people and judge unbelievers. Supported by these pillars, who would want to have anything to do with the sin that God forgives through Jesus' death and judges at his return?

6, 7. So then, let us not be like others, who are asleep, but let us be alert and self-controlled. For those who sleep, sleep at night, and those who get drunk, get drunk at night.

Paul continues to expand on the comparisons that he has made earlier. People who do not reckon with Jesus' return are like those who *sleep* or *get drunk at night.* They are insensitive to and unconscious of spiritual truth. They are unresponsive to the stern reality of God's coming judgment.

8. But since we belong to the day, let us be self-controlled, putting on faith and love as a breastplate, and the hope of salvation as a helmet.

In contrast to those who live as if asleep or drunk, Christians are to live as faithful soldiers on sentry duty. They are alert, watchful, and prepared. In all matters

HOW TO SAY IT

Amos. AY-mus.

Azerbaijan. Ah-zer-bye-SHAHN.

Ephesians. Ee-FEE-zhunz.

Isaiah. Eye-ZAY-uh.

rapere (Latin). rap-EAR.

Thessalonians. THESS-uh-LO-nee-unz.

Thessalonica. THESS-uh-lo-NYE-kuh.

DAILY BIBLE READINGS

Monday, Apr. 19—Live to Please God (1 Thessalonians 4: 1-7)

Tuesday, Apr. 20—Live Quietly (1 Thessalonians 4:8-12)

Wednesday, Apr. 21—The Lord Will Return (1 Thessalonians 4:13-18)

Thursday, Apr. 22—He Will Come as a Thief (1 Thessalonians 5:1-5)

Friday, Apr. 23—Be Alert (1 Thessalonians 5:6-11)

Saturday, Apr. 24—Encourage the Faint-hearted (1 Thessalonians 5:12-18)

Sunday, Apr. 25—Prayer for Blamelessness at Christ's Coming (1 Thessalonians 5: 19-28)

Father, bring to our minds again the hope to which we have been called. Empower us to live in light of that hope! In Jesus' name, amen.

they are *self-controlled*. Such self-control comes only when a person submits in faith to the God who will bring judgment. Putting on the armor of God is how the submissive believer becomes self-controlled. Paul compares God's provision for the Christian with armor in Romans 13:12 and Ephesians 6:10-17 as well.

The means to godly self-control are the three great Christian virtues of *faith*, *love*, and *hope*. Faith directs the believer to submit to God's truth, confident that God is right in all that he says. Love directs us to act to benefit others rather than to indulge our selfish desires. Hope enables us to endure the hardships that faith and love entail, knowing that God will bring salvation in the future. *Hope of salvation* is not just a belief that we have "a chance" to be saved, but is a confident expectation that God will certainly fulfill his promise to save.

C. FULFILLING GOD'S PURPOSE (vv. 9-11)

9. For God did not appoint us to suffer wrath but to receive salvation through our Lord Jesus Christ.

God's holiness demands that he judge and punish sin. Even so, he does not delight in punishing sinners but seeks to forgive them. Yet such mercy cannot be taken for granted. It is awful to treat God's grace as something cheap by continuing to sin because of the promise of forgiveness. Rather, if sin makes God's *wrath* necessary, we must recoil from it. We must live according to the purpose for which God appointed us: not to be punished, but to be saved.

Likewise, we must understand the reality of God's judgment from the vantage of his gracious purpose to save. Final judgment is real, and the danger of "falling asleep" and being surprised by judgment like an unbeliever is also real. But God has given us every protection because he intends to save us, not judge us. We can therefore be confident, not anxious and worried.

10. He died for us so that, whether we are awake or asleep, we may live together with him.

When we speak of God's purpose, we should remember what he did to accomplish it. When Jesus died for us, he became a substitutionary sacrifice: he died in place of the people who deserved to die. If God will do that to save sinners, surely he will provide everything they need to come to the goal of their salvation!

Paul continues to speak of waking and sleeping here, but now he has returned to the comparison between death and sleep that he used in 1 Thessalonians 4:13-15. He repeats his earlier point that God will be faithful to his promise. Even death cannot keep him from saving his people and uniting them in his presence forever.

11. Therefore encourage one another and build each other up, just as in fact you are doing.

Just as he does in 4:18, Paul tells his readers to remind each other of the practical value of understanding Jesus' return. For the believer, it is a source of joy, encouragement, and motivation. It shows us what he created us for and how we need to live out his purpose in the world. So Paul tells us to use this message constantly with each other, so that God's saving purpose can be fulfilled in all of us.

CONCLUSION

As it is sometimes presented, Jesus' return can seem strange and fantastic, like science fiction. For many Christians, it seems frightening. When we really see what Paul says in this passage, we understand that it is neither. Jesus' return is the purposeful end of everything God has done, the climax of his program. For the believer it means the fulfillment of our fondest hopes and healing of our deepest hurts. It changes life from hopeless self-indulgence to hopeful, purposeful

Discovery Learning

This page contains an alternative lesson plan emphasizing learning activities. Classes desiring such student involvement will find these suggestions helpful. The next page is a reproducible activity page to further enhance discovery learning.

LEARNING GOALS

After participating in this lesson, each student will be able to:

1. Tell what Paul said about Christ's return and how Christians ought to live in anticipation of it.

2. Explain how hope in Christ's return brings comfort, even when loved ones die before that event.

3. Evaluate his or her feelings about the Lord's return and express them verbally or artistically.

INTO THE LESSON

Choice One: Agree/Disagree. Ask your class to respond to the following agree/disagree statements designed to encourage learners to express their understandings of, and their feelings toward, the return of Christ. Say, "I will read each statement and then count to three. On three, indicate your response by raising your right hand if you agree with the statement, or your left hand if you disagree." (This activity is included in the student booklet.)

1. The idea of Christ's return causes me to be afraid.

2. The Scriptures tell us the approximate time of the return of Christ.

3. When a Christian dies, his or her soul sleeps until Jesus comes again.

4. Signs will precede the return of Christ.

5. The concept of the return of Christ should cause people to be alert and ready.

6. Christians will be surprised at the return of Christ.

7. Anticipating the return of Christ is a source of encouragement and joy for me.

Choice Two: Write a Letter. Read the letter printed below to your class. Then ask, "How would you respond to Erica's questions?" Allow class members to give possible responses.

"Dear Friend, I am really confused about the second coming of Christ. Some books I have read are so dogmatic about details of the return of Christ. Is it possible to know when Jesus will return? What signs will precede the return of Christ so that Christians will be ready? What passages in the New Testament can I read to find answers? Please help. Your friend, Erica."

(This is included in the student booklet.)

Make a transition by saying, "Today's lesson text looks at the questions posed to Erica that we have been answering. As we study today's lesson, watch for other answers for Erica."

INTO THE WORD

Choice One: Bible Quiz. Have class members write a Bible quiz on today's text, trying to write a question for each verse. Assign this to be done in pairs, or have the whole class work together, as you write the questions for all to read.

A sample question from 1 Thessalonians 4:13: "True or False—Christians grieve at the death of a loved one just like anyone else." Or 1 Thessalonians 5:8 may suggest, "What three things should Christians do in anticipation of the second coming of Christ?"

Choice Two: Guest Speaker. Many congregations have a "resident expert" on the second coming. Ask your preacher or an elder to suggest a guest speaker. Your "expert" will enjoy the opportunity to expound on this oft-misunderstood topic; the class will enjoy hearing someone else. Be aware that this "expert" may present views that create disagreement in the class; you can use that for further discussion.

INTO LIFE

Choice One: Write a Letter. Ask class members to write a letter to "Erica" (see "Into the Lesson" above) and answer her questions from today's lesson. Provide paper and pens. Or have your class members write encouragement and joy to someone (such as a missionary, military personnel, or someone incarcerated), based on the text. Have addresses, envelopes, and postage ready.

Choice Two: Responsive Reading. Lead your class in a responsive reading, using ideas from today's text. Since Paul uses the phrase, "Encourage one another" twice in the text, you might want to use the phrase, "Encourage one another with these words," as a refrain after each verse in the style of Psalm 136. You might start with something like this:

"Brothers, we do not want you to be ignorant about those who fall asleep, or to grieve like the rest of men, who have no hope."

"Encourage one another with these words."

"We believe that Jesus died and rose again and so we believe that God will bring with Jesus those who have fallen asleep in him."

"Encourage one another with these words."

Continue on through 1 Thessalonians 4:13-17; 5:1-10. Suggest that every class member use these words this week.

The Second Coming

This chart compares the two images that Paul used in explaining the second coming of Christ. As you study the text, fill in the four columns of this chart by writing *yes* or *no* in each box.

Descriptions	Birth Pains	A Thief in the Night	Second Coming for Believers	Second Coming for Unbelievers
Anticipated and expected				
Anticipated with fear				
Anticipated with joy				
Sudden and decisive				
Exact time unknown				
Calls for alertness				
Calls for Preparation				
Avoidable				

Anti-Ignorance Facts

Paul wrote that he did not want us to be ignorant about the second coming of Christ. Make a list of facts about the second coming that every believer should know. Share your list with a friend.

REFLECTING HIS GLORY

WHY TEACH THIS LESSON?

Some mirrors tell the truth and some don't. My bathroom mirror, for example, always tells me the truth. It has never failed to provide me with an exact representation of my image—usually to my dismay! Other mirrors, however, are not nearly so accurate. For example, the curved mirror on the outside of my car door does not tell the truth. It never has and it never will. That's why its designers had to include the warning, "Objects in mirror are closer than they appear."

As God calls us to reflect his glory in our lives, which of these two mirrors are we most like? Do you know people who should be labeled with a warning, "This person is actually much closer to Christ than he or she appears to be"? Paul's challenge of two thousand years ago is still valid: God's glory is to be seen in the lives of people transformed in his image, people who are to live out their calling by his power. Today's lesson will help us to do just this.

INTRODUCTION

A. PRACTICE WHAT YOU PREACH

The story made the nightly news as one of those "would-you-believe-it?" segments at the end of the show. A jewelry company named "Love Your Neighbor" was suing a homeless charity called "Love Thy Neighbor" for trademark infringement. The similar names, said the jewelry company, confused customers. The company demanded that the charity pay monetary damages for lost sales and stop using the "trademarked" name.

We can laugh or shake our heads at such outrages. But we all know too many examples of people whose claim to godliness is contradicted by their actions.

B. LESSON BACKGROUND

Paul knew of such examples, too. As he wrote his second letter to the Thessalonians, he realized that these infant Christians were far from perfect. Yet he saw in them evidence of the Lord's work in their lives. They were the genuine article—not perfect people, but people whose lives gave glory to the Lord who had saved them.

After Paul's first letter to the Thessalonians, many things seemed to have become worse in their lives. They had faced persecution, but now it seemed to become more intense. Such experiences probably prompted some to doubt. If Christians were being persecuted, was God still faithful to them? Furthermore, some of the problems that Paul had addressed in his first letter were still continuing. In particular, some Christians who had been taking advantage of others' generosity still refused to work when they were able. Paul wrote 2 Thessalonians largely to correct these ongoing problems.

But a church with problems is not a failure. Whatever needed correcting in their beliefs and actions, the Thessalonian Christians were still showing the glory of God through lives transformed by the gospel. So Paul offers commendation to them and thanks to God for their lives, even as he prays that they (and he) will continue to glorify the Lord Jesus until he returns.

DEVOTIONAL READING:
EPHESIANS 1:3-14

BACKGROUND SCRIPTURE:
2 THESSALONIANS 1–3

PRINTED TEXT:
2 THESSALONIANS 1:3, 4, 11, 12;
2:13–3:4

LESSON AIMS

After participating in this lesson, each student will be able to:

1. Summarize Paul's description of how the Thessalonians would glorify God by living by and growing in their faith.

2. Tell why it is important for believers to reflect God's glory in the way that they live.

3. State one specific action he or she can take this week to reflect God's glory.

May
2

KEY VERSE

But we ought always to thank God for you, brothers loved by the Lord, because from the beginning God chose you to be saved through the sanctifying work of the Spirit and through belief in the truth.—2 Thessalonians 2:13

I. THANKSGIVING AND PRAYER (2 THESSALONIANS 1:3, 4, 11, 12)

A. FAITH FOR TRIALS (vv. 3, 4)

3. We ought always to thank God for you, brothers, and rightly so, because your faith is growing more and more, and the love every one of you has for each other is increasing.

In 1 Thessalonians 1:2, 3, Paul had commended the church for its active faith, love, and hope. Here he repeats his commendation of their *faith* and *love*. The measure of their growth in these two areas is impressive because it comes despite hardships that the church has faced. The church may have been discouraged by its struggles, but Paul sees its growth as all the more significant because of it. When we understand that the gospel begins with the message of the cross, we realize that God's work in our lives will take place in the midst of hardship rather than apart from it.

For all this, Paul believes that he *ought* to *thank God.* Giving thanks to God is not just something that Christians do when they feel like it. Those belonging to the body of Christ, who understand the cross of Christ, are obliged to thank God for his work in Christians' lives even when circumstances seem less than joyful.

4. Therefore, among God's churches we boast about your perseverance and faith in all the persecutions and trials you are enduring.

When Paul says he is boasting about the Thessalonians to other *churches,* this is not self-glorifying boasting, but God-glorifying boasting (see Romans 3:27; 2 Corinthians 10:17). Paul is sharing the good news that God's work is continuing among his people.

To do such boasting in the midst of suffering takes a keen eye of faith. Paul's eye of faith focuses on the Thessalonians' *perseverance,* an active quality that endures difficulty with firmness. He also commends their *faith*—not just the faith that they had when they first believed in Jesus, but their ongoing faith that has remained firm in *trials* that have come since. Real faith under trial always demonstrates staying power based on trust in God.

Suffering through *persecutions* from others along with various trials has become the soil in which the Thessalonians' faith has taken root. Such difficulties could have been a threat to their faith. Instead, suffering has made their faith grow stronger. Compared to their difficult circumstances, their faith stands out all the more! God is often best glorified in circumstances that seem most difficult.

The Thessalonians' suffering prompts Paul to remind them of something: God promises to punish those who refuse to repent of their opposition to him and his people (see 2 Thessalonians 1:5-10, not in today's text). But God's judgment is not his only response to his people's suffering. His other response is his promise to strengthen them. Paul counts on that promise as he explains his prayers for the Thessalonian Christians in verses 11, 12 (next).

WHAT DO YOU THINK?

Thinking about Paul's example, what obligation do we have to thank and praise our fellow Christians? How might their growth depend on our doing those two things?

DYING FOR ONE'S FAITH

Most Christians in Western Europe and North America really don't know much about persecution. We talk about being "persecuted" when an atheist tries to get prayer out of schools or sues to have a cross removed from a public square, or when a movie or TV show portrays Christians in a less-than-complimentary light.

It's a far different picture elsewhere in the world. The church was repressed for decades in Communist countries, sometimes with deadly violence. More recently the persecution has been in Muslim countries in Africa, Asia, and the Middle East. In the aftermath of America's response to Muslim terrorists, Christians' lives have been at risk in many nations that have a strong Islamic presence.

Take Pakistan, for example. In that country sixteen worshipers at a Catholic church died in gunfire on October 28, 2001. Five were killed at a Protestant service on March 17, 2002. On August 5, 2002, two Christians were murdered in an attack on a Christian school. Four days later, four nurses at a Christian hospital were killed as they left a prayer service. Ironically, most of their patients were poor Muslims.

This puts persecution in a different light! In Thessalonica as in threatening places today, true Christians respond with renewed faith and commitment to the Lord, who gave his life for them. How do you suppose Western Christians would respond if pressed in similar circumstances?   —C. R. B.

Visual for lesson 9. *Let this simple visual remind your learners that God is glorified even in our "small" services.*

B. PRAYER FOR CHRIST'S GLORY (vv. 11, 12)

11. With this in mind, we constantly pray for you, that our God may count you worthy of his calling, and that by his power he may fulfill every good purpose of yours and every act prompted by your faith.

Paul's constant prayer for these Christians is that what God has begun in them he will by his faithfulness bring to completion. The Thessalonians, like all Christians, had been called by God through the good news of Jesus to belong to him forever (see 1 Thessalonians 2:12). Persecution and suffering might make believers think that God had abandoned them since they had received their *calling*. But Paul knows that God does no such thing. God's *purpose* is to make his people his forever. He will see that purpose through to its end.

Like most Christians, the Thessalonians may be troubled by their own sense of failure and unworthiness. Paul prays not that they actually will be worthy of God's call (which is impossible), but that God will *count* them *worthy*. God's favor does not come by merit, and no one can earn it. But by his grace God promises to treat those with faith in Christ as if they are worthy, despite the fact that they are sinners. Being counted worthy is the foundation of all of God's work in the lives of his people.

12. We pray this so that the name of our Lord Jesus may be glorified in you, and you in him, according to the grace of our God and the Lord Jesus Christ.

What happens when Christians cooperate with God in what he is doing in their lives? Christ is *glorified*. When Christ returns, his glory will be seen by all (2 Thessalonians 1:10). In the meantime, his glory is to be seen in the lives of people transformed in his image and living out their calling by his power.

II. SAVED AND SANCTIFIED (2 THESSALONIANS 2:13-17)

A. REMEMBERING THE INITIAL CALL (vv. 13, 14)

13. But we ought always to thank God for you, brothers loved by the Lord, because from the beginning God chose you to be saved through the sanctifying work of the Spirit and through belief in the truth.

In 2 Thessalonians 2:1-12 (not in our text for today), Paul has been discussing the ongoing problem of evil in the world. Now he shifts gears to focus again on the people of God, who have been *saved* from that evil. He repeats his thanksgiving from the beginning of the letter, again saying that he has an obligation *to thank God* despite what seems like bad circumstances. Those circumstances do not lessen Christ's love for his family, even though they sometimes make his love difficult to see.

Being *loved by* Christ and being chosen by God are different expressions of the same essential idea in this verse. Both mean that Christians belong to God and can depend on his power to see them through to the end. However, it is important to understand the relationship between our faith and God's choosing. God

WHAT DO YOU THINK?

If the deeds of God's people are to reflect his glory and character, what lies have you "told" about God lately by your behavior? How can you correct this?

does not choose people and then cause them to believe as a result of being chosen. Rather, it's the other way around: he chooses people to be with him for eternity because they believe. We are saved through *belief in the truth*.

God's choosing means that Christians receive the blessings of salvation. In this regard, Paul stresses the work of the Holy *Spirit*. The Holy Spirit brings sanctification, that is, making believers to be the holy people of God. When the Holy Spirit enters a person's life, the Spirit identifies or marks that person as one who belongs to God. But that identity carries the need to imitate the holiness of God—to become holy in thought and behavior as well as in identity. Saved people can never stay the way they were before. When they live out their holy identity by imitating God's holiness, they reflect his glory in the world.

14. He called you to this through our gospel, that you might share in the glory of our Lord Jesus Christ.

The message of the *gospel* calls people to all that Paul has mentioned: belonging to God's people, being saved from judgment, being made holy by the Holy Spirit—all based on faith in the message of *Christ*. The *gospel* "call" is not a mysterious experience. It is the summons of the gospel message that addresses our deepest needs and most difficult problems. We hear it when we listen to the message that *Jesus*, the Son of God, died and rose for our sins.

God's purpose in the gospel call is that by believing in Christ we should share in Christ's own *glory*. Part of the wonder of the gospel is that God willingly shares his glory with his people. They participate in his victory in the world and enjoy the benefits of it. That is true both in the present and in the future. In the present we enjoy the blessings of life in the Holy Spirit and fellowship with each other as God's people. We may suffer in this age, but so did the Christ whose glory we share.

When Jesus returns, his glory will be fully revealed. We will be gathered to him at that time and he will be known to all as his people. In the meantime, we are to live in a way that demonstrates his glory to the world.

B. HOLDING FAST TO THE TEACHINGS (v. 15)

15. So then, brothers, stand firm and hold to the teachings we passed on to you, whether by word of mouth or by letter.

So then sums up what Paul has just written. If the gospel calls Christians to reflect the glory of God, then they must remain *firm* in that calling to see it through to its goal. They need to be firm because of the opposition that they will continue to face as God's people in a hostile world. If they fail to remain firm, they are working against the purpose of God.

The teachings that were *passed on* to the Thessalonians refers to the instructions and facts about Christ (what we might call Christian tradition) that the Thessalonian Christians had learned by word of mouth from Paul and his associates in ministry, or by letters such as 1 and 2 Thessalonians. So to remind these Christians to remain true to the teachings is to tell them to remain true to the original gospel that they had received. As we think about our lives and practices, we need to know the difference between Biblical teaching—the original, authentic Christian tradition—and our own customs, habits, and preferences.

THE COST OF TRADITION

A few hundred people live in a Havasupai village in a remote branch of the Grand Canyon. This village is seventy-five miles by road from Peach Springs, and then eight miles by mule path. Residents have a few modern comforts, such as electricity and telephones. But the U.S. Mail still comes in its traditional way: by

WHAT DO YOU THINK?

Even though "saved people can never stay the way they were," we all know people who show little or no difference after their conversion. Why do some Christians make such dramatic changes for the better while others fail?

mule train, as it has for more than one hundred years. Everything the Havasupai use or eat comes to their village in this way.

Such mail delivery is expensive! For example, postage for fresh water costs more than the water itself. A typical shipment of five hundred cases of soda costs two thousand six hundred dollars. Food, clothes, wheelbarrows, computers, the usual letters and cards, and even Christmas trees get "mailed" into the village by mule.

It costs a lot to maintain tradition. To the Havasupai, it's apparently worth it. But what is the value of tradition to Christians? It depends on what traditions we're talking about. The traditional teachings Paul referred to formed the unchanging core of the gospel, not "the way we've always done things," as we normally think of tradition. "Tradition" can be a positive and necessary identifying link to the past. Or, in the form of "tradition-alism," it can make the gospel an irrelevant vestige of bygone days. We must be wise enough to discern the difference. The future of the church depends on it!   —C. R. B.

C. COUNTING ON GOD'S PROVISION (vv. 16, 17)

16, 17. May our Lord Jesus Christ himself and God our Father, who loved us and by his grace gave us eternal encouragement and good hope, encourage your hearts and strengthen you in every good deed and word.

"Standing firm and holding on" is a tough assignment when the world is filled with evil. So Paul moves quickly from his command to stand firm to a confident prayer for God's help to overcome in the struggle.

Paul begins this prayer by mentioning *Christ* emphatically. Doing so allows us to understand how God helps us hold on. If Christ endured the cross for our salvation, he can certainly provide what we need to endure opposition and hold firmly to the gospel. Further, Christ is the *Lord* of glory (see verse 14). That means he has unlimited power to help his people.

Paul also refers here to God as *Father*, underlining what we can expect from him. As Father, he gives his children exactly what they need (see Luke 11:11-13). He is the God who has already given his people *eternal encouragement and good hope* through grace. Because that help comes from God, it can never end.

Our Lord's encouragement includes reassurance in difficult times, but it goes beyond that sense to include help to overcome difficulties and to move forward. To encourage the *heart* means more than consoling the feelings; it means strengthening the believer's will to act on what is right and true.

We can understand the rest of these two verses in the same way. To *strengthen* means to make believers firm in their convictions. This leads them to say and do what is right and good. God certainly will see his purpose through to its end at Christ's return. Until then, he will enable believers to live as his people. We will bring him glory in our deeds and words, as we live holy lives, until his glory is fully revealed.

III. MESSAGE AND DELIVERANCE (2 THESSALONIANS 3:1-4)

A. PRAY FOR THE MESSAGE (v. 1)

1. Finally, brothers, pray for us that the message of the Lord may spread rapidly and be honored, just as it was with you.

In several of his letters Paul not only speaks of his prayers for the readers, but also asks for their prayers for him (Romans 15:30-32; Ephesians 6:19-20; Colossians 4:3). Here he asks for prayer in a way that means not just praying once but praying repeatedly. Such prayer expresses the reliance on God that the gospel demands.

HOW TO SAY IT

Colossians. Kuh-LOSH-unz.
Corinthians. Kor-IN-thee-unz.
Ephesians. Ee-FEE-zhunz.
Havasupai. Ha-vuh-SOO-pie.
Thessalonians. THESS-uh-LO-nee-unz.
Thessalonica. THESS-uh-lo-NYE-kuh.

DAILY BIBLE READINGS

Monday, Apr. 26—We Have an Inheritance in Christ (Ephesians 1:7-14)

Tuesday, Apr. 27—Your Faith Is Growing (2 Thessalonians 1:1-5)

Wednesday, Apr. 28—Christ Glorified by His Saints (2 Thessalonians 1:6-12)

Thursday, Apr. 29—Called to Obtain Glory (2 Thessalonians 2:13-17)

Friday, Apr. 30—The Lord Will Strengthen You (2 Thessalonians 3:1-5)

Saturday, May 1—Imitate Us (2 Thessalonians 3:6-10)

Sunday, May 2—Do Not Be Idle (2 Thessalonians 3:11-18)

WHAT DO YOU THINK?

Again, we see the importance of prayer for Paul. If we don't pray for our church leaders, church members, and church programs, then how much of the blame is ours when they fail?

WHAT DO YOU THINK?

Describe times when you have not fit in with the world's established gods and customs. In what ways did you turn (or could you have turned) those times into opportunities to demonstrate "God's established order"?

PRAYER

Dear Father, help us to hang on! When the world distracts us, teach us to lift our gaze to eternity. May we be yours forever. In Jesus' name, amen.

THOUGHT TO REMEMBER

"Our present sufferings are not worth comparing with the glory that will be revealed in us" (Romans 8:18).

He asks for prayer first that the gospel can *spread rapidly* toward God's goal of salvation for all. Paul also desires prayer that the gospel will *be honored.* The gospel spreads rapidly and is honored when it is believed and obeyed. This is what has happened with the Thessalonian Christians. Though they have faced discouragements and problems, their life in the gospel has honored or glorified the gospel. This reminds us again of the glory of Christ, revealed at present in his people and in its fullness at his return.

B. PRAY FOR DELIVERANCE (vv. 2-4)
2. And pray that we may be delivered from wicked and evil men, for not everyone has faith.

Lawlessness and *evil* will oppose God's work until Christ returns. Then they will be defeated utterly. But God is already overcoming them as the gospel goes forward. So Paul asks for prayers that God would continue to overcome his opponents as they opposed Paul. In effect, Paul says, "Continue to *pray* 'Deliver us from the evil one' on my behalf."

3. But the Lord is faithful, and he will strengthen and protect you from the evil one.

Confidence in prayer comes from knowing the faithfulness of God. Many people do not have faith, but God is always *faithful.* He will always deliver his people and see his purpose through to its end.

Paul expresses this confidence in a way that reminds us how God proves himself faithful. He will keep his people from *evil,* not by removing them completely from its presence (until Christ returns), but by enabling them to overcome evil by his strength.

4. We have confidence in the Lord that you are doing and will continue to do the things we command.

Paul has good reason to be confident about the Thessalonian Christians. Despite persecutions, they have held to their faith.

But Paul's ultimate confidence is in God himself. God has been at work in the Thessalonian Christians in the past, strengthening them to bring him glory. He has been with Paul in the past, enabling him to proclaim the gospel and bring God glory. He was faithful to his Son, Jesus Christ, raising him from the dead. He has always been faithful to all of his people. We can count on him now. We can count on him in the future. We can count on him forever.

CONCLUSION
The story of God's people often reads like a story of failure. We need only to recall the failures of Moses, David, and Peter to realize the truth of this statement. Quite frankly, our faith sometimes fails. We struggle with sin. We wrestle with evil. Paul, who at one time persecuted the church, knew this all too well. Hopefully, we are able to overcome our failures and move forward in the work for Christ and his kingdom. But sadly, some believers succumb to the pressures of the world and forsake the Lord altogether. Demas was just such a one—he even went to Thessalonica! (See 2 Timothy 4:10.)

Yet God is glorified when his people live out their imperfect faith. He continues to change them and strengthen them so that they reflect his glory more and more. His glory is perfected in our weakness. At Christ's return, he will glorify his people through his Son.

When we know what God is doing and where he is taking us, we will be ready to reflect his glory more clearly until Christ comes again. What will you do this week to "polish your mirror" to better reflect that

Discovery Learning

This page contains an alternative lesson plan emphasizing learning activities. Classes desiring such student involvement will find these suggestions helpful. The next page is a reproducible activity page to further enhance discovery learning.

LEARNING GOALS

After participating in today's class session, each student should be able to:

1. Summarize Paul's description of how the Thessalonians would glorify God by living and growing in their faith.

2. Tell why it is important for believers to reflect God's glory in the way that they live.

3. State one specific action he or she can take this week to reflect God's glory.

INTO THE LESSON

Choice One: Case Study. (This activity is also included in the student book.) Read the following case study aloud to introduce the lesson. Or ask a class member to read it: "David and Beverly have been church members for several years. They attend church regularly, but it does not seem to have an impact on the way they live. Beverly is a self-confessed gossip. Dave's language at work and his ribald jokes make him popular with the guys, but where is his influence for Christ? Doesn't God and shouldn't we expect more from Beverly and Dave?"

Make a transition to the lesson saying, "What does God expect from believers in regard to lifestyle? As we look at our text today, watch for what God expects."

Choice Two: Debate. Ask two students in advance to prepare a debate. One will affirm the proposition, "God expects Christians to glorify him by the way they live." The other will refute the proposition, arguing that since every person sins and falls short, the pressure to conform is too powerful; and besides, God does not need us to glorify him—he is altogether glorious already.

INTO THE WORD

Choice One: Group Discussion. Divide your class into four groups to discuss the four sections in today's text. Assign each group to develop a list of ways that God is glorified through the lives of believers. Each group is to select a leader and a recorder who will list the group's findings. Ask each group to share its list. You might ask the groups to mark their assigned text in the manner suggested in the "Scripture Marking" section of the reproducible page that follows.

Choice Two: Interview. Conduct an "interview with the apostle Paul," as you would if he visited your class. Prepare the questions and discuss as a group

how he might answer them. Study each verse and frame a question that might be suggested by the content. For example, 2 Thessalonians 1:3 can suggest the question, "What are your personal feelings about the people in the church at Thessalonica?" Paul could answer, "I am always thanking God for each one of them. I am so pleased that their faith and love are both increasing."

Choice Three: Acrostic. Write the words *Glorify God* vertically on a page of newsprint. Then ask your class to list things that glorify God that can be tied into the phrase. For example, "Good deeds" could be written next to a "G." (This is included in the student book.)

INTO LIFE

Choice One: Write a Prayer. In his epistles Paul records many of his prayer concerns for people. Write and pray a Paul-like prayer for a young Christian. For example, based on 1:3, 4 you might pray, "Lord, I thank You for (Harold) because his faith is growing more and more and his love for all the brothers is increasing. All the leaders are proud of his perseverance and faith in all the persecutions and trials he is facing." (This activity is included in the student book.)

Choice Two: Brainstorm. Lead your class in a brainstorming session to compile a list of ways that Christians can glorify God today. Use the appropriate section of the reproducible page. Paul makes general statements in the text like, "every good purpose," "every act prompted by your faith," and "every good word and deed." What you want to create is a list of specific and practical means of giving glory to God. Tell your class that the purpose is to generate as many ideas as possible, so you will not stop to evaluate or discuss ideas. Encourage them to call out things as rapidly as they can be written down. Have two people ready with markers and large pieces of paper taped to the wall.

After the brainstorming period, go back and put stars beside the items your class thinks are the most plausible and realistic projects. Then select one that your class can do together that would give glory to God. For example, your class might list "Feed the hungry." One way to accomplish this would be to open a soup kitchen. Or perhaps your class could raise funds for an existing soup kitchen and then volunteer as a group to staff a specific meal each month.

Scripture Markings

Inexpensive markers are available in a variety of colors and they make a great Bible study method. But most people would not want to mark up their Bible. Mark the printed text below according to the following instructions.

1. Use a yellow marker to highlight the three phrases "every good purpose of yours," "every act prompted by your faith," and "every good deed and word."

2. Highlight in blue the words or phrases that show how Paul felt about the Thessalonians, like "thank God for you" or "brothers."

3. In green mark each phrase that identifies something that gives glory to God. For example, "faith is growing more and more"; "your perseverance and faith in all the persecutions and trials you are enduring."

4. Highlight in red the commands, such as, "stand firm" and "hold to the teachings."

2 Thessalonians

1 [3]We ought always to thank God for you, brothers, and rightly so, because your faith is growing more and more, and the love every one of you has for each other is increasing. [4]Therefore, among God's churches we boast about your perseverance and faith in all the persecutions and trials you are enduring. . . . [11]With this in mind, we constantly pray for you, that our God may count you worthy of his calling, and that by his power he may fulfill every good purpose of yours and every act prompted by your faith. [12]We pray this so that the name of our Lord Jesus may be glorified in you, and you in him, according to the grace of our God and the Lord Jesus Christ.

2 [13]But we ought always to thank God for you, brothers loved by the Lord, because from the beginning God chose you to be saved through the sanctifying work of the Spirit and through belief in the truth. [14]He called you to this through our gospel, that you might share in the glory of our Lord Jesus Christ. [15]So then, brothers, stand firm and hold to the teachings we passed on to you, whether by word of mouth or by letter. [16]May our Lord Jesus Christ himself and God our Father, who loved us and by his grace gave us eternal encouragement and good hope, [17]encourage your hearts and strengthen you in every good deed and word.

3 [1]Finally, brothers, pray for us that the message of the Lord may spread rapidly and be honored, just as it was with you. [2]And pray that we may be delivered from wicked and evil men, for not everyone has faith. [3]But the Lord is faithful, and he will strengthen and protect you from the evil one. [4]We have confidence in the Lord that you are doing and will continue to do the things we command. [5]May the Lord direct your hearts into God's love and Christ's perseverance.

Ways I Can Glorify God

Use the three phrases below to make lists of ways you can glorify God.

Every good purpose of yours	Every act prompted by your faith	Every good deed and word
_____	_____	_____
_____	_____	_____
_____	_____	_____
_____	_____	_____
_____	_____	_____

Living Expectantly
Unit 2: Visions of Hope
(Lessons 10-13)

WORSHIPING THE LAMB

LESSON 10

WHY TEACH THIS LESSON?

About twenty years ago, John MacArthur wrote an insightful book entitled *The Ultimate Priority*. It described the supreme importance of worship. Today's lesson offers us much the same idea: as the Lamb makes his presence known in the book of Revelation, nothing seems to be more important than worship!

Sadly, however, many Christians seem to have a rather ho-hum attitude toward worship. They do not prepare themselves for Sunday morning by getting enough sleep the night before. They read the Sunday morning comics rather than preparing themselves spiritually to enter into God's presence in a special way. The result, sometimes, is all too clear. Today's lesson from the book of Revelation is just what we need to adjust our outlook on the importance of worship.

INTRODUCTION

A. INTO THE PRESENCE OF GOD

Have you ever had trouble worshiping and serving in the church? On Sunday morning, do you find it difficult feeling or believing that you're really in the presence of God? Today the book of Revelation will give you the opportunity to come into his presence in a unique way!

When we are aware of God's presence, we can worship and serve profoundly in spirit and in truth. And Revelation is indeed a book of truth! Here we can learn more about the relationship of Father, Son, and Spirit to one another. The book of Revelation teaches us truth about Jesus, who is given many identifying titles: the faithful witness, the first begotten of the dead, the prince of the kings of the earth, Alpha and Omega, the beginning and the end, the first and the last. In addition to the titles there are many actions picturing what Jesus has done for all Christians, his servants, so that they can know the blessings of being in a relationship with him.

Whatever helps we may use in our worship services—worship leader, praise team, words on a screen, songbooks, musical instruments of all sorts—cannot be substituted for a real sense of the presence of God. And bringing us into God's presence is where the book of Revelation truly shines! No other book in the Bible can kindle the mind and heart of the Christian for worship better than the book of Revelation.

B. LESSON BACKGROUND

To understand any passage of Scripture properly, we must get an overview of the context in which it stands. This is especially important for passages in the book of Revelation because the author (the apostle John) develops a vocabulary to be used throughout, and the message of the book builds upon this vocabulary.

John makes clear from the outset that this is a message revealed by Jesus Christ himself (Revelation 1:1, 5). But not only is the message from him, it is also about him. We see Christ in the midst of the seven golden lampstands in 1:20, which are identified as the seven churches of Asia. Christ is the one who knows the circumstances of the seven churches—their strong points, their weak points,

---

DEVOTIONAL READING:
REVELATION 4:1-11

BACKGROUND SCRIPTURE:
REVELATION 4, 5

PRINTED TEXT:
REVELATION 5:1-10

LESSON AIMS

After participating in this lesson, each student will be able to:

1. Describe the unique position of the Lamb as the one who is worthy of worship.

2. Explain why the focus of one's worship and life must be on the Lamb.

3. Express worship to the worthy Lamb.

May
9

KEY VERSE

"Worthy is the Lamb, who was slain, to receive power and wealth and wisdom and strength and honor and glory and praise!"
—Revelation 5:12

everything! He challenges them (and us) to be overcomers of those things that would destroy a proper relationship with him.

There is blessing for the overcomers, but judgment for the failures. The form of the message carries a likeness of the Old Testament prophets. Those prophets proclaimed God's message for the people to repent. Their message was conditional. If the people repented, then there would be blessing from God. If not, God must pronounce judgment—penalty for rejecting his word.

With each of the letters to the churches is the closing command that they must heed what the Spirit says. The reader thus becomes aware that the Holy Spirit's ministry is a part of this whole matter. When the Spirit is called the "seven Spirits" of God (Revelation 1:4; 3:1; 4:5; 5:6), we do not count Spirits, but rather we consider his "sevenfold" potential to convict and encourage the faithful Christian.

In chapter 4 we move to a vision of the throne room of God. The focus of attention is on the one seated upon the throne. John indicates that he himself was brought right into God's presence so that he could see things from God's vantage point. It became John's responsibility to present the facts so that his readers would understand. We come to greater understanding when we identify with John by being where he is, as well as seeing and hearing the things he does.

One important thing John discovers in chapter 5 is the existence of a sealed book. This book does not exist for its own benefit—rather, it points to Christ.

I. WHO IS WORTHY? (REVELATION 5:1-5)

A. SEALED BOOK (v. 1)

1. Then I saw in the right hand of him who sat on the throne a scroll with writing on both sides and sealed with seven seals.

As chapter 5 opens, our attention falls upon the *scroll* that is in God's *right hand*. This book is entirely filled with a message. The fullness is indicated by the description of being written *on both sides*. It is also heavily sealed under someone's authority. John uses the word *seven* more than fifty times in the book of Revelation. Very frequently, "seven" shows us "the full value" of what is under discussion. Hence, the reader desires to know this full message, but only the one of proper, full authority can open it.

B. IMPORTANT QUESTION (v. 2)

2. And I saw a mighty angel proclaiming in a loud voice, "Who is worthy to break the seals and open the scroll?"

To break the seals and to *open the scroll* are two ways of saying the same thing. To do one is to do the other. The *mighty angel* in charge for the moment kindles our anticipation, for not just anyone dare open it. The call of this angel is able to reach to the farthest limits in seeking someone of proper office before God. Is it possible to find someone with sufficient authority?

C. DEEP GRIEF (vv. 3, 4)

3, 4. But no one in heaven or on earth or under the earth could open the scroll or even look inside it. I wept and wept because no one was found who was worthy to open the scroll or look inside.

Although the shattering call of the angel rings through every corner of the universe, no answer comes back. There is no response, at least at first. This fact causes John much grief because he apparently senses that the message of the sealed *scroll* can give him help and hope for his needs. So he gives in to despair since no one immediately steps forward claiming the right to open this scroll.

HOW TO SAY IT

Asia. AY-zhuh.
Ephesians. Ee-FEE-zhunz.
Isaiah. Eye-ZAY-uh.
Jeremiah. Jair-uh-MY-uh.
Judah. JOO-duh.
messianic. mess-ee-AN-ick.
Philippians. Fih-LIP-ee-unz.

UNWORTHY!

It was an amazing decision: at the height of the 1996 college football season, Robert Carothers, President of the University of Rhode Island, suspended all seventy-two football players, thus forfeiting an upcoming game with rival University of Connecticut. The reason? Six team members had rushed into a fraternity house and beat up three residents while twenty-five teammates surrounded the house to ensure that no one escaped.

The National Collegiate Athletic Association said that in its long history no team had ever forfeited a game for such a reason. Some complained because the action jeopardized the team's playoff chances. But the president became a hero to many who had been saddened and sickened by the attitude of many sports "heroes" who thought themselves immune to the requirement of decent conduct. "This is not about football," Carothers said. "This is about character." President Carothers's suspension of the team said, in effect, that the team was not worthy to carry the university's name and colors onto the field.

When we talk in terms of human worthiness before God, we always must conclude, "No one is worthy." Not one of us is worthy in and of ourselves to carry the "name and colors" before him. Sin has made this tragically so. Does this fact make you weep as it did John?   —C. R. B.

D. VITAL ANSWER (v. 5)

5. Then one of the elders said to me, "Do not weep! See, the Lion of the tribe of Judah, the Root of David, has triumphed. He is able to open the scroll and its seven seals."

Revelation 4:4 mentions twenty-four elders in the throne room. *One of the elders* serves as the spokesman for God, or as a "master of ceremonies" to give encouragement at this critical situation. This elder announces that there is indeed one who is worthy *to open the scroll*. This worthiness is indicated first by two messianic titles: *the Lion of the tribe of Judah* (cf. Genesis 49:9) and *the Root of David* (cf. Isaiah 11:1, 10; Jeremiah 23:5; 33:15). These titles are coupled with the action of prevailing or overcoming. The next verse tells us why.

II. HE IS WORTHY! (REVELATION 5:6-10)

A. THE LAMB COMES (v. 6)

6. Then I saw a Lamb, looking as if it had been slain, standing in the center of the throne, encircled by the four living creatures and the elders. He had seven horns and seven eyes, which are the seven spirits of God sent out into all the earth.

The elders of Revelation 4:4 and the four beasts of 4:6b-8 are still in the throne room, but now the focus of attention shifts to *a Lamb*. This is the first of more than thirty uses of "Lamb" in Revelation. The apostle John (who writes the book of Revelation) is already aware of the application of this term to Jesus (see what this apostle wrote earlier in John 1:29, 36).

The fact that this Lamb *had been slain* brings to mind the suffering servant of Isaiah 53. Even so, he is now standing alive and ready to act. The Lamb has *seven horns* of power. No literal lamb has horns, so this is a figure. A lamb is normally thought of as a docile, meek animal, but these horns of power are very fitting in the midst of God's *throne* room. There seems to be a bit of a paradox as power and submissive sacrifice are coupled together.

The Lamb also has *seven eyes*. These are equated with the *seven Spirits* of God, which we have already discussed in the Lesson Background. This sevenfold Spirit communicates with all the earth, not just with the seven churches of Asia in chapters 2 and 3. This verse shows us that the Lamb has a tie with God who sits on his throne, as well as with the Spirit who functions on behalf of people. The

WHAT DO YOU THINK?

How much of a gap is there between the Lamb's worthiness to open the scroll and that of "the best of the rest" of the universe? Why is that important to you?

WHAT DO YOU THINK?

Verse 6 places the spotlight on the Lamb. What are some ways we can put the spotlight on the Lamb in everything we do?

WHAT DO YOU THINK?

We note that a "bit of a paradox" exists in Jesus as both Lion and Lamb, "as power and submissive sacrifice are coupled together." How can we exhibit a similar "paradox" in our lives of service?

DAILY BIBLE READINGS

Monday, May 3—*He Is Coming With the Clouds (Revelation 1:4-8)*

Tuesday, May 4—*He Holds the Seven Stars (Revelation 2:1-7)*

Wednesday, May 5—*Words of the Son of God (Revelation 2:18-29)*

Thursday, May 6—*He Has Conquered (Revelation 3:14-21)*

Friday, May 7—*Holy Is the Lord God Almighty (Revelation 4:1-11)*

Saturday, May 8—*Who Is Worthy? (Revelation 5:1-5)*

Sunday, May 9—*The Lamb Is Worthy (Revelation 5:6-14)*

WHAT DO YOU THINK?

How has the "song" you have sung as a Christian been "new"? What noticeable difference has becoming a Christian made between the "old you" and the "new you"?

entire Godhead (Father, Son, and Holy Spirit) is united in the redemptive work. Even so, the achievement of the Lamb draws our attention and our praise here. The Lamb is worthy of our worship! He is ready to act (again) on our behalf.

B. THE LAMB ACTS (v. 7)

7. He came and took the scroll from the right hand of him who sat on the throne.

Anticipation heightens. Hope is about to become fulfilled. There is no question as to the Lamb's relationship with *him who sat on the throne*. Neither is there any question as to the Lamb's right to the book. Its message will assist John and all other suffering servants. This includes us, even though at this point the "suffering" aspect may not seem personal. It is, however, very personal for John, who is in exile on the island of Patmos "because of the word of God, and the testimony of Jesus" (Revelation 1:9).

C. THE LAMB WORSHIPED (vv. 8-10)

8. And when he had taken it, the four living creatures and the twenty-four elders fell down before the Lamb. Each one had a harp and they were holding golden bowls full of incense, which are the prayers of the saints.

When *the Lamb* receives the sealed scroll from the hand of God, the conduct of the *living creatures* and the *elders* is that of worship. It is proper for John and the readers to join in with them. The *harps* are for praise, and the *golden bowls full of incense* are equated with *the prayers of the saints*. Passages such as Ephesians 1:1 and Philippians 1:1 remind us that all Christians are "saints." This means that the prayers of saints are our prayers, too!

We will have to wait until the fifth seal is opened in Revelation 6:9, 10 to learn what the prayers of the saints have to do with the message of the sealed scroll. There we will see that the message concerns those who were "slain because of the word of God." The suffering of the faithful servants called forth God's vengeance on the wicked, and the servants are given the means to sustain themselves through suffering. See also the opening of the seventh seal in Revelation 8:1-4.

9. And they sang a new song:

> *"You are worthy to take the scroll*
> *   and to open its seals,*
> *because you were slain,*
> *   and with your blood you purchased men for God*
> *   from every tribe and language and people and nation.*

Many folks who have been to church for years don't like to learn any new songs. They're content to stick with their "old favorites"! But in God's heavenly throne room we see those gathered singing *a new song* (see also Revelation 14:3).

The word *new* doesn't just mean "different." Rather, it signifies a "changed quality" of songs that have been sung before. See also the changed quality of the "new name" in Revelation 2:17 and the "new Jerusalem" in 3:12.

This song of praise expresses appreciation of a person's relationship with God under the new covenant. That changed relationship has been brought about by the saving work of Christ in forgiving sin through blood, making righteousness available. It is the providing Christ—the "Rock" of 1 Corinthians 10:4—who will disclose the message of the sealed *scroll*, a message designed to preserve this relationship that we have with God through Christ. No other relationship can equal it, regardless of how strong human bonds may be.

Robert E. Coleman is right when he adds that "It is called 'a new song' because that which Christ has accomplished is wholly different and superior to the old covenant; nothing like it has ever existed before. New works of grace call forth new songs of praise" (*Songs of Heaven*).

A New Song

New musical idioms often seem strange and (sometimes) shocking. The twentieth century saw the advent of jazz and rock 'n' roll. Perhaps strange at first, both are now well-established forms of musical expression.

However, one of the strangest "new songs" in secular music was John Cage's "4'33"." It was first performed for a gathering of modern, cutting edge artists at Woodstock in 1952, and it was too outrageous even for them to accept. Some walked out during the performance.

The piece lasted for four minutes and thirty-three seconds (hence the name). The pianist played nothing, but merely closed and opened the piano keyboard lid and turned several pages of blank musical score while timing it all with a stopwatch. Even stranger is one reviewer's comments: "4'33" wasn't at all easy for Cage to write. Although it was initially conceived in 1947, the piece wasn't written until 1952, and then only after long and careful deliberation."

Late in the twentieth century, we saw Christian music metamorphose from hymns and gospel songs to the "praise music" of contemporary worship services. Dismay and disdain not unlike the response to John Cage's "4'33"" characterize the reaction of many Christians to the new music.

But the "new song" of which the apostle John writes is new more for its message than for its style: out of all who have ever lived, one has finally been found who is worthy to open the book of life. That one is our Lord Jesus Christ who has brought redemption to reality. This is a song worth singing throughout eternity!

—C. R. B.

Visual for lesson 10. *This calligraphy will help reinforce today's Key Verse. Who is worthy? He is worthy!*

10. *"You have made them to be a kingdom and priests to serve our God, and they will reign on the earth."*

This verse, a part of the "new song," also presents the blessings of this relationship with God. To be made kings and priests is similar to Revelation 1:6, which tells us what Jesus Christ has achieved in making "us *to be a kingdom and priests to serve* his God and Father."

The king-kingdom idea carries throughout the Bible. For Christians, our position in God's kingdom is a present reality that has eternal significance; it reaches its fulfillment in Heaven itself. What a privilege it is to have God's provision and protection in his kingdom! We allow this protection to become a reality when we show our submission to him and depend on him.

Yet this privilege, as others, holds a corresponding responsibility: we are priests to minister for God on behalf of our needs and the needs of others (1 Peter 2:5, 9). What access, what protection, what relationship, what responsibility! Praise the Lord!

Also, we know what it is to reign with Christ. We have become united in the likeness of his death and his resurrection, and thus live and *reign* with him (cf. Romans 6:3-7). John discusses this idea again in Revelation 20:6. What assurance it is knowing that our relationship with him includes reigning with him! Praise the Lord again!

And Christ is indeed praiseworthy. The ground of praise is Christ's death and resurrection, and the blessings thereby brought to those who accept his redemptive work. He has met our need. He is the One who has the answer to the problems of his people, his suffering servants.

The fifth chapter of Revelation closes with the picture of God's triumphant jubilation as coming from the four living creatures, the twenty-four elders, the

What Do You Think?

Now that we have become "priests," how can we live out our priestly calling in the coming week?

[Romans 12:1; Philippians 4:18; and 2 Timothy 4:6 may help with this question.]

thousands of angels, and the inhabitants of the universe. The great act of homage closes as it began: with the response of the central characters. God shows that he is worthy of worship. And all those of us who view this scene now add our "amen." Worthy is the Lamb to receive our worship! Amen! Come, Lord Jesus!

CONCLUSION

As we consider the visions that God provided John, it is important to note what one sees and what one hears. When we put these elements together, we should have a clear understanding of what the visions mean. The visions are not intended to be mysterious or vague or subject to anyone's opinion. They are revelations from God, who allowed John to remove the "cover" so that we can see and understand.

If we can think of today's lesson text as a scene in an act of a drama, we will instinctively realize that it is essential that all parts be kept in their proper sequence. In that way we will be able to understand the author's intent. As we meditate on the scene, we realize that the dominant figure is the Lamb. His description gives us an insight into his nature, his role, and his relationships.

As we find ourselves drawn into the scene, we identify with John in sensing the meaning of all the imagery. We are reassured and comforted to be in the presence of the Lamb, who cares about our need and can act to meet that need. This need and the desire for assistance is brought into focus as we consider what the message of the sealed book might be.

Our anticipation is heightened, for we know that only the Lamb has the right to open the seven-sealed scroll. This scroll holds an assuring message for John and all the rest of the suffering servants—then and now (see Revelation 6:1–8:5). Christians, praise the Lamb!

Are you hurting today because things do not seem to be going well at church, even though you are serving faithfully? Do you wonder whether anyone understands how desperate you feel, knowing your spouse is terminally ill? Are you grief-stricken because your position has been cut at work? A great number of circumstances that bring us hurt cause us to cry out, "It's just not fair!"

True, it may not be fair. But we are not promised that situations and events in this life will always be fair. What we are promised is that the Lamb (whose own death wasn't "fair") is present to provide what we need at such an hour. It is especially comforting to remember that he will be with us in the hour of our death, as we journey to his arms. Hence, we can sing "the new song" of praise to the Lamb—our Lamb!

During the past two decades, there has been an ongoing discussion and debate in many churches as to style of music to be used in worship. The emphasis has been such that some Christians could conclude that music is the central feature of our assemblies and our worship. Such an issue is not only divisive in the church, but it is also taking our focus away from what the vital matter is in worship.

The real matter is not hymn or praise choruses, guitars, pianos, or organs, padded pews or chair arrangements, worship ministers or song leaders—or all the various helps we want to emphasize. The foundational requirement, rather, is a real sense of the presence of the Lamb, an understanding of who he is, and a perception of our relationship with him. It is he who is worthy of praise!

When we let things that we have incorporated into our worship services take our minds and hearts away from the Lamb, we need to repent and return to the worship of the one who is worthy of our devotion. In this way we will not withhold our commitment and service to him. If we repent, then there is blessing. If we do not, the result is judgment.

Discovery Learning

This page contains an alternative lesson plan emphasizing learning activities. Classes desiring such student involvement will find these suggestions helpful. The next page is a reproducible activity page to further enhance discovery learning.

LEARNING GOALS

After participating in this lesson, each student will be able to:

1. Describe the unique position of the Lamb as the one who is worthy of worship.

2. Explain why the focus of one's worship and life must be on the Lamb.

3. Express worship to the worthy Lamb.

INTO THE LESSON

For these activities you will need the following: (1) a long sheet of paper with a ribbon to be wrapped around it as a scroll; (2) a "special" chair (throne) that is different from the rest of the chairs in the room; (3) a sheet of paper with the words *Perfect Person* written on it; (4) a tape or CD copy of the song "Watch the Lamb" by Ray Boltz.

Before the class arrives, prepare the scroll with the words of the songs found in Revelation 5:9, 10, 12, and 13. Set the special chair apart from the other furniture in the class, and attach the sheet of paper with the words *Perfect Person* to this chair. Wrap the scroll with a ribbon and place it on the seat of the chair.

As you begin the class, say, "Write the name of the person in the class who is most worthy to sit in this special chair." This will likely result in some discomfort for the students because there is not a person in the class who is "perfect" or even "most worthy."

Say, "Obviously, not one of us could be seated in this chair as a perfect person. Only Christ can sit here."

INTO THE WORD

As a volunteer reads Revelation 5:1-10, tell the class to listen carefully for the word used for the One who is worthy. Ask, "Why is the word *Lamb* used of Jesus?" Allow the students time to respond and discuss possibilities. Say, "This word *Lamb* is used extensively in the book of Revelation, beginning with chapter 5. It is a special designation set aside for the one worthy to open the scroll."

Form small groups and assign the following texts: *Group 1*—Exodus 12:1-14; *Group 2*—Luke 22:7-16; *Group 3*—Revelation 6:16; 12:10-12; Revelation 17:12-14; and Revelation 21:22-27. Tell the students to make a list of characteristics and purposes of the lambs or Lamb based on these texts.

Have a member of each group report their findings. The first two groups have texts that focus on the idea of a lamb as sacrifice in the Passover. The Revelation texts provide several characteristics, such as wrathful (6:16), conqueror, King of kings (17:14), and dwelling place (21:22).

Ask, "Given these characteristics and purposes of the Lamb, why is He and He alone to be worshiped?" The response should mirror the characteristics and purpose: He should be worshiped because He is Lord of lords; He is our dwelling place; He alone provides the perfect and final sacrifice.

If you have time, you can enhance your discussion by being ready to note how the Scriptures refer to Jesus as the Lamb in other passages. Isaiah 53:7 and 1 Peter 1:19 are examples.

INTO LIFE

Have the students return to their groups. Say, "List ways our focus in worship is often diverted away from the Lamb." After a short time, ask a representative from each group to present the ways a person may be distracted in worship. These may include such distractions as food and drink in the sanctuary, style of music, or family conflict on the way to church. As each is presented, identify how it may affect a person's worship.

Note that worship does not occur only in the church building. The image of a slain lamb standing recalls the image of the "living sacrifice" mentioned in Romans 12. Worship is a way of life, and our way of life, our worship, is to be directed toward the Lamb. Make another list of distractions, this time of those things that can distract us from a life of worship.

Encourage students to write down one issue that distracts them from worship in the assembly and one issue that distracts them from a life of worship. Ask them to write the words, "Not Worthy" across this sheet of paper as if voiding a check. Direct the students' attention to the reproducible page that follows; suggest they use it as their personal follow-up to today's study.

Open the scroll placed on the chair and read the words aloud to the class. As the song "Watch the Lamb" by Ray Boltz plays, have the students pray for wisdom in worshiping the Lamb without distraction. If this song is not accessible, sing a hymn or chorus focused on worshiping the Lamb (e.g., "Thou Art Worthy").

Finally, say, "We will leave this chair with the opened scroll to remind us of the focus of the book of Revelation throughout the remaining three weeks."

Acrostic

Reflecting on the Scripture from Revelation printed below, use the words *Worthy is the Lamb* to indicate different aspects of worship necessary in your life of worship. One entry is given to get you started.

REVELATION 5:9, 10

"You are worthy to take the scroll
   and to open its seals,
because you were slain,
   and with your blood you purchased
      men for God
   from every tribe and language and peo-
      ple and nation.
You have made them to be a kingdom and
      priests to serve our God,
   and they will reign on the earth."

REVELATION 5:12

"Worthy is the Lamb, who was slain,
   to receive power and wealth and wisdom
      and strength
   and honor and glory and praise!"

REVELATION 5:13

"To him who sits on the throne
   and to the Lamb
be praise and honor and glory and power,
   for ever and ever!"

W _____

O _____

R *Reverence* _____

T _____

H _____

Y _____

is the

L _____

A _____

M _____

B _____

Living Expectantly

Unit 2: Visions of Hope

(Lessons 10-13)

RECEIVING GOD'S SALVATION

LESSON 11

WHY TEACH THIS LESSON?

A few months ago, I signed up for a program that is designed to help protect me from the crime of "identity theft." Now, if a thief somehow gains access to my personal information, then he or she (supposedly) will not be able to use my good credit for criminal purposes by pretending to be me. Perhaps you have heard the horror stories of this actually happening. Identity theft is a frightening prospect!

But there will be no possibility of identity theft when we stand before Christ. On that great day the identities of the true Christians will be clear for all to see. Until then, however, the true Christians undergo suffering as they are mixed with other groups. We are heartened when we realize that this is only temporary. Today's lesson will remind us that our eternal reward will make all our sufferings worthwhile. Since God's "seal" is always upon us, what have we to fear?

INTRODUCTION

A. WHAT SALVATION COSTS

Robert E. Coleman tells a story of a traveler who was always on the lookout for unusual things in each city he visited. In one particular town, he noticed a curious spire atop a public building. Upon closer inspection the man noticed that the wall bore a stone figure of a lamb about two-thirds of the way up. Upon inquiry, the traveler discovered that the replica marked the spot where a workman had lost his balance and had fallen while the building was under construction.

But the worker wasn't killed, as a local resident related. When the mason fell, he providentially landed on a lamb that was on its way to slaughter along with several others. The lamb's body provided enough "cushioning" to break the man's fall and save his life (at the cost of the lamb's own life). The builder was so impressed with the event that he had the image of a lamb placed there as a lasting tribute. If you had been that traveler, what would your reaction have been?

B. LESSON BACKGROUND

When we saw the Lamb in Revelation 5, we saw him standing, ready to act. We also saw an image of the Lamb having been slain. The reality of the Lamb's suffering was obvious. Both his suffering and readiness to act were for our benefit.

As the story unfolded, the Lamb began to act as he took the sealed book in order to open it and reveal its desired message (Revelation 5:5, 8). The book held an assuring message for John and all the rest of us who are suffering servants "because of the word of God and the testimony of Jesus" (1:9).

In the first five messages of the sealed book the reality of suffering is obvious. But more than that, the reader understands that the suffering church in her faithfulness asks for judgment upon sin. All the aspects of the throne room scene combine to assure us that God and the Lamb will execute this righteous judgment. That judgment is only on the wicked who have not repented. The message of the sixth seal emphasizes just how serious this judgment shall be (6:12-17).

In the series of images, the reader is aware that the entire message is building to a climax. As we cross into chapter 7, we realize that it is "intermission time"

DEVOTIONAL READING:
REVELATION 3:7-13

BACKGROUND SCRIPTURE:
REVELATION 7

PRINTED TEXT:
REVELATION 7:1-3, 9, 10, 13-17

LESSON AIMS

After participating in this lesson, each student will be able to:

1. Tell how the believer's relationship with the Lamb provides protection, salvation, and comfort.

2. Relate the blessings of this relationship to the trials one faces in life, and describe the victory that results.

3. Identify a personal trial for which he or she will seek the Lord's help and comfort.

WHAT DO YOU THINK?

In what ways can we pay "a lasting tribute" to the Lamb who saved our lives, as the appreciative mason did? Following that, what do we do to prepare for the reaction of others?

May 16

KEY VERSE

"For the Lamb at the center of the throne will be their shepherd; he will lead them to springs of living water. And God will wipe away every tear from their eyes."

—*Revelation 7:17*

in this act of the play we are watching. During this intermission, the reader can reassess his or her relationship with the Lamb, knowing his salvation and his protection.

Here in John's "theater" is a scene that will help to strengthen our patience. The sixth seal left us with a scene that was quite bleak; but as happens so often in this book, the scene changes when the picture looks the bleakest. The scene of chapter 7 is a refreshing interlude, for the reader is given a graphic pledge of God's protection for his church through her trials.

Unless the Lamb's salvation and protection are real, Christians may break under the stress of their trials. We can learn much from the scene, understanding that tribulation does not come from God. We comprehend the protection and the strength provided by the Lord. The reader, along with John, becomes involved in the scene so that he or she knows the personal and practical nature of what is seen and what is heard.

I. RESTRAINT AND SEAL (REVELATION 7:1-3)

A. ANGELS PROTECT THE CHURCH (v. 1)

1. After this I saw four angels standing at the four corners of the earth, holding back the four winds of the earth to prevent any wind from blowing on the land or on the sea or on any tree.

This fourfold nature of the wind creates a kind of "fullness of opposition" to God's people as the four horses and their riders did in the opening of the first four seals of the sealed scroll (Revelation 6:1-8).

God's protection is seen as *four angels standing,* ready to serve God and his people. To make the picture all-inclusive, they are positioned *at the four corners of the earth.* It is not stated in this fashion to convey the idea that the earth is flat. Rather, the figure shows a full defense from all directions.

The series of the potential recipients of the wind seems somewhat unusual: the *land,* the *sea,* and *any tree.* In identifying the realm where people live, John probably uses this series so that the reader will not be tempted to take it too literally and try to cite a particular geographical location at a certain time in history. A tree is a natural object to select for observing the reality of opposition, the wind. Do not we do the same thing if someone asks us if the wind is blowing, or how strong it is? We look to the nearest tree to check the movement of the leaves or the branches. Thus, the use of *tree* helps us to know the expression is figurative, but real.

It is the ministry of the angels to hold back the wind. Hence, the Christian perceives that there is no way any opposition need destroy one's relationship with Christ. It is foolish to ask what would happen if the angels were to let go. We know that God is in control, and the four angels will not weaken.

What assurance this is for all Christians, realizing God's power is greater than that of the opposition! This imagery should remind us that things are not always what they seem to be. Even though Christians know what it means to hurt as they go about their day-to-day encounters, they must know also that the reality of the suffering is not a sign that God has abandoned them. There are two sides to the Christian experience. The security must be as real as the suffering. The scene helps to get this point across.

HOW TO SAY IT

Corinthians. Kor-IN-thee-unz.
Ephesians. Ee-FEE-zhunz.
Ezekiel. Ee-ZEEK-ee-ul or Ee-ZEEK-yul.
Isaiah. Eye-ZAY-uh.

PROTECTION FROM THE WIND

The wind: sometimes it is a refreshing, gentle breeze; sometimes, the destructive frenzy of a tornado or hurricane. Even between these two extremes it can have amazing power. You may have seen film clips of the collapse of "Galloping Gertie," a suspension bridge across Tacoma Narrows in Washington State. Gentle winds through the Narrows would cause the bridge to rise and fall several feet so that drivers would lose sight of cars ahead of them.

Then, early in the morning of November 7, 1940—just four months after its completion—winds reaching forty-five miles per hour began to twist the roadway over a twenty-eight-foot arc from side-to-side—a ninety-degree movement. For thirty minutes the bridge twisted violently before collapsing into the waters below.

It is this destructive power of the wind that John alludes to when he notes that the four angels are holding back the metaphorical winds that could bring suffering to the people of God. The forces of evil—whether natural, human, or demonic—may twist the surface of life beneath us and toss us violently from side to side. But it is only to a limited degree and for a limited time. John assures us that the power of God is a stabilizing force, our ultimate protection and our hope for eternal refuge. It is a protection available to the Christian, and no one else.   —C. R. B.

B. ANGELS SEAL THE CHURCH (vv. 2, 3)

2. *Then I saw another angel coming up from the east, having the seal of the living God. He called out in a loud voice to the four angels who had been given power to harm the land and the sea:*

The spotlight now falls on *another angel*, who comes *from the east*. This phrase could be translated more literally as "from the rising of the sun." This is another expression for the radiance of God's glory. The angel's *loud voice* relays instructions to *the four angels* seen holding back the four winds from the servants of God. There is no mistaking the commanding nature of this voice. The next verse helps us understand the meaning of *the seal of the living God*.

3. *"Do not harm the land or the sea or the trees until we put a seal on the foreheads of the servants of our God."*

When we read *do not harm the land or the sea or the trees* our thought is not on "place," but on "people," as the context indicates. This *harm* is delayed until God's servants can be sealed and protected. The idea of sealing the people of God is a figure found in the Old Testament (cf. Song of Solomon 8:6; Ezekiel 9:4).

Sealing is also a figure used in the New Testament of the presence of the Holy Spirit (cf. 2 Corinthians 1:22; Ephesians 1:13; 4:30). It is a mark of ownership, and thus provides authentication, security, and protection. Revelation 9:4 shows us God's wrath against those who are not sealed.

II. MULTITUDE AND PROCLAMATION (REVELATION 7:9, 10)

A. APPEARANCE OF MANY (v. 9)

9. *After this I looked and there before me was a great multitude that no one could count, from every nation, tribe, people and language, standing before the throne and in front of the Lamb. They were wearing white robes and were holding palm branches in their hands.*

Following the "sealed servants" of Revelation 7:3 and the "144,000" of 7:4-8 (not in today's text), the reader is shown another identification for God's people: *a great multitude*. When we place these three values together we see John's way of indicating "kind" or "quality" of those in the scene.

Whether we think of this group as "numbered" (144,000) or "without number," we should not miss John's intent to show us the bigger picture: twenty-first-century Christians are just as much a part of this group as those in John's day. When we read the messages to the seven churches in Revelation 1:9–3:22, for example, we understand that the apostle's intent is for the message to be for all churches of all time (including our time).

For this multitude, nationality and language are irrelevant! As we see them *before the throne and in front of the Lamb*, they are ready to worship. Part of being

WHAT DO YOU THINK?

Knowing that you have been "sealed," how secure and protected do you feel? Realizing that feelings are deceptive, how do we manage those times of trial when God seems distant?

[Some passages that can enrich your discussion include Romans 8:28; 1 Corinthians 10:13; 2 Corinthians 1:10; 2 Timothy 4:18; James 1:2-4; and 1 Peter 1:6, 7.]

ready for this festive celebration is wearing the right clothes (cf. Matthew 22:11, 12). To be dressed in *white* is a common characteristic of those who overcome through Christ (Revelation 3:4, 5, 18; 6:11; 7:13, 14). Their actions involve having palms *in their hands*. *Palm branches* are often a part of a scene of festive joy (John 12:13). They are appropriate for the expression of praise and worship that follow.

The Changing "Face" of the Church

As the early church expanded, Christianity became primarily a white, Western religion, and it remained so for centuries. But after World War II, the church began to break out of this small box. What amazing changes are taking place today! Consider, for instance, that of the world's estimated four hundred million evangelical Christians, 70 percent are non-Western, living in Africa, Asia, Oceania, and Latin America.

In 1960, more than half of all who claimed to be Christians lived in North America and Europe. Around 1970, Christianity's "center of gravity" began moving south and east. By 1990, only 38 percent of all Christians lived in Western nations. That figure is now down to only about 30 percent!

The church is growing at a much slower rate in the Western nations than elsewhere in the world. To put it another way, the "face" of Christianity is changing. No longer is it white and Western; now it is brown, black, and yellow.

As the affluent and self-satisfied West has turned its back on Christian values, the rest of the world has found the answer to the soul's deepest needs. Today the church looks more and more like the picture John paints for us in our text for today, with members from "every nation, tribe, people and language." May we continue to spread the gospel to the uttermost parts of the world!   —C. R. B.

B. Ascent of Praise (v. 10)

10. And they cried out in a loud voice:

> "Salvation belongs to our God,
> who sits on the throne,
> and to the Lamb."

When Christians see what their relationship with *God* and *the Lamb* really means, the natural reaction is praise and worship. The Lamb has provided our salvation, which includes forgiveness, righteousness, and assurance with the presence of the Holy Spirit. He provides all we need. What do we have to worry about?

III. IDENTITY AND SERVICE (REVELATION 7:13-17)

A. John Questioned (vv. 13, 14a)

13, 14a. Then one of the elders asked me, "These in white robes—who are they, and where did they come from?"

I answered, "Sir, you know."

Now John finds himself personally involved in the vision. As one of the elders asks him to identify those dressed *in white robes,* John has not forgotten the previous scenes. In those scenes he saw Christ dressed in white, the overcomers promised robes of white, and the twenty-four elders on twenty-four thrones with their robes of white and their crowns of gold. As John now ponders the great multitude dressed in white robes, he undoubtedly also remembers the slain saints under the altar, satisfied with their white robes and their rest for a little time.

The question that the elder asks of John means that John is being challenged to draw "the bottom line" and comprehend the meaning. When John replies to the elder *Sir, you know,* the implication is something like "you know that I understand."

What Do You Think?

What strategies might we use to ensure that in our next affliction we will have a song instead of (or along with) a tear?

B. ELDER REPLIES (vv. 14b-17)

14b. And he said, "These are they who have come out of the great tribulation; they have washed their robes and made them white in the blood of the Lamb.

The reply of the elder, who serves as spokesman in the scene, then reinforces the meaning for the reader. The ones clothed in *white* robes are overcomers. *The great tribulation* is a "trial" they have experienced or are experiencing as their faith is tested. They are clothed in righteousness in God's presence because of their faith in the salvation provided by Christ. In casting their allegiance with him, they have *washed their robes* in *the blood of the Lamb.* What availing faith!

Daniel 12:1 speaks of a great "time of distress," and Matthew 24:21 also warns of "great distress." These passages may refer to specific periods in history. But before we get carried away with too much speculation of "when" and "where," let us remember that all Christians are tested. Each of us goes through some kind of great tribulation. Each of us has personal struggles in a sin-sick world, as John had in his day. But those struggles will come to an end, as we see in the next verse.

15. Therefore,

> "they are before the throne of God
>   and serve him day and night in his temple;
> and he who sits on the throne will spread his tent over them.

The uncountable multitude from verse 9 is observed standing ready to serve *before the throne.* This service is *day and night*—a picture of continued service, growth, and appreciation of the presence *of God.*

What blessings there are in that presence! We are learning in the scenes to appreciate this presence and relationship in the here and now, especially in the ministry of the Holy Spirit. If people do not enjoy being in God's presence now and serving him continually in the church, they surely could not enjoy Heaven. Unless Christians come to an understanding of the presence of God, they will make a sham of faith and the church. Our faith is not real if we do not know the blessings of his presence. The more we overcome in this life through his power, the greater will be our comfort in the life to come.

16. "Never again will they hunger;
> **never again will they thirst.**
> **The sun will not beat upon them,**
> **nor any scorching heat.**

This verse sets forth figures that express the reality of hurt, trials, or suffering common to Christians. The very necessities of physical life can be the occasion for trial. Food, water, clothing, shelter—all are basic.

There are times when it may seem that we don't have much assurance of these physical necessities. In such times we can find ourselves put to the test as to whether we will stay faithful amidst our suffering and lack. When we hurt, the presence and the protection of the Lamb can seem far away and not quite real. The image from our next verse gives us something to hold on to in such times.

17. "For the Lamb at the center of the throne will be their shepherd;
> **he will lead them to springs of living water.**
> **And God will wipe away every tear from their eyes."**

The figure that we have become familiar with from chapter 5 onward is the metaphor of Christ as *the Lamb.* In a way, it may seem paradoxical that the Lamb is also a *shepherd* who shall feed them. But remember that when we first saw the Lamb in last week's lesson he stood ready to minister even though he appeared to have been slain. The hurt brought to the Lamb may have caused the onlooker to wonder whether there might be someone greater than he.

DAILY BIBLE READINGS

Monday, May 10—Deliverance Belongs to the Lord (Psalm 3:1-8)

Tuesday, May 11—The God of My Salvation (Psalm 25:1-5)

Wednesday, May 12—My Rock and My Salvation (Psalm 62:1-6)

Thursday, May 13—On God Rests My Deliverance (Psalm 62:7-12)

Friday, May 14—Through Jesus Is Forgiveness of Sins (Acts 13:32-39)

Saturday, May 15—Salvation Belongs to Our God (Revelation 7:1-10)

Sunday, May 16—Before the Throne of God (Revelation 7:11-17)

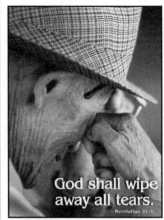

God shall wipe away all tears.
— Revelation 21:4

Visual for lessons 11 and 13. *Use this visual to remind your learners that God is the great tear-wiper.*

WHAT DO YOU THINK?

Do you have trouble believing that "Heaven has already started for the Christian"? In what ways is this really true in your personal life?

[Hebrews 6:4, 5 and 1 Peter 2:3 can stimulate your students' thinking on this question.]

WHAT DO YOU THINK?

What are some ways that the Lamb has been a "shepherd" and a "great tear-wiper" in your life? What "great tribulation" are you feeling right now that needs his tender, loving care?

PRAYER

Thank you, God, for being the loving, caring Father that you are. Because of the Lamb, we know you have seen our needs and are able to meet those needs. And because of the Lamb we are never alone, no matter what kind of situation tests our faith.

Father, it is because of the Lamb that we understand both sides of our Christian experience: our hurting and our protection. We know that testing is very real, but we are thankful that your provision strengthens us. Because of Christ, we smile amidst our tears. In the name of the Lamb we pray, amen.

THOUGHT TO REMEMBER

Our hurt is real, but so is the Lamb's power.

But being able to overcome his own ordeal means that he is the very one who has the power to help us in our time of trial. The Lamb's ability to help us is no assurance that we shall bypass trial and suffering. It is a guarantee, however, that we shall triumph because of our relationship with the Lamb.

Because he lives, we live. Heaven has already started for the Christian. Eternal life (the Lamb's kind of life) began for the new Christian when he or she became united with Christ and was raised to "live a new life" (Romans 6:3-5). As a result, Christians know what it is to live and reign with Christ even now.

Many Old Testament passages speak of God's provisions (e.g., Psalm 23; Isaiah 49:10, 11; Ezekiel 34:23). In the New Testament we see Christ himself providing for our needs. This fact comes alive when we see him in the midst of the seven golden lampstands of Revelation 1, as the Lamb with seven horns and seven eyes in Revelation 5, and as the Good Shepherd protecting the flock of God in John 10. In the verse before us we have a chance to see his gracious provision made more vivid than anywhere else in Scripture. We share his tent, his food and *water*, and his supply for all our needs.

When we realize "where we are," somehow we are not as threatened and the pain is not as severe. The stubbed toe of the child somehow seems less painful in the security of the parent's arms. In like manner, God is the great tear-wiper! What love and security in his presence!

RETURN OF STOLEN PROPERTY

In 1960 Audrey Wheeler left her purse at a restaurant. It contained her ID card, several pictures of her family, a copy of Psalm 23 from her father's funeral, and her pay envelope with a week's pay in cash. A thief took the money and left the rest, which somehow ended up in the kitchen wall of the café. It was found forty years later when the building was demolished.

When Wheeler recovered her purse at the police station, it was in surprisingly good condition considering the time and the place where it had been hidden. As she pulled out each of the lost treasures, she and her sisters spent several hours talking about the memories that each item brought forth. The women agreed that the memories triggered by the pictures were far more important than the lost cash, although at the time it had been a lot of money.

The innocence of the human race was stolen in the Garden of Eden. Our relationship with God that was lost in the fall was far more valuable than anything Adam and Eve hoped to gain. We still suffer from their mistaken quest today.

But John tells us about a new Heaven. There everything that has been stolen by sin shall be renewed in the presence of God. All our hurt and misery shall be wiped away. In fact, through the work of Christ God already is giving us a taste of the new Paradise that he is preparing for us. With such a great gift at hand, does it really make any sense to continue in sin?   —C. R. B.

CONCLUSION

Because of God's salvation provided in the Lamb, Christians have the assurance of a right relationship with God. His dwelling place brings protection; throne or tent are essentially the same. Where God is and what results from his presence are the necessary things to understand. All this means is that we need not worry about why Christians suffer, or the timing of the Lord's return and the end of the world. Our relationship with God is restored and real right now, and any trial is temporary and bearable. His presence makes it that way!

We shall not, and dare not, let anything interrupt this relationship. Thus, our hearts are kindled for praise, and we echo the words of the great multitude: "Salvation belongs to our God, who sits on the throne, and to the Lamb!"

Discovery Learning

This page contains an alternative lesson plan emphasizing learning activities. Classes desiring such student involvement will find these suggestions helpful. The next page is a reproducible activity page to further enhance discovery learning.

LEARNING GOALS

After this lesson each student will be able to:

1. Tell how the believer's relationship with the Lamb provides protection, salvation, and comfort.

2. Relate the blessings of this relationship to the trials one faces in life and describe the victory that results.

3. Identify a personal trial for which he or she will seek the Lord's help and comfort.

INTO THE LESSON

Ask several students to name the person from whom they have experienced the most helpful shepherding. This person does not have to be living. Students may indicate people such as a parent, close relative, classmate from high school, close friend, elder, spouse, or an employer. Ask, "What characteristics of this person make him or her so helpful?" List these characteristics for all to see.

Ask, "When you have faced difficult times in your life, what has this person provided?" Write responses on the board. After taking all of the responses, identify each as helping through (1) providing comfort or (2) providing protection. (*Examples of comfort responses include: crying with the person, coming to visit, or simply being available. Examples of protection responses include standing up for someone in the presence of criticism, making sure the person was not in the same situation again, providing the basics of life: food, clothing, shelter.*)

Say, "The Lamb as our Shepherd provides us with both the ultimate comfort and absolute protection, regardless of the severity of the trials we face."

INTO THE WORD

Say, "This particular section of Revelation is quite involved, and students often miss the point in the details." Tell the students to read through Revelation 7:1-8, focusing on every detail they can find. After they have finished reading, ask students to list these details aloud while you write them. (*Details will include four angels, four corners, four winds, angel from the east, seal on foreheads, 144,000, and 12,000 from each of the twelve tribes.*) Ask, "Give some examples of times you have heard or seen any of these details used as the focus of a study or presentation of Revelation." You can provide an initial example of the focus of Jehovah's Witnesses on 144,000 people who are saved. When examples are stated, do not let students pursue them in detail.

Say, "Often people stop at the details and completely miss what this text is intended to be: a very encouraging text." Have students read Revelation 7:9-17 with a view to the "big picture." When they have finished, have each student write a short summary of this section. Ask for volunteers to read their summaries. A sample summary is: "People of every background who have experienced severe trials will receive salvation and rest, ultimately standing before the Lamb in worship."

INTO LIFE

Read the commentary on verse 14, page 321: "Daniel 12:1 speaks of a great 'time of distress,' and Matthew 24:21 warns of 'great distress.' These passages may refer to specific periods in history. But before we get carried away with too much speculation of 'when' and 'where,' let us remember that all Christians are tested. Each of us goes through some kind of great tribulation. Each of us has personal struggles in a sin-sick world, as John had in his day. But those struggles will come to an end."

Say, "In reviewing this text we see the inevitability of trials and the assurance of victory in salvation." Have each student recall, without dwelling on the details, several of the most difficult trials he or she has faced throughout life, writing each one on the left side of a sheet of paper. On the right side each should then write how his or her relationship with the Lamb has affected the experience of this trial. An example of a difficult trial might be extended unemployment. A strong relationship with Christ during this period could include trust in God's provision. Ask volunteers to report on how they have faced difficulties within the context of a relationship with Christ. Ask some to volunteer experiences they have had dealing with trials outside of a relationship with Christ. Have each student write down one current trial that he or she needs to address by completing the following sentence: A great trial in my life is. . . .

After reading from the scroll (from lesson 10), ask students to write a prayer to the Lamb concerning this specific trial. Encourage the students to seek the Lord's help and comfort through prayer and through God's people in the days ahead.

Direct the attention of the learners to the reproducible activity on the following page. Encourage them to use it as a follow-up for today's study. It provides an opportunity for personalizing the grand truths in the text.

Trials in the Stages of Life

It is not unusual for each stage of development to include different types of "trials." Below are five columns, one for each stage of development. List the difficult times you experienced during each of these ages. Speculate as to what "trials" might lie ahead in those stages of life you have not yet experienced.

Childhood	Adolescence (13-21)	Young Adult (22-40)	Middle Adult (41-65)	Older Adult (66+)

Answer the following questions for the most difficult event in one or more of the life stages cited above.

1. How did my relationship with Christ influence me during this difficult time?

2. What kind of impact did other Christians have on me during this difficult time?

3. What could I do to help others through difficult life experiences?

4. How might I better prepare for a difficult experience in the future?

ENDURING WITH THE SAINTS

WHY TEACH THIS LESSON?

One of my favorite sayings is, "You have to deal with reality!" Some people are not good at dealing with reality, however. Rather than facing issues squarely and working through the pain, such folks may pretend that certain problems in life will "just go away" as soon as something extraordinary happens. They think their problems will all be over, for example, when they win the lottery.

But our sufferings are real, and each of us has a cross to bear (Luke 9:23). Christians must not pretend otherwise. We realize, however, that the future reality of eternal life makes our earthly sufferings worthwhile. God has said so. And he is the one who gives us strength to solve, work through, or patiently endure our problems in the here and now. Today's lesson provides us with the reminder that we all need in this regard.

INTRODUCTION

A. OUR MOST PRECIOUS POSSESSION?

In his book *Songs of Heaven* Robert E. Coleman passes along a story from Henri Nouwen about a Lutheran bishop who was sent to a Nazi concentration camp during World War II. While there, an SS officer tried to force a confession from the man by beating him. Although the intensity of the torture increased, it could not break the man's silence. The infuriated officer, pounding his victim even harder, finally shrieked, "But don't you know that I can kill you?" The man looked in the eyes of his torturer and said, "Yes, I know—do what you want—but I have already died."

Instantly, as though paralyzed, the officer could no longer raise his arm. It seemed as though power over the man had been taken from that officer. All the cruelties had been based on the assumption that the man's physical life was his most precious possession. But it wasn't.

B. LESSON BACKGROUND

The book of Revelation strengthens Christians to be victorious over all those forces that oppose them and attempt to destroy their relationship with the Lamb. This divine drama—properly seen, understood, and applied—blesses the viewer or reader. The drama begins by showing us Christ in the midst of the churches (Revelation 1–3). The church as a whole asks for judgment on the sin that causes her to suffer (4–11). After that comes the climax of victory for the faithful, and God's wrath for the wicked (12–22).

Throughout this drama we are reminded that there is a "greater reality" beyond that of our temporary earthly existence. This "revelation of Jesus Christ" (Revelation 1:1) reminds us of God's glory and power. He is present with faithful Christians. He is willing and able to protect us for eternity. But God is also able to

DEVOTIONAL READING:
2 TIMOTHY 2:3-13
BACKGROUND SCRIPTURE:
REVELATION 14
PRINTED TEXT:
REVELATION 14:6-13

LESSON AIMS

After participating in this lesson, each student will be able to:

1. Contrast the punishment of the wicked with the blessings of the faithful.

2. Explain how God's judgment for sin gives him glory and avenges the faithful.

3. Praise God for his justice and mercy.

KEY VERSE

This calls for patient endurance on the part of the saints who obey God's commandments and remain faithful to Jesus. —Revelation 14:12

May
23

bring judgment on the ones who deserve it. That judgment is sure and full; none of the wicked will escape it.

Chapter 14 presents both the reality of that judgment and God's protection of Christians. God is faithful to his Word. He will not abandon his own.

As an expression of his active relationship with us, the Lamb is standing in God's dwelling place. God's people (by the figure "144,000," the same sealed group of chapter 7) are identified by having the Father's name on their foreheads (14:1). The sights and sounds of the scene are reinforced by the "new song" of the faithful because of what is made possible by virtue of their relationship with the Lamb (14:3). They are in the protective presence of the throne.

These who are purchased or redeemed are introduced to the reader as "first-fruits to God and the Lamb" (14:4). The Old Testament offering of the firstfruits was a trusting experience in faith. Through this faith experience the worshiper would learn what God is like. The worshiper believed God would supply a full harvest. The firstfruits belonged to God just as the whole harvest did. The faithful, like the firstfruits offering, belong to God. They have faith that God will provide all that they need—for eternity.

I. EVERLASTING GOSPEL (REVELATION 14:6-8)
A. MESSAGE TO EVERYONE (vv. 6, 7)
6. Then I saw another angel flying in midair, and he had the eternal gospel to proclaim to those who live on the earth—to every nation, tribe, language and people.

The scene now changes to focus on a series of angels and their messages. We need not try to identify these angels concerning whether or not they already have had a ministry in connection with the Revelation of Jesus Christ. After all, God has a great host of angels to assist in his purposes. Remember that Jesus, on the night he was betrayed, said that he could call on "twelve legions" of angels (Matthew 26:53).

The series of angelic messages has to do with *the eternal gospel*. In Revelation 14:3, 4, just before our text begins, we can see what this gospel means for those who have been redeemed "from the earth" and "from among men." These are the ones who sing the "new song," knowing the quality of life with the Lamb. Their faithfulness is one side of the gospel. The flip side is the judgment of the unfaithful. This is something of a repeat of the opening of the fifth seal in Revelation 6:9-11. There we see the protected position of the slain servants under the altar, calling out for the judgment of the wicked. (See also Matthew 12:41, 42 and 2 Thessalonians 1:4-10.)

The gospel message of the glorified Christ is a two-edged sword (Revelation 1:16; 2:12), even for Christians; the gospel corresponds with the message of "the little scroll" that to John was both sweet and sour (10:9-11). Throughout the book of Revelation we have occasion to see both sides of the gospel in the lives of the faithful: it means both protection and suffering for God's people. The suffering is brought by sin, which comes from various directions.

But the gospel requires also that this suffering not go unavenged. This message before us shows the just recompense in the eternal gospel. This is a message to all *who live on the earth*.

7. He said in a loud voice, "Fear God and give him glory, because the hour of his judgment has come. Worship him who made the heavens, the earth, the sea and the springs of water."

Those hearing the message must *worship* God. They must *fear God and give him glory*. He is Almighty God, the powerful Creator (Exodus 20:11; Psalm 146:6). Christians gladly worship him. God's enemies, however, prefer to worship "the beast" of Revelation 13. They stubbornly resist the truth, even though they must be aware of the certainty of the judgment of God for their evil deeds.

B. MESSAGE OF JUDGMENT (v. 8)

8. A second angel followed and said, "Fallen! Fallen is Babylon the Great, which made all the nations drink the maddening wine of her adulteries."

The *second angel* in this series now speaks his judgment message. This message centers on the figure of *Babylon*. This is a term that kindles in the minds of those first readers a picture of a mighty foreign power that had brought captivity to the people of God (2 Chronicles 36:20). In the first century A.D., that great city no longer existed in its literal, historical sense. Yet the hurt that the Babylonian Empire caused in centuries past still could serve as a figure of speech for the enemies of God's people (cf. 1 Peter 5:13).

The angel qualifies *Babylon the Great* as *fallen* (cf. Isaiah 21:9). All prestige of the past is seen as sham. The proud lie prostrate under the judgment of God. Nothing is hidden from him.

There is no question that what the wicked receive is their just due, for they have made all nations *drink* of the *wine* of the wrath of her *adulteries* (cf. Jeremiah 51:7-9; Revelation 18:2, 3). Judgment has come as a consequence of their debauchery before God. They willingly received what they were offered. It tasted so good and felt so good at the time—sin is like that—yet it ended in wrath. What an aftertaste!

THE MIGHTY ALWAYS FALL

Darius the Great was one of the most powerful emperors in the ancient world. From 522 to 486 B.C., he ruled over an empire that stretched from the Indus River in what is now eastern Pakistan, west to what is now Turkey, and south to the area covered by modern Egypt. He built the royal city of Persepolis (in what is modern Iran), built a road system that is still in use, and established a postal system that was far ahead of its time.

In October 1971, Iran's Shah Reza Pahlavi held an opulent celebration in Persepolis to commemorate the founding of the Persian Empire some twenty-five centuries previously. Of course, it was a celebration that commemorated the Shah's reign as well! But only eight years later, that reign was over when radical Islamic clerics took control. The Shah was forced to flee into exile with what little he could salvage of his tattered claims to imperial glory.

Cyrus, a predecessor of Darius, had conquered Babylon in 539 B.C. The remains of that city were a part of Darius's empire. But as Babylon had fallen to a Persian conqueror, so also the time came for the Persian Empire to fall to Alexander the Great. Centuries later, the Shah's time came as well. And so it goes!

John uses Babylon as a symbol of the arrogance of power and opposition to God. The fates of Darius, the Shah, and a thousand others teach us that all earthly kingdoms are temporary. God will use the nations of the world as he wills, and he will condemn those who oppose him. Rulers and nations neglect these truths at their peril. God still writes on the pages of history.   —C. R. B.

II. EVERLASTING PUNISHMENT (REVELATION 14:9-11)

A. IDENTITY OF THE CONDEMNED (v. 9)

9. A third angel followed them and said in a loud voice: "If anyone worships the beast and his image and receives his mark on the forehead or on the hand,

The *third angel* now declares the wicked to be those who worship *the beast and his image*. The repetition reassures the reader that unrepentant sinners cannot escape the wrath of God. Revelation 7:3 and 9:4 tell us that Christians are "sealed"

WHAT DO YOU THINK?

How does it affect you to read about God's vengeance—his "boiling anger," ready to erupt like a volcano?

DAILY BIBLE READINGS

Monday, May 17—In the World You Face Persecution (John 16:29-33)

Tuesday, May 18—Endure to the End (Matthew 10:16-22)

Wednesday, May 19—Many Will Fall Away (Matthew 24: 9-14)

Thursday, May 20—Be Faithful to the Task (Matthew 24:45-50)

Friday, May 21—Our Hope in the Risen Lord (1 Corinthians 15:12-20)

Saturday, May 22—We Have Victory Through Christ (1 Corinthians 15:54-58)

Sunday, May 23—A Call for Endurance (Revelation 14:6-13)

to receive God's protection. The wicked are, in a sense, also "sealed"—they are marked folks, doomed to destruction (Revelation 16:2). To worship the beast and his image is idolatry, pure and simple (cf. 13:12-17; 14:11).

B. FATE OF THE CONDEMNED (vv. 10, 11)

10. ". . . he, too, will drink of the wine of God's fury, which has been poured full strength into the cup of his wrath. He will be tormented with burning sulfur in the presence of the holy angels and of the Lamb.

The wine of God's fury will be *poured* out on the same, meaning the condemned of verse 9. The images of pouring and fire and *burning sulfur* may remind John's readers of the volcanic eruption of Mt. Vesuvius that had destroyed the cities of Pompeii and Herculaneum in A.D. 79. That destruction does not compare, however, with the expression of God's righteous anger for sin that is to come.

There is to be blessing for the faithful and dire penalty for the wicked. The *wrath* that is *poured full strength* means that God's judgment is not watered down. The wicked will receive no less than what they deserve. Their sin has doubled back on them.

When we imagine the pungent smell of burning sulfur and the pain that fire causes, we sense the full dimensions of the scene. The wicked are not punished off in a corner somewhere, but receive their punishment in the presence of the holy angels, and in the presence of the Lamb. The wicked are not in fellowship with the righteous—their unrighteousness is clear for all to see. This makes them worthy of God's wrath.

Those attracted to the world are going to perish with the world. Anyone who chooses to serve the devil must expect to suffer the consequences that the devil will suffer (Revelation 20:10, 13-15; 21:8).

11. "And the smoke of their torment rises for ever and ever. There is no rest day or night for those who worship the beast and his image, or for anyone who receives the mark of his name."

Another dimension of the doom for the wicked is pictured as fire sending up *smoke* as evidence of the consuming power that is present; however, this fire never runs out of fuel. This fiery punishment lasts *for ever and ever* (also Revelation 20:10).

We are cautioned, therefore, to be on guard so that the temptations confronting us daily do not have an overpowering appeal. They may come from peer pressures—no age is exempt. Our pride may be the stumbling block. Prestige in the community may seem to be more important than the moral issues involved. In our day all kinds of sins are so common that we are tempted to think that if "everyone is doing it," then it must not be so bad. After all, this is the twenty-first century—aren't we "enlightened"?

If we are drawn back into sin, we must realize what group we are becoming part of: the opposers of God's people and God's work. In such a situation we are subject to the wrath of God if we do not repent and change our lifestyle. Sin unforgiven calls forth due judgment.

"POMOBABBLE"

John Leo, a commentator on the social and political peculiarities of Western society, has come up with the term pomobabble. The term refers to postmodern explanations of right and wrong that, in reality, explain away the existence of ultimate truth. Postmodernism says truth doesn't exist and all values are simply a way for those in power to stay there.

Fortunately, some people are beginning to see through the haze. Writing satirically to point out the logical holes in such folly, Alan Sokal, a physicist at New York University, wrote a pomobabble article arguing that gravity is simply a "social construct"—that is, a value society has accepted because it is useful. *Social Text* magazine did not realize the article was a hoax, and printed it. Professor Sokal then wrote to the editors and said that anyone who believes gravity to be a "social construct" should come to his apartment and jump out the window—from the twenty-first floor (*U.S. News & World Report,* March 15, 1999).

One of the most dangerous forms of pomobabble is seen in the area of morality. For quite some time now we have been told that morality is merely what society has agreed upon, nothing more nor less. But the fires of Hell are not a "social construct." Those whose "smoke of their torment rises for ever and ever" will be the ones to find this out the hard way. Make sure you're not one of them.   —C. R. B.

III. EVERLASTING REWARD (REVELATION 14:12, 13)

A. OBEDIENT AND FAITHFUL (v. 12)

12. *This calls for patient endurance on the part of the saints who obey God's commandments and remain faithful to Jesus.*

This verse provides us a key for interpreting not only this series of angelic messages, but also the entirety of this Revelation of Jesus Christ. Revelation 13:10 offered a similar encouragement: "*This calls for patient endurance and faithfulness on the part of the saints.*"

In the everyday activities of life, we find our faith and our relationship to Christ tested. It is not always easy to make the right choices, especially in unanticipated or unique circumstances. The appeal is strong; the test so real. To assist us in having the patience we need to endure, we have the everlasting gospel hidden in our hearts. It is a ready resource. Since we are aware of "both sides," we want to do whatever it takes to maintain our all-important relationship with Christ.

In a way, we need to set our minds on considering an active plan in dealing with the hard choices and tests. An active plan begins with backing up to get a full view of what is happening. Is it of God, of the devil, or of my own selfishness? Will my choice strengthen my relationship with Christ or weaken it? How will the results of my choice affect the ones who look to me as an example? It takes active resistance on our part to develop patience. We are resolved to do whatever it takes to stay *faithful.*

Many of life's difficulties can be linked to a lack of will and a failure to consider the outcome. We are thankful that God does not permit us to be tempted beyond what we are able to bear (cf. 1 Corinthians 10:13). The devil cannot really make us do the wrong thing. God is for us, and his Spirit is all-powerful. But we must yield our spirit to his. It takes an act of our will.

Also, our overview enables us to consider the final outcome. If we join the enemy by foolish choices, we can expect due penalty. We can know blessing only when we are willing to do "all that it takes" to keep our relationship with the Lamb. Only then can we anticipate the time when there will be no more tests.

In overcoming the obstacles that stand in the way of holiness, we need proper motivation—that motivation is eternal life. To gain that prize we have to continue to keep the *commandments* of God and hold on to the faith of Jesus. We are strengthened in these when we participate in godly endeavors in the church and in relationships with those who provide insight, encouragement, and accountability. All in all, we must resolve to do whatever it takes to endure with the saints. We can win with Christ!

PRAYER

Thank you, God, for the clarity of your Word. Its light makes it possible for us to have a full view of your work. We are so grateful that that work includes us. We know that our lives will not always be easy. But we are thankful for the help of your Holy Spirit and the Lamb. May we be able and willing to assist fellow Christians when they, too, are tempted. Because of the Lamb and in his name we pray, amen.

WHAT DO YOU THINK?

Do you agree with the lesson writer that our sins are "foolish choices"? Why, or why not?

"Blessed are the dead which die in the Lord."
Revelation 14:13

This visual illustrates both the sobering reality and marvelous comfort of Revelation 14:13.

WHAT DO YOU THINK?

What do you think happens to those who "die in the Lord" but who have no labors to rest from, and no works to follow them? Or is such a situation even possible? Explain.

WHAT DO YOU THINK?

What tools do you see Satan using in your own life to try to draw you into apostasy? How do you stay on guard?

THOUGHT TO REMEMBER

"The Lamb will overcome them because he is Lord of lords" (Revelation 17:14).

B. LABOR AND REST (v. 13)

13. Then I heard a voice from heaven say, "Write: Blessed are the dead who die in the Lord from now on."

"Yes," says the Spirit, "they will rest from their labor, for their deeds will follow them."

The *voice* that John hears *from Heaven* is comparable to the voice "from the throne" (Revelation 16:17; 19:5). Either expression indicates it is God's voice, and this message is to be heard and heeded. This fact is strengthened as John is told to *Write*. It is not that John has to be told this because he is old and absent-minded, but rather because there is significance to the message that must not be missed.

One side of the message that has been presented is the assurance of due judgment of the wicked. The other side of the everlasting gospel, the counterpart, is the reward of the righteous. This reward is not in dollars and cents. Neither is it based on any of our "merits." All is by God's grace through relationship with the Lamb.

This reward will mean the absence of those things that bring toil and trouble. It is truly *rest from* the labors "by the sweat of your brow" (Genesis 3:19). The effect of such rest does not mean that our works are forgotten. Quite the contrary! Christians have the assurance that their godly works do follow them into eternity (Luke 19:11-19).

We do well to remember, though, that not all works of service done in the name of Christ are of equal value before God (see 1 Corinthians 3:10-15). It is even possible to get so careless in our Christian walk that we "lose it all." Apostasy was very real in the first century—the devil used every tool he could. Whether the occasion was the Nicolaitans, false apostles, the prophetess Jezebel, or any other false teacher, people were being drawn away from the truth (Revelation 2:14-16, 20-23).

It is possible to be an overcomer with the Lamb! We do well to identify with John in this scene, as well as in the kinds of choices John makes. Only then can there be a proper sense of security, assurance, and confidence of our relationship with God.

CONCLUSION

The message of Christ is indeed "a sharp double-edged sword" (Revelation 1:16). There are two sides. The one is God's protection, and the other is the reality of hurt. The message of the slain souls under the altar (6:9) has two sides. These faithful servants of God know the reality of suffering. But they are also very much alive, knowing God's presence and protection "under the altar."

The everlasting gospel of Revelation 14 gives us another opportunity to consider both sides. We are protected, yet we still suffer. But our suffering is temporary since there is sure punishment for the wicked opposers of God and his people. As a result, the faithful are rescued from their great trials. The punishment is personal; each one who deserves it receives fully what is due. The blessing is also personal; each faithful servant will know rest from trials since each one has demonstrated patient endurance.

Faithful servants are overcomers. Overcomers are ones who know the strengthening afforded by God's presence. Even in this life we know something of what Heaven is like. Even when we are experiencing opposition, we can lift up our eyes to catch a glimpse of Heaven where trials are no more. Even now we know the presence of the Lamb. He provides and protects, even though we are not yet entirely shielded from hurt. His grace is sufficient for us to be overcomers!

Discovery Learning

This page contains an alternative lesson plan emphasizing learning activities. Classes desiring such student involvement will find these suggestions helpful. The next page is a reproducible activity page to further enhance discovery learning.

LEARNING GOALS

After participating in this lesson, each student will be able to:

1. Contrast the punishment of the wicked with the blessings of the faithful.

2. Explain how God's judgment for sin gives him glory and avenges the faithful.

3. Praise God for his justice and mercy.

INTO THE LESSON

As students arrive hand, each a copy of the reproducible page that follows and direct the student's attention to the top timeline. Ask them to write in major events throughout that span of history that can be considered terrible trials or "tribulations" and those that are blessings. These may include invention of the airplane, wars, medical discoveries, the Great Depression, the Holocaust, the spread of totalitarian regimes, "ethnic cleansing," and attacks on the World Trade Center. Ask, "How does a person deal with any of these traumatic events?"

Say, "Viktor Frankl, survivor of the Nazi death camps and a psychiatrist, found that spiritual life could deepen even in the midst of the trauma of a concentration camp. He discovered that those people who could remain focused on some meaning beyond the severe trials of the camps tended to survive longer and be less affected by the trauma than those without any such meaning. In his classic book, *Man's Search for Meaning*, he reports that he came to realize he had to learn and teach despairing men that 'it did not really matter what we expected from life, but rather what life expected from us.'"

Say, "By substituting the word *God* for *life* in this quote, we find a capsule of the message of our text for today and, perhaps, the book of Revelation itself: "It does not really matter what we expected from God, but rather what God expected from us." Display this statement for the students.

INTO THE WORD

Form two groups. Tell the first group to read Revelation 14 and determine how a faithful person is identified. (*Among the characteristics of these people are these: not defiled, pure, followed the Lamb, and did not speak falsehood.*) The other group should read the same text and determine ways by which a wicked person is identified. (*These*

are characterized as worshiping the beast and the image of the beast and receiving the mark of the beast.*) Ask both groups to report.

After this reading, the first group will read the text again, recording all of the blessings that the faithful will receive. (*These include the ability to sing a new song and to rest from their labors.*) Tell the other group to read the same text a second time and record all the punishments the wicked will receive. (*These include torment and no rest.*) Ask both groups to report.

Have both groups compare their findings from the Revelation text with what is presented in Matthew 25:31-46, by answering the following questions:

1. How do the faithful and wicked compare with the sheep and goats?

2. How are the faithful and wicked identified in Matthew as compared with Revelation?

3. How does keeping or obeying God's commandments in Revelation 14:12 fit with the King's response to the righteous in Matthew 25:40?

Using the students' comparisons, clarify that the Matthew and Revelation texts together provide the image of Jesus as Judge. Point out that the faithful are characterized by their response of obedience based on faith.

INTO LIFE

Say, "It is not unusual for people to claim they believe in Heaven but not in Hell. This text is clear that there are two very different destinations for people. God has expectations for us, and how we respond to those expectations will be factored into God's righteous judgment."

Ask students to state expectations that God has for every individual according to his Word. A general example is to live in a way that is worthy of the gospel (Philippians 1:27). A more specific example is to watch what one says (James 1:26). Write these for all to see.

Ask students to consider these and privately note any in which they have not been obedient. Say, "If God judged us without any mercy, we all would be lost. Yet, God has demonstrated his mercy in providing his Son as the Lamb. The faith we have in the Lamb of justice and mercy allows us to endure."

Read the the scroll from lesson 10. Lead the class in a corporate prayer praising God for his justice and his mercy, especially toward those who believe. Read James 5:7-11 as a conclusion to the time of prayer.

Trials and Blessings

Using the time line below record any specific world events that can be seen as trials or blessings in our lifetime. You might also include any trends (not specific events; examples may include the changing divorce rate, the increased interest in service by young people) that indicate trials or blessings.

Use the time line below to record specific events and trends that are unique to your life. (Examples may include the birth of a child or a severe illness.)

1. How have these events and trends affected the world? Nation? Community? Your family? You?

2. How have these events and trends affected your faith life, specifically?

3. What sort of trials and blessings do you anticipate in the near and distant future?

4. How might you best prepare to face trials in life and receive the blessings offered by God in eternity?

5. How might you help others prepare?

DWELLING WITH GOD

LESSON 13

WHY TEACH THIS LESSON?

Consider the case of a young couple that has fallen into the trap of "transition thinking." The house that they're living in right now is not what they really intend as their ideal housing situation. No, no, their current house is only a "transition house" until that next promotion at work allows them to buy something better.

Transition thinking is a double-edged sword. It is quite dangerous if it focuses only on that which is earthly (cf. Luke 12:16-21). But transition thinking can be a great blessing when it causes us to lift our sights to eternity, when it causes us to anticipate that last great transition when we will dwell with God forever. Such a thought is almost beyond comprehension. It is a concept that will give your learners hope, no matter what temporary situation they're mired in at the moment.

INTRODUCTION

A. THE BIG STUFF

"Don't sweat the small stuff!" more than one person has advised. "And it's all small stuff," someone else added. There is a lot of truth in those two observations. Everything in this world that is temporary is "small stuff." This fact becomes amazingly clear when we have an eternal perspective or outlook on our earthly lives.

But that same eternal perspective reminds us that there is some "big stuff" as well. That "big stuff" includes everything that God thinks is important: love, holiness, righteousness, forgiveness—the list goes on!

The ultimate "big stuff" for every human being is his or her eternal destiny. How sad to see so many people drifting unconcerned in their quagmires of sin. Today's lesson challenges us to lift our gaze to the future, our eternity. When we do, we can find it surprisingly easy to let go of the temporary pleasures of sin. What a blessing God has prepared for his faithful people!

B. LESSON BACKGROUND

The "future realities" for both the righteous and the unrighteous come across vividly in the book of Revelation! Those marked by the Lamb receive full blessing. Those opposed to God, who are marked by the beast, receive full judgment. Beyond any doubt the reader must know that he or she needs to maintain a right relationship with the Lamb.

That relationship is not based on what we see in our lifetimes, but on the full revelation of Christ. The scenes and messages of the book of Revelation reassure us that we will be able to handle any present suffering. The divine power that is with us is much greater than the demonic power that is against us.

We see the end result of demonic power in Revelation 20:11-15, just before today's text. There the spotlight falls upon the wicked, who receive the Judge's condemnation. The fact that unrepentant people deserve their judgment is shown by the record of the works of their lives as recorded in "books." These books of God's knowledge are thorough and contain no mistakes.

DEVOTIONAL READING:
REVELATION 22:1-5

BACKGROUND SCRIPTURE:
REVELATION 21:1–22:5

PRINTED TEXT:
REVELATION 21:1-7, 22-27

LESSON AIMS

After participating in this lesson, each student will be able to:

1. Identify the rewards for the righteous that are associated with Heaven.

2. Give reasons to support the idea that being with God is the best part of Heaven.

3. State one way that he or she will become more aware of living daily in God's presence.

KEY VERSE

And I heard a loud voice from the throne saying, "Now the dwelling of God is with men, and he will live with them. They will be his people, and God himself will be with them and be their God."
—Revelation 21:3

May
30

This part of the victory scene of Revelation 20 may seem sad to us. We cannot picture the victory of the faithful, however, without also being aware of the flip side: the judgment of the unrighteous and the unfaithful. We see in the Revelation of Jesus Christ what it means to be in fellowship with the Lamb, as well as what it means to be his opponent. It is not hard to choose to be an overcomer with the Lamb. He is our great resource of strength. With him by our side we, too, shall be victorious! Whether that victory is a long time in coming or is to arrive soon doesn't really matter. It's the ultimate, eternal victory that counts.

Our challenge today, then, is to be as faithful as John wanted his first-century readers to be. If we are, then our lives will demonstrate godliness to this generation and to the next. If we are not, then judgment awaits.

The book of Revelation makes all this clear to us. The closing scenes of this book bring this message to a climax and motivate us to faithfulness. Rather than seeking more revelation, as some today foolishly do, may we devote ourselves to understanding and applying the revelation that God has already given us. When we do, rich blessings surely await.

I. IN A NEW SITUATION (REVELATION 21:1-7)

A. NEW CREATION (vv. 1, 2)

1. Then I saw a new heaven and a new earth, for the first heaven and the first earth had passed away, and there was no longer any sea.

The transitional phrase *then I saw* juts forth in the text. This phrase extends as a point to hang our hope upon, as nails fastened in a sure place (cf. Ezra 9:8; Ecclesiastes 12:11; Isaiah 22:23). Throughout the book of Revelation we have been alert both to what is seen and what is heard, for the message is the combination of these two.

This scene here is that of *a new heaven and a new earth* in contrast to *the first heaven and the first earth*. In John's vision of the future, the old situation has passed away. This will be a realization of Isaiah 65:17.

This present world has been good, but it is not sufficient for the eternal structure. It groans under the weight of sin (Romans 8:22). In 2 Peter 3:10, 12, the apostle tells us how this physical world will be destroyed. Even the Garden of Eden was not complete enough to provide the fullness of relationship that God has in view for his people. The word *new* emphasizes quality.

We see another contrast between the old and the new creations with the image there is no more *sea*. The sea was a figure of great threat in the minds of ancient people. The sea separates John from his loved ones as he is exiled on the island of Patmos (Revelation 1:9). It is from the sea that "the beast" of Revelation 13:1 comes with his purpose to overcome the saints. For John and his contemporaries, the sea is the epitome of evil, of all things bad and harmful.

Thus the situation that John pictures is one in which all opposition is gone—anything that would trouble the servants of God or anything that would separate them from God. The relationship in "a new heaven and a new earth" is realized in its fullness without "sea."

WHAT DO YOU THINK?

Thinking about the statement, "This present world has been good," what are some of the best things in this earthly life? How will they be improved in Heaven? What joy of Heaven are you most anticipating?

"NO MORE SEA"

In May 2002, Richard Van Pham sailed from Long Beach, California, toward Catalina Island, usually visible just twenty-six miles off the coast. Pham was tired and went below deck to sleep—not normally a good idea since his route would cross a busy shipping channel. But it was an even worse idea on that particular evening.

When Van Pham awoke in the morning, he discovered that the wind had changed, a storm had broken his mast and torn his sails, and he was drifting far off course. Neither his outboard motor nor his two-way radio were working. He spent the next three-and-one-half months adrift, surviving on fish, sea turtles, and sea gulls. (His verdict on the taste of sea turtle meat was "excellent!" and sea gulls "taste like chicken.")

The U.S. Navy discovered Van Pham drifting about two hundred fifty miles west of Costa Rica, or about twenty-five hundred miles from home. Inadequate preparation for the journey, inattention, and rough weather turned the sea, which had been his friend, into an enemy that almost took his life.

For John, the island of Patmos was not a romantic place where one could watch the day fade away as the sun sank picturesquely into the sea. No, the sea for John separated him from fellow Christians. When he rejoices that "there was no more sea," he uses the sea partly as a symbol of his loneliness that will be destroyed in Heaven's glorious reunion of the saints. Both "seafarers" and "landlubbers" can look forward to that reunion.   —C. R. B.

2. I saw the Holy City, the new Jerusalem, coming down out of heaven from God, prepared as a bride beautifully dressed for her husband.

The scene of "renewal" continues in such a marvelous way! John's first-century readers know about old Jerusalem, of course, with all its unholiness and injustice. Even now in the early twenty-first century we can see that earthly Jerusalem is a place torn by violence and fear.

What a refreshing contrast it is, then, to anticipate *the new Jerusalem!* (See also Revelation 3:12.) Abraham hoped to see this city (Hebrews 11:8-10, 16).

Not only is the city new, it is also *holy* and *prepared as a bride* adorned *for her husband*. The text expresses the rejoicing there is in the climax of the marriage. Faithfulness has been pledged and tested. The beautiful result is that bride and husband are thus to dwell together forever. The resulting fellowship is worth all earthly struggles! (See also Revelation 19:7.)

This new city affords protection and security as contrasted with the fear of the sea (21:1). It is God's doing. The bride portrays the blessed response to God's gracious action: a prepared people brought into an eternal relationship because of faithfulness to the Lamb. God's action and our response unite to form a relationship greater than that which has ever been known.

B. NEW RELATIONSHIP (vv. 3, 4)

3. And I heard a loud voice from the throne saying, "Now the dwelling of God is with men, and he will live with them. They will be his people, and God himself will be with them and be their God.

When we read of *the dwelling of God*, the Old Testament tabernacle comes to mind. We recall the tent of meeting in Moses' day, God's presence, the system of sacrifices, and all that God provided to cause people to desire a relationship with him. The twelve tribes of Israel in the Old Testament did indeed learn something of what it meant to be the people of God (Leviticus 26:11, 12).

However, it is only the true Israel (cf. Romans 9:6; Galatians 6:16) that will know the fullness. It is only in Christ that people have become able to comprehend the real meaning of the kingdom of God, a meaning that was beyond the grasp of the Old Testament kings and prophets. We in Christ have learned the meaning of submission to the King and the benefit of his protection. We will learn still more when Christ returns.

4. He will wipe every tear from their eyes. There will be no more death or mourning or crying or pain, for the old order of things has passed away."

We see the fullness of God's care as God himself wipes away our tears (Isaiah 25:8; Revelation 7:17). No comforting parent can rival him!

WHAT DO YOU THINK?

Which figure in this lesson presents to you a more powerful image of the church: the figure of "the bride" or the figure of "the city"? Why?

God shall wipe away all tears.
~ Revelation 21:4

Visual for lessons 11 and 13. *Use this visual to illustrate verse 4 of the lesson text.*

Not only does John picture the removal of tears, but he also lists more things from our experience that indicate the hurts we have felt from our struggle with opposition. The words *death*, *mourning*, *crying*, and *pain* bring to mind issues of suffering and separation. But the time is coming when "the enemy" that brought us such things is no more! All those former things that belong to *the old order* are passed away. Those things were temporary, but the "new" are eternal.

C. New Assurance (v. 5)

5. He who was seated on the throne said, "I am making everything new!" Then he said, "Write this down, for these words are trustworthy and true."

The source of the message—he that sat *on the throne*—underscores the extreme importance of what is said. What is *new* implies a contrast with what was "first." This is an important fact regarding what it means for God to be with his people. The old creation will not just be "fixed up." It is even more than a restoration of the Garden of Eden. It is new! At that time "our lowly bodies" will be "like his glorious body" (Philippians 3:21). Those who know the "new life" (cf. 2 Corinthians 5:17) can become the "new Jerusalem" (cf. Galatians 4:25, 26; Hebrews 12:22-24).

The message gives divine assurance. There may not yet be all the answers concerning "how" and "when," but we know "for whom" this message is given. It is for the overcomers, those who triumph over suffering.

As we have heard along with John the command to write, we know the value and the usefulness of the message. Just as the one who gave them is "Faithful and *True*" (Revelation 19:11), so also are his words.

D. New Inheritance (vv. 6, 7)

6. He said to me: "It is done. I am the Alpha and the Omega, the Beginning and the End. To him who is thirsty I will give to drink without cost from the spring of the water of life.

Again we see titles used to identify the glorified Christ of Revelation 1. He who is "the faithful witness" (1:5) is also the *Alpha* and *Omega* (1:8; 22:13)—the first and last letters of the Greek alphabet. His identification as *the Beginning and the End* is very similar to "the First and the Last" in 1:17. He is the source of life, both earthly and eternal. Many of the titles throughout the book of Revelation keep the reader aware of the reality. Everything is assured—*It is done!*

However, the protection of Christ is only for those who take their thirst to the fountain of *the water of life*. People feel longings for various things and they often attempt to satisfy those impulses in sinful ways. Those unrepentant people are not included here. It is only God's true people who will receive this benefit. Some benefit already has been realized—we are experiencing it right now. The Eternal One who has spoken is the one who has invited us to share this water of life.

The idea of "water" as a figure of God's care is not new. See Psalm 65:9; Isaiah 41:17, 18; 55:1; Jeremiah 2:13; Zechariah 13:1; John 4:13, 14; 7:37, 38. This figure is also found in Revelation 7:17 at the close of a grand scene depicting God, his people, and the absence of all opposition. In our present context we have opportunity to have this theme amplified as we view the city in all its beauty. Amidst the imagery we must not forget we are viewing God with his people.

As Much As We Want, And It's Free!

Years ago, a small Midwestern town put in a municipal water system. Water meters seemed to be a needless expense; citizens numbered only a few hundred, and the town had its own lake. But soon it was discovered that someone, disgruntled

---

What Do You Think?

What improvements over the Garden of Eden do you most anticipate in your heavenly home? Why?

How To Say It

Alpha. AL-fa.

Corinthians. Kor-IN-thee-unz.

Ecclesiastes. Ik-LEEZ-ee-AS-teez.

Ezekiel. Ee-ZEEK-ee-ul or Ee-ZEEK-yul.

Galatians. Guh-LAY-shunz.

Hebrews. HEE-brews.

Isaiah. Eye-ZAY-uh.

Leviticus. Leh-VIT-ih-kus.

Omega. O-MAY-guh or O-MEE-guh.

Patmos. PAT-muss.

Zechariah. ZEK-uh-RYE-uh.

with local politics, was entering vacant houses and turning on the faucets so that they would run continuously. Water meters soon followed!

That petty act was a symbolic precursor to the water problems the world is now facing. The world's population boom increases the need for irrigation water if that population is to be fed. Next, throw in the need for green lawns and golf courses so desert cities in affluent cultures will seem like "home" to people moving there from wetter climes. All this translates into growing demands on the supplies of water.

But the water problem for the less affluent parts of the world is more basic: one in five people in the world do not have access to safe drinking water! In China and the Indian subcontinent, the two most populous regions in the world, the rivers are polluted to the point of endangering health and life.

However, John's promise regarding Heaven is that the pure water of life will be free to all for eternity. He uses water—the very stuff of life itself—as a symbol of the magnificence of the preparations God is making for us. And there won't be any water meters!
—C. R. B.

7. "He who overcomes will inherit all this, and I will be his God and he will be my son."

We must stress again that the result we see is only for those that overcome through the power of the Lamb. Not all will accept or keep a place in God's family as Christians, the church. It is noteworthy to check the listing in Revelation 21:8 of those whose end is the second death. Their end is eternal separation from God—the opposite of the inheritance of the faithful, God with his people (cf. 2 Corinthians 6:16).

II. IN THE PRESENCE OF GOD (REVELATION 21:22-27)

A. Temple and Lamb (vv. 22, 23)

22. I did not see a temple in the city, because the Lord God Almighty and the Lamb are its temple.

The focal point of Old Testament worship was the *temple*. God put his glory there (1 Kings 8:11), but also took that glory away because of wickedness (Ezekiel 10). The laying anew of the temple's foundation in Ezra's day was a time of great joy and weeping (Ezra 3:10-13). The completion of the second temple in 515 B.C. was also a time of high emotion (Ezra 6:13-18).

But no temple experience of the old covenant can match what is being described here! The fullness of the picture gives us *God* and *the Lamb*. From Revelation 4 and 5 and following we were made conscious of the vital role of the Lamb to make our relationship with God possible. There is no "curtain" to separate God from people as in the old temple. The Lamb has removed it (cf. Mark 15:38). This is the great worship experience we desire—all barriers are gone. Now we are in the very presence of God.

23. The city does not need the sun or the moon to shine on it, for the glory of God gives it light, and the Lamb is its lamp.

The Old Testament experience was good, but it was not complete. When we see the city of God now, we see it in its wholeness. God provided lights to benefit us in this world (Genesis 1:16). Yet what they provided in part is now seen in fullness (cf. Isaiah 60:19, 20; Revelation 22:5). Here is the eternal safety and security!

B. Nations and Gates (vv. 24, 25)

24. The nations will walk by its light, and the kings of the earth will bring their splendor into it.

Try to imagine all the dignity, power, and greatness of all the mighty rulers of all time. If you can do that, you might have something of a composite picture to

Daily Bible Readings

Monday, May 24—The Lord Almighty Reigns (Revelation 19:6-10)

Tuesday, May 25—A New Heaven and Earth (Revelation 21:1-7)

Wednesday, May 26—John Sees the Holy City (Revelation 21:9-14)

Thursday, May 27—God's Glory Is its Light (Revelation 21:22-27)

Friday, May 28—There Will Be No More Night (Revelation 22:1-5)

Saturday, May 29—I Am Coming Soon! (Revelation 22: 6-10)

Sunday, May 30—I Am the Alpha and Omega (Revelation 22:12-17)

PRAYER

Father, your glory is beyond description! We have a better grasp of it as we see the goal of our faith in this lesson. We long to be home with you. But right now, Father, we want to share the message so that we can bring others with us. Help us to do so in the name of the Lamb, amen.

help you understand the glory of God. The phrase *the nations* does not refer to everyone who has ever lived. Rather, it refers to the faithful ones who will share the presence of God and his glory.

BRINGING THE NATIONS TOGETHER IN PEACE

In 1899, the International Peace Conference was held in The Hague to develop a forum for settling international disputes peacefully. Fifteen years later, World War I erupted. The League of Nations was founded in 1919 at the end of that war, but less than twenty years later World War II had begun.

The world tried again in 1945. That was the year that delegates from fifty nations met in San Francisco to sign the charter for the United Nations. Since then, world leaders have addressed the UN, but often with a spirit of belligerence. One of the most famous examples of this occurred in a 1960 session of the UN, attended by U.S. President Eisenhower, Britain's Macmillan, the Soviet Union's Khrushchev, Cuba's Castro, India's Nehru, Yugoslavia's Tito, Egypt's Nasser, and many others. The session is remembered for Khrushchev's act of pounding his shoe on the desk in rage.

When the kings of the earth bring their glory to Heaven's gathering of which John writes, it will be in a far different spirit. All people there—whether great or humble—will give honor to the Lamb of God. The Prince of Peace will, at last, have brought the world together. Come again, Lord Jesus!　　　　　　　—C. R. B.

25. On no day will its gates ever be shut, for there will be no night there.

How dark a city often was in ancient times! City gates would be shut securely at night lest enemies plunder the defenseless inhabitants under cover of darkness. Our scene reminds us that the threat of enemies is gone for people in the presence of God. He offers constant light and complete protection. It is eternal day with God and his people. (See Isaiah 60:11; Zechariah 14:7; and Revelation 22:5.)

WHAT DO YOU THINK?

Will you feel secure in the "gated community" of Heaven if the gates are never closed? Why, or why not?

C. GLORY AND HONOR (vv. 26, 27)

26. The glory and honor of the nations will be brought into it.

Rays of *glory* seem to stream in from all sectors. Because of the Lamb, all the nations have been blessed. Salvation has reached unto the uttermost part of the earth (cf. Acts 1:8). Grace given to the faithful returns from them as praise and *honor* and glory for the Lamb upon the throne, for he is "King of kings and Lord of lords" (Revelation 19:16). God shows himself as God by achieving his purposes in bringing us to himself. Here is glory!

27. Nothing impure will ever enter it, nor will anyone who does what is shameful or deceitful, but only those whose names are written in the Lamb's book of life.

The holy city has nothing *shameful or deceitful*. All things are pure and holy as God and redeemed humanity live together (Isaiah 52:1). It is the Lamb who has made such conditions possible. There is complete separation from the wicked. The *names* recorded *in the Lamb's book of life* (cf. Philippians 4:3) gain the promise of Revelation 21:7: "He who overcomes will inherit all this." These are those who know full relationship with God.

WHAT DO YOU THINK?

Christians have their names written in the "book of life," even though we have done sinful things. What will you have to say about such things when you meet your Savior face-to-face?

CONCLUSION

All the details of "the city" have helped us as Christians to comprehend what it means to be "the wife of the Lamb." We have no doubts about God's protection and provision. We desire to enter into the city to dwell with him forever. Knowing the result, we are equipped to handle the present tests to our faith. We are ready to worship and to serve the Lamb.

THOUGHT TO REMEMBER

Heaven makes it all worthwhile!

Discovery Learning

This page contains an alternative lesson plan emphasizing learning activities. Classes desiring such student involvement will find these suggestions helpful. The next page is a reproducible activity page to further enhance discovery learning.

LEARNING GOALS

After participating in this lesson, each student will be able to:

1. Identify the rewards for the righteous that are associated with Heaven.

2. Give reasons to support the idea that being with God is the best part of Heaven.

3. State one way that he or she will become more aware of living daily in God's presence.

INTO THE LESSON

Prior to today's class session take an informal survey of several children, asking them, "What is Heaven like?" Record their responses with video or audio.

As students arrive, give each one a copy of the reproducible activity "My Vision of Heaven" from the next page. If some have trouble coming up with ideas, suggest they complete this sentence: "My vision of Heaven is. . . ." Report the responses you have received from the children you asked in preparation for this class. After that, ask several classmembers to relate their "visions."

Say, "There are almost as many different human ideas of Heaven as there are human beings, it seems. The idea of what awaits us has occupied the thoughts of writers and filmmakers for many years. In fact, *Newsweek*'s August 12, 2002, cover was entitled 'Visions of Heaven.'" (If you have access to that issue, consider sharing what is included.) "To separate fact from opinion and imagination, let's see how Heaven is presented in chapter 21 of Revelation."

INTO THE WORD

Have the students read Revelation 21:1-7, 22-27 in order to complete the sentence, "The vision of Heaven presented in Revelation 21 is. . . ." Students may summarize how Heaven is described in this text or write a single word that captures the essence of the text. As students respond, direct their attention to these concepts: (1) Heaven has some rewards such as the ceasing of pain, sorrow, and death; (2) Heaven, as presented in Revelation 21, is not quite as tailored to each individual as many of us tend to think, since the idea of God residing with people (21:3) is a key concept in this text; (3) Heaven does not have the physical boundaries we have come to associate with life and living, such as a temple (21:22), celestial bodies for light (21:23), and night

(21:25). A look at the texts listed on the second part of the reproducible page, "A New Testament View of Heaven," can complete this "view."

Ask, "What is the focus of Revelation 21:22, 23?" This is an opportunity to revisit the previous points. God and the Lamb are the temple. God and the Lamb provide the light. The focus in these verses is on God and the Lamb. Mention that this focus on God coupled with the idea of God residing with people (21:3) demonstrates the value of God's presence in a biblical concept of Heaven. Though moving from pain and suffering into rest (see Hebrews 4) is often the focus of a human concept of Heaven (and even mentioned in Scripture; see Revelation 21:4), the everlasting presence of the eternal God and the Lamb are what should truly draw the believer's gaze heavenward.

INTO LIFE

Say, "It is difficult for a finite person to describe something eternal. That is what we try to do with Heaven." Remind the students of the concept of dwelling with God in Heaven. Ask students to provide occasions and experiences in which they have been aware of God's presence. These may include such biblical history as the exodus or the incarnation, but it may include personal history as well. Identify ways in which we can know that God has been present in the examples provided.

Ask, "If God is indeed present in this world and not only a distant God who has removed himself from us, how can we become more aware of his presence?" Have students work in pairs to brainstorm ideas. (*Possible ideas include waking up with the first thought on one's mind being a prayer, noticing the handiwork of God's creation more intentionally and verbalizing it, and seeing contacts with people as opportunities to do ministry—service, evangelism—for God.*) Have one of each pair volunteer what he or she considers a particularly good idea of his or her partner.

Say, "Revelation 21 concerns eternity and begins to give us an idea of the value of dwelling with God. Yet, we remain on earth in anticipation of that eternity." Ask students to review the ideas suggested earlier concerning how to be more aware of God's presence. Instruct each student to select and write down one way in which he or she will commit to becoming more aware of living in God's presence. Conclude the lesson by once again reading the verses from the scroll used in lesson 10.

My Vision of Heaven

In the space provided, draw a picture, write a poem, or create a collage that expresses your concept of Heaven:

A New Testament View of Heaven

Look up the following Scriptures to see how Heaven is described in various New Testament books:

Matthew 5:34

Philippians 3:17-21

Matthew 22:23-33

Hebrews 8:1, 2

John 14:1-4

Revelation 4:1, 2

Acts 7:48-50

Revelation 8:1

Acts 7:54-56

Revelation 11:11-19

Summer Quarter, 2004

Special Features

	Page
Faithful in Doctrine and Life...John W. Wade	342
A Merciful and Faithful High Priest	343
The Old Covenant Compared With the New Covenant	344

Lessons

Hold Fast to the Faith

(Hebrews)

Unit 1: Encouraged to Be Faithful

June	6	Faithful to the Son....................................*Hebrews 1:1-9; 2:1-4*	345
	13	Following the Author of Our Salvation ....*Hebrews 2:5-18*	353
	20	Faithful Through Obedience..............................*Hebrews 3:12–4:2, 9-13*	361
	27	Jesus: The Great High Priest..............................*Hebrews 4:14–5:10*	369

Unit 2: Strengthened to Be Faithful

July	4	Faithful to Teaching..*Hebrews 5:11–6:12*	377
	11	Faithful to the New Covenant ....*Hebrews 8:6-13*	385
	18	Roll Call of the Faithful ....*Hebrews 11:1-13*	393
	25	Faithful and Disciplined..................................*Hebrews 12:1-13*	401

Guidelines for the Church's Ministry

(1, 2 Timothy; Titus)

August	1	Select Good Leaders ....*1 Timothy 3:1-13; 5:17-19*	409
	8	Be Ministers of Godliness...*1 Timothy 4:7–5:8*	417
	15	Handle God's Word Rightly ....*2 Timothy 2:1-15*	425
	22	Remain Faithful..................................*2 Timothy 3:1-5, 12–4:5*	433
	29	Do Good Works ....*Titus 2:7, 8, 11–3:10*	441

About These Lessons

Championship sports teams are very skilled at playing both defense and offense. Our summer lessons offer us a great mix of these two concepts for the Christian life. We will learn how to remain faithful (defense) while making sure the church is ready to light the world (offense). Join the training!

Jun 6

Jun 13

Jun 20

Jun 27

Jul 4

Jul 11

Jul 18

Jul 25

Aug 1

Aug 8

Aug 15

Aug 22

Aug 29

Faithful in Doctrine and Life

by John W. Wade

This quarter's lessons provide an interesting mix of doctrinal studies and surveys dealing with practical application. During June and July we will discover the doctrinal foundation for our faith as we see the writer of Hebrews comparing and contrasting certain points of the Mosaic covenant with the new covenant. In August we move to what are commonly called "the Pastoral Epistles," namely 1 and 2 Timothy and Titus.

HOLD FAST TO THE FAITH

UNIT 1: *ENCOURAGED TO BE FAITHFUL*

JUNE

Lesson 1 sets forth Christ's unique relationship with God. Once Jesus had provided cleansing for sin, he sat down at the right hand of his Father. With all that God has done for us, how can we not be "Faithful to the Son"?

Lesson 2 discusses Christ's humanity. His kinship with the human race gives him an eternal appeal—an appeal that none other could possibly have. What could be more important than "Following the Author of Our Salvation"?

Lesson 3 reminds us that Christianity promises the rest and blessings of Heaven. But in order to receive this great blessing, we must remain faithful. Shall we not be "Faithful Through Obedience" to the very end?

Lesson 4 emphasizes Christ's work as our great high priest. Because of his unique position, shall we not approach the throne of grace with the assurance that we will be helped by "Jesus: The Great High Priest" in our own time of need?

UNIT 2: *STRENGTHENED TO BE FAITHFUL*

JULY

Lesson 5 is a vital study for Christians who may have an emotional attachment to Christianity, but understand little about what the Bible actually teaches. How can we be "Faithful to Teaching" when we don't know what the teaching really is?

Lesson 6 reminds us that in the Christian era God deals with us through a new covenant. This covenant is not based on our efforts but those of Christ. With all that Christ has done for us, will we be "Faithful to the New Covenant"?

Lesson 7 reviews the exploits and troubles of some of the great heroes of the faith. Will we follow their examples of faithfulness and be counted in the "Roll Call of the Faithful" on God's great, final day?

Lesson 8 causes us to consider God's discipline in our lives. This is a study much needed in pleasure-driven cultures. With eternity before us, how can we not be "Faithful and Disciplined" in the here and now?

GUIDELINES FOR THE CHURCH'S MINISTRY

AUGUST

Lesson 9 begins our next unit with Paul's instructions to Timothy, his younger colleague in ministry, regarding selection of elders and deacons. If we fail to "Select Good Leaders," how can the ministry of our churches have any credibility?

Lesson 10 sets forth Paul's instructions to Timothy to train himself in godliness and put his spiritual gifts to good use. If our leaders neglect their spiritual gifts, how can they "Be Ministers of Godliness"?

In **Lesson 11** Paul warns Timothy about what is and isn't useful in a Christian leader's life and in the teaching process. How can the gospel move forward if we do not "Handle God's Word Rightly"?

Lesson 12 offers us Paul's warning that many will become unholy and rebellious. This calls for patience and persistence in ministry. What will we say to God on the judgment day if we do not "Remain Faithful" to our callings?

Lesson 13 winds up our summer studies with a reminder from the short book of Titus that God's salvation is intended for everyone. But if we fail to "Do Good Works," can we really claim to be part of the body of Christ?

Sound doctrine should always result in changed lives that glorify God. We pray that the Lord will bless you to achieve this goal as you teach these lessons.

A Merciful and Faithful High Priest

LEVITICAL PRIESTS	JESUS AS PRIEST
Many	One
Of the tribe of Levi	Of the tribe of Judah
Offered animal sacrifices (over and over)	Offered Himself (once)
In the order of Aaron	In the order of Melchizedek
Sacrificed for their own sins and the sins of others	Sacrificed for the sins of others; He was sinless
Served only for a limited time	Serves eternally
Served only as priests	Serves as both Priest and King
Served in a physical, temporal tabernacle	Serves in a spiritual, eternal tabernacle
Functioned under a weak and terminal covenant	Serves in a strong and endless covenant

OLD COVENANT BY MOSES	NEW COVENANT IN JESUS
temporary	eternal
national	universal
priests from the tribe of Levi	priests from all in the covenant
sinful men as high priests	Jesus as only and sinless high priest
sealed by the blood of animals	sealed by the blood of the Lamb of God
repeated sacrifices necessary	a single and final Sacrifice
high priest enters into Holy of Holies for the people	High Priest enters Heaven to welcome the people
written on stones by the hand of God	written on hearts by the Spirit of God

FAITHFUL TO THE SON

WHY TEACH THIS LESSON?

Advances in technology have made counterfeiting a very tempting "profession" to enter. Governments around the world use that same technology to beat counterfeiters at their own game. The fundamental idea is to ensure that the only currency accepted as genuine is that which originated from the proper place.

When it comes to religion, Satan is the master counterfeiter. He likes to use all the newest tricks he can in order to draw people away from Christ. But Jesus is "the genuine article" because it is only he who "is the radiance of God's glory and the exact representation of his being" (Hebrews 1:3). Today's lesson will help us to reject all substitutes as we look forward to an eternity with him.

INTRODUCTION

A. "HOW SHALL WE ESCAPE?"

Just outside the town where I grew up, a big barn sat near one of the main roads. Painted on its side in large letters visible to all who drove by were these words from Hebrews 2:3: "How shall we escape, if we neglect so great salvation?" *(King James Version)*.

Through the prophets and others chosen to lead the Israelites, God began to prepare the way for his fuller revelation through his Son. Through his Son, God opened the very gates of Heaven, making salvation possible for all. For those who foolishly reject him "no sacrifice for sins is left, but only a fearful expectation of judgment and of raging fire that will consume the enemies of God" (Hebrews 10:26, 27). This may not be what sinners want to hear, but it is certainly clear!

There is a sequel to this story. Recently I drove by the barn and noticed that all the words had been painted over. No longer were those who passed by challenged to give thought to their spiritual status. Perhaps this is a modern parable on the condition of the spirituality in our times. The secular world no longer worries or even cares about its relationship with God. And worse, even many who call themselves Christians show little real concern about God's uncompromising demands that his followers live pure and holy lives. But painting out words on a barn will not obliterate his timeless commandments.

B. LESSON BACKGROUND

Commentators have suggested that the epistle to the Hebrews "begins like a treatise, proceeds like a sermon, and closes like a letter." Although some controversy has surrounded this book, it occupies a crucial place in the New Testament.

The main controversy about Hebrews deals with its authorship. In the past many ascribed this book to Paul. However, there are some serious problems with attributing it to that great apostle. Unlike the epistles that bear Paul's name, Hebrews is unsigned. Nor can we give an exact date for its writing. It seems obvious, however, that it was written before A.D. 70. The Romans destroyed Jerusalem and the temple in that year, ending the worship services that had been conducted. Had Hebrews been written after that date, the writer almost certainly would have mentioned it because of the book's subject matter at various places.

DEVOTIONAL READING:
COLOSSIANS 1:14-20
BACKGROUND SCRIPTURE:
HEBREWS 1:1–2:4
PRINTED TEXT:
HEBREWS 1:1-9; 2:1-4

LESSON AIMS

After participating in this lesson, each student will be able to:

1. List the reasons why Jesus is superior to all others in revealing God to us.

2. Explain the honor that is due Jesus as God's Son, the author of our salvation.

3. Make a statement of faith in Jesus as the Son of God.

KEY VERSE

The Son is the radiance of God's glory and the exact representation of his being.
—Hebrews 1:3a

We are not told of the specific destination of this epistle. But clearly it seems to be aimed at Jewish Christians, specifically those then living in Palestine. The purpose of the letter was to encourage them to remain faithful in spite of the persecutions they had endured. The writer seems concerned that they might be tempted to abandon Christianity and return to Judaism. For that reason *better* is a key word throughout the letter. Christ is better than the fathers who had spoken in the past or the angels. Further, Christians have a better hope (7:19), a better covenant based on better promises (8:6), a better sacrifice (9:23), and in Heaven a better inheritance (10:34).

I. GOD HAS SPOKEN (HEBREWS 1:1-9)
A. THROUGH THE PROPHETS (v. 1)
1. In the past God spoke to our forefathers through the prophets at many times and in various ways,

A fundamental proposition of both Judaism and Christianity is that God has spoken to the human race. Our God is not some remote, obscure deity who observes our activities from afar with little or no involvement. How reassuring, and at the same time sobering, to realize that he is not just "out there," but is also here with us.

The fact that God has spoken *at many* different *times* means that he has never locked himself into a predictable timetable for his numerous revelations. But one thing is sure: he always has revealed himself when humanity has needed it.

There has also been a great variety of *ways* through which God has spoken. He has, of course, used people *(the prophets)*—sometimes speaking to them in an audible voice, at other times through dreams or visions. But he has also used other means of getting his message to the *forefathers*. He revealed his will through a burning bush (Exodus 3:2), through a pillar of fire and a pillar of cloud (Exodus 40:38), and even through a donkey (Numbers 22:22-35).

B. THROUGH HIS SON (vv. 2, 3)
2. . . . but in these last days he has spoken to us by his Son, whom he appointed heir of all things, and through whom he made the universe.

These last days may refer to the closing days of the old covenant that, with the coming of Christ, was no longer binding on the people. It seems best, however, to take this as referring to the new covenant, which ushers in the final stage of God's dealings with sinful humanity. Although nearly two thousand years have passed since these words were written, we need to keep in mind that God doesn't count time as we do, for "with the Lord a day is like a thousand years, and a thousand years are like a day" (2 Peter 3:8).

Combining verses 1 and 2, we see a clear contrast between God's previous revelations and his revelation through his Son, Jesus Christ. That contrast was made quite clear on several occasions during Jesus' earthly ministry. On the mount of transfiguration, for example, Moses (representing the law) and Elijah (representing the prophets) appeared with Jesus. Both the law and the prophets were important parts of God's revelation. But in conclusion God spoke, "This is my Son, whom I love; with him I am well pleased. Listen to him!" (Matthew 17:5).

The importance of the Son's message is affirmed when we see that the Father has appointed Jesus to be heir of all things. Jesus is "firstborn over all creation" (Colossians 1:15). The "all things" that Jesus has created according to John 1:3 constitute *the universe*. Jesus affirmed his own preexistence in John 8:58. God's main purpose for speaking to "our forefathers through the prophets" through the centuries was to prepare for the coming of his Son.

Suppose a fellow believer came to you and said, "Say, a friend gave me this book. He says it's 'another testament of Jesus Christ.' Maybe we need to see what it says and add that to our teachings at church." How would you respond to your friend's suggestion? How does today's text help you in your answer?

"The Eagle Has Landed"

The words from July 20, 1969, are still burned in my memory: "Houston, Tranquility Base here. The Eagle has landed." My astonishment and elation as a fourteen-year-old knew no limits when, six hours later, Astronaut Neil Armstrong descended a ladder to become the first human in history to set foot on another celestial body.

The twenty-one hours those adventurers spent on the surface of the moon came back to us in grainy black-and-white, but we could see it all: the lunar module sitting proudly upon the surface, an astronaut coming down the ladder from the module, the panoramic views—so many images! Astronaut Edwin "Buzz" Aldrin called the view one of "magnificent desolation."

The astronauts didn't make it to the moon simply in the lunar module, however. Many years of planning and building had produced the Saturn V booster rocket. After launch, that rocket would shed successive stages until it was gone—leaving only the command, service, and lunar modules. The booster rocket existed for a specific purpose, and it performed its job well.

Judges, prophets, and kings all made their appearance before Christ arrived. They were the successive "stages" over the centuries that pointed to his coming. But they've served their purpose and have dropped away. Now it is Christ alone to whom we look—the one who is "at the right hand of the Majesty in Heaven."

When the Son of God set foot on planet earth, we can imagine that what he saw around him was a picture of "magnificent desolation." It was magnificent because "He came to that which was his own," but desolate because "his own did not receive him" (John 1:11). As we look to him today, may we remember that there are many in our world of magnificent desolation who still need him.   —R. L. N.

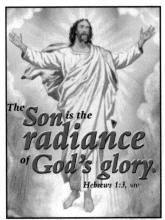

Visual for Lesson 1. *This glorious visual will remind your learners of the majesty of their Savior.*

3. The Son is the radiance of God's glory and the exact representation of his being, sustaining all things by his powerful word. After he had provided purification for sins, he sat down at the right hand of the Majesty in heaven.

This verse summarizes some of the more important aspects of the relationship between the Father and *the Son*. First of all, the Son is like the Father in *the radiance* of his *glory*. John 1:14 affirms this same idea: "We have seen his glory, the glory of the One and Only, who came from the Father."

Second, the Son shares with the Father the power to sustain *all things*. That is, Christ is involved in the power that upholds all created things. Third, he has by himself purged our *sins*. Through his death on the cross he has paid the price required by God's holiness and justice (Romans 3:21-26). Finally, he sat down on the right hand of the Majesty on high, indicating his eternal reign with the Father. (See also Hebrews 8:1; 10:12; 12:2; Revelation 3:21.) There is no glory or power greater than Jesus.

C. Superiority of His Son (vv. 4-9)

4. So he became as much superior to the angels as the name he has inherited is superior to theirs.

The recipients of Hebrews were being tempted to return to the Judaism that they had left to become Christians. One of the main thrusts of this letter was to encourage them to hold fast in their new faith. One argument that the writer uses is to show that the Son is *superior to the angels*. During the centuries between the Old and New Testaments, Jewish writers created much speculation about the work of angels. Although angels are heavenly beings and are messengers for God, they are inferior to the Son because they have not received his more excellent name, that is, Son of God. The next several verses give us more reasons for the Son's superiority.

Visuals for These Lessons

The visual pictured in each lesson (such as the one above) is a small reproduction of a large, full-color poster included in the Adult Visuals *packet for the Summer Quarter. The packet is available from your supplier. Order No. 492.*

HOW TO SAY IT

Bethlehem. BETH-lih-hem.
Demas. DEE-mus.
Deuteronomy. Due-ter-AHN-uh-
    me.
Elijah. Ee-LYE-juh.
Judaism. JOO-duh-izz-um or
    JOO-day-izz-um.
messianic. mess-ee-AN-ick.
scepter. SEP-ter.
Septuagint. Sep-TOO-ih-jent.

5. For to which of the angels did God ever say,

> "You are my Son;
>   today I have become your Father"?

Or again,

> "I will be his Father,
>   and he will be my Son"?

The writer demonstrates the superiority of the *Son* over *the angels* by using a series of quotations from the Old Testament. The writer knows that the Christian readers of Jewish background accept these Scriptures as God's authoritative Word.

The first quotation is from Psalm 2:7 (also found in Acts 13:33 and Hebrews 5:5). This psalm is widely recognized both in Judaism and in Christianity as being messianic. *You are my Son* was not spoken to the angels, but only to the Christ.

The second quotation is from 2 Samuel 7:14, which is identical to 1 Chronicles 17:13. This prediction originally applied to future–King Solomon, but the writer of Hebrews now applies it to Jesus as well. Solomon was in the line of David, as is Jesus (Matthew 1:1, 6).

6. And again, when God brings his firstborn into the world, he says,

> "Let all God's angels worship him."

Firstborn does not refer to some hypothetical remote period when the Son did not exist (indeed, he has existed from eternity past). Rather, it refers to the incarnation, when the baby Jesus was born in Bethlehem. *Let all God's angels worship him* is from Deuteronomy 32:43 in the Septuagint, the ancient Greek translation of the Old Testament, which doesn't read the same way either in the earlier Hebrew or in English versions. (Perhaps your copy of the *New International Version* explains this in a footnote.) Luke 2:14 confirms for us that angels said, "Glory to God in the highest" at the birth of Jesus.

THE ONLY LEADER WORTHY OF WORSHIP

Today is the sixtieth anniversary of the D-day invasion, which led to the defeat of Adolf Hitler and his henchmen. Hitler grew up a penniless vagabond on the streets of Vienna, Austria. After serving as a soldier in World War I, he came into contact with the National Socialist German Workers' Party (Nazis) while living in Germany.

The Nazis were a handful of malcontents and radicals on the fringe of society. Hitler asserted himself into their leadership and transformed the Nazis into a political force. Through political scheming and his considerable ability as an orator, Hitler campaigned so effectively that he eventually enlisted about a third of Germany under the Nazi banner.

By March 23, 1933, Hitler was dictator of Germany. On May Day of that year, he held a rally of one hundred thousand workers and delegates from German labor unions at Tempelhof airport in Berlin. With the help of Nazi symbols, special lighting effects, and Hitler's fiery oratory, the cheering workers were mesmerized. Hitler was, in effect, worshiped as a type of "savior." The sobering and deadly events over the course of the next twelve years would make the error of this adulation plain to all.

Human leaders are fallible and will always disappoint us—perhaps not on the scale of a Hitler, but they will disappoint us nevertheless. Only Jesus is worthy of worship. Following the example of angels, we should worship no one but God (Revelation 19:10; 22:8, 9). Jesus Christ is God, and he will never deceive us. He will never disappoint us. Only he can show us the way to eternal life.   —R. H.

PRAYER

Almighty God, we thank you for allowing us to share in all the joys and blessings that come to us through our Christian faith. Give us the wisdom and determination to pass this faith on to our children and to all others who have not known these joys and blessings. Through Christ we pray, amen.

7. In speaking of the angels he says,

> *"He makes his angels winds,*
>   *his servants flames of fire."*

This quotation is from Psalm 104:4. This verse shows the contrast between Jesus, whom God calls his "Son" (in verse 5), and the *angels,* who are ministering spirits (cf. Hebrews 1:14). The Son is to be worshiped (verse 6), but the angels are to serve.

8, 9. But about the Son he says,

> *"Your throne, O God, will last for ever and ever,*
>   *and righteousness will be the scepter of your kingdom.*
> *You have loved righteousness and hated wickedness;*
>   *therefore God, your God, has set you above your companions*
>   *by anointing you with the oil of joy."*

These two verses are a quotation from Psalm 45:6, 7. There the psalmist praises the glory and might of *God.* The writer of Hebrews, inspired by God, takes these verses and applies them quite appropriately to *the Son* of God.

Since the *throne* of the Son is *for ever and ever,* it is secure, eternal, and can never be threatened. Because God is holy, He, on the one hand, loves *righteousness* and, on the other hand, must hate *wickedness.*

Being anointed with *oil* is a majestic picture of the Son's position above his *companions.* See Exodus 28:41; 1 Samuel 10:1; and 1 Kings 19:16 for Old Testament examples of *anointing* someone to an office of high service.

II. WE MUST LISTEN (HEBREWS 2:1-4)

A. IMPORTANCE OF HEEDING (v. 1)

1. We must pay more careful attention, therefore, to what we have heard, so that we do not drift away.

The word *therefore* is crucial in this epistle. It is often used to mark a conclusion that logically follows statements that have preceded it. Thus when we see the word, we ought to be alert to the practical applications that accompany it.

Here the writer exhorts his readers to *pay* close *attention* to the things that they *have heard.* These things include the gospel message that they had received while they were still Jews living under the law. Also included are sermons and lessons they have heard that have helped them grow toward maturity in the faith.

While many of the Jewish Christians had suffered persecution because of their faith, this does not seem to be the problem addressed here. The author apparently is not concerned that the readers will openly and dramatically renounce Christianity and return to Judaism. The real danger is that the readers will carelessly, little by little, *drift away.*

That danger remains as real today as it was in the first century. Rarely does a Christian publicly renounce his or her faith. He or she is much more likely to drift away slowly. We see it when a person who once attended worship services every Sunday begins to attend only once or twice a month (cf. Hebrews 10:25). Eventually that person shows up only for special occasions, such as Christmas and Easter, or sometimes not at all.

Several factors may contribute to this slipping away—family, business, and recreation interests are possibilities. A growing unwillingness to make the effort to live up to the high standards of Christianity is also a danger. When we see this pattern developing in a person, the church and its leadership need to make efforts to restore that person.

WHAT DO YOU THINK?

  What are some examples of those who have "drifted away" from the faith? What can help people avoid "faith drift"?

  [Advise caution in using real names!]

B. Punishment for Disobedience (vv. 2, 3)

2, 3. For if the message spoken by angels was binding, and every violation and disobedience received its just punishment, how shall we escape if we ignore such a great salvation? This salvation, which was first announced by the Lord, was confirmed to us by those who heard him.

The message spoken by angels most likely refers to the law given at Mount Sinai. No mention of angels is made in the Exodus account of Moses receiving the law at that time. But the writer apparently has access to information not mentioned there. In Galatians 3:19 Paul speaks of the law being "put into effect through angels by a mediator." See also Stephen's final words in Acts 7:53.

The writer of Hebrews uses the involvement of angels in law-giving to make a vital point. Those who disobeyed the law were justly punished—that is, they lost their hope of *salvation.* Since this was true of those who violated the old covenant, how much more certain will it be the punishment of those who violate the terms of the new covenant, which has been established by the death of God's own Son! Notice, too, that this stern warning is not directed at those who arrogantly and blatantly reject the Son. Instead, this warning is directed at those who could become guilty of neglect of the offer of salvation that they already have accepted. This is the "drift away" that the writer has just mentioned in verse 1.

This warning is so important that we should not move on too quickly. God had revealed his law to Moses, and the old covenant remained in force for centuries. Now the new covenant has been revealed through the Lord. Step by step throughout his three-year ministry, Christ had begun to set forth the terms of this new covenant. In Matthew 13:3-9, 18-23, Jesus mentioned various types of responses to his message. The writer of Hebrews is issuing a warning to those who have heard and accepted that message, but now may be drifting away. How can they possibly escape punishment if they drift away after having heard the truth?

There are times when the best way to deal with persons who are in danger of slipping away is with soft words and gentle persuasion. But there are also times when they must be confronted bluntly—as the writer of Hebrews does here!

C. Evidence to Believe (v. 4)

4. God also testified to it by signs, wonders and various miracles, and gifts of the Holy Spirit distributed according to his will.

As God has revealed his word across the centuries, he has confirmed it through *signs, wonders, and various miracles.* Throughout his earthly ministry, Jesus performed miracles that confirmed his message (John 20:30, 31).

As a further and continuing support for that message, our Lord sent *the Holy Spirit* after he had departed (John 14:26). Peter refers to this support when he notes that the message he preached was by the power of "the Holy Spirit sent from heaven" (1 Peter 1:12). How can we ignore a salvation that comes through miraculous signs—signs that can be only from God Almighty?

CONCLUSION

Teaching the exclusive truth of the Christian faith is crucial. Ideally this ought to begin in our homes. Unfortunately, many parents do not feel capable of doing a good job of passing on their faith to their children. Even though most of us are not professional educators, we need to understand that there are many important things each of us can do—praying at mealtimes, having a Bible study with our children, and emphasizing Christian values in our conversations are examples.

Let us all make a firm commitment that we will not allow Christianity to slip away because of our neglect.

What Do You Think?

Why do you think people "ignore such a great salvation" that can be had in Christ? How do we help people examine their false assumptions?

What Do You Think?

How can we communicate the need for salvation to people who don't believe in the concept of punishment? How does the "good news" of the gospel make little sense unless one also has the "bad news" of sin and its consequences as background?

What Do You Think?

How would you discuss with a skeptic the evidence that exists to establish the truth of the Christian faith?

Thought to Remember

God has spoken, and we must listen.

Discovery Learning

This page contains an alternative lesson plan emphasizing learning activities. Classes desiring such student involvement will find these suggestions helpful. The next page is a reproducible activity page to further enhance discovery learning.

LEARNING GOALS

After this lesson each student will be able to:

1. List the reasons why Jesus is superior to all others in revealing God to us.

2. Explain the honor that is due Jesus as God's Son, the author of our salvation.

3. Make a statement of faith in Jesus as the Son of God.

INTO THE LESSON

Prepare an activity sheet titled "The Supremacy of Jesus." Print the following instructions on the sheet. "The book of Hebrews ascribes some wonderful superlatives to Jesus. Read some of them in 1:1-9, and fill in the blanks below. Then use the letters in the boxes to discover the 'key word' for the book of Hebrews."

Follow these instructions with the acrostic below.

KEY WORD: _ _ _ _ _ _ _

Clues:

1. Jesus is the exact representation of [God's] _____ (1:3). *Being*

2. Jesus is _____ of all things (1:2). *heir*

3. Jesus' name that he has _____ is superior to that of angels (1:4). *inherited*

4. Jesus' righteousness will be his _____ (1:8). *scepter*

5. God has _____ to us by his Son (1:2). *spoken*

6. The angels _____ Jesus (1:6). *worship*

(Key word: *Better*.)

Begin the lesson by giving the handout to individuals, teams, or small groups. (This activity is also in the student book "Discovery Learning" page.)

Make the transition to Bible study by telling the class that our study of Hebrews will unveil a Jesus that is better than anything else that life has to offer, better than any god ever imagined.

INTO THE WORD

Prepare a short lecture on the background of the epistle to the Hebrews. Use notes in the Lesson Background on pages 345, 346 and on verses 1 and 2. Use the following words on a visual or the chalkboard as an

outline: "*Author, Date, Specific Destination, Purpose, Better, The Past, Last Days.*"

The following three activities may be provided to as many groups of four or five people as your class has. Each group will do only one and should be given a sheet of poster board and a marker. Prepare written instructions for each group as follows.

Activity #1. Read Hebrews 1:1-9. Remember that the purpose of the book is to show that Jesus is better than, or superior to, angels, prophets, Moses, priests, and the entire Old Testament system. On the poster board list every phrase or word that describes Jesus' superiority. From your list select three or four of these descriptions and share the significance of each with the entire class.

Activity #2: Begin your study by reading Hebrews 2:1-4. This passage and other numerous reminders in this book encourage Christians to hold on to the core of their faith. Christians are still tempted by heretical doctrines. Discuss and select what your group considers the core doctrines of Christianity that must be preserved and taught. List them and be prepared to tell the rest of the class why these are important.

Activity #3. Read Hebrews 2:1-4. Complete the activity "Stay Anchored," noting your responses on the poster. (Provide this group with a copy of the reproducible page that follows.)

Allow each group to report. If you have several groups doing each activity, have one person from each group report only one or two answers.

INTO LIFE

Read aloud the conclusion of the lesson commentary (page 350). Ask, "How would you define *postmodernism*?" (Be prepared with a definition that you have found on the Internet, in dictionaries, or in theological references.) Then ask the following questions. "How is it a threat to the core values of Christianity?" "How does this definition of postmodernism describe our nation or our way of thinking? Give examples." Use the second activity on the reproducible page, "Christ Is Supreme," to lead a discussion of the relevancy and application of Christ's supremacy as it relates to the issues noted there.

Close with a chain prayer. Ask for three "links" or persons to (1) thank God for Jesus, (2) ask help for Christian homes, and (3) ask help for churches in teaching core Christian values.

Stay Anchored!

Hebrews 2:1 tells us to "pay more careful attention . . . so that we do not drift away." There are many "riptides" in today's world that can make it easy to drift away from the Lord. In the drifting waves below, jot a few of these pressures and "tides" that make us gently and slowly drift away from God's grace.

Christ Is Supreme

The first part of today's text, and all of the epistle to the Hebrews, makes it clear that Jesus is better than the prophets, angels, Moses, and priests of the Old Testament system. What does the reality of the supremacy of Christ mean to the following?

TODAY'S WORLD RELIGIONS

TODAY'S CHURCH

TODAY'S CHRISTIAN

FOLLOWING THE AUTHOR OF OUR SALVATION

Jun
13

LESSON 2

WHY TEACH THIS LESSON?

We watch with fascination as demolition crews use explosives to bring down old buildings and stadiums in preparation for something that will be new and better. Sometimes *construction* cannot occur unless there is first a *destruction*.

Jesus came to earth to "construct" something better for us: a new covenant that brings us salvation. In the process he destroyed the work of the devil, which had held us in slavery to sin (Hebrews 2:14, 15). How sad it is to see so many today who continue to sit amidst the rubble of the devil's destroyed work! Today's lesson will present an opportunity for your students to make sure they're not among them.

INTRODUCTION

A. VITAMINS AND GOD

As early as 1500 B.C., observers were aware of an affliction we call *scurvy*. The health problems that this malady causes became very widespread among sailors by the A.D. 1500s. That was "the age of sail," when humanity was pushing restlessly into remote corners of the world on long sea voyages. Victims of scurvy suffered from inflammation of the gums and mouth. In severe cases the teeth would loosen and fall out. The disease brought indigestion, physical weakness, and hemorrhaging of various bodily organs. One report claims that ten thousand sailors died from this affliction between A.D. 1580 and 1600.

For a long time no one had any idea what caused this problem. But gradually observers came to realize that the affliction was due to some kind of dietary deficiency. In 1747 a ship's physician noticed that adding citrus fruit to the diets of those afflicted with scurvy cured the malady. It was only in the early twentieth century, however, that we learned that scurvy is caused by a deficiency in Vitamin C (ascorbic acid). Now we knew the true nature of the cure—and the prevention!

We face a similar situation in the spiritual realm. All about us we see those suffering from the worst of all diseases—sin. Lying, murder, and adultery are all symptoms of a dire spiritual affliction. Many are ignorant of the cause of their troubles, and so they haven't the slightest idea where to look for its cure. Some feel a sense of need and desperately turn to religious fads and frauds to fill their yearning. Often this results in treating only the symptoms and not the disease itself.

If people only realized that God, as he has revealed himself through Christ, supplies for our every spiritual need! In order for vitamins to strengthen us physically, they must be taken into the body in one form or another. In order for God to meet our eternal needs, we must allow him to come into our lives through Christ.

B. LESSON BACKGROUND

Today's lesson text picks up where last week's left off. In that lesson we were reminded of how God had revealed himself to humanity in various ways across

DEVOTIONAL READING:
PHILIPPIANS 2:5-11
BACKGROUND SCRIPTURE:
HEBREWS 2:5-18
PRINTED TEXT:
HEBREWS 2:5-18

LESSON AIMS

After participating in this lesson, each student will be able to:

1. Describe how Christ's sacrifice makes reconciliation with God and atonement for our sins.

2. Explain the significance of Jesus' incarnation.

3. Express gratitude to God for his redemptive act through Jesus.

KEY VERSE

For this reason he had to be made like his brothers in every way, in order that he might become a merciful and faithful high priest in service to God, and that he might make atonement for the sins of the people.
—Hebrews 2:17

Lesson 2 Notes

the centuries. As the high point of earlier revelations, God finally had revealed himself in the ultimate through his Son, the long-awaited Messiah. The writer of Hebrews established the fact that the Son was superior to the angels and thus properly commanded mankind's full attention. We continue that theme today.

I. CHRIST'S SUPERIORITY (HEBREWS 2:5-9)
A. World's Subjection (v. 5)
5. It is not to angels that he has subjected the world to come, about which we are speaking.

The Son was involved in the creation of the physical world (John 1:3; Colossians 1:16; Hebrews 1:2). He also has power over *the world to come.* The writer of Hebrews is firmly convinced that when Christ came in the flesh, he inaugurated a new era. The new era will reach its fulfillment when Jesus returns in triumph to bring about the new heavens and new earth—the world to come. (See also Mark 10:30; Ephesians 1:21; Hebrews 6:5.) *Angels* are, and forever will be, involved and active in this new era, but there is no doubt that the Son is in charge.

B. Psalmist's Testimony (vv. 6-8)
6, 7. But there is a place where someone has testified:

> *"What is man that you are mindful of him,*
>   *the son of man that you care for him?*
> *You made him a little lower than the angels;*
>   *you crowned him with glory and honor*

To say *there is a place* may strike us as a strange way to quote Scripture! But we need to remember that in those days the Scriptures were not conveniently divided into chapters and verses as our Bibles are today. Further, the readers would be familiar enough with this passage (which is Psalm 8:4-6) that they did not need book, chapter, and verse to recognize that it came from the Scriptures.

Many Bible students believe that this part of Psalm 8 has two "layers" of interpretation. First, the psalmist (David) speaks of man in the strictly human sense. In this sense the word *man* is generic, referring to males and females. At the same time the psalmist may be speaking prophetically of a specific man: the Messiah who was to come. Note the phrase *son of man,* which Jesus used to describe himself in the Gospels (cf. Daniel 7:13). On the other hand, this phrase is also used extensively in the book of Ezekiel to refer to that prophet's frailty and mortality.

The writer of Hebrews quotes from this section of Psalm 8 in a context that many believe maintains these same two "layers" of interpretation. First, it applies to Jesus (cf. v. 9). At the same time the phrase "son of man" as used in Psalm 8:4 (and as reapplied here in Hebrews 2:6) can refer to mortals.

The question *What is man?* is just as relevant today as it was when it was originally written. Many today consider humans to be no more than the product of a long evolutionary process. If true, this means that we are unique only because we have superior mental capacities that allow us to exploit the rest of nature.

But neither the psalmist nor the writer of Hebrews sees it that way. Humans have unique worth in God's sight. We are *a little lower than the angels* in that we are subject to some restrictions that angels do not face while we are on the earth. As humans, our physical bodies are limited to existence in a physical world. In our physical bodies we must face physical death. Jesus took on these same limitations when he came as a man, making him also a little lower than the angels for a while.

But there's more to the story. Being *lower than the angels* is a temporary condition both for Christ (in the first century) and for us. We are made in the image of

How to Say It

Belarus. Beh-lah-ROOS.
Colossians. Kuh-LOSH-unz.
Eisenhower. EYE-zen-how-er.
Ezekiel. Ee-ZEEK-ee-ul or Ee-ZEEK-yul.
Isaiah. Eye-ZAY-uh.
Messiah. Meh-SIGH-uh.
Natasha. Nuh-TASH-ah.
sovereignty. SOV-er-in-tee or SOV-ran-tee.

God (Genesis 1:26), but the Bible says nothing of the sort for angels. After Christ's return, we shall judge angels (1 Corinthians 6:3).

After Christ's resurrection and ascension into Heaven, his earthly limitations disappeared when he was *crowned* with *glory and honor* and set over all the works of God's hands. This status, of course, exceeds the rule we were given over creation (again, Genesis 1:26). The theme of Christ's humiliation followed by his glorification and reception of absolute sovereignty occurs several times in the book of Hebrews (7:27, 28; 8:1; 9:12, 24; 10:12, 13; and 12:2).

8. *". . . and put everything under his feet."*
In putting everything under him, God left nothing that is not subject to him. Yet at present we do not see everything subject to him.

On God's great, final day, the world will be in subjection to the redeemed of humanity (1 Corinthians 6:2, 3). Even so, all things ultimately will be subjected to Christ, or put *under his feet*. Those final victories are not immediately obvious to us. Limited as we are by human frailties, it may appear to us that Satan is triumphant. On every hand we see much evidence that he is in charge and is winning. Even in our own lives we sometimes feel this way.

Yet when we seem almost completely overwhelmed by evil, this is the verse that can give us the hope we need. In the end, "our side wins" for all eternity!

C. CHRIST'S SACRIFICE (v. 9)

9. But we see Jesus, who was made a little lower than the angels, now crowned with glory and honor because he suffered death, so that by the grace of God he might taste death for everyone.

Much of the language here is a repeat of verse 7. By coming in the flesh, Jesus was somehow made to be *a little lower than the angels*. His humiliation became even greater when he suffered and died. As a result of all this, he was *crowned with glory and honor*. Paul expresses this same idea in Philippians 2:8, 9. On more than one occasion, Jesus mentioned to his disciples that he must experience *death* (Matthew 17:22, 23; Mark 10:45).

As a result of his suffering, he was exalted and given a name "above every name" (again, Philippians 2:9). His sacrificial death was not to benefit just one race or one nation, but was intended for *everyone*. As a result, we have a responsibility to share this good news with the entire world.

II. CHRIST'S WORK AND POSITION (HEBREWS 2:10-18)

A. WORK OF SALVATION (v. 10)

10. In bringing many sons to glory, it was fitting that God, for whom and through whom everything exists, should make the author of their salvation perfect through suffering.

All things are for *God* and by him. This reflects a statement made in Romans 11:36: "For from him and through him and to him are all things." As part of the Father's work, *it was fitting* for God to bring *many sons to glory*. Everything that God does is fitting and appropriate. At times we may have doubts about certain actions of God, but our doubts reflect on us and on our finite weaknesses rather than on God's wisdom.

Right here is where the Jewish leaders of Jesus' day got into trouble. Their concept of what the Messiah would be like and what he would do led them to reject Jesus because he did not fit their preconceived pattern. But we ourselves are sometimes guilty of defining what we think God is like or what we think he "ought" do in given situations. We may assert, for example, that a loving God would not send sinners to Hell, but that assertion flies in the face of clear biblical teachings to the contrary. Rather than projecting our own opinions on God, we would be wise to allow the Scriptures to speak for God's attributes and attitudes.

The author of their salvation refers to Christ. The word *author* captures the idea that Jesus is the creator or producer of salvation for those who come after him in seeking it. In this capacity Christ is more than just an example for others to follow. He is also the one who created the trail.

A vital part of the author's task was to be made *perfect* through sufferings. This does not mean that Christ was ever less than morally perfect. Rather, the idea of "perfect" here is to "make complete." Under the law, God required the sacrifice of animals for sin. But that was only a temporary solution (Hebrews 10:4). Now under the new covenant God requires the suffering of his Son to deliver us from our sins. This is the sense in which the Son was "made complete" (perfect). We may find this concept difficult to understand, but this is another example where we should accept the wisdom of God rather than depending on our own wisdom.

His Suffering, and Ours

John K. Huk tells us of events concerning the time when Communists controlled the area just east of Poland known as Belarus. At first, the Communists intentionally sought out Christians to operate their stores and farms because they knew they could be trusted. By the 1930s, however, this had changed. Many believers were imprisoned; others lived under the cloud of persecution.

Take the case of Natasha, a young girl whose father worked as a laborer. The father was never jailed, but he knew that he would never be promoted. He also knew that no member of the family would be permitted to go to college. The family attended church openly near Minsk. The congregation repeatedly petitioned the government for registration that was never given.

On Natasha's first day in high school, her mother sent her off with a prayer, knowing what was likely to happen. Natasha came home nearly in tears late in the afternoon. "They assembled the students together," Natasha said. "Before the whole school the principal called me to the platform. As I stood there he kept yelling at me, 'Look at you. Our country has given you your schooling. Our country has educated you and assisted your development as a citizen. And what have you become? A believer. You have turned away from your country's principles and have become a believer. You should be ashamed.'"

Mother wrapped her arms around the girl and tried to comfort her. "I am not harmed," Natasha said. "It was difficult, but I knew my time had come."

The suffering of Christ completed his work to deliver us from the penalty of sin. Reflecting on his suffering makes our own suffering seem more endurable. We know it is temporary. Our own suffering for his Name can complete our walk with him.　　　　　　　　　　　　　　　　　　　　　　　　　　—R. H.

B. Position of Brother (vv. 11-13)

11. Both the one who makes men holy and those who are made holy are of the same family. So Jesus is not ashamed to call them brothers.

What a glorious thing to know that Christ considers us to be *brothers!* (See also Mark 3:33-35 and Romans 8:29.) He is able to do this because we have been *made holy* by his blood. We are made holy as we are set apart for God's purposes.

Through his sufferings *Jesus* Christ has paid the penalty necessary to bring God and humanity back together. As a result, you and I as Christians are a part of his *family*—we are all of one (Romans 8:17). This places a heavy responsibility upon us to live up to the high standards that he has set for us as members of the body of Christ. We are his heirs, an idea Paul introduces in Romans 8:17.

What Do You Think?

Throughout history there have been swings in attitude in regard to our relationship with Jesus. To some he is almost untouchably removed from his followers. In reaction to this some think of Jesus almost as casually as a "good ol' boy" who lives next door. On a scale with "untouchable" at one end and "buddy" at the other, where would you rank the proper relationship between Jesus and his followers? Why?

12, 13. He says,

> "I will *declare your name to my brothers;*
> *in the presence of the congregation I will sing your praises.*"

And again,

> "I will *put my trust in him.*"

And again he says,

> "Here am I, and the children God has given me."

The writer now uses three quotations from the Old Testament to show that our inclusion in Christ's family is not a new idea. The first comes from Psalm 22:22.

Notice that the family relationship (*brothers*) that the writer introduces takes place in the context of the church. How important it is that we develop our congregations into solid "families"! To do that, we first have to learn to have the proper relationship with Christ.

The second and third references come from Isaiah 8:17 and 8:18. Together these verses express the idea of trusting God just as Isaiah realized how his own family had been used by God to reveal his will to Israel. Again, the importance of Christ's family as brothers must not be missed as we become more and more sanctified for his work.

C. WORK OF DESTRUCTION (vv. 14-16)

14. *Since the children have flesh and blood, he too shared in their humanity so that by his death he might destroy him who holds the power of death—that is, the devil—*

Our struggle with Satan is a spiritual struggle (Ephesians 6:12). But because we are partakers of *flesh and blood,* Satan directs many of his attacks upon us through the flesh. Thus if Christ was to be tempted "in every way, just as we are" (Hebrews 4:15), it was necessary that he join us in the flesh.

Through his physical death and resurrection, Christ destroyed *the power of death* wielded by *the devil.* For this reason Paul can hail Christ's resurrection with these triumphant words: "Where, O death, is your victory? Where, O death, is your sting?" (1 Corinthians 15:55).

15. . . . *and free those who all their lives were held in slavery by their fear of death.*

People dread the idea of being *in slavery* or bondage. For many, death is the most feared slave master—feared because its bondage seems so final. But because of our Lord's victory over the devil, we can view death as a defeated enemy. Christ is now the one who holds the "keys of death and Hades" (Revelation 1:18).

16. *For surely it is not angels he helps, but Abraham's descendants.*

Christ's birth was heralded by *angels,* but he did not come as an angel. When Jesus was born, he came as a human—specifically as a Jew in the seed of Abraham. This is true in the sense that Abraham was his physical ancestor (Matthew 1:2). Yet all Christians are *descendants* of Abraham in the more important spiritual sense (see Romans 4:9-16; 9:6-8). Jesus came as "one of us"!

D. POSITION OF HIGH PRIEST (vv. 17, 18)

17. *For this reason he had to be made like his brothers in every way, in order that he might become a merciful and faithful high priest in service to God, and that he might make atonement for the sins of the people.*

The writer's thoughts now move to the high priesthood of Christ (cf. Hebrews 4:14–5:10; 8:1-6). In the Old Testament the high priest was selected from among the people—he was one of them (Hebrews 5:1). In similar fashion Christ was in all things fully human.

WHAT DO YOU THINK?

The book of Hebrews features many Old Testament allusions and quotations, as we see in our text. What are some things our church can do to make sure it does not neglect the study of the Old Testament?

WHAT DO YOU THINK?

Do you as a Christian fear death? Should you? Why, or why not?

A Merciful and Faithful High Priest	
LEVITICAL PRIESTS	JESUS AS PRIEST
Many	One
Of the tribe of Levi	Of the tribe of Judah
Offered animal sacrifices (over and over)	Offered Himself (once)
In the order of Aaron	In the order of Melchizedek
Sacrificed for their own sins and the sins of others	Sacrificed for the sins of others; He was sinless
Served only for a limited time	Serves eternally
Served only as priests	Serves as both Priest and King
Served in a physical, temporal tabernacle	Serves in a spiritual, eternal tabernacle
Functioned under a weak and terminal covenant	Serves in a strong and endless covenant

Visual for lesson 2. *Use this tabular chart to discuss the attributes of our "merciful and faithful high priest."*

WHAT DO YOU THINK?

In the early history of the church, some emphasized the deity of Jesus to the exclusion of his humanity. What kind of problems could this viewpoint cause if it began to spread in our church today?

WHAT DO YOU THINK?

We often think of temptation as being strongest where we are the weakest. Thus, some people draw the mistaken conclusion that Jesus' temptations were not very "tempting": he had no weakness to exploit, so he faced no strong temptation. How would you respond to such a claim?

PRAYER

Most gracious Father, we lift up our voices in prayer to you, knowing that you have provided for our every need. We especially thank you that you have given us Jesus Christ as our great high priest, enabling us to become reconciled to you. In his name we pray, amen.

THOUGHT TO REMEMBER

By the grace of God, Christ has tasted death for every one of us.

When the *high priest* stood before the altar in Old Testament times to offer up the sacrifices, he was bridging the chasm between God and humanity—the separation that had been created by sin. Under the terms of the new covenant, Christ serves in a similar but infinitely more effective capacity. This reconciliation between God and humanity was not cheap, however. The cost to Christ was his suffering and death on the cross.

18. Because he himself suffered when he was tempted, he is able to help those who are being tempted.

Christ identified with us in every important struggle of our existence. Because he *was tempted,* yet without sin, he knew the pain that sin can bring; thus *he is able* to provide *help* and strength for us when we face temptation. When we pray for forgiveness for our sins, we are not praying to some distant and aloof god who does not feel our pain. Instead, our prayers arise to one "who has been there." Our prayers are to the God who has felt the pain of sin more than we can possibly imagine.

COMBAT EXPERIENCE?

Sometimes we feel that our leaders don't really know what it is like to live where we live. Dwight Eisenhower was never in combat, yet his orders meant life or death to those under his command. He asked repeatedly to be sent overseas to fight during World War I, but his requests were denied. He spent the entire war in the U.S., training troops who would be sent into combat.

After that war ended, Eisenhower served with distinction on various staff jobs, but felt he would never be given the opportunity of a command. By 1941 he was a colonel. The Army Chief of Staff liked his work and promoted him to brigadier general and then to major general. Eisenhower eventually became Supreme Commander for the D-day invasion. On December 20, 1944, he was a five-star general.

How did a man who never saw combat relate to the men under his command? Anyone who has seen the photos of "Ike" talking to the GIs can see that this man from a little town in Kansas understood the hopes and fears of the average soldier.

Yet Jesus understands our hopes, fears, and needs infinitely better than any human leader can. Jesus faced personal "combat" with Satan. Jesus knew poverty, rejection, pain, even death. He is Creator, Ruler, and Redeemer. If people are willing to put their trust in an Eisenhower for an earthly cause, should they not be even more willing to trust Jesus for their eternity?   —R. H.

CONCLUSION

We live in a world where suffering abounds. Suffering may be physical, but often the more serious and sustained suffering we endure is emotional and spiritual in nature. Modern science has made great strides in developing medicines and techniques that eliminate much of our physical suffering. Counselors have also developed strategies that reduce emotional suffering. With all of these resources available, we are able to avoid a great deal of suffering in our daily lives.

Since we are so concerned about avoiding suffering, we are always amazed when anyone chooses to suffer. As a result, we applaud those who heroically risk pain and suffering for some great cause. Examples include soldiers serving their country or someone risking his or her life to save another from danger.

If these people are worthy of our praise, how much more we should stand in utter amazement that our Lord should leave his heavenly throne and come into this world to suffer humiliation and the cross for us! Also amazing is the fact that many continue in rebellion against him (John 1:11). Sometimes ignorantly, but more often knowingly and arrogantly, we have defied him. And yet our Lord came and "died for our sins according to the Scriptures" (1 Corinthians 15:3).

Discovery Learning

This page contains an alternative lesson plan emphasizing learning activities. Classes desiring such student involvement will find these suggestions helpful. The next page is a reproducible activity page to further enhance discovery learning.

LEARNING GOALS

After participating in this lesson, the student will be able to:

1. Describe how Christ's sacrifice makes reconciliation with God and atonement for our sins.

2. Explain the significance of Jesus' incarnation.

3. Express gratitude to God for his redemptive act through Jesus.

INTO THE LESSON

Option #1. Early in the week recruit a volunteer to give a three- or four-minute report on the disease "scurvy" and the importance of vitamin C. Give that person a bottle of vitamin C and an orange to use as visual aids. Also give a photocopy of the introduction to today's lesson commentary and an article from an encyclopedia about scurvy. After the report is completed, make the transition to Bible study by using the concluding remarks in the lesson commentary Introduction.

Option #2. Ask people to name their favorite authors and the type of books they write. List the names on a poster board. Make the transition to the lesson by saying, "Hebrews introduces us to another author." Tell the class Jesus is called the "author" of our salvation in 2:10. Hebrews 2 unpacks a wonderful glimpse of Jesus' purpose in coming to earth and his relationship with us.

INTO THE WORD

Ask people to work in reading teams of four or five people. Give each team a written copy of one of the following assignments. Distribute to all teams (except team #1) a copy of the entire lesson commentary for today's study. Give teams 1 and 2 a Bible dictionary also.

Reading Team #1. Your key word is *incarnation*. Read Hebrews 2:5-18, and then read the article in the Bible dictionary about "incarnation." Define *incarnation* and identify notes of significance for believers. Select a spokesperson to report your findings.

Reading Team #2. Your key words are *lower* and *higher*. Read Hebrews 2:5-18. Clarify and explain how Jesus is both "lower" and "higher." Also explain why we needed someone with flesh and blood—not an angel—to die in our place. Select a spokesperson to share your findings.

Reading Team #3: Your key words are *reconciliation* and *atonement*. Define these words and state how these words define or influence our relationship with God.

How do these words connect with the picture of Jesus as the "author" of our salvation? Select a spokesperson to share your findings.

Reading Team #4. Your key word is *make(s)*. Read Hebrews 2:5-18. Explain the significance of each use of the word or how each of the following happens: v. 11, makes us holy; vv. 11, 14-18, makes us brothers or family; v. 17, makes atonement. Select a spokesperson to share your findings with the class.

Allow each team's spokesperson to report. If you have more than one group on the same task, ask one team to report and others to add to comments already made.

INTO LIFE

The following activity may be done as a whole class activity or in the small groups used earlier. Display four poster boards, each with one of the following headings: "Jesus' Incarnation," "Jesus, Author of Salvation," "My Reconciliation," and "Celebrate Sanctification." Tell the class or groups, "You are worship directors selecting songs for four different worship services, focusing on the theme assigned. Music helps us celebrate and give thanks. Determine appropriate choruses or songs for your song service." Have a stack of hymnbooks and chorus books available.

Conclude this study on a devotional note. Give each person a copy of the reproducible page that follows. Allow a few minutes for each to "develop his snapshots" in the "Non-Digital Snapshots" exercise at the top of the page. Ask those who will to describe their snapshots with the words or sketches they have used on their sheets.

To individualize today's study, refer each learner to the second activity on the reproducible page, "Experiencing Atonement." Suggest that each use this in the coming week in one of his or her personal devotional times.

Repeat as a group the verse appearing at the bottom of the reproducible (2 Corinthians 5:21). Once it is generally known, do a "pass-along" activity wherein one person starts the verse (for example, "God made him who had no sin") and then says the name of another class member who will add a phrase/clause (for example, "to be sin for us") and then "pass the verse along" to another until it is complete. Repeat until all have the verse reasonably well fixed in mind.

Non-Digital Snapshots

Hebrews 2:5-11 brings wonderful mental images to mind. Perhaps you can help capture these "snapshots" and make them personal to you.

HOLY MEN

Verse 11 reminds us that Jesus has the power to make individuals holy. Make a word picture of holiness by writing words that describe your concept of holy ones.

My "snapshot" of holy ones

REPRESENTING ATONEMENT

The word *atonement* is a special word for Christians. Draw a simple picture representing atonement for sins.

My "snapshot" of atonement

Experiencing Atonement

In the space below use words or draw a picture to express your personal reaction to enjoying atonement.

"God made him who had no sin to be sin for us, so that in him we might become the righteousness of God" (2 Corinthians 5:21).

FAITHFUL THROUGH OBEDIENCE

LESSON 3

Jun
20

WHY TEACH THIS LESSON?

Will it be safe to travel on an airplane that makes it 98 percent of the way to its destination? Could you survive by swimming only 95 percent of the way across a deep lake? Can an athlete win by running 99 percent of the race?

In all of these examples, only 100 percent will do. The same is true of the Christian life. To gain eternal life requires that "we hold firmly till the end the confidence we had at first" (Hebrews 3:14). We show our firm hold by means of our obedience to Christ. The history of God's people shows us, unfortunately, many examples of those who did not make it to the finish line. Today's lesson tells us how and why to avoid being one of those.

INTRODUCTION

A. FAITHFUL UNTO DEATH

In the early morning hours of February 26, 1852, the British troopship *H.M.S. Birkenhead* was sailing off the coast of Africa. Over six hundred were on board—soldiers, sailors, women, and children. Suddenly the ship struck a hidden reef and began to take on water. It was soon obvious that the ship could not be saved, and the soldiers gave a ready hand to the sailors who were beginning to lower the lifeboats. By order of the commanding officer, women and children had priority in the limited number of boats.

As the survivors pulled away from the ship, the last view they had of the sinking vessel was that of the soldiers still standing at attention until the commanding officer ordered them to save themselves by any means possible. All of the women and children survived, but many of those still on board who could not swim continued to stand in military formation as the ship went down.

Over four hundred fifty soldiers and sailors died that day, including the commanding officer and the ship's captain. Their sacrifice and self-discipline were memorialized as "the Birkenhead drill" by Rudyard Kipling (1865–1936) in his poem "Soldier an' Sailor Too":

> To take your chance in the thick of a rush,
>   with firing all about,
> Is nothing so bad when you've cover to 'and,
>   an' leave an' likin' to shout;
> But to stand an' be still to the Birken'ead drill
>   is a [very] tough bullet to chew,
> An' they done it, the Jollies—'Er Majesty's Jollies—
>   soldier an' sailor too!

Those who lost their lives that day could not be called martyrs for the cause of Christ. Yet their resoluteness is similar to what Christians have demonstrated

DEVOTIONAL READING:
2 CORINTHIANS 5:16–6:2

BACKGROUND SCRIPTURE:
HEBREWS 3:12–4:13

PRINTED TEXT:
HEBREWS 3:12–4:2, 9-13

LESSON AIMS

After participating in this lesson, each student will be able to:

1. Cite the dangers of falling away from the faith and the rewards for remaining faithful.

2. Explain why God expects faithful obedience from his people.

3. Memorize one passage of Scripture to encourage faithful living.

KEY VERSE

We have come to share in Christ if we hold firmly till the end the confidence we had at first.   —Hebrews 3:14

LESSON 3 NOTES

down through the centuries. In the struggle between God and the forces of evil, a few of us may be called upon to perform dangerous duties for our Lord. In most situations God seems to ask us to perform the routine and outwardly humdrum tasks that appear to be anything but heroic. In all cases, however, God requires us to remain steadfast under every pressure—faithful unto death itself!

B. LESSON BACKGROUND

The previous two lessons presented some facts that are fundamental to the Christian faith. God has spoken to humanity—first to "our forefathers" through the prophets, and now "in these last days" through his Son. The Son is one with the Father, "the radiance of God's glory and the exact representation of his being" (Hebrews 1:1-3). That makes the message that he brings unique.

Another vital point is that the Son is superior to the angels. Yet he humbled himself, taking on flesh, that he might through his suffering and death destroy the devil (2:14). Finally, he stands in the presence of God as our great high priest to make reconciliation for our sins (2:17).

Now comes the "so what?" point. If all these things are true—and they are— so what? Today's lesson gives us an answer to that question. Hebrews 2:3, from two lessons ago, began to provide us with some of the answer by pointing out that there is no escape for us if we neglect the great salvation he offers. Today's lesson enlarges on this answer by urging the people to defend themselves against the sin of unbelief. That message is just as demanding on us today as it was when it was first written because both blatant, overt unbelief and the casual, noncommitted kind of "practical unbelief" are rampant.

I. EXHORTATION TO FAITHFULNESS (HEBREWS 3:12-19; 4:1, 2)
A. DON'T HARDEN HEARTS (3:12-19)
12. See to it, brothers, that none of you has a sinful, unbelieving heart that turns away from the living God.

Satan is always seeking to undermine our faith, weaken it, and ultimately destroy it. Sometimes he uses forceful frontal attacks, challenging people's faith through threats and physical torture. More often, however, he uses various clever tricks to erode faith slowly, wearing it away so gently that we are scarcely aware of it until we face a real crisis and find ourselves helpless.

In the four verses previous to this one, the readers are reminded of their forefathers in the wilderness. They had witnessed God's hand upon the Egyptians, and yet they rebelled against him. We may wonder how in the face of God's mighty works they could still fall into unbelief, but we have only to look into our own lives to find the answer. Their punishment was that "they shall never enter my rest" (Hebrews 3:11; cf. Psalm 95:11) That "rest" refers to the promised land, which almost an entire generation did not live to see.

The writer uses this history to warn his readers that they will also lose their rest (i.e., Heaven) if they harden their hearts. Going back into Judaism is also departing *from the living God*, since that would mean rejecting God's most profound revelation: his Son.

13. But encourage one another daily, as long as it is called Today, so that none of you may be hardened by sin's deceitfulness.

In the previous verse the readers were addressed as "brothers," indicating that they were members of a family. As such, they had a special responsibility to exhort or encourage one another to remain faithful.

This exhortation was to be daily, and for good reason. Satan is relentless in his efforts to tempt, and so we need help and encouragement regularly and

WHAT DO YOU THINK?

Some people view salvation as holding a ticket to Heaven—once they have it, they can do as they please because no one can take away their "ticket." What is the danger of such a view?

frequently to resist him. Through its deceitfulness sin promises so much but delivers only disaster. Christian fellowship is vital in helping avoid this snare (see Hebrews 10:25).

THE TRIUMPH OF THE TEN THOUSAND

In 401 B.C. ten thousand Greek soldiers found themselves deep in enemy territory, leaderless, and with no food, scant weapons, and no source of supplies. They had enlisted in the army of Cyrus, named after Cyrus the Great, the conqueror of Babylon of some one hundred eighty years previous. The latter Cyrus had amassed an army of more than one hundred thousand. Many were Asiatics (barbarians), with ten thousand Greeks forming the fighting core. Cyrus was fighting his brother for their dead forefather's Persian throne.

Cyrus fought the Persians at Cunaxa and won, but he was killed in the battle. With his death the barbarian allies melted away, leaving the ten thousand Greeks to fend for themselves. Their leaders went to a conference with the Persians under guarantee of safe passage, but only one came back, stabbed and beaten. As he died, he gasped out the truth that the Persians had murdered all their officers.

Xenophon, one of the ten thousand, called a council of the lesser officers who had not been invited to that conference. "Do not despair," he told them. "We are Greeks. We are free men who can think for ourselves."

Hungry and isolated, the ten thousand marched homeward. They skillfully defeated the Persians whenever they attacked. With each crisis Xenophon would call an assembly, explain the situation, and ask for suggestions. "Whoever has a better plan, let him give it."

One day they heard a roaring sound. An ambush? Ten thousand weary soldiers came to the ready. No, it was not the enemy, it was the welcome sound of the sea. From here they could easily make it home.

How many examples from history do we need to tell us what we already know: that we need to stick together, to help each other, to "encourage one another daily"?
—R. H.

14. We have come to share in Christ if we hold firmly till the end the confidence we had at first.

We have the precious privilege of being, in a sense, partners with Christ. We *share* in his kingdom. But there is a condition that must be met to keep our position: we must be steadfast until *the end*. How we begin the race is important, of course. But how we finish it is vital. All of us know of those who started well in Christ's kingdom, but for one reason or another fell out of the race (cf. 2 Timothy 4:7). Some became weary and did not have the spiritual stamina to finish. Others were distracted by the worthless toys that Satan dangled before them.

15, 16. As has just been said:

> "Today, if you hear his voice,
>   do not harden your hearts
> as you did in the rebellion."

Who were they who heard and rebelled? Were they not all those Moses led out of Egypt?

Verse 15 is a quotation from Psalm 95:7, 8. It reminds those of Jewish background of their long history. At the time Hebrews was written, this history, stretching back to Abraham, covered about two thousand years. History can be a powerful teaching instrument, provided that people learn from it. Unfortunately, the Jewish people did not learn the lessons from history they should have learned. But are we any different?

WHAT DO YOU THINK?

What does it mean for a person to become "hardened" and how does it happen? What has caused you to become a little hardened at times? How did you overcome it?

Hold Fast! Hold Firmly!

from Hebrews 3:14; 4:14

Visual for lessons 3 and 4. *Leave this image posted this week and next to remind your learners to hold on!*

Do not harden your hearts is an encouragement for the readers to avoid the mistakes of their forefathers in the wilderness. The readers undoubtedly have heard the account of the exodus many times, but the writer calls their attention to it in order to make an application to their current situation. God had blessed the Israelites in many ways when he used *Moses* to lead them *out of Egypt.* Yet in spite of these blessings, they had provoked God by hardening their *hearts.* However, not all that came out of Egypt fell into this trap. Caleb and Joshua were exceptions (Deuteronomy 1:36, 38). May we have their faithfulness!

17. And with whom was he angry for forty years? Was it not with those who sinned, whose bodies fell in the desert?

This verse reflects Numbers 14:29, 32. That passage was written before the punishment took place. And it indeed came true. The sin of those *whose bodies fell in the desert* was a failure to listen and to heed (Numbers 14:22). This led to unbelief, as our next verses show.

18, 19. And to whom did God swear that they would never enter his rest if not to those who disobeyed? So we see that they were not able to enter, because of their unbelief.

Those who perished in the wilderness and were not able to enter into the promised land were punished because of *unbelief.* Yet God did not expect the ancient Israelites to have a blind faith—quite the opposite! They had seen God's glory and miracles (again, Numbers 14:22). Their failure to believe was thus inexcusable. Now that we have the Son, is our own unbelief any less inexcusable?

B. DON'T FALL SHORT (4:1, 2)

1, 2. Therefore, since the promise of entering his rest still stands, let us be careful that none of you be found to have fallen short of it. For we also have had the gospel preached to us, just as they did; but the message they heard was of no value to them, because those who heard did not combine it with faith.

Chapter 4 begins with a dire warning based on the history the writer has just reviewed. Most Israelites did not survive to reach the (earthly) promised land because of unbelief. But an even worse fate would befall the readers of Hebrews if they should turn away from God: eternal exclusion from Heaven.

The Hebrew Christians have heard the good news of Christ's atoning death and have accepted it. In a similar way, the Israelites who were led out of Egypt had *heard* (and seen) the good news that a better life awaited them once they escaped the bonds of slavery. Unfortunately, this good news did not profit them because their actions were not combined *with faith.* This is the writer's first of more than thirty uses of the word *faith.* What an important concept this is, then and now!

II. PROMISE OF REST (HEBREWS 4:9-11)

A. FUTURE SABBATH (vv. 9, 10)

9, 10. There remains, then, a Sabbath-rest for the people of God; for anyone who enters God's rest also rests from his own work, just as God did from his.

In Hebrews 4:3-8 (not in our text for today) the author continues with Old Testament quotations and examples. Verse 9 begins the logical conclusion to all this, as we see that important transition word *then.*

The *Sabbath-rest* mentioned here is, of course, Heaven. This idea looks back to creation, when God, after six days of creative activity, rested on the seventh day (Genesis 2:1-3). It looks forward to the time when we rest from our earthly works (Revelation 14:13).

This does not mean, however, that we are to look forward to our heavenly rest as a place where we will do nothing. The Scriptures give us only a few hints

WHAT DO YOU THINK?

Since we live among people who believe all sorts of things, how can we communicate that it is only certain beliefs that allow us to "enter his rest"? How do you make sure that you don't fall into false beliefs or unbelief in this regard?

WHAT DO YOU THINK?

How can we as Christians use the Old Testament concept of "Sabbath rest" for our lives today—if at all? How do we avoid the mistaken notion that Sunday is the "Christian Sabbath"?

[Make sure your learners consider Colossians 2:16 in this discussion.]

of what Heaven will be like, but we certainly have reason to believe that we will be active there.

B. PRESENT EFFORT (v. 11)

11. Let us, therefore, make every effort to enter that rest, so that no one will fall by following their example of disobedience.

As the author exhorts the readers to *make every effort to enter that rest*, the suggestion is not that they are to work to "earn" their salvation. That idea is foreign to New Testament teaching. Salvation comes through God's grace (Ephesians 2:8, 9). God's Son has done all the work necessary for us to enter Heaven. Yet faith without works is dead faith (James 2:26). So we work to the glory of God to show where our allegiance lies.

The readers' Jewish forefathers had fallen in the wilderness because they weren't willing to step out on faith to do the work of entering the promised land. That work of faith would have realized that it was actually God working behind the scenes to defeat the enemies. Their failure is an example of unbelief.

III. POWER OF GOD (HEBREWS 4:12, 13)

A. SWORD THAT PENETRATES (v. 12)

12. For the word of God is living and active. Sharper than any double-edged sword, it penetrates even to dividing soul and spirit, joints and marrow; it judges the thoughts and attitudes of the heart.

The concept of God's *word* sometimes refers to Christ himself, as in John 1:1 or Revelation 19:13. Here, however, it refers to God's revelation, written down as Scripture. The *word of God* is not just a book, which may do little more than gather dust on a shelf. It is involved in the work of judging and guiding those who carry it in their hearts and heed it.

The illustration of this power is a comparison with a sword (cf. Ephesians 6:17), specifically a *double-edged sword*. Such a sword "cuts both ways" and is powerful in all kinds of situations (cf. Proverbs 5:3, 4; Revelation 1:16; 2:12). Just as a sharp sword in the hands of a skilled fighter can shatter bones *and marrow*, so the Word may penetrate the inner workings of our spirits.

We may be able to hide our thoughts and intentions from those about us, but we cannot hide them from the Word. The Word not only guides our actions, it also judges whether or not we pay heed to that guidance.

B. SIGHT THAT PENETRATES (v. 13)

13. Nothing in all creation is hidden from God's sight. Everything is uncovered and laid bare before the eyes of him to whom we must give account.

Whether on the highest mountain, beneath the deepest sea, or behind the thickest wall, we cannot escape God's penetrating vision. This constant surveillance prepares us for the time when we stand before the heavenly judgment throne. When the Lord returns, he "will bring to light what is hidden in darkness and will expose the motives of men's hearts" (1 Corinthians 4:5). Wise is the person who lives life as if God were watching every move—which he is.

PEOPLE WATCHING

Do you enjoy watching people? Perhaps you have noticed how people react to one another in restaurants. At one table is a particular couple; you may see her glancing around the room, her eyes never quite meeting his. That is just as well, because he is intent on his meal. They've not exchanged a word for ten minutes. Over in a corner sits another couple. Both people lean across the table. Each responds to

---

DAILY BIBLE READINGS

Monday, June 14—*Do Not Harden Your Hearts (Psalm 95: 6-11)*

Tuesday, June 15—*The Israelites Rebelled in the Wilderness (Deuteronomy 1:22-33)*

Wednesday, June 16—*Obedience to God Brings Blessing (Deuteronomy 11:22-32)*

Thursday, June 17—*We Are Ambassadors for Christ (2 Corinthians 5:16–6:2)*

Friday, June 18—*Hold Your Confidence Firm (Hebrews 3: 12-19)*

Saturday, June 19—*We Who Believe Enter God's Rest (Hebrews 4:1-5)*

Sunday, June 20—*Make Efforts to Enter That Rest (Hebrews 4:6-13)*

WHAT DO YOU THINK?

Have you ever felt yourself being "cut" (judged) by God's "double-edged sword"? What was it like for you, and how did you react?

How to Say It

Babylon. BAB-uh-lun.
Caleb. KAY-leb.
Cunaxa. Koo-NAK-suh.
Cyrus. SIGH-russ.
Deuteronomy. Due-ter-AHN-uh-me.
Joshua. JOSH-yew-uh.
Persian. PER-zhun.
Santayana. San-tuh-YAH-nuh.
Xenophon. ZEE-nuh-fun.

Prayer

Help us, Father, to learn how to please you through obeying you. Guide us as we seek to find your will for us, and then give us the strength, knowledge, will, and stamina to serve you in ways that will be pleasing to you. Help us avoid distractions that can keep us from the obedience that you require. Because of Jesus and in his name, amen.

Thought to Remember

"Ask for the ancient paths, ask where the good way is, and walk in it" (Jeremiah 6:16).

what the other says. Both laugh. Which pair is likely to be the couple married twenty-five years? Which pair is likely to be dating or newly married?

Researchers tell us that gestures and "body language" can reveal much. But body language can also be misleading. A youth minister was concerned about one member of the Youth Committee. Every time the youth minister spoke during a committee meeting, this man would frown and tilt his head. "He doesn't like me," thought the youth minister. Months later the youth minister realized that the man had difficulty hearing; the furrowed brow and tilted head were simply the result of his attempt to hear.

Outward gestures can be revealing, but also can be superficial and misleading. God, however, is not fooled by any body language. No secrets can be kept from him. We cannot "schmooze" our way into favor with the God who knows our innermost secrets. Do you live your life with this truth in mind?   —R. H.

CONCLUSION

A. Quitters

One of the most grueling and demanding events in sports is the marathon. In an Olympic game several years ago, the winner of the women's marathon and others had already crossed the finish line, and the television cameras were ready to move on to another event. Suddenly one more runner staggered into the stadium and onto the track, totally exhausted. All she could do was stumble around the track, unable even to run in a straight line. It looked as if she would collapse at any moment, but she did manage to cross the finish line.

Later, a reporter asked her why she didn't quit when it was obvious that she could not win a medal. She replied, "I didn't spend all those months training only to come here to quit." Although she won no medals for her efforts, she won the respect of all who heard her willingness to carry on when totally exhausted with no hope of winning.

The Christian life is not a hundred-yard dash. It is not something to be finished very quickly with all speed and no stamina. Rather, it is a marathon, lasting a lifetime. Unlike an Olympic marathon, however, there are no silver or bronze medals for those who finish second or third in the race of life. The eternal reward goes instead to all those who finish the race—but they must finish! That was what the writer of Hebrews was trying to tell the readers.

One who competes in a race must spend countless hours practicing and conditioning. Some who become Christians and later drop out of the race are those who never quite understood all that was involved in the commitment they made. They take their commitment rather lightly and thus are not seriously involved in Bible study, church attendance, and Christian service. Thus they simply lack the spiritual stamina to run such a demanding race. Others simply may grow weary in well doing (cf. Galatians 6:9). Still another factor is Satan, who attempts to turn us aside by all kinds of things—material possessions, fame, physical comfort, even friends and family. Hebrews 12:1 warns against such distractions.

B. History as Bunk?

"History is more or less bunk," Henry Ford remarked in 1916. Unfortunately, many share this view. The prophets of ancient Judah and Israel, however, often referred to their past as a basis for their messages of warning and of hope. More often than not, the people closed their hearts to the prophets' words. The writer of Hebrews was doing all that he could to prevent that from happening again.

George Santayana (1863–1952) observed that those who do not remember the past are doomed to repeat it. That is the warning of the writer of Hebrews to the first-century readers—and to us.

Discovery Learning

This page contains an alternative lesson plan emphasizing learning activities. Classes desiring such student involvement will find these suggestions helpful. The next page is a reproducible activity page to further enhance discovery learning.

LEARNING GOALS

After this lesson each student will be able to:

1. Cite the dangers of falling away from the faith and the rewards for remaining faithful.

2. Explain why God expects faithful obedience from his people.

3. Select and memorize one passage of Scripture to encourage faithful living.

INTO THE LESSON

Through the entire session display a poster that will not be used until the lesson application. The poster should read, "Let us not become weary in doing good, for at the proper time we will reap a harvest if we do not give up" (Galatians 6:9). Prepare and display a second poster titled "Faithful Unto Death," with the often-used wedding vows: "Will you love, comfort, honor, and keep him (her), in sickness and in health, and forsaking all others be faithful to him (or her) so long as you both shall live?"

Divide the class into groups of two or three. Have each student tell his or her group of a couple whose marriage demonstrates these wedding vows. After a few minutes, ask two of the groups to tell of one of their models of marriage faithfulness to the entire group. Make the transition to Bible study by explaining that God often uses the model of faithfulness in marriage as an illustration of how he wants to enjoy a rich relationship with Christians, who are his bride.

INTO THE WORD

Give a brief lecture introducing today's study, based on the Lesson Background from page 362. Emphasize the "So What?" portion of the Introduction in your comments.

Answer the following discussion questions (divided into the three major subjects of today's text) in groups of four or five people or as a whole class. Use a printed handout with space for answers. If you do this as a whole class, explain that space is included for notes to encourage retention and understanding. Also, if you do this as a whole class, read the text for each discussion before asking the questions.

God's Demand for Faithfulness (3:12-19; 4:2)

1. God expected faithfulness from the Israelites. The writer of this passage reminds us of one time when they failed. As a group, recall or retell the story of the exodus, their wanderings, and the promised land. (Ask a "scribe" to outline these events on a poster or marker board.)

2. Who did not get to enter the promised land? Why not?

3. What does Hebrews 4:2 teach about the practical side of faith?

4. What message is God giving today's believers in this passage?

Snapshots of the Reward for the Faithful (4:9-11)

1. Why would God use the word picture of "rest" as his snapshot of our heavenly reward?

2. Look up Hebrews 11:10 and 11:16 for two other word pictures of Heaven that God chose to use. Why did he choose these "snapshots"?

3. What other word pictures of Heaven can you recall that God has used in his Word? What is your favorite "snapshot"? Why?

God's Word as a Sword (4:12, 13)

1. As the writer speaks of God's Word, what may be the significance of mentioning a sword with two sharp edges?

2. Look at the last half of verse 12. What is God's lesson to us about his Word in this verse?

3. Why is God's omniscience (v. 13) mentioned in conjunction with his Word?

INTO LIFE

Say, "The Christian has temptations or issues, just as a husband or wife do, that may lead to unfaithfulness." Ask the class to brainstorm temptations, issues, or life events that face people the age of your class and that may lead toward unfaithfulness to God. Ask a class member to write these in view. Then ask class members to note mentally any of the situations that are a particular danger to him or her. Direct learners to the reproducible page for a "Personal Evaluation" of faithfulness.

Point to the poster of Galatians 6:9. Give each person a three-by-five card to write the Galatians 6:9 words. As all write, repeat the words several times together as a class. Ask the learners to memorize the words by repeating them several times each day all week, as an encouragement to faithful living.

Personal Evaluation of My Faithfulness ✏

Reading today's Scripture automatically calls us to a personal evaluation of our faithfulness to God. Use the following evaluation guide to help your self-evaluation. Mark an "X" on the line at a point indicating your personal evaluation. Then identify an area of your life where you will make a commitment to a more faithful lifestyle.

KEEPING GOD FIRST IN MY LIFE

✏Unfaithful ├────┼────┼────┼────┼────┼────┼────┤ Very Faithful

TEACHING MY FAMILY/FRIENDS OF GOD'S EXPECTATION FOR FAITHFUL LIVING

✏Unfaithful ├────┼────┼────┼────┼────┼────┤ Very Faithful

FAITHFUL IN VOLUNTEERING MY TIME TO HIS SERVICE

✏Unfaithful ├────┼────┼────┼────┼────┼────┤ Very Faithful

FAITHFUL IN SHARING MY MATERIAL WEALTH

✏Unfaithful ├────┼────┼────┼────┼────┼────┤ Very Faithful

FAITHFUL IN BIBLE STUDY

✏Unfaithful ├────┼────┼────┼────┼────┤ Very Faithful

FAITHFUL IN MY WORSHIP LIFE

✏Unfaithful ├────┼────┼────┼────┼────┤ Very Faithful

I plan to honor God by improving my faithfulness to him by doing the following:

Hold Fast to the Faith
Unit 1: Encouraged to Be Faithful
(Lessons 1-4)

JESUS: THE GREAT HIGH PRIEST

WHY TEACH THIS LESSON?

The world places a premium on "having friends in high places" in order to get things done. But such "friends" usually expect something in return for their favors. This often tawdry and underhanded game is described by various euphemisms such as "one hand washes the other," "dancing with the one who brought you," and "you scratch my back and I'll scratch yours."

How sad to be involved in such game playing yet overlook the fact that Jesus is in the highest possible position, and he calls us friends. He is our great high priest, able to do far more for us than anyone in a position of influence on earth ever can. And there is nothing he expects us to do to earn his favor. In fact, it is he who has done all the work necessary to repair the broken relationship between people and God. Today's lesson will bring these facts back to mind, and challenge us to live up to our own priesthood as well.

INTRODUCTION

A. THAT OTHERS MIGHT LIVE

On the afternoon of January 13, 1982, Air Florida's flight 90 began its take-off roll down the runway of Washington's National Airport. But shortly after becoming airborne, the plane stalled because of ice on its wings and plunged earthward. It hit a bridge jammed with commuters and then sank into the icy Potomac River.

Rescue personnel were soon on the scene, and a helicopter hovering low overhead dropped a line to tow people to shore. Yet one of the few survivors visible in the water consistently refused to take the lifeline. Instead, he passed it on to someone else each time the helicopter returned.

That man was later identified as Arland D. Williams, Jr. He was trapped by a jammed seat belt and refused to have the helicopter spend time trying to pull him free when others needed help just as much. Mr. Williams eventually lost own battle to survive and *Time* magazine said, "If the man in the water gave a lifeline to the people gasping for survival, he was likewise giving a lifeline to those who observed him."

In a much more profound way, Christ did so as well. The "eternal lifeline" he passes to us comes at the price of his own life. Unlike the *Time* magazine conclusion, however, there is no distinction between "the people gasping for survival" and "those who observed him." All people are drowning in sin and need this great high priest to intervene on their behalf.

B. LESSON BACKGROUND

The priesthood was an important part of the covenant that God revealed to Moses. Priests were "go-betweens"—representing people to God and God to the

DEVOTIONAL READING:
HEBREWS 7:21-28
BACKGROUND SCRIPTURE:
HEBREWS 4:14–5:10; 7
PRINTED TEXT:
HEBREWS 4:14-16

Jun
27

LESSON AIMS

After participating in this lesson, each student will be able to:

1. Describe the work of Jesus on our behalf as our great high priest.

2. Tell some of the ways that we are blessed by having Jesus as our high priest.

3. Acknowledge an area of temptation and seek Jesus' help in overcoming it.

KEY VERSE

Therefore, since we have a great high priest who has gone through the heavens, Jesus the Son of God, let us hold firmly to the faith we profess.

—Hebrews 4:14

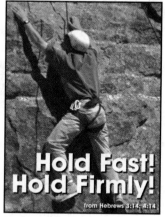

Visual for lessons 3 and 4.
Use this visual to remind your learners that our great high priest expects us to hold on!

WHAT DO YOU THINK?

What are some things that you have had to do personally to "hold firmly to the faith" that you profess?

people. The law required that members of the priesthood be drawn from the descendants of Aaron (Numbers 3:10), who was from the tribe of Levi (Exodus 4:14). The concept of one man's being the "high" priest begins to be seen in Leviticus 16:32 and 21:10. The high priests were sometimes looked to as leaders or advisors to the political leaders.

In the tabernacle and later in the temple, the high priest normally presided over the offering of sacrifices. The high priest came before God not only as the chief mediator between God and those whom the priest represented, but also as a sinner himself. Some sacrifices were so sacred that they could be offered only by the high priest (Leviticus 16; Hebrews 9:7). What a responsibility!

The high priests unfortunately became overly involved in the political processes in the period between the Old and New Testaments. In about 174 B.C., ungodly rulers began to select at their whim the men to fill that office. As a result, high priests were sometimes implicated in corrupt activities. The high priest in Jesus' day is a good example. Clearly, something better was needed. The old covenant, designed to be temporary, needed to be replaced.

I. HEAVENLY HIGH PRIEST (HEBREWS 4:14-16)

A. IMMORTAL (v. 14)

14. Therefore, since we have a great high priest who has gone through the heavens, Jesus the Son of God, let us hold firmly to the faith we profess.

Once again the word *therefore* shows us that what comes next is the logical conclusion to the previous verses, which were part of last week's lesson. The writer already has established in Hebrews 3:1 that *Jesus* is a high priest. Now we have the further description *great high priest*.

This description sets Jesus in contrast to Aaron and those who followed him as priests. Those priests were all fallible human beings. Since they all died, their services as priests were limited to their own brief life spans.

Our great high priest, by contrast, can no longer die. He is able to serve as our high priest in Heaven for eternity. The phrase *gone through the heavens* speaks to the majesty and glory of Jesus Christ in this regard. Some suggest that this idea refers to Christ's ascension (Acts 1:9) during which he passed through the "immediate" heaven and on into the "ultimate" Heaven (cf. 2 Corinthians 12:2).

Since our great high priest indeed has gone through the heavens, it would be foolish not to *hold firmly to* our Christian *faith*. Some of the first-century readers may be tempted to return to Judaism, and the writer now underscores the earlier exhortations for Christians to remain true to their commitment.

B. SYMPATHETIC (v. 15)

15. For we do not have a high priest who is unable to sympathize with our weaknesses, but we have one who has been tempted in every way, just as we are—yet was without sin.

The idea that our *high priest* was fully human was discussed in lesson 2 (Hebrews 2:17). Here the same concept is expressed as a double negative: *we do not have a high priest who is **unable** to sympathize with our weaknesses*.

On many occasions we may have sympathized with others caught in painful situations. We can extend to them our encouragement, but unless we've "been there and done that," then it's difficult to know the depth of their pain. Because Christ has come in the flesh, he indeed has "been there and done that."

To be *tempted in every way, just as we are* does not suggest that Christ faced every single temptation that we will ever face. But he has indeed experienced temptations that come through the flesh and those that come through pride (e.g., Matthew 4:1-11). Jesus was besieged by Satan himself, but resisted all temptations successfully. So even though Jesus was unscarred by sin, he can empathize with us and strengthen us when we are tempted.

C. APPROACHABLE (v. 16)

16. *Let us then approach the throne of grace with confidence, so that we may receive mercy and find grace to help us in our time of need.*

Under the Mosaic covenant only the high priest could enter the Holy of Holies to offer the yearly sacrifice of blood (Leviticus 16:29-33). All others were forbidden to enter the Holy of Holies on pain of death. But Christ's sacrifice on the cross changed all of that. At the time of his death the heavy curtain that separated the Holy of Holies from the Holy Place was torn from top to bottom, symbolically opening it for all believers to enter in (Mark 15:38).

We enter when we *approach the throne of grace with confidence.* One normally might approach the throne of a king with an overwhelming sense of fear, not knowing how the king will react. But when we come before him, we can do so with confidence because he extends grace to us. When we come *in our time of need,* we have every reason to believe that he will hear us and respond.

II. ISRAEL'S HIGH PRIEST (HEBREWS 5:1-4)

A. HUMAN (v. 1)

1. *Every high priest is selected from among men and is appointed to represent them in matters related to God, to offer gifts and sacrifices for sins.*

Under the Mosaic covenant the *high priest* was chosen from among the descendants of Aaron to oversee the priestly mission before *God.* God did not send an angel or some other heavenly being to carry out this mission. It was most appropriate for the high priest to be one of the people whom he would *represent.* For this reason it was necessary for Christ to come in the flesh that he might represent the entire human race before God.

The main task of these high priests was *to offer* both *gifts and sacrifices for sins.* This idea covers a wide range of things presented to God, both plant and animal. How this same idea applies to Jesus is an important topic in the book of Hebrews.

B. GUILTY (vv. 2, 3)

2. *He is able to deal gently with those who are ignorant and are going astray, since he himself is subject to weakness.*

A high priest ideally had to become "all things to all people" if he were to fulfill his ministry. Any priest had to meet very exacting standards for the specialized priestly ministry (see Leviticus 21:1–22:16). However, the priests' concentration on holiness tended to isolate them from those who were *ignorant* or were *going astray,* meaning the wayward and worldly. So how could the high priest—or any priest—maintain the high standard of holiness that God demanded, yet still *be able to deal gently with* ordinary people?

The earthly high priest was best able to do this because *he himself* was *subject to weakness.* Although always searching for greater holiness, the most godly high priests were still able to "connect with" those under his spiritual care because he shared their weaknesses and knew the power of temptation.

The arrogant religious leaders of Jesus' day, however, wanted nothing to do with "sinners." We see their attitude come out as they react to Jesus' association with the outcasts and the misfits of society (Matthew 9:11). Those leaders accused him of being "a glutton and a drunkard, a friend of tax collectors and 'sinners'" (Matthew 11:19). Jesus' compassion stands in stark contrast with their

WHAT DO YOU THINK?

How does Jesus comfort you in your weaknesses? How have you comforted fellow Christians in their weaknesses?

WHAT DO YOU THINK?

How much confidence do you have in approaching "the throne of grace"? On what do you base your confidence?

HOW TO SAY IT

Aaronic. Air-AHN-ik.
Abraham. AY-bruh-ham.
Annas. AN-nus.
Caesar. SEE-zur.
Caiaphas. KAY-uh-fus or KYE-uh-fus.
Charlemagne. SHAR-luh-main.
Corinthians. Kor-IN-thee-unz.
Corsican. KOR-suh-ken.
Galatians. Guh-LAY-shunz.
Gethsemane. Geth-SEM-uh-nee.
Hebrews. HEE-brews.
Isaiah. Eye-ZAY-uh.
Leviticus. Leh-VIT-ih-kus.
Melchizedek. Mel-KIZ-eh-dek.
Mosaic. Mo-ZAY-ik.
Napoleon. Nuh-POH-lee-un.
Philippians. Fih-LIP-ee-unz.
Potomac. Puh-TOE-mick.

SOLUTION TO PUZZLE ON P. 376

(Unused letters have been removed from the grid below to help you find the letters that form the given words.)

```
D E S I G N A T E D
  O S I R R H   S   H
N M F A A     E O B E Y
    T E B C   U A L
S E   R E R S P T D
U M E L C H I Z E D E K
F P   E   Y N F       F   P
F T G E N T L Y I   O E
E E H E A V E N S C R
R D         S     F E
E           S   E V S
D               C   E
  S A L V A T I O N R
```

arrogance and corruption; Jesus promised that they would be punished severely (Mark 12:38-40).

3. This is why he has to offer sacrifices for his own sins, as well as for the sins of the people.

Under the Mosaic covenant, the high priest offered *sacrifices* not only *for the sins of the people* but also *for his own sins* (Leviticus 9:7; 16:6). However, we are told that "it is impossible for the blood of bulls and goats to take away sins" (Hebrews 10:4). Eventually a perfect sacrifice would be required. Only Christ could provide that, by sacrificing himself. Here is where we see a sharp difference between the old covenant priesthood and the priesthood of Christ. Christ did not offer sacrifice for himself because he committed no sin.

C. CALLED (v. 4)
4. No one takes this honor upon himself; he must be called by God, just as Aaron was.

The high priesthood in ancient Israel was a most honored and respected office, second only to that of the king. Yet even kings were not allowed to perform the tasks of priests (e.g., 2 Chronicles 26:16-21). Under God's plan, one did not come to the position of high priest as the result of a popular election, a military coup, or political conniving. A person who occupied this office was *called by God*.

History does not give us much specific information about how high priests were chosen, but in some way God's hand was involved in the process. Of course we know from history that the hand of God was sometimes circumvented, and on occasion rascals and scoundrels occupied the office. This was certainly true during Jesus' ministry when Annas and Caiaphas were high priests (Luke 3:2).

III. PERFECT HIGH PRIEST (HEBREWS 5:5-10)
A. SON OF GOD (v. 5)
5. So Christ also did not take upon himself the glory of becoming a high priest. But God said to him,

> "You are my Son;
> today I have become your Father."

Christ did not come to earth to glorify *himself.* Instead, "being found in appearance as a man, he humbled himself and became obedient to death—even death on a cross!" (Philippians 2:8). It was God who glorified him (2:9-11).

On at least two occasions, God publicly declared Jesus to be his *Son* (see Matthew 17:5 and Luke 3:22). The latter part of the verse before us is from Psalm 2:7, which prophetically looked forward to the glorification of God's Son when he came as a man. Psalm 2:7 is also used in Acts 13:33 and Hebrews 1:5.

GREEDY FOR GLORY

"Ambition," said Napoleon, "is so natural to me, so innate . . . that it is like the blood that flows in my veins." Born in 1769, young Napoleon lived in the shadow of his older brother Joseph, the favorite of their parents. Napoleon chafed under this neglect and learned to obtain by charm what he could not otherwise have.

Through his brother's influence, Napoleon was appointed lieutenant colonel in the Corsican National Guard, then became captain in the French army. He was made brigadier general at age twenty-four after helping put down a revolt. The government promoted him to major general after he provided leadership during another period of intense unrest.

Using his intelligence, his ability to judge people and situations, and his capacity for prolonged hard work, Napoleon schemed his way into more power. This led to military campaigns throughout Europe and the foundation of an empire. Napoleon crowned himself Emperor of France on December 2, 1804.

Contrast Napoleon's self-aggrandizement with Jesus, who "did not take upon himself the glory." Perhaps Napoleon recognized this as well when he observed, "Alexander, Caesar, Charlemagne, and I founded empires. But on what did we rest the creations of our genius? Upon force. Jesus Christ founded his empire upon love; and at this hour millions of people would die for him." May we follow in the footsteps of Christ, not the Napoleons of the world.   —R. H.

B. ORDER OF MELCHIZEDEK (v. 6)
6. *And he says in another place,*

"You are a priest forever,
*   in the order of Melchizedek."*

The previous verses have been comparing and contrasting the high priesthood of Christ with the high priesthood of the old covenant. Now the writer introduces a new element: *Melchizedek.* This man is a mysterious figure, living in the time of Abraham. Melchizedek preceded Aaron and Moses by several hundred years. Not only was Melchizedek a priest of some kind, he was also "king of Salem" (Genesis 14:18). When Abraham returned from a successful campaign, he was greeted by this Melchizedek, who pronounced God's blessings upon Abraham. Abraham, in turn, paid tithes to Melchizedek (Genesis 14:19, 20).

The Aaronic priesthood originated in the tribe of Levi. Since Christ was of the tribe of Judah, he could not be a *priest* of the Aaronic order in the biological sense. But this restriction was set aside because Christ was a priest *in the order of Melchizedek.* This does not mean that Christ was a descendant of Melchizedek. Rather, it means that Christ was a priest of a similar kind. See Psalm 110:4; Hebrews 6:20; 7:17.

C. GIVER OF SUBMISSION (vv. 7, 8)
7. *During the days of Jesus' life on earth, he offered up prayers and petitions with loud cries and tears to the one who could save him from death, and he was heard because of his reverent submission.*

Christ's intercessory work of a priest began while he was still on earth as he offered up prayers and supplications *with loud cries and tears.* This refers to Christ's prayers in the Garden of Gethsemane. While the Gospel accounts do not mention loud crying and tears, they do make it clear that his prayers in the garden were deeply emotional (Matthew 26:36-46; Mark 14:32-42; Luke 22:39-46).
8. *Although he was a son, he learned obedience from what he suffered*

This verse poses something of a problem. If Christ was perfect (and he was) and if he was always obedient (and he was), then why did he have to learn *obedience* by suffering? We begin to arrive at an answer by remembering Jesus' humanity. When Jesus came into the world as a baby, He, somehow, was able to set aside temporarily some of his divine knowledge and characteristics. Thus it could be said that he "grew in wisdom and stature" (Luke 2:52).

Leon Morris adds that Jesus "*learned obedience* by actually obeying." Jesus came not only ready to act, he *did* act. In so doing, he obeyed the will of the Father. That obedience purchased our salvation!

THE PURPOSE OF PAIN
What if there were no pain? Dr. Paul Brand, who has worked with lepers in India, tells how tragic it is when that disease destroys nerves so that the victims no longer

WHAT DO YOU THINK?

What was a time that you prayed with strong emotions? Do you think your emotions made a difference in how God answered your prayers? Why, or why not?

WHAT DO YOU THINK?

Our text says that Jesus "learned obedience from what he suffered." Although it's often inappropriate to compare ourselves with Jesus, in what ways have you learned obedience by suffering?

DAILY BIBLE READINGS

Monday, June 21—*Melchizedek Blessed Abraham (Genesis 14:11-20)*

Tuesday, June 22—*The Lord Is a Priest Forever (Psalm 110: 1-7)*

Wednesday, June 23—*Our High Priest Knows Our Weaknesses (Hebrews 4:14–5:4)*

Thursday, June 24—*Jesus Learned Obedience Through Suffering (Hebrews 5:5-10)*

Friday, June 25—*A Priest Not Through Physical Descent (Hebrews 7:11-17)*

Saturday, June 26—*The Guarantee of a Better Covenant (Hebrews 7:18-22)*

Sunday, June 27—*Jesus Holds a Permanent Priesthood (Hebrews 7:23-28)*

PRAYER

Our Father, we come before you as believers. Yet we must pray that you will help our unbelief. Strengthen our faith and our zeal so that we can trust more fully in him who is our mediator before you. In the name of our great high priest we pray, amen.

THOUGHT TO REMEMBER

"You are . . . a royal priesthood" (1 Peter 2:9).

feel pain. Think about how the various parts of the foot absorb the weight and pressure of each step as we walk. Sometimes the toes take the brunt, then the side of the foot, then the heel. Without even thinking about it, we adjust our walk accordingly. But a leper can walk five miles and cause bleeding ulcers on his feet simply because the foot feels no pain and allows repeated pounding upon the same areas of the foot.

Hospital patients who are paralyzed or comatose need to be turned frequently for the same reason: no spot on the body can endure repeated pressure and remain undamaged. The pain of a sprained ankle alerts the brain that, "Hey, I need some recovery time! Give me a break." Why pain? Pain indicates that something is wrong and prods us to take corrective action.

Jesus felt pain, too. But it was our pain that he felt. "Feeling our pain" is more than a cliché, and is more than his mere identification with us. Pain for Jesus meant that something was wrong. That "something" was *sin*.

The ultimate pain Jesus felt was the penalty for sin he endured as he hung upon the cross. "By his wounds we are healed" (Isaiah 53:5). Will we embrace him today, or will we be like those "whose consciences have been seared as with a hot iron" (1 Timothy 4:2)—unable to feel the pain of sin and its welcome relief through Jesus?
    —R. H.

D. AUTHOR OF SALVATION (vv. 9, 10)

9, 10. *. . . and, once made perfect, he became the source of eternal salvation for all who obey him and was designated by God to be high priest in the order of Melchizedek.*

Once made perfect doesn't mean that Jesus was ever "imperfect." As Leon Morris explains, "There is a perfection that results from having actually suffered; it is different from the perfection that is ready to suffer." As a result of suffering, Jesus *became the source of eternal salvation*. What a breathtaking promise: salvation that stretches into the far reaches of eternity!

But this promise is not universal; it does not extend to everyone. It is extended only to *all who obey him.* Here we are brought back to a central theme of the Hebrews epistle: faithful obedience to God through Jesus Christ. No other religion offers eternal life. Returning to Judaism would be a tragedy of the greatest proportion (Galatians 3:1–4:7; 5:1-6).

CONCLUSION

In two thousand years of church history, from time to time there have arisen teachers and leaders who have taught that it is possible for a Christian to reach a level of maturity in which he or she is able (eventually) to live a sinless life. Practical experience, however, tells us something quite different.

Struggle as we may against temptations, we often fail and fall into sin. The apostle Paul had experiences like ours. In Romans 7:19 he wrote: "the evil I do not want to do—this I keep on doing." In despair he cried out, "What a wretched man I am! Who will rescue me from this body of death?" (Romans 7:24).

Paul found the answer in Jesus Christ. And so may we. Coming in the flesh, the Son of God was tempted "in every way, just as we are" (Hebrews 4:15) by the same kinds of temptations that we meet. Yet he was without sin, and, as our great high priest, offered himself as a sacrifice to pay sin's penalty.

At times in our struggle against sin we feel almost overwhelmed by the power of the devil. But we have good reason to take courage because we have a Savior who has not only paid sin's price, he has also experienced our struggles against temptation. Even if we are unable to achieve moral perfection in this life, we know that we are able to enter eternity through his grace.

Discovery Learning

*This page contains an alternative lesson plan emphasizing learning activities. Classes
desiring such student involvement will find these suggestions helpful. The next page
is a reproducible activity page to further enhance discovery learning.*

LEARNING GOALS

After participating in this lesson, the student will be able to:

1. Describe the work of Jesus on our behalf as our great high priest.

2. Tell some of the ways that we are blessed by having Jesus as our high priest.

3. Acknowledge an area of temptation and seek Jesus' help in overcoming it

INTO THE LESSON

Ask a man or woman in your class who enjoys drama to come to the class dressed in a Bible times costume. This person will give a brief lecture on the tradition and role the high priest played in Jewish life. He or she should tell of background and requirements for the role, their leadership responsibilities, their function in worship and sacrifices, and their role as mediator between man and God. The lesson background in the lesson commentary will be an excellent brief summary. However, a Bible dictionary will be very helpful in preparing for this introduction.

Make the transition by reminding the class that a key word in Hebrews is *better* or *superior.* Today we will discover that Jesus not only is superior to that old system, but that he becomes a very personal high priest acting on our behalf.

INTO THE WORD

Have a volunteer read Hebrews 4:14–5:10 aloud. Tell the group we will do three brief exercises to help us grasp the grand truths of this revelation of Jesus. Provide paper and pens to each person or to study teams of two persons. After each exercise, ask people to report their findings as you write their answers on a marker board or poster. (The same general learning can be examined by using the reproducible activity "Searching for the Right Words" section of the page.)

First exercise: Read the text and find every descriptive word or phrase describing Jesus as our high priest. We are especially interested in words that help us understand his stature or his role. Example: *great* (4:14). *Other answers may include these: without sin (4:15), sympathetic to our weaknesses (4:15), offering sacrifices on man's behalf (5:1, 3), compassionate (5:2), called by God (5:4), made perfect (5:9), and more.*

Second exercise: Scan the printed text and list the blessings that come to us because of Jesus' work as high priest. *Examples: He sympathizes with our weaknesses (4:15); we can confidently approach God's throne (4:16); mercy and grace (4:16); eternal salvation (5:9).*

Third exercise: This is the "so what?" exercise. Look at the text searching for responses expected from us as subjects to the high priest. What are we expected to do? *Answers include that we are to hold firmly to our faith (4:14) and to obey our high priest (5:9).*

Prepare and give a brief lecture for Hebrews 4:14. Remind the class that the key word for Hebrews is *better.* Three points for this mini-lecture are that Jesus is better than the Jewish priesthood because he is immortal; he makes intervention for us in Heaven, rather than in the temple Holy of Holies; and he is the divine Son of God.

INTO LIFE

To apply this lesson to life the first activity focuses on our responsibilities as Christ's priesthood. The second celebrates and honors Christ as our great high priest.

First, show a poster with the words "Royal Priesthood (1 Peter 2:9)" on it. Leave room on the poster to write class responses. Tell the class that, while we celebrate Jesus as our high priest, we also need to remember that Christians are called to be a "royal priesthood." Ask the group, "How do Christians fulfill the duties of a royal priesthood? What is God expecting of us as we fill this role?" List the class responses. After completing this exercise, remind the class that our text asks us to hold fast to our faith and to be obedient to our high priest. One way to do that is to fulfill our role as a royal priesthood.

Then tell the group we should celebrate Christ's position as high priest. We will do that by making an acrostic around the words *high priest.* Give teams of two people sheets of poster board and a marking pen. Ask them to write the letters of the words *High Priest* vertically. They are to build the acrostic with words describing Jesus' role and the blessings he offers as our high priest. (This activity is offered in the *NIV Bible Student* "Discovery Learning" page.)

Conclude this study by asking two people to pray. One is to thank God for his wisdom in appointing Jesus as our high priest. The second is to express commitment to being obedient to our high priest as members of the royal priesthood.

Searching for the Right Words

Today's Scripture holds wonderful words that describe Jesus as our great high priest. It also reveals wonderful blessings to us and calls us to respond to his majesty. Listed below are some of the precious words of this text. Find them in the word search puzzle. Note: Where phrases are listed, find the underlined word in the puzzle. (See page 372 of *The NIV Standard Lesson Commentary* for hints for the solution.)

DESCRIPTIONS OF JESUS, OUR HIGH PRIEST	BLESSINGS TO US	THE RESPONSE EXPECTED
Great (4:14)	Mercy (4:16)	Hold firmly (4:14)
Son of God (4:14)	Grace (4:16)	Obey (5:9)
Gone through the heavens (4:14)	Help (4:16)	
Tempted like us (4:15)		Deal gently (5:2)
Sinless (4:15 paraphrased)		
Offers gifts and sacrifices (5:1)		
A priest forever (5:6)		
The order of Melchizedek (5:6)		
Suffered (5:8)		
Source of salvation (5:19)	Eternal salvation (5:9)	
Perfect (5:8)		
Designated by God (5:10)		

```
D E S I G N A T E D P L Z
K O S I R R H T S V H C L
N M F A A W E O B E Y X Z
K T E B C L U A L P N F C
S E U R E R S P T D Z A Z
U M E L C H I Z E D E K E
F P S E O Y N F J H F W P
F T G E N T L Y I W O E I
E E H E A V E N S C R X X
R D C Y Q A S I X F E Q J
E N Z U B V S U E D V S E
D U G B W K Q C P B E N O
H S A L V A T I O N R B T
```

Good News Gazette

What good news would you like to share with the world from this Scripture? Write three paragraph topics you would include in an article about this good news.

FAITHFUL TO TEACHING

LESSON 5

WHY TEACH THIS LESSON?

Today the United States of America celebrates the two hundred twenty-eighth anniversary of her "Declaration of Independence." We might wonder whether any person living in the year 1776 could possibly have envisioned the far-reaching implications of that document—not just for the United States, but for the entire world!

As interesting as those implications are, today your learners can do something even more important: they can make (or renew) a "Declaration of *Dependence*" to the king of the universe. But words of dependence and allegiance by themselves are not enough. We must show our trust in him by following his teaching. Today's lesson prepares your learners not only to do that, but also to understand our king's teaching in more profound ways.

INTRODUCTION

A. STUNTED GROWTH

In an era before the most modern surgical techniques, a beautiful baby was born to a certain couple. The baby seemed quite normal and healthy in every respect. For the first few months he grew and learned to do the things that growing babies do. But after a few more months his parents noticed that his head was not growing in proportion to his body. Before long his cooing and laughter ceased and a blank look came over his face.

A medical examination revealed that there were no fissures in the bone structure of the baby's head. The cranial bones were fused together at birth and thus could not expand to accommodate a growing brain. With the brain so compressed, it could not develop, and the boy became severely retarded. Modern medicine might have been able to correct this problem, but in those days that was not a possibility.

The spiritual problems that the first readers of the book of Hebrews faced were rather like this. When they had first become Christians, there was every reason to believe that they would continue to grow and become mature Christians. But something had stunted their spiritual growth.

B. LESSON BACKGROUND

The previous lesson dealt with the fact that Christ is our great high priest. It was reassuring to learn that we have a high priest who was touched with all the infirmities of the flesh, tempted just as we are, and yet without sin. As the sinless Son of God, he can make intercession for us to the Father.

We assume that the Hebrew Christians had some understanding of this very important doctrinal truth. But the problem was that they were not always living as if they understood the responsibilities that accepting these truths brought. It was reasonable to expect them to experience growth from spiritual infancy to spiritual maturity. It is obvious that this had not happened to many of them. They were still surviving on "milk" (the rudiments of the gospel truth) when they should have been thriving on "meat" (the deeper things of the gospel).

DEVOTIONAL READING:
PSALM 119:97-106

BACKGROUND SCRIPTURE:
HEBREWS 5:11–6:20

PRINTED TEXT:
HEBREWS 5:11-14; 6:1-12

Jul
4

LESSON AIMS

After participating in this lesson, each student will be able to:

1. Cite characteristics of spiritual immaturity and spiritual maturity.

2. Describe some of the risks of prolonged spiritual immaturity.

3. Identify one step or action he or she will take toward greater spiritual maturity.

KEY VERSE

Therefore let us leave the elementary teachings about Christ and go on to maturity.
—Hebrews 6:1a

Fortunately, however, there was a straightforward cure for the problem: move on to the "meat"! Do we really even need to point out that this problem that plagued the first-century Christians is just as much an issue today?

I. PROBLEM STATED (HEBREWS 5:11-14)

A. THEIR LETHARGY (v. 11)

11. We have much to say about this, but it is hard to explain because you are slow to learn.

In verses previous to this (which were in last week's lesson), the writer set forth certain aspects of Christ's priesthood, comparing and contrasting it with the old Aaronic priesthood. Then the writer injected the idea that Christ's priesthood is of the order of Melchizedek, that mysterious priest-king who ministered to Abraham (Genesis 14:18-20). We know little about Melchizedek except that his "priesthood" was distinct from the Aaronic priesthood, which was established by the law.

The writer of Hebrews apparently wants to explore this idea in greater detail, but the readers aren't ready for it. A good teacher usually senses when his or her students are not ready to pursue a subject further. Although addressing the readers through the written word rather than in a classroom presentation, the writer somehow realizes that they are not ready for the next step in the lesson. Quite frankly and bluntly, they are *slow to learn!*

B. THEIR STAGNATION (vv. 12, 13)

12. In fact, though by this time you ought to be teachers, you need someone to teach you the elementary truths of God's word all over again. You need milk, not solid food!

We don't know how long the recipients of this letter have been Christians. But evidently it was long enough that by now they *ought to be teachers.* Perhaps they were second-generation Christians. If so, that could explain their laxness, since second-generation converts can lack the zeal that motivated their parents.

But no matter what generation of Christians we are in, the Great Commission makes every Christian a teacher (Matthew 28:19, 20). There are, of course, different kinds of teachers. Some teach formally before a class. Not all are gifted to teach in this way, but everyone can teach informally on a one-to-one basis.

But even at this informal level, the teacher must have information and insight to share with others (1 Peter 3:15). Perhaps as important as being able to share information is the teaching one does in his or her lifestyle. A bad example can cancel out dozens of good lessons.

It works the other way around, too: good examples aren't much use if there is not a thoughtful reason to back them up. It seems that these Hebrew Christians lack an understanding of the fundamentals of the faith and thus need to take a refresher course. What happened the first time that they were taught these things? Did they not pay attention?

Or did they fail to understand some of the principles that were being taught and thus are not able to relate them effectively to other aspects of their lives? Do other things in their lives now distract them, consuming the time that should be spent in Christian spiritual growth?

In short, why are they still stuck drinking *milk* when they should have moved on to *solid food* by now? These questions are still appropriate when we try to analyze why Christians repeat this problem today!

13. Anyone who lives on milk, being still an infant, is not acquainted with the teaching about righteousness.

WHAT DO YOU THINK?

Why do you think that many Christians lack an urgency in learning the truths of the faith? How does the church contribute to the problem? What ill effects result from Christians remaining in the "elementary school" of the faith for so many years?

The references to *milk* and solid food in verses 12 and 13 describe two different levels of learning (cf. 1 Corinthians 3:2). Babies thrive on milk for the first several weeks of their lives; for them to try to eat solid food would be impossible and even dangerous. Adults, on the other hand, might drink milk, but they are able to eat a varied diet that includes food with more substance. Indeed, good physical health requires that we move away from a milk-only diet as we grow.

C. THEIR NEED (v. 14)

14. But solid food is for the mature, who by constant use have trained themselves to distinguish good from evil.

The distinction between spiritual maturity and immaturity is not just one of learning information about Christianity. That is the simple part of spiritual growth. Far more important is how information is applied in real-life situations.

A mature Christian has learned *to distinguish good from evil.* Some evil is easy to recognize. Examples are behaviors that the Bible clearly teaches are sinful, such as adultery. But distinguishing between good and evil is not always so clear-cut. The issue of eating meat that had been sacrificed to idols in 1 Corinthians 8 is an example of a "gray area" situation. As we work our way through that passage, we are impressed by how much discernment Paul shows. We need to have this kind of discernment as well.

THE NEED TO KEEP GROWING

Henry Ford is both famous and infamous. He started out as a machinist's apprentice in Detroit while still in his teens, repairing clocks as a sideline. An avid reader, he studied engineering in what little spare time he had. When his apprenticeship was over, he worked repairing steam engines for Westinghouse. He became chief engineer of the Edison Illuminating Company at the age of thirty.

Determined to apply the potential of the internal combustion engine to the horse-drawn wagon, he experimented with a one-cylinder engine he had made himself. Then he put a two-cylinder engine on a light carriage in June 1896. One thing led to another, and on June 16, 1903, he organized the Ford Motor Company. Henry Ford's idea was to make cars that more people could afford. By 1915, his company had sold fifteen million Model Ts.

But all was not well. Henry Ford, the creative innovator, stopped growing in wisdom. He failed to understand the changing automobile market. Competitors' cars were faster, more comfortable, and available in some color other than black. Sales of Fords declined. Finally, in 1928, Ford introduced the Model A. Despite its innovations, Ford's share of the auto market continued to decline. By 1940 it was less than 20 percent.

Henry Ford did not trust his leaders. He went so far as to form an internal department to check up on his employees and their private lives. He became increasingly eccentric, almost tyrannical, until his death in 1947. Henry Ford shows the tragedy of stagnation. The consequences were serious for him personally, for his family, and his company. Far more serious are the consequences if we as Christians neglect to keep growing spiritually.   —R. H.

II. SOLUTION OFFERED (HEBREWS 6:1-6)

A. GROWTH IN MATURITY (vv. 1-3)

1. Therefore let us leave the elementary teachings about Christ and go on to maturity, not laying again the foundation of repentance from acts that lead to death, and of faith in God,

The writer of Hebrews now moves us toward a solution. Leaving *the elementary teachings about Christ* is not to suggest that the Hebrew Christians abandon

Let us leave the elementary teachings about Christ and go on to maturity.
Hebrews 6:1, NIV

Visual for lesson 5. This photograph can remind your class that learning "elementary" things is only a foundation for greater maturity.

HOW TO SAY IT

Aaronic. Air-AHN-ik.
Abraham. AY-bruh-ham.
bulimia. buh-LEE-me-uh.
Corinthians. Kor-IN-thee-unz.
Hebrews. HEE-brews.
Melchizedek. Mel-KIZ-eh-dek.
Pentecost. PENT-ih-kost.
Zechariah. ZEK-uh-RYE-uh.

DAILY BIBLE READINGS

Monday, June 28—*There Is No Other Gospel (Galatians 1:6-12)*

Tuesday, June 29—*Stand Firm in Christ's Freedom (Galatians 5:1-10)*

Wednesday, June 30—*Don't Abandon Your Confidence (Hebrews 10:32-39)*

Thursday, July 1—*Your Decrees Are My Meditation (Psalm 119:97-101)*

Friday, July 2—*Your Word Is a Light (Psalm 119:102-106)*

Saturday, July 3—*Move on to Solid Food (Hebrews 5:11–6:3)*

Sunday, July 4—*Do Not Become Sluggish (Hebrews 6:4-12)*

these principles. This *foundation* is rather like the ABCs. A child who learns these in kindergarten does not abandon this knowledge when he or she enters the first grade and begins to read. The alphabet provides the foundation upon which reading skills are built. The principles mentioned here provide the foundation upon which a Christian grows toward spiritual *maturity.*

Peter, in his sermon on the day of Pentecost, proclaimed some of these basic principles. That sermon set forth Jesus as the Christ, the promised Messiah, who had been slain on the cross but had been raised from the dead. Peter made it clear that his listeners shared in the guilt for that *death.* When they cried out and asked what they must do, Peter responded with instructions for repentance and baptism (Acts 2:38). Their *repentance from acts that lead to death* meant that they had to turn away from Judaism that sought God's favor through observing the law. Instead, they had found God's grace through faith in Jesus Christ.

2. . . . instruction about baptisms, the laying on of hands, the resurrection of the dead, and eternal judgment.

Take a close look at the four topics listed in this verse. If asked to explain them, could you do it? These are some of the "milk" issues of spiritual growth. Those who are still stuck on understanding these will have a hard time moving on to Christian maturity!

Baptisms here is plural, suggesting that a part of knowing basic doctrine is being able to distinguish between Christian baptism and the various ceremonial washings performed by Jews of that day. *The laying on of hands* may refer to the action of the apostles by which the Holy Spirit was imparted to some first-century believers (Acts 8:14-18). The laying-on of hands was also used to recognize those who had been selected for offices in the church (1 Timothy 4:14; 2 Timothy 1:6).

The resurrection of the dead and *eternal judgment* are foundational doctrines that naturally go together. The resurrection mentioned here is the general resurrection of all the dead, who then must face the judgment. For Christians this will be a wonderful experience that brings joy. But to the unsaved it will bring only fear, despair, and condemnation (John 5:28, 29). This is basic!

3. And God permitting, we will do so.

This verse sums up the previous two verses, which urged the readers to move beyond the basic principles. It also serves as a transition for the verses that follow.

B. DANGER OF APOSTASY (vv. 4-6)

4. It is impossible for those who have once been enlightened, who have tasted the heavenly gift, who have shared in the Holy Spirit,

Those who have once been enlightened refers to those who had heard the gospel and responded to it as Peter instructed on the day of Pentecost (Acts 2). While three thousand who heard that sermon repented and were baptized, not everyone there that day responded positively.

Yet those who submitted to Peter's instructions received such rich blessings! Those blessings included tasting *the heavenly gift* of eternal life as they received the gift of *the Holy Spirit.*

There were other gifts as well: the joy of associating with other Christians in worship and the joy that comes from Christian service are just two. But with these blessings came some serious responsibilities, as we shall see later.

5. . . . who have tasted the goodness of the word of God and the powers of the coming age,

This continues the list of blessings the readers had received since becoming Christians. *The word of God* includes the Old Testament, especially those portions that predict the coming of the Messiah.

This *word* also includes the preaching of the inspired apostles. It would not necessarily have included much of the New Testament yet, because much of it had not been written, and what had been written had not been widely circulated.

6. . . . if they fall away, to be brought back to repentance, because to their loss they are crucifying the Son of God all over again and subjecting him to public disgrace.

We are frightened to read the conclusion of verses 4-6: for those who *fall away*, it is impossible to bring them *back to repentance*. Across the centuries scholars have debated the meaning of these verses.

Certainly this verse does not mean that a person cannot be restored to God's favor after committing one or even many sins. Otherwise, all of us would stand under eternal condemnation! The description here does not fit that of a careless backslider whose love for the Lord grows cold.

This same issue is discussed in Hebrews 10:26-31 (see also 1 John 5:16, 17). Perhaps the most accurate interpretation is that the one who is under this severe condemnation is a former believer who has openly and maliciously rejected Christ. This would be someone who has done so in such a blatant manner that he or she has "recrucified" *the Son of God . . . subjecting him to public disgrace*. In effect such people are joining with those who crucified Jesus in the first place.

CHANGE IS POSSIBLE

Stephen Arterburn tells the stories of Marisa, Mark, and Ben. Marisa's brother told her she was "ugly, dumb, and fat" when she was only six. Dad was gone much of the time and offered her no encouragement. To relieve her pain she buried herself in her mother's spicy novels, creating an image of herself as the sexy heroine. Marisa had her first sexual experience at age thirteen, progressed to a series of illicit relationships, to bulimia, three abortions, and genital herpes.

Mark began collecting skin magazines as a teenager and soon was deeply into pornography. One day he skipped school, took a bus downtown, and visited a theater that showed triple-X films. After he married, he traveled for his business; adult bookstores, adult movies in his hotel room, and "men's clubs" became regular fare while on the road.

Ben, though married, progressed from adult bookstores to soliciting prostitutes. For months he hid his behavior, but one night the police arrested him. "Donna," he began when he called home, "I'm in trouble." She dreaded to hear the rest.

Three people; the same problem in different dimensions. Can those who have fallen so low recover? They can if they want to. Ben did. He and Donna are together and have a strong marriage; his addiction is under control. Marisa contemplated suicide, but has become a strong person in her own right and no longer engages in the former behaviors. Mark is still where he was, only worse. Two of the three wanted to change; one did not.

Wanting to change made the difference. If we turn away from Christ's power to change us permanently, what hope is there? —R. H.

III. ILLUSTRATIONS AND CONFIDENCE (HEBREWS 6:7-12)
A. REAP WHAT IS SOWN (vv. 7, 8)
7. Land that drinks in the rain often falling on it and that produces a crop useful to those for whom it is farmed receives the blessing of God.

People in the first century lived closer to nature than those in industrialized societies do today, and so writers frequently based their illustrations on agriculture. Some of our Lord's most notable parables were based on agricultural practices. The point that the author is making here is quite obvious: the *land* that is properly tilled and bears a good harvest makes the farmer happy. In the same way, a Christian whose life bears good fruit has God's approval and *blessing*.

WHAT DO YOU THINK?

Have you known someone who rejected his or her Christian faith, but later repented and confessed Christ anew? What was that person's renewed faith like? What did the church do to strengthen that person?

PRAYER

Most Holy God, we thank you for the wondrous promise of eternal life. May we grow in the knowledge that we need to achieve the spiritual maturity necessary for lifelong faithfulness. In Jesus' name, amen.

8. But land that produces thorns and thistles is worthless and is in danger of being cursed. In the end it will be burned.

The crop from the second soil is quite different—*thorns and thistles*—even though both soils received the rain. How they were treated determined their crop yield. The first soil is carefully tilled to eliminate weeds. The other is neglected, with disastrous results. One who lives a life dedicated to the service of the Lord will be blessed. One who misuses his or her potential, on the other hand, faces a terrible fate: to *be burned.*

B. Expect Better Things (vv. 9, 10)
9. Even though we speak like this, dear friends, we are confident of better things in your case—things that accompany salvation.

After the thunder and lightning comes the sunshine. Clearly, the author does not believe that the readers have fallen into the apostasy being warned against. The writer believes *better things* of them. On occasion, God's messengers must bring words of dire warning, but these are but the backdrop for God's blessings.
10. God is not unjust; he will not forget your work and the love you have shown him as you have helped his people and continue to help them.

Two points are worth noting here. First, God is just and will remember their *work and the love* they *have shown him* (cf. Mark 9:41). Second, they have *helped his people* and continue to minister them. Hebrews 10:32-34 gives us an idea of what some of those good works were. When we minister to the needs of others, we minister to the Lord. In Matthew 25:31-46 Jesus clearly indicates that how we treat others will be a factor in our final judgment.

C. Avoid Laziness (vv. 11, 12)
11, 12. We want each of you to show this same diligence to the very end, in order to make your hope sure. We do not want you to become lazy, but to imitate those who through faith and patience inherit what has been promised.

The writer's desire is not just a vague, general feeling; it is aimed at *each one of the readers personally.* They were doing well up to a point, and so the writer encourages them to continue their efforts *to the very end.* We sometimes fail to encourage the faithful as much as we ought. We need to realize that even the most faithful sometimes become "weary in doing good" (Galatians 6:9).

But with the note of encouragement comes a warning not *to become lazy.* After that the section shifts back to a positive emphasis, ending with the practical suggestion to look to others who *through faith and patience inherit what has been promised.* Perhaps the writer is thinking of Abraham, as in Hebrews 11:8. Such pillars of faith are examples even today.

CONCLUSION
Yogi Berra once observed that a game is "not over until it's over." What is true of a game of baseball is certainly just as true of a Christian life. Just as it is possible for a baseball team to lose the game in the last half of the last inning, the writer of Hebrews warns the readers that it is possible to fall away even if one has made a good start in the Christian life. As expressed in a previous lesson, life is much more like a marathon than a hundred-yard dash. We must persist to the end! The writer repeats this theme in Hebrews 12:1, 2. Spiritual growth helps us endure.

The apostle Paul, imprisoned and facing execution, gives us an example of steadfast faith: "I have fought the good fight, I have finished the race, I have kept the faith. Now there is in store for me the crown of righteousness, which the Lord, the righteous Judge, will award to me on that day" (2 Timothy 4:7, 8).

Discovery Learning

This page contains an alternative lesson plan emphasizing learning activities. Classes desiring such student involvement will find these suggestions helpful. The next page is a reproducible activity page to further enhance discovery learning.

LEARNING GOALS

After this lesson the student will be able to:

1. Cite characteristics of spiritual immaturity and spiritual maturity.

2. Describe some of the risks of prolonged spiritual immaturity.

3. Identify one step or action he or she will take toward greater spiritual maturity.

INTO THE LESSON

Before class begins, mount a six-and-a-half-foot-long banner vertically on the wall before students arrive. This may be made from strips of poster board or by using a roll of white freezer paper. On the banner make the markings of a ruler and supposed measurements taken as a child was growing toward adulthood. At the top of the banner write "It'll Stunt Your Growth!"

Begin the class session by mentioning the banner and asking, "What did grandmother tell us would stunt our growth?" (*Coffee and cigarettes are common answers.*)

Next, tell the class, "Of more concern for adults are immature attitudes and behavior." Ask the class to identify characteristics of an immature adult. Mention the following categories: emotional, academic, social, decision-making. List responses on a marker board. Then add the words *spiritual immaturity* as a category. Say, "God's Word will help us identify characteristics of spiritual maturity and help us reach it."

INTO THE WORD

Option 1: Distribute a copy of the reproducible activity page that follows. Give students time to complete the puzzle individually, or work on the puzzle as a class.

Option 2: Prepare a study guide with the following headings and questions. This activity will be accomplished better in small groups of two to five people than as a whole class. The study groups will need a fairly large block of time. The headings, assignments, and questions are as follows.

Characteristics of the Spiritually Immature

Jot down the characteristics or descriptions of spiritually immature Christians you find in the text. See Hebrews 5:11, 12, 13; Hebrews 6:11, 12.

What basic doctrines are known even by the immature?

What are the risks of continuing spiritual immaturity? Explain the illustrations (Hebrews 6:4-8).

Characteristics of the Spiritually Mature

Note descriptions of spiritually mature Christians in Hebrews 5:14; 6:1; 6:11, 12. What positive, encouraging note concludes these remarks?

Groups will not need to report their findings, since all have studied the same text and questions. Instead, ask the following discussion questions:

1. Why are the doctrines listed in the text considered "basic," something even the immature should know?

2. Using this as a measure of maturity and immaturity, what needs do you see for our church?

INTO LIFE

On the reverse of the handout, have printed six of these "growth-o-meters." Only one should have a sample arrow drawn on it.

Ask the class to brainstorm a list of characteristics they see in spiritually mature people (from today's text or others). Write the responses on a poster board. After you have created a long list, give each person five colored dots to place on the five characteristics they believe are most important demonstrations of spiritual maturity. This will require some movement of class members, so ask them to do this quickly. If you have a large class, you may display a second identical list on another side of the room and ask half the class to use it.

To make the lesson personal, ask each class member to write each of the top five characteristics selected by the class on top of one of the large "growth-o-meters" on the back of his or her study guide. (The one with an arrow is an example. The students should use the five without arrows.) All are to use this for a self-evaluation, drawing arrows to indicate how they judge their spiritual maturity. Then ask each class member to select one area to become a focus in improving his or her spiritual maturity in the next several weeks. Ask each student to place a check mark by the "growth-o-meter" selected and to note one activity or action that will begin his or her commitment to this area of spiritual growth.

Puzzled No More!

Use Hebrews 5:11–6:12 to complete the crossword puzzle. Pencil the chapter and verse beside each clue. This exercise will help you understand this wonderful Scripture encouraging spiritual maturity.

ACROSS

1. Our goal, according to this Scripture text.
3. Diligence will make this sure.
4. Make mine solid!
5. A product of worthless land.
6. Another product of worthless land.
8. Solid food is for this kind of believer.
11. Christians have been _____.
14. The land drinks this.
15. A kind of learner which, unfortunately, describes some believers.
17. Those who will be resurrected.
18. The end for land that bears only thorns and thistles.
19. Not a characteristic of God.

21. A farmer always hopes for a good one.
22. The type of spiritual food for the mature believer.
23. Description of one with poor spiritual discipline.

DOWN

2. One of the very basic Christian doctrines.
5. Mature believers should be carrying this role.
7. The kind of gift that believers have tasted.
9. A description of land that only produces weeds.
10. Another word for basic.
12. What believers "have tasted" of the Word of God.
13. Those who fall away subject Christ to public ___.
16. The laying on of _____.
20. Food for the spiritually immature.

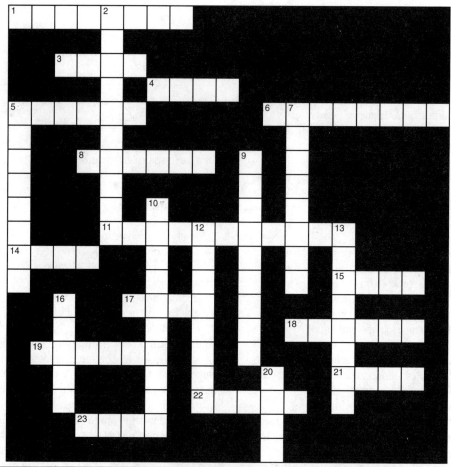

FAITHFUL TO THE NEW COVENANT

LESSON 6

WHY TEACH THIS LESSON?

My wife and I have been searching for a house to buy, and we've looked through dozens of homes. Since I want to erect a fence to keep the pets in the yard, one question I always ask is, "What is the community covenant involving fences in this neighborhood?" The last thing I want to do is buy a house without this crucial bit of information. Violating a community covenant has legal implications, not to mention creating bad will with the neighbors!

Covenants have their origin with God himself. He is the first covenant-maker. To be within the community of the redeemed for eternity we must know, understand, and submit to the terms of his new covenant. Does it make any sense to think we can have eternal life without knowing God's requirements? Today's lesson will help your learners ensure their eternity by reflecting on God's new covenant and its superiority to the old.

INTRODUCTION

A. NEW COVENANT

Hong Kong, located just at the southern tip of China, existed for many years as a British colony. Under this "covenant" the people enjoyed the rights and privileges of British citizenship. As a result, Hong Kong grew to become one of the busiest and most prosperous cities in Southeast Asia. But in 1997 Great Britain's lease on the colony expired and Hong Kong reverted to Communist China.

As that date approached, many citizens became apprehensive about the future, and rightly so. They knew about some of the tragic conditions the Communists had brought to China. China offered a new contract, or covenant, that promised that the people could retain some of the rights and privileges that they had enjoyed under the British. But looking at the oppressive conditions on the mainland, no one was sure that the Communists would keep their promises. In the years since then Hong Kong has not been totally incorporated into mainland China, but the citizens are living under new restrictions that limit some of their freedoms.

How different it is with God's new covenant! It is superior to the old in every way. The old covenant was one of law. It set standards that people in their weakness could not meet. By contrast, the new covenant is one of grace. The standards are not any lower, but now we have a means of forgiveness when we fall short.

B. LESSON BACKGROUND

A covenant can be thought of as an agreement or contract between two parties. Each party assumes certain obligations or responsibilities. Such an agreement may be made between two individuals, two countries, or between God and people. When people make covenants or contracts with each other, there is a certain give-and-take as they negotiate terms.

DEVOTIONAL READING:
HEBREWS 10:5-18

BACKGROUND SCRIPTURE:
HEBREWS 8, 9

PRINTED TEXT:
HEBREWS 8:6-13

Jul
11

LESSON AIMS

After participating in this lesson, each student will be able to:

1. Contrast the elements of the old covenant God had with Israel with the new covenant God has with Christians.

2. Explain how the new covenant is superior to the old.

3. Identify one person to whom he or she can explain the benefits of the new covenant.

KEY VERSE

The ministry Jesus has received is as superior to theirs as the covenant of which he is mediator is superior to the old one, and it is founded on better promises. —Hebrews 8:6

OLD COVENANT BY MOSES	NEW COVENANT IN JESUS
temporary	eternal
national	universal
priests from the tribe of Levi	priests from all in the covenant
sinful men as high priests	Jesus as only and sinless high priest
sealed by the blood of animals	sealed by the blood of the Lamb of God
repeated sacrifices necessary	a single and final Sacrifice
high priest enters into Holy of Holies for the people	High Priest enters Heaven to welcome the people
written on stones by the hand of God	written on hearts by the Spirit of God

Visual for lesson 6. *Post this chart to help your learners see the stark differences between the old and new covenants.*

WHAT DO YOU THINK?

In what ways have you personally benefited from Christ's "superior ministry"?

WHAT DO YOU THINK?

God found fault with those who lived under the old covenant. Today, do you think that God is finding fault with you as you live under his new covenant? Why, or why not?

[Be sure the learners consider Romans 6:1-4; 1 Peter 1:15, 16; 1 John 1:9; and Jude 4 in this discussion.]

But this is not the case with covenants between God and people. In those instances God establishes all the terms; then he expects us to submit to them. For example, when God put Adam and Eve in the Garden of Eden, he made certain things very clear. They were to dress the garden and keep it. In return, they could expect to enjoy the fruit of all the trees except one. When they broke the covenant, they were expelled from the garden, never to return.

Much later, when God began to unfold his plans to send his Son into the world as the Savior, he entered into a covenant with Abraham, then called Abram (Genesis 12). The Mosaic covenant followed. Except for prophetic references to a "new covenant" (as in Jeremiah 31:31-34), this is, of course, the most significant covenant mentioned in the Old Testament. It is much more detailed than the earlier covenants, with laws and restrictions that covered a whole range of situations. Further, it was for a whole nation of Israel. Having led the Israelites out of bondage in Egypt, God entered this covenant with his people at Mount Sinai, with Moses acting as the mediator (Exodus 19, 20).

But in the hundreds of years that followed the Sinai experience, an unfortunate pattern developed. For a time the people would be obedient to the terms of the covenant, and then they would fall away, either through neglect or outright rebellion. Then God would send a messenger, usually a prophet but sometimes a king, to stir a revival. The people would then return to the covenant, but before long the vicious cycle would start all over again. Even after returning from the horrors of exile, God's people kept embracing sin. Clearly something better was needed.

I. NEW COVENANT HAS COME (HEBREWS 8:6-8a)

A. THE NEW IS BETTER (v. 6)

6. But the ministry Jesus has received is as superior to theirs as the covenant of which he is mediator is superior to the old one, and it is founded on better promises.

In previous lessons we have learned that Christ is our great high priest. Hebrews 8 now teaches us more about his functions in that capacity. For starters his *ministry* is *superior to* the ministry of the priests who served under the old *covenant*. The most obvious reason for this superiority, of course, is that he is the Son of Almighty God. As the *mediator* of a better covenant we can think of Jesus as a "go-between" (1 Timothy 2:5).

The new is superior to *the old* in the fact that the new covenant is *founded on better promises*. Abraham was promised that he would have numerous descendants and receive God's physical blessings. Under the Mosaic covenant the people were promised a land of their own, which eventually they were able to possess. But these blessings, as precious as they were, were temporal, confined to this earth. The better promises that come through Christ are eternal.

B. THE OLD WAS INADEQUATE (vv. 7, 8a)

7, 8a. For if there had been nothing wrong with that first covenant, no place would have been sought for another. But God found fault with the people and said:

There was nothing really wrong with the *first covenant*, as far as what it was designed to do. The problem was in its application, and *God found fault with the people* who should have kept that covenant. We are told that the law was "weakened by the sinful nature" (Romans 8:3). People simply did not live up to the high standards required by the Mosaic law.

But didn't God know of this human weakness when he gave the law? Of course he did. But if God knew of this human weakness, then why did he give people a law that he knew they would not (or could not) keep? The law served several purposes, but the most important was to prepare us for the coming of Christ (see Galatians 3:24). Since it is through the law that "we become conscious of sin" (Romans 3:20), it is the law that shows us our need for the forgiveness that is available only in Jesus. The old covenant law provided a receptive context in which Christ would carry out his ministry. Thus it is apparent that from the beginning God planned a new covenant that would supersede the Mosaic covenant. (See Ephesians 1:4; 1 Peter 1:19-21.)

II. NEW COVENANT WAS PREDICTED (HEBREWS 8:8b-13)

A. WHY WE NEED IT (vv. 8b, 9)

8b. *"The time is coming, declares the Lord,*
> *when I will make a new covenant*
with the house of Israel
> *and with the house of Judah.*

This is the beginning of a lengthy quotation from Jeremiah 31:31-34. Some consider these verses to be the single most important passage in the Old Testament! From the beginning God knew the weaknesses of the law. So God began to make provisions for this problem hundreds of years before Christ came.

Early in Jeremiah's career as a prophet, during the reign of good King Josiah, there was hope that the people might return to God (2 Kings 21:24–23:25). But before lasting changes could be made in the life of the nation, King Josiah and the country of Judah were caught up in the international struggles of that day. Assyria, which had been the dominant power in the area stretching from Babylon to Egypt, was being challenged by her enemies. Josiah was killed in one of the battles of this struggle (2 Kings 23:29), and the kings of Judah who followed him were either corrupt or weak.

Note that both *the house of Israel* and *the house of Judah* are to be included in this new covenant. In 931 B.C., following the death of King Solomon, the kingdom of Israel divided itself into Israel (the northern kingdom) and Judah (the southern kingdom).

Following that division, the house of Israel had been scattered among foreign lands (2 Kings 17:6). As Jeremiah wrote, the house of Judah had been partially taken into captivity in Babylon, with a much more extensive exile to follow in a few years. Yet the new covenant is intended for both of these broken parts, for the whole house of unbroken Israel (cf. Romans 9–11)—and for the rest of the world, too (see Isaiah 42:6; 49:6).

9. *"It will not be like the covenant*
> *I made with their forefathers*
when I took them by the hand
> *to lead them out of Egypt,*
because they did not remain faithful to my covenant,
> *and I turned away from them, declares the Lord.*

The ancient Jews honored Abraham, looking to him as their father (John 8:33, 39). He was the beginning of the Hebrews as a distinct people. Although he was childless until he was a very old man, his descendants became a great nation just as God had promised (Genesis 12:2).

Even so, the Jews looked to the exodus as their beginning as a separate and distinct nation. This event left a lasting impression on their national psyche that the centuries could not erode. They realized that they had not escaped *Egypt* through their own efforts. This had been accomplished through the mighty acts of God. They realized that they were helpless until God *took them by the hand* and led them to freedom.

HOW TO SAY IT

Abram. AY-brum.
Abraham. AY-bruh-ham.
Assyria. Uh-SEAR-ee-uh.
Babylon. BAB-uh-lun.
Corinthians. Kor-IN-thee-unz.
Ephesians. Ee-FEE-zhunz.
Galatians. Guh-LAY-shunz.
Jeremiah. Jair-uh-MY-uh.
Josiah. Jo-SIGH-uh.
levitical. leh-VIT-ih-kul.
Midianite. MID-ee-un-ite.
Mosaic. Mo-ZAY-ik.
Solomon. SOL-o-mun.
Uzziah. Uh-ZYE-uh.
Wiesenthal. VEE-sehn-tall.

But memories of God's blessings in the past were not enough to keep the Israelites *faithful to* God's *covenant* that he had *made with their forefathers*. It is easy enough for us to be critical of the ancient Jews because they failed to live up to the covenant. But as Christians are we any better? Are we not at times just as unfaithful to our rich heritage of blessings that we have received from God?

FALLEN HEROES

After lengthy study, Professor Bobby Clinton of Fuller Seminary concluded that fewer than 30 percent of Bible leaders "finished well" (*Current Thoughts & Trends,* September 2002, p. 2). Examples to support Professor Clinton's conclusion are not hard to find. Gideon, whose three hundred men routed the Midianite army, made an idol (Judges 8:22-27). Solomon, the wisest person who ever lived, introduced the idolatry that ultimately destroyed his nation (1 Kings 11:1-13).

King Uzziah is another example. After ascending to the throne at age sixteen, he sought the Lord sincerely at first. He defeated the Philistines, rebuilt several towns he took from them, and repulsed his Arab enemies as well. Uzziah's fame spread as far as Egypt because he had become very powerful (2 Chronicles 26:1-15).

Then pride took over. Being so arrogant that he felt no place to be off limits to him, Uzziah entered the holy temple to burn incense before the altar in violation of the law. The results were frightening (2 Chronicles 26:16-21).

When the leaders of God's people lapse into disobedience, is there any doubt that people will follow their example? (See Jeremiah 44:17.) Praise God that he has sent to us our ultimate, sinless leader: Jesus Christ. He is the author of the new covenant, and he is the leader who never fails to set the proper example in helping us submit to that covenant that leads to eternal life. Follow him!   —R. H.

B. WHAT IT DOES (vv. 10-12)

10. *"This is the covenant I will make with the house of Israel*
    after that time, declares the Lord.
I will put my laws in their minds
    and write them on their hearts.
I will be their God,
    and they will be my people.

A *covenant* or a contract is in effect as long as both parties honor its provisions. But when either party fails to meet its obligations, the agreement is broken. This happened very early in the history of the Mosaic covenant, even while the people were still in the wilderness. Yet God gave them another chance, and then another, and then another.

Finally, the time had come for the new covenant. The writer continues to quote from Jeremiah in making the case. Certainly it would be *with the house of Israel* (meaning both Judah and Israel). But the new covenant includes many others, as noted in comments to verse 8b, above (see also Romans 10:12).

More than five hundred years before the writing of Hebrews, the prophet Jeremiah had predicted that after a certain length of *time* the new covenant would go into effect. This prophecy is fulfilled in the birth, death, and resurrection of Christ, and in the outpouring of the Holy Spirit on the day of Pentecost. The new covenant is not a covenant written on tablets of stone (Exodus 20). Rather, it is a covenant in which God puts his *laws in their mind* and *on their hearts.*

In Old Testament times as well as today, the word *heart* could mean much more than the physical organ that pumps the blood through the body. It was used to describe the seat of human emotions and human will. To accept God's new covenant and live under its precepts, one must do much more than just understand it. While understanding the covenant is essential, this understanding

DAILY BIBLE READINGS

Monday, July 5—*I Will Make a New Covenant (Jeremiah 31: 31-37)*

Tuesday, July 6—*Jesus, Mediator of a Better Covenant (Hebrews 8:1-6)*

Wednesday, July 7—*God's Laws Written on Our Hearts (Hebrews 8:7-13)*

Thursday, July 8—*The Blood of Christ Secured Redemption (Hebrews 9:1-12)*

Friday, July 9—*The Blood of Christ Purifies Us (Hebrews 9: 13-18)*

Saturday, July 10—*Christ's Sacrifice Removes Sin (Hebrews 9:23-28)*

Sunday, July 11—*Christ's Single Offering Perfects Us (Hebrews 10:10-18)*

must lead to an emotional commitment to it (Acts 2:37). This commitment, in turn, must lead to an act of the will to live up to the covenant's requirements.

Under the old covenant God had again and again demonstrated to the people that he was the one and only God. Unfortunately, the people were enticed by false gods and as a result often turned their backs on him. In this verse the writer assures us that under the new covenant God will restore that broken relationship. *I will be their God, and they will be my people.*

11. *"No longer will a man teach his neighbor,*
    or a man his brother, saying, 'Know the Lord,'
because they will all know me,
    from the least of them to the greatest.

The phrases *no longer will a man teach his neighbor, or a man his brother* mean that people will have direct access to God under the new covenant. We do not need to go through the human intermediaries—the priests of the levitical system—that was a feature of the old covenant (cf. Isaiah 54:13; John 6:45; Hebrews 4:16; 10:19-22).

Of course, a teaching function still exists under the new covenant as the New Testament makes clear in 1 Corinthians 12:28, 29 and Ephesians 4:11, 12. Under the new covenant every Christian is a priest (1 Peter 2:9). In this capacity we have not only the opportunity but also the obligation to study and understand the new covenant.

12. *"For I will forgive their wickedness*
    and will remember their sins no more."

Under the old covenant the day of Atonement was a high point in the year (Leviticus 16). It reminded the people that the sacrifices and offerings made throughout the year were not enough to atone for *their sins.* But even this important day was itself not enough, for the blood of bulls and goats cannot take away sin (Hebrews 10:4).

An outstanding feature of this new covenant, on the other hand, is God's permanent forgiveness. Because Christ takes the sin penalty upon himself, God takes away the sins of his people. What a privilege to serve a God who no longer remembers our iniquities! The writer quotes from this section of Jeremiah in Hebrews 10:16, 17 as well (see also Romans 11:27). When Christ returns, *all* Christians will *know* him in the fullest sense of Jeremiah's original prophecy.

SEEKING FORGIVENESS

Simon Wiesenthal had been an architect before the Nazis confined him in a concentration camp in Poland. One afternoon he was cleaning rubbish out of a hospital for wounded German soldiers being brought in from the Eastern Front. A nurse took him to the bedside of Karl, a dying SS trooper. The boy's head wrapped in bandages oozing pus.

Karl, knowing that Wiesenthal was Jewish, grabbed his hand and began to tell his story. Karl had been fighting in a Russian village where his group rounded up several hundred Jews. He and his companions had been ordered to set cans of gasoline in the house and then to fill the house with as many of the Jews as the house could hold. About two hundred were crammed inside and the doors locked.

Karl and the other soldiers tossed grenades in the windows, setting the house afire. They shot anyone who tried to escape. Karl told of a man who jumped from the second story with his clothes on fire, holding a child in his arms. The child's mother jumped next. All three were shot as they tried to crawl away.

Sobbing, Karl asked Wiesenthal to forgive him, saying that only if he were to obtain forgiveness from a Jew could he go to his grave in peace. Could Wiesenthal forgive him? Wiesenthal turned and left the room, with no word of forgiveness.

WHAT DO YOU THINK?

How could an observer notice by your actions that you have accepted the new covenant? What actions are typical of one who has made that commitment?

WHAT DO YOU THINK?

How would you counsel a fellow believer who just can't shake his or her sense of guilt?

[Psalm 103:12; Romans 4:5; 1 Corinthians 15:9; and Galatians 1:13 can be part of your counseling.]

Our sins have mocked the holiness of God, in whose image we are created. But God has made forgiveness available to all. Through Christ, he forgives and remembers our sins no more. His Holy Spirit strengthens us for greater holiness daily. Even so, do we continue in sin?

—R. H.

C. THE "BOTTOM LINE" (v. 13)

13. By calling this covenant "new," he has made the first one obsolete; and what is obsolete and aging will soon disappear.

The transition from the old to the *new* covenant was not instantaneous. The change took place over several decades. It began with the birth of Jesus. The process continued through the ministry of John the Baptist, through Jesus' own ministry, and through Jesus' death, resurrection, and ascension. The outpouring of the Holy Spirit on the day of Pentecost was another crucial point in the process.

From that point on the new covenant has been in effect, and the old covenant cancelled. The book of Hebrews seems to be written from the perspective that temple sacrifices are continuing, however (see Hebrews 10:11), so this book probably was written before A.D. 70. In that year came the destruction of Jerusalem and its temple. With that destruction the old covenant will finally *disappear.*

CONCLUSION

As we look back to the first century, when Christ came bringing the good news of salvation, we may wonder why everyone did not immediately respond to this wonderful message. Through his teaching, his miracles, and especially through his resurrection, Jesus gave ample proof of his identity.

There are several reasons why not everyone accepted the message that Jesus brought. Those most violent in their rejection were the religious leaders. They enjoyed prominent positions and perks. They were respected by most of the people, and they were able to live comfortably above the poverty-level experiences of many others. Those leaders were not always happy with the Roman rule that had been imposed upon them, but they had learned to make the necessary concessions to live with the situation. In their security they took a dim view of anyone who might threaten this delicate balance (John 11:48).

There were others who, though also not especially happy with the power arrangements as they existed, were unwilling to accept the gospel because it meant making a personal change. Most of us, especially as we grow older, find ourselves resistant to change. Change brings the threat of the unknown. For many throughout history, the unknown seemed to be more dangerous than the situation they were in—even if they are not entirely happy with the present situation. This may have been the case with many of the Hebrew Christians who may have been considering going back into Judaism.

Some who might have been interested in becoming Christians undoubtedly were deterred by the threat of persecution. They had seen what had happened to others who had been beaten, imprisoned, and even killed. Their hearts may have been touched by the blessings offered by the new covenant, but the price was too high. Some who were interested in becoming Christians were persuaded by friends or family against taking that step.

Human nature has not changed in the two thousand years since Christ walked the earth. Some refuse to surrender to the call of Christ because they do not want to risk their places of prominence or profit. Others are afraid of change of any kind. While most of us are not kept from becoming Christians because of fear of persecution, there are places in the world where that is a real threat. The parable of sower (Matthew 13:1-9) still confronts us today. What type of "soil" are you?

WHAT DO YOU THINK?

Since the old covenant is now obsolete, do you bother studying the Old Testament? Why, or why not?

[Romans 15:4 and Hebrews 8:5; 10:1 may challenge your learners' thinking here.]

PRAYER

We give you thanks, O Lord, that you have allowed us to live under the new covenant. Help us gain a better understanding of both the responsibilities of the new covenant and the blessings that we can enjoy under it. May we never yield to the temptations to abandon it and the wonderful personal relations with you it affords us. In our Savior's name we pray, amen.

THOUGHT TO REMEMBER

May others see in us the joy of the new covenant!

Discovery Learning

This page contains an alternative lesson plan emphasizing learning activities. Classes desiring such student involvement will find these suggestions helpful. The next page is a reproducible activity page to further enhance discovery learning.

LEARNING GOALS

After this lesson each student will be able to:

1. Contrast elements of the old covenant God had with Israel with the new covenant God has with Christians.

2. Explain how the new covenant is superior to the old one.

3. Identify one person to whom he or she can explain the benefits of the new covenant.

INTO THE LESSON

Display this statement as students arrive: "A covenant is a treaty or an agreement between two parties, each of which assumes certain obligations and responsibilities." Take these visual aids to class: a wedding license and a credit purchase agreement (a loan agreement for a house, appliance, or automobile). Begin the class by telling the students, "Ours is a culture of covenants. While we may not often use the word *covenant*, it is still a great description of major decisions in our lives." Review the definition of *covenant* you have on display. Show the two examples you brought to class. Ask the class to cite obligations or responsibilities that come from each of the two.

Make the transition to Bible study by telling the class, "God has made several agreements with people down through the years. However, his greatest covenant is one that has an impact on every life in this classroom."

INTO THE WORD

Introduce the lesson with a brief lecture based on the lesson commentary "Lesson Background." Use the following words in a list as visuals for this mini-lecture: *Adam and Eve, Noah, Abraham, Mosaic covenant, a better covenant.*

Give the students a handout that has a large heading: "Enjoying _ _ _ _ _ _ _   _ _ _ _ _ _ _ _ _" (or refer to the "Discovery Learning" page in *NIV Bible Student*). Include the following instructions: "Read Hebrews 8:5-13. Use the following clues to find words in this passage to fill in the blanks. Then use the letters in boxes to complete our major heading and discover our blessing in Christ."

"[Moses] was about to ❏ _ _ _ _ the tabernacle" (v. 5).

But the ministry _ ❏ _ _ _ has obtained is . . . superior (v. 6).

If there had been nothing wrong with the _ _ _ _ ❏ covenant . . . (v. 7).

I will make a new _ _ _ _ _ _ _ _ ❏ with the house of Israel (v. 8).

I took them by the hand to lead them out of ❏ _ _ _ _ (v. 9).

They did not ❏ _ _ _ _ _ faithful (v. 9).

I will ❏ _ _ my laws in their minds (v. 10).

I will . . . _ ❏ _ _ _ [my laws] on their hearts (v. 10).

They will be my _ _ _ ❏ _ _ _ _ (v. 10).

They will all know ❏ _ (v. 11).

I will _ _ _ _ ❏ _ _ _ their wickedness (v. 12).

What is _ _ ❏ _ _ _ _ _ and aging will soon disappear (v. 13).

By calling this covenant "_ ❏ _," . . . (v. 13).

[I] will remember their ❏ _ _ _ no more (v. 12).

(*Answers: build, Jesus, first, covenant, Egypt, remain, put, write, people, me, forgive, obsolete, new, sins. Heading: Better Promises.*)

Under this exercise, write: "After filling in the blanks on the headline, write a few ways the blessing described in the heading is true."

After students have completed the exercise, distribute copies of the reproducible activity "Share Your Thoughts" from the next page. Allow time for completing the activity; then discuss the results.

INTO LIFE

Make a poster with the heading "Covenant Blessings." Under those words make two columns headed "Old Covenant" and "New Covenant." First, ask the students to list in the first column some of the blessings and requirements of the old Mosaic covenant between God and Israel. Ask them to list in the second column some of the blessings God brings to his people with the new covenant and what God expects from his people today. Ask learners to make prayer notes on the "Prayer and Praise" section of the reproducible page.

Tell the class, "Suppose you were expected to tell someone how and why the new covenant is better than the old." Ask the class to work in pairs and list reasons on the back of their handout of ways the new covenant is superior and why this is important. After a few minutes, have members share their answers. Close the class by reminding the class that a covenant is an agreement. Ask "What is God's expectation of us? What are some of the things he would like from his people in 2004?"

Share Your Thoughts

Read Hebrews 8:6-13. Write a word or two describing your thoughts or reactions to the verses noted in the "thought bubbles" provided. You may describe a profound discovery to you, a question, a new and wonderful description, or a decision resulting from that passage.

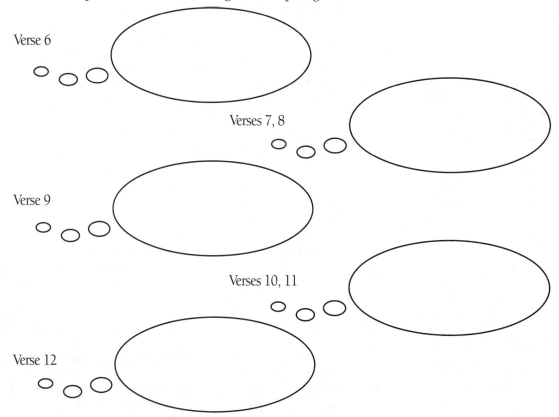

Verse 6

Verses 7, 8

Verse 9

Verses 10, 11

Verse 12

My Prayer and Praise!

Here is your opportunity to thank God for the superior covenant he offers you. You may either write a prayer or write some notes about the themes of your prayer.

Hold Fast to the Faith
Unit 2: Strengthened to Be Faithful
(Lessons 5-8)

ROLL CALL
OF THE FAITHFUL

LESSON 7

WHY TEACH THIS LESSON?

Nations around the world memorialize their fallen heroes in various ways. Statues, monuments, and shrines are almost too numerous to count. Technology has even allowed impressive "virtual memorials" on the Internet. Such memorials are important because they remind us of honorable sacrifice.

The writer of Hebrews has created for us a memorial as well. This memorial, found in chapter 11, reminds us of the actions of those heroes of the faith who have gone before. It also reminds us that others will remember our lives in certain ways after we are gone. Today's lesson will help your learners understand the importance of leaving their own legacies of faith to those that follow. Eternal life—both our own and that of those who come later—will depend on it!

INTRODUCTION

A. MORTGAGE ON THE FUTURE

In the Second Punic War (218–202 B.C.) the famous Carthaginian leader Hannibal invaded Italy. He subsequently defeated in several battles the best armies the Romans could put in the field. The citizens of Rome were alarmed, to say the least. Nothing but the walls of their city stood between them and total defeat.

The Roman leaders wavered in their counsel, some arguing for terms of peace and others for continued resistance. Legend has it that one courageous citizen stepped forward with an unusual idea: he offered to purchase the very parcel of land upon which Hannibal's tent stood. When asked the reason for his unusual offer, he is said to have replied, "Fellow Romans, I am taking a mortgage on the future." (Compare Jeremiah 32:1-15, 42-44.) The confident attitude of this citizen is said to have been instrumental in rallying the Romans and stiffening their resistance. Hannibal eventually withdrew.

Today we will see the writer of the Hebrew epistle "call the roll of the faithful." As we read it, we are struck by how they maintained faith in the face of dismal prospects. In hopeless conditions they took a mortgage on the future.

B. LESSON BACKGROUND

The book of Hebrews is a book that *warns* (Hebrews 2:1-4; 3:7-19; etc.). We don't know all the reasons that the readers may have had for wanting to abandon Christianity, but fear of persecution or hardship is very likely.

The writer of this epistle marshals several arguments to convince the readers to remain true to their Christian faith. The new covenant is better than the old in having a better high priest, a better sacrifice, and a better hope. Now in Hebrews 11 the inspired writer turns to Jewish history to demonstrate that great heroes of the past had faced all kinds of challenges to their faith. But they had prevailed in spite of the danger.

DEVOTIONAL READING:
HEBREWS 11:17-26
BACKGROUND SCRIPTURE:
HEBREWS 11
PRINTED TEXT:
HEBREWS 11:1-13

LESSON AIMS

After participating in this lesson, each student will be able to:

Jul 18

1. Briefly recount the stories of the Bible heroes in today's text and tell how they demonstrated faith.

2. Tell a personal story of how a difficult time in life helped his or her faith to grow.

3. Identify someone who is experiencing difficulty and at least one specific way he or she can encourage that person's faith.

KEY VERSE

Without faith it is impossible to please God, because anyone who comes to him must believe that he exists and that he rewards those who earnestly seek him. —Hebrews 11:6

Logical arguments are useful in any discussion of the Christian faith, even essential. But perhaps the most forceful argument for the power of faith in God is to look at the examples of those who have triumphed over all kinds of difficulties in their efforts to remain true to him. The author of Hebrews selects a variety of past heroes of the faith to make just such an argument. In many ways Abraham is the greatest of those examples. The example of Abraham would be especially forceful to Jewish Christians, who looked to him as their father in the faith.

I. NATURE OF FAITH (HEBREWS 11:1-3)

A. DESCRIPTION OF FAITH (vv. 1, 2)

1. Now faith is being sure of what we hope for and certain of what we do not see.

This is certainly one of the most important verses in the entire Bible. Eternal life depends on *faith*. If we do not understand what faith is, we may well forfeit our *hope* for the life to come. Faith as described here conveys the idea of confidence in what one believes. Faith is not just vague wishful thinking; it is the complete confidence that God's promises will be fulfilled.

Right here is where modern believers have a great advantage: we can look at centuries past and see that God has indeed kept all his promises. This evidence of things that we can see in the pages of the Bible and in history provides us with the ability to be *sure of what we hope for.* Our faith is not a blind faith.

2. This is what the ancients were commended for.

The ancients were those who had lived in the past (cf. Hebrews 1:1). Not all of these *were commended* however. Adam and Eve were expelled from the Garden of Eden for rebellion. Cain was the first murderer. But some were obedient and received God's blessings as a result. It was by faith that these were able to serve in such a way that they received God's approval (see verses 4 and following, below).

B. FAITH IN CREATION (v. 3)

3. By faith we understand that the universe was formed at God's command, so that what is seen was not made out of what was visible.

Where did the earth and the other heavenly bodies come from? How did they get here? From the primitive savage who looked into the starry heavens, to modern scientists who use the Hubble telescope to search the vast reaches of space, humanity has looked for explanations.

Some modern scientists scoff at biblical answers as superstition of pre-modern thinking (cf. Genesis 1; Psalm 33:6, 9). They insist that they alone can give us scientific answers (cf. 2 Peter 3:5). For example, some propose the "Big Bang" theory for the beginnings of *the universe.* Even if this theory were true, it does not tell us where the original matter and energy came from to produce the great explosion. At this point the scientist has to fall back on some kind of *faith* to tell us about the origins of matter and energy.

Since both Christians and non-Christians must rely on faith to answer these ultimate questions, we have a right to ask whose faith is more valid. Which is more reasonable: to have faith that the material used to form the universe somehow just "always existed," or to have faith in a God who is able to create things from nothing?

II. FAITH OF VARIOUS PEOPLE (HEBREWS 11:4-13)

A. ABEL (v. 4)

4. By faith Abel offered God a better sacrifice than Cain did. By faith he was commended as a righteous man, when God spoke well of his offerings. And by faith he still speaks, even though he is dead.

WHAT DO YOU THINK?

How would you respond to the claim that faith is "accepting something that you have no good reason to think is true"?

The account of *Cain* and *Abel* is found in Genesis 4:1-15. Both brothers brought sacrifices to God. Cain brought "of the fruits of the soil," while Abel brought "fat portions from some of the firstborn of his flocks." God accepted Abel's sacrifice, but rejected Cain's. This so angered Cain that he murdered his brother.

This verse gives us a clue regarding God's viewpoint. We are told that Abel offered *a better sacrifice* because he was *righteous*. It is evident that the problem was not with the sacrifice itself, whether animal or grain. The important issue was that of attitude.

Abel offered his sacrifice *by faith* with a humble heart, while Cain offered his grudgingly or arrogantly. As a result of his godly example, Abel still speaks to us *even though he* has been *dead* for thousands of years.

B. ENOCH (vv. 5, 6)

5. *By faith Enoch was taken from this life, so that he did not experience death; he could not be found, because God had taken him away. For before he was taken, he was commended as one who pleased God.*

There are two men named *Enoch* in Genesis. Genesis 5:21-24 allows us to conclude that the Enoch being discussed was the son of Jared and the father of Methuselah. The most important information we learn about him in that passage is that he "walked with God" (v. 24). This is significant because in Enoch's day most people were walking away from God, not with him.

Enoch's faith is the reason the writer of Hebrews mentions him as an example. As a result of his faith, Enoch *did not experience death* in the usual sense, for "God took him away" (again, v. 24; compare the case of Elijah in 2 Kings 2:11).

Because of this unusual event, numerous Jewish myths had sprung up about Enoch. As interesting and fanciful as some of these are, we need not dwell on them and miss the main point the author is making: Enoch walked *by faith* and as a result was pleasing to God. Jude 14, 15 mentions a prophecy of Enoch.

6. *And without faith it is impossible to please God, because anyone who comes to him must believe that he exists and that he rewards those who earnestly seek him.*

This very important verse indicates the reason that the actions of Abel and Enoch are worthy of being mentioned in this context of *faith*. Abel and Enoch did not simply *believe* that God *exists*. Belief is important, but it does not go far enough by itself (see James 2:19). Abel and Enoch were among the few that *earnestly* sought God. As a result, they did indeed *please God*.

All of us are painfully aware that there are times and situations when it is difficult to see any tangible evidence that God really does reward his followers. But with the evidence of history and the eye of faith we can look beyond our immediate situations and see the eternal blessings that he has in store for us.

C. NOAH (v. 7)

7. *By faith Noah, when warned about things not yet seen, in holy fear built an ark to save his family. By his faith he condemned the world and became heir of the righteousness that comes by faith.*

When God looked upon *the world* in Noah's day, he saw that it was terribly evil and corrupt. So he made the decision to cleanse it with a flood (Genesis 6:11-17). We don't know exactly how God spoke to Noah, but we do know that he ordered him to build *an ark*. Noah "did everything just as God commanded him" without any record of hesitation or questioning (Genesis 6:22).

Part of God's message to Noah was a warning *about things not yet seen*. This is where faith comes in, and Noah really demonstrated it when he set out to build

WHAT DO YOU THINK?

With Abel as an example, what do you think God is looking for in a sacrifice from you that would be pleasing to him?

WHAT DO YOU THINK?

Thinking about how Abel continues to "speak" to us today, in what ways would you want your Christian example to "speak" to others long after God has called you home?

[Enrich your discussion by considering 2 Timothy 1:5 and 1 Peter 2:12.]

God rewards "them that diligently seek him."

from Hebrews 11:6

Visual for lesson 7. *This poster will remind your learners of the importance of diligence in the Christian walk.*

such a huge vessel. This was a tremendous undertaking, and most likely he had to carry it out in an atmosphere of ridicule from friends and neighbors. Nor was it a simple weekend project. By some calculations, this task took decades. During that time this "preacher of righteousness" (2 Peter 2:5) was unable to save any but his own family (Genesis 7:13; 1 Peter 3:20). It took a lot of faith to continue preaching under those discouraging circumstances.

A JOB WELL DONE

At the beginning of a project we often can see only dimly where it will lead. That was certainly true of Dokie Hampton's work. Before her death Dokie was a member of "The Quilters," a group of women who met regularly in Mabel Winkler's basement making quilts. Typically, they would begin in the morning, stop to eat lunch, then work on through the afternoon.

Their work was extraordinary, with hundreds and hundreds of stitches in each quilt and many separate patches of material carefully arranged and skillfully joined. These quilts were not only practical, they were works of art. Buyers gladly paid premium prices for such excellent work.

Stitching was something Dokie did quite well. In fact, she worked for a company in Akron, Ohio, sewing material to tailor-make men's suits to the wearer's exact specifications. Each stitch had to be absolutely secure so that the material would not tear. More importantly, every stitch had to be airtight! These suits were to be worn in a vacuum. If one of Dokie's stitches leaked air, the man wearing the suit could die. Who needed such clothing? American astronauts.

Dokie was one of a select handful of seamstresses assigned this task. She had only a vague notion of how her work would be used. But later on Dokie better understood the reason behind the request as she and millions of others watched on television.

Safely inside the ark on the day the rain started pouring down, Noah better understood the instructions God had given him. But the understanding came *after* faith. How much faith are we exercising today?   —R. H.

D. ABRAHAM, PART 1 (vv. 8-10)

8. By faith Abraham, when called to go to a place he would later receive as his inheritance, obeyed and went, even though he did not know where he was going.

The writer now causes us to consider the life of *Abraham* as an example of one who lived by faith. The Bible tells us more about the life of Abraham than the other heroes previously mentioned, and Jews look to Abraham as the father of their nation.

Abraham lived with his father and other members of his family in Ur of the Chaldeans, located on the lower Euphrates River (modern Iraq). Abraham accompanied his father when he moved to Haran (Genesis 11:27-32).

God *called* Abraham *to go to a place he would later receive as his inheritance* after his father died. Since Abraham was seventy-five years old, it took no little faith for him to leave Haran (Genesis 12:4). When God called him out, God didn't give him a carefully marked road map showing the route he was to take and his final destination (Genesis 12:1). Rather, he *went, even though he did not know where he was going.* Abraham didn't question God—he obeyed!

9. By faith he made his home in the promised land like a stranger in a foreign country; he lived in tents, as did Isaac and Jacob, who were heirs with him of the same promise.

For the rest of his life Abraham lived as a nomad *in the promised land.* That land remained a land of promise, not only for him, but also for his son *Isaac* and grandson *Jacob* (Genesis 35:27). Only centuries later were Abraham's descen-

DAILY BIBLE READINGS

Monday, July 12—*Abraham Did Not Weaken in Faith* (Romans 4:13-22)

Tuesday, July 13—*Abel and Enoch Had Faith* (Hebrews 11:1-6)

Wednesday, July 14—*By Faith Noah Built an Ark* (Hebrews 11:7-12)

Thursday, July 15—*They Desired a Heavenly Country* (Hebrews 11:13-19)

Friday, July 16—*Isaac, Jacob, Joseph Had Faith* (Hebrews 11:20-26)

Saturday, July 17—*By Faith Moses Led the Israelites* (Hebrews 11:27-31)

Sunday, July 18—*Others Commended for Their Faith* (Hebrews 11:32-40) dants able to claim that land as God intended under *the same promise.* Abraham and his family *lived in tents,* indicating a nomadic lifestyle.

10. For he was looking forward to the city with foundations, whose architect and builder is God.

When he left Haran, Abraham may have envisioned building a *city* in the promised land, where he could have a permanent dwelling place. But by faith he had a nobler vision: a city *with foundations,* built by God. Abraham saw beyond the nomadic life that was to be his lot on earth. He saw instead the promise of a heavenly home. The writer of Hebrews will expand on this "city" in 11:16; 12:22; and 13:14.

E. SARAH (v. 11)

11. By faith Abraham, even though he was past age—and Sarah herself was barren—was enabled to become a father because he considered him faithful who had made the promise.

It may surprise us that *Sarah* is mentioned as a model of a faithful person. In fact, she doubted God's promise that *Abraham* would have heirs through her. At one point she encouraged her husband to take her handmaid as a secondary wife so that Sarah could "build a family through her" (Genesis 16:1-3). Later, when God sent three messengers to Abraham, Sarah overheard them tell him that she would have a son. On hearing it, she "laughed to herself" (Genesis 18:12).

Yet at some point her *faith* began to grow. Perhaps her attitude began to change as she watched Abraham faithfully try to carry out the Lord's mandate. We need to realize that our faith can be contagious. When others see our faithful lives, they can catch some of that faith.

F. ABRAHAM, PART 2 (v. 12)

12. And so from this one man, and he as good as dead, came descendants as numerous as the stars in the sky and as countless as the sand on the seashore.

As a result of God's power and Abraham's faith, his descendants became *as numerous as the stars in the sky* and as the *sand* which is *on the seashore.* The fulfillment of this promise is so important that this imagery is used in several Bible passages (Genesis 15:5; 22:17; 32:12; Exodus 32:13; Deuteronomy 1:10; 10:22). Paul discusses Abraham's profound faith in this regard in Romans 4:18, 19.

MODERN HEROES OF THE FAITH

"My first thought was that I should kill those rebels," says Vidya Sharma. Vidya lives in Katmandu, Nepal. Vidya had just learned that Maoist rebels had murdered his younger brother.

The trek to his brother's village took Vidya three days. Maoists had repeatedly threatened him, but Vidya had never considered that they would harm his family members. Rebels had come to his brother's house in the village of Toli about 11:00 P.M. and had thrown a small bomb through a window of the family home, wounding several.

The Communists broke into the house, kicking and beating indiscriminately. Yelling at Vidya's aged parents, they demanded, "Why did you permit your son to become a Christian?" Their son was the only Christian in this Hindu village. The Maoists ordered everyone out of the house and set off a much larger bomb, destroying everything. Then they shot Mahesh, Vidya's twenty-two-year-old brother.

Like the earlier Khmer Rouge in Cambodia, Maoist rebels in Nepal ranged through the countryside with their "purification" campaign, annihilating anyone they felt was against them. Because Christians generally favor democracy and believe in certain God-given rights, the Maoists saw them as enemies.

HOW TO SAY IT

Abraham. AY-bruh-ham.
Cambodia. Kam-BOH-dee-uh.
Carthaginian. Kar-thuh-JIN-ee-un.
Chaldeans. Kal-DEE-unz.
Elijah. Ee-LYE-juh.
Enoch. E-nock.
Euphrates. You-FRAY-teez.
Hannibal. HAN-nuh-bull.
Haran. HAIR-un.
Isaac. EYE-zuk.
Jacob. JAY-kub.
Jared. JAIR-ed.
Khmer Rouge. Kuh-MER Roozh.
Methuselah. Muh-THOO-zuh-luh.
Punic. PEW-nik.
Ur. Er.
Vidya Sharma. VID-yuh SHAR-muh.

Through prayer Vidya's anger has gone, but his determination to continue his Christian work is stronger than ever. His family has suffered, his brother is dead, and his life is still threatened. But Vidya Sharma continues his important witness for Christ in this far-off spot in Southeast Asia, convinced that God knows his situation and that God's reward will far outweigh any present difficulties. May our own lives be just as faithful.

—R. H.

G. SUMMARY (v. 13)

13. All these people were still living by faith when they died. They did not receive the things promised; they only saw them and welcomed them from a distance. And they admitted that they were aliens and strangers on earth.

Foresight is a vital part of faith. That's what it means for these heroes to be able to see *the things promised . . . from a distance.* For example, Jesus said that "Abraham rejoiced at the thought of seeing my day" (John 8:56). The way these heroes lived their lives acknowledges the fact that they were *aliens and strangers on earth* (cf. Genesis 23:4; 47:9; Psalm 39:12). As Christians we also are to acknowledge that we are but strangers and aliens on this earth (cf. 1 Peter 2:11).

CONCLUSION

Occasionally we hear people say, "I don't take anything on faith." This is an absurd statement, for every day in countless ways we live by faith. For example, when we receive our direct deposit pay stub, we have faith that the money actually went to the bank. When we approach a bridge while driving, do we stop, pull off the road, and check the safety of the bridge? Of course not. Without even a thought we drive across the bridge. We have faith in the engineers who planned the bridge and the crews who built it.

In most situations faith does not come instantaneously, but must develop over time. Faith grows out of evidence from the past. Over the years we have lived in several different places and have had many different neighbors, some good and some otherwise. Several months ago a new neighbor moved in next door. He was a total stranger, and I had no basis for forming an opinion about him. Before long we learned that he was a Christian and that we shared many common interests. As we learned more about him, our faith in one another grew. Now we work together on all kinds of projects on his property and on mine, and I value him as a trusted friend. I have faith that he will not break our trust.

Much the same can be said about how we develop a relationship with God and acquire faith in him. As small children we learn about God in the home and at church. This learning usually comes slowly, a little bit at a time. The rate of our learning depends on many factors, both internal and external.

We may accept Christ and become Christians at some point along the way. But that does not mean that the growth of our faith stops. Conversion is but one step—an important step to be sure—in the process of becoming mature Christians. Our faith grows through our own experiences and by observing the lives of others. That growth is not always a smooth, upward curve. Often it proceeds by jerks and starts—frequently upward, but sometimes downward as well.

If, like Abraham, we continue to look for the "city with foundations, whose architect and builder is God," we will not be disappointed in the end. Among those aging saints who are more mature in their faith, we see a calm, assured trust in God that grows out of a lifetime of following him. Theirs is a faith that looks ever forward. This is the message the writer of Hebrews was trying to get across to the first-century Jewish Christians. It is a message for every generation.

WHAT DO YOU THINK?

In what ways are you like (or unlike) those mentioned in Hebrews 11:13, who "did not receive the things promised" but "only saw them and welcomed them from a distance"?

WHAT DO YOU THINK?

In what ways do you (or do you not) consider yourself to be a "stranger" and "alien" on earth?

PRAYER

Gracious God, we thank you for the lives of the faithful whom you have portrayed in Scripture to serve as examples. May we be encouraged by these faithful examples to grow in our faith toward Christian maturity. May we serve in turn as faithful examples to others. In Jesus' name, amen.

THOUGHT TO REMEMBER

Faith is the victory!

Discovery Learning

This page contains an alternative lesson plan emphasizing learning activities. Classes desiring such student involvement will find these suggestions helpful. The next page is a reproducible activity page to further enhance discovery learning.

LEARNING GOALS

After participating in this lesson, each student will be able to:

1. Briefly recount the stories of the Bible heroes in today's text and tell how they demonstrated faith.

2. Tell a personal story of how a difficult time in life helped his or her faith to grow.

3. Identify someone who is experiencing difficulty and at least one specific way he or she can encourage that person's faith.

INTO THE LESSON

Write the words *FAITH MODELS* at the top of a marker board or poster board. Ask the class to name friends or acquaintances they would say are models of faith. As you add each suggested name to the list, ask others why they think that one has been chosen as a model of faith. (An exercise similar to this is in the student book, *NIV Bible Student*.)

God knows that models of faith are inspirational and motivational. Make the transition to Bible study by saying, "Many of our models and the models God chose are people who demonstrate great faith in adverse circumstances. This study should help arm us for times when Satan is attacking our personal lives."

INTO THE WORD

This Bible study lends itself to two topics: the nature of faith and the necessity of faith. Study groups will use handouts to focus on these. Use the front of the handout to write the assignment for one group and the back to write the assignment for the other. Divide the class into groups of no more than five people each, identifying each group as a "1" or a "2." (If you choose, use the handouts as discussion guides in a whole-class activity.)

Group 1. Distribute handouts and direct attention to the side labeled "The Nature of Faith." The instructions under the heading should be, "Read Hebrews 11:1-13 and answer the following questions.

"A. Verse one is a classic description of faith. One writer says this is one of the most important verses in the Bible. Why or how is this true?

"B. Faith is often modeled when life circumstances are most challenging. How was the faith of the persons mentioned in our text (listed below) demonstrated, and in what circumstances? Abel (v. 4), Enoch (v. 5 and Genesis 5:17-24), Noah (v. 7), Abraham (vv. 8-13), Sarah (vv. 11, 12).

"C. As time allows, discuss how hope and faith differ."

Group 2. This group's heading should read "The Necessity of Faith." Write the following assignment: "Read today's text, Hebrews 11:1-13. Focus on the teaching in verse 6, and answer the following questions.

"A. Without faith it is impossible for us to please God. Why is faith so important for a healthy relationship with God?

"B. Faith usually grows out of experience. Illustrate this principle for the class with any example you wish. (*A simple one is to have someone turn on/off the lights; experience teaches us that the lights will go on/off using the switch. What does this principle teach us about faith in God?*)

"C. Explain or illustrate how faith continues to grow after a person becomes a Christian. What are the dangers for believers if faith does not continue to develop throughout life's walk?"

After the groups report, give a brief summary based on the lesson commentary on verse 13.

INTO LIFE

Say, "We have seen biblical models who have demonstrated faith as they faced difficult circumstances. As they did, we learn from our experiences and become encouragers to other people facing life's challenges.

Distribute copies of the reproducible activity "We, Too, Can Model Faith" from the next page. Ask the learners to explain why or how the faith of a person may be tested in each circumstance cited on the activity sheet. (They can record their ideas in the second column.) Ask how Christians who have faced similar challenges and yet remained faithful could encourage such a person. If your class shares such things easily, ask volunteers to tell of personal experiences from which their faith has grown and enabled them to encourage others. End this testimonial moment by asking each student to identify one difficult personal event that has equipped him or her to help others. Allow prayer groups to pray for each other's faithful witness in matters both easy and difficult.

As you close the session, call attention to the reproducible activity "My Experience and Faith." Encourage the students to complete this activity on their own sometime during the week.

We, Too, Can Model Faith

Faith is often tested and modeled in difficult circumstances. Many models in Hebrews 11 are mentioned because they remained faithful in dismal circumstances. Listed below are a few times or ways faith may be tested in a believer's life today. In the second column, write how or why this circumstance might prove challenging to a believer's faith. In the third column write a possible testimony that a believer who has gone through such a trial may be able to give.

CIRCUMSTANCE	HOW/WHY FAITH MAY BE CHALLENGED	A POSSIBLE TESTIMONY BY THE "EXPERIENCED"
Open-heart Surgery		
Major Financial Setback		
A Son Announces He Is Homosexual		
A Husband & Wife Discover They Cannot Have Children		
A Spouse Is Discovered To Be Having an Affair		
A Daughter Is Killed in an Automobile Accident		

My Experience and Faith

Probably as you look back on dismal circumstances in your life, you can see where God was at work. As a result of those experiences, your faith has grown.

In the heart at the right, jot down two or three of those life experiences that have pushed your faith to the edge and have helped you to grow.

As you note these experiences, remember the responsibility to share your faith experiences as implied in the first exercise on this page.

Hold Fast to the Faith

Unit 2: Strengthened to Be Faithful
(Lessons 5-8)

FAITHFUL AND DISCIPLINED

LESSON 8

WHY TEACH THIS LESSON?

Most parents realize that their children need to be disciplined. But there is disagreement regarding the proper methods. Are spankings effective, or do they do more harm than good? What about using "time out" exclusively? The arguments go on and on. Whatever *method* is used, the *outcome* of parental discipline should be the same: a child who will have self-discipline later as an adult.

A child who is never disciplined is done a great disservice. Likewise, we should expect our heavenly Father to discipline us. It is his discipline that enables us to produce a "harvest of righteousness" (Hebrews 12:11) as we grow in spiritual maturity. Today's lesson will help us see this vital connection.

INTRODUCTION

A. FROM JUNK TO JEWELRY

An uncut diamond is scarcely a thing of beauty. Its odd shape and dull appearance completely conceal its true value from the untrained observer.

Then the apparently worthless bit of rock is placed in the hands of a skilled diamond cutter. He or she may spend hours cleaving the stone (cutting it in two) with special tools and then many more hours cutting, grinding, and polishing the stone before it can be mounted in a piece of jewelry. Were the stone a living thing and sensitive to pain, it might well complain of this cruel treatment. Yet when this treatment has been completed, the diamond is no longer a dull and worthless piece of stone, but a brilliant and precious jewel.

Sometimes God handles us as "diamonds in the rough." He allows suffering to come into our lives—suffering that we often cannot understand or appreciate. Yet, when it is all over—perhaps many years later—we can see that God, the master diamond cutter, was working all along to fashion us into precious jewels. The cutting and grinding have shaped us into masterpieces.

B. LESSON BACKGROUND

In last week's lesson the writer of Hebrews offered us a list of some heroes of the faith. Our study ended with Abraham, but the list is actually much longer, continuing through Isaac, Jacob, and Moses (Hebrews 11:20-29). Then the writer mentions some of the judges down to the time of Samuel and David. Other heroes are not named, but some of their sufferings are listed: fury of the flames, edge of the sword, jeering, floggings, imprisonment, being sawn in two, and other violent mistreatment (11:34-37).

Obviously, all these heroes had human shortcomings. Yet each in a personal way exemplifies a trust in God that serves as an example for those who follow.

I. THE RACE OF LIFE (HEBREWS 12:1-3)

A. THE TASK BEFORE US (v. 1)

1. *Therefore, since we are surrounded by such a great cloud of witnesses, let us throw off everything that hinders and the sin that so easily entangles, and let us run with perseverance the race marked out for us.*

DEVOTIONAL READING:
1 PETER 4:12-19
BACKGROUND SCRIPTURE:
HEBREWS 12
PRINTED TEXT:
HEBREWS 12:1-13

LESSON AIMS

After participating in this lesson, each student will be able to:

1. Identify the basic elements necessary to run a good spiritual race.

2. Express the importance of being patient and persistent when facing hardship.

3. Identify an impediment to a good spiritual race that he or she would like to lay aside.

Jul
25

KEY VERSE

Endure hardship as discipline; God is treating you as sons. —Hebrews 12:7

As we think about *such a great cloud of witnesses* that surrounds us, we must ask, "Which way is the witnessing going?" In Hebrews 11 the author has just given us examples of heroes of the faith. As we read that list, we could say that their accomplishments and hardships serve as witnesses to spur us on.

But the writer more likely is intending to say that those heroes themselves are now witnessing us as we work for Christ. In this case the picture is that of an athletic stadium where the runners and other athletes perform before a vast, cheering crowd. Such a crowd can be a great encouragement to the participants in an athletic contest. As Christians we see this crowd with the eye of faith.

We can also acknowledge at this point that we are always surrounded by earthly witnesses. Some of them are on our side, and some are antagonistic. Although the writer is not referring to present-day witnesses, we should nevertheless remember to conduct ourselves in such a way that we will not bring reproach to God's name.

What Do You Think?

Who is watching you "run the race" of the Christian life? How does knowing that they are watching affect your behavior?

Proper conduct requires that we *throw off everything that hinders and the sin that so easily entangles.* These are really two separate ideas. Athletes, then as now, carry nothing in a race that will slow them down. Many things in life may serve as distractions from fully devoted service to Christ, although such things might not be classified as *sin* in and of themselves. An example could be spending too much time surfing the Internet (even if visiting only wholesome web sites). We must learn to shed such baggage as we "travel light" in our Christian service.

Rejecting sin is even more important. Sin saps our physical, emotional, and spiritual strength. Sin compromises our witness to non-Christians. Although we all fall back into sin at times, we cannot run a victorious race if we remain there.

What Do You Think?

What sorts of things hinder you as you run the race of faith? How do you deal with them?

We also do well to remember that the Christian life is a marathon, not a sprint. Athletes train differently for a short dash than for a long-distance run. A good start out of the blocks and a sustained burst of speed are crucial for very short races. The training required to develop those skills do little to help the long-distance runner, however. *Perseverance* and endurance are much more important for the marathoner.

Thinking Ahead

Akio Morita, cofounder of the Sony Corporation, once rejected a deal that would have made a lot of money for his company. Soon after Sony was formed, the Bulova company offered to buy one hundred thousand of Sony's transistor radios. The deal was worth more than ten times the value of Morita's company, but he declined.

Why? Even though accepting the offer would have put cash in Morita's pocket, he knew it would have done nothing for Sony because Bulova wanted to put their own name on the radios. Morita wanted to sell Sony products, not products with someone else's name on them.

In his letter of refusal Morita told the Bulova company that in fifty years the name Sony would be as well known as the name Bulova, and that the radio that he had helped create would be one step toward that goal. Had he been thinking only of the short-term, Morita might have taken the offer. But because he was thinking long-term, he did not. History shows the wisdom of Morita's decision.

The writer of Hebrews encourages us to remain faithful to the long-term goal, no matter how appealing short-term distractions may be. Many leaders in the secular world grasp this concept. Do we in the church understand it as well as they?—R. H.

B. The Example Before Us (vv. 2, 3)

2. Let us fix our eyes on Jesus, the author and perfecter of our faith, who for the joy set before him endured the cross, scorning its shame, and sat down at the right hand of the throne of God.

If our goal is to become Christlike, we must look to *Jesus* as both our model and our inspiration. The word *author* can be understood as "pioneer" or "trailblazer." Those terms appropriately suggest that he has gone ahead to mark the path for those who will follow.

As the *perfecter of our faith* Jesus has completed that which is necessary for a victorious life. He did this by enduring *the cross.* He was willing to undergo that shame because he knew the joy of doing God's will.

That joy is complete now that he sits *at the right hand of the throne of God* (Hebrews 1:3, 13; 8:1; 10:12). This indicates that he has been restored to the glory that he knew before he came into the world.

3. Consider him who endured such opposition from sinful men, so that you will not grow weary and lose heart.

The Hebrew Christians are facing ridicule and persecution. The solution is to look to Christ. Under persecution, he was unwavering in his commitment to serve God. Looking to him is the prevention to becoming *weary and* losing *heart.*

II. THE DISCIPLINE OF THE FATHER (HEBREWS 12:4-11)

A. STRENGTH AND ENCOURAGEMENT (vv. 4-10)

4. In your struggle against sin, you have not yet resisted to the point of shedding your blood.

Christians are under constant "inward" attack by Satan; these attacks, of course, must be met and rejected. But many will have to face physical persecution for their faith as well. At the point in time that the author writes, the Hebrew Christians apparently have not yet experienced such persecution. They undoubtedly know about the deaths of Stephen (Acts 7:54-60) and James (Acts 12:2), but they themselves *have not yet resisted to the point of shedding* their own *blood.* But "not yet" can mean that martyrdom looms as a real possibility, and the readers have to be ready for it.

5, 6. And you have forgotten that word of encouragement that addresses you as sons:

> "My son, do not make light of the Lord's discipline,
>   and do not lose heart when he rebukes you,
> because the Lord disciplines those he loves,
>   and he punishes everyone he accepts as a son."

Every parent must deal with the problem of disobedience when rearing children. It is a serious mistake to allow disobedience to go uncorrected. To do so encourages more disobedience, to the ultimate harm of the child. Today we see all too many cases where parents have abdicated their obligation to correct their children. The results are tragic for both the parents and the children.

We certainly are not suggesting that child abuse is ever appropriate, but many of us who are older can remember when a paddling at the hands of parents or teachers had tremendous value in correcting our behavior. We need to remember that even our Lord learned "obedience from what he suffered" (Hebrews 5:8). We may not be able to understand the full theological implications of that verse, but we can understand the practical application of it to our own lives. If our Lord had to learn obedience by suffering, how much more does that concept apply to us?

The Old Testament shows us that the children of God confronted him with their disobedience time and again. God did not let their disobedience go unpunished. With that fact undoubtedly in mind, the writer now injects a quotation from Proverbs 3:11, 12 to make sure that the readers remember the connection between suffering and being a child of God.

WHAT DO YOU THINK?

How has attention to Jesus helped you endure the hardships that can come as a result of Christian faith?

WHAT DO YOU THINK?

Although almost no one in modern North America is threatened with death for Christian faith, what are some examples from around the world of Christians currently facing the prospect of martyrdom? What should you do about this sobering reality?

Proverbs 3:11, 12 is a passage that the readers undoubtedly have heard before. It expresses a theme designed to help the readers recall that the many things their ancestors had suffered from other nations came because of disobedience (e.g., Deuteronomy 8; Jeremiah 31:18). The suffering of the Israelites came about many times when God deliberately raised up enemies as a means of punishment.

The writer wants the readers to understand that regardless of what the future might hold, God still loves them. The sufferings that they are to undergo may be the result of evil persecution or chastisement from God for sinful disobedience. If it is to be the latter, the readers should realize that God's chastisement grows out of love; it is neither vindictive nor based on a desire for revenge.

In those dark times when God punishes his wayward children, we must not forget that his actions grow out of love, out of concern to keep us on the narrow path (Matthew 7:14). If we forget this, we are likely to become bitter and resentful, crying out in self-pity, "Why me, God, why me?" When we were being punished for our misdeeds as children, it was not always obvious to us at the time that our parents loved us. In fact, we often resented both the punishment and them. Only as the years passed and we achieved a certain level of maturity did we come to realize that they punished us because they loved us.

7. Endure hardship as discipline; God is treating you as sons. For what son is not disciplined by his father?

This thought reinforces verse 6. When we accept chastening and realize its ultimate purpose, we rejoice in knowing that this is the process he is using to help us maintain a special relationship with him. He is dealing with us *as sons.* (See Proverbs 13:24.)

8. If you are not disciplined (and everyone undergoes discipline), then you are illegitimate children and not true sons.

The writer makes this next point quite sharply. All first-century Jews know that illegitimate sons do not have the same legal rights and privileges that the legitimate sons have regarding the parents' estate. Those who have been *disciplined* and have accepted it are the ones who are the legitimate *sons* of God. But those who have not been so chastened are *illegitimate children.*

Parents naturally will discipline their own children as appropriate. But parents are not obligated to discipline children who are not under their legal care. When certain people receive no corrective discipline from God, that is proof of their status as "outsiders." They are not members of God's family and are not eligible to receive his eternal inheritance. Rejoice that you are not one of them!

9. Moreover, we have all had human fathers who disciplined us and we respected them for it. How much more should we submit to the Father of our spirits and live!

Not all children grow to respect their parents who *disciplined* them. Sometimes their parents had punished them harshly or unfairly, or without showing any love in the process.

Usually, however, children do grow up to respect their parents. That respect is likely to grow as the children themselves become parents and have to deal with their own offspring. If we as children have grown to respect our parents for the love they showed us and the sacrifices they made for us, *how much more should we respect our heavenly Father* for all that he has done for us?

10. Our fathers disciplined us for a little while as they thought best; but God disciplines us for our good, that we may share in his holiness.

The chastening we received from our parents lasted for only *a little while*—that is, a few years at most. They did it according to the best knowledge that they had.

Unfortunately, they sometimes made mistakes in disciplining us. But not so with God. He deals with us wisely, seeing beyond the present to the future that

WHAT DO YOU THINK?

What are some ways that you are grateful for how your parents disciplined you as a child? How would you have been different if they hadn't? What parallels do you see to their discipline and God's?

[Be cautious with this question, as it may present an opportunity for some to express bitterness toward parents who were harsh in their discipline.]

he has in store for us. He does it so that *we may share in his holiness.* Because he is holy, he wants us to be holy as well (1 Peter 1:16).

B. HARDSHIP AND HARVEST (v. 11)

11. No discipline seems pleasant at the time, but painful. Later on, however, it produces a harvest of righteousness and peace for those who have been trained by it.

No right-thinking person is likely to seek punishment! But when we understand and accept punishment as a part of God's plan, then we will enjoy *a harvest of righteousness and peace.* This frees us from the bitterness and resentment that often results from suffering. With such freedom comes greater devotion to the Master. God's discipline is for our eternal good. God disciplines his people out of love (Revelation 3:19).

III. THE NEED TO GET MOVING (HEBREWS 12:12, 13)

A. STRENGTH, NOT FEEBLENESS (v. 12)

12. Therefore, strengthen your feeble arms and weak knees.

Runners in the marathon, which is a distance of more than twenty-six miles, speak of a certain point in the race where they "hit the wall." That point is usually around the twenty-mile mark. At that point they suddenly are overwhelmed by the feeling that every ounce of energy in their bodies has been exhausted and they can't go any farther. The winners, of course, somehow reach down and find the strength to finish.

The writer seems to be describing Christians who have "hit the wall." They believe that they have exhausted every ounce of their spiritual energy and can't make it to the finish line. *Feeble arms and weak knees* in a runner are signs of exhaustion. Runners look for these signs in their competitors and, seeing them, take new courage.

We can be certain that Satan is watching for every sign that might indicate that Christians are completely exhausted and will become easy prey for him. Here the faltering Christians are encouraged to put every bit of energy into one last effort to make the finish line. (See Isaiah 35:3.)

B. HEALING, NOT LAMENESS (v. 13)

13. "Make level paths for your feet," so that the lame may not be disabled, but rather healed.

Our lesson text concludes with a reference to Proverbs 4:26. *The lame* refers to weaker Christians. The stronger Christians are to help them. They do this by making *level paths* for *feet* to follow; those Christians who have greater spiritual maturity have a responsibility that the less mature Christians be *healed*, and that none of them would *be disabled.* Undoubtedly this includes setting a good example. Christian leaders will give an account for how well they lead God's flock (Hebrews 13:17).

TEACHING BY EXAMPLE

Whit Criswell was ready to commit suicide when preacher Wayne B. Smith came to Whit's house. Whit owed $380,000, which he had embezzled from his own bank. He had spent all the money, and more, on gambling. After a long discussion Wayne prayed. Before he left he told Whit, "If you need anything, call me; I'll always be your friend."

Criswell went to the state prison for two years. "Wayne came to see me," Whit says. "When I was released to [a halfway house], Wayne came by to take me to a revival at the church. Afterward he invited me to go eat with him and the guest speaker and the musical group."

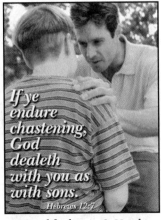

If ye endure chastening, God dealeth with you as with sons.
Hebrews 12:7

Visual for lesson 8. *Use this visual to remind your learners of the benefits and significance of discipline.*

DAILY BIBLE READINGS

Monday, July 19—Happy Are Those God Disciplines (Psalm 94:8-15)

Tuesday, July 20—The Lord Your God Disciplines (Deuteronomy 8:1-5)

Wednesday, July 21—Run With Perseverance (Hebrews 12:1-6)

Thursday, July 22—Discipline Yields the Fruit of Righteousness (Hebrews 12:7-11)

Friday, July 23—Make Straight Paths for Your Feet (Hebrews 12:12-17)

Saturday, July 24—Watch How You Treat God's Grace (Hebrews 12:18-24)

Sunday, July 25—Offer God an Acceptable Worship (Hebrews 12:25-29)

HOW TO SAY IT

Abraham. AY-bruh-ham.
Deuteronomy. Due-ter-AHN-uh-me.
Hebrews. HEE-brews.
Isaac. EYE-zuk.
Isaiah. Eye-ZAY-uh.
Jacob. JAY-kub.
Jeremiah. Jair-uh-MY-uh.
Moses. MO-zes or MO-zez.

PRAYER

Dear Father, we thank you for sending your Son to set the example of faithful service, regardless of what it cost him in suffering and shame. Teach us to lay aside the weights that hinder us and to run with perseverance the race of life. In our Lord's name we pray, amen.

THOUGHT TO REMEMBER

When you feel weary, remember that cloud of witnesses.

After Whit was allowed to go home, Wayne kept dropping by. He asked Whit to go places with him: hospital calling, a trustees' meeting at Wayne's alma mater, a sermon study group, and speaking engagements. Wayne also invited Whit to do volunteer work in the church, and he accepted. Before very long Wayne invited Whit to join the church staff. Today Whit Criswell is minister of his own church, which has grown from one hundred fifty to over seven hundred under his leadership.

Showing is always better than talking in the Christian life. Jesus wasn't "all talk"; he showed us how to live. It's up to us to pass that example along.   —R. H.

CONCLUSION

A. THE TRAILBLAZER

Many of us have thrilled to the stories of Daniel Boone, who made his way from Virginia across the Appalachian Mountains into what later became the states of Tennessee and Kentucky. As he traveled through the wilderness, he blazed a trail so that others could follow him into the rich lands in the West. He blazed that trail by chopping chunks of bark from large trees along the path he took. All one had to do to follow his trail was to watch for the blaze marks.

Several years ago I was involved in blazing some trails through a large wooded tract that our Christian camp was developing. We were modern Daniel Boones, but with a difference. We didn't chop patches of bark off the trees to blaze our trails, but rather we used the brightly colored plastic tape that is preferred by surveyors. We simply tied them around trees as we made a way through the woods. The tape could be seen readily by anyone wishing to follow the trail.

Jesus Christ, our divine trailblazer, has done a far better job than either Daniel Boone or we. When he blazed the trail to Heaven, he was the one who knew the way. He also knew our weakness and the problems we would face during our journey. On the night that he was betrayed, he said to his disciples, "I am the way and the truth and the life. No one comes to the Father except through me" (John 14:6). May we have the courage and the strength to follow him no matter what the cost. May we also renew our failing devotion to him when God disciplines us.

B. "HITTING THE WALL"

Earlier we mentioned the expression "hitting the wall" as used by marathon runners. It is that point in the race when a runner suddenly feels that he or she can't go any farther.

Situations like that may develop in one's Christian life. One reaches a point of feeling unable to go on; the temptation is to drop out. That was the danger that the writer saw developing in the lives of some of the Jewish Christians who would be first to read the book of Hebrews.

That "wall" could be caused by several things. One potential hazard was ridicule and persecution. The Jewish Christians had not yet "resisted to the point of shedding [their] blood," but that possibility was very real in their day. In some parts of the world today that is a very real threat.

Another potential cause for dropping out is weariness (Galatians 6:9). Some people spend their entire lives serving a certain congregation. Then they come to retirement and retire from everything. Still another "wall" that some Christians hit is self-centeredness. They become so wrapped up in the busyness of personal and congregational life that they never seem to have time for true ministry: visiting the sick, feeding the hungry, etc. When people are active in helping others, that wall evaporates.

Discovery Learning

This page contains an alternative lesson plan emphasizing learning activities. Classes desiring such student involvement will find these suggestions helpful. The next page is a reproducible activity page to further enhance discovery learning.

LEARNING GOALS

After this lesson each student will be able to:

1. Identify the basic elements necessary to run a good spiritual race.

2. Express the importance of being patient and persistent when facing hardship.

3. Identify an impediment to a good spiritual race that he or she would like to lay aside.

Several sections on the reproducible activity page that follows can be used with the plans below. Compare the ideas here and there, and select those most useful with your class.

INTO THE LESSON

Plan an interview with a present or former runner or coach of runners. If possible, have this person dress for a race. Questions for the interview include (1) Tell us about the clothing people often wear for running. Why is this important? (2) What kind of preparation and training goes into getting ready for running a long distance race? How is this different from training for sprints? (3) What enemies of runners make races difficult?

Thank the person interviewed. Make the transition to Bible study by telling the class we are going to talk about running a race, but not one that competes against other persons. It is a race that is a test of spiritual endurance.

INTO THE WORD

Prepare and display three posters, each with one of the following headings: "In the Grandstands," "Preparations for the Race," and "Race Strategy." Read the Scripture text together, asking all to watch for words and phrases important to each heading on the posters.

Ask the learners to review the Scripture and call out ideas for each topic. Write their answers on the posters. The following answers may be included:

IN THE GRANDSTANDS

A great cloud of witnesses (v. 1)

PREPARATIONS FOR THE RACE

Throw off everything that hinders and entangling sins (v. 1)

Expect suffering (vv. 4, 5)

Strengthen arms and knees (vv. 12, 13)

RACE STRATEGY

Persevere (v. 1)

Keep looking at Jesus (v. 2)

Endure hardship and discipline (vv. 7, 8)

After these have been listed, use the following "key word" activity to interpret the Scripture. Have one of each of the following "key words" written on a slip of paper that has been rolled up and tied with yarn or colored string. Ask teams of two people to select one of these "mini-scrolls." Each team is to open and explain the concept or significance this key word has in today's study. The "key words" to be written on the scrolls (one per scroll) are as follows:

Cloud of witnesses (v. 1.)

Everything that hinders (v. 1)

Perseverance (v. 1)

Author and Perfecter (v. 2)

Opposition (v. 3)

Blood (v. 4)

Hardship (v. 7)

Sons (vv. 7-10)

Pleasant or painful (v. 11)

Paths (vv. 12, 13)

INTO LIFE

Prepare the following full-page handout for each person. Answer most of these questions and assignments as a whole class. However, give a few moments for individuals to respond to the personal questions or tasks.

HEARING CHEERING!

We all love to have people cheering us on—even in our spiritual race of life. Who are some of the people typically cheering Christians on in their spiritual race? List them here.

Now, name one or two special people who are in your cheering section.

RATS IN THE RACE!

Our Scripture tells us there are hindrances or impediments a Christian must lose in order to run a successful race. What are some of the common weights believers find strapped to their ankles that may impede this race?

Circle one or two that keep you from running well.

FINISHING FINE!

How would you define or picture a person who has finished life's race well? What habits, patterns, or values do you see in this top-notch spiritual athlete?

Circle one of these qualities that you would like to practice more in this week's race. Look for ways to let this habit or quality blossom in your life as you run the race.

The Coach's Instructions

Let's allow Hebrews 12 to be our coach in running life's spiritual race. What tips do you find coming from our coach in the following verses? Space is given for at least two tips packed into verse #1.

v. 1 _____

v. 1 _____

v. 2 _____

v. 3 _____

v. 4 _____

v. 7 _____

v. 9 _____

v. 12 _____

v. 13 _____

Rate Your Race

Using the following scale as number one being poor and number five being excellent, indicate how well you feel you are doing in life's spiritual race by circling a number: 1=poorly, 5=well

My Cheering Section*	1	2	3	4	5
Eyes Fixed on Jesus	1	2	3	4	5
Persistence	1	2	3	4	5
Endure Hardship	1	2	3	4	5
Submit to Discipline	1	2	3	4	5

*People who provide spiritual support, encouragement, etc.

A Rat in the Race!

God teaches that we must remove things from our lives that will impede running the spiritual race well. What is one of these weights that you know you must shed in order to run well? Write or draw it in the box below.

Help From Another Coach

Sometimes we need to have someone to help us organize the race. If it would be helpful to have someone to whom you are accountable in shedding the "rat" you identified above, whom would you ask? Identify that person here, call that person, meet for lunch, tell him or her your need, and pray together.

SELECT GOOD LEADERS
LESSON 9

WHY TEACH THIS LESSON?

Two years ago the financial markets were rocked by a series of accounting scandals. As investigators unraveled the tangled webs of deceit, they found many disturbing things. Notable was the sheer arrogance of certain corporate leaders who (apparently) thought that the houses of cards they were constructing would endure.

The church is not immune to misconduct and incompetence from her own leaders, as we all well know. The church cannot win the world for Christ if her leaders bear the taint of wrong motives and spiritual immaturity. Today's lesson speaks not only to the church's current and future leaders, but also to those charged to support them—in other words, everyone!

INTRODUCTION

A. THE NEED

Leadership is one of the hot-button issues of our time. You cannot peruse the business section of a bookstore without seeing many books on the subject. It is of crucial importance in the church as well. There are nearly as many books on leadership in the average Christian bookstore as there are in a secular bookstore.

No one in the business world would dispute the significance a leader has on an organization. Certainly no one on a sports team would dispute it either. Enter the world of the military and you will find agreement there as well. This lesson is about Paul's advice to Timothy on how to choose good leaders for the church.

B. LESSON BACKGROUND

A first-century man named Timothy received two important letters that bear his name. Timothy was Paul's son in the faith (1 Timothy 1:2). Evidently Paul had no children of his own, but Timothy was like a son to him.

Paul met Timothy, who was already a disciple, while on a missionary journey (Acts 16:1-5). Timothy became one of Paul's most trusted associates. Paul typically gave Timothy challenging assignments (1 Corinthians 4:17; 16:10; Philippians 2:19, 22; 1 Thessalonians 3:2). This may explain the need for the letters of 1 Timothy and 2 Timothy.

These two letters plus Titus are grouped together in the Scriptures and are commonly referred to as the Pastoral Epistles. They live up to their designation! Paul not only gives advice on how a church is to be pastored (shepherded), he also does some pastoring himself with Timothy and Titus.

One important area where these two disciples required the apostle's counsel concerned the issue of church leaders. As the first-century church expanded, it began to require more structured leadership in local congregations.

One distinct New Testament office is that of "elder." This office is also known as an "overseer" or "bishop." (The Greek words *presbyteros* and *episkopos* that lie behind our English translations mean the same thing in Acts 20:17, 28 and Titus 1:5, 7). Over the centuries the word *bishop* has come to mean someone in authority over several churches, but that concept is not found in the New Testament.

DEVOTIONAL READING:
ACTS 20:17-32

BACKGROUND SCRIPTURE:
1 TIMOTHY 3:1-13; 5:17-19

PRINTED TEXT:
1 TIMOTHY 3:1-13; 5:17-19

LESSON AIMS

After participating in this lesson, each student will be able to:

1. Describe the two basic offices in the early church.

2. List some of the essential qualities that church officers are expected to possess.

3. Write a letter of appreciation to a church leader who is faithfully fulfilling the required duties of the office.

Aug
1

KEY VERSE

They must keep hold of the deep truths of the faith with a clear conscience.—1 Timothy 3:9

LESSON 9 NOTES

Elders were also known as pastors or shepherds (Ephesians 4:11). Today, the term *pastor* is often used to designate a preaching minister, but in the New Testament it was a term used for the office of elder.

Another office was that of deacon. This is a Greek word that means "servant" in a general sense, but in certain contexts it refers to a specific office of the church. At some point in the expansion of first-century Christianity, local churches came to have both elders (or bishops or overseers) and deacons (see Philippians 1:1).

I. QUALITIES OF ELDERS (1 TIMOTHY 3:1-7)

Paul gives a long list of qualities that provide a profile of a great Christian leader. Some are very similar to one another and therefore related. There is also a great deal of overlap with Titus 1:6-9.

A. DESIRE (v. 1)

1. Here is a trustworthy saying: If anyone sets his heart on being an overseer, he desires a noble task.

When Paul relates this true saying, is he quoting an old adage, quoting a previous teaching of his own that Timothy is familiar with, or creating a new saying as he writes? We can't be sure. What's most important is the truthfulness of the saying itself: it is indeed an honorable thing to desire to be a Christian leader. There is such a thing as selfish ambition (Luke 22:24-27), but that is not the same as the humble desire and willingness to lead.

B. BLAMELESS AND FAITHFUL (vv. 2a, 2b)

2a. Now the overseer must be above reproach,

The general idea of being *above reproach* cannot, of course, be taken as an absolute—otherwise we would expect leaders to be perfect! It is more the idea that no one should look at a prospective elder and think, "Oh, no! Not him!" Perhaps what Paul specifically means by "above reproach" can be found in the list that follows.

2b. . . . the husband of but one wife,

This phrase has sparked much debate. Most students agree that it means that an elder must be, or must have been, married. Is Paul making that an absolute requirement? If so, neither he nor Jesus could have been an elder. (And, of course, neither of them was an elder!) There is no doubt that some qualities of pastoral care are learned best in family life.

What of those who were once married but are no longer? Very few believe Paul means to exclude widowers. Literally, *husband of but one wife* is a "one-wife man" or even a "one-woman [kind of] man." (The word for *wife* in the Greek is simply the word for woman.) We can be certain that a bigamist, or man with a mistress, could not be considered. The issue the church struggles with today is whether or not a divorced man may be an elder. If we take this to mean "a one-woman [kind of] man," then the issue is the man's own personal faithfulness. Even if a man's wife has been unfaithful, he may still very well be a one-woman man.

Many churches look at this issue on a case-by-case basis. What is indisputable is that the quality of a person's marriage affects his ability to lead.

C. DISCIPLINED AND HOSPITABLE (vv. 2c, 2d)

2c. . . . temperate, self-controlled, respectable,

This verse continues with virtues that almost speak for themselves. Being *temperate* and *self-controlled* both point to the ability to control one's desires. (See also Titus 1:8.) *Respectable* includes the idea of living an honorable life.

WHAT DO YOU THINK?

The lesson writer refers to leadership "qualities." How would that be different from seeing Paul's list as "qualifications"? How would this distinction help in addressing some of the troublesome issues that arise in connection with some of the traits listed?

WHAT DO YOU THINK?

What do you think about having divorced men serve as elders or in paid ministry positions? What dangers are present when divorced men are allowed to hold such positions? What dangers are present when they are not?

2d. . . . hospitable,

Hospitable is literally to be a "lover of strangers." It refers to the willingness to give food or shelter to travelers or visitors. Traveling prophets and evangelists were in particular need of such hospitality. Paul himself was a recipient of this type of kindness. (See Romans 12:13; Titus 1:8; Hebrews 13:2; 1 Peter 4:9; contrast 2 John 10.)

D. COMMUNICATOR (v. 2e)
2e. . . . able to teach,

Being *able to teach* does not require an elder to be a distinguished orator or dynamic speaker. But he should be able to explain the gospel, at least in a private setting. Teaching is a spiritual gift listed in Romans 12:7 and Ephesians 4:11.

E. NOT ADDICTED (v. 3a)
3a. . . . not given to drunkenness,

Wine was common in the ancient world, and its dangers were well known then as now. Passages such as Proverbs 21:17; 23:20, 21, 29-32 are very plain on the dangers of alcohol. There are practical and spiritual reasons for modern Christians to practice total abstinence, but that subject is not addressed here. Paul's restriction logically may be extended to all unhealthy addictions to the various legal and illegal drugs that confront us in news reports every day.

F. TEMPERAMENT (v. 3b)
3b. . . . not violent but gentle, not quarrelsome, not a lover of money.

There is a certain overlap between the ideas of being *violent* and *quarrelsome*, and the latter can lead to the former. We perhaps should not see these ideas as unconnected from the discussion of drunkenness earlier in this verse when we consider that those who abuse alcohol are frequently the ones who get into fights. Those who are not convinced of this need only watch one or two episodes of the TV show *Cops* to be persuaded otherwise!

Someone who is *a lover of money* undoubtedly is in violation of the Tenth Commandment (Exodus 20:17). We should be careful to remember that the acquisition of wealth is not a sin in and of itself. But both those who need money and those who already have plenty are in danger of developing a sinful attitude. See 1 Timothy 6:10.

G. ORDERLY FAMILY (vv. 4, 5)
4, 5. He must manage his own family well and see that his children obey him with proper respect. (If anyone does not know how to manage his own family, how can he take care of God's church?)

Once again there is a point of controversy here. Does this verse mean that the elder must have *children*, or is Paul simply discussing the typical or normal situation? There are men today who will not allow themselves to be considered for the office of elder because they take what Paul says quite literally.

It is certainly true that lessons learned from managing one's *own family* can affect how well a man serves as an elder. If a church leader has not displayed leadership in his home, he will find it difficult to exercise leadership in the *church*. Many leadership and interpersonal skills learned in the home will work in the church.

H. SPIRITUAL MATURITY (v. 6)
6. He must not be a recent convert, or he may become conceited and fall under the same judgment as the devil.

Visual for lesson 9. *This poster will remind your learners of God's expectations for church leaders.*

WHAT DO YOU THINK?

Paul says an elder is not to be a "novice." How long does someone have to be a Christian to be no longer a novice? What factors other than time need to be considered?

DAILY BIBLE READINGS

Monday, July 26—Select Those Full of the Spirit (Acts 6: 1-7)

Tuesday, July 27—Paul Didn't Shrink From His Ministry (Acts 20:17-24)

Wednesday, July 28—Keep Watch Over the Flock (Acts 20: 25-31)

Thursday, July 29—Remember Your Leaders (Hebrews 13: 7-17)

Friday, July 30—An Overseer Must Be Above Reproach (1 Timothy 3:1-7)

Saturday, July 31—Deacons Must Be Serious (1 Timothy 3: 8-13)

Sunday, Aug. 1—Good Leaders—Worthy of Double Honor (1 Timothy 5:17-22)

If we take the Greek word translated *recent convert* and pronounce it in English it comes out as our word *neophyte*. The danger of selecting a recent convert or neophyte to be elder is quite clear, and the Bible talks about the issue of pride (being *conceited*) in numerous places (e.g., Proverbs 11:2; 13:10; 16:18; Romans 12:16). Spiritually mature believers truly know what it means to bear the responsibility of being an elder. This knowledge will create the humility that a leader needs.

I. GOOD REPUTATION (v. 7)

7. He must also have a good reputation with outsiders, so that he will not fall into disgrace and into the devil's trap.

Leaders should be respected. This should be true not just among Christians, but also by the community as a whole. Can the church really have a good witness if its leaders are known scoundrels?

The devil's trap is probably the sin of pride (see v. 6, above). It is assumed that the besetting sin of the devil, the sin that caused him to be cast from Heaven, was pride.

THE HIGH ROAD TO LEADERSHIP

Allen Iverson of the Philadelphia 76ers is recognized as much for his behavior off the court as his play on the court. Known as one of the "bad boys" of the NBA, he maintained this image in July, 2002, when he was charged with four felony and ten misdemeanor counts in conjunction with an alleged attack on his estranged wife.

The Reebok company, which extended an existing contract with Iverson in 2001 for fifty million dollars, did not even flinch when the charges were announced. Instead, a Reebok spokesman said, "It is Allen's celebrity status, not the facts, that continue to fuel these proceedings." Alan Brown, a sports marketing agent, said, "It might even help sales. Yes, it's the bad boy image, but the bad boy image unfortunately right now is what sells, and he's the best bad boy out there."

In a world that looks more to image than character, the church must hold true to God's Word in regard to leadership. Nowhere is this more important than in the selection of leadership for the local congregation.

What a leader does "off the court" affects the work in leading the church of the Lord Jesus. Character qualities such as being disciplined, peaceable, and above reproach are necessary in a world that too often values the opposite.   —A. E. A.

II. QUALITIES OF DEACONS (1 TIMOTHY 3:8-13)

The Greek word *deacon* occurs nearly one hundred times in the New Testament, in various forms. Often it means simply "servant" in a general sense.

But here Paul uses this word to refer to a specific office of the church. Many students think that the very first deacons are listed in Acts 6:1-6, although the specific word *deacon* does not occur there. Many of the qualities of deacon overlap with the qualities of elder, so it will not be necessary to discuss those that are repeated.

A. RESPECTABLE AND SINCERE (vv. 8a, 8b)

8a. Deacons, likewise, are to be men worthy of respect,

An important way for a deacon to become *worthy of respect* is by conducting himself with dignity and seriousness . Can you imagine what it would be like for a church to have deacons who took nothing seriously, who had a flippant attitude toward everything?

8b. . . . sincere,

A godly deacon is *sincere*; he is not someone who says one thing to one person and something completely different to another.

B. NOT ADDICTED (v. 8c)

8c. . . . not indulging in much wine, and not pursuing dishonest gain.

See the previous discussion in verse 3, above. Although elders have the greater authority, deacons must meet the same high standards.

C. HAVING A PURE CONSCIENCE (v. 9)

9. They must keep hold of the deep truths of the faith with a clear conscience.

The *deep truths* that were a great mystery to those who lived in Old Testament times have now been more fully revealed as the gospel of Christ (Romans 16:25, 26). What was once hidden is now made known (Colossians 1:26). Paul desperately wants all believers to know these truths (Ephesians 3:1-6). Deacons need to understand these great *truths of the faith* and believe them *with a clear conscience.*

D. TESTED (v. 10)

10. They must first be tested; and then if there is nothing against them, let them serve as deacons.

Some students think that the idea of *being tested* suggests that an apprenticeship for deacons is appropriate. Whatever means of testing is used, the end result must be that *nothing* can be said *against* potential deacons, as was required for potential elders (see v. 2, above).

E. FAMILY CONDUCT (vv. 11-13)

11. In the same way, their wives are to be women worthy of respect, not malicious talkers but temperate and trustworthy in everything.

The conduct of *their wives* will reveal the quality of a potential deacon's home life. As with elders, a deacon is very unlikely to be able to take care of the church if his home life is chaotic (see v. 4, above, and vv. 12, 13, next).

12, 13. A deacon must be the husband of but one wife and must manage his children and his household well. Those who have served well gain an excellent standing and great assurance in their faith in Christ Jesus.

Again, the ideas here mirror what Paul has already said in verse 4, above. After reminding Timothy that deacons are also to be good husbands and fathers, Paul commends deacons for their significant work. Does the mention of an *excellent standing* and *great assurance* speak to the deacon's being respected in the eyes of God, the eyes of the church, or the eyes of the community? It could be all three.

We should pause to note that there is nothing in these verses to indicate that the office of *deacon* is to be considered some kind of stepping-stone to the office of elder. Some might remain deacons for the rest of their lives. Each office has a purpose in the church. The two have different functions, but both are important.

III. CHURCH'S RESPONSIBILITIES (1 TIMOTHY 5:17-19)

Godly leaders are so important! Churches must not neglect their obligations to them.

A. SHOW APPRECIATION TO LEADERS (vv. 17, 18)

17, 18. The elders who direct the affairs of the church well are worthy of double honor, especially those whose work is preaching and teaching. For the Scripture says, "Do not muzzle the ox while it is treading out the grain," and "The worker deserves his wages."

Notice that *elders* are the ones *who direct the affairs of the church*, and it appears that certain ones of those early elders were to receive some kind of *double honor.* The Scripture that Paul uses to back this up is Deuteronomy 25:4.

WHAT DO YOU THINK?

If it was the "elders" who labored in the preaching of the word in the New Testament church, why do we have paid preachers today? What advantages do you see in having a paid preacher instead of a preaching eldership? What advantages can you see in having preaching elders instead of a paid preacher? How do Acts 21:8 and 2 Timothy 4:5 speak to these questions?

PRAYER

Gracious Father, thank you for the privilege of service in your church. Help us each to accept the responsibility that comes with the privilege. In Jesus' name, amen.

THOUGHT TO REMEMBER

No church will grow beyond its leaders.

The way Paul uses this passage, both here and in 1 Corinthians 9:7-12, gives us the idea that the double honor includes some kind of pay. It seems that in many first-century churches, at least some elders may have served in full-time positions. This supports the concept of paid ministry.

Although all Christians are ministers in a general sense, some are paid and have responsibility to serve full-time. But financial compensation is probably only half of this double honor. The other half that these elders are to receive is the honor of respect.

HONOR TO WHOM HONOR IS DUE

Selecting leaders with high integrity and good character is vital for the success of a church. But an often-overlooked ingredient in the successful church is the need for good followers.

Good followers show respect for their leaders. Sadly, however, respect for authority has eroded in modern culture. Not only is this evident with regard to leaders in government or schools, but also is apparent in the church. Resigning from church roles, withholding of offerings, missing church services, and maligning the character of the church leader is evidence of poor "followership" and lack of respect.

In all areas of life respect for those over you is vital. In the battle for Europe during World War II, Major General George S. Patton was loyal to his commanding officer, General Dwight Eisenhower, even though at times he was so disgusted with his superior that he wouldn't speak to him. During the Korean War, however, General Douglas MacArthur failed to show proper respect to President Harry S. Truman.

MacArthur ignored the chain of command in military decision-making and began writing letters to the Veterans of Foreign Wars as well as to the Speaker of the House about what the United States should do in Korea. So President Truman fired him. As Truman explained, avoidance of World War III while containing aggression was a difficult line to walk, but that was the policy the United States had decided upon. No soldier, not even a five-star general, could challenge that policy without disturbing an essential element of democratic government.

Just as a nation is dependent upon the proper lines of respect for smooth operation, so a church needs people who respect and honor those in leadership positions. Without proper lines of respect and authority a nation is vulnerable to attacks from its enemies. And without the adherence to proper respect to appropriate authority within the church, Satan himself, the ultimate enemy, will attack and destroy.

—A. E. A.

B. SHOW FAIRNESS TO LEADERS (v. 19)

19. Do not entertain an accusation against an elder unless it is brought by two or three witnesses.

Leaders will always receive criticism. Sometimes they will even be the subject of slander. However, no *accusation* should be entertained unless *two or three witnesses* support it. This is consistent with Old Testament law (Deuteronomy 17:6; 19:15) and is consistent with what Paul told the church at Corinth (2 Corinthians 13:1).

CONCLUSION

Everyone agrees that leadership is complex. Some seem to exercise it intuitively. Others have to study, practice, make mistakes, and grow. While there is much the church can learn from the world on leadership techniques, the church must remember that its leaders operate by a different set of rules. There is no institution quite like the church. There is no authority quite like Christ. That is the reason we need Paul's advice. That's the reason we need the Holy Spirit's strength.

Discovery Learning

This page contains an alternative lesson plan emphasizing learning activities. Classes desiring such student involvement will find these suggestions helpful. The next page is a reproducible activity page to further enhance discovery learning.

LEARNING GOALS

After this lesson each of your students will be able to:

1. Describe the two basic offices in the early church.

2. List some of the basic qualities that church officers are expected to possess.

3. Write a letter of appreciation to a church leader who is faithfully fulfilling the required duties of the office.

INTO THE LESSON

To begin the class, distribute copies of the reproducible activity "Church Leader of the Year" from the next page. Or make copies of the following open-ended statements and give each student a copy.

1. My idea of a good elder is . . . .

2. To be a good deacon, a man must . . . .

Whichever activity you choose, allow two or three minutes for the students to write some ideas. Then ask volunteers to share their work. Tell your class that today's lesson will deal with Paul's word to Timothy on characteristics of good leaders for the church.

INTO THE WORD

Divide your class into an equal number of groups composed of four to six students per group. Half of your groups will do Study A, about elders, below. The other half will do Study B, about deacons. (In the student books, space is provided for this activity.) Otherwise, copy the lists onto a two-column chart and provide a chart to each group. After they finish their work, discuss each group's findings with the whole class, comparing them with earlier comments in the Into the Lesson exercise. Column one will list Qualifications; column two will provide space to list Values.

STUDY A

Read 1 Timothy 3:1-7, then complete this chart, indicating the value to the church and to the elder of each qualification below:

Qualifications: Sets his heart on the office; above reproach; husband of but one wife; temperate; self-controlled; respectable; hospitable; able to teach; not given to drunkenness; not violent; not a lover of money; not quarrelsome; manages his family well; has obedient and respectful children; not a recent convert; has a good reputation. Values: (for example, if an elder "sets his heart on the office," he will not have to be recruited nor convinced; he will be more likely to persist in service; for example, if a leader is "above reproach," there will be no disagreement as to his suitability for spiritual leadership, and he will be a good model of righteousness to those within the church and those without.)

STUDY B

Read 1 Timothy 3:8-13, then complete this chart, indicating the value to the church and to the deacon of each qualification below:

Qualifications: worthy of respect; sincere; not indulgent in wine; not pursuing dishonest gain; has a clear conscience; tested; has a wife who is worthy of respect, not a malicious talker, temperate, and trustworthy; has but one wife; manages his children and household well. Values: (for example, if a deacon is "worthy of respect," people will be more likely to follow him in service projects; if he is "not indulgent in wine," he is demonstrating the self-control that is a primary fruit of the Spirit.)

After reviewing the qualifications of church leaders, turn your class's attention to a discussion of the church's responsibilities to those leaders in 1 Timothy 5:17-19.

INTO LIFE

For the hypothetical situations described below, ask your class to suggest Scriptural answers.

1. An elder has been accused of serious wrongdoing by another member. How should the church handle the situation to be fair to all involved—the elder, the accuser, and the congregation?

2. An elder in your congregation has faithfully served in the position for over twenty-five years—much longer than anyone in the congregation's history. What would be an appropriate way to honor him and encourage him for his distinguished service? (See "Happy Anniversary!" on the reproducible page.)

3. A young man has let it be known that he would like to be elected to the office of deacon. How should your congregation evaluate his qualifications? (Secure a copy of your congregation's bylaws or policy on selecting leaders to compare it to the class's response.)

4. A well-qualified, mature member of your congregation has been nominated to be an elder, but another member has objected because the candidate is a widower and no longer "the husband of one wife." How should the leadership deal with such an objection?

Church Leader of the Year

You have been invited to a banquet to honor the "church leader of the year," an outstanding non-professional church leader from your fellowship of churches. What qualities or activities do you expect to hear extolled in the presentation of this award? List some of them below.

Happy Anniversary!

An elder in your congregation has faithfully served in the position for over twenty-five years—much longer than anyone else in the congregation's history. Use the space below to list some ideas for ways to honor him and encourage him for his distinguished service.

_____   _____

_____   _____

_____   _____

_____   _____

_____   _____

BE MINISTERS OF GODLINESS

LESSON 10

WHY TEACH THIS LESSON?

Bookstores are heavily stocked with all the latest works on management and leadership. Authors and publishing houses try to persuade us that if we don't stay current on leadership trends, then we're behind the times. The Internet bookstore Amazon.com will offer you over twelve thousand "hits" if you search for books on the topic of leadership on its Web site. Woe to the leader who isn't aware of the latest and greatest in management theory!

Church leadership, however, is not an "idea of the month club." Church leadership finds its basis in a set of unchanging fundamentals that must be mastered. Undergirding these fundamentals is the foundation of godliness. Without godly leaders, nothing good can happen in the church. This truth is just as important to the twenty-first century church as it was to the first-century church. It is a truth to learn (or relearn) in today's lesson.

INTRODUCTION

A. TO THE GYM, TO THE CHURCH, OR BOTH?

Have you noticed how many gyms and health clubs there are around you? Have you seen the advertisements for exercise gadgets and diet programs on television, in magazines, and even on little signs posted on utility poles? No one would suggest that it is wrong to pursue good health. Good nutrition and exercise are important—even good stewardship of our lives. But Paul reminds us that whatever commitment we give to physical well-being is secondary to spiritual training.

This is just one of the issues Paul tackles in the lesson before us. He will also deal with matters of church dynamics, relationships, and doctrinal purity. A healthy church pays close attention to such issues. Our "spiritual workout" today will prepare us to witness and grow for Christ as Timothy did nearly two thousand years ago.

B. LESSON BACKGROUND

Last week we studied a list of characteristics or qualities that should be present in potential leaders in the church. This week we study a passage that forced Timothy to take a long look at himself and his ministry. It is important for us to remember that these letters to Timothy are like personal notes to him—we are reading his mail.

Paul was not afraid to give Timothy the difficult assignments and the tough advice. This is what equips Timothy to deal with issues that pose challenges in the local church. As a younger minister, Timothy faced many hurdles in leading and relating to the various groups within his congregation.

Today's lesson is more than good advice from one long-dead man to another about a situation from ancient history. Those who minister to the church today have faced (or will face) many of the same challenges of the first-century church. Church leaders still need to develop the spiritual maturity and interpersonal skills that Paul urged on Timothy.

DEVOTIONAL READING:
2 PETER 1:3-11
BACKGROUND SCRIPTURE:
1 TIMOTHY 4:6–5:16
PRINTED TEXT:
1 TIMOTHY 4:7-16

LESSON AIMS

After participating in this lesson, each student will be able to:

1. Identify the qualities demonstrated by a faithful servant of God.

2. Express the importance of spiritual training in the life of a Christian servant.

3. Devise a spiritual training program that he or she will follow.

Aug
8

KEY VERSE

For physical training is of some value, but godliness has value for all things, holding promise for both the present life and the life to come.
—1 Timothy 4:8

I. LIFESTYLE OF THE GODLY MINISTER (1 TIMOTHY 4:7-10)

A. GO INTO TRAINING (vv. 7-9)

7. Have nothing to do with godless myths and old wives' tales; rather, train yourself to be godly.

Today we still use the expression *old wives' tales*. It refers to the stories older women might tell their children or grandchildren at night. These are made-up stories, intended to entertain and delight the children. In this passage the phrase probably refers to old legends—made-up stories, false teachings that came from sources other than the inspired apostles—that should not be confused with the gospel. (See also 1 Timothy 1:4; 6:20; 2 Timothy 2:16; and Titus 1:14.)

Clearly Paul is ridiculing such stories. Instead of bothering with such nonsense, Timothy is to focus on something much better: training *to be godly.* Paul would like to see Timothy—and all Christians—replace worthless chatter with spiritual disciplines that result in drawing closer to God and his truth.

8. For physical training is of some value, but godliness has value for all things, holding promise for both the present life and the life to come.

The phrase *is of some value* indicates that *physical training* does have a degree of worth, but it is more important to train oneself spiritually. The Greek word Paul uses here for *training* is the word that eventually gave us our English word *gymnasium.* The use of this word, along with certain other illustrations, suggests that Paul was a sports fan. Or at least he recognized the significance of illustrations dealing with athletics. The Greeks had originated the Olympic games, and Timothy's proximity to Greek culture while in Ephesus (1 Timothy 1:3) would make such illustrations particularly meaningful.

Paul compared the Christian life with a race in 1 Corinthians 9:24-27; Galatians 2:2; 5:7; and 2 Timothy 4:7. Although physical training has positive, earthly consequences, spiritual training has consequences for the life that now is, and of that which is to come.

WHAT DO YOU THINK?

Paul says that godliness is valuable not only in terms of "the life to come"—that is, Heaven—but also for "the present life." How have you found godliness to make your life better?

TRAINING FOR THE LONG RUN

Olympic athletes are known for the strict training regimen that they endure in preparing for the games. One such Olympian was Emil Zatopek (1922–2000), a Czech army officer who competed in the 1948, 1952, and 1956 summer games.

Zatopek did not look like the traditional distance runner. At five feet, eight inches and 145 pounds, he is spoken of as being a scrawny man with a frail frame. As he ran, he looked as if he labored for every step and would collapse from exhaustion at any moment. His style was not the classic distance runner's style either. His head bobbed from side to side, his arms flailed wildly, and his face was contorted as if he were in pain.

The training regimen Zatopek followed was not a normal pattern either. Developing his own routine, he ran at night wearing heavy boots. Preparing for the 10,000-meter race, he would run five times 200 meters, twenty times 400 meters, and five times 200 meters without sitting between runs. Instead he jogged between sets. Trainers scoffed at his efforts.

But Zatopek was rewarded when he won the 10,000-meter race in 1948. He was rewarded again in 1952 when he won an Olympic triple crown—races of 5,000 meters, 10,000 meters, and the marathon. Interestingly, Zatopek had never run the marathon before, but he won it in Olympic record time. His training made the difference between victory and defeat.

The Christian life is not a sprint. It is a distance run. All runners in this race are not the same. But the important lesson learned from Zatopek is to set a regimen of spiritual growth and then "run with perseverance the race marked out for us" (Hebrews 12:1).   —A. E. A.

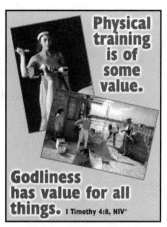

Visual for lesson 10. *Use this visual to remind your learners that we must not neglect our practice of godliness.*

9. This is a trustworthy saying that deserves full acceptance

Paul uses the formula *this is a trustworthy saying* (or something very similar) in 1 Timothy 1:15; 3:1; 2 Timothy 2:11; and Titus 3:8 as well. This phrase introduces some kind of saying or proverb that is well known to Timothy, something from Paul's preaching that is familiar, or a new saying that Paul is creating as he writes.

In any case, we are curious about whether this faithful saying refers to what was taught previously in verse 8 or to what follows in verse 10. We are not sure. It would appear, however, that verse 8 best reflects the kind of proverb that would qualify as a "faithful saying."

B. TRUST GOD (v. 10)
10. . . . (and for this we labor and strive), that we have put our hope in the living God, who is the Savior of all men, and especially of those who believe.

The words used here to describe Christian travail are very strong. To *labor and strive* suggests that we give our all to the task. Paul may be referring specifically to a leader's ministry in the church, but some think that he is speaking of the more general need of all Christians to strive for a life of godliness.

Either possibility honors the living God. The phrase *who is the Savior of all men* does not mean that God saves all people, but that he makes salvation available to all because of the cross. Salvation ultimately comes to *those who believe,* and not to unbelievers.

II. DUTIES OF THE GODLY MINISTER (1 TIMOTHY 4:11-16)
A. TEACHING AND MODELING (vv. 11, 12)
11. Command and teach these things.

Some things, says Paul, need to be addressed with authority. That is the reason he can say *command . . . these things.* Paul will later tell Timothy how to command, but here he is stressing the importance of impressing truth on the congregation. These are not just suggestions! But for Timothy to *command and teach* may pose a certain problem, as the next verse shows.

12. Don't let anyone look down on you because you are young, but set an example for the believers in speech, in life, in love, in faith and in purity.

The Greek word for *young* or youth can be used for a man who is of age to serve in the military. Some calculate that Timothy may be about thirty years old. Will his relative youth be a problem in teaching the older folks in his congregation? Perhaps!

So Paul recommends some ways to overcome this potential problem. The first concerns the way Timothy is to communicate: he is to *set an example . . . in speech.* How often our tongue can get us into trouble! (See James 3:1-12.) On the other hand, well-chosen words can heal and encourage.

Second, Paul says Timothy should be an example *in life.* Timothy's lifestyle certainly is to include everything he would do *in love, in faith, and in purity.* These are not new concepts in Paul's writings. He stresses them numerous times, in various ways (e.g., 1 Corinthians 13; 2 Corinthians 6:3-10; 1 Thessalonians 1:3). Timothy's age will not be a problem if he demonstrates spiritual maturity. A church leader who does not give attention to the areas Paul lists is certain to fail no matter what his age; a bad example ruins credibility.

B. MINISTERING AND SUSTAINING (vv. 13, 14)
13. Until I come, devote yourself to the public reading of Scripture, to preaching and to teaching.

WHAT DO YOU THINK?
Why is it necessary to follow a command with teaching?

WHAT DO YOU THINK?
Are most young people in your congregation looked on as good examples? Why, or why not? How can we encourage them to be the kind of example Paul encourages Timothy to be?
[Be careful not to allow this discussion to become a blame-the-bad-parents session!]

HOW TO SAY IT

Czech. Check.

Corinthians. Kor-IN-thee-unz.

Emil Zatopek. EE-mil Zuh-TOE-peck.

Ephesus. EF-uh-sus.

Lystra. LISS-truh.

Nehemiah. NEE-huh-MY-uh.

presbytery. PREZ-buh-ter-ee.

synagogue. SIN-uh-gog.

Thessalonians. THESS-uh-LO-nee-unz (Th as in thin).

Titus. TIE-tus.

Paul tells Timothy to give attention *to the public reading of Scripture.* Sadly, this is not often emphasized in many churches today. But public Scripture reading can have a powerful effect (see Nehemiah 8:1-12). Emphasis is also to be given to *preaching* and *teaching*.

This is a picture of some aspects of worship in the early church. There is a time for Scripture reading as well as a time to preach and teach what has been read. The early church often reflects the customs of the Jewish synagogue. In the synagogue it was standard practice to give words of explanation after the reading of Scripture.

With preaching or exhortation there is always a note of persuasion and decision (e.g., Acts 2:14-41). With teaching the emphasis is on the material itself—namely the facts of Scripture (e.g., Luke 24:27). We need both!

14. Do not neglect your gift, which was given you through a prophetic message when the body of elders laid their hands on you.

Timothy had been blessed in a certain way by the *elders.* We don't know when or where this happened, but it could have been at Ephesus (1 Timothy 1:3) or even Lystra (Acts 16:1). We're not even sure about the nature of the special *gift* with which Timothy was endowed. The important thing to Paul is that Timothy actually use his spiritual gifts. Why should God give a gift to a person who has no intention of using it? Such a person may as well not have the gift at all.

The phrase *laid their hands on you* has often been seen as an ordination, although this verse does not call it as such. Still, it appears very much as if this event was a precursor to what later would be called ordination. Acts 8:18; 1 Timothy 5:22; 2 Timothy 1:6; and Hebrews 6:2 also discuss the practice of laying on of hands.

C. DILIGENCE AND PERSEVERANCE (vv. 15, 16)

15. Be diligent in these matters; give yourself wholly to them, so that everyone may see your progress.

The ministry that Timothy is involved in requires him to be totally absorbed. This complete commitment means that he will continue to grow spiritually in order that his *progress* may be obvious to all.

16. Watch your life and doctrine closely. Persevere in them, because if you do, you will save both yourself and your hearers.

Paul exhorts Timothy to give attention to both his *life and doctrine* or teaching. Many Christian leaders and servants get these out of balance. We have all met people in the church who know the Bible book, chapter, and verse but have not learned how to apply it appropriately. As a result, they bear no fruit (Luke 13:6-9).

There also are others who live out the Christian lifestyle, but show little or no interest in matters of doctrine. They are the ones who say, "Give us something practical! Don't bother us with tedious doctrine." Such people are spiritually shallow and may fall prey easily to false doctrine (cf. Matthew 13:5-7). A balanced Christian and a balanced leader will be concerned with both doctrine and practical application. That kind of leader will bless those who are led.

III. SKILLS OF THE GODLY MINISTER (1 TIMOTHY 5:1-8)

A. RELATING TO MEN OF ALL AGES (v. 1)

1. Do not rebuke an older man harshly, but exhort him as if he were your father. Treat younger men as brothers,

Respect for those who are *older* was very much a part of the fabric of the ancient world. Even so, there may be times when a younger leader needs to

WHAT DO YOU THINK?

What is the difference between behaving in such a way that "everyone may see your progress" and "showing off"? What caution would you advise for someone who wants to take Paul's words to heart?

[Matthew 5:16 and 6:1-4 will be important for this discussion.]

disagree with those who are older. When this happens, the principle of treating the older man like a *father* is helpful.

To recognize someone as a father and others as *brothers* is the imagery of a family. When times of disagreement come, the family still has to stay together. This requires skill on the part of Timothy and all church leaders today.

REVIVING RESPECT

John Donne's classic "Meditation 17," written in 1624, reminds us that "No man is an island, entire of itself; every man is a piece of the continent, a part of the main." To emphasize this thought, Donne states that "if a clod be washed away by the sea, Europe is the less." That sounds drastic in a modern culture that puts a premium on certain people, such as celebrities and sports stars, while treating unborn infants with contempt.

Unfortunately, even in the church there is sometimes a lack of respect and regard for one another. A young person may look down upon an older person because of the heritage and traditions the older person holds. A senior saint may look down on the young because of music tastes or dress styles that are different. Fear, lack of knowledge, or outright arrogance may be the cause of these divisions within the church.

But in the end everyone really wants to be liked and respected. In his 1936 classic *How To Win Friends and Influence People*, Dale Carnegie agrees with the apostle Paul on the necessity of doing those things that make for harmony among people. Carnegie gives six principles to live by so that others will like you. These include the following:

• Be genuinely interested in other people.
• Smile.
• Remember that a person's name is to that person the sweetest and most important sound in any language.
• Be a good listener. Encourage others to talk about themselves.
• Talk in terms of the other person's interests.
• Make the other person feel important—and do it sincerely.

These simple principles will help Christians fulfill the admonition of Paul to young Timothy on how to live in community with others. This type of community living makes for a harmonious church with a glorious future.   —A. E. A.

B. RELATING TO WOMEN OF ALL AGES (v. 2)

2. . . . *older women as mothers, and younger women as sisters, with absolute purity.*

The same basic principle from verse 1 is also applied to the *women* of the church. Paul adds the reminder that these relationships should be pursued with all *purity*. This extra caution is due to the fact that members of the opposite sex are involved. This surely needs to be heeded in our own day as well.

C. RELATING TO WIDOWS OF ALL AGES (vv. 3-8)

3. *Give proper recognition to those widows who are really in need.*

The churches of Timothy's day evidently take seriously the responsibility of supporting financially the *widows* in the Christian community. Widows have a very difficult time supporting themselves in the ancient world. The Scripture groups "widows and orphans" together in numerous places to describe those who are most vulnerable. (e.g., James 1:27). The church takes care of the physical needs of widows. In exchange for the financial support, these widows probably perform certain duties to help support the work of the local congregation.

When Paul says to help *widows who are really in need*, he probably means that the church should take special interest in those widows who have absolutely no

DAILY BIBLE READINGS

Monday, Aug. 2—Become Slaves to Righteousness (Romans 6:19-23)

Tuesday, Aug. 3—Pursue Holiness (2 Corinthians 6: 14–7:1)

Wednesday, Aug. 4—Train Yourself in Godliness (1 Timothy 4:6-10)

Thursday, Aug. 5—Be an Example to Believers (1 Timothy 4:11-16)

Friday, Aug. 6—Honor Widows, Older Persons (1 Timothy 5:1-8)

Saturday, Aug. 7—Pursue Righteousness, Godliness (1 Timothy 6:11-16)

Sunday, Aug. 8—Do Good, Store Up Treasure (1 Timothy 6: 17-21)

WHAT DO YOU THINK?

Paul gives special instructions about how Timothy should treat women "with absolute purity." What specific safeguards should men use when working or serving with women in today's church?

PRAYER

Father, help me to evaluate myself. Help me to behave properly in my personal life as well as in the way I relate to people. May I do it all in Jesus' name and for his glory, amen.

WHAT DO YOU THINK?

Suppose a church member tells you his wife is in a nursing home with Alzheimer's. Her health care costs are soaring. He says, "I have been advised to get a divorce so the nursing home cannot take all of my assets. I still love her, but what good will it do if I lose everything? She will never get any better. Besides, she doesn't even know me anymore. The marriage is already dead!" How would you advise your friend?

THOUGHT TO REMEMBER

Church leadership begins with holiness.

one else to support them or look after them. After all, some widows may have adult children nearby. Others may be childless or have lost their children in infancy or childhood. The latter are truly desolate. A widow's own family members have the first responsibility to support the one in need.

4. But if a widow has children or grandchildren, these should learn first of all to put their religion into practice by caring for their own family and so repaying their parents and grandparents, for this is pleasing to God.

These women had supported their *children,* and it is now incumbent upon them to return the favor. Jesus had harsh words for those who refused to support *their parents* (Mark 7:9-13).

5. The widow who is really in need and left all alone puts her hope in God and continues night and day to pray and to ask God for help.

Paul maintains that the Christian *widow* is in a unique position to trust *in God* and *pray.* Her tragic circumstance can bring her closer to God. It is the kind of widow who gives herself wholly to God who is a prime candidate for the church's "widow list." This kind of widow is represented by Anna in Luke 2:36, 37. This elderly woman was constantly helping and praying in the temple.

6. But the widow who lives for pleasure is dead even while she lives.

Deserving *widows* should not be living for earthly *pleasure,* Paul warns. The situation he is referring to most likely concerns the behavior of some younger widows. The situation is so desperate for widows that some give themselves over to a sinful lifestyle, either as prostitutes to gain money, or to fornication in the attempt to find a husband or benefactor. Paul wants all widows to be true to the Christian requirements. He has more to say about the status and conduct of widows in 1 Corinthians 7.

7. Give the people these instructions, too, so that no one may be open to blame.

Paul's plan will keep family members from being *open* to the charge that they are dishonoring their mothers. It will also keep the widows from the charge that they are taking advantage of the church. When corruption is allowed to creep in, the church becomes ineffective and loses its witness.

8. If anyone does not provide for his relatives, and especially for his immediate family, he has denied the faith and is worse than an unbeliever.

This is quite an indictment! What could be worse than denying *the faith?* The kind of insensitive behavior in view here surely denies both the letter and spirit of the teaching of Jesus (again, see Mark 7:9-13).

Conditions are different today, with pensions, government social insurance, and the like. Even so, Christ expects his people to take responsibility for the care of their family members. Christian mercy should be expressed first and foremost to those closest to us. If we don't do that, then we are not likely to show mercy to anyone else.

CONCLUSION

There is no doubt that service of any type is a complex matter. This is particularly true in church leadership. Those serving in that capacity not only need to understand the Scriptures, they also need to understand people. Ministry is for God and to God, but it is exercised in a setting of community.

The sheer difficulty of the task requires those who serve the church in both leadership and nonleadership positions to call forth their best. This involves not only the best in terms of personal piety, but also all the wisdom and sensitivity needed to deal with people. It is a rare person who can do it all well, but they do exist. Some do it well intuitively and some do it well after years of trial and error. But it's something we can all improve upon!

Discovery Learning

This page contains an alternative lesson plan emphasizing learning activities. Classes desiring such student involvement will find these suggestions helpful. The next page is a reproducible activity page to further enhance discovery learning.

LEARNING GOALS

After participating in this lesson, each of your students should be able to:

1. Understand the importance of spiritual training in the life of a minister.

2. Appreciate the importance of a minister developing people skills.

3. Evaluate his or her own competence in these areas.

INTO THE LESSON

To begin the class, ask your students to draw a picture of their ideal preacher. The picture may be realistic or abstract or even a stick figure depending on the skill of the artist. The important thing is to represent qualities that make a "perfect" preacher. You will need to provide paper and colored pencils or even crayons for the exercise. If you use the student books, space is also provided there for this activity. The reproducible page also has space at "Wanted: The Perfect Preacher." To get learners started suggest they include such elements as "large hands."

Allow several minutes for your class to finish their drawings, then ask volunteers to share their work with the class and indicate which features are most important to them. Make a list of those important characteristics on the chalkboard, then tell your class that, as last week's lesson examined the qualities of elders and deacons, this lesson will discuss the qualities and duties of preachers.

INTO THE WORD

Pair off your students to study today's text, 1 Timothy 4:7–5:8. Each pair will read the text, then make two lists. One will be a list of the positive traits and activities Timothy was encouraged to have or do. The other will list the negative traits or activities Timothy was to avoid. You will need to provide paper for this activity or point your class to their student books where there is space for the exercise. Their lists should look something like this:

POSITIVES

1. Training to be godly (4:7)

2. Labor and strive (v. 10)

3. Set an example in speech, life, love, faith, purity (v. 12)

4. Give attention to public reading, to preaching, to teaching (v. 13)

5. Be diligent/wholly devoted to Paul's teaching (v. 15)

6. Watch your life and doctrine (v. 16)

7. Exhort elders as fathers and treat older women as mothers, and young men and women as brothers and sisters (5:1, 2)

8. Give proper recognition to needy widows (v. 3)

9. Teach people to be blameless (v. 7)

NEGATIVES

1. Have nothing to do with godless myths and old wives' tales (4:7)

2. Don't let anyone look down on you because you are young (v. 12)

3. Don't neglect your gift (v. 14)

4. Don't rebuke an older man harshly (5:1)

Using the lesson commentary and the following questions, discuss the importance of each positive and each negative trait or activity on the list.

1. What did Paul mean when he wrote, "Train yourself to be godly"?

2. To what "old wives' tales" did Paul refer?

3. How does one "strive"?

4. How can a young preacher overcome presumptions about his youth?

5. Why did Paul emphasize public reading, preaching, and teaching?

6. Why was Paul adamant about how the preacher should treat different age groups in the church?

INTO LIFE

Ask your students to imagine that they are personal spiritual trainers for your minister or ministers. Working in pairs again, they should devise a specialized weeklong training program for him/them, using today's text as a guideline. The program should include the following basic elements, plus any other duties and exercises they believe are necessary or beneficial: devotional time, study time, sermon and lesson preparation time, family time, recreation/personal time, administrative duties, group worship and group study time, and visitation time. After listing all the elements of the program, your teams should allocate them to the Monday through Sunday chart with hourly blocks from 6 a.m. to 11 p.m., that appears on the reproducible page as "Spiritual Fitness Training Schedule." (Make copies of this chart at 130-135% to make writing on it easier.) Discuss what the students see happening as they make their charts.

Wanted: The Perfect Preacher

In the space provided, write a want-ad for your ideal preacher. Be sure to include the qualities he needs to have to meet your expectations.

Go back and put a checkmark (✔) by each one you believe is on God's qualification list.

Spiritual Fitness Training Schedule

In the following chart fill in some of the important and constant elements of your own spiritual fitness regimen.

	MON	TUE	WED	THU	FRI	SAT	SUN
6:00 A.M.							
7:00 A.M.							
8:00 A.M.							
9:00 A.M.							
10:00 A.M.							
11:00 A.M.							
12:00 N.							
1:00 P.M.							
2:00 P.M.							
3:00 P.M.							
4:00 P.M.							
5:00 P.M.							
6:00 P.M.							
7:00 P.M.							
8:00 P.M.							
9:00 P.M.							
10:00 P.M.							

HANDLE GOD'S WORD RIGHTLY

LESSON 11

WHY TEACH THIS LESSON?

A preacher on a cross-country flight was witnessing to the non-Christian woman in the seat next to him. However, to every statement the he made the woman would respond, "Well, that's just your opinion." Each time his counter-response would be, "You are correct in saying that that is my opinion. But that's not the real issue is it? The question really is, 'Is the statement I just made *true*?'" After several rounds of dialogue with these identical endings, the woman, beginning to smile, knew what was coming next and changed her reply.

This woman had a *postmodern* outlook. This viewpoint claims that there is no truth that is "external," or true for everyone—there is only truth that is "internal" or relative to each individual. But that is not the apostle Paul's outlook! He went to a martyr's death because of certain things he knew to be true for everyone. God expects Christians to labor, suffer, and contend for truth. Today's lesson shows us the way!

INTRODUCTION

A. NOTHING BUT THE TRUTH?

Today's lesson text speaks to us in two areas of life where we need reminders. First, it reminds us how blessed we are to have the Bible so accessible to us. Before the invention of the printing press, handwritten copies of the Bible were too expensive for the average person to own. Today, we can choose from a dizzying array of Bible versions and study aids in all price ranges.

Some areas of our world still do not have that kind of access. A man once spoke to a congregation with a distressing story about distributing Bibles with a Christian organization in a third-world country—and running out. People were pleading for Bibles with tears in their eyes. They begged the men to come back. Some of the children tore their Bibles so they could give parts to friends. It is easy to forget how blessed we are to have access to the Scriptures.

Second, today's text also speaks to us at a philosophical level. It assumes that there is such a thing as truth and that we can know truth. This is a foreign concept in a world that has largely rejected the concept of objective or absolute truth. Paul believed that truth existed and that God had revealed it. This lesson also reveals that Paul believed that sharing God's truth was worth the cost and sacrifice.

B. LESSON BACKGROUND

The lesson presents to us Paul in his old age, facing a martyr's death (2 Timothy 4:6; Philemon 9). He is concerned that his protégé Timothy continue the same plan for spreading the gospel that Paul himself had followed.

Timothy had learned of faith from his mother and grandmother. He had learned the fullness of the Christian gospel from Paul himself. Timothy had

DEVOTIONAL READING:
PSALM 119:9-16

BACKGROUND SCRIPTURE:
2 TIMOTHY 2

PRINTED TEXT:
2 TIMOTHY 2:1-15

LESSON AIMS

After participating in this lesson, each student will be able to:

1. Describe the example set by a good soldier, athlete, or farmer, as explained in today's text.

2. Tell how regular Bible study can help the believer to demonstrate the qualities typified by soldiers, athletes, and farmers.

3. Identify one obstacle he or she will overcome in order to be faithful in studying God's Word.

Aug
15

KEY VERSE

Do your best to present yourself to God as one approved, a workman who does not need to be ashamed and who correctly handles the word of truth.
—2 Timothy 2:15

shared Paul's hardships. Many were deserting the gospel (2 Timothy 1:15; 4:10a), but not Timothy.

The conviction of truth undoubtedly was what kept Timothy faithful. In this lesson we will see how Paul admonished Timothy to make sure that truth is passed on regardless of personal consequences. The stakes were just too high to do otherwise.

I. LABORING FOR THE TRUTH (2 TIMOTHY 2:1-7)

A. WE ARE TEACHERS (vv. 1, 2)

1. You then, my son, be strong in the grace that is in Christ Jesus.

Timothy's strength is not to be found in himself; it is a supernatural strength that comes from *Christ Jesus.* This may be something of a relief to Timothy, who some believe tends to be timid (1 Corinthians 16:10; 2 Timothy 1:7). The work of the gospel needs supernatural help. There is simply no other way to face the challenge.

2. And the things you have heard me say in the presence of many witnesses entrust to reliable men who will also be qualified to teach others.

Paul wants Timothy to continue the tradition. Like a relay runner passing a baton, Timothy is to pass on to others the same faith that was passed to him. His mother, grandmother (2 Timothy 1:5), and finally Paul himself had first shared it with him; those whom Timothy instructs will then pass it on to others.

When Paul says that Timothy heard him share the gospel in front *of many witnesses,* we need not spend too much time wondering who those specific witnesses were. This is probably a general reference to the many times when Timothy heard Paul expound the gospel before various groups of people.

Paul continues from here to compare the Christian worker with three other kinds of workers. In certain respects, Christian workers are to be like soldiers, athletes, and farmers.

B. WE ARE SOLDIERS (vv. 3, 4)

3. Endure hardship with us like a good soldier of Christ Jesus.

No one knows *hardship* like a *soldier,* particularly soldiers in the ancient world. Paul has learned much about a soldier's life since he has spent considerable time in the company of soldiers while in prison. Conditions "on the road" are tough, and the soldiers are away from home for long periods of time. Add to that the threat of death, and you recognize the extraordinary commitment of the soldier.

God's men and women are to have that same kind of commitment. We are all soldiers for the cause of Christ (Philippians 2:25; Philemon 2). Paul uses military images about as frequently as sports images. (See 1 Corinthians 9:7 and Ephesians 6:10-17.)

ENDURING HARDSHIP

The difficulties and hardships faced by soldiers are many and varied. There is separation from family, the discomforts of sleeping on hard ground, exposure to the elements, and meals consisting of cold food—not to mention the constant threat of injury or death at the hands of the enemy!

Consider the paratroopers who took part in the D-day invasion in 1944. Enlisted paratroopers carried an average of seventy pounds of equipment, while officers averaged ninety pounds of gear. Adding the weight of their parachutes, each man weighed in at between ninety and one hundred twenty pounds over his body weight. These paratroopers were dropped behind enemy lines to secure needed targets. They knew that if the accompanying sea-borne assault failed, there would be no rescue.

HOW TO SAY IT

Colossians. Kuh-LOSH-unz.

Corinthians. Kor-IN-thee-unz.

Ephesians. Ee-FEE-zhunz.

Messiah. Meh-SIGH-uh.

Nehemiah. NEE-huh-MY-uh.

Philemon. Fih-LEE-mun or Fye-LEE-mun.

Philippians. Fih-LIP-ee-unz.

Titus. TIE-tus.

Much planning and preparation went into that drop. However, heavy fog and enemy gunfire made it impossible to drop the paratroopers precisely as planned. Both the 82nd and the 101st Divisions suffered heavy losses. In spite of these hardships, both divisions were able to put together units and continue the invasion. Heroic efforts in the face of hardships are what led to making D-day the beginning of the end of World War II.

The Christian soldier is also faced with many hardships. For some it is leaving home and family behind for service. For others it is the extra weight of concern for the ministry of the church. For many it is witnessing the casualties of fellow Christian soldiers who fall to the assaults of the enemy. But the good soldier of the cross endures the hardships and continues the march to victory. Does that description fit you?   —A. E. A.

4. No one serving as a soldier gets involved in civilian affairs—he wants to please his commanding officer.

Taking the vow or oath of enlistment means that a full-time soldier puts *civilian* priorities behind. *No one* can serve two masters. Just as a soldier puts aside the entanglements of the civilian world, so the Christian puts aside the entanglements of the secular world.

Paul does not mean by this that we can totally divorce ourselves from the secular world. Paul himself did secular work as a tentmaker so that he could serve the church without charge (Acts 18:3). Not every Christian can make a living from doing church work. Christians cannot avoid the responsibilities of the workaday world. Neither can we avoid the responsibilities of home life. If we were to be totally divorced from community life, we would have no one with whom to share the gospel! (See 1 Corinthians 5:9, 10.) What is forbidden is allowing oneself to be distracted by secular concerns.

Another thing that soldiers know how to do is to follow lawful orders and *please* their commanders. Soldiers who do not follow orders are useless at best and a danger to their fellow soldiers at worst. Those serving in God's kingdom must have a sense of duty as soldiers for him.

C. WE ARE ATHLETES (v. 5)

5. Similarly, if anyone competes as an athlete, he does not receive the victor's crown unless he competes according to the rules.

Another group that knows well what sacrifice means is that of the world-class *athlete.* Here Paul uses another of his sports analogies (see also last week's lesson).

This verse describes the winner of a race who receives his *crown* of victory. The crown or wreath awarded in the Olympic games of Paul's day corresponds with the gold medal of the modern Olympiad.

Competitors have a chance to win only if they compete *according to the* established *rules.* This could refer to the rules of training, but more likely it means the rules of the competition itself. The Christian must also always be aware of his or her commitment to the rules of the Lord. Just because we have been saved by grace does not mean we are free to ignore the moral laws of God. We still live under authority.

D. WE ARE FARMERS (vv. 6, 7)

6. The hardworking farmer should be the first to receive a share of the crops.

A *farmer* also demonstrates the type of qualities needed in Christian leadership and service. The farmer knows how to work hard, to be patient, and to cooperate with nature and trust God.

WHAT DO YOU THINK?

We all know Christians who are entangled "in civilian affairs." How is your life different because of your faith? How have you kept yourself from worldly entanglements?

SOLUTION TO PUZZLE ON P. 432

(Unused letters have been removed from the grid below to help you find the letters that form the given words.)

```
        S E S S E N T I W
R E I D L O S T       Y N
C O M P E T E S     T I
H         L     I A
A     H   W O R K M A N
I   F T     O   E N D U R E
N   A       H R       E D
E R I G H T E O U S N E S S E
D   T U       C     E P I
L   H A       R     R T E F
E   F         O   V   I C I
P   U         W A   M T L
S A L V A T I O N     B A U
O           T       U S Q
G N I R E F F U S     S Q
```

Many of the most important things in life operate by a sowing-and-reaping rule from farming. A farmer does not reap on the same day that the seeds are sown. Crop growth takes time! In the world of spiritual development, education, and even health, we do well to operate with the patience of the farmer—trusting that in the end we will reap rewards.

The good news is that the faithful farmer is *first to receive* the reward *of the crops.* Just as a farmer eats of his or her own crops, the Christian benefits personally from the development of holiness of life.

7. Reflect on what I am saying, for the Lord will give you insight into all this.

Timothy is not to brush over Paul's words lightly, as if they were optional. Instead, Timothy is to consider those words carefully and expect to receive understanding in all things as a result. This involves the interaction of Timothy's own patient reasoning and the work of the Holy Spirit. This is the same interaction necessary for us to understand and apply the Bible today. The three analogies of soldier, athlete, and farmer also appear in 1 Corinthians 9:7, 24-27. If Timothy will reflect on these things, the Lord will give him understanding.

Before moving on, let's take one more look at the figures Paul uses. There is something important that sustains all those that Paul uses in his illustrations; that something is hope. The good soldier sacrifices in the hope of victory, the athlete competes in the hope of a crown, and the farmer labors with the hope of a future harvest.

While there is definitely sacrifice, discipline, and hard work in the Christian life, there is also great hope. Paul himself expresses this hope as he approaches the end of his life (see 2 Timothy 4:6-8).

II. SUFFERING FOR THE TRUTH (2 TIMOTHY 2:8-13)

A. CHRIST SUFFERED (v. 8)

8. Remember Jesus Christ, raised from the dead, descended from David. This is my gospel,

An important part of identifying *Jesus* as the Messiah is to recall that he is a descendant of *David* (Matthew 1:1; Romans 1:3). Paul not only describes Jesus in terms of his ancestry, but also in terms of his great victory over death. It is not a *dead* Christ that Timothy is to concentrate on. Neither is Timothy to think that he serves a Christ who never suffered death. Timothy is to remember the entire truth and therefore celebrate a risen Savior (Romans 1:4; 1 Corinthians 15:4, 20). We, too, must use these essential facts as anchor points for our faith.

B. PAUL SUFFERED (vv. 9, 10)

9. . . . for which I am suffering even to the point of being chained like a criminal. But God's word is not chained.

Paul points out that in his own situation he is being persecuted as *a criminal* for his faith in Jesus Christ (cf. Acts 16:23; Ephesians 3:1; Philippians 1:12-14). As in the case of Jesus, Paul is treated this way even though he has committed no crime.

Yet Paul can see that even though he himself is *chained,* the gospel goes on unchained. What a perspective! Time after time people have tried to silence truth by silencing the messenger. It does not work. God's message is far more powerful than any earthly messenger. God's truth can never be imprisoned.

10. Therefore I endure everything for the sake of the elect, that they too may obtain the salvation that is in Christ Jesus, with eternal glory.

The elect are the Christians. God has foreseen their faith from eternity past, and has chosen them to spend eternity in Heaven with him. But obtaining this salvation and eternal *glory* happens only through *Christ Jesus.* Paul has indeed endured all things *for the sake of* this group (2 Corinthians 6:3-10; 11:23-33). His upcoming martyrdom will be one more thing he will *endure* for the elect's sakes.

C. WE SUFFER (vv. 11-13)

11. Here is a trustworthy saying: If we died with him, we will also live with him;

We have discussed the phrase *trustworthy saying* in previous lessons (cf. 1 Timothy 1:15). Here the phrase serves as a lead-in to what may be a hymn or poem of the early church.

The phrase *if we died with him* leads us to wonder when it was that we died with Christ. The answer is that we died with Jesus when we became Christians. Paul told the Roman Christians that when they were baptized they "were baptized into his death" (Romans 6:3). In some way, it is in the water of baptism that we join Jesus in death, "buried with him through baptism" (Romans 6:4; cf. Colossians 2:12). Some think that these passages refer to baptism by the Holy Spirit (Matthew 3:11). These two baptisms could be thought of as two sides of a single coin—inseparable.

Following Christ's death "to sin" (Romans 6:10), we consider ourselves "dead to sin" (6:11). If this interpretation is correct, then to be dead with him refers to dying with Christ at the time of our conversion.

However, there are some who believe that in this context Paul is talking about "daily dying" to sin rather than the initial conversion. It is interesting to note that in Romans 6:11-14 Paul indicates that our original death to sin gives rise to what may be called a daily dying to sin. So both could be in mind here as well.

For the Christian, death gives way to life, and there are two ways we *live with him.* One is in the future resurrection (Romans 6:5). This will be a marvelous thing, but Paul would have us understand that we live with Jesus now also. We are already alive in Christ (Romans 6:11).

12. . . . if we endure, we will also reign with him. If we disown him, he will also disown us;

It is also important to Paul that Christians commit for the long haul. They must *endure.* Those who suffer and endure (cf. Luke 9:23) are to take heart through the promise that they *will also reign with* Jesus (Revelation 22:5). This should resonate with any Christian undergoing persecution. Suffering is temporary; reigning with Christ is eternal.

The second part of this verse is a solemn warning. Perhaps people had already wilted under the pressure of the persecution. But regardless of the persecution, if we reject or disown Jesus, he will disown us. In Matthew 10:33 Jesus says essentially the same thing

GOD IS THERE

What is the source of suffering? The most basic answer is that suffering results from living life in a fallen world. Even for the follower of Christ there is pain and suffering because of this body of flesh in which we live. But a deeper issue we face as Christians is, "Where is God when we suffer? Has he abandoned us to face the pain and pressure on our own?"

Bob Russell, in a sermon delivered following the terrorist attacks in New York and Washington on September 11, 2001, helps us deal with these questions. Russell says, "Where was God last Tuesday? The same place you parents are when your sixteen-year-old gets in the car and drives off, and you say, 'Oh, I hope he listens to what I said.' [He was] the same place the father of the prodigal son was when his son was hurting in the far country—standing on the front porch, watching and hoping he would come back. [He was] the same place he was when his

Study to show thyself approved unto God, a workman that needeth not to be ashamed, rightly dividing the word of truth.
2 Timothy 2:15

Visual for lesson 11. *One way we can present ourselves approved to God is by studying his Word. A Bible study group can help!*

DAILY BIBLE READINGS

Monday, Aug. 9—Keep God's Precepts Diligently (Psalm 119:1-6)

Tuesday, Aug. 10—Treasure God's Word in Your Heart (Psalm 119:9-16)

Wednesday, Aug. 11—Believers Encourage Apollos in the Word (Acts 18:24-28)

Thursday, Aug. 12—Entrust Teachings to Faithful People (2 Timothy 2:1-7)

Friday, Aug. 13—God's Word Is Not Chained (2 Timothy 2:8-13)

Saturday, Aug. 14—Rightly Explain the Word of Truth (2 Timothy 2:14-19)

Sunday, Aug. 15—The Lord's Servant, an Able Teacher (2 Timothy 2:20-26)

PRAYER

Dear Father, help me to appreciate the privilege of having access to your Word and your gospel. Remind me, too, of my obligation to study and share that Word. May I show my devotion to Jesus by laboring faithfully on his behalf. In Jesus' name, amen.

WHAT DO YOU THINK?

What "trivial matters" have caused strife in churches? Who is responsible for keeping the church focused on eternal matters when these trivial issues pop up? What can you do to help people keep the right perspective?

WHAT DO YOU THINK?

What would cause a "workman" to be "ashamed"? What specific safeguards can we put in place to be sure we are not unworthy workers?

Son was dying on the cross and people were gloating over his death—waiting in the shadows, knowing there would be victory and resurrection."

Since God has promised never to leave us or forsake us—and this includes times of pain and suffering—it is our task as followers of the truth of God's Word to remain faithful. Paul encourages us with the reminder that, "For our light and momentary troubles are achieving for us an eternal glory that far outweighs them all" (2 Corinthians 4:17).   —A. E. A.

13. . . . *if we are faithless, he will remain faithful, for he cannot disown himself.*

The final line of this poetic section gives us a beautiful view of God's faithfulness. Even if people are *faithless* and they don't believe and obey, God will still be *faithful* because it is his nature. See also Numbers 23:19; Romans 3:3, 4; and Titus 1:2.

III. CONTENDING FOR THE TRUTH (2 TIMOTHY 2:14, 15)

A. FAITHFUL IN WITNESS (v. 14)

14. *Keep reminding them of these things. Warn them before God against quarreling about words; it is of no value, and only ruins those who listen.*

If we tell a person something only once, it might not stick. Memory is fragile, and people need reminders (see 2 Peter 1:12; 3:1; Jude 5). In light of certain problems, Paul wants Timothy to help his congregation remember the great truths of the faith. Timothy will do this as he warns *them before God.*

Perhaps some in Timothy's church have created an environment where people strive or go to war over *words.* It's not that words aren't important. The gospel is communicated with words! Paul is describing, rather, a situation where people are arguing over trivial matters (cf. 1 Timothy 6:4; Titus 3:9).

B. FAITHFUL IN THE STUDY (v. 15)

15. *Do your best to present yourself to God as one approved, a workman who does not need to be ashamed and who correctly handles the word of truth.*

If Timothy does what Paul tells him, he will be *a workman who does not need to be ashamed,* since he will have done what is expected. What is expected is that Timothy will be one *who correctly handles the word of truth.* It is Timothy's responsibility to do his job of teaching the Scriptures well. He must do his best to be accurate and clear as he teaches the Word of God (cf. Nehemiah 8:8).

CONCLUSION

When we witness to people and try to convince them to become Christians, we often stress the benefits. We often talk of the happiness and joy that comes to those who give their lives to Christ. In so doing, we sometimes make the mistake of making Christianity sound easy.

But Jesus never said it would be easy. Paul never said it would be easy. It is fulfilling, but not easy. Jesus warned people that they must take up a cross if they want to be Christians (Luke 9:23). Paul says in today's text that Timothy must sacrifice and work hard for the cause. There are some things worth sacrificing for. The Christian life is one of them.

In particular, our lesson today suggests that our great striving should be directed toward the ministry of the Word. This can mean preaching, but there are other ways to fulfill this admonition. For Timothy, who labored in the ministry of the Word as a vocation, no doubt it had special meaning. But there are many ways people can share God's Word, even if they are volunteer ministers.

Christians need the kind of all-consuming dedication that Paul speaks of in this lesson. His words to Timothy are his words to us!

THOUGHT TO REMEMBER

Be an approved worker.

Discovery Learning

This page contains an alternative lesson plan emphasizing learning activities. Classes desiring such student involvement will find these suggestions helpful. The next page is a reproducible activity page to further enhance discovery learning.

LEARNING GOALS

After this lesson each of your students will be able to:

1. Describe the example set by a good soldier, athlete, or farmer, as explained in today's text.

2. Tell how regular Bible study can help the believer to demonstrate the qualities typified by soldiers, athletes, and farmers.

3. Identify one obstacle he or she will overcome in order to be faithful in studying God's Word.

INTO THE LESSON

To begin the class, distribute copies of a three-column handout containing the headings "SOLDIER," "ATHLETE," and "FARMER." Ask your students to complete the chart by listing several traits a person would need to perform well in each profession. (For example, the soldier needs a submissive and obedient spirit; the athlete needs a competitive drive and self-discipline; the farmer needs faith and hard work.)

Ask students to reveal their answers; then briefly discuss similarities of the traits of each occupation, such as dedication and perseverance. Say, "Today's lesson will compare the Christian life to each of these professions. Let's see how we can complete our spiritual responsibilities in a noble and honorable way."

INTO THE WORD

Ask a volunteer to read 2 Timothy 2:1-15 aloud. Distribute the "Word Search" activity from the next page, and allow students time to complete it in order to familiarize them with the text. Then divide your class into pairs of students and assign to each pair one of the two exercises below. After the studies are finished, have each pair report its findings.

EXERCISE 1

Read 1 Corinthians 9:7, 24-27 and 2 Timothy 2:1-7 and complete the following statements:

1. A Christian is like a soldier in the following ways:
2. A Christian is like an athlete in the following ways:
3. A Christian is like a farmer in the following ways:

EXERCISE 2

Read 2 Timothy 2:8-13; 2 Corinthians 11:23-27; 1 Peter 2:12-24 and complete the following statements:

1. Jesus suffered for mankind in the following ways:
2. Paul suffered for the church in the following ways:

3. Christians are to suffer for their faith in the following ways:

After a brief discussion, use the lesson commentary and explain how God expects Christians to contend faithfully for the truth of the gospel (see 2 Timothy 2:14, 15) no matter what the circumstances. In particular, tie together the idea of laboring and suffering for Scriptural truth with the idea of faithfully passing on that truth to other non-Christians and Christians.

INTO LIFE

Distribute copies of the reproducible activity "The Christian Life Is Like a . . " from the next page. Allow four or five minutes; then discuss the students' answers.

Then tell the students you'd like their input on some case studies. For each scenario below your class should identify ways to solve the problem while upholding the absolute truths of Scripture discussed in today's lesson and general Christian principles.

1. Dave is running for Congress for the first time. He has always been a staunch pro-life advocate, but his campaign manager wants him to moderate his views (or at least to avoid the issue) so he can broaden his support in a tight race. What should he do?

2. Heather has risen to a prominent position in the accounting department of a major corporation. She has become aware that her employer is overstating the company's profits in its quarterly reports to hide the corporation's financial woes and to keep its stock price from falling. What should she do?

3. Samantha has been trying to lead her neighbor to Christ. This morning the woman called and begged Samantha, "If my husband asks, tell him we were out shopping together last night. I don't want him to know where I was." What should Samantha say?

4. Michael is fully scheduled for the coming weekend with a variety of good activities for and with his family and service projects for his local congregation. A college friend calls him with the offer of free tickets to the opening football game of their alma mater in an adjoining state. How should Michael respond?

After classmembers discuss responses to these situations, challenge class members to identify other such situations—either hypothetical or actual—where a Christian must make a difficult choice while upholding Christian principles.

Word Search

All the words in the list to the left are found in 2 Timothy 2:1-15. Look across, up, down, and diagonally, and draw a line around each word as you find it.

Athlete
Authority
Chained
Competes
Crown
Endure
Faithful
Gospel
Qualified
Remain
Respect
Righteousness
Salvation
Servant
Soldier
Submit
Suffering
Witnesses
Workman

```
D R C J S E S S E N T I W N E
R E I D L O S T E I K Y T N N
C O M P E T E S S M T A I E S
H R I C N L I E D I S A N N K
A K N T H E W O R K M A N S Y
I I F T J M E O S E N D U R E
N B A K R S H T R A N K E E D
E R I G H T E O U S N E S S E
D E T R U N S T C K O E E P I
L S H A N N T X R Y S R T E F
E S F E K N I M O N V T I C I
P U U S K N E S W A X S M T L
S A L V A T I O N T R Z B K A
O N K R T O T T I U R K U N U
G N I R E F F U S E C C S N Q
```

See page 427 for solution.

The Christian Life Is Like a . . .

Paul's three analogies for the rigors of the Christian life are in today's text: soldier, athlete, farmer. What figure from your vocational experience would you compare to the demands of living and growing in Christ? Suggest one and then describe the ways in which a comparison may be made.

Guidelines for
the Church's Ministry
(Lessons 9-13)

REMAIN FAITHFUL

LESSON 12

WHY TEACH THIS LESSON?

Is there anyone who isn't aware that we live in an age of political correctness? A hallmark of this outlook can be found in the concept of *tolerance* that (along with its close cousin *diversity*) tells us we are not to judge the lifestyles and cultural practices of others. Behaviors are not to be seen as "bad" or "good," merely "different."

But in order to remain faithful to God we must be able to recognize good and evil. This requires spiritual maturity in being able to judge or discern between behaviors. Further, we must recognize the right and ability of God's word to sit in judgment and conquer evil thoughts and actions. This requires spiritual maturity. Today's lesson starts (or continues) us on the road to maturity in these two areas.

INTRODUCTION

A. DON'T COUNT IT OUT

The infamous agnostic Robert G. Ingersoll (1833–1899) once declared that the Bible would soon be in the morgue. But the Bible lives on more than one hundred years after Ingersoll himself went to the morgue. Before Ingersoll, the French philosopher Voltaire (1694–1778) predicted that in a hundred years the Bible would be an outmoded and forgotten book. Fifty years after Voltaire was gone, his house was owned and used by a Bible society.

It has been popular from time to time to suggest that the Bible is obsolete and will ultimately be rejected. Nevertheless, the Bible stays on the bestseller list year after year. Those who sound its death knell eventually are the ones who end up in the grave.

Don't ever count the Bible out. There will always be some passages here and there with which we struggle (cf. 2 Peter 3:16), but the Bible has proven itself to be relevant from generation to generation.

B. LESSON BACKGROUND

Last week we looked at the Bible from the perspective of the church leader, who is to teach it faithfully, accurately, and clearly. This week we will look at the incredible power of the Bible itself, the power to counter any false teaching.

Scholars are not positive about the identity of the false doctrine that threatens the church as Paul writes the Pastoral Epistles of 1 Timothy, 2 Timothy, and Titus. Some think it to be a non-Christian religious system called *gnosticism*. Others believe the problem was some kind of *Judaizing*.

Gnostic comes from a Greek word that means knowledge. The gnostics got their name from their belief that they had a secret knowledge of God and his plans. Gnostics also thought all flesh to be evil. This led some to deny themselves anything good, even legitimate pleasures. (Paul may be writing against this viewpoint in 1 Timothy 4:3.) Other gnostics proposed they could commit all kinds of sins in the flesh as long as they kept their spirits clean.

Some gnostic ideas resembled Christian ideas in a superficial way, so certain ideas could have crept into the church almost unnoticed for a time. Even though

DEVOTIONAL READING:
1 JOHN 5:1-5
BACKGROUND SCRIPTURE:
2 TIMOTHY 3:1–4:8
PRINTED TEXT:
2 TIMOTHY 3:1-5, 12-17; 4:1-5

LESSON AIMS

After participating in this lesson, each student will be able to:

1. Produce a profile of the wicked people described in today's text.

2. Explain how faithfulness in teaching the Bible provides an antidote to wickedness.

3. Plan to share the Word of God with someone who needs to hear it.

KEY VERSE

But you, keep your head in all situations, endure hardship, do the work of an evangelist, discharge all the duties of your ministry.

—2 Timothy 4:5

Aug
22

gnosticism wasn't really all that prominent during Paul's life, early forms of it may already have been developing, particularly in Ephesus, where Timothy lived (1 Timothy 1:3). John, who also ministered in Ephesus, seemed to be concerned about this doctrine in his letters.

Judaizing is the belief that Christians must follow the Jewish law in addition to believing in Christ. If this is the false doctrine that Paul has in mind, then the false teachers are urging an undue commitment to Jewish traditions (see Galatians 2:14; 1 Timothy 1:4; and Titus 1:14).

Even if neither of these two problems is around much today, Paul's warnings allow us to understand the problems that false religious ideas can cause in our twenty-first-century congregations. What is important to us isn't so much the specific false doctrine in question, but the power of the Word of God to defeat *any* false doctrine or heresy. False doctrines have come and gone as the centuries have passed, but the Bible never has lost its authority.

I. CHARACTERISTICS OF EVIL PEOPLE (2 TIMOTHY 3:1-5, 12, 13)
A. THEIR CONDUCT (vv. 1-4)
1. But mark this: There will be terrible times in the last days.

It is important to understand what Paul means by *the last days*. This concept was originally developed in the Old Testament, where it referred to the time when God would balance the scales of justice when he intervened to uphold his holiness. When in distress, people hoped for and prayed for "the day of the Lord" to come. It was to be a day of joy for the faithful and judgment for the wicked.

The New Testament writers applied this concept to the time after Christ's first coming. Peter, on the day of Pentecost, said that the last days had arrived (Acts 2:16, 17). The writer of Hebrews speaks of what has happened "in these last days" (Hebrews 1:2). John says "this is the last hour" (1 John 2:18). See also 1 Timothy 4:1 and 2 Peter 3:3.

The idea that the last days had arrived led some in the first century to maintain that Jesus would come back within just a few years. However, the concept of "the last days" does not require that. It is clear that Paul is talking to Timothy about a present problem, not a future one. It is a problem that will become even more severe as time passes.

2. People will be lovers of themselves, lovers of money, boastful, proud, abusive, disobedient to their parents, ungrateful, unholy,

Paul commences on a list of about nineteen vices that evil people possess (cf. Romans 1:29-31). Some of these vices are what we might call "external sins," visible for all to see. Others are more "internal," being sins of thoughts and attitudes. Many of them overlap one another.

This verse begins with what may be seen as the beginning of all sin: people being *lovers of themselves*. Is it not the foundation of sin to be so impressed with ourselves that we believe we know more than God? Christianity requires that we must put self aside and recognize that God is greater.

Covetousness, or loving *money*, is also listed. God thinks this problem to be serious enough to include a prohibition of it in the Ten Commandments (Exodus 20:17). Covetousness is essentially a selfish desire for money or material wealth. Money itself is not evil, but love of money is (1 Timothy 6:10).

Next on the list are those who are *boastful*. This is closely related to being *proud* (cf. Proverbs 16:18; James 4:6). Another word we could use is "conceited." One humorist tried to sum up this problem by noting that conceit is the weirdest disease because it makes everyone sick except the one who has it!

agnostic. ag-NAHSS-tick.
gnostic. NAHSS-tick.
gnosticism. NAHSS-tih-SIZZ-um.
heresy. HAIR-uh-see.
Judaizing. JOO-day-ize-ing.
Judas Iscariot. JOO-dus Iss-CARE-e-ut.
Pentecost. PENT-ih-kost.
polygamous. puh-LIH-guh-mus.
polytheistic. PAH-lee-thee-ISS-tick.
Voltaire. Voll-TARE.

While amusing, this is not really true. The one who has this problem is suffering from a spiritual disease. Such a person is more than a mere irritation.

Abusive carries the idea of being slanderous toward God, or blasphemous. All slander is evil (see v. 3, next), but it is supremely dangerous to slander God.

As with covetousness, we are warned all the way back in the Ten Commandments that to be *disobedient to their parents* is a sin (Exodus 20:12). Those who doubt that society has slipped in this regard need only spend a few hours "people watching" at a shopping mall to be convinced otherwise!

Interestingly, ingratitude—being *ungrateful*—is seen as a vice on the same plane as the rest. Many of us would be prone to not recognize ingratitude as a sin at all. To be unthankful ultimately reveals an improper attitude toward God.

This verse concludes by noting the problem of being *unholy*. The word used here stresses a lack of fellowship with God (see 1 Timothy 1:9).

3. . . . without love, unforgiving, slanderous, without self-control, brutal, not lovers of the good,

Verse three continues the list of vices. *Without love* refers to a lack of family affection. This is a problem that Paul discusses in Romans 1:31 as well.

It follows that if people are without love, they will also be *unforgiving*. More literally, this word means "without a treaty." It paints us a picture of relationships with irreconcilable differences.

The term *slanderous* comes from the same root as the word *devil*. The devil is the ultimate slanderer, and we help his cause when we engage in this activity.

Without self-control can also convey the idea of being "without strength." The lack of strength Paul is talking about is absence of moral fortitude.

The next quality is *brutal*, or literally "untamed." No doubt a person who does not control his or her anger and other emotions can be like a brutal beast. Such people are unpredictable in their actions, and the damage they can wreak may be very great.

Those who are *not lovers of the good* are condemned for having a corrupted view of life. We may not always be able to do good, but we ought at least to love good.

4. . . . treacherous, rash, conceited, lovers of pleasure rather than lovers of God—

The sobering meaning of *treacherous* is all too clear. There is nothing quite so painful as to be betrayed by someone whom you thought to be on your side. This word describes Judas Iscariot in Luke 6:16.

To be *rash* is the idea of being "reckless" (see Acts 19:36). The original word gives us a picture of someone falling head forward.

The next quality, *conceited*, describes someone who thinks too highly of himself or herself. This overlaps the idea of being boastful or proud from verse 2 (see also Romans 12:3).

Those who are *lovers of pleasure rather than lovers of God* are, in effect, idol worshipers. Anything that we put on the throne of our hearts instead of God is an idol.

B. THEIR RELIGION (v. 5)

5. . . . having a form of godliness but denying its power. Have nothing to do with them.

The evil people Paul talks about are not devoid of religion. In fact, casual observers might judge them to be very religious. But it is just *a form of godliness*. They go through the motions of religion, but they are not Christian. Even though they like the form their religion takes, they deny it has any real *power*. "They claim to know God, but by their actions they deny him" (Titus 1:16).

WHAT DO YOU THINK?

We assume that Paul is writing to adults. So we may be surprised to read "disobedient to their parents" in his list of vices. To what extent should an adult Christian continue to obey his or her parents? Why?

WHAT DO YOU THINK?

What are some evidences that one has "a form of godliness" but lacks substance in his or her faith? How might any of us suffer from this condition to some extent? How can we avoid it?

C. THEIR RUTHLESSNESS (vv. 12, 13)

12. In fact, everyone who wants to live a godly life in Christ Jesus will be persecuted,

Those who have been Christians for some time realize that God has not promised his people magical protection from persecution. Passages such as Matthew 16:24; John 15:20; and Acts 14:22 warn us otherwise.

13. . . . while evil men and impostors will go from bad to worse, deceiving and being deceived.

The presence of Christianity will not make *evil* people better if they don't want to be made better. The presence of the Christian witness simply may make such people more determined to *go from bad to worse*. Not only will these people be *deceived*, they will deceive others. The ability to lie to others and to themselves is a fundamental quality of evil people.

II. ABILITY OF SCRIPTURE TO CONQUER EVIL (2 TIMOTHY 3:14–4:5)

A. LEGACY OF THE WORD (vv. 14, 15)

14. But as for you, continue in what you have learned and have become convinced of, because you know those from whom you learned it,

Timothy must not be led astray by false teachers! The gospel is not just something that Timothy "knows about"; rather, it is something that has convinced him of truth. One reason for his confidence is that he can trust those who first taught him. See the next verse.

15. . . . and how from infancy you have known the holy Scriptures, which are able to make you wise for salvation through faith in Christ Jesus.

Timothy was taught *from infancy* by his grandmother and his mother (2 Timothy 1:5). Young Jewish children were often taught Scripture verses when they were very young. The Old Testament stresses the importance of teaching God's Word to children (see Deuteronomy 4:9). The Old Testament *Scriptures* that Timothy had learned helped prepare him for later *faith* in Jesus (cf. John 5:39).

B. ORIGIN OF THE WORD (v. 16a)

16a. All Scripture is God-breathed.

All Scripture ultimately comes from God. Working through human writers, God is the author and source. Second Peter 1:21 tells us a bit about how this inspiration took place. We can take comfort in the fact that "the Scripture cannot be broken" (John 10:35).

THE BIBLE STANDS

On one of his old history books a student once wrote, "In case of famine, eat this book; it's full of baloney! In case of flood, stand on this book; it's dry!" The world sees the Bible in much the same way: an outdated and often erroneous history book.

A nineteenth-century writer, commenting on the reliability of the Bible, states, "People for two millennia have been refuting and overthrowing this book, and yet it stands today as solid as a rock. Its circulation increases, and it is more loved and cherished and read today than ever before. People make about as much impression on this book as a man with a tack hammer would on the pyramids of Egypt.

"The hammers of infidels have been pecking away at this book for ages, but the hammers are worn out, and the anvil still endures. If this book had not been the book of God, men would have destroyed it long ago. Emperors and popes, kings and princes and rulers, scholars and intellectuals, have all tried their hand at it; they die and the book still lives."

What accounts for such durability and esteem for the Bible? Simply this: it is the Word of God. The apostle Peter reminds us that "prophecy never had its origin in

WHAT DO YOU THINK?

What does it matter "of whom" someone has learned the truth of the gospel? What challenge is implied here for parents and teachers?

DAILY BIBLE READINGS

Monday, Aug. 16—Rejoice in Persecution (Luke 6:20-26)

Tuesday, Aug. 17—By Endurance You Will Gain Life (Luke 21:12-19)

Wednesday, Aug. 18—Avoid Lovers of Pleasure (2 Timothy 3: 1-9)

Thursday, Aug. 19—Continue in What You Have Believed (2 Timothy 3:10-15)

Friday, Aug. 20—Be Persistent in Proclaiming the Word (2 Timothy 3:16–4:4)

Saturday, Aug. 21—I Have Kept the Faith (2 Timothy 4: 5-10)

Sunday, Aug. 22—The Lord Gave Me Strength (2 Timothy 4:11-18)

the will of man, but men spoke from God as they were carried along by the Holy Spirit" (2 Peter 1:21).

For one who believes in the inspiration of the Bible, it naturally follows that the Bible is the authority for living. To claim that the Bible is inspired by God yet reject its authority for daily living is a contradiction.   —A. E. A.

C. PURPOSE OF THE WORD (vv. 16b, 17)

16b, 17. . . . and is useful for teaching, rebuking, correcting and training in righteousness, so that the man of God may be thoroughly equipped for every good work.

Scripture is valuable for so many things! For those who will allow it, Scripture can bring rebuke and correction for all the problems listed in 2 Timothy 3:1-5.

When Paul says that the purpose of Scripture is to make us *thoroughly equipped for every good work,* he means that we will be given all we need to be mature Christians and to meet the demands of God.

D. URGENCY OF THE WORD (vv. 1, 2)

1. In the presence of God and of Christ Jesus, who will judge the living and the dead, and in view of his appearing and his kingdom, I give you this charge:

To invoke the names of *God* and the *Christ Jesus* in this manner means that the *charge* that Paul has for Timothy is very important.

2. . . . Preach the Word; be prepared in season and out of season; correct, rebuke and encourage—with great patience and careful instruction.

The charge to *Preach the word* seems straightforward. But Paul doesn't have in mind "only when it's convenient"! To preach the Word *in season and out of season* means that Timothy should be prepared to preach the Word at all times, whether it is convenient or not. The same goes for us.

Notice Paul says that preaching includes correcting, rebuking, and encouraging. There are preachers who specialize in correcting and rebuking, but rarely do any encouraging. Others *encourage* but never *rebuke.* Biblical preaching requires that we do both. And just as God has shown *great patience* to us (2 Peter 3:9), so our preaching is to be done with patience.

THE PRIORITY OF PREACHING

Preaching holds a prominent place in spreading the gospel message. This has been the case throughout the history of the church. It was at the preaching of Peter on the day of Pentecost that the church was born. Philip the evangelist went to Samaria proclaiming the gospel (Acts 8:5).

The apostle Paul said, "When I preach the gospel, I cannot boast, for I am compelled to preach. Woe to me if I do not preach the gospel!" (1 Corinthians 9:16). The ultimate challenge for preaching given in Scripture is Paul's rhetorical question of Romans 10:14: "How, then, can they call on the one they have not believed in? And how can they believe in the one of whom they have not heard?"

Some would say that preaching is outdated in our world today. In *Prescription for Preaching,* Woodrow Kroll addresses this issue when he asks, "Are conditions today any different which would make the gospel message irrelevant? You might venture an answer in the affirmative. Clothes are different, styles are different, customs are different, therefore people must be different. But you are wrong. The Bible doesn't deal with clothes, styles, or customs. It deals with man's sin and God's provision for man's sin."

Kroll goes on to note that our universal sin problem remains the same, despite ever-changing clothing styles and customs. A universal problem requires a universal cure: faith in Christ. That's what makes the gospel message relevant even in the twenty-first century.   —A. E. A.

WHAT DO YOU THINK?

If the Bible is all that verses 16 and 17 say it is, then we ought to spend considerable time in studying it! What are some ways you can realize these benefits from the Bible? What specifically do you do to know and understand its message?

PRAYER

Dear Father, I desire to know your Word, share your Word, and order my life by your Word. May that commitment bear fruit in my life and my church. In Jesus' name, amen.

Visual for lesson 12. *This poster will remind your learners of their lifelong task in preparing for church leadership.*

E. ALTERNATIVES TO THE WORD (vv. 3-5)

3. For the time will come when men will not put up with sound doctrine. Instead, to suit their own desires, they will gather around them a great number of teachers to say what their itching ears want to hear.

This is a bit of a repeat from 1 Timothy 4:1-3. This warning to Timothy is ours as well: some people will be interested only in what they *want to hear,* not what they need to hear. That's what it means to have *itching ears.*

4. They will turn their ears away from the truth and turn aside to myths.

Paul also discusses the problem of *myths* in 1 Timothy 4:7 and Titus 1:14. During the time between the Old and New Testaments, Jewish writers had created a great many fanciful tales. Greek myths went back even farther than that.

But the New Testament writers always insist that their teachings rest on historical foundations, unlike those myths and legends. If Jesus did not actually live, die, and rise from the dead, then what hope do we have? (See 1 Corinthians 15:12-19.)

5. But you, keep your head in all situations, endure hardship, do the work of an evangelist, discharge all the duties of your ministry.

Once again, Paul cautions Timothy to be prepared to *endure hardship* as he carries out his evangelistic ministry. The word *evangelist* is related to the word *gospel.* When Timothy does *the work of an evangelist,* he will be "telling the good news."

Acts 21:8 and Ephesians 4:11 tell us that certain people were called evangelists in the early church. Some think that an evangelist filled an office similar to that of an elder or a deacon, but this is uncertain since there are so few uses of this term in this kind of context. Someone designated as an evangelist must surely have spent most of his time sharing the gospel with unsaved people. As Timothy preaches, he is to do this as well.

CONCLUSION

Educators extol the virtue of lifelong learning. They rightly remind us that we can never know everything, that there is always more to learn, and that we need to continue to grow. The same can be said of Bible study. Even if you began studying as a child, you can always learn more of God's will from that greatest of all books.

No less an intellect than U.S. President John Quincy Adams (1767–1848) spoke of his love for, and study of, the Bible. He made it his practice for many years to read through the Bible once a year. His plan was to read four or five chapters every morning immediately after waking up. He gave a full hour to this study and described it as "the most suitable manner of beginning the day." He went on to say that with "reference to revelation, to history, or to morality, it is an invaluable and inexhaustible mine of knowledge and virtue."

Unfortunately, however, many people today never do much reading of *anything,* let alone the Bible. They may scan the newspaper or the Internet for information, but this hardly counts as the genuine mental exercise of reading. As Chuck Colson noted, we are becoming an "aliterate" society, meaning a society composed of people who *can* read, but simple choose not to because it's too much work.

But if we are to love God with all our mind (Mark 12:30), we must know what he has to say. This knowledge has its greatest effect on us when we read it directly for ourselves from his Holy Word. A good way to begin is to use a "one-year Bible" that is conveniently divided into three hundred sixty-five daily readings. Following the example of Adams, let us commit to reading and studying the Bible daily.

Discovery Learning

This page contains an alternative lesson plan emphasizing learning activities. Classes desiring such student involvement will find these suggestions helpful. The next page is a reproducible activity page to further enhance discovery learning.

LEARNING GOALS

After this lesson each of your students should be able to:

1. Produce a profile of the wicked people described in today's text.

2. Explain how faithfulness in teaching the Bible provides an antidote to wickedness.

3. Plan to share the Word of God with someone who needs to hear it.

INTO THE LESSON

Distribute copies of the agree-disagree statements following; ask your students to record their opinions for each. (This exercise is reproduced in the student books.)

(1) The greatest threat to the church today is false doctrine. (2) If the Bible is not Holy Spirit inspired, we cannot depend on it for spiritual guidance. (3) The world will get better and better until the Lord returns. (4) The gospel is the only hope of salvation for the world.

Discuss students' answers briefly, noting their views. Tell your class, "Today's lesson deals with the need for Scriptural power to counter false teaching in the last days before Christ returns."

INTO THE WORD

Use the lesson background section to explain the threat of gnosticism and its doctrines. Next, divide your class into several small groups to complete the two exercises that follow. Space for these exercises is provided in the student book.

Exercise 1. Ask each group to use the information from 2 Timothy 3:1-9, 12, 13 to produce a profile of the heretics depicted there by describing both their conduct (see vv. 1-4, 6-9, 12, 13) and their false religion (see v. 5).

After your groups finish their profiles, ask each to report their findings to the class. Summarize their answers on the board or on an overhead transparency; then go on to Exercise 2.

Exercise 2. Using the information from Exercise 1, plus Paul's teaching in 2 Timothy 3:14–4:5, explain the church's appropriate response to the conduct and religion of the heresy discussed earlier. Specifically ask, "How is the Bible an antidote to immoral conduct?" and "How does the Bible help us to detect and correct false teaching?"

Distribute copies of the the reproducible activity "Sound Advice Even Today" from the next page. This will both summarize the text and begin to make application. The next activity will take the application farther.

INTO LIFE

Finally, ask your students to use today's lesson plus the Scriptures indicated to critique the doctrines of the imaginary cults described below.

Steve's High-flying Extraterrestrial Cult denies the existence of the Trinity, teaching that God is one being, the Chief Executive Officer (CEO), among other beings he created who exist in the "Upper Story." The CEO created this world and its inhabitants as a kind of lab experiment. Jesus was an Upper Story Being (USB) who came to earth in a UFO and took control of a human body to show others how to attain the Upper Story. To do that, a human must become a disciple of a USB, such as Jesus, while he is in a human body. Then, when the USB leaves earth, he takes his disciples with him, forever, to the Upper Story. *RESPONSES: (1) There is only one true God (1 Corinthians 8:4-6). (2) Man is not a lab rat, but was made in God's image (Genesis 1-2; Job 37:16). (3) Jesus is not a USB, but the Son of God in the flesh (John 1:1-14; Colossians 2:9). (4) Salvation comes not by being a disciple of a USB, but by faith in the person and work of Jesus Christ (Acts 4:10-12; Romans 3:25, 26).*

Joe's Polytheistic Polygamous Cult teaches that there are an infinite number of gods, and all were once human beings before they became divine. Each worthy human today can also become a god by believing in Jesus. His nature and will are revealed in the Bible and in The Book of Joe, given to Joe by Jesus' Father, the God whom humans are to worship. The Book of Joe is the Father's final revelation to man and is superior to the Bible, where the two disagree. The Book of Joe says that whoever believes in Jesus as he is revealed in that book will become a god after death. Husbands and wives will be married forever and will continue to have children in the hereafter. Faithful believers will have planets to colonize. *RESPONSES: (1) There is only one true God (Isaiah 44:6-8); (2) God was never a mere mortal, and humans cannot become divine (1 Timothy 6:15, 16); (3) The Bible is God's final revelation to man before the return of Christ and the end of the world (Hebrews 1:1-3; Jude 3); (4) Marriage and procreation are for this life only (Luke 20:27-38).*

Sound Advice Even Today

Today's Key Verse is Paul's advice (command!) to Timothy who faces hard times. Look at the three key elements and make a personal judgment as to how you are doing.

> **Keep your head in all situations, endure hardship, do the work of an evangelist, discharge all the duties of your ministry.** —2 Timothy 4:5

KEEP YOUR HEAD

In what kinds of situations are you most likely to lose your head?

What can Christ and his Spirit do to help you keep it on your shoulders?

ENDURE HARDSHIP

What hardships would be most likely to sidetrack your faith and ministry?

____ Economic Loss   ____ Anti-Christian Persecution   ____ Physical Health

____ World Conflict   ____ Family Trauma   ____ Other: _____

WORK AND DISCHARGE YOUR DUTIES

What do you see as the duties you have been assigned by God? List them and then evaluate your performance on a scale of 1="Complete Fulfillment" to 6="Still on the 'To Do' List."

Duties	My Evaluation
_____	1 2 3 4 5 6
_____	1 2 3 4 5 6
_____	1 2 3 4 5 6
_____	1 2 3 4 5 6
_____	1 2 3 4 5 6
_____	1 2 3 4 5 6

DO GOOD WORKS

LESSON 13

WHY TEACH THIS LESSON?

At funerals, you see three kinds of people: the physically dead, the spiritually dead, and the spiritually alive. The physically dead are unable to do any further works (either good or bad) on this earth. God has "closed the book" on their earthly lives—nothing can be added or subtracted. Those who are physically alive but spiritually dead, however, still have an opportunity to accept Christ and "produce fruit in keeping with repentance" (Matthew 3:8). Those who are both physically and spiritually alive are the ones busy "yielding a hundred, sixty, or thirty times" what has been sown in their hearts (Matthew 13:23).

All of us are destined to end up in the first of these three categories (unless the Lord returns first). Until that time, we have a choice as to which of the other two categories will mark our lives. Today's lesson shows us just how clear that choice is. As we learn, let us also keep in mind that the time is short. For some of us, it is much shorter than we may imagine.

INTRODUCTION

A. DO NOTHINGS

There is an old story about a preacher who came to visit an elderly couple in their home. The wife could not hear much and therefore missed some of the conversation. After a while she asked the visiting preacher, "Now, what is it you do?" Her husband replied, "Oh, ma, he don't *do* nothing. He's a preacher."

Titus was not to be a do-nothing preacher. While Paul will remind him of the beauties of God's grace, Titus will also be told how important it is to remain committed to good deeds.

Christianity has struggled constantly about the relationship between grace and works. This lesson will help us put that issue into perspective. The church has also struggled with the relationship between doctrine and practical Christian living. This lesson will help us in that area as well.

B. LESSON BACKGROUND

Many of the subjects covered in the two letters to Timothy are also covered in Titus. Some even see the letter to Titus as a kind of condensed version of 1 Timothy. It would not be surprising that Paul would say similar things to two of his key lieutenants.

An interesting comparison between Timothy and Titus may be made on the issue of circumcision. In Galatians 2:1-5 we learn that certain Jews expected Titus, a Greek, to be circumcised according to the Old Testament law. Since Titus was a Gentile, however, Paul would not require him to undergo a Jewish practice. Such a requirement would serve to bring Gentile converts into bondage in opposition to the "freedom we have in Christ Jesus" (Galatians 2:4).

Timothy, on the other hand, was a Jew because his mother was Jewish. Therefore, Paul knew that it was expedient to circumcise him (Acts 16:1-3). There was no point in creating an unnecessary roadblock in Timothy's witness to his fellow Jews.

DEVOTIONAL READING:
JAMES 1:19-25
BACKGROUND SCRIPTURE:
TITUS 2:1–3:11
PRINTED TEXT:
TITUS 2:7, 8, 11-15; 3:1-10

LESSON AIMS

After participating in this lesson, each student will be able to:

1. Make a list of all the commands for action that Paul gave Titus in the lesson text.

2. Explain how good works demonstrate appreciation for the salvation we have through Jesus Christ.

3. Name one of Paul's commands that he or she will put into practice this week.

KEY VERSE

In everything set them an example by doing what is good. In your teaching show integrity, seriousness and soundness of speech that cannot be condemned.
—Titus 2:7, 8a

Aug
29

LESSON 13 NOTES

Titus must have had a strong connection to the church at Corinth, for Paul mentions him several times in 2 Corinthians. We know that Titus traveled with Paul and Barnabas on a very sensitive mission to Jerusalem (Galatians 2:1). Paul must have trusted Titus a great deal.

Paul's letters charged Timothy to correct certain problems in Ephesus. Similarly, Titus is to provide leadership on the island of Crete (Titus 1:5). The problems on Crete, however, do not seem to be as severe as those in Ephesus. The church or churches on Crete were newer, whereas Ephesus had a more established church.

I. DISCIPLINES OF A GODLY LIFE (TITUS 2:7, 8, 11–3:2)

A. WILLINGNESS TO BE AN EXAMPLE (vv. 7, 8)

7. In everything set them an example by doing what is good. In your teaching show integrity, seriousness

We often profit by having *an example*—someone to model the behavior or practice we wish to perform. What a compliment to Titus, that Paul thought him up to the challenge of being that example! (See also 1 Timothy 4:12; 1 Peter 5:3.)

Beyond his example in *doing what is good,* Titus is to be an example in commitment to trustworthy *teaching.* Even though some Christians are often frustrated or bored with the study of basic biblical principles, we must recognize their importance. Our deeds need a solid doctrinal foundation. Without such a foundation, false doctrine can take over. When that happens, our deeds can become worthless or even evil.

Handling *teaching* with *integrity* and *seriousness* is vital. The latter does not mean that Christians are to be grim people. Rather, it is a reminder that teaching and preaching Scripture is serious business.

8. . . . and soundness of speech that cannot be condemned, so that those who oppose you may be ashamed because they have nothing bad to say about us.

The instruction to preach with *soundness of speech* probably refers to Paul's concern that Titus's preaching be above reproach. While the word *seriousness* in verse 7 refers to the manner of teaching, *soundness of speech* probably refers to the content of what is communicated.

What is certain is that if someone teaches what is good and true, then others cannot condemn the message. At least they cannot do so with any credibility. Titus is to speak with such integrity that his opponents will be ashamed to criticize him (cf. 1 Peter 2:15).

B. STRENGTH TO SAY "NO" (vv. 11, 12)

11, 12. For the grace of God that brings salvation has appeared to all men. It teaches us to say "No" to ungodliness and worldly passions, and to live self-controlled, upright and godly lives in this present age,

Although God was gracious to people in Old Testament times, his *grace* comes into distinct focus in the person of Jesus Christ. It is this quality Paul has in mind when he speaks of how *the grace of God that brings salvation has appeared* to us all. This does not mean that all people will receive that grace. The grace has appeared to all, but we must accept it.

God's grace not only saves us, it also teaches us various things. Some would say that grace teaches us to sin more and more since we know we will be forgiven. Paul disagrees strenuously with that idea (Romans 6:1-4). Instead, Paul would argue that the presence of God's grace gives us the strength *to say no* to sin.

Ungodliness and worldly passions are closely related. It is a foolish person who builds his or her life on the things of the world—things that we will surrender at

WHAT DO YOU THINK?

Who has been a significant example of the Christian life for you? How have you tried to follow that example? In what ways have you tried to be a good example for others?

A Pattern of Good Works
from Titus 2:7

Visual for lesson 13. *Let this visual remind your learners that there is no such thing as being a "part-time" example.*

death (cf. Luke 12:16-21). The way some people live, you would think they were going to live a few years in Heaven and an eternity on earth!

Instead of having such a worldly attitude, we are to be *self-controlled* and *upright* so our *lives* will be *godly*. We do well to remember, "For everything in the world—the cravings of sinful man, the lust of his eyes and the boasting of what he has and does—comes not from the Father but from the world" (1 John 2:16).

JUST SAY NO

In the early 1980s Nancy Reagan, First Lady of the United States, was appalled when she learned of the prevalence of drug and alcohol abuse among children. In an effort to curb this problem she launched a campaign called "Just Say No." The campaign began at an elementary school in Oakland, California, and spread across the country. It was a simple message: "When someone offers you drugs, just say no." TV ad campaigns picked up the theme. Grocery bags carried the message as well.

Yet some poked fun at the message saying that it was simplistic and therefore unrealistic. T-shirts said, "I said no to drugs, but they wouldn't listen." Others called the campaign a waste of money, dismissing it as simply a "feel good" message.

In the final analysis, however, the most effective way to stop a problem is never to let it start. It is not that *just saying no* is too simple; it is that people think they can dabble a little in the drug culture and then can say *no* when they feel they have gone too far. But that is what is unrealistic.

The old adage is true: "If you play with fire, you're going to get burned." Whether it is dabbling in drugs, alcohol, illicit sex, witchcraft, cheating on taxes, or any other sin, the best way to keep from being burned is to say no at the very outset. Simple? Yes. Simplistic? No. Effective? Most definitely!   —A. E. A.

C. READINESS FOR THE LORD'S RETURN (v. 13)

13. . . . while we wait for the blessed hope—the glorious appearing of our great God and Savior, Jesus Christ,

Having talked about the implications of Jesus' first coming, Paul now moves to the subject of the second coming. When a community in ancient times knew a king was coming, they would prepare for that visit. When we as Christians live "self-controlled, upright, and godly lives" (v. 12, above), we will be ready for the arrival of our King. Jesus' return will be the realization of our *blessed hope*. This passage offers us a definitive statement of the divinity of *our great God and Savior, Jesus Christ*. (See also John 20:28; Romans 9:5; Hebrews 1:8; and 2 Peter 1:1.)

D. REALIZATION OF GOSPEL TRUTH (v. 14)

14. . . . who gave himself for us to redeem us from all wickedness and to purify for himself a people that are his very own, eager to do what is good.

This verse speaks to the very heart of the gospel message! When Christ *gave himself for us,* he took the penalty that the Father had decreed for our sin. The one who did this is the one who will return (v. 13, above) to claim his *people*. We show our faith in him by our *good* works until he returns (Ephesians 2:10).

E. REMINDER OF DUTY (v. 15)

15. These, then, are the things you should teach. Encourage and rebuke with all authority. Do not let anyone despise you.

Paul now returns to his challenge of Titus 2:1. It is similar to the challenge to Timothy in 2 Timothy 4:2. Since the message that Titus has been given to proclaim comes from an apostle, it is a message of *authority*. As long as Titus can remember this, no one will be able to intimidate him into silence or into thinking otherwise.

WHAT DO YOU THINK?

"Ungodliness and worldly passions" seem to be at the heart of much of the entertainment industry. Movies, television, magazines, and other media display increasing amounts of immorality. Even the "good guys" participate. How can a Christian "deny" such ungodliness and still stay in touch with the culture?

WHAT DO YOU THINK?

But some people will despise anything and anyone affiliated with God or morality. How do we know when to avoid confrontation in order not to be "despised," and when to stand up and let the ungodly "despise" our godly position?

[Ephesians 4:15 and 1 Peter 4:14-16 will be important in your discussion.]

DAILY BIBLE READINGS

   Monday, Aug. 23—Generosity Glorifies God (2 Corinthians 9:10-15)

   Tuesday, Aug. 24—Let Your Light Shine Before Others (Matthew 5:11-16)

   Wednesday, Aug. 25—Elders Should Teach Those Younger (Titus 2:1-5)

   Thursday, Aug. 26—Be a Model of Good Works (Titus 2:6-10)

   Friday, Aug. 27—Be Zealous for Good Deeds (Titus 2:11-15)

   Saturday, Aug. 28—Be Ready for Every Good Work (Titus 3:1-6)

   Sunday, Aug. 29—Good Works Are Excellent and Profitable (Titus 3:7-11)

F. HUMILITY OF A GOOD CITIZEN (3:1, 2)

1. Remind the people to be subject to rulers and authorities, to be obedient, to be ready to do whatever is good,

Since we are citizens of a heavenly kingdom, we may get the idea that we are exempt from the rules of earthly governments. But both here and in Romans 13:1-7 Paul tells us otherwise. The governing authorities may not be not Christian rulers, but we are to obey them nonetheless. (See also 1 Peter 2:13-17.)

Christians know that without some kind of law to govern social behavior, chaos will result. So Christians obey the government. This obedience, however, is not absolute. We would not obey the government in those cases where the government tries to force us to do something against God's will (see Acts 4:19; 5:29).

Paul describes earthly governments as *rulers and authorities*. Paul uses this terminology to refer to demons in Ephesians 6:12, but in the case at hand he means earthly, secular rulers.

2. . . . to slander no one, to be peaceable and considerate, and to show true humility toward all men.

Christians are not *to slander* anyone, even their enemies. Not only are Christians to speak no evil, they are also not to lash out physically. Titus is also told to show *humility*. This does not mean weakness, but rather carries the ideas of being self-controlled and gentle (cf. Matthew 5:5). In the verses that follow, Paul lists several motivations for a life of godliness.

II. MOTIVATION OF THE GODLY LIFE (TITUS 3:3-10)

A. FUTILITY OF OUR PAST (v. 3)

3. At one time we too were foolish, disobedient, deceived and enslaved by all kinds of passions and pleasures. We lived in malice and envy, being hated and hating one another.

How desperate our situation was without Christ! We *were foolish*, but beyond that we were stubbornly *disobedient*. To make the situation even worse, we were *deceived*. We know that before we accepted Christ, we were just as sinful as our neighbors (cf. Ephesians 4:18, 19). This fact should keep us from having a sense of pride. What we need instead is gratitude that God can change lives. In the state we were in previously, it was so much easier to give in to *passions* as well as *malice and envy*. Many who give way to *hating* end up being hated by others.

B. COMPLETENESS OF OUR SALVATION (vv. 4-7)

4. But when the kindness and love of God our Savior appeared,

The kindness and love of God appeared in the midst of our hopelessness in the person of Jesus Christ. As the next verse shows, this was not of our doing.

5. . . . he saved us, not because of righteous things we had done, but because of his mercy. He saved us through the washing of rebirth and renewal by the Holy Spirit,

Notice the concept of grace that is presented clearly here when we are told that *because of his mercy* Jesus *saved us*. We are not saved because we are so good or so lovable (see Ephesians 2:8, 9; 2 Timothy 1:9). The verse then speaks of *the washing of rebirth* as well as the *renewal by the Holy Spirit*. Some think that *washing of rebirth* refers to an "inner, spiritual cleansing." Others think that Paul is referring to water baptism. Indeed, it would be difficult to imagine Titus not thinking of water baptism when he reads this phrase (see also Acts 22:16; Ephesians 5:26).

Water, of course, has no power to wash away sins. It's just water. Neither does the person administering the baptism have any such power. As a result, we can conclude that Paul speaks of *washing of rebirth* in the sense that we are saved *in* the waters of baptism, but not *by* those waters (cf. Colossians 2:12).

This viewpoint upholds the importance of grace. When a person submits to baptism, it is part of an appeal for grace and a time to receive grace—it is not an attempt to earn salvation. Baptism apart from personal faith and repentance means nothing.

It is the Holy Spirit who brings about our renewal. Mere human effort cannot do this. Peter connected water baptism with receiving "the gift of the Holy Spirit" in his sermon on the day of Pentecost (Acts 2:38).

BEAUTY AND THE BEAST

Some consider the fairy tale *Beauty and the Beast* to be the most beloved love story of all time. The foundational theme of the story has been used in many movies and books throughout the years. It is the story of a spoiled prince who snubs an old beggar woman at his castle because of her unattractive appearance.

The woman warns the prince not to make judgments by appearance. Repeatedly she returns to the castle, but each time the prince turns her away. After her final dismissal, the old woman turns into a beautiful princess. She also casts a spell on the prince that turns him into a beastly looking creature. The only way to erase the ugliness of his appearance is that he learn to love another and earn her love in return. The rest of the story is a familiar one of the triumph of love over appearance.

And it is an illustration of grace as well. How ugly we were in our sin! Our sin-marred appearance was repulsive to God. But the God of grace saw beyond the ugliness of sin and he loved the unlovely. Christians often quote that most fundamental of Bible truths from John 3:16: "For God so loved the world. . . . " Unfortunately, we don't often grasp how much love that took.

There is a twist to this story of grace that we must not overlook. The beast in the fairy tale had to learn to express love to win the beauty to himself. God, on the other hand, was the beautiful one who made the first step by expressing love to ugly and sinful humanity by giving his Son for us. Paul puts it this way: "But God demonstrates his own love for us in this: While we were still sinners, Christ died for us" (Romans 5:8).

A God who demonstrates such beautiful love deserves the best we "redeemed beasts" have to offer. And those around us having the beastliness of sin need to be pointed to the beautiful Savior.   —A. E. A.

6. *. . . whom he poured out on us generously through Jesus Christ our Savior,*

The word *whom* refers to the Holy Spirit. The outpouring of the Holy Spirit occurred on the day of Pentecost, just mentioned with verse 5, above. Since that great day each Christian has received the gift of the Holy Spirit's indwelling (Acts 2:39). Jesus promised that he would ask the Father to send the Holy Spirit (John 14:16, 17). Notice also that our God is not one who gives sparingly. God gives abundantly and *generously.*

7. *. . . so that, having been justified by his grace, we might become heirs having the hope of eternal life.*

To be *justified* means to be declared righteous (Romans 3:21-26). As a result Christians also have *become heirs* (Galatians 3:29). This is a sign of the great love that God has for us, that he would number us as his children. But there is more: to be justified and to be made heirs means having the certain *hope of eternal life.* What a God we serve!

C. IMPORTANCE OF GOOD DEEDS (vv. 8-10)

8. *This is a trustworthy saying. And I want you to stress these things, so that those who have trusted in God may be careful to devote themselves to doing what is good. These things are excellent and profitable for everyone.*

HOW TO SAY IT

Abraham. AY-bruh-ham.
Barnabas. BAR-nuh-bus.
Colossians. Kuh-LOSH-unz.
Corinthians. Kor-IN-thee-un.
Crete. Creet.
Ephesians. Ee-FEE-zhunz.
Galatians. Guh-LAY-shunz.
gnostic. NAHSS-tick.
gnosticism. NAHSS-tih-SIZZ-um.
heresy. HAIR-uh-see.
heretic. HAIR-uh-tik.
Lech Walesa. Lek Wuh-LEN-suh.
Titus. TIE-tus.

PRAYER

Dear Father in Heaven, I thank you for bringing Heaven's blessings to earth. Help me to make this earth more heavenly, even as I strive to help prepare people for Heaven. It is so easy to talk like a Christian—help me also to live like one, too. In the name of Jesus I pray, amen.

This verse begins with the statement that we have seen in previous lessons: *This is a trustworthy saying.* Again, it can refer to a proverb that Titus already knows well, to some teaching that Paul has emphasized repeatedly, or to a new teaching that Paul is creating as he writes.

The things that Paul has to say next are so important that he wants Titus to *stress* them to his readers, who must be careful *to devote themselves to doing what is good.* "For we are God's workmanship, created in Christ Jesus to do good works, which God prepared in advance for us to do" (Ephesians 2:10). To recognize that Christian deeds are both *excellent and profitable* is to say not only that there is something inherently good about those deeds, but also that there are practical benefits. The one doing the deeds and the one receiving them both benefit.

9. But avoid foolish controversies and genealogies and arguments and quarrels about the law, because these are unprofitable and useless.

As with the previous instructions to Timothy in 2 Timothy 2:14, 16, 23, Paul warns Titus not to get involved in trivial matters. If the heresy Paul is concerned about is gnosticism, then these *genealogies* may have been gnostic genealogies. If the problem is a Jewish heresy, then the genealogies may be attempts to connect people with Old Testament characters and heroes. John the Baptist made it plain that biological descent from Abraham doesn't make a person more favored before God (Matthew 3:9). The fact Paul talks about *quarrels about the law* supports the idea that the heresy was a Jewish one.

10. Warn a divisive person once, and then warn him a second time. After that, have nothing to do with him.

A *divisive person* person may be one who ends up splitting the church over the "unprofitable and useless" issues of verse 9, above. Divisive people may be very articulate and persuasive, but end up doing more harm than good. Titus is to warn such a person twice about the damage being done to the church.

If the person keeps it up after two warnings, the result is not to be merely that Titus would give him "the cold shoulder." Something more formal, a kind of church discipline, is in mind here. This shows how dangerous Paul thought a divisive person could be and how precious is the unity of the church (see Romans 15:5, 6).

CONCLUSION

The great Polish political reformer and Nobel Prize winner Lech Walesa said, "Words are plentiful; deeds are precious." Paul might well agree! But Paul may also admonish us to understand what he told Titus. Words and deeds go together. One confirms the other. Deeds without words can be interpreted in contradictory ways to those who observe them. Words without deeds may be judged insincere or hypocritical.

We Christians preach and teach God's Word. We also have Christian deeds as a natural result of the grace we have experienced. We glorify God when our words and our deeds reinforce one another. Jesus challenges us to let our light "shine before men" (Matthew 5:16). We do this in both word and deed. This is not to bring glory to us, but so that others will give glory to the Father who is in Heaven.

John Wesley (1703–1791) revealed his code of living this way: "Do all the good you can, by all the means you can, in all the ways you can, in all the places you can, at all the times you can, to all the people you can, as long as ever you can." That is a difficult challenge, but one worth adopting. In light of all God has done for us, that is the best way to live.

Discovery Learning

*This page contains an alternative lesson plan emphasizing learning activities. Classes
desiring such student involvement will find these suggestions helpful. The next page
is a reproducible activity page to further enhance discovery learning.*

LEARNING GOALS

After this lesson each of your students will be able to:

1. Make a list of all the commands for action that Paul gave Titus in the lesson text.

2. Explain how good works demonstrate appreciation for the salvation we have through Jesus Christ.

3. Name one of Paul's commands that he or she will put into practice this week.

INTO THE LESSON

Ask your students to name as many activities as they can that require personal discipline to be successful. (This exercise is also found in the student book.) Answers may include dieting, exercise, Bible reading. As your students suggest activities, list them on the board. When they finish, ask them to categorize the answers as activities requiring physical discipline (P), mental discipline (M), moral or ethical discipline (E), spiritual discipline (S), or some combination of the above (C). Ask volunteers to suggest which activities require the most discipline and why. After discussing their responses, tell your class that today's lesson will deal with the importance of developing Christian discipline.

INTO THE WORD

Using material in today's Lesson Background, give a brief lecture on Titus and the situation that led Paul to write the epistle addressed to him.

For the next part of the lesson, divide your class into three groups (or multiples of three). Give the groups these assignments:

GROUP 1

Using a photocopy of today's printed text, mark each verse in the following way.

1. Put a plus sign (+) beside each verse that tells the reader to do something.

2. Put a minus sign (–) beside each verse that tells the reader to avoid doing something.

3. Put an exclamation point (!) beside each verse that contains a promise to the reader, or indicates something that God has done for us.

Say, "Some verses may receive more than one mark." *Their results should look like this: 2:7 (+); 8 (+, –); 11 (!); 12 (–, +); 13 (+, !); 3:1 (+); 2 (–, +); 3 (–); 4 (!); 5 (!); 6 (!); 7 (!); 8 (+); 9 (–); 10 (+).*

GROUP 2

Using a photocopy of today's printed text, mark each verse in the following way.

1. Put an asterisk (*) beside each verse that tells us how we should/should not behave toward others.

2. Put an ampersand (&) beside each verse that tells us how we should/should not behave toward God.

3. Put a pound sign (#) beside each verse that tells us how God behaves toward us.

Note: some verses may receive more than one type of mark. *Their results should look like this: 2:7 (*, &); 8 (*); 11 (#); 12 (&, *); 13 (&, #); 3:1 (*); 2 (*); 3 (&, *); 4 (#); 5 (#); 6 (#); 7 (#); 8 (*); 9 (&, *); 10 (*)*

GROUP 3

Write a verse-by-verse paraphrase of today's text, to capture the meaning of Paul's words. For example, 2:7 might be rendered, "Be a model to others by doing good deeds at every opportunity and by being sound, serious, and sincere in the way you follow Biblical doctrine."

When your groups complete their assignments, review their work in this manner: first, have someone from Group 3 read the group's paraphrase of a verse, then have Groups 1 and 2 indicate how they marked the verse. Finally, discuss the verse's meaning.

Direct attention to the "Christian Growth" activity on the reproducible page that follows. Ask learners to fill it in as a group, based on their studies just finished.

INTO LIFE

After discussing the text, ask students to complete the following "Christian Discipline Inventory," also printed in the student book. Beneath each statement give them four choices: "Always, Usually, Sometimes, Never."

1. I consciously try to be a model to others by my good deeds and commitment to Biblical truth.

2. I watch the things I say and do because I don't want anyone to use my behavior as an excuse to criticize the Lord or his church.

3. I am eagerly looking for the return of Christ.

4. I try to be a good citizen so the government won't have an excuse to persecute the church.

5. I avoid wasting my time on doctrines not clearly taught in the New Testament.

Distribute copies of the reproducible activity "A Code of Living" from the next page; use this to close.

Christian Growth

Dave is a new Christian who wants to develop a Christian lifestyle. What are the rungs he should take up the "ladder of Christian discipline"? Write some suggestions on the "rungs" of the ladder below.

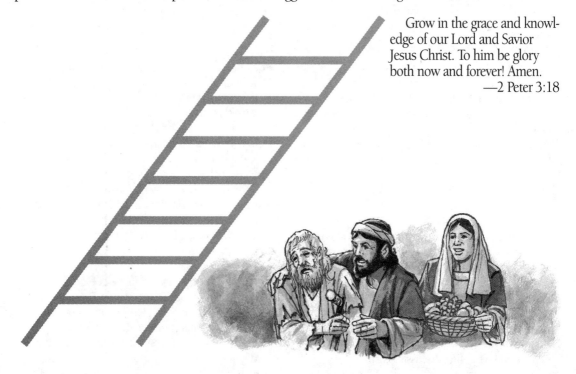

Grow in the grace and knowledge of our Lord and Savior Jesus Christ. To him be glory both now and forever! Amen.
—2 Peter 3:18

A Code of Living

John Wesley said, "Do all the good you can, by all the means you can, in all the ways you can, in all the places you can, at all the times you can, to all the people you can, as long as ever you can." Join with several fellow students to make a list of benevolent programs or services offered by your congregation to do good for members and for non-members. Beside it, make a second list of programs your congregation could be doing.

Benevolent Works We Are Doing

Benevolent Works We Could Do

_____   _____

_____   _____

_____   _____

_____   _____

_____   _____